BK 872. D836C V2
COMPLETE ROMAN DRAMA
1942 .00 FP /DUCKWORTH,

3000 057417 20025
St. Louis Community College

D1272138

872 D836c FP v. 2
DUCKWORTH
COMPLETE ROMAN DRAMA
8.00

INVENTORY 98

INVENTORY 1985

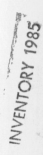

THE COMPLETE ROMAN DRAMA

THE RANDOM HOUSE

Lifetime Library

THE
Complete Roman Drama

ALL THE EXTANT COMEDIES OF PLAUTUS AND

TERENCE, AND THE TRAGEDIES OF SENECA,

IN A VARIETY OF TRANSLATIONS

EDITED, AND WITH AN INTRODUCTION, BY

GEORGE E. DUCKWORTH

Associate Professor of Classics, Princeton University

IN TWO VOLUMES

VOLUME TWO

RANDOM HOUSE . NEW YORK

COPYRIGHT, 1942, BY RANDOM HOUSE, INC.

MANUFACTURED IN THE UNITED STATES OF AMERICA

BY H. WOLFF, NEW YORK

CONTENTS · VOLUME I

CONTENTS · VOLUME II

COMEDIES

TRAGEDIES

APPENDIX

THE PLAYS OF PLAUTUS (*Continued*)

XVIII
STICHUS

CHARACTERS IN THE PLAY

PANEGYRIS, *wife of* EPIGNOMUS
PAMPHILA, *sister of* PANEGYRIS *and wife of* PAMPHILIPPUS
ANTIPHO, *an aged Athenian, their father*
GELASIMUS, *a parasite*
CROCOTIUM, *maid to* PANEGYRIS
PINACIUM, *slave boy of* PANEGYRIS
EPIGNOMUS, *a young Athenian*
PAMPHILIPPUS, *his brother*
STICHUS, *slave of* EPIGNOMUS
SANGARINUS, *slave of* PAMPHILIPPUS
STEPHANIUM, *maid to* PAMPHILA

DIDASCALIA[1]

The *Stichus* of Titus Maccius Plautus. Taken from the Greek play of Menander, *The Brothers*.[2] Acted at the Plebeian Games in the plebeian aedileship of Gnaeus Baebius and Gaius Terentius. Produced by Titus Publilius Pellio. Music, on Tyrian flutes throughout, by the slave of Marcus Oppius. Presented in the consulship of Gaius Sulpicius and Gaius Aurelius.[3]

ACROSTIC ARGUMENT

An old man rebukes his daughters because they persist in remaining faithful to their husbands, two impoverished brothers who are abroad, and refuse to give them up. They find the proper words to appease him and he allows them to keep the husbands they have. Enriched again, the husbands return from across the sea. Each one retains his own wife, and a holiday is given to Stichus.

INTRODUCTION

THE *Stichus,* presented in 200 B.C., is unique among the plays of Plautus. It has no real plot, but is composed of a succession of scenes which fall into three groups; these might be entitled "The Abandoned Wives," "The Homecoming or The Disappointed Parasite," and "The Slaves' Carousal." Each part has its own tone; the action progresses from serious comedy to farce, and from farce to burlesque. Stichus, the slave who gives his name to the play, is prominent only in the final part. The comedy contains neither intrigue nor recognition—the two motives which are found, either singly or in combination, in the plots of most Roman comedies. In the *Stichus* two sisters yearn for the return of their husbands; the husbands, who are brothers, arrive and are welcomed by their father-in-law. The reunion between husbands and wives is not portrayed on the stage.

In spite of its careless construction and its lack of dramatic movement, the play is not lacking in interest. Many of the individual scenes have vigour and humour, and the characters are well drawn, particularly the two wives who, like Penelope in the *Odyssey,* await faithfully the return of their husbands, their father who wishes them to divorce their husbands and remarry, and the parasite Gelasimus who is so eager to profit by the homecoming of the two brothers. J. W. Duff calls the play "an interesting social document"; its main purpose seems to be the portrayal of certain social types and certain aspects of ancient life. The two brothers celebrate their homecoming with a banquet but the banquet is held inside. What the audience sees on the stage is the celebration of Stichus and Sangarinus with their joint-sweetheart. The final scenes with their song and dance and drunkenness are in a sense a parody of the doubtlessly more restrained festivities of their masters being held within the house.

Gelasimus is one of the best of Plautus' parasites; his desire to auction off his wares and his futile attempts to get a dinner from each of the returning husbands provide much amusement, as does the father's desire for a music girl, so thinly disguised under his fable of the man "just like me." Pinacium, who brings back the good tidings of the return, is amusing as a running slave, and has many characteristics of

3

Paegnium in *The Girl from Persia*. There is nothing elsewhere in Plautus quite like the revelry of the slaves in Act Five; the conclusion of *The Girl from Persia* is somewhat similar, but it has as an added purpose the discomfiture of Dordalus. The orgy in the *Stichus* has no structural value; it is a portrayal of life below stairs and the burlesque treatment is purely for its own sake.

To evaluate such a play as the *Stichus* is difficult. It has been called "dull," "one of Plautus' poorest plays," "excellent in its parts, impossible as a whole." Structurally it has no complication and no denouement, and hardly deserves to be considered a comedy. Yet there is plenty of wit and humour in the various scenes. It is surprising to learn from the didascalic notice that the Greek original was *The Brothers* (the *Adelphoe*) of Menander, who was the greatest of the dramatists of Greek New Comedy. This Greek play was not the original of Terence's *The Brothers*. The two Roman plays have no similarity whatsoever, and there is good evidence that Menander composed two plays of the same title. In spite of many ingenious conjectures, it is impossible to tell how much Plautus omitted from his Menandrian original and how much he added from other sources or himself invented.

STICHUS

(SCENE:—*A street in Athens in front of the houses of* EPIGNOMUS, PAMPHILIPPUS, *and* ANTIPHO.)

Act One.   Scene I

(*Enter* PANEGYRIS *and* PAMPHILA *from* EPIGNOMUS' *house.*)

PANEGYRIS (*resignedly*): It seems to me, sister, that Penelope must have been very melancholy, being, as it were, a grass widow for such a long time. Surely we are in a position to sympathise with her, what with our own husbands also away and their affairs turned over to us— a constant cause of concern, as is but right.

PAMPHILA (*stoically*): It's our duty, all right, and we're doing nothing more than our conscience tells us. But come here, sister, and sit down a while; I want to go into detail with you about this business of men.

PANEGYRIS (*startled*): What's that? Surely everything's all right, isn't it?

PAMPHILA (*as they seat themselves*): I should certainly hope so. But this is the thing that bothers me, sister, that our father, who the entire city admits stands unrivalled in honesty, should now be playing the part of a "public enemy," harming our husbands without reason and wanting to separate us from them. That's the thing that makes me sick of life; it's the cause of my grief no less than of my grey hairs. (*Sobbing.*)

PANEGYRIS (*reassuringly*): Now wait a minute, don't cry; you're just treating yourself the way your father threatens to treat you. I hope he will be better disposed to us than that, because, if I know him, he's just joking. Why, he wouldn't realise your fears for all the cheese on the moon.[4] And what if he did? We should have no right to be annoyed, for his action wouldn't be without grounds. After all, you know, our husbands left home three years ago.

5

PAMPHILA: Yes, that's true.

PANEGYRIS: And they don't let us know whether they're still alive, let alone in good health. We're ignorant of their whereabouts, their activities, their general state. And what's more, they don't return.

PAMPHILA: So that's what's troubling you, sister, that you're doing your duty, while they're shirking theirs?

PANEGYRIS: That's the story.

PAMPHILA: Well, now, you just keep quiet! Don't you dare let me hear that again from you.

PANEGYRIS: Why not?

PAMPHILA: Because, in my opinion, every sensible person should look after his own affairs. And even though you are the older, I'm warning you to keep your own business in mind. What if our husbands are worthless and don't treat us as they should? We must employ every energy to remember our own duty, lest this contagion of indolence spread.

PANEGYRIS: I guess you're right. I'll keep quiet.

PAMPHILA: Just see that you remember.

[PANEGYRIS: Sister, I don't want people to say that I'm unmindful of my husband. His regard for me certainly isn't wasted. Goodness me! I'm really grateful for his kindness. After all, I have no grievances over my marriage, and I wouldn't want it otherwise. But still, our father holds full power over us, and we must follow out the commands of our parent.

PAMPHILA: I realise that, and it grieves me terribly to think about it, for he's pretty clearly revealed his attitude already.

PANEGYRIS: Then we must consider what's the best thing for us to do.]⁵

Act One.   Scene II

(*Enter* ANTIPHO *from his house.*)

ANTIPHO (*to the servants within*): A servant who's always neglecting his work until he's told about it and doesn't think of doing it himself is a good-for-nothing servant. Yet you always think of coming around for your gastronomical allowance on the first of every month. Why are you so poor at thinking about your household duties? Now if each thing isn't put in its proper place before I return, I'll give you something to think about—a good dose of oxhide. Humph! Why, it seems as if I were living with hogs instead of human beings. Just see to it that my house is clean before I return. I won't be long; I'm merely going over to my elder daughter's. If anyone gives me a call, you know where to reach me; but I'll soon be back.

PAMPHILA (*to* PANEGYRIS): What'll we do, sister, if our father takes a stand against us?

PANEGYRIS: We'll have to put up with his plans, since he has the parental prerogative. I think our course must be determined by submission rather than by opposition. If we seek it as a favour, I hope we can obtain it from him. We can't oppose him without calling down the worst shame and disgrace upon our heads—and that's a thing I wouldn't do; nor would I want you to do it. We'd better implore him. And if I know him, he's open to entreaty.

ANTIPHO (*to himself, uncertain as to his procedure*): I'm not quite sure how I'll broach the matter to them—whether I should befuddle them, say, by pretending that I never had anything against them, or as if I had suspected that they were to blame. Or maybe I ought to treat them lightly, or perhaps threateningly. I know them well enough to realise there'll be a dispute if they choose to remain here rather than get married again. No, I won't do that! What good does it do me to quarrel with my own children, especially at my age? And besides, I don't think they're deserving of such treatment. No, sir, I don't want a rumpus. I believe the thing will work out best if I do this: I'll pretend that they've been up to some kind of mischief. I'll simply scare the souls out of them, and then I'll bring up the matter and reveal my sentiments about it. It's going to take a lot of talking, all right. But now I'll go in. (*As he approaches* PANEGYRIS' *house*) Look! The door's open now.

PAMPHILA (*to* PANEGYRIS): I'm sure I just heard father's voice.

PANEGYRIS: Yes, that's who it is. Let's captivate him with a kiss as he enters. (*They rise to greet him.*)

PAMPHILA: Good morning, father. (*They shower him with kisses.*)

ANTIPHO (*grouchily*): And the same to you. Stop that! Sit down!

PAMPHILA: Surely you don't mind a kiss?

ANTIPHO: I've had enough of your kisses.

PANEGYRIS: Why do you say that, father? Tell me.

ANTIPHO: Because it makes my breath salty.

PAMPHILA (*pointing to their bench*): Sit down here, father.

ANTIPHO (*gruffly*): Nope, I won't sit there; you sit there. I'll sit on this seat.

PANEGYRIS: Wait a minute, here's a cushion.

ANTIPHO (*more pleasantly*): You're taking good care of me. There, I'm well enough cushioned. Sit down.

PAMPHILA (*bringing another cushion*): Permit me, father.

ANTIPHO: What's the purpose?

PANEGYRIS (*making him comfortable*): There is a purpose.

ANTIPHO (*relaxing*): Have your own way. Now, that's enough, I say.

PAMPHILA (*as the sisters seat themselves*): Why, daughters can't ever take too good care of their parents. Whom ought we to esteem more than you? And next to you, father, our husbands, to whom you were willing to give us in wedlock.

ANTIPHO: You're acting just as good wives ought to act, when you have the same regard for your absent husbands as you would if they were present.

PAMPHILA: It's but our duty, father, to revere those who have chosen us as their companions.

ANTIPHO (*as if about to broach a weighty matter*): Say, there's nobody snooping around here, is there?

PANEGYRIS: There's no one here but us.

ANTIPHO (*very seriously*): Well, I want your advice. You see, I'm un-tutored in the affairs and ways of woman, and so I'm coming to you as a pupil does to his teachers. With what characteristics should women be endowed to be the ultimate in womanliness? I want each of you to tell me.

PAMPHILA: What's this? You're coming here to us to inquire about the ways of women?

ANTIPHO: Well, you see, I'm looking for a wife, now that your mother is dead.

PAMPHILA (*shocked*): It certainly won't be hard to find one with characteristics inferior to our mother's. And you won't find one anywhere under the sun who's better than she was.

ANTIPHO: Well, my question still stands before the two of you.

PAMPHILA (*in amazement*): Gracious, father! Why—why, I'll tell you the necessary characteristics, that is, if they're to be according to my notion.

ANTIPHO: Good! Speak your mind.

PAMPHILA: I'm thinking about those women who walk about the town and yet take care that not a single gossip can busy herself over them.

ANTIPHO (*to* PANEGYRIS): And now it's your turn to speak.

PANEGYRIS: What do you want me to say, father?

ANTIPHO: Why, in what way a woman may best show herself to be excellent in character.

PANEGYRIS: When she can restrain herself from doing wrong, even though the temptation is strong.

ANTIPHO: Hm-m! That's a good answer. (*To* PAMPHILA) Your turn now; tell me, which makes the better wife, a winsome maid or a widow?

PAMPHILA: Well, so far as I know, (*trying to confuse the issue*) of many malignities, the minimum of malevolence makes the minimum of misery.

ANTIPHO (*somewhat puzzled*): How can a woman shun shortcomings?

PAMPHILA: Why, by taking care in advance of what she'll not regret later.

ANTIPHO (*to* PANEGYRIS): What kind of woman seems to you to be the wisest?

PANEGYRIS: The one who can keep her head when things are going well and who still maintains her dignity after a reversal of fortune.

ANTIPHO (*laughing*): Ha, ha! This, my dears, has indeed proved a very charming examination of you and your own traits of character. (*More seriously*) But this is the real reason I've come to confer with you: my friends have persuaded me that I ought to take you two back home.

PAMPHILA: But we're the ones whose interests are at stake, and we advise you quite differently. Either you should not have given us, in the first place, to husbands you didn't approve of, or now it's not right for you to take us away from those husbands when they are absent.

ANTIPHO: Am I to allow you girls to stay married to beggars, as long as I live?

PAMPHILA: The one you term beggar is dear to me. A king is always beloved by his own queen. And my opinion is the same in my present poverty as it was when I was wealthy.

ANTIPHO: Brigands and vagrants—you esteem them all, don't you?

PAMPHILA: You didn't marry me to money, I hope, but to a man.

ANTIPHO: Well, why wait for men who've been away now for three years? Why not make a first-class marriage instead of this useless union?

PANEGYRIS: It's folly, father, to lead unwilling hounds to the chase. A wife proves to be an enemy when she's married against her will.

ANTIPHO: Then you've both made up your mind that you're not going to follow your father's orders?

PANEGYRIS: We are following them—by remaining steadfast in the marriages you originally arranged.

ANTIPHO (*rising*): Good-bye. I'm going to my friends to explain your resolution.

PANEGYRIS: And they'll honour us the moɔ for it, I believe; that is, if those friends of yours have any honour themselves.

ANTIPHO: Just see that you take care of your own affairs as best you can.

PANEGYRIS (*elated*): Oh, I like that! Now you're talking—with such advice! Now we'll pay attention to you. (*To* PAMPHILA, *as* ANTIPHO *departs*) Come on, sister, let's go inside.

PAMPHILA: Sorry, I have a house of my own to look after. Don't forget; if any news should arrive from your husband, let me know. (PAMPHILA *goes into her house.*)

PANEGYRIS (*calling after her*): You know our compact—we'll inform each other as the news breaks. (*Calling to her maid inside*) Crocotium, ho, Crocotium!

(*Enter* CROCOTIUM *from* PANEGYRIS' *house*)⁶

Go and fetch that sponger of a Gelasimus. I want to send him to the
harbour to see if, by chance, a ship has put into port recently from Asia.
I already have one servant sitting at the port watching every day, but
I simply must have someone inform me from time to time. Now, hurry
up and get back as soon as possible. (PANEGYRIS *goes into her house.*)

Act One.   Scene III

(*Enter* GELASIMUS, *bewailing his fortune.*)

GELASIMUS (*to himself, not seeing* CROCOTIUM): Oh-h-h! I suppose my
mother must have been Hunger herself; never, no, sir, never since I
was born have I had enough to eat. No one will ever do more justice to
his mother than I do—as much as I hate to do it. [Nor has anyone ever
done more than I do for my mother Hunger.]⁷ Whereas she carried me
in her belly for ten months, I've carried her in mine for more than ten
years. And besides, she carried me when I was only a tiny tot—certainly a cinch for her! But the Hunger I'm carrying around in my
belly is certainly not small. Gad, it's annoying! In fact, this time it
beats all previous records for size. Why, I have to put up with my
pangs every day, and yet I can't get mother to come out into a life of
her own. I don't know what to do! I've often heard it said that an elephant usually stays pregnant for ten years; I guess this Hunger of
mine must have come from elephant seed. She's been clinging to my
insides now for years and years. Hm-m! If anyone's looking for a
clown, I'll fill the bill with all my paraphernalia; all I'm concerned
about is relief from my stomach trouble. My father called me Gelasimus
when I was quite small and I've lived up to my name ever since. (*Grinning*) A real Laughing Jackass, you see! (*More seriously*) Then too, I
got this name because of my poverty; after all, it was really poverty
that gave me the dignity of a profession—Sir Gelasimus, Master Jester!
Ha, ha! Yes, sir, poverty teaches all the crafts to anyone she lights
upon. My father told me that food was dear when I was born. I suppose that's the reason I'm so hungry now. But generosity's the keynote
of my family—that's why I would never think of refusing anyone who
invites me to eat. It's tough that one kind of speech has departed from
men. Golly, but that was a first-rate and appropriate kind of speech,
to my way of thinking: "Come now, you simply must come to dinner.
No excuses! Please don't refuse. Is it convenient? I won't let you go
until you come and have dinner with me." But now they've found a

substitute for that speech, and, God, it's vicious and vile! "I'd love to have you over for dinner, but I'm dining out myself." I'd just like to see such speeches get their backs broken; but if such a person should dine at home, the phrase would disappear *in toto*. These speeches make me learn foreign habits; no auctioneer for my profession; I've got to be my own crier and proclaim I'm for hire.

CROCOTIUM (*aside, catching a glimpse of* GELASIMUS): Ah, there's that sponger I'm supposed to bring back. I'll just eavesdrop a little to hear his line before I speak to him.

GELASIMUS (*looking over the audience*): This place is just teeming with busybodies whose only interest is the other fellow's business. They don't give a damn for their own affairs. When they know that someone's having an auction, they run right up and demand the reasons for it: whether it be bankruptcy, a real estate proposition, or a divorce and return of the dowry. And yet, I guess, the whole bunch of them deserves to be bad off. Personally I don't care. I'll announce the reasons for the auction and then let them rejoice in my downfall. For no one is curious without hoping for the worst. So here goes! (*Addressing the audience*) This is why I'm announcing the auction; I'm a wretched man, I've suffered dreadful losses. My possessions have made me poor—the host of drinks, now gone from mortal sight—the many dinners whose deaths I have mourned—the cups of honey-wine—the midday luncheons, all the ones I missed these last three years! I've grown old and miserable from sorrow and suffering. In truth, I'm almost dead from hunger.

CROCOTIUM (*aside*): He's simply a scream when his stomach's screaming for food.

GELASIMUS: Now I've made up my mind I'm going to have an auction. Everything must go; I won't keep a thing myself. (*Addressing the audience as an auctioneer*) Just step up, please! Step up! Free gifts for all present! Now here we have some funny stories. Do I hear a bid? What am I bid for these funny stories? (*No response from the audience*) A dinner? (*Silence*) Come, come now! Does anyone offer a lunch? (*More silence*) Bless you, they're yours for a lunch or a dinner. (*Looking at a spectator*) Hm-m, did I see you nod? (*No response*) You can't do better anywhere else. I won't let any other parasite have better goods. Let me see. Here I have some Greek rubbing alcohol. What am I bid? (*Silence*) Why, this can be taken internally or externally. I'll make a bargain: I'll throw in some jibes, some blarney, and some sycophantic silliness free of charge. Who wants to buy a rusty strigil, a lusty flask, or an empty parasite who will hold your table crumbs?

(*Silence*) Don't you patrons understand? I've got to get rid of this stuff quickly so I can pay my church dues to Hercules.

CROCOTIUM (*aside*): Well, I must say there's nothing worth much at that auction. Hunger's taken possession of the very depths of his stomach. I'll have a talk with him.

GELASIMUS (*aside, seeing her*): Who can this woman be coming towards me? Oh, I know, it's Epignomus' maid, Crocotium.

CROCOTIUM: Good morning, Gelasimus.

GELASIMUS (*mournfully*): That's not my name.

CROCOTIUM: Goodness, it was too your name.

GELASIMUS: To be sure, it was, but I lost it from overuse. Circumstances have changed it to Crumchaser.

CROCOTIUM (*holding her sides*): Oh! You certainly made me laugh today.

GELASIMUS: When? Where?

CROCOTIUM: Just now, when you were crying that auction.

GELASIMUS: Damnation! Did you listen to that?

CROCOTIUM: Yes. It just suited you, too.

GELASIMUS: Where are you going now?

CROCOTIUM: To you.

GELASIMUS: Why me?

CROCOTIUM: Panegyris ordered me to ask you to come along back to her house.

GELASIMUS (*with new vigour*): Hallelujah! I certainly will with all haste. (*Rubbing his hands and licking his lips*) Is—uh—is the—uh—meat for the sacrifice all broiled? How many chops has she put on the grill?

CROCOTIUM: Why, she's not making any sacrifice.

GELASIMUS: What? What? No sacrifice? No chops? What in the world can she want with me then?

CROCOTIUM: She wants to speak to you about some wheat, I think about ten pecks of wheat.

GELASIMUS (*hopefully*): Oh, yes, I'm to ask her for it?

CROCOTIUM: Oh, no, she'd like to borrow it from you for our use.

GELASIMUS (*somewhat coldly*): You just tell her I've got nothing to give or lend. Why, I don't own a damned thing but this old coat. And besides, I've even sold my tongue. Tell her that!

CROCOTIUM: Oh, so your tongue is gone now, eh?

GELASIMUS: Sure, so far as the phrase "I'll give" is concerned. But look here, there's one in my stomach that can still say "How good!"

CROCOTIUM: "Good for nothing!" Humph! That's what you mean.

GELASIMUS: The same to you, it says.

CROCOTIUM: Well, are you coming, or not?

GELASIMUS: Of course I'm coming. Go home and tell her I'm on the way now. Hurry! (*To himself, as* CROCOTIUM *goes into* EPIGNOMUS' *house*) I wonder why she sent for me. She never did that before—no, sir, not since her husband left. What in the world can it be? Well, it won't cost anything to see what she wants. (*Looking down the street*) Oh! There's her lackey Pinacium. Just look at that. Look at the attitude the boy's striking. Isn't it cute? My, my, just like in a picture! Gad, that fellow doesn't do so badly, either. Many a time he's ladled the wine out in little cups in the loveliest manner.

Act Two.   Scene I

(*Enter* PINACIUM, *with fishing equipment.*)

PINACIUM (*skipping along and singing*):
    The messenger of Jove ne'er brought his sire
        Such news of joy as to my dame I bring.
    With gladsomeness and glee my heart's afire;
        My mood forbids that I do aught but sing.

    I am the messenger of news so bright,
        My heart with mirth and music overflows.
    Trip it, Pinacium, prove with footstep light
        You've reached the height where fame, where glory
           glows.

Now you can give your mistress help in need
Before her lord Epignomus' return.
As a good wife she loves her lord indeed
And for his coming all her senses burn.

Oho! Pinacium, dance and trip and sing;
Heed not another's wondering, questioning glance.
Push him aside and let your laughter ring,
E'en though he be a king that blocks your dance.

GELASIMUS (*aside*): Now what the hell has gotten into Pinacium that
makes him skip along in such a carefree way? Why, he's carrying a
fishing rod and some tackle.

PINACIUM (*coming to a stop and reflecting to himself*): You know, I
believe it'd be better if my mistress would send me some envoys with
gifts of gold and chariots to carry me—after all, she's the one that's
asking for the news. I simply can't proceed any farther on foot. So I'm
going back to where I came from. (*He returns to his starting point*) To
my way of thinking, it's her business to come to me. I guess she thinks
that what I know is nothing at all. Well, the news I'm bringing from
the harbour is so good, the gladness so great, that my mistress herself,
unless she knew of it, would scarcely dare to ask the gods for it. And
is this the unattended reception I get? I hope not. It's certainly not
cricket! It would really seem better if she'd come herself and meet me
and beg for my news. A lucky person like me has every right to be
proud. (*Pausing*) Yet, come to think of it, how would she know I knew
this? I guess in the long run it'd be better to return and tell her the
whole story. This way I'll relieve her of a lot of worry, and at the same
time I'm strengthening her bliss, I'll be lengthening my ancestral record
of good deeds. (*With more self-confidence*) Why, I'll make the prowess
of Agamemnon's herald look like nothing. Messengers? I'll outdo them
all. And at the same time I can keep in practice for the Olympic games.
(*Starting to run*) But this place won't do! The track's too short, damn
it! (*Arriving at* EPIGNOMUS' *house*) Oho! The door's shut. Well, I'll go
and knock. (*He beats on the door*) Get this door open! Hurry up! Hey,
get a move on in there! Come on, open up and stop fooling around. God,
but they're slow! Just see how long I've been standing here knocking!
Are you taking a nap or something in there? I know what I'll do—see
which is the stronger, the door or my elbows and feet. Whew! I wish
this door had run away from home; it would sure catch it from me
then. (*He pounds until he's exhausted*) Can't pound any more—all

worn out! Just one last crack! (*He gives the door all he's got*) There, take that!

GELASIMUS (*aside*): Hm-m! I'll just go up and say "Hello" to him. (*To* PINACIUM) Good morning.

PINACIUM: Good morning, yourself.

GELASIMUS (*searching for a subject of conversation*): So you've turned fisherman, eh?

PINACIUM: How long ago didn't you eat?

GELASIMUS (*ignoring* PINACIUM's *rudeness*): Where have you been? (*Looking at the basket*) What d'ye have there? Why the hurry?

PINACIUM: None of your business.

GELASIMUS: What's in that basket?

PINACIUM: Snakes for your dinner.

GELASIMUS: Say, what's eating you?

PINACIUM: If you had any manners, you'd let me alone.

GELASIMUS (*infuriated*): Can't I get the truth out of you?

PINACIUM: Sure. You aren't going to eat today.

Act Two.   Scene II

(*Enter* PANEGYRIS *from the house.* PINACIUM *steps aside.*)

PANEGYRIS: Heavens, who's breaking down the door? Where is he? (*She sees only* GELASIMUS) Oh, so you're the culprit, you're the heavy artillery, eh?

GELASIMUS (*pleasantly*): Good morning. At your service, ma'am!

PANEGYRIS: Some service, I must say, battering down my door like that.

GELASIMUS: Don't blame me. Your own servant did it. I was merely coming here to see what you wanted with me. And I really took pity on this poor door.

PINACIUM (*ironically*): And so you attempted to save it.

PANEGYRIS: Who's that? He sounded quite close to us.

PINACIUM: Pinacium.

PANEGYRIS: Where is he?

PINACIUM (*stepping up*): Give me your attention, Panegyris, and get rid of that penniless parasite.

PANEGYRIS (*shocked*): Pinacium!

PINACIUM: That's what my forefathers christened me.

PANEGYRIS: What are you doing?

PINACIUM: You're asking what I'm doing?

PANEGYRIS (*growing impatient*): Well, why not?

PINACIUM (*indifferently*): What have you to do with me?

PANEGYRIS: Oh, getting high hat, you rascal? Pinacium, speak to me this instant!

PINACIUM: Then order my guards to let me go.

PANEGYRIS: What guards?

PINACIUM: You're asking me? Weariness has me completely in her clutches.

PANEGYRIS: Well, it's quite evident that it's not holding your tongue.

PINACIUM (*somewhat downhearted*): Golly, how I did run, coming back from the port, just for your sake!

PANEGYRIS (*eagerly*): And you've got some good news?

PINACIUM: And how! You just can't imagine the news I've got.

PANEGYRIS: Oh, I'm saved.

PINACIUM: And I'm dead. Fatigue has sucked up the very marrow of my bones.

GELASIMUS: Hell, what about me? Hunger's chewed up the very marrow of my belly.

PANEGYRIS: And did you meet anyone?

PINACIUM: Oh, many people.

PANEGYRIS: The man?[8]

PINACIUM: Hundreds of them. But among all of them there wasn't a single one more worthless than this fellow. (*Indicating* GELASIMUS.)

GELASIMUS (*furious*): Is that so? I've had enough of his insults. Now listen here, if you annoy me again—

PINACIUM: Yes, I know. You'll stay very hungry.

GELASIMUS (*subsiding*): I'll persuade myself to think you're speaking the truth.

PINACIUM (*to* PANEGYRIS, *officiously*): This place must be cleaned up. (*Calling to the servants within*) Hey, in there, bring out some brooms and a long stick, too. I want to ruin the spiders' webs and sweep them all down.

GELASIMUS: Why, the poor things will freeze after that.

PINACIUM: What? You think they're in the same boat as yourself, with only one suit of clothes, eh? (*As the slaves bring out the brooms*) Here, take that broom.

GELASIMUS (*obeying*): Oh, well, all right.

PINACIUM (*sweeping*): I'll work here, you take care of that side.

GELASIMUS: I'll do it.

PINACIUM (*calling at the door*): Will someone bring out a bucket of water?

GELASIMUS (*aside*): He's a regular Director of Public Health and Sanitation without being elected.

PINACIUM (*handing the bucket to* GELASIMUS): Now, you hurry up and paint the ground; sprinkle in front of the house.

GELASIMUS: Yes, sir.

PINACIUM: It ought to be finished by now. Here, I'll knock the spiders off the door and walls. (*He seizes the pole and does so.*)

GELASIMUS (*to* PANEGYRIS): This is housecleaning time, all right.

PANEGYRIS: I can't make this out at all. Perhaps some guests are coming.

PINACIUM (*to the servants within*): You cover the couches!

GELASIMUS (*aside*): Well, that's a good start. Dinner couches, eh?

PINACIUM (*calling orders as he chases spiders*): Some of you cut wood! And clean the fish here in my basket, some of you! (*To others*) Your job'll be to get down the ham and the sweetbreads.

GELASIMUS (*delighted*): Golly, but that chap knows how to do things.

PANEGYRIS (*to* PINACIUM): Goodness! You don't pay much attention to your mistress, do you?

PINACIUM: I do, too. I've let everything else go just to accommodate you.

PANEGYRIS: What about the errand, then, that I sent you to the harbour on? Come on, tell me.

PINACIUM (*still engaged with the spiders*): All right. When you sent me down to the harbour, the radiant sun was just rising out of the sea. I was asking the customs collectors there if any ship had come in from Asia and they said no; just at that moment I spied a Cyprian vessel. Gee, I don't think I've ever seen a bigger one. With full sail she came right into port, riding on a fair breeze. Well, we were asking each other whose ship it might be and what its cargo was, when I noticed your husband Epignomus and his slave on board.

PANEGYRIS (*excited*): What's that you say? Epignomus?

PINACIUM: Your husband.

GELASIMUS (*aside*): And my happiness!

PINACIUM: I tell you, he's come.

PANEGYRIS: Did you really see him yourself?

PINACIUM: I sure did! And you should've seen the silver and gold that ship's carrying.

GELASIMUS: Hurrah! Wonderful! (*With renewed vigour*) By gad, I'll certainly use the broom now. With pleasure! (*He sweeps furiously.*)

PINACIUM: And a great quantity of wool and purple cloth.

GELASIMUS (*aside*): Just the thing to keep my belly warm.

PINACIUM: And ivory and golden couches.

GELASIMUS (*aside*): Oh, how royally I'll recline at banquets!

PINACIUM: Then too, he's got Babylonian goods on board, rich carpets and tapestries—a whole cargo of fine stuff.

GELASIMUS (*aside*): This is too damned wonderful for words!

PINACIUM: Yes, and to continue, he's bringing lute girls and flute girls and harp girls. And are they beautiful!

GELASIMUS (*aside*): Splendid! After I tipple, I'll trifle. That's just when I'm at my best.

PINACIUM: And then, he's brought quantities of perfume of various kinds.

GELASIMUS (*aside*): No jokes for sale now! The auction's all off! I've become an heir. To hell with those rascally auction-goers! Nice going, Hercules, for the increase in tithes I promised you. There's some hope now of getting that dastardly Hunger of mine out of my belly.

PINACIUM (*looking at* GELASIMUS): Oh, yes, and I forgot to say, he's brought some parasites along with him.

GELASIMUS (*suddenly deflated*): Ouch! I'm sunk!

PINACIUM: And they're very clever, too.

GELASIMUS: Damn it! I'll unsweep all the sweeping I've done.

PANEGYRIS: Did you see my sister's husband, Pamphilippus?[9]

PINACIUM: No.

PANEGYRIS: Didn't he come back?

PINACIUM: Yes, Epignomus said he came back at the same time. But I rushed back here as quick as I could to announce this nice scoop of news.

GELASIMUS (*aside*): The jokes I just took off the market are back on sale again. Those horrible people can again rejoice at my downfall. Hercules, you've certainly messed this up. Infallibility of the gods— humph!

PANEGYRIS: Go inside, Pinacium, and bid the servants prepare the altar for me to make a sacrifice. (*To* GELASIMUS, *as* PINACIUM *goes in*) And good-bye to you, sir!

GELASIMUS: Don't you want me to assist in the arrangements?

PANEGYRIS: No, thank you; I have enough servants inside. (*She goes into the house.*)

GELASIMUS (*to himself*): Well, Gelasimus, old boy, things look pretty dark for you now, if the one brother isn't here and the other who has come doesn't help any. I'll go back home and learn some flashes of wit from my books. If I don't get rid of those parasites he's bringing, I'm just plain sunk! (GELASIMUS *departs sadly.*)

Act Three.   Scene I

(*Enter* EPIGNOMUS *and* STICHUS, *followed by music girls and slaves.*)

EPIGNOMUS (*reverently*): To Neptune and the goddesses of weather I am gratefully indebted for my prosperous and safe return home. And thanks to Mercury also, who helped me in my business and quadrupled my wealth with the profits. (*Looking towards his house*) Those whom I made to grieve when I went away will now rejoice at my arrival. I've already met my father-in-law Antipho and have returned again into his good graces—a good example of what money can do. When he sees that I've returned in triumph and am bringing home with me a great deal of wealth, he greets me in friendly fashion right there on the vessel. No mediating party, either! And today he's scheduled to have dinner with my brother and me. Both of us were in the same port yesterday but my ship set out a little bit earlier this morning. (*Advancing towards the door of his house*) Come on, Stichus, lead these girls inside that I've brought back with me.

STICHUS: Sir, whether I mention this or not, I know you're aware of all the hardships I've endured along with you. Now I wish I could have just this one day of respite from those many miseries. This is the day of my homecoming, and it's fitting I celebrate a thanksgiving feast.

EPIGNOMUS: What you're demanding is but fair and just. You may have it, Stichus. I won't bother you all day. Go where you like and do what you please. For my part, I'll set you up with a jug of old wine.

STICHUS: Grand! I'll have a girl friend for the day.

EPIGNOMUS: Ten, if you like—but the bill'll be yours.

STICHUS: Just one thing more—

EPIGNOMUS: What is the one thing? Tell me.

STICHUS: May I go out to dinner?

EPIGNOMUS: Oh, I think so, if you're invited.

STICHUS: Gee, sir! This is neat! Invitation or not, I really don't care.

EPIGNOMUS: Where are you dining today?

STICHUS: Look, here's the story. My girl Stephanium lives next door. She's your brother's maid. Well, she and I have reserved a table at a dinner party given at her fellow slave's, Sangarinus the Syrian's, going Dutch, of course. She's seeing both of us; we're rivals, all right.

EPIGNOMUS: Well, first help bring these girls inside. Then the day's all yours. (EPIGNOMUS *goes into his house.*)

STICHUS (*calling after him*): I'll take the blame, if I don't paint the town red. (*To himself*) Well, I guess I'll cross over through the garden to my sweetheart and move in for the night. I'll pay my share and leave orders for a dinner to be cooked at Sangarinus'. Or else I'll go and provide the provisions myself. I'm sure that Sangarinus will soon arrive with his master. The servant who doesn't get to a dinner party on time deserves a good beating. He'd soon beat it home on time, then. I must see now that all's prepared. Gee, I'm taking too much time. (*To the audience*) You good people mustn't be amazed that we slaves drink, love, and arrange dinner parties. It's perfectly legal in Athens. (*To himself*) But come to think of it, this house has another door in the back, and they use the back part of the house more anyway. I'll go that way for the provisions and return with them the same way. There's a pathway connecting the houses; it runs through the garden. (*To the retinue*) Come on, everybody, follow me! (*Aside*) Boy, what I won't make of this day! (*All go into* EPIGNOMUS' *house.*)

Act Three.   Scene II

(*Enter* GELASIMUS *with renewed confidence.*)

GELASIMUS (*to himself*): I've been looking through my books, and I'm positive I can hold on to my patron with my jokes. Now I'll take a peep to see if he's arrived from the harbour yet. That'll give me a chance to captivate him with my stories and jokes as soon as he arrives.

(*Enter* EPIGNOMUS *from his house.*)

EPIGNOMUS (*looking down the street*): Why, that's the parasite Gelasimus I see coming towards me. That's just who it is.

GELASIMUS (*to himself, not seeing* EPIGNOMUS): When I left the house, all indications were for a prosperous day. Right in front of me, I saw a weasel grab off a mouse. That certainly prophesies something—prosperity, no doubt! This is the way I interpret it: just as the weasel found its daily bread, I hope to get mine, too. There you have it! (*Looking towards the house*) Why, that's Epignomus standing over there. (*He rushes towards him*) Oh, Epignomus, how glad I am to see you back! Oh, how I must weep for joy over you! Have you been keeping well?

EPIGNOMUS (*somewhat coldly*): I've felt fine, thanks.

GELASIMUS: Here's to your health, with a full—belly.

EPIGNOMUS: That's very kind of you. May the gods fulfill your wish!

GELASIMUS: I'd like to dine with you, to celebrate your safe homecoming.

EPIGNOMUS (*pretending to misunderstand*): Well, actually, I'm already engaged. Thanks just the same, though.

GELASIMUS: Well, promise it.

EPIGNOMUS: It's all settled.

GELASIMUS: Oh, come on, promise!

EPIGNOMUS: It's a thing that can't be changed.

GELASIMUS: I'll be simply thrilled, honest I will!

EPIGNOMUS: I know that. When the proper occasion comes, I'll see to it.

GELASIMUS: It's an occasion right now.

EPIGNOMUS: I can't do it, I tell you.

GELASIMUS: Why do you refuse me? Come on, give in! I'm all ready now.

EPIGNOMUS: Oh, go on; you run along and pick up another guest for yourself today.

GELASIMUS: Why don't you promise?

EPIGNOMUS: If I could, I'd not refuse.

GELASIMUS: Well, I certainly promise you one thing. I'll be charmed to accept, if you should promise.

EPIGNOMUS: Good-bye. (*He turns to go inside.*)

GELASIMUS (*holding him*): Is it really all arranged?

EPIGNOMUS: Yes, it's arranged, all right. I shall dine at home.

GELASIMUS: Well, since you won't promise to come to my place, and since this line of argument doesn't get us anywhere, I'll try another approach. I'll speak right out. Do you wish me to come to your house for dinner?

EPIGNOMUS: Yes, if I could; but nine strangers are coming to dine with me.

GELASIMUS: Oh, I don't have to be accommodated on a couch. You know I'm well acquainted with the bench.

EPIGNOMUS: But these guests are public orators, outstanding gentlemen, who have come from Ambracia as ambassadors of their people.

GELASIMUS: All the more reason you should place these eminent statesmen at the highest part of the table, and a low-down person like me at the lowest.

EPIGNOMUS: It'd be out of the question for you to be admitted in the presence of orators.

GELASIMUS: Heavens, I'm an orator myself, but business is bad. Perhaps there will be some leavings tomorrow—

EPIGNOMUS (*interrupting*): Good-bye. (*He goes into the house.*)

GELASIMUS (*to himself*): Oh, I'm ruined, utterly ruined! No doubt about it! The world's smaller than before by one Gelasimus. I've made up my mind never to trust a weasel again. Why, there never was a more shifty beast—it just slinks around from place to place ten times a day. Was I so foolish as to base my auspices on this creature, when it was a matter of life and death? The only thing to do now is to summon my friends and figure out by what statute I must—starve to death. (GELASIMUS *departs.*)

Act Four.   Scene I

(*Enter* ANTIPHO *and* PAMPHILIPPUS *from the direction of harbour.*)

ANTIPHO: The gods bless me and preserve my daughters for me, Pamphilippus! I'm certainly glad to see that you and your brother have both returned here to your native land, and that your affairs have turned out so well.

PAMPHILIPPUS (*rather coldly*): I'd want a bond from you, Antipho, if I didn't see that you were friendly towards me. But now that I find you're friendly, I'll trust your sincerity.

ANTIPHO: I'd ask you in to dinner, but your brother told me, when he invited me to his place, that you also were to dine with him today. It would have been much more appropriate for me to have been the host to you two than for me to be his guest. But I don't want to offend him. Nor do I want to win your favour merely with words; tomorrow you'll both come to my house along with your wives.

PAMPHILIPPUS: Then to mine the following day. He already asked me yesterday to come today. Well, Antipho, I've made my peace with you at last, eh?

ANTIPHO: Since you've been as successful as you and your friends could wish, all is peace and harmony between us now. After all, you know, a man's financial status largely governs the number of his friends. If he is secure financially, his friends will likewise be secure. But if his finances begin to totter, his friends totter also. Friends and wealth go hand in hand.

(*Enter* EPIGNOMUS *from his house.*)

EPIGNOMUS (*calling to those inside*): I'll soon be back. (*To himself*) It's a great pleasure, when you've been away from home for a long time, to return and find nothing to annoy you. My wife has taken care of my household during my absence in such a way that she's stripped me completely clean—of anything annoying. (*Seeing the others*) But look, there's Pamphilippus walking along with his father-in-law.

PAMPHILIPPUS: How's everything, Epignomus?

EPIGNOMUS: How about yourself? How long since you put into port?

PAMPHILIPPUS: Not long after you.

EPIGNOMUS: And now he (*indicating* ANTIPHO) is calm and peaceful, eh?

ANTIPHO: More so than the sea you two have crossed.

EPIGNOMUS: You haven't changed much! (*To* PAMPHILIPPUS) Say, brother, shall we unload the ship today?

PAMPHILIPPUS: Come, come, not so fast! Let's have a good time instead, and take a load on for a change. How soon will dinner be ready? I went without lunch today.

EPIGNOMUS: Come on inside and take a bath.

PAMPHILIPPUS: I'm headed home to do my duty by the gods and my wife. When I've attended to what I want, I'll drop over here right away.

EPIGNOMUS: But wait, your wife's bustling about inside here with her sister.

PAMPHILIPPUS: So much the better; there'll be less delay. I'll be here in a moment. (*He starts towards his house.*)

ANTIPHO (*stopping him*): Before you leave, I want to tell Epignomus a little fable, while you're still here.

PAMPHILIPPUS: By all means.

ANTIPHO: Once upon a time there was an old man—just like me. He had two daughters—just as I have. They were married to two brothers —just as mine are to you.

EPIGNOMUS (*to* PAMPHILIPPUS): I wonder where this fable is going to end.

ANTIPHO: The younger brother had a lute girl and a flute girl, imported from abroad—(*looking at* EPIGNOMUS)—just as you do. The old man was a widower—just like me.

EPIGNOMUS (*amused*): Go on, go on! (*To* PAMPHILIPPUS) This fable certainly has plenty of point.

ANTIPHO: Then the old man addressed the brother who owned the flute girl—just as I'm addressing you—

EPIGNOMUS: Continue! I'm all ears.

ANTIPHO: "I gave you my daughter," he said, "to provide you with entertainment at nighttime. Now it seems but right that I receive a girl from you to pass the night with."

EPIGNOMUS: Who says that? The one just like you?

ANTIPHO: Yes, just as I'm saying it to you. "Why, I'll give you two," the young man said, "if one isn't enough. And if two aren't sufficient, the number'll be raised to four."

EPIGNOMUS: Now I wonder who says that. The one just like me?

ANTIPHO: The very one who's just like you. Then the old man—just like me—continued: "Give me four of them, if you're willing, by all means, provided you throw in the grub so that they don't plunder my pantry."

EPIGNOMUS: Just imagine an old man so stingy as to say that—to demand food of the fellow who's contributing the girls.

ANTIPHO: Just imagine a young man so unfair as to deny even a grain of wheat when he was asked. Heavens! That old man was only doing the right thing; he had given his daughter a dowry, and he should get one for his flute girl.

EPIGNOMUS: Hm-m! That young man was certainly clever to refuse to give an endowered concubine to the old man.

ANTIPHO: The old man wanted to fix up the matter about the food, if he could. Well, he wasn't successful. So he said he wanted to close the deal under any circumstances. "Closed," said the young man. "Very kind of you," said the old man, "Are we agreed?" says he; "I'm ready to comply," says the other. (*Turning towards* EPIGNOMUS' *house*) But now I'm going in and congratulate my daughters on your arrival. Then I'll go and take a Turkish bath—a good way to reduce my yearage, you know. After my bath I'll be at dinner, reclining in leisure. (ANTIPHO *goes into* EPIGNOMUS' *house.*)

PAMPHILIPPUS (*laughing*): What a masterpiece that Antipho is! A damned good story he told, all right! Even now the old rascal takes himself for a youngster. He can have a girl—to sing him to sleep at night. Frankly, I don't see what else he could do with one. (*Changing the subject*) But how's our parasite Gelasimus getting along? Still in good health?

EPIGNOMUS: I saw him just a few minutes ago.

PAMPHILIPPUS: How's he conducting himself?

EPIGNOMUS: Hungrily as ever.

PAMPHILIPPUS: Why didn't you ask the man to dinner?

EPIGNOMUS: Hell, I don't want to go into bankruptcy on my arrival. (*Spies* GELASIMUS *down the street*) Well, there he is! The wolf in the story! Right here before our eyes, anxious to eat.

PAMPHILIPPUS: Let's kid him along.

EPIGNOMUS: You took the words right out of my mouth.

Act Four.   Scene II

(*Enter* GELASIMUS.)

GELASIMUS (*to the audience*): Now to take up where I left off—since I left here, I've taken counsel with my friends and relatives. They strongly advise me to cut my throat today—with my appetite. But wait, is that Pamphilippus I see with his brother Epignomus? Why, it certainly is. I'll accost him. (*Rushing up to them*) O Pamphilippus, how I've longed for you! The life of my life! The joy of my salvation! How are you? Golly, I'm glad you've returned home.

PAMPHILIPPUS: A cordial greeting to you, Gelasimus.

GELASIMUS: You've been well, I hope?

PAMPHILIPPUS: I've felt fine, thanks.

GELASIMUS: Gad, I'm delighted to hear it. Gad, how I'd like to have a thousand bushels of silver right now!

EPIGNOMUS: What would you do with it?

GELASIMUS: I'd invite him (*pointing to* PAMPHILIPPUS) to dinner, and not you.

EPIGNOMUS: You're only spoiling your own chances—saying such a thing.

GELASIMUS: Well, then, I'd invite you both. Actually, it's not my bad intentions that keep me from inviting you to my house, but I just haven't got a thing at home. You're well aware of that, no doubt.

EPIGNOMUS: By Jove, I'd love to invite you, but I haven't any room left.

GELASIMUS: Oh, it wouldn't hurt any for me to stand. I can take it—down to my stomach.

EPIGNOMUS: No, but there's a chance—

GELASIMUS (*eagerly*): What's that?

EPIGNOMUS: A chance, when the guests are gone, that you may come—

GELASIMUS: To hell with you!

EPIGNOMUS: That you may come and wash the dishes.

GELASIMUS: The devil take you! (*With renewed hope*) What do you have to say, Pamphilippus?

PAMPHILIPPUS: Why, I've already promised to dine out.

GELASIMUS: What? Dine out?

PAMPHILIPPUS: Certainly. Dine out.

GELASIMUS: How the devil can a tired man like you want to dine out?

PAMPHILIPPUS: Do you have a better suggestion?

GELASIMUS: Sure. Why don't you order supper cooked at home and retract your acceptance?

PAMPHILIPPUS (*surprised*): I should dine at home alone?

GELASIMUS: Oh, no, not alone; invite me.

PAMPHILIPPUS: Why, he'd be highly indignant, especially when he's entertaining on my account.

GELASIMUS: It's very simple, you know, to get yourself excused. Follow my advice, have the dinner prepared at home.

EPIGNOMUS: I won't put up with his deceiving that man today.

GELASIMUS: Is this any of your business? Do you think I don't see what you're up to? (*To* PAMPHILIPPUS) Now look here, take care of yourself! That man there is trying to wolf your estate. You know how men are assaulted in the streets at night.

PAMPHILIPPUS: Well, I guess I must order more attendants to accompany and defend me.

EPIGNOMUS (*to* GELASIMUS): He won't go now, he just won't, and it's your fault for urging him not to go out.

GELASIMUS (*to* PAMPHILIPPUS): All you need to do is to go home and order a dinner promptly cooked up for me and you and your wife. Do that and you won't complain of being deceived.

PAMPHILIPPUS: Well, Gelasimus, I'm afraid that you'll have to go hungry during our dinner party this evening.

GELASIMUS: Then you really are going out to dinner?

PAMPHILIPPUS: Yes, with my brother next door.

GELASIMUS: It's all settled?

PAMPHILIPPUS: All settled.

GELASIMUS: God, but I hope you get pelted with a stone!

PAMPHILIPPUS: I'm not afraid. I'll go through the garden and won't appear in public.

EPIGNOMUS: What d'ye say, Gelasimus?

GELASIMUS: Oh, you've invited statesmen—you can have 'em.

EPIGNOMUS: But this concerns you.

GELASIMUS: Well, if it really does concern me, I'm ready.

EPIGNOMUS: By Jove! You know, I believe there may still be room for one like you to lie in.

PAMPHILIPPUS: There's no question in my mind; it should be done.

GELASIMUS (*again hopeful*): Oh, you light of the community!

EPIGNOMUS: That is, if you're able to squeeze yourself in.

GELASIMUS: Why, even between iron bars. Just a teeny, weeny bit of space, enough for a puppy-dog—that's enough space for me.

EPIGNOMUS: I'll arrange it some way or other. Come along.

GELASIMUS (*as they pass* EPIGNOMUS' *door*): In here?

EPIGNOMUS: Oh, no, in jail. You certainly wouldn't better yourself in here. (*To* PAMPHILIPPUS) Come on now, let's go.

PAMPHILIPPUS: I'm just going to do service to the gods. Then I'll be right over to your house. (PAMPHILIPPUS *goes into his own house.*)

GELASIMUS: Well, where do we go now?

EPIGNOMUS: Man, I've already told you—you're headed for the jail.

GELASIMUS (*resignedly*): If you order it, I'll go even there.

EPIGNOMUS: Great Jehoshaphat! This fellow would be resigned to an execution, if there were a dinner or a lunch in the offing.

GELASIMUS: That's the way I am. I'm willing to fight with any damned thing except hunger.

EPIGNOMUS: As long as you were our parasite, my brother and I were broke.

GELASIMUS: I'm not to go to your house?

EPIGNOMUS: No. I've seen enough of your brand of good luck. I don't want any donkey like you making a monkey out of me. (EPIGNOMUS *goes into his house.*)

GELASIMUS (*to himself*): They're gone, all gone! Oh, Gelasimus, take counsel with thyself. Me? Yes, thee. With myself? With thyself. Behold the high cost of living! Behold the passing of man's altruism and humanitarianism! Yea, even see how the labour of clowns availeth nothing, and their very vocations are exploited. Never, by Jove, shall anyone gaze upon me tomorrow as a living man. For now I'll load my throat with a dose of hempen rope. I'll keep 'em from saying "he died of hunger." (GELASIMUS *trudges dolefully down the street.*)

Act Five.   Scene I

(*Enter* STICHUS *from* PAMPHILIPPUS' *house with a table and benches. He puts them down somewhat unsteadily, and looks around.*)

STICHUS (*to himself*): It's certainly very funny, to my way of thinkin', that people keep lookin' out for someone they're waitin' for, 'specially, by Jove, when the person they want doesn't come any faster for all that. Well, I guess I'm in the same boat, waitin' here for Sangarinus. He won't come a bit faster, even so. If that fellow doesn't come soon, I'll have my party all alone by myself. Soon as I bring that jug of wine out here from my house, I'll take my seat. The day's meltin' away like snow, damn it! (*He goes into* EPIGNOMUS' *house.*)

Act Five.   Scene II

(*Enter* SANGARINUS *from the direction of the harbour.*)

SANGARINUS (*lightheartedly*): Hail, Athens, thou queen-mother of Greece! How glad I am to see this city, the longed-for abode of my master. My only thought is my sweetheart Stephanium; I wonder how she is and what she's doing. However, I gave orders to Stichus to say "hello" for me and to tell her I'd arrive today, so she'd get the dinner ready in time. But look, there's Stichus now!

(*Enter* STICHUS, *carrying his jug which is no longer full.*)

STICHUS (*to himself*): Nice goin', master; you certainly did well to give your servant Stichus this gift. Oh boy, oh boy, oh boy! I bear the pleasures of the world in this jug—yes, sir—the laughter, jokes, kisses, dances, endearments, good fellowship—all of 'em, right here in the jug.

SANGARINUS: Stichus!

STICHUS (*seeing the other*): Oho!

SANGARINUS: How're you doing?

STICHUS: Wunnerful, Sangarinus, my charmin' fellow. I'm just bringin' you and me a companion—ole Bacchus himself. God, yes! The dinner's all cooked, the house's all ours—you see, the dinner party's at my master's house. Your master and his wife and Antipho are there with Epignomus, and—look at the gift I got. (*Handing him the jug.*)

SANGARINUS (*taking a long drink*): Who dreamed about gold?

STICHUS: What difference does that make to you? Go in now, hurry and get cleaned up.

SANGARINUS: I have cleaned up.

STICHUS: Fine! Follow me inside then.

SANGARINUS: I'm coming, all right.

STICHUS: Let's get completely soaked today. Away with those foreign customs! Let's stand by our native Athens. Follow me.

SANGARINUS: I'm coming. Such a homecoming as this pleases me. That foretaste certainly tasted good. (*They enter* PAMPHILIPPUS' *house.*)

Act Five.   Scene III

(*Enter* STEPHANIUM *from* EPIGNOMUS' *house.*)

STEPHANIUM (*to the audience*): Spectators, my purpose is not to confuse any of you, just because I come out of this house, when I really live there. (*Pointing to* PAMPHILIPPUS' *house*) I'll let you in on the secret. I was called here from home a little while ago, for after the arrival of the men was announced, we all had to hurry in here—covering couches and cleaning up the house, you know. Nevertheless, in the midst of this work, I kept in mind my two boy friends, Stichus and fellow-servant Sangarinus, and so managed to get their dinner cooked. Stichus got the food; I'm doing the rest. He also gave the orders. Now I'm leaving here and will attend to my sweet homecomers. (*She goes into* PAMPHILIPPUS' *house.*)

Act Five.   Scene IV

(*Enter* SANGARINUS *and* STICHUS, *laden with food. Both have obviously
had more to drink.*)

SANGARINUS: Come on, come on, bring it all outside. Form the dish
brigade! Stichus, I make you the Master of the Jug. I'm determined to
try all sorts of things with our banquet today. (*Putting the food on the
table*) Golly, but it's delightful for us to have it here! Whoever goes
by I want to be called in to give us a hand—with our merrymaking.

STICHUS: Tha's all right with me, jus' so everybody brings his own
wine. (*Pointing to his jug*) Nobody's gonta get jolly today from this
but us. Le's have another drink all alone by ourselves.

SANGARINUS: This is a banquet, I mus' say! Certainly ample, considering our resources, what with nuts, beans, figs, olives,[10] lupinulets, and
little pieces of pastry.

STICHUS: It's enough; 's better for a slave to do things modestly than
too liberally—jus' as his money permits. People with heaps of money
can drink out of ewers, tankards, and loving cups, but we mus' drink
from our ole Samian jug. (*Fondling the jug*) 'Sall right. We drink
jus' the same, we do our duties jus' as our wealth permits. (*They do
their duty by the jug.*)

SANGARINUS: Come now, decide where we're to lie.

STICHUS: You take the head of the table. And besides, so you'll know,
I'll split it up with you this way. See! You keep whichever territory
you wanna take now.

SANGARINUS: What tha' hell is this "territory" talk?

STICHUS: Well, do you prefer to take command of Water or of Wine?

SANGARINUS (*diving for the bench in front of the wine*): The wine,
of course—tha's very clear. But now, while our girl is delayin'[11] and
adornin' herself, le's have some fun ourselves. I appoint you General
Chief of Staff over this banquet.

STICHUS: Say, a charmin' thought jus' came to me. We're like the
Cynics; we're usin' benches instead of couches.

SANGARINUS (*stretching out*): Well, anyway, this is much nicer. But
in the meantime, General, why's this tankard failing us? Tell me, how
many cups do we have to a drink?

STICHUS: As many as the fingers on your hand. There's an old song about it:

> Pour either five or three;
> But four must never be.

SANGARINUS: Here's to your health! (*Preferring a stronger drink*) Say, if you're smart, you won't mix more than one-tenth water in that wine. (*They pour and drink.* SANGARINUS *bursts into song*)

> To you good luck—luck to us all;
> The best for you and me I call.
> The very best, Stephanium,
> We hope and pray on you will fall.

STICHUS: Well, drink, if you're goin' to drink!

SANGARINUS: Oh, I'm not backward. (*Drinking eagerly.*)

STICHUS (*drinking*): Golly, but thish party'sh complete. All we need'sh our lil sweetheart. Tha'sh all that ishn't here. Yeshir, thish's a cute lil party. Here'sh a cup for you; you've got the wine.

SANGARINUS: Say, I could do with a piece of steak.

STICHUS: Now if wha'sh here ishn't good enough for you, nothing will be good enough for you! Here, have some water.

SANGARINUS: Tha'sh a nice expresshun. Anyway, I don' care for dainties. (*He pours out a drink and hands it to the stage musician*) Have a drink, maestro! Well, come on, if you want it, drink 'er down! Don' be bashful. What the hell are you so particular about? You see you've got to drink it—go on, take it, I say. You won't have to pay for it; the government'll take care of all that. You shouldn't be so backward; jus' pull those pipes away from your mouth.

STICHUS (*noticing* SANGARINUS' *increasing unsteadiness*): When he'sh had 'ish drink, follow my 'xample or set yourshelf one. Don' wanna drink thish all up. Why, we'd be uselessh after that. My, my, thish jug gets empty fast.

SANGARINUS (*to the musician*): Now, what? Even though you were cautioush, it didn't hurt you. Come on now, maestro, you've had your drink; take up your pipes again! Lessee those cheeks swell out like a serpent! Come on, Stichus, whoever gets out of step paysh for a drink.

STICHUS: Tha'sh a wunnerful idea. We mush' obey a fair order like that.

SANGARINUS: All ri', then, watch me! (*He cuts a caper as the musician plays*) Now if you mix that number up, I get your drink.

STICHUS: Tha'sh a very fine and honesh' agreement. Watch, here'sh my first number! (*He makes an effort and dances and sings*)

> Neat and cute it is, pal—rivals, yet like brothers;
> One stein will do for both, boy—our maiden's one another's.
> Two hearts that beat as one, then—I'm you and you are I;
> If she's with you or she's with me no jealousy I spy.

(*They sing and dance around several times.*)

SANGARINUS: Oh, dear, tha'sh enough now. I don' wanna get tired of it. Le's play some other game.

STICHUS: How about callin' out our girl. She'll give ush a dance!

SANGARINUS: B-Brilliant idea!

STICHUS (*calling at the door*): Stephanium! Oh, you sweet, lovable, charmin' Stephanium, come on out to your sweethearts. You're bee-ootiful enough for me now.

SANGARINUS: He meansh super-super-bee-ootiful.

STICHUS: Come on out and make ush playful chaps still more playful.

SANGARINUS (*calling, as he and* STICHUS *support each other*): We're back and we've been waitin' for you to come out, Stephanium dear. Oh, you're sweet ash honey! If we're welcome and you like ush both, won't you come out?

Act Five.   Scene V

(*Enter* STEPHANIUM *in all her glory.*)

STEPHANIUM: I'm at your service, dears. As Venus loves me, I would've come out the same time you did, but I wanted to fix myself up 'specially just for you. But I suppose that's natural with a woman; after she's bathed and scrubbed and bedecked and massaged, she still feels a mess. A mistress can repel lovers by her sloppiness a lot easier than she can appeal to them by her daintiness.

STICHUS: Doesn't she say the cutest thingsh?

SANGARINUS: Her words are love inshpired.

STICHUS: Sangarinus, oh, Sangarinus!

SANGARINUS: Wha'sh the matter?

STICHUS: I'm achin' from head to foot.

SANGARINUS: Did ya say in the head? Now, ishn't that too bad?

STEPHANIUM: On which side shall I lie?

SANGARINUS: Which side d'ye want?

STEPHANIUM: I'd like to be beside both of you. You know, I love you both.

STICHUS: Humph! A run on the bank, so far ash I'm concerned.

SANGARINUS: And my freedom'sh all gone.

STEPHANIUM: Come, my dears, give me room to recline, if you want me.

STICHUS: Want you?

STEPHANIUM: I want to be with both of you.

STICHUS: Oh, dear! I'm hopelesshly losh'! (*To* SANGARINUS) Wha' about you?

SANGARINUS: Did you say something?

STICHUS: Heavensh! We can't get through the day without her dancing. (*To* STEPHANIUM) Come now, my lil honey-sweet, dance. I'll be your partner.

SANGARINUS (*struggling to his feet*): Hell, you won't get rid of me that way. I'll put on an act tha'sh a real act. I want to feel nish, too.

STEPHANIUM: Well, if I must dance, you'd better give the maestro something to drink.

STICHUS: Certainly—a drink for all of ush.

SANGARINUS: Here ya are, maestro, first of all. (*Pouring him a drink*) And as soon as you've drunk it, keep your old custom and quickly strike up some soft, sweet, seductive song. Just make us tingle to our very finger-tips. (*Passing the jug to* STICHUS) Here, put some water in it.

Act Five.   Scene VI

SANGARINUS (*to the musician*): Here, take thish. (*As the musician drinks it quickly*) That *wush* good, wushn't it? You didn't wait that time. (*To* STEPHANIUM) Jus' a minute, my little cutie, give me a kiss while he's drinkin'.

STICHUS: Hey, what are you tryin' to make out of her? A common whore? Nish girlsh shouldn't give kisses standin' up! Hurray! Hurray! Serves the thief right! (*He pushes them over and a chase ensues.*)

SANGARINUS (*to the musician*): Come on, maestro, puff out your cheeks. A sweet lil ditty now. Give us a new song for some old wine. (*There is a general melee on the stage.*)

Act Five.   Scene VII

SANGARINUS: What Ionian dancer or acrobat could equal this? (*He flies through the air in a great leap.*)

STICHUS (*recovering from a similar gymnastic gyration*): Well, what if you did beat me that time. Dare me again!

SANGARINUS: Come on, try this one. (*He turns a tremendous tailspin.*)

STICHUS: You—you, try this one! (*He takes a gigantic jump.*)

SANGARINUS: Hippity!

STICHUS: Skippity!

SANGARINUS: Rippity!

STICHUS: Whew!

SANGARINUS: Now, both together—calling all dancers, calling all dancers! We can't get along without this any more than a mushroom can without rain!

STICHUS (*exhausted*): Come on, let's go inside. We've danced enough for our wine! And you, good spectators, give us your applause and then have a party of your own at home.

1. Of the plays of Plautus, only the *Stichus* has the *didascalia,* or official notice of the production. A short fragment of the *didascalia* of the *Pseudolus* has survived.

2. This play was not the Menandrian original of Terence's comedy, *The Brothers.*

3. The Stichus was presented in November, in the year 200 B.C.

4. Literally, "for all the fabled mountains of Persia made of gold."

5. This passage is bracketed by Lindsay; it does not occur in the Ambrosian Palimpsest, the earliest of the Plautine manuscripts.

6. It is not certain that Crocotium enters at this point and remains on the stage unobserved during Gelasimus' entrance monologue. The instructions of Panegyris may be directed to Crocotium inside; if so, Crocotium enters at the end of Gelasimus' first speech.

7. Lindsay brackets this verse as a variant of the preceding line.

8. Panegyris means *virum* in the sense of "husband"; Pinacium understands it in the sense of "man."

9. Lindsay reads *Pamphilum* here.

10. The text of this verse is corrupt.

11. The text is corrupt here; *cessat,* the emendation of Goetz and Schoell, has been adopted.

XIX
THE THREE PENNY DAY

CHARACTERS IN THE PLAY

LUXURY and POVERTY, *who speak the Prologue*
MEGARONIDES, *an old gentleman of Athens*
CALLICLES, *his friend*
LYSITELES, *a young Athenian, son of* PHILTO
PHILTO, *father of* LYSITELES
LESBONICUS, *friend of* LYSITELES
STASIMUS, *slave of* LESBONICUS *and* CHARMIDES
CHARMIDES, *father of* LESBONICUS *and friend of* CALLICLES
A SWINDLER

ACROSTIC ARGUMENT

.   Charmides, going abroad, entrusts a buried treasure and all his affairs to his friend Callicles. During his absence his son squanders his property, and even sells their house; Callicles buys it. The young man's sister is asked in marriage, although she has no dowry. Callicles wishes to give the girl a dowry and so, to avoid criticism, he arranges for a man to say that he is bringing money from her father. When this man gets to the house, Charmides has already returned and has some fun with him. His children then marry.

INTRODUCTION

The Three Penny Day (the *Trinummus*) is based on *The Treasure* by Philemon. It is one of Plautus' quieter comedies and like *The Captives* portrays the actions of refined and virtuous people. There are no grotesque characterisations and no coarse jests. The comedy is far more Terentian than Plautine in its quiet humour and illustrates the wide variety of interest to be found in Plautus' plays. The work as a whole is even more sedate than *The Captives* for it has no parasite to interrupt the more serious action of the play and add a touch of farce to the proceedings.

The Three Penny Day is primarily a play of character rather than action. Charmides during his absence from home has entrusted the welfare of his children and his property to his friend Callicles. When Lesbonicus, the spendthrift son of Charmides, plans to sell his father's house, Callicles is forced to buy it, since Charmides has revealed to him the existence of a secret treasure there. Callicles' purchase is misunderstood by his neighbours, among them Megaronides. Lysiteles wants to marry Lesbonicus' sister, but without the usual dowry, and Philto, Lysiteles' father, agrees. These characters are all nice people and talk and act in a reasonable manner. Callicles is a devoted friend who looks after the interests of the absent Charmides, and Megaronides is worried about the reputation of Callicles. The play contains much moralising, especially on the part of the righteous Philto whose many "wise saws" are too numerous to be taken seriously. His son Lysiteles is an upright young man—almost painfully so—and his long *canticum* on love (Act Two, Scene I) recalls Philolaches' monody in *The Haunted House,* Act One, Scene II. Even the wasteful Lesbonicus has the financial welfare and the reputation of his sister at heart. Stasimus, the impudent slave, yearns for the return of Charmides before the old man's property is entirely consumed—somewhat inconsistently, since he has aided Lesbonicus in spending it.

The conflict in the play is between Lysiteles and Lesbonicus and concerns the dowry which Lesbonicus wants to give his sister; it is Callicles' desire to provide a dowry for the girl that leads to the one piece of trickery in the play—the hiring of a swindler who will pretend to come from Charmides with the money. The deception is not successful since Charmides returns unexpectedly from abroad and confronts his supposed messenger. This scene (Act Four, Scene II) is excellent and undoubtedly the most amusing in the play; the false messenger gives a fantastic account of his travels and thinks that the man he meets has "Charmidised" himself merely in order to get the money. The jests of Megaronides and Callicles about their wives and Stasimus' attempt to keep Philto from accepting Lesbonicus' farm also provide considerable humour.

The ending of the play is rather abrupt and it has been suggested that Plautus shortened the conclusion of his original. Certainly the marriage of Lesbonicus to the daughter of Callicles is sudden and unmotivated. Lysiteles, like Callidamates in *The Haunted House* (the original of which is also attributed to Philemon), secures pardon for his spendthrift friend. But Charmides' forgiveness is on a higher moral plane than that of Theopropides, who was won over chiefly by Callidamates' promise to pay for Philolaches' extravagances.

Although *The Three Penny Day* is far less characteristic of Plautus than many other comedies, it has been considered through the ages as one of its author's best works. It was the basis of Cecchi's *La Dote* (1550), Destouches' *Le Trésor Caché*, and Lessing's *Der Schatz* (1750). Colman's *The Man of Business* (1774) combined elements from *The Three Penny Day* and Terence's *Phormio*.

THE THREE PENNY DAY

(SCENE:—*A street in Athens in front of the houses of* CALLICLES *and* MEGARONIDES; LESBONICUS, *who has recently sold his father's house to* CALLICLES, *has reserved for himself an apartment in the rear with a private entrance; the house of* PHILTO *is nearby.*)

Prologue

(*Enter* LUXURY, *followed by* POVERTY.)

LUXURY: Follow me this way, my daughter, that you may do your duty.

POVERTY: I am following you, but I don't have any idea of our destination.

LUXURY (*halting in front of the house where* LESBONICUS *lives*): It's right here. See, this is the house. Go right in now. (POVERTY *enters the house, and* LUXURY *addresses the audience*) Now, that no one of you may be confused, I'll put you on the right track with a few words— that is, if you promise to give me your attention. And now, if you'll listen carefully, I'll tell you first of all who I am, and who the woman was that just went inside. In the first place, Plautus gave me the name Luxury, and he decided that this woman Poverty should be my daughter. But learn now why she entered this house at my suggestion, and give attentive ear while I inform you. There is a certain young man who lives in this house; with my assistance he has wasted his father's property. Since I see that he has nothing left with which to support me, I have given him my daughter to spend his life with. But don't expect me to give you the plot of this play; the old men who will appear on the stage will reveal the story to you. The name of this play in the original Greek is *The Treasure;* Philemon wrote it. Plautus translated it into a foreign tongue[1] and named it *The Three Penny Day,* and he asks of you that the play be

43

allowed to keep this name. That's all I have to say. Good-bye, and listen in silence. (LUXURY *departs.*)

Act One.　Scene I

(*Enter* MEGARONIDES, *somewhat troubled.*)

MEGARONIDES (*to himself*): To criticise a friend for a fault that deserves it is a thankless task, but there are times when it's useful and profitable. And so today I'm going to criticise a friend of mine soundly, for a fault that soundly deserves it; I do it unwillingly, but my honour wills that I do it. Why, a regular plague has attacked moral standards here, and almost all of them are half-dead already. And while they've been languishing, evil practices meanwhile have been springing up in abundance like well-watered plants. There isn't anything cheap these days except evil practices; but you can haul in a heavy harvest of them, all right. There's a group of men here who think they get a lot farther by gaining the favour of a few than by considering what's advantageous for all. In this way, sound practices are sacrificed to this gaining of favour which in many matters is a hateful hindrance, holding back both the public and private welfare.

Act One.　Scene II

(*Enter* CALLICLES *from his house.*)

CALLICLES (*to his wife inside*): I want our Household God to be honoured with a wreath. Pay him worship, my wife, that this house may prove to be happy, favourable, fortunate, and lucky for us—(*aside, as he closes the door*) and that I may see you dead and gone as soon as possible.

MEGARONIDES: This is the man that's become childish in his old age— committing a fault that deserves censure. I'll go up to him.

CALLICLES (*looking around*): Whose voice do I hear nearby?

MEGARONIDES: A well-wisher's, if you're the sort of person I want you to be; but if you aren't, it's the voice of an antagonist, and an angry one, at that.

CALLICLES: Good day, my friend and confrere! How are you feeling, Megaronides?

MEGARONIDES: Good day to you, Callicles, to be sure.

CALLICLES: Feeling well? Have you been well?

MEGARONIDES: Yes, I've been pretty well.

CALLICLES: What about your wife? Is she well?

MEGARONIDES: Better than I want her to be.

CALLICLES (*grinning*): I'm delighted for your sake, by Jove, that she is alive and well.

MEGARONIDES: Damn it! I suppose you're happy whenever I have any misfortune.

CALLICLES: Well, I want all my friends to have the same thing I have.

MEGARONIDES: Oho, you rogue! And how's your own wife?

CALLICLES: Immortal. She's alive and will keep right on living.

MEGARONIDES: Heavens! What wonderful news! I pray the gods that she may successfully survive you.

CALLICLES: My prayer exactly, by heavens—provided that she could be your wife.

MEGARONIDES: Do you want us to change wives? I take yours and you take mine? You wouldn't be cheating me a bit, I'll guarantee.

CALLICLES: Indeed! You'd have caught me off my guard, I suppose.

MEGARONIDES: You'd know damned soon what you'd done, I can assure you.

CALLICLES: Keep the one you've got. "The evil that we know is the best." If I should take one now that I don't know, I wouldn't know what to do.

MEGARONIDES: Right you are. "A happy life means a long life." (*More seriously*) But give me your attention and stop this silly nonsense. I'm coming here to see you for a special reason.

CALLICLES: What's that?

MEGARONIDES: To give you a good sound reprimanding, with many withering words.

CALLICLES (*innocently*): Me?

MEGARONIDES: There isn't anyone else here except you and me, is there?

CALLICLES (*looking around*): Not a soul.

MEGARONIDES: Then why do you ask if it's you I'm going to reprimand? Unless you think I'm going to berate myself. (*Losing his temper*) Look here! If your decent conduct of other days is decaying within you, [if you wish to change your character to different ways,]² or if different ways are altering that character of yours and you're giving up old ways and chasing after new ones, you'll infect all your friends with a painful ailment—they'll be sick at the sight and sound of you.

CALLICLES: What in the world has made you talk like this?

MEGARONIDES: Because all decent men and women ought to try to keep themselves clear of suspicion and guilt.

CALLICLES: They can't do both.

MEGARONIDES: What do you mean?

CALLICLES: You ask? I'm the keeper of my own conscience and I can shut out guilt; suspicion is stored in the mind of other people. Suppose now that I should suspect you of having stolen the crown from the head of the statue of Jupiter on the Capitoline, from the statue that stands on the very summit of the temple; if you hadn't done it, and still I wanted to suspect you of it, how could you prevent me from having my suspicions? But I'd like to know what's on your mind.

MEGARONIDES: Do you have any friend or acquaintance with sound common sense?

CALLICLES: Well, I'll tell you frankly; there are some I know to be friends, some I suspect of it, and some whose natures and feelings I can't understand well enough to tell whether they belong to my friends or my enemies. But you are the truest friend of all my true friends. If you know that I've done anything unwittingly or wrongfully and you don't accuse me of it, you're the one to be severely reprimanded.

MEGARONIDES: I realise that, and your complaint is just, if I've come here to you for any other reason.

CALLICLES: I'm awaiting whatever you have to say.

MEGARONIDES: Well, first of all, common gossip is saying nasty things about you everywhere; your fellow-citizens are calling you Filthylucregrabber; and then there are others, too, who are calling you an old vulture; they say you don't give a damn whether you devour foreigners or fellow-citizens. When I hear people say these things about you, I'm tortured and miserable.

CALLICLES: This is in my control, Megaronides, and then again it isn't. I can't keep them from saying it; I can keep them from saying it with justification.

MEGARONIDES: Was Charmides here a friend of yours?

CALLICLES: He was and still is. And to convince you that this is true, I'll give you this evidence. After this son of his squandered his property and Charmides realised that he was being plunged into poverty, his wife being dead and their daughter now a grown maiden, and since he was about to go on a trip to Seleucia, he entrusted to my care his unmarried daughter and all his affairs, and that worthless son of his. I hardly think he would have thought so much of me, if he hadn't been a friend of mine.

MEGARONIDES: Look here! About that young man that you see is worthless, who was entrusted to your care and keeping—why don't you reform him? Why don't you make him a decent citizen? It would have been a lot better to devote your efforts to that and to make him more virtuous, if you could, than for you to be a sharer in his ill-repute and to add your own wrongdoing to his.

CALLICLES: What have I done?

MEGARONIDES: What a rascal does.

CALLICLES: That's not my way.

MEGARONIDES: You bought this house from the young man, didn't you? Why are you silent? This house, I mean, where you're living now.

CALLICLES: I bought it, and paid the money for it, forty minae, to the young man himself.

MEGARONIDES: You gave him the money?

CALLICLES: Certainly, and I don't regret it.

MEGARONIDES (*angrily*): God! The rotten care the youth is entrusted to! So in this way you gave him a sword to kill himself with, eh? What's the difference? Isn't it just the same thing when you put money in the hands of a young man that's love-crazy and ungovernable, so that he can finish erecting the edifice of folly already begun?

CALLICLES: Shouldn't I have paid him the money?

MEGARONIDES: Of course not. You should neither buy anything of him, nor sell anything to him, nor give him any chance to become worse. You've cheated the fellow entrusted to your care, have you not, and driven out of his own house the father who put him in your keeping? (*In a disgusted tone*) Hell! Fine keeping that is! And wonderful care! Get this man to act as guardian; he's good at feathering his own nest!

CALLICLES (*calmly*): Megaronides, you overwhelm me with your accusations, and they're most unexpected; the result is that I must now entrust to you what was secretly trusted to my discretion, faith, and fidelity, something that I was to tell no living soul and not to let leak out.

MEGARONIDES: Anything trusted to me you'll pick up just where you laid it down.

CALLICLES: Look around and make sure that no one can overhear us. (MEGARONIDES *does so*) Look around again, I beg of you.

MEGARONIDES: I'm listening, if you have anything to say.

CALLICLES: If you'll keep quiet, I'll tell you. (*In a lower tone*) When Charmides was about to go abroad from here, he revealed to me a treasure in this house, buried here in a certain room. (*Anxiously*) But look around.

MEGARONIDES (*doing so again*): There's no one.

CALLICLES: It was about three thousand gold Philippeans. He and I were alone, and he begged me with tears in his eyes in the name of friendship and honour not to reveal this to his son nor to anyone else from whom word of it could leak out and get to him. Now if he returns here in safety, I'll restore his property to him; if anything should happen to him, I at least have the means to give a dowry to his daughter who was entrusted to my care, and I can manage to give her the sort of marriage she deserves.

MEGARONIDES: Ye immortal gods! How quickly with a few words you have made me a different person from the one that came to you! (*Eagerly*) But keep right on with your story, as you started.

CALLICLES: Why tell you how his wisdom and my loyalty and the whole secret were almost completely ruined by that worthless young rascal?

MEGARONIDES: How was that?

CALLICLES: I was away in the country for a mere six days; during my absence and without my knowledge, without even consulting me, he posted a sign and advertised the house for sale.

MEGARONIDES: Our wolf was all the more hungry and had his mouth open all the wider; he was watching for the dogs to go to sleep; he wanted to carry off the whole entire flock.

CALLICLES: By heaven, he'd have done it, too, if this old dog hadn't caught a scent of it first. But now I want to ask you something, in turn. What was it my duty to do? Let me know that. Was it right for me to reveal the treasure to him, contrary to what his father had begged me to do? Or was I to permit someone else to become the owner of the house? Wouldn't the money belong to the man who bought the house? Instead, I bought the house myself, I paid out the money on account of the treasure, so that I could turn it over intact to my friend. And so I really didn't buy the house for myself or for my own enjoyment; I bought it back again for Charmides, and paid for it out of my own pocket. This is my story. Whether I've acted rightly or wrongly, Megaronides, I admit that I've done this. Well, here are my misdeeds! Here is my avarice for you! It's on account of this that people spread slanderous reports about me.

MEGARONIDES: *Arrêtez-vous!* You've overwhelmed your reprimander; you've tied my tongue; I haven't a thing to say in reply.

CALLICLES: Now I beg you to assist me with word and deed and take a share in this task of mine.

MEGARONIDES: I promise you my assistance.

CALLICLES: Then where will you be a little later?

MEGARONIDES: At home.

CALLICLES: Anything else you wish?

MEGARONIDES: That you be faithful to your trust.

CALLICLES: With all sincerity. (*He prepares to depart.*)

MEGARONIDES (*calling after him*): But tell me this.

CALLICLES: What is it?

MEGARONIDES: Where's that young fellow living now?

CALLICLES: He reserved an apartment in the rear, when he sold the house.

50   *Plautus*   [195-229]

MEGARONIDES: Just what I wanted to know. Go on now. (*Calling again*) But tell me this. What about the girl now? At your house, I suppose?

CALLICLES: That's right. I'm taking as good care of her as of my own daughter.

MEGARONIDES: That's the right way to act.

CALLICLES: Anything else you want to ask me before I leave? (*He goes into his house.*)

MEGARONIDES (*calling after him*): Good-bye. (*To himself*) There's certainly nothing more silly or stupid, more smooth-tongued or gossipy, more impudent-tongued or perjured than these everlasting city folk that they call dandies. Yes, and I set myself down in one and the same category with them, for I believed the false tales of those fellows who pretend to know everything and who actually know nothing. Why, they know what everyone has in his mind or is going to have; they know what the king has whispered in the ear of the queen; they even know what Juno has talked about with Jupiter. Things that don't exist and never will—they still know them all. They don't give a damn whether truly or falsely they praise or blame anyone they wish, provided they know what they choose to know. Everybody was saying that Callicles here didn't deserve to be a citizen or to be alive, since he had stripped this young man of his property. And after hearing the words of these tattle-tales, I went rushing forth in my ignorance to rebuke an innocent friend. The authority for each tale they tell ought to be traced to its very source; and if there isn't any authority, then the talebearer should be fined and punished; if this were done, the general public would be a lot better off. Then there'd be few people, I guarantee, who'd know what they don't know, and they'd keep their silly chitter-chatter to themselves. (MEGARONIDES *goes into his own house.*)

Act Two.   Scene I

(*Enter* LYSITELES *in great distress.*)

LYSITELES (*to himself*): Many things are going round and round in my head at the same time, and I'm getting grief for myself as I think about them; I'm fretting and tormenting and tiring myself, for this mind of mine is now a damned hard taskmaster. But this isn't clear or well thought out, which way of life is better to follow, which I should consider would give more stability for spending one's life. I don't know whether to devote myself to love or to business; or which alternative will provide more pleasure for living my life. (*Reflecting*) I'm really not clear about the matter. The only thing to do, I guess, is to examine both courses at the same time, and to be both judge and advocate in this trial. That's what I'll do; I like the idea. First of all, I'll describe how the arts of Love run their course. Love never expects to have any man come rushing into his toils except those of base desires; these are the men he seeks and pursues; he coaxes them along cunningly and works against their best interests. He's wheedle-wordy, rapacious, mendacious, dainty-loving, greedy, wanton; he's a despoiler, an alluring corrupter of men into whorehouse-haunters, and when penniless a pryer into secrets. As soon as the lover is pierced by the barbed kisses of the one he loves, his property straightway floats outside and flows away. "Give me this, my honey," says she, "if you love me, please do." And then the poor goose says, "Of course, my darling; I'll give you that, and anything more that you want." Then she strikes him as he's hanging there; now she asks for more; this isn't enough damage, so she demands still more, for eating and drinking and spending. The lover is allowed to have her for a night; then the whole household is brought in—the wardrobe woman, the masseur, the cashier, the fan bearers, the sandal carriers, the singing girls, the jewel-keeper girls, the to-messengers and fro-messengers, and all of them devour his bread and board. The lover in his hospitality spends his last cent. And when I think over in my mind how little a man's worth when he's in want—away with you, Love! I don't like you, I have no use for you. No matter how sweet it is to eat and drink, Love still provides bitterness, enough to make us wretched. The lover avoids the forum, avoids his relatives, avoids his own most innermost thoughts, and people no longer wish to consider him their friend. In a thousand ways he must be shunned, O Love; he must be kept off and held off afar, for the man who has fallen in love has perished more completely than if he took a leap from a ledge. Away with you, Love; keep your own property for yourself,[3] Love, and never be a friend of mine! There are others that you can still make worried and wretched, men that you have enslaved to your power. (*Making a firm decision*) Now I'm determined to devote myself to virtuous deeds, even though it does involve a great deal of labour. These are the things that good men wish to gain —wealth, confidence, honour, fame, and favour; these are the rewards of the righteous. And so I'd far rather live with upright men than with deceitful scoundrels.

Act Two. Scene II

(*Enter* PHILTO.)

PHILTO (*looking around*): Where did that fellow betake himself when he went out of the house?

LYSITELES: Here I am, father; command me as you wish. I won't delay you, and I won't hide myself in some corner out of your sight.

PHILTO (*very righteous*): You'll be acting consistently with the rest of your life, if you show proper respect and affection for your parent. My son, I don't want you to have any conversation with worthless men either in the streets or in the forum, none whatever. I know what the moral standards of this age are; a bad man wants a good man to be bad, to be like himself. Bad men throw our standards into disorder, into confusion. This insatiate horde, grasping, greedy, covetous men, consider sacred things profane and public things private. This grieves me, this torments me, this it is that I harp on day and night for you to avoid. The only things they think it right to keep hands off are the things their hands can't reach; as for the rest—grab it, hide it, clear out, lie low! Such sights bring tears to my eyes, that I have lived to see such a race of men as this. Why didn't I die first and descend to the dead? Why, these men praise the manners of our ancestors, and then besmirch the very men they praise. I'll excuse you from following practices like these or staining your character with them. Follow my example and live by the good old standards, do the things I advise you to do. I haven't any use for these filthy, disorderly practices with which our gentlemen disgrace themselves. If you carry out these injunctions of mine, many a good maxim will take root in your breast.

LYSITELES (*patiently*): From my earliest youth all the way to my present age, father, I have always been subservient to your injunctions and your precepts. As far as my own nature was concerned, I considered that I was free; but from the standpoint of your parental control, I deemed it proper that my inclinations should be subservient to your wishes.

PHILTO: The man who struggles with his inclinations from his earliest youth, whether he is to be the sort his inclinations think proper, or the sort that his parents and relatives wish him to be—well, if his inclinations conquer the man, it's all up with him; he serves his inclinations, not himself. But if the man has overpowered his inclinations, then he will be called conqueror of conquerors as long as he lives. My son, you have reason to rejoice, if you have conquered your inclinations instead of their conquering you. It's much better for you to be the man you ought to be than to be the man that pleases your inclinations; those who conquer their inclinations will always be considered more worthy than those enslaved to their inclinations.

LYSITELES: I have always esteemed your maxims as a protection for my tender youth; I have taken particular pains, father, not to go to any den of iniquity, not to go roaming around at night, not to take from another person what is his, and not to cause you any grief. I have ever kept your precepts in good repair by my own correct conduct.

PHILTO: Why make a fuss about it? The good that you've done was done for yourself, not for me. My life is almost over; it's you that your conduct chiefly concerns. The upright man is one who is dissatisfied with himself, no matter how upright and virtuous he may be; the man who is well satisfied with himself is neither upright nor virtuous; the man who disapproves of himself has an innate desire for decent conduct. Roof over your good deeds with other good deeds, so that the rain won't come through.

LYSITELES: That's why I said this, father, because there's a certain matter about which I want to get your permission.

PHILTO: What is it? I'm eager now to give my assent.

LYSITELES: There's a young man here of noble family, a friend and companion of mine, who hasn't managed his affairs with much care and caution, father; I want to do him a favour, if you have no objection.

PHILTO (*ironically*): Out of your own funds, I suppose?

LYSITELES: Of course; for what's yours is mine, and all mine is yours.

PHILTO: What about this fellow? Is he broke?

LYSITELES: Quite broke.

PHILTO: Did he have money?

LYSITELES: Yes, he *had* some.

PHILTO: How did he lose it? Was he engaged in public contracts or maritime commerce? Was it by trading, or did he lose it dealing with slaves?

LYSITELES: None of these.

PHILTO: How then?

LYSITELES: It was his generosity, father, I assure you; furthermore, he did lose some of it in luxurious living, indulging his—inclinations.

PHILTO (*with heavy sarcasm*): Gad! What a fine friendly introduction to a man, who has lost his money in no honest way and now is broke! I don't want a fellow with such a character to be a friend of yours.

LYSITELES: He doesn't mean to do any wrong; that's why I want to relieve his poverty.

PHILTO: It's not doing a beggar a good turn to give him something to eat and drink; you merely lose what you give him and prolong his life for more misery. I don't say this because I'm unwilling to do what you wish and do it gladly; but when I apply this saying to that man of yours, I'm warning you to pity others in such a way that others won't have to pity you.

LYSITELES: I'm ashamed to desert him and deny him aid in his trouble.

PHILTO: My word, it's better to be shamed than blamed, even though the words do have the same number of letters.

LYSITELES (*insistent*): Well for heaven's sake, father, we have plenty of property properly acquired, thanks to the gods and our forbears and your own efforts. You ought not to blame yourself for doing a service to a friend; on the contrary, you ought to be ashamed if you don't do it.

PHILTO: If you have considerable wealth and take something away from it, does it become greater or less?

LYSITELES: Less, father; but don't you know the song that they often sing at the stingy cuss who parts with nothing?
"I hope you lose what you have got;
I hope you get what you have not.
Your money brings to you no fun,
Nor does it help out anyone."

PHILTO: I know of course that they often do that; but, my son, the real part-with-nothing is the man who has nothing with which to play his part.

LYSITELES: Thanks to the gods, father, we have both enough for our own enjoyment, and to enable us to be generous to our friends.

PHILTO: Gad! I can't deny you anything you wish. Whose poverty do you wish to relieve? Speak out frankly to your father.

LYSITELES: It's young Lesbonicus, the son of Charmides; he lives there. (*Pointing to the house of* CALLICLES.)

PHILTO: You mean the fellow who devoured what he had, and even what he didn't have?

LYSITELES: Don't upbraid him, father. Many things happen to a man whether he wants them or not.

PHILTO (*indignantly*): Good heavens, my boy! That's not so; you don't usually talk this way. The wise man, I assure you, moulds his own fortune; not many things happen to him that he doesn't want, unless he's a bungling moulder.

LYSITELES: The man who wants to be a skilful moulder of the course of his life needs considerable experience in moulding; but this fellow is still very young.

PHILTO: Wisdom isn't acquired by age, but by character. Age serves merely to flavour wisdom, while wisdom provides age with sustenance. But come now, tell me. What do you wish to give him?

LYSITELES: Why, not a thing, father. Only don't you prevent me from accepting whatever he gives me.

PHILTO (*puzzled*): And in that way will you be relieving his poverty, by accepting something from him?

LYSITELES: In just that way, father.

PHILTO: Damn it! I'd like to have you explain the method to me.

LYSITELES: Very well. Do you know what his family is like?

PHILTO: Why yes; a very fine one.

LYSITELES: He has a sister, a fine young woman of marriageable age. I want to marry her, father, without a dowry.

PHILTO (*aghast*): A wife without a dowry?

LYSITELES: That's right. In this way you'll gain his undying gratitude, at no cost to yourself; and there's no way in which you can give him more suitable assistance.

PHILTO: Am I to let you marry a wife without a dowry?

LYSITELES: You must do it, father; and in this way you'll bring great honour to our family.

PHILTO (*yielding*): I can quote many wise saws, and eloquently, too; this old head of mine holds many old and ancient sayings. But now that I see you are winning friendship and favour for our family, I decide as you wish, in spite of my earlier opposition. You have my permission; ask for the girl, marry her.

LYSITELES: The gods preserve you for me! But to this favour add one more thing.

PHILTO: Well, what is this one thing?

LYSITELES: I'll tell you. You go to him, you win him over, you ask for the girl.

PHILTO: Just listen to that now!

LYSITELES: You'll finish the business much more quickly. Everything you do will be final. In an affair like this one word of yours will bear more weight than a hundred of mine.

PHILTO: Well, well! As a result of my kindness, I've brought this bother on myself! (*More pleasantly*) All right, I'll assist you.

LYSITELES: You're a delightful person! This is the house; he lives here; his name is Lesbonicus. Go on, please attend to the matter. I'll wait for you at home. (*He departs.*)

Act Two.   Scene III

PHILTO (*to himself as he approaches* LESBONICUS' *door*): This situation isn't the best possible one, and it's not quite as I think it ought to be; but still it could be a great deal worse. There's one thing, though, that comforts me as I think about it—the man who thinks only of his own wishes when he's making plans for his son is a perfect fool; he makes himself wretched, without making matters a bit better. He's making heavier weather for his old age by stirring up such an unseasonable storm. (*Stopping*) But there, the door where I was headed for is opening. Lesbonicus and his slave are coming out at just the right time. (*He steps back.*)

Act Two.   Scene IV

(*Enter* LESBONICUS *and* STASIMUS; *they do not see* PHILTO *at first.*)

LESBONICUS: It's less than fifteen days since you received forty minae from Callicles for this house; isn't that right, Stasimus?

STASIMUS: When I think it over, I seem to recall that it happened.

LESBONICUS: What's become of the money?

STASIMUS: Eaten up, drunk up; gone up in smoke; gone down the drain. The fish man got it, the baker, the butchers, the cooks, the green-grocers, the perfumers, the poultry men; it was consumed quickly. Gad! It disappeared in every direction as quickly as when you throw poppy seeds to ants.

LESBONICUS: But heavens! Less than six minae was spent on those items.

STASIMUS: What about the money you gave to harlots?

LESBONICUS: I'm including that in the amount.

STASIMUS (*grinning*): And the money I cheated you of?

LESBONICUS: Ah! That's the biggest item of all.

STASIMUS: Well, you can't get a clear idea of your money, if all you do is spend it; unless you're convinced that your money lasts for ever.

PHILTO (*aside*): He's pretty slow and stupid, to balance his accounts now after he's squandered the money; that's something he should have thought of earlier.

LESBONICUS: I still don't see at all clearly how to account for the money.

STASIMUS: Gosh! The account is clear enough to see; it's the money that's vamoosed. Didn't you receive forty minae from Callicles? And he took over formal ownership of the house, didn't he?

LESBONICUS: Quite so.

PHILTO (*aside*): My word, it looks as if our new relative has sold his house; when his father comes back from abroad, he'll have a place with the beggars at the gate, unless he can crawl into his son's belly.

STASIMUS: And then you paid Olympicus the banker a thousand drachmae, which you owed him on account; and you had just been dunned for the debt.

LESBONICUS: To be sure, it was money I pledged to pay.

STASIMUS: You'd better say, "money I did pay"; and it was for that young fellow you used to say was rich.

LESBONICUS: That's right.

STASIMUS: So that the money was wasted.

LESBONICUS: That's right, too. When I saw the pitiful state he was in, I had pity on him.

STASIMUS: You have pity for others, but no pity or shame for yourself.

PHILTO (*aside*): It's time for me to approach. (*He advances towards them.*)

LESBONICUS (*seeing him*): Isn't this Philto coming toward us? By gracious, it is he.

STASIMUS (*to* LESBONICUS): Golly! I'd like to have that fellow for a slave of mine; just think of the money he has.[4]

PHILTO: Philto wishes a hearty good day to both master and slave, to Lesbonicus and Stasimus.

LESBONICUS: The gods give you, Philto, every blessing you desire. How is your son?

PHILTO: He wishes you well.

LESBONICUS: The same for him, to be sure.

STASIMUS (*aside*): That phrase, "he wishes well," is worthless, unless the person does well. I've got wishes, too, to be free; I wish in vain. He (*indicating his master*) might wish to be a decent sort; it would be a useless wish.

PHILTO: My son has sent me to you to propose a bond of marriage and friendship between our two families. He wants to marry your sister; I'm in hearty agreement and desire it also.

LESBONICUS: This isn't like you—to mock at my misfortunes, when you're so fortunate.

PHILTO: I'm a man; you're a man. God bless me, I haven't come here to make fun of you, and I don't think it decent to do so. What I've said is the truth: my son begged me to ask that your sister be his wife.

LESBONICUS (*firmly*): It's right for me to recognise the state my circumstances are in. The position of my family is not on a level with yours. Go hunt some other marriage arrangement.

STASIMUS (*aside to* LESBONICUS): Are you out of your mind and your wits completely, to reject this match? It looks to me that you've found a friend here to fight your battles for you.

LESBONICUS (*in an angry aside to* STASIMUS): Oh, go to the devil, won't you?

STASIMUS: Hell! If I did start to go, you'd stop me.

LESBONICUS (*stiffly, to* PHILTO): This is my final answer, Philto, unless you want me for something else. (*Prepares to leave.*)

PHILTO: I trust, Lesbonicus, that you will be more kindly disposed to me than I now find to be the case. To indulge both in foolish words and foolish work, Lesbonicus, isn't a sound procedure in this life of ours.

STASIMUS (*to* LESBONICUS): By golly, he told the truth there.

LESBONICUS (*to* STASIMUS): I'll knock out your eye, if you speak another word.

STASIMUS: Damn it! I'll speak anyway. If I can't speak with two eyes, I'll do it with one.

PHILTO: Do you say this now, that your position and resources are not on a level with ours?

LESBONICUS: That's what I say.

PHILTO: What about this? Suppose you went to a temple banquet, where what they call a public feast is served, and your partner on the couch happened to be a rich man, whose clients heaped up an abundance of dainties on the table; suppose you wanted something from the food heaped up there for him, would you eat it, or would you go without your dinner there on the couch beside the rich man?

LESBONICUS: I'd eat it, if he didn't forbid me to.

STASIMUS: By Jove, I'd eat it even if he did forbid; I'd stuff both cheeks and cram it down, and whatever pleased him I'd pluck by preference, and I wouldn't let him have a mouthful of my vital victuals.

No one ought to be bashful at the table, for there men decide about the most important matters of existence.

PHILTO (*smiling*): Right you are.

STASIMUS: And I'll tell you frankly: I'll get out of the way of your rich man on the street, on the sidewalk, or in public office; but when it comes to belly-matters, I'm damned if I'll move out of his way this far (*with a gesture*), unless he beats me up first with his fists. With the cost of living what it is, a dinner is a legacy without encumbrances.

PHILTO: Always be sure to consider this, Lesbonicus, that the best thing of all is to be the best sort of person yourself; if you can't do that, keep as close to the best sort as possible. And now, Lesbonicus, I want you to accept and consent to this match that I'm proposing and asking of you. The gods are rich, wealth and position befit the gods; but we poor mortals, when once we have breathed forth our trifling little life, are rated with an equal rating in Hades—the beggar and the plutocrat alike.

STASIMUS (*aside*): It's a wonder that you can't take your wealth there with you. When you're dead, you can be just as dead as the name implies.

PHILTO: And so that you'll realise now that position and wealth don't mean a thing and that we don't underrate your good will, I ask you to give your sister to my son without a dowry. May the match turn out happily! (*As* LESBONICUS *does not reply*) Am I to consider her betrothed? Why don't you answer?

STASIMUS: Ye immortal gods, what an offer!

PHILTO: Why don't you say, "May it turn out happily; I'm willing"?[5] You'll say it, won't you?

STASIMUS: Confound it! He used to say "I'm willing," when there was no need of it; now, when it is necessary, he can't say it.

LESBONICUS: I'm very grateful to all of you, Philto, for considering me worthy of being connected with your family. And although this fortune of mine has suffered sadly as a result of my folly, we still have a farm near the city; I shall give that to my sister as a dowry. It's the only thing that my riotous living has left me, except my life.

PHILTO: But I assure you, I don't want a dowry.

LESBONICUS: I'm determined to provide one.

STASIMUS (*aside to* LESBONICUS): Master, do you want to deprive us of the nurse that nourishes us? Don't do that, please. What will we live on in the future?

LESBONICUS (*to* STASIMUS): Keep still, won't you? Do I have to account to you for my actions?

STASIMUS (*aside*): We're utterly undone, unless I think up something. (*Beckoning to* PHILTO) Philto, I want a word with you.

PHILTO: Why, yes, if you want something, Stasimus.

STASIMUS: Step this way a bit. (*He draws him aside.*)

PHILTO: Very well.

STASIMUS: I'm telling you this in secrecy; I don't want you to let my master or anyone else know about it.

PHILTO: Trust me freely with anything you please.

STASIMUS: I warn you, by gods and mortals, not to let that farm belong to you or your son. I'll give you my reasons for this.

PHILTO: Gracious! I'm anxious to hear them.

STASIMUS: Well, in the first place, when the land's being ploughed, the oxen drop dead in every fifth furrow.

PHILTO (*incredulous*): Oh, get out!

STASIMUS: Why, the entrance to Hades is in that farm of ours. Then too, the grapes rot on the vines before they're ripe.

LESBONICUS (*aside, thinking his slave is persuading* PHILTO *to accept the dowry*): He's convincing the fellow, I do believe. He may be a rascal, but he's not disloyal to me.

STASIMUS (*to* PHILTO): And listen to the rest of the story. Moreover, when there's a very heavy harvest of grain everywhere else, that farm produces three times less than you sow.

PHILTO: Ah! Just the spot where bad habits ought to be sown, if they can be killed off in the sowing.

STASIMUS: And there's never a single owner of that field who doesn't have his affairs turn out terrible for him. Some of the owners went into exile, others died, others hanged themselves. And look at the present owner now—they've made a grand slam against him.

PHILTO: To the devil with a farm like that!

STASIMUS: You'd say "to the devil with it" a lot more, if you heard everything. Why, every other tree is blasted with lightning; the hogs all die with the quickest kind of quinsy. The sheep get the mange; they're as bare of wool as—look!—this hand of mine. You know what a hardy race Syrian slaves are; but not a one of 'em survives if he stays on that farm six months; they all drop off with the midsummer complaint.

PHILTO (*concealing his amusement*): I believe it's as you say, Stasimus. But the Campanian race far surpasses the Syrians in endurance. However, judging from your description, that farm is certainly the ideal spot for all the public enemies to be sent to. People talk about the Isles of the Blest, where all the people gather who have lived good lives; contrariwise, it seems proper that evildoers be packed off to that farm, (*with mild scepticism*) if it *is* the way you describe.

STASIMUS: It's Calamity's own hangout; why say more? Look for any kind of trouble whatsoever, and you can find it there.

PHILTO (*sharply*): But you, by gad, can find it there, and elsewhere too.

STASIMUS (*unruffled*): Don't tell him, please, that I told you this.

PHILTO: Oh, you've told it to safe enough ears.

STASIMUS: Why, he's just crazy to get rid of the farm, if he can find someone to pull a fast one on.

PHILTO: Well, by Jove, that farm will never belong to me.

STASIMUS: No, sir, not if you're wise. (*Aside, as* PHILTO *rejoins* LESBONICUS) Jove! What a clever job of frightening the old fellow away from the farm! For we haven't a thing to live on, if master loses that.

PHILTO: Here I am back again, Lesbonicus.

LESBONICUS: Tell me, please, what did he say to you?

PHILTO: What do you suppose? He's a man, he wants to be free; but he hasn't the money to give.

LESBONICUS: And I want to be rich, but it's a useless wish.

STASIMUS (*aside*): You had your chance, if you'd been willing; now, when nothing's left, you don't have a chance.

LESBONICUS (*partly overhearing*): What are you muttering to yourself, Stasimus?

STASIMUS: About what you said just now. If you'd been willing earlier, you would be; now you're wishing for it too late.

PHILTO (*to* LESBONICUS): No arrangement can be made with me about the dowry. You handle the matter with my son in any way you wish. (*Formally*) I now ask you to give your sister to my son. May the match turn out happily! (*As* LESBONICUS *hesitates*) What now? Are you still considering it?

LESBONICUS (*reluctantly*): Well, have your way! Since you wish it so: may the gods bless the match! I'm willing.[5]

STASIMUS: I'm damned if anyone has ever awaited the birth of a son as long as I've awaited the birth of that "I'm willing." May the gods prosper all your plans.

PHILTO: I hope so.

LESBONICUS: And now, Stasimus, you go to my sister here in Callicles' house; tell her how we've made these arrangements.

STASIMUS: I'll be glad to go.

LESBONICUS: And congratulate my sister.

STASIMUS: To be sure.

PHILTO: You come along with me, Lesbonicus, so that we can decide on the wedding day with Lysiteles. And at the same time we'll confirm this agreement. (PHILTO *departs.*)

LESBONICUS (*to* STASIMUS): You tend to those orders of mine; I'll be back here shortly. Tell Callicles to meet me.

STASIMUS: Go on now, won't you?

LESBONICUS: He's to see what must be done about the dowry.

STASIMUS: Go on now!

LESBONICUS: For I'm determined not to let her marry without a dowry.

STASIMUS: Just you go on now!

LESBONICUS: And indeed, I'll never let her suffer for—

STASIMUS: Get out now!

LESBONICUS: —my own recklessness.

STASIMUS: Go on now!

LESBONICUS: The only fair solution seems to be that, for my sins,—

STASIMUS: Go on now!

LESBONICUS: —I should be the one to suffer.

STASIMUS: Go on now!

LESBONICUS: Oh, father, shall I ever see you again?

STASIMUS (*with increasing vehemence*): Go on now! Go on now! Go on now! (*To himself, as* LESBONICUS *departs*) There, at last I got him to go. (*With a sigh of relief*) The gods love us! It's a bad business handled in a damned good way, that is, if the farm is safe for us; but there's still considerable uncertainty about what will happen to it. If he makes over the farm, I'll get it plenty—right in the neck, for I'll have to carry his shield, his helmet, and his pack in foreign service. He'll flee from the city when the wedding's over, and be off somewhere or other, right on the road to ruin; he'll be off to Asia or Cilicia to serve as a soldier. (*After a pause*) Well, I'll go where I was ordered to, even though I hate the house ever since Callicles kicked us out of our own home. (*He enters the house of* CALLICLES.)

Act Three.   Scene I

(*Enter* CALLICLES *and* STASIMUS *from the former's house.*)

CALLICLES: What's this you've just said, Stasimus?

STASIMUS: That my young master Lesbonicus has just betrothed his sister. (*Impertinently*) There, that's what.

CALLICLES: Betrothed her to whom?

STASIMUS: To Lysiteles, Philto's son; without a dowry, too.

CALLICLES: Marry her into such a wealthy family without a dowry? I just can't credit what you say.

STASIMUS: Rot! You never give any credit, anyway. But if you don't credit this, I'll credit—

CALLICLES: What?

STASIMUS: —myself with not giving a damn.

CALLICLES: How long ago was it done? Where?

STASIMUS: Why, here in front of this door. "Right lately," as they say in Praeneste.

CALLICLES (*with irony*): And now that he's ruined, Lesbonicus has become thriftier than when he was wealthy, eh?

STASIMUS: In fact, Philto came of his own accord to ask her for his son.

CALLICLES: God! This will be a terrible disgrace, if the girl doesn't get a dowry. (*Aside*) Damn it! I see that I just have to take a hand in this matter. I'll go visit my reprimander and get his advice. (*He goes into the house of* MEGARONIDES.)

STASIMUS (*to himself*): I've got a pretty good idea, a good inkling, why he hurried off so fast; he wants to get the farm away from Lesbonicus, just the way he did the house. Oh, poor master Charmides, how your property is being wrecked in your absence! Oh, if I could only see you safely home again, that you could take vengeance on your enemies— and reward me for my devotion to you, both past and present! It's awfully difficult to find a friend in the true meaning of the term, one to whom you can entrust your cares and then go to sleep without a worry. (*Looking down the street in the direction of* PHILTO's *house*) But there comes our new son-in-law with his new relative. There's some sort of disagreement between them. They're both walking fast; master's ahead and Lysiteles is clutching his cloak. They've stopped—quite *comme il faut*. I'll withdraw a bit. I'm anxious to hear what these two relatives have to say. (*He steps back.*)

Act Three.   Scene II

(*Enter* LYSITELES *and* LESBONICUS; *they do not see* STASIMUS.)

LYSITELES: Stand still! Don't turn away and hide your face from me.

LESBONICUS: Can't you let me go my own way?

LYSITELES: I'd let you go, Lesbonicus, if it seemed to your advantage, if it would bring you fame or honour.

LESBONICUS: You're doing the easiest thing in the world.

LYSITELES: What's that?

LESBONICUS: Injuring a friend.

LYSITELES: That's not my way, and I never learned how.

LESBONICUS (*bitterly*): What a learned person for one who didn't learn how! How would you act, if some one had taught you to be a bother to me? You pretend to do me a good turn; you do me a bad one, instead, and give me bad advice.

LYSITELES: I?

LESBONICUS: Yes, you.

LYSITELES: How am I doing you a bad turn?

LESBONICUS: Because you're doing what I don't want.

LYSITELES: I'd like to look after your own best interests.

LESBONICUS: Are you better at that than I am? I've got some sense, I can consider pretty well what is to my own interests.

LYSITELES: Is this showing sense, to refuse a favour from a friend?

LESBONICUS: I don't consider it any favour, if the recipient doesn't want it. I know and realise what I have to do; my mind's still functioning, and I won't be won aside by your words from paying heed to public opinion.

LYSITELES: Look here! I can't restrain myself from telling you what you deserve to hear. Did your ancestors hand down to you this fine name of yours just for this purpose, that you could ruin with riotous living what they had won by their upright conduct? Why, your father and your grandfather provided you with an easy and level road to honour, that you might be the protector of the good name of your descendants; but you've made the road a hard one by your wrong-doing and your idleness and your foolish conduct. You've preferred to put your love affairs ahead of serious things. And now do you think you can cover up your faults in this manner? Ah! It just isn't possible. Get some decency in your mind, I urge you, and drive out that laziness of yours. Devote yourself to your friends in the forum, instead of devoting yourself to your mistress in bed, as you usually do. And that's why I'm awfully anxious for you to keep that farm of yours, so that you'll have something to help you to reform, without the citizens who dislike you perpetually plaguing you because of your poverty.

LESBONICUS: I agree with everything you've said, I'll even set my seal on it. I've ruined my father's property and the good name of my forebears. I knew all the time how I ought to live, but I was a poor fool and couldn't do it. Caught by the power of passion, wedded to easy living, I fell upon evil days. (*With an air of finality*) But I'm very grateful to you now, for you deserve it.

LYSITELES: But I can't let you disregard my efforts in this way or be so contemptuous of my advice.⁶ And at the same time, I'm grieved that you show so little sense of shame. And finally, if you don't listen to me and do what I say, you'll be so concealed behind your worse self that Honour can't locate you, and you'll be buried away in obscurity when you especially want to be eminent. To be sure, Lesbonicus, I know that noble nature of yours pretty well. I know that you haven't sinned of your own volition, but love has warped your reason. I too understand all the ways of Love. For Love is just like an aerial torpedo—there's nothing that flies more quickly; and he makes men's moods mooning and moody. The more a thing's approved, the less pleasing it is; if it isn't approved, it's pleasing. If something's scarce, you want it; if there's a plentiful supply, then you don't; if a man tries to stop you, he urges you on; if he tries to persuade you, he prevents you. It's awfully wretched lodgings you'll get if you put up at the sign of Cupid. But I advise you again and again to consider carefully what you want to do. If you keep on with your present endeavours, you'll set your family tree on fire, and then you'll have a perfect passion for some water to put it out; and if you find some— (*sarcastically*) with the common sense that lovers usually show—you won't leave even a spark to brighten up your family hearth.

LESBONICUS: That's easy to find; you can always get fire, even from an enemy. But upbraiding me as you are, you're driving me from my faults to an even worse course. You're urging me to let you marry my sister without a dowry. No, sir! It isn't proper for me, after I've squandered so much of my father's property, still to be wealthy and have a farm; why, that sister of mine would be impoverished, and she'd have a right to hate me for it. A man who loses the respect of his own relatives will never be esteemed by other people. I shall do just what I said; I don't want you to trouble yourself any more.

LYSITELES (*holding him back*): And is it so much better for you to be plunged into poverty for your sister's sake? Is it better for me to have the farm than for you to have the means of carrying out your obligations?

LESBONICUS: I don't want you to worry so much about relieving my poverty; I'd rather have you keep me from being defamed, even though I am destitute; I don't want people to spread the rumour around that I've given you my sister for a concubine instead of a wife, if I should give her to you without a dowry. Would anyone be considered a viler person than I? Such gossip as this would glorify you and besmirchify me, if you married her without a dowry. You'd get the honour and good repute, I'd get just the reproaches.

LYSITELES (*sarcastically*): Do you think you'll get the highest office in the state, if I take your farm from you?

LESBONICUS: I neither wish it nor expect it nor think so; but there's some honour when a man of shame does his duty.

LYSITELES: To be sure, I know what you're thinking of; I see it, sense it, understand it. This is your intention: after you've bound our families by marriage and given up the farm and don't have a thing left to live on, you'll flee from the city without a cent; when the wedding's over, you'll run away, deserting your country, your relatives, your connections, your friends. People would say that you had been driven away from here by my doing and my greed. Don't imagine that I will permit a thing like this to happen.

STASIMUS (*joining them*): I can't keep from shouting, "Bravo! Bravo, Lysiteles! Encore!" The victory is easily yours. This fellow is defeated; your performance definitely wins. (*To* LESBONICUS) He acts the part better and composes better lines; so I'll just fine you a mina for your stupidity.[6]

LESBONICUS (*in anger*): How'd you happen to interrupt us and burst into the middle of our discussion?

STASIMUS (*impudently*): Footwork—I'll go the same way I came.

LESBONICUS (*turning his back on* STASIMUS): Come along home with me, Lysiteles, and we'll talk over the matter at greater length there.

LYSITELES: I'm not in the habit of doing things in secret. I'll tell you how I feel about it: if your sister marries me without a dowry, as I consider the proper arrangement, and you don't go away from here, then what's mine will be yours; but if you're differently disposed—good luck to you in whatever you do, but I'll never be your friend on any other terms. My decision is just that! (LESBONICUS *enters his apartment in the rear of* CALLICLES' *house.*)

STASIMUS: Why, he's gone. Listen, Lysiteles! I'd like a word with you. (*To himself, as* LYSITELES *goes down the street without replying*) And now he's gone too! Stasimus, you're all that's left. What am I to do now? Why not buckle up my baggage and sling my shield on my back, and have some heels hammered on my slippers? It can't be helped. I'll be a soldier's drudge before long, I can see that. When my master has put himself[6] on the pay-roll of some king, I suppose that in comparison with the greatest warriors he'll be a fierce—deserter; and what spoils he will capture there—the man that meets my master. Then too, as soon as I have my bow and quiver and arrows ready, and my helmet on my head—I'll take a peaceful little nap in the tent. Now I'll go to the forum. Five days ago I lent a talent to a fellow;[7] I'll ask it back, so that I'll have something to take with me for travelling expenses. (*He departs in the direction of the forum.*)

Act Three.   Scene III

(*Enter* MEGARONIDES *and* CALLICLES *from the former's house.*)

MEGARONIDES: According to your story, Callicles, it's absolutely necessary for the girl to receive a dowry.

CALLICLES: Heavens! It would hardly be decent of me to let her marry without a dowry, when I have her money in my possession at home.

MEGARONIDES (*nodding his approval*): Yes, there's a dowry ready for her at home. Unless you want to wait until her brother arranges for the wedding without it. You could go to Philto afterward and say that you were giving her a dowry, and doing it out of friendship for her father. (*Reflecting*) But there's this difficulty; I'm afraid that such an offer might expose you to public disfavour and discredit; they'd say that you had a special reason for being generous to the girl. They'd pretend that her father had given you the dowry which you gave her, that your generosity came from that source, and that you hadn't turned it over to her intact just as you received it, but that you had kept part of it for yourself. (*Pausing*) But it's a very long time now to await the arrival of Charmides. And meanwhile the fellow's desire to marry her may vanish. And this match is such an excellent one for her.

CALLICLES: All these points occur to me too, damn it! Consider whether this possibility seems more useful, more helpful—for me to go to Lesbonicus himself and explain the situation to him. (*Reflecting*) But how could I reveal the treasure now to that young hothead, who's interested only in love affairs and wild living? Not at all, by Jove! Not at all! Why, I know for certain he'll gobble down the very spot where the money's buried. And I'm afraid to dig, lest he hear the noise and track down the treasure, if I say I'm providing the dowry.

MEGARONIDES: How then can the dowry be drawn out on the sly?

CALLICLES: We'll wait for a suitable opportunity, and in the meantime you ask for a loan from some friend or other.

MEGARONIDES: Is it possible to get money from some friend or other?

CALLICLES: Of course.

MEGARONIDES: Nonsense! Immediately you'd run into that same reply: "I? Why, I don't have a damned thing to lend."

CALLICLES (*as if in reply to the friend's refusal*): And, damn it! I'd rather have you tell me the truth than lend me the money.

MEGARONIDES (*as an idea strikes him*): Look here! See if this scheme suits you.

CALLICLES: What scheme?

MEGARONIDES: A clever one, in my opinion; I just thought of it.

CALLICLES: What is it?

MEGARONIDES: Have some one hired as soon as possible, to pretend he's a foreigner.

CALLICLES: What is he supposed to do then?

MEGARONIDES: Have the man dressed like a foreigner to the very life; let him have a strange appearance, such as isn't seen here; he's to be a mendacious-talking rascal—

CALLICLES: What is he supposed to do then?

MEGARONIDES: —full of deceit and impudence—

CALLICLES: And what then?

MEGARONIDES: He's to come to the young fellow as though from his father in Seleucia, and bring greetings from his father; he's to say that the father is alive and well, prospering in his business dealings, and intending to return soon. Our trickster will bring two letters—which we'll compose and seal—as though from the father; he'll give one to Lesbonicus and say that he wants to give the other to you.

CALLICLES: Come, come! Keep on talking!

MEGARONIDES: He's to say that he's bringing some gold to the girl from her father to be her dowry and that the father ordered him to give the gold to you. Now do you understand?

CALLICLES: Quite well; I'm listening with great pleasure.

MEGARONIDES: And then finally you'll give the gold to young Lesbonicus when the girl is married.

CALLICLES: Jove! How cleverly contrived!

MEGARONIDES: In this way the young man won't have any suspicion when you've dug up the treasure; he'll think the gold was brought to you from his father, but you'll be getting it from the treasure.

CALLICLES: A smart scheme! Excellent, in fact! I'm rather ashamed, though, to take up swindling at my time of life. But when he brings the letters all sealed, [but when he's brought the letters all sealed,]² don't you think the young man knows the seal on his father's ring?

MEGARONIDES: Hush, won't you? A thousand reasons can be raked up to explain that: he lost the one he had and had a new one made. Even if he brings the letters unsealed, he can say they were unsealed at the custom house for inspection. In a matter of this sort, it's mere idleness to waste time in talk; we could spin out words about it forever. Go on and get the treasure now; be quick and quiet about it! Get every male and female slave out of the house. And listen, will you?

CALLICLES: What is it?

MEGARONIDES: Be sure to keep this a deep secret from your wife, too. For there isn't a single damned thing that she can keep to herself. (*As* CALLICLES *hesitates*) What are you standing there for? Why don't you get away from here and get going? Open it up, take out as much gold as we need for this purpose, then bury it again at once; and do it quietly, just as I said. Get everybody out of the house.

CALLICLES: I'll do that.

MEGARONIDES: And really, we're talking far too much; we're wasting the day, when we need to be in a hurry. There's nothing to be afraid of about the seal; just leave that to me. That's a clever excuse I mentioned—that the letters were examined by the customs officials. Then, too, don't you see what time of day it is? What do you think that young rake is doing, with his nature and disposition? He's been drunk for a long time; he'll be in a state to agree to anything. And then, the best argument of all, this man of ours will say he's bringing money, not applying for it.

CALLICLES (*convinced*): That's quite enough.

MEGARONIDES: I'll hire some swindler in the forum, and fix up the two letters, and send him here to the young fellow properly primed.

CALLICLES: Well, I'll go in and do my duty; you tend to yours. (*He enters his house.*)

MEGARONIDES (*calling after him*): I'll have it tended to in the trickiest possible style. (*He departs in the direction of the forum.*)

Act Four. Scene I

(*Enter* CHARMIDES *from the harbour.*)

CHARMIDES (*overjoyed at his arrival*): To thee, O Neptune, brother of Jupiter and Nereus,[8] mighty ruler of the mighty main, joyfully and jovially I render recognition, and I give my grateful gratitude to thee and thy salty waves, in whose hands was all power over my property and my life, since they have brought me back from their realm to my native city.[6] And so to thee, Neptune, above all other gods, I utter and express my deepest gratitude. Men say that thou art savage and severe, voracious in thy habits, revolting, unsightly, unendurable, frenzied. I have experienced quite the opposite, for on the deep I found thee calm and gentle, exactly as I wished. And long ago I happened to have heard that this was thy glory—well known it is among mortals—that thy practice was to spare the poor, to ravage and wreck the rich. Ah! I praise thee; thou knowest how it's just and proper to treat mankind; this is worthy of the gods; may they always be benign to beggars. Faithful thou hast been, although people repeat that thou art faithless. Had it not been for thee, I know full well thy satellites would have foully dissevered and dispersed my wretched body, and all my property likewise, far and wide over thy dark-blue waters. For just like dogs, not otherwise, the raging tempests roared around the ship, the rain and waves and angry blasts were set to snap the mast, to tear the yards, to rip the sails, had not thy generous grace been given to me. But now away from me! Determined I am henceforth to give myself to a life of leisure. Enough have I gained in my weary struggles to procure wealth for my son. (*More calmly, as he looks down the street*) But who is this queer-looking fellow coming up the street just as I return. A strange sort of garb he has! In spite of my desire for home, I'll wait to see what he's about.

Act Four.   Scene II

(*Enter the* SWINDLER *from the forum.*)

SWINDLER (*to himself*): I'm calling this day *The Three Penny Day,* for I've hired out my services on a swindling scheme today for that amount. I'm arriving from Seleucia, Macedonia, Asia and Arabia—countries that I never set eye or foot on. Just look at the wretched business that poverty brings a miserable mortal to! The idea of being obliged for the sake of three pennies to say that I've received these letters from a man that I don't know anything about; I don't know him, and I don't really know whether or not he was ever born at all.

CHARMIDES (*aside, observing his large hat*): Jove! This fellow belongs to the mushroom family; he covers himself all up with his head. He has something of an Illyrian look about him, judging from the clothes he's coming in.

SWINDLER: The fellow that hired me took me home after he hired me, told me what he wanted, explained to me and instructed me in advance what I was to do and how to do it. Now if I add a few touches, my employer will get all the better bargain in his swindling-job. I'm outfitted just as he fitted me out; that's the way money works. He borrowed this costume from the property manager at his own risk, too. If I can diddle the old fellow out of this costume now, I'll give him reason to believe that I'm a damned good swindler without his instructions.

CHARMIDES (*aside*): The more I examine this man, the less I like his looks. It's a wonder if the fellow isn't a sleepy-slicker[9] or a cutpurse. He's examining the neighbourhood, he's looking around and surveying the houses. Damned if I don't believe he's spying out the spot that he can come and rob later. (*Moving nearer*) I'm even more anxious to see what he's up to; I'll watch him closely.

SWINDLER: This is the locality that my employer pointed out to me, and (*pointing*) that's the house where my swindles must be set in motion. I'll go knock on the door. (*He approaches the door.*)

CHARMIDES (*aside*): Why, he's making a beeline right for our house. It looks to me as if I'd have to spend the night of my arrival wide awake, damn it!

SWINDLER (*knocking*): Open up here! Open up! Hey, is anyone tending to this door?

CHARMIDES (*stepping up to him*): Young man, what are you after? What do you want? Why are you knocking on that door?

SWINDLER (*insolently*): Look here, old man! I've been assessed, and gave the collector a complete accounting. I'm trying to find the whereabouts of a young fellow named Lesbonicus in this neighbourhood, and also another man, about as white-headed as you are; the man who gave me these letters said his name was Callicles.

CHARMIDES (*aside*): It's certainly my son Lesbonicus that he's looking for, and my friend Callicles, to whom I entrusted my children and my property.

SWINDLER: Inform me where these people live, father, if you know.

CHARMIDES (*annoyed and uneasy*): What do you want them for? Who are you? Where's your home? Where do you come from?

SWINDLER (*smoothly*): So many questions at one time! I don't know what to answer first. If you'll question me calmly and separately about each single point, I'll let you know about my name and my business and my journeys.

CHARMIDES: I'll do as you wish. Come now, first of all give me your name.

SWINDLER: That's a difficult task you're beginning with.

CHARMIDES: How so?

SWINDLER: Because, father, if you started your journey before daybreak from the first part of my name, it would be bedtime before you reached the end of it.

CHARMIDES (*amused*): From what you say, that name of yours requires travelling expenses.

SWINDLER: My other name's a little shorter, about the size of a little wine flask.

CHARMIDES: And what is that name, young man?

SWINDLER: "Presto"—that's my name, the everyday one.

CHARMIDES: Gad! What a tricky name! Just like your saying "Presto!" if I entrust anything to you. "Presto"—and instantly it's gone. (*Aside*) This fellow's a slick swindler, all right. (*Aloud*) Look here, young man!

SWINDLER: What is it?

CHARMIDES: Tell me, those men you're looking for—what do you want of them?

SWINDLER: The father of the young fellow, Lesbonicus, gave me these two letters (*showing them*). He's a friend of mine.

CHARMIDES (*aside*): Now I've caught him in the act. He says I gave him these letters. I'll have some fine fun with him.

SWINDLER: Now if you pay attention, I'll tell you what I began to say.

CHARMIDES: I'm all attention.

SWINDLER: He told me to give this letter to his son Lesbonicus, and he wanted me to give the other one to his friend Callicles.

CHARMIDES (*aside*): He's up to some deception here, so damned if I don't indulge in a bit of counterdeception. (*Aloud*) Where was the father?

SWINDLER: Getting along prosperously.

CHARMIDES: But where?

SWINDLER: In Seleucia.

CHARMIDES: And you received these letters from him?

SWINDLER: With his own hands he put them into my hands.

CHARMIDES: What does this man look like?

SWINDLER: He's about a foot and a half taller than you are.

CHARMIDES (*aside*): A pretty kettle of fish! I'm taller when I'm absent than when I'm present. (*Aloud*) You know the man?

SWINDLER: A queer question, when I'm in the habit of dining with him.

CHARMIDES: What's his name?

SWINDLER (*forgetting the name*): It's the—the name of a fine gentleman, by Jove!

CHARMIDES: I want to hear the name.

SWINDLER: It's—oh, hell!—it's—it's—oh, damn me!

CHARMIDES (*innocently*): What's the trouble?

SWINDLER: I just now swallowed the name without realising it.

CHARMIDES: I don't care for a person who keeps his friends shut up inside his teeth.

SWINDLER: And the name was on the tip of my tongue right now.

CHARMIDES (*aside*): I was lucky to forestall this fellow today in time.

SWINDLER (*aside*): I'm caught in the act, confound it!

CHARMIDES: Have you thought up the name yet?

SWINDLER (*aside*): Heavens and earth! Damned if I'm not ashamed of myself!

CHARMIDES: Just see how well you know the man!

SWINDLER: As well as I do myself. You often look for the very thing you hold in your hand and see with your eyes. I'll think it up letter by letter. The name begins with C.

CHARMIDES: Callias?

SWINDLER: No.

CHARMIDES: Callippus?

SWINDLER: No.

CHARMIDES: Callidemides?

SWINDLER: No.

CHARMIDES: Callinicus?

SWINDLER: No.

CHARMIDES: Callimarchus?

SWINDLER: It's no use. But I don't give a hang about it anyway; I remember enough for my own purposes.

CHARMIDES: But there are lots of people here with the name of Lesbonicus; if you don't tell me the father's name, I can't point out the men you're looking for. What does it sound like? Perhaps we can get it by guessing.

SWINDLER: It sounds like this: Chares, maybe? Or Charmides?

CHARMIDES: It isn't Charmides, is it?

SWINDLER: That's the very name. And I hope the gods damn him!

CHARMIDES (*sternly*): I told you a little while ago; it's better for you to speak well of a friend than ill of him.

SWINDLER: But didn't the worthless wretch keep hiding there between my lips and my teeth?

CHARMIDES: Don't abuse a friend in his absence.

SWINDLER: Then why did that lazy fellow stay in hiding?

CHARMIDES: If you had called him by name, he'd have answered. But where is he?

SWINDLER (*romancing freely*): I left him at the court of Rhadamas in Monkeysia.

CHARMIDES (*aside*): Can anyone be sillier than I am, inquiring about my own whereabouts? But nothing's dissuitable for this affair. (*Aloud*) See here! What about this question? What places have you visited?

SWINDLER: Why, very astonishing ones, astoundingly so.

CHARMIDES: I'd like to hear about them, if you don't mind.

SWINDLER: Really, I'm just dying to describe them. First of all, we sailed to Pontus to the land of Arabia.

CHARMIDES: Aha! So Arabia is in Pontus, eh?

SWINDLER: Of course. Not the Arabia that produces frankincense, but the one where wormwood grows, and poultry-marjoram.

CHARMIDES (*aside*): What a wonderful liar this fellow is! And I'm an even greater fool to ask him about my travels, when I know about them and he doesn't; except that I want to find out where he'll finally end up. (*Aloud*) But look here! Where did you go after that?

SWINDLER: Pay attention, and I'll tell you. To the head of the river that arises in heaven under the throne of Jupiter.

CHARMIDES: Under the throne of Jupiter?

SWINDLER: That's what I say.

CHARMIDES: In heaven?

SWINDLER: And right in the middle of it, too.

CHARMIDES: Well, well! And so you really climbed up to heaven?

SWINDLER: Why, we were carried in a little fishing boat right upstream against the current.

CHARMIDES: Well, well! And you even saw Jupiter?

SWINDLER: The other gods said that he had gone to his country estate to dole out rations to the slaves. Then, after that—

CHARMIDES: Then, after that— I don't want you to tell me a thing.

SWINDLER: . . .[10] damn it, if you annoy me.

CHARMIDES: For no decent person ought to tell how he made the trip from earth to heaven.

SWINDLER: I'll do as I see you wish. But direct me to the men I'm looking for, the men I must deliver these letters to.

CHARMIDES: See here! If you chanced to catch sight of this same Charmides, the fellow you say gave you these letters, would you recognise him?

SWINDLER: Gad! You must think I'm a silly goose, not to be able to recognise the person I've spent my life with. Or would he be so foolish as to entrust to me a thousand gold Philippeans and ask me to deliver them to his son and his friend Callicles, in whose hands he said he had left all his property? Would he entrust it to me if he didn't know me and I didn't know him awfully well?

CHARMIDES (*aside*): I certainly want to try swindling this swindler now, to see if I can trick him out of the thousand Philippeans that he said I gave him; I don't know who the fellow is and I never laid eyes on him before today. Would I entrust gold to such a chap? Why, if my life were to depend on it, I'd never trust him with a lead nickel. But I must come upon him with cunning. (*Aloud*) Hey, there, Presto! I want a few words with you.

SWINDLER: A few hundred, if you wish.

CHARMIDES: Do you have the gold you received from Charmides?

SWINDLER: Yes, a thousand gold Philippeans, paid out at the bank by his own hand.

CHARMIDES: You're sure you received it from Charmides himself?

SWINDLER (*indignantly*): It's queer that I didn't get it from his father or his grandfather, who are dead.

CHARMIDES: Young man, just give me that gold.

SWINDLER (*in amazement*): Give it to you? What gold?

CHARMIDES: The gold you admitted receiving from me.

SWINDLER: Receiving from you?

CHARMIDES: That's what I say.

SWINDLER: Who are you?

CHARMIDES: I am Charmides, the man who gave you the thousand gold coins.

SWINDLER: By Jove, you are not, and you never will be today, as far as this gold is concerned, anyway! Get out of here, you swindler! You're trying to swindle a swindler.

CHARMIDES (*firmly*): I am Charmides.

SWINDLER: It won't do you any good if you are, by heaven, because I'm bringing no gold. Pretty clever of you, to creep upon me at just the right time! As soon as I said I was bringing gold, you became Charmides; you weren't before I mentioned the gold. You can't get away with it. So just as you Charmidised yourself, go and get un-Charmidised again.

CHARMIDES: Who am I then, if I'm not the person I am?

SWINDLER: What concern is that of mine? As long as you're not the man I don't want you to be, you can be anyone you wish, for all I care. Just now you weren't the man you were; now you've become the man you weren't then.

CHARMIDES: If you're going to do it, do it.

SWINDLER: Do what?

CHARMIDES: Return the gold.

SWINDLER: You're dreaming, old man.

CHARMIDES: You admitted that Charmides gave you the gold.

SWINDLER: To be sure, on paper.

CHARMIDES (*angrily*): Will you hurry to get out of this neighbourhood at once, or not, you sleepy-slicker,[9] before you get a thorough thrashing on the spot?

SWINDLER: What for?

CHARMIDES: Because I'm really Charmides, the man you've been lying about, the man you said gave you the letters.

SWINDLER: Oho! I ask you now, are you the man?

CHARMIDES: I certainly am.

SWINDLER: You don't say so! You're really he?

CHARMIDES: I really am Charmides, I say.

SWINDLER: Well, well! So you're really he?

CHARMIDES: The realiest he there is. Now get out of my sight!

SWINDLER: Well now, seriously, in honour of your arrival, you must receive—a flogging at my wish and that of the new police commissioners.[11]

CHARMIDES: So you're getting abusive too?

SWINDLER: Why no; since you've arrived safely— the gods destroy you, if I care a damn whether you'd been destroyed before you got here. I've got my money for this job, and to hell with you! I don't care a straw who you are and who you aren't. I'll go now and report to the man who gave me the three pennies, so that he'll know he's wasted his money. I'm going. Bad health to you, and fare ill! I hope all the gods confound you, Charmides, for coming back from abroad. (*The* SWINDLER *departs.*)

CHARMIDES (*to himself*): Now that he's gone away, I seem to have the time and opportunity to speak freely. I've been stung with anxiety for some time now, wondering what business that fellow had in front of my house. That letter brings up battalions of fears in my breast, and then the thousand gold pieces—what do they mean? Damn it! A bell never goes tinkle-tinkle of its own accord; if no one tugs it or touches it, it's still, it's silent. (*Looking in the direction of the forum*) But who's this I see down the street, breaking into a run? I want to observe what he's up to. I'll step back here. (*He withdraws.*)

Act Four.   Scene III

(Enter STASIMUS *from the forum, running and somewhat unsteady.)*

STASIMUS *(to himself)*: Stasimus, make haste with all speed, get home to your master's house, or something frightful will happen suddenly to your shoulder blades, through your own stupidity. Lively now, let's hasten! It's been a long time since you left home. Just look out for yourself that the tinklepot game[12] doesn't get you with blows of bull's-hide on your back, if you're missing when master wants you. Don't stop running now. *(He pauses and looks at his hand)* Damnation, Stasimus! You're a worthless wretch! Did you really leave your ring in the wine-shop after the wine had warmed your whistle? *(Turning)* Back you go, run back to get it back, while you can.

CHARMIDES *(aside)*: Whoever this fellow is, his throat is his taskmaster; it's teaching him the art of running.

STASIMUS *(to himself)*: Aren't you ashamed of yourself, you good-for-nothing? To have lost your memory after three guzzles! Or was it because you were drinking there with honest fellows, who could easily keep their hands off other people's property? Close-fist was there, Cocktail, Catch-crumb, Crib-ring, Cakeling[13]—clatter-eyes and clatter-shins, all of them, and fetter-galled rascals, too. Do you think you can get your ring back from men like that? Any one of 'em could steal the sole of a shoe right off a runner when he was running.

CHARMIDES *(aside)*: God bless me! What an old master of a thief!

STASIMUS: Why go after what's gone? I'd just be adding extra toil to my loss, as a sort of additional bonus. Why don't you consider what's lost is lost? *(Turning again)* Swing about! Back again to your master!

CHARMIDES: This man's not a runaway slave, anyway; he thinks of home.

STASIMUS: How I wish the old-fashioned standards, the old-fashioned thrift, were held in greater esteem today than evil practices!

CHARMIDES *(aside)*: Ye immortal gods! He's really beginning to put forth royal reforms! He longs for the old-fashioned ways; he loves them just as his forefathers did, you can be sure of that.

STASIMUS: Nowadays it's the practice to have no regard for what is proper, but—but merely what is pleasing. Corruption is the common practice, and the laws are lax; it's the common practice that permits you to drop your shield and flee from the enemy; it's become the practice to seek office as a reward for wrongdoing.

CHARMIDES (*aside*): A shameless practice, indeed!

STASIMUS: It's become the practice to pass over sound citizens.

CHARMIDES (*aside*): Oh, a worthless practice!

STASIMUS: Why, the common practices have now placed the laws in their power, and they've got them more under control than—children have their parents. The unhappy laws are hung on the wall with iron nails; it would be a great deal better to have our evil practices fastened there.

CHARMIDES (*aside*): I'd like to approach and accost him; but it's fun to hear him, and I'm afraid, if I speak to him, that he'll begin to talk about something else.

STASIMUS: And law gives no protection from these present day practices; law is subservient to 'em, and they proceed to plunder both what's sacred and public.

CHARMIDES (*aside*): Damnation! A painful punishment ought to be given to these practices.

STASIMUS: And shouldn't things like this be punished by the state? For such men are public enemies and do injury to the state as a whole; by their own dishonest conduct they destroy confidence in the honesty of those who have done no wrong; for people judge their character by the character of the others. And how did this idea occur to me? My own experience just reminded me of it. If you give anyone a loan, it's lost and no longer your own; when you ask it back, you find that your kindness has turned your friend into an enemy. If you begin to press him for it, you have a choice of two things: either you'll lose your loan or you'll lose your friend.[14]

CHARMIDES (*aside*): Why, this is my slave Stasimus.

STASIMUS: Take my own case: I made a loan of a talent, and with that talent I bought an enemy and sold a friend. But I'm all the greater fool for worrying about public matters instead of my immediate interest— guarding my back. I'm going home. (*He turns towards* LESBONICUS' *door.*)

CHARMIDES: Hey, there, you! Stand still! Listen here!

STASIMUS (*without looking back*): Hey, there, you! I won't stand.

CHARMIDES: I want you!

STASIMUS (*not looking*): What if I don't want you to want me?

CHARMIDES: Ah! You're acting awfully rudely, Stasimus.

STASIMUS (*not looking*): You'd better buy yourself a person to order around.

CHARMIDES: Damn it! I did buy one and paid the money down, too. but if he won't obey my order, what am I to do?

STASIMUS (*not looking*): Punish him plenty.

CHARMIDES: Good advice; I've decided to do it.

STASIMUS (*not looking*): That is, unless you're obligated to him.

CHARMIDES: If you're a good slave, I'm obligated to you; if not, I'll do as you suggest.

STASIMUS (*not looking*): What concern of mine is it whether you have good slaves or bad slaves?

CHARMIDES: Because you have a share in both the good and the bad.

STASIMUS (*not looking*): That latter share I leave to you; just put the other share down on my account, the good share.

CHARMIDES: You'll get it, if you deserve it. Look back at me. I am Charmides.

STASIMUS (*turning around*): Eh? Who's this that mentioned the best man alive?

CHARMIDES: The best man alive himself.

STASIMUS: Sea and earth and heavens! Ye gods, protect me! Can I believe my eyes? Is it he, or is it not? It is, it certainly is, it is most assuredly! O my most longed-for master, the best of health to you!

CHARMIDES: And to you, Stasimus!

STASIMUS: That you are safe—

CHARMIDES (*interrupting*): I know, and I believe you. But drop the rest of it. Answer me this: how are my children, my son and my daughter that I left here?

STASIMUS: They're alive and well.

CHARMIDES: You mean both of them?

STASIMUS: Yes, sir.

CHARMIDES (*fervently*): Then the gods wish me to be safe and saved! (*Going towards the door of* CALLICLES' *house*) The rest of the things I want to know I'll ask you at my leisure inside. Let's go in. Come along.

STASIMUS (*in alarm*): Where are you going?

CHARMIDES: Where would I go, except home?

STASIMUS: Now—

CHARMIDES: Now, what?

STASIMUS: That's not our house.

CHARMIDES (*amazed*): What's this you say?

STASIMUS: Your son sold the house—

CHARMIDES: Ruination!

STASIMUS: —for silver minae, paid down in cash—

CHARMIDES: How many?

STASIMUS: Forty, sir.

CHARMIDES: Good God! Who bought it?

STASIMUS: Callicles, the man you entrusted your affairs to; he moved here to live and kicked us outside.

CHARMIDES: Where's my son living now?

STASIMUS: Here in this rear apartment.

CHARMIDES (*in despair*): I'm completely done for!

STASIMUS: I thought you'd take it hard when you heard about it.

CHARMIDES (*dramatically*): I've sailed the mighty main midst countless dangers, at the peril of my life I've preserved myself from pirates aplenty, and I've returned in safety. Now, back home, I'm ruined and wretched, on account of the same ones for whom I've been struggling at my time of life. Oh, the bitterness of it takes my breath. Stasimus, hold me up.

STASIMUS (*supporting him*): Do you want me to get you some water?

CHARMIDES: They should have poured water on my property, when it was gasping for breath.

Act Four.   Scene IV

(*Enter* CALLICLES *from his house, in working clothes.*)

CALLICLES: What's this uproar I hear in front of my house?

CHARMIDES: O Callicles, O Callicles, O Callicles! What sort of friend did I entrust my property to?

CALLICLES: One who is upright and faithful and loyal and most devoted. My greetings to you, and I'm delighted that you have returned safely. (*He whispers a few words in* CHARMIDES' *ear.*)

CHARMIDES (*learning the truth about the house*): I believe so, if everything is as you say. But what's the meaning of this garb of yours?

CALLICLES: I'll tell you. (*In a lower tone*) I was digging up the treasure inside to get a dowry to give your daughter. But I'll explain this and all the rest of it to you inside. Come along.

CHARMIDES: Stasimus!

STASIMUS: Huh?

CHARMIDES: Run swiftly to Piraeus and make one long race of it! You'll see the ship there that we came in on. Bid Sangario to tend to the unloading of the things I ordered, and you stay with him. The duty has already been paid at the custom house; there's no need for delay. Go on, step lively, and get back here in a hurry!

STASIMUS: I'm there and back here too.

CALLICLES (*to* CHARMIDES): You follow me inside.

CHARMIDES: I'm right with you. (CHARMIDES *and* CALLICLES *go inside.*)

STASIMUS (*to himself*): Well, this one man has remained a faithful friend to my master and hasn't yielded an inch from his devotion and loyalty; he's the one person, I suspect, that's kept faith. But I believe that he's had a lot of trouble over the matter. . . .[10] (STASIMUS *departs in the direction of the harbour; a short time is supposed to elapse before the next Act.*)

Act Five. Scene I

(*Enter* LYSITELES, *overjoyed.*)

LYSITELES (*to himself*): Here's the man preeminent among all men, the one who's outstanding in joys and pleasures! All the delights I desire befall me at the right time! The things I want pursue me, stand by me, chase after me, and joy follows upon joy! Stasimus, the slave of Lesbonicus, just now met me at home; he told me that his master Charmides had arrived from abroad. Now I must meet him quickly, that the father may confirm with his greater authority the arrangement I've made with his son. I'll go. (*Listening*) But the door is creaking; that means an awkward delay. (*He steps back.*)

Act Five. Scene II

(*Enter* CHARMIDES *and* CALLICLES *from the house.*)

CHARMIDES (*in great earnestness*): There never was and never will be, and I don't think there is now, any man on earth whose faith and fidelity towards a friend can equal yours. Why, if it hadn't been for you, he would have unhoused me from this house.

CALLICLES: If in any way I have acted well towards a friend or been devoted to his best interests, I don't feel that I have deserved praise, I merely think I have been free from fault. For a gift that's bestowed outright upon a man is lost at once; that which is lent can be recalled whenever you wish.

CHARMIDES: It's just as you say. But I can't wonder enough at this— that he betrothed his sister into such a fine family.

CALLICLES: Yes; it's Lysiteles, the son of Philto.

LYSITELES (*aside*): Why, he's mentioning my name.

CHARMIDES: It's an excellent family he's got into.

LYSITELES (*aside*): Why not speak to them at once? (*Changing his mind*) But I'll wait a bit, I think, for he's beginning to talk on just the right topic.

CHARMIDES: Damn!

CALLICLES: What's the matter?

CHARMIDES: I forgot to mention this to you inside just now. When I arrived a little while ago, I ran into some sort of trickster, a very supercolossal swindler. He said that he was bringing to you and my son Lesbonicus a thousand gold pieces that I had given him. I didn't know who he was and I'd never laid eyes on him anywhere before. (*As* CALLICLES *bursts out laughing*) But what are you laughing about?

CALLICLES: He came at my instigation, to pretend to bring me money from you that I could give as a dowry to your daughter; when I gave her the money I had on hand, I wanted your son to think it had come from you; I didn't want him to find out the truth in any way, that your treasure was in my possession, and then bring suit against me to claim it as part of his father's property.

CHARMIDES: Clever, by gad!

CALLICLES: Megaronides, our devoted friend, devised the scheme.

CHARMIDES: Well, I'm delighted with the deception! My hearty approval!

LYSITELES (*aside*): Why do I stand here like a fool, afraid to break in on their conversation, instead of doing what I intended to do? I'll speak to the men. (*He approaches them.*)

CHARMIDES (*to* CALLICLES): Who is this fellow coming towards us?

LYSITELES: Best greetings from Lysiteles to Charmides, his father-in-law!

CHARMIDES (*genially*): The gods give you whatever you wish, Lysiteles!

CALLICLES (*smiling*): Don't you consider me worthy of a greeting?

LYSITELES: Of course; my greetings to you too, Callicles. But it's right for me to put him first—"the shirt is closer than the coat."

CALLICLES (*to them both*): I hope that heaven will give your plans a happy outcome.

CHARMIDES: I hear that my daughter has been betrothed to you.

LYSITELES: If you have no objection.

CHARMIDES: Why, no! I have no objection.

LYSITELES: Then do you promise me your daughter as my wife?

CHARMIDES: I promise her, and a thousand gold Philippeans as a dowry.

LYSITELES: I don't care about the dowry, sir.

CHARMIDES (*smiling*): If she is pleasing to you, the dowry that she gives you must please you too. In short, you won't get what you want, if you don't take what you don't want.

CALLICLES (*to* LYSITELES): That's a just plea.

LYSITELES: He'll win his case, with you as advocate and judge. (*To* CHARMIDES) Do you promise to give me your daughter on those terms?

CHARMIDES: I promise.[15]

CALLICLES: And I likewise promise.

LYSITELES (*overjoyed*): Blessings on you, my kinsmen!

CHARMIDES (*sternly*): And yet, confound it, there are some things that I'm angry at you about.

LYSITELES (*in surprise*): What have I done?

CHARMIDES: You've permitted my son to be a rotter.

LYSITELES: If this happened with my approval, you have just cause to be angry at me. But permit me to gain from you one thing that I want.

CHARMIDES: What is it?

LYSITELES: I'll tell you. If he has acted foolishly in any way, please pardon him. Why do you shake your head?

CHARMIDES: I'm tortured at heart and I'm afraid.

LYSITELES: Why on earth are you?

CHARMIDES: I'm tortured because he is the sort of youth I don't want him to be. I'm afraid, if I refuse your request, that you will think I don't hold you in sufficient esteem. Well, I won't be hardheaded about it. I'll do as you wish.

LYSITELES: You're a grand person. I'll go and call him out. (*He hurries to* LESBONICUS' *door.*)

CHARMIDES: It's a shocking thing, if one isn't allowed to punish evil-doing as it deserves.

LYSITELES (*knocking*): Open up here, open up quickly, and call out Lesbonicus, if he's at home. It's an urgent matter, and I want to see him at once. (*He knocks again.*)

(*Enter* LESBONICUS *from his house.*)

LESBONICUS (*angrily*): Who the devil's made such a thundering noise to get me outside?

LYSITELES: Your friend and well-wisher.

LESBONICUS: Is everything all right? Tell me.

LYSITELES: Just fine. I'm happy that your father's returned safely from abroad.

LESBONICUS: Who says he has?

LYSITELES: I do.

LESBONICUS: Have you seen him?

LYSITELES: Yes, and you may see him likewise. (*He points to* CHARMIDES.)

LESBONICUS: Oh, father, father dear, blessings on you!

CHARMIDES: And many blessings on you, my son!

LESBONICUS: If I've caused you any anguish, father—

CHARMIDES (*generously*): Nothing has happened; have no fear. My affairs have prospered, and I'm back safe and sound—if only you're willing to be an upright youth. (*As* LESBONICUS *nods his willingness*) A wife's been arranged for you, the daughter of Callicles here.

LESBONICUS: I'll marry her, father, her and anyone else you want me to.

CHARMIDES (*laughing*): Although I was angry with you, one affliction is quite enough for one man.

CALLICLES: Oh, no! It isn't enough for him. Why, it wouldn't be enough, if he should marry a hundred wives for his sins.

LESBONICUS: But from now on I shall live a decent life.

CHARMIDES: Good words; if you'll only act accordingly.

LYSITELES: There's no reason, is there, why I shouldn't marry to-morrow?

CHARMIDES: None at all. (*To* LESBONICUS) And you be ready to marry the day after.

THE ACTORS: Give us your applause.

1. Plautus preserves the Greek atmosphere here by referring to Latin as "a foreign tongue."

2. Lindsay brackets this passage as a later addition.

3. This is an amusing use of the regular Roman formula of divorce, by which the wife received back her dowry.

4. A slave's money was legally the property of his master.

5. Literally "I promise"; the formal betrothal was similar to the terms of a verbal contract; see note 15.

6. The text is corrupt here.

7. The loan by a slave of so large a sum is of course purely imaginary, and the Roman audience would so understand it.

8. Charmides' mythology is inaccurate; Nereus was not the brother of Jupiter and Neptune.

9. The meaning of *dormitator* is uncertain; it has been explained both as "one who sleeps by day and steals by night," and "one who talks foolishly in his sleep."

10. There is a short lacuna here.

11. Since the new aediles ("police commissioners") entered office in March and the Megalensian Games, held in April, did not have dramatic productions until 194 B.C., this play must have been produced in the last decade of Plautus' life.

12. *Cottabus* ("tinklepot") was a game in which a few drops of wine were thrown into a brazen vessel in such a way that they made a ringing sound.

13. The comic names invented by Stasimus are thus translated by Freeman and Sloman in their edition of the play.

14. Cf. Polonius in *Hamlet*, Act One, Scene III:
> "Neither a borrower nor a lender be:
> For loan oft loses both itself and friend."

15. The betrothal here follows the legal phraseology of the *sponsio*, or verbal contract.

XX
TRUCULENTUS

CHARACTERS IN THE PLAY

DINIARCHUS, *a young Athenian*
ASTAPHIUM, *maid of* PHRONESIUM
TRUCULENTUS, *slave of* STRABAX
PHRONESIUM, *a courtesan*
STRATOPHANES, *a soldier*
CYAMUS, *a Thracian slave belonging to* DINIARCHUS
STRABAX, *a country youth*
CALLICLES, *an aged Athenian*
A MAID *belonging to* CALLICLES
SURA, *a hairdresser*

ACROSTIC ARGUMENT

Three young men are madly in love with one and the same woman—one a country youth, another a city youth, the third a soldier from abroad. In order to rake in a heavy haul from the soldier, she secretly passes off as her own a child of unknown parentage. A slave tries with force and harshness to keep harlots from squandering the savings of his master, but even he is softened. The soldier arrives and gives costly gifts because of the child. Finally the father of the ravished maiden learns all the facts, and it is agreed that the man who raped her shall marry her; the courtesan who has posed as the child's mother gives back the child to its father.

INTRODUCTION

THE *Truculentus* is an unusual play. Like *The Three Penny Day* it is concerned primarily with the delineation of character, but in this instance the characters are unpleasant and unsympathetic. The *Truculentus* presents a picture of the life of a courtesan and her treatment of her lovers. To Phronesium young men exist only as a source of wealth and she plays each against the other in order to increase the lavishness of their gifts. The already bankrupt Diniarchus, the soldier Stratophanes, and the country youth Strabax vie with each other in their attempts to win her favour. The portrayal of these characters and especially of the mercenary Phronesium and her equally crafty maid Astaphium is cruel and vivid. The gruff servant Truculentus who gives his name to the play, although his role is a minor one, is interesting as an ancient forerunner of Mrs. Malaprop.

The play includes the motives of trickery and recognition but they are secondary to the dramatist's main purpose. Phronesium pretends to be the mother of a baby to increase the plunder she gets from Stratophanes. Her feigned convalescence and apparent disdain of the soldier's gifts create a situation full of grim humour. Stratophanes' fury at being scorned and his altercation with Diniarchus' slave are effectively displayed. One unusual feature of the soldier is that, unlike other Plautine warriors, he has no desire to boast of his exploits. When Diniarchus is revealed as the father of the baby, he departs to marry the child's mother, promising Phronesium that he will visit her from time to time. The play closes with the soldier and Strabax frantically outdoing each other in their efforts to win over the courtesan—"a fool and a madman competing for their own ruin," is Astaphium's cynical comment. Phronesium promises to divide her favours between them—an unpleasant ending matched in Roman comedy only by the agreement of Phaedria in Terence's *The Eunuch* to use Thraso's infatuation for Thais as a source of revenue.

The *Truculentus* is the comedy which, along with the *Pseudolus,* is said to have brought pleasure to Plautus in his old age. Estimates of the play in modern times have varied widely. The immorality of the play and its sordid plot have been sharply condemned. Yet the effect of the play is far more striking than that of many other Plautine comedies. Paul Lejay considers it the one satiric comedy which Plautus wrote and says that his other plays would amuse the spectators but the *Truculentus* would make them think. W. M. Lindsay calls it "one of Plautus' cleverest plays," and P. J. Enk refers to it as a masterpiece. Whatever the attitude of the individual critic will be, the *Truculentus* stands alone among Roman comedies for its bitter treatment and sardonic humour and for its lifelike portrayal of one unpleasant aspect of ancient society.

TRUCULENTUS

(SCENE:—*A street in Athens in front of the house of* PHRONESIUM *and the town house of the father of* STRABAX.)

Prologue

Plautus seeks a very small section of your large and pleasant city, to which he may transport Athens without the aid of architects. Well, now! Will you give it to him or not? They nod assent. Then I shall obtain it from you without delay.[1] What if I should ask for something from your private property? They nod dissent. Excellent, by Jove! The good old customs still abide with you, to have a ready tongue for saying "No." But let's discuss the matter for which we came here. This stage before us shall be Athens while we perform this comedy. A woman named Phronesium dwells here (*pointing to her house*). Her character befits this present age: she never demands from her lover—what's been already given, but she sees to it that there's nothing left of what he has left; she begs and carries it off, as is the way of women. All the women do this, as soon as they perceive that men are in love with them. This woman pretends to the soldier that she has given birth to a child; she wants to sweep away his property to the very last cent. Why say more? . . .[2]

Act One. Scene I

(*Enter* DINIARCHUS.)

DINIARCHUS (*to the audience*): An entire lifetime isn't really long enough for a lover to learn how many roads there are to destruction. And Venus herself, in whose hands lie the sum and substance of lovers, will never instruct us in calculation of this sort—how many ways there are to deceive a lover, how many methods of destroying him, how many enticements to entice him. And how many blandishments there are, how many angry moods, how many gifts to be presented![3] The gods protect us! Whew! And all the lying that has to be done, in addition to the

95

gifts! In the first place, then, there's the yearly allowance; that's her first haul, and for that three nights are granted. Meanwhile she asks for money or wine or oil or wheat to find out whether you're generous or thrifty. It's just like dropping a casting net into a fish pond; when the net has gone to the bottom, the fisherman draws up the rope; when the net's been cast, he makes sure that the fish doesn't get away; moving the net here and there, he keeps the fish entangled until he gets it out of the water. It's the same way with a lover, if he gives what is asked and is generous rather than thrifty. More nights are added and in the meantime he swallows the hook; if once he's drained a drink of undiluted love and the draught has gone deep into his breast, at once the lover's done for, and his fortune and his credit as well. If a harlot happens to be angry at her lover, the lover's doubly ruined; he's lost both his fortune and his peace of mind; if another man is more desirable to her, he's likewise ruined; if the nights he spends with her are few, his peace of mind is ruined; if the nights are many, the lover's happy, but his fortune's ruined. Before you give one thing, she's ready to ask for a hundred; a gold trinket's been lost, or a cloak torn, or a maidservant bought, or a silver bowl, or a bronze bowl, or a couch, or a little Greek casket, or there's always something the lover must furnish his wench with.[4]

And while we're ruining our fortunes, our credit, and ourselves, we take great pains to conceal our actions and keep them dark, so that our parents and relatives won't know about them. But if we should inform them of our deeds instead of concealing things, they would restrain our fiery blood at the appropriate time, and we could pass on to our descendants the wisdom of the past; then, I'd guarantee, there'd be no more pimps and harlots, and there'd be a lot fewer spendthrifts than there are at present. As things are now, there are almost more pimps and harlots than there are flies in the heat of the summer. Why, if they aren't anywhere else, there are enough pimps and harlots sitting around the bankers' booths to make a considerable number; I'm quite sure there are more harlots there than scale-weights. And what value the pimps are at the bankers' I don't know, except to be used as account books, where the money lent out may be put down; I'm referring to money paid out; don't think I mean money paid back. In short, in this great nation of many people, now that the state is peaceful and quiet and our enemies have been defeated, everyone who has the price to pay must have a love affair.

Now, take my own case: Phronesium, the courtesan who dwells here, has completely driven her name from my heart, [Phronesium, for phronesis means wisdom.][5] I used to be first and foremost with her, I admit, and that's a damned disastrous position for a lover's cash. Then

she found another person who could give her more, a Babylonian soldier, and since he was a greater spendthrift, she moved him into my
position, although the hussy said she hated and detested him. It's said
now that he'll soon arrive from abroad; so she's cooked up this plot:
she pretends that she has given birth to a child and that the soldier is
the baby's father; that's to get rid of me and enable her to live a gay
life with the soldier. That's why the slut needs a palmed-off child! Does
she fancy she can deceive me? Did she think she could hide it from
me, if she'd been pregnant? It was the day before yesterday that I returned to Athens from Lemnos, where I'd gone on a public mission.
(*As* PHRONESIUM'S *door opens*) But here's her little maid Astaphium!
I've had some traffic with that young lady, too. (*He withdraws.*)

Act One.   Scene II

(*Enter* ASTAPHIUM *from* PHRONESIUM'S *house.*)

ASTAPHIUM (*to servants within*): Listen at the doors and look after the
house, so that no visitor goes away more heavily laden than when he
came; don't let anyone that came to us empty-handed leave the house
with his hands full. (*To herself*) I know the ways of men; that's what
the young ones are up to these days. Five or six jolly fellows come in
to visit the harlots; their plans are prepared; when they get inside, one
of them keeps kissing his mistress constantly, while all the others turn
into kleptomaniacs; but if they see anyone watching them, they devise
some trick to delight the observer with their jests and games. Often they
stuff away a lot that belongs to us; they act just like sausage-makers.
(*To the audience*) That's what happens, confound it, and some of you
spectators know that I'm not lying. It's a brave exploit for them to get
plunder from us plunderers. But gracious me! We pay these robbers of
ours back in their own coin in a lovely fashion; why, they look on while
we heap up their property, and they even bring it to us of their own
accord.

DINIARCHUS (*aside*): She's whipping me with words like that, for I
brought property of mine here.

ASTAPHIUM (*answering someone within*): I remember. To be sure, I'll
bring him back with me to our house, if he's at home. (*She moves away.*)

DINIARCHUS: Hallo there! Astaphium, wait a minute, before you leave.

ASTAPHIUM (*without turning*): Who calls me back?

DINIARCHUS: You'll find out; look back here.

ASTAPHIUM (*still not turning*): Who is it?

DINIARCHUS: A man who wants you all to have lots of good things.

ASTAPHIUM (*as before*): Give them to us, if you want us to have them.

DINIARCHUS: You'll have them, I promise. Just look back here.

ASTAPHIUM (*as before*): Oh, dear, whoever you are, you're bothering me to death.

DINIARCHUS: Stop, you worthless wretch!

ASTAPHIUM (*as before*): My good sir, you're a nuisance. (*Turning*) Is that Diniarchus? Why, it certainly is.

DINIARCHUS: I'm glad to see you.

ASTAPHIUM (*indifferently*): The same to you.

DINIARCHUS: Give me your hand and walk along with me.

ASTAPHIUM (*advancing*): I'm your servant and obedient to your command. (*She holds out her hand.*)

DINIARCHUS (*shaking her hand*): How are you?

ASTAPHIUM: In good health, and so's the man whose hand I'm holding. Since you've arrived from abroad, a dinner must be given.

DINIARCHUS: That's nice of you; a kind invitation, Astaphium.

ASTAPHIUM: Please now, let me go where mistress ordered.

DINIARCHUS (*releasing her hand*): Off with you then. But look here!

ASTAPHIUM: What do you want?

DINIARCHUS: Tell me where you're going. Who is it? Who are you fetching?

ASTAPHIUM: Archilis the midwife.

DINIARCHUS: You're a clever hussy; you smell of the training you've had. I've caught you in an open lie, you slut.

ASTAPHIUM: How is that, please tell me.

DINIARCHUS: Because you said you were going to bring "him," not "her." Now you've turned the man into a woman. A sly deceiver you are! Now tell me, Astaphium. Who is this fellow? A new lover?

ASTAPHIUM: I think you're a man of considerable leisure.

DINIARCHUS: Why do you think that?

ASTAPHIUM: Because you attend to other people's affairs without charging them for your food and clothing.

DINIARCHUS: You people have provided me with the leisure.

ASTAPHIUM: How's that, I'd like to know?

DINIARCHUS: I'll elucidate. I lost my property at your house; you're the ones that robbed me of my occupation. If I'd kept my property, I'd have some business to keep me occupied.

ASTAPHIUM: Do you think that you can farm on the public lands of Venus or of Love on any other terms than by becoming a man of leisure?

DINIARCHUS: Phronesium was the public land farmer, not I; your explanation is all twisted. Why, she's taken away my cattle, contrary to the legal terms of my pasturage tax.

ASTAPHIUM: Most persons who mismanage their property do the same thing you're doing; when they haven't anything to pay their taxes with, they find fault with the tax officials.

DINIARCHUS: My pasturage contract with you is turning out badly. Now, for a change, I'd like to have a nice little bit of plough-land at your place, as much as my resources permit.

ASTAPHIUM: This field of ours is for pasture, not ploughing. People who want plough-land had better go to boys for it; They're accustomed to being ploughed. We girls have this bit of public land, but those others are the real publicans.

DINIARCHUS: I know both types very well.

ASTAPHIUM: Gracious me! That's why you are a man of leisure—because you went wrong in that direction and this too. But with which do you prefer to have dealings?

DINIARCHUS: You're more impertinent, but they're full of perjury. Whatever one gives them is lost and they don't even benefit by it. If you girls get something, at least you drink and feast it away. In short, they're shameless, while you are worthless and conceited.

ASTAPHIUM: All this abuse you heap upon us is really directed against yourself, Diniarchus, instead of us and them.

DINIARCHUS: How is that?

ASTAPHIUM: Here's the reason: a man who criticises another's faults ought himself to be spotless. You don't get anything from us, wise guy; we may be worthless, but we can get it from you.

DINIARCHUS (*sadly*): Oh, Astaphium, that isn't the way you used to talk to me; you were flattering then, when I still possessed what is now in your possession.

ASTAPHIUM: When a man's alive, you may know him; when he's dead, let him rest in peace. I knew you as long as you were alive.

DINIARCHUS: You don't consider me dead, do you?

ASTAPHIUM: Tell me please, how could you be more so? You used to be her favoured lover, but now you bring your sweetheart nothing but complaints.

DINIARCHUS: Damn it! It's your own fault; you girls were in such a hurry to get your plunder. You should have done it more leisurely, so that I could last longer for you.

ASTAPHIUM: A lover is like an enemy's city.

DINIARCHUS: How do you make that out?

ASTAPHIUM: It's the best thing for his sweetheart to have him sacked as soon as possible.

DINIARCHUS: I admit that, but a friend is very different from a lover. Heavens! The oldest friend's the best thing a person can have. And confound it! I'm not dead yet; I still have some land and houses.

ASTAPHIUM (*changing her tone*): Well for heaven's sake! Why are you standing here in front of the door like a stranger and a foreigner? Go right in; you're not a stranger, no indeed! Goodness me! There isn't a person today that she loves more with her heart and soul, (*aside*) if you really do have some land and houses.

DINIARCHUS: Your tongues and talk are steeped in honey; your deeds and your hearts are steeped in gall and bitter vinegar. You utter sweet words with your tongues, but your hearts are filled with deeds of bitterness.

ASTAPHIUM: If lovers don't give us presents, I haven't learned how to talk.

DINIARCHUS: . . . I haven't learned how to talk either.[1]

ASTAPHIUM: You shouldn't talk this way, you soul of generosity. Leave that to these miserly men who struggle against their own inclinations.

DINIARCHUS: You're a tricky wench, just as enticing as ever!

ASTAPHIUM: How eagerly we awaited your return from abroad! Heavens! Mistress is so anxious to see you.

DINIARCHUS: How's this, now?

ASTAPHIUM: You're the only one she loves of all her lovers.

DINIARCHUS (*aside*): Well done, lands and houses! You've come to my aid at the right time. (*Aloud*) Look here, Astaphium.

ASTAPHIUM: What do you wish?

DINIARCHUS: Is Phronesium inside now?

ASTAPHIUM: She is for you, whatever she is for the others.

DINIARCHUS: Is she well?

ASTAPHIUM: Oh, my, yes! And she'll be still better, I hope, when she sees you.

DINIARCHUS: This is our greatest fault, this is the thing that ruins us when we're in love: if we're told what we want to hear, even when it's an obvious lie, we're fools enough to believe it the truth, and then we let our righteous anger drop.[6]

ASTAPHIUM: Oh, come now! That's not so.

DINIARCHUS: You say she loves me, eh?

ASTAPHIUM: Why, you're her one and only.

DINIARCHUS: I heard that she's had a baby.

ASTAPHIUM: Oh, Diniarchus, please hush!

DINIARCHUS: What's the matter?

ASTAPHIUM: Poor me! I shudder whenever there's any mention of the childbirth; you almost lost your Phronesium. Go on in, please, and see her. But you'll have to wait; she was in her bath; she'll soon be out, though.

DINIARCHUS: See here, you. How could she have a baby when she was never pregnant? That belly of hers never showed signs of swelling, to the best of my knowledge.

ASTAPHIUM: She didn't let you know about it; she was afraid that you'd urge her to have an abortion and cause the death of the baby.

DINIARCHUS: Damn it! Then that Babylonian soldier is the baby's father, and she's awaiting his arrival now.

ASTAPHIUM: Yes, they say the soldier will soon be here, according to the message he sent. I'm surprised that he hasn't arrived already.

DINIARCHUS (*hesitating*): Shall I go in, then?

ASTAPHIUM: Of course. Just as boldly as in your own home. Dear me! You're one of the family, Diniarchus, even now.

DINIARCHUS: How soon will you be back?

ASTAPHIUM: In just a minute. The place I'm headed for isn't far away.

DINIARCHUS: Be sure to come back quickly. In the meantime, I'll wait here in your house. (*He goes into the house of* PHRONESIUM.)

Act Two. Scene I

ASTAPHIUM (*to herself*): Ha, ha, ha! I can relax now, since that pest of mine has gone inside. At last I'm alone. Now I can speak as freely as I want to and say just what I wish and please. The poor sap! My mistress has already sung a dirge over his property. Those lands and houses of his are mortgaged to pay for Love's estate. But my mistress does talk over frankly with him her most important plans, and he's considered more as a friend on the advisory board than a person on active duty. He gave while he could; now he has nothing. We have what he had, and what we had he now has. That's the way things happen in life. Fortunes are in the habit of changing quickly, life is uncertain; we remember him when he was rich, and he remembers us when we were poor; our memories have shifted. Anyone would be a fool to marvel at this. If he's impoverished, we must put up with it; he had his love, he got his just deserts. It's a sin for us to pity men who mismanage their property. A bawd who knows her business ought to have good teeth, she ought to smile on each newcomer and speak alluring words, with evil plans in her heart and fair words on her tongue. A courtesan should resemble a briar bush; any man she touches should suffer plenty of pain. She ought never to listen to a lover's pleas, but should send him off home as a deserter when he no longer has anything to give her. Only a man who hates his own money will ever be any good as a lover. As long as he can pay, he can love; when his money runs out, he can turn to another occupation; when he has nothing, he should be reasonable and yield his place to those who have. His gifts are useless unless he desires to give again; the man who's forgotten the gift he just gave is the one loved at our house. The proper lover is one who forgets all else and then squanders his money too. The men complain that we always treat them badly and that we're so greedy. How are we? And in what way do we treat them badly? Goodness me! No lover has ever given enough to his sweetheart, and God knows we've never received enough, and no girl has ever asked enough. When a lover runs out of gifts and says he hasn't anything more to give, we believe his word alone, and we don't have enough for ourselves, when he doesn't have enough to give. We ought always to be on the watch for new givers, who have untouched treasures to make their gifts from. Take for instance the country youth who lives here (*indicating the house of* STRABAX). My goodness! What a charming person he is, and what a generous giver! Why, just last night he jumped over the garden wall and visited us, without his father knowing it. He's the man I want to meet. But his slave is a terribly savage fellow; when he sees any one of us come near the house, he shouts at us and scares us away as if he were shooing geese from a corn bin. He's such a bumpkin. Well, come what may, I'll knock at the door. (*Knocking*) Does anyone have charge of this door? Is anyone coming out here? (*She steps back, as the door opens violently.*)

Act Two.   Scene II

(*Enter* TRUCULENTUS *in a temper.*)

TRUCULENTUS: Who the devil is banging on our door like a battering-ram?

ASTAPHIUM (*sweetly*): It's I. Look here at me.

TRUCULENTUS: What "I" do you mean?

ASTAPHIUM: Don't you think I'm "I"?

TRUCULENTUS: Why do you come near this house or do this hammering?

ASTAPHIUM: Good health to you.

TRUCULENTUS (*gruffly*): Enough of your good health. Don't want it. Ain't healthy anyway. I'd rather be sick than have any of your good health. What I want to know is, what's your business here at our house?

ASTAPHIUM (*calmly*): Hold, don't be distressed.

TRUCULENTUS: Hold your mistress yourself, confound you![7] That's what you're in the habit of doing. You shameless slut, getting fresh with a farmer and making indecent suggestions.

ASTAPHIUM: I said "distress"; you changed one letter in your reply. (*Aside*) This fellow is certainly truculent.

TRUCULENTUS (*overhearing*): Woman, you're still abusing me, eh?

ASTAPHIUM: How am I abusing you?

TRUCULENTUS: Well, you're calling me truculent. See here, if you don't get out of here right now or tell me at once what you want, I'm damned if I don't trample you underfoot, woman, just the way a sow does her litter of pigs.

ASTAPHIUM (*in disgust*): This is plain farmyard talk, all right.

TRUCULENTUS: The monkey stock is something to be more ashamed of. Have you come here to flaunt yourself, with your bones all bedecked, just because you've dyed your cloak the colour of smoke, you whore? Think you're pretty, eh, just because you've got brass bracelets?

ASTAPHIUM: Now I like you, when you speak so gruffly to me.

TRUCULENTUS (*beginning to weaken*): What about that question I asked you? (*Seizing her hand*) Do you carry brass rings around with you to claim property with? (*Eyeing her*) I'll bet you those Victories on your earrings are made of wood.

ASTAPHIUM: Don't touch me.

TRUCULENTUS (*recovering*): Touch you? So help me holy weeding-hoe, I'd rather go back to the country and embrace a broad-horned ox and spend an entire night with it on the straw, than have a hundred nights with you given me, dinners and all. You taunt me with the country, eh? Well, you've found a man that's ashamed of indecency. Damn it, woman, what business do you have at our house? What do you keep running here for, every time we come to the city?

ASTAPHIUM: I want to meet your women folks.

TRUCULENTUS: What women folks are you talking about? There isn't even a female fly in the house.

ASTAPHIUM: There's no woman living there?

TRUCULENTUS: They've gone to the farm, I tell you. Get out.

ASTAPHIUM: What are you shouting for, you lunatic?

TRUCULENTUS: By golly, if you don't make haste and hurry away from here, that hair of yours that's so nice and slick, so frizzled and frilled and perfumed, I'll yank right out of your brain.

ASTAPHIUM: What in the world for?

TRUCULENTUS: Because you dared to come near our door all scented and perfumed, and—and (*weakening again*) because you've got your cheeks covered with rouge so prettily.

ASTAPHIUM: Goodness me! I merely blushed with fright because you shouted so.

TRUCULENTUS: Is that so? You blushed, eh? Just as if there's any part of your body that can take any more colour, you minx. You've covered your cheeks with red paint and the rest of your body with white clay. You're all shameless creatures.

ASTAPHIUM: And just how have we shameless creatures wronged you people?

TRUCULENTUS: I know more than you think I know.

ASTAPHIUM: Please tell me, what is it you know?

TRUCULENTUS (*angrily*): How master's son Strabax is being ruined at your house, how you're luring him on to wickedness and wrongdoing.

ASTAPHIUM: If you were in your right mind, I'd say, "It's downright slander." No one is in the habit of being ruined at our house; it's their property they ruin. When their property's ruined, they can depart in safety if they wish. And I don't know that young man of yours, anyway.

TRUCULENTUS: Oh, is that so? What does the garden wall say, as it grows a brick lower every night, where he's travelled the road to destruction on his way to your house?

ASTAPHIUM: The wall's an old one; there's nothing strange about the old bricks tumbling down.

TRUCULENTUS: Old bricks tumbling down, is it? By Jove, may never a mortal man believe me again on two things,[8] if I don't tell my old master about these doings of yours.

ASTAPHIUM: Is he as savage as you are?

TRUCULENTUS: Well, he didn't make his money by giving handouts to harlots; he got it by thrift and hard work. And now it's being carried secretly over to your place, you shameless creatures. That's what you use for eating, anointing, imbibing. Me keep quiet about it? Damned if I don't go right now to the forum and tell the old man about these goings on. I don't want my hide to harvest a crop of misfortunes I didn't plant. (TRUCULENTUS *departs.*)

ASTAPHIUM (*to herself*): My goodness! If this fellow lived on mustard, I shouldn't think he could be so snappish. But he certainly seemed devoted to his master. Well, however savage he is, I hope a little coaxing, urging, and other courtesan-like tricks can change him; I've seen other wild beasts tamed.[1] Now I'll go back to see my mistress. (*As* PHRONESIUM's *door opens*) Well, there's that pest of mine coming out. He looks dejected. He still hasn't met Phronesium.

Act Two. Scene III

(*Enter* DINIARCHUS *from* PHRONESIUM's *house.*)

DINIARCHUS (*to himself*): Fish spend their whole lives bathing, but I don't think they take as long to bathe as Phronesium here. If women could be loved as long a time as they spend in their baths, all lovers would become bathkeepers.

ASTAPHIUM: Can't you endure waiting even a little while?

DINIARCHUS: Damn it! I'm worn out already with waiting. I need a bath myself, I'm so confounded tired. You go in, Astaphium, please, and tell her I'm here. Urge her to hurry up, convince her she's been bathing long enough.

ASTAPHIUM: All right. (*Going.*)

DINIARCHUS: And listen, will you?

ASTAPHIUM (*stopping*): What do you want?

DINIARCHUS: The gods damn me for calling you back! Didn't I just tell you to go?

ASTAPHIUM: What did you call me back for, then, you worthless wretch? You've made a mile's delay for yourself. (*She goes into the house.*)

DINIARCHUS (*to himself*): I wonder why she was standing out here so long in front of the house; she's on the lookout for someone; the soldier, probably. He's the one they're eager for now. They're just like vultures, foreseeing three days beforehand the day when they're going to have a good meal. They're all gaping for him, their minds are all fixed on him. When he gets here, nobody will pay any more attention to me than if I'd been dead for the past two hundred years. What happiness there is in holding on to one's cash! Damn me for a poor fool! I realise my fault, now that I've ruined my fortune. But now, if any large and juicy legacy should come my way, now that I know the sweet things and bitter things that money can bring, damned if I wouldn't save it and live so thriftily that (*weakening, as he glances at* PHRONESIUM's *house*) inside a few days I wouldn't have a cent left. That's the way I'd refute the people who criticise me now. But I see the door is opening; it's like a whirlpool and swallows up anything that comes within its bolts.

## Act Two.	Scene IV

(*Enter* PHRONESIUM, *attended by maids.*)

PHRONESIUM (*sweetly*): Tell me, please, you don't think my door will bite, do you? Is that why you're afraid to come in, darling?

DINIARCHUS (*aside*): See the spring! All flowers and fragrance! How it gleams and glistens!

PHRONESIUM: Why are you so rude on your return from Lemnos, Diniarchus, that you don't give your sweetheart a nice kiss?

DINIARCHUS (*aside*): Oh, Lord! Now I'm in for punishment, and it'll be terrible, too.

PHRONESIUM: Why did you turn away?

DINIARCHUS: How do you do, Phronesium?

PHRONESIUM: How are you? Will you dine with us today, now that you've arrived safely?

DINIARCHUS: I've accepted an invitation.

PHRONESIUM (*disappointed*): Where are you dining?

DINIARCHUS (*succumbing*): Wherever you say.

PHRONESIUM: It'll please me if you dine here.

DINIARCHUS: And me even more, I assure you. You'll spend today with me, won't you, Phronesium dear?

PHRONÆSIUM: I'd like to, if it were possible.

DINIARCHUS (*as if servants were present*): Bring me my sandals. Quick! Away with the table!

PHRONESIUM: I beg of you, are you in your right mind?

DINIARCHUS (*staggering away*): Gad! I can't drink now, I feel so faint!

PHRONESIUM: Wait; something'll be done. Don't go away.

DINIARCHUS (*recovering*): Ah! A dash of cold water! Now I feel better. (*To the imaginary servants*) Take away my sandals, give me something to drink.

PHRONESIUM (*smiling*): Dear me! Just the same as you used to be. But tell me, did you have a good trip?

DINIARCHUS: Surely; an excellent one, for it brought me here to you and gave me a chance to see you.

PHRONESIUM: Embrace me.

DINIARCHUS (*doing so*): Gladly! Ah-h-h! This is sweeter than sweet honey. This is why, O Jupiter, I'm more fortunate than you!

PHRONESIUM: Won't you give me a kiss?

DINIARCHUS: I'd rather give you ten. (*Beginning to kiss her.*)

PHRONESIUM: There, that's why you're poor. You promise me more than I ask of you. (*She holds him off.*)

DINIARCHUS: I wish you'd been as sparing of my money in the first place as you are now of your kisses.

PHRONESIUM: If I can possibly save you anything, I certainly want to do it.

DINIARCHUS: You're bathed now, aren't you?

PHRONESIUM: Gracious, yes! At least to my own satisfaction. I don't look dirty to you, do I?

DINIARCHUS: Heavens, no! Not to me anyway. But there was a time, when I was prosperous, when we seemed rather dirty to each other. But what's this I've heard upon arriving about your actions, this new trick that you've been up to during my absence?

PHRONESIUM (*innocently*): What do you mean?

DINIARCHUS (*with sarcasm*): Well, in the first place, I'm delighted that you've had a child and come through it safely.

PHRONESIUM (*to her maids*): Go into the house, girls, and close the door. (*To* DINIARCHUS, *when they have gone*) There's no one left now but you to hear what I have to say. I've always entrusted my most important plans to you. (*In a lower tone*) In fact, I haven't had a child and I wasn't pregnant; I just pretended to be. I don't deny that.

DINIARCHUS: Darling mine, on account of whom?

PHRONESIUM: On account of the Babylonian soldier, who kept me as a wife the year that he was here.

DINIARCHUS: I had suspected that. But what's the point of it? What was the advantage of the pretence?

PHRONESIUM: So there'd be a bond, a tie to bring him back to me again. Now he's just sent me a letter; he says he's going to find out how much I think of him: if I let this child of ours live and bring it up, he'll give me all his property, he says.

DINIARCHUS: I'm pleased to hear that. What's your plan, now?

PHRONESIUM: Now that the tenth month is almost here, mother told the maids to go in different directions and to hunt out and locate a baby, boy or girl, that could be passed off as mine. Why waste words? You know our hairdresser Sura?

DINIARCHUS: The one who lives across from your house? Of course.

PHRONESIUM: As she was working around from family to family, she got on the track of a baby boy. She brought me the baby secretly and said it had been given to her.

DINIARCHUS: What a sly baggage she was! And now the woman that gave birth to the child first isn't the mother, but you are by a second birth.

PHRONESIUM: You understand the whole matter perfectly. And now, according to the message the soldier sent me, he'll be here himself before long.

DINIARCHUS: So meanwhile you're taking care of yourself as if you'd just been in labour, eh?

PHRONESIUM: Why not, when the business can be so beautifully managed without any labour? It's the proper thing for everyone to be smart in his own profession.

DINIARCHUS: But what will become of me when the soldier arrives? Can I live, deprived of you?

PHRONESIUM: When I get from him what I want, I won't have any trouble finding a way to stir up enough discord to disrupt our arrangement. And after that, my darling, I'll be with you forever.

DINIARCHUS: Jove! I'd prefer a bed with you forever.

PHRONESIUM (*laughing*): Well, today, I must offer a sacrifice in behalf of my baby. It should be done on the fifth day.

DINIARCHUS: I suppose it should.

PHRONESIUM: Don't you want to give me some little gift?

DINIARCHUS: Damned if you don't make me feel prosperous again, darling, when you ask me for something.

PHRONESIUM: That's the way I feel when I get it.

DINIARCHUS: You'll have a gift, I'll see to that. I'll send my slave boy here with it.

PHRONESIUM: Please do so.

DINIARCHUS: Be satisfied with it, whatever he brings.

PHRONESIUM: Goodness! I won't be sorry to receive your gift; you'll see to that, I'm sure.

DINIARCHUS: Anything else you wish of me?

PHRONESIUM: Yes, come back to see me when you have time. Good-bye.

DINIARCHUS: Good-bye. (*To himself, as* PHRONESIUM *goes into her house*) Ye immortal gods! To do what she's just done for me isn't like a woman in love, it's more like a devoted and trusting pal; she confided to me the substitution of the child, a thing no girl would confide to her own sister. Now she's opened up her very soul to me; she'll never be faithless to me as long as she lives. Shouldn't I love her? Shouldn't I wish her well? I'll cease to love myself rather than fail to love her. Shouldn't I send her a gift? Why, I'll go this moment and have five minae sent her, besides having a mina's worth of food brought her. I'd rather have things well with her, who wishes me well, than with myself, since I bring all sorts of evil on myself. (DINIARCHUS *departs.*)

Act Two.   Scene V

(*Enter* PHRONESIUM *from her house, attended by maids who place a couch for her before the doorway.*)

PHRONESIUM (*to servants within*): Nurse that baby, girls. (*To herself*) Ah, what troubles we poor mothers have, what torture we endure! (*Reflecting*) Gracious, what a wicked scheme it is! And when I think the matter over, well—we're considered much less cunning than our natures really are. I speak for myself first, home-taught, that's what I am. Oh, the mental anxiety, the pangs in my heart, for fear the baby will die and—kill off my scheme. Now that I'm called a mother, I'm all the more eager to have it live. I was bold enough to undertake the scheme, now I must carry it out. It's a sinful thing I've started on, through my greed and love for gain; I've taken on myself the labour pangs of others. Still, one shouldn't enter on any sort of crafty game unless it's carried out with cunning and care. (*To the audience*) Now you can all see for yourselves the negligée that I've come out in; I'm pretending that I'm still ailing from the childbirth. If a woman starts to do something bad and doesn't carry it through to completion, she feels sick, she feels worn out, she feels just plain miserable. If a woman starts to do something good, she soon becomes disgusted with it. Very few women grow weary of doing something bad, and very few finish doing anything good; it's much less burdensome for a woman to do wrong than to do right. I'm a bad one myself, and it comes from my mother's training and my own baddish nature; I pretended to the Babylonian soldier that I was pregnant, and now I want him to know that my badness was well planned. He'll be here before long, I suppose. I've purposely taken precautions to lie here in this costume as though recovering from childbirth.[1] (*To the maids*) Some myrrh, please, and light a fire on the altar; I must worship Lucina. (*As the maids obey the orders*) Place it here, and go out of my sight. (*She moves towards the couch*) Oh, Pithecium, help me to lie down; come here, assist me! (*As she is made comfortable on the couch*) Ah! That's the way a new mother should be. Take my sandals, Archilis; throw a coverlet over me. (*Calling inside*) Where are you, Astaphium? Bring me out some herbs and some dainties. Bring water for my hands. (ASTAPHIUM *comes out, obeying the orders. The other maids go into the house*) Dear me! I wish the soldier would come now.

Act Two. Scene VI

(*Enter* STRATOPHANES, *followed by an orderly and two slave girls.*)

STRATOPHANES (*to the audience*): Spectators, don't expect me to praise my prowess; not by speech but by actions am I accustomed to announce my valorous deeds. Well I know that many military men have been monstrous liars. I could mention Homeronides[9] and a thousand after him who have been convicted and condemned for their fictitious battles. [The man who convinces a hearer more than an observer deserves no praise.][5] I have no use for the fellow who is praised by hearers more than by observers. One eyewitness is worth more than ten hearsays. The hearers say what they hear, the observers really know. And I have no use for warriors that city fops praise and the soldiers are silent about, nor for those whose tongues at home are sharp enough to blunt the edge of swords. Why, the brave bring far more benefit to the people than do the eloquent and clever. Valour easily finds for itself a fluent eloquence. An eloquent citizen without valour I'd consider like a hired mourner who praises others but can't praise herself. Well, after ten months' absence I'm returning to Athens to see my sweetheart; I left her pregnant here from my embrace, and I want to see how she fares.

PHRONESIUM (*to* ASTAPHIUM): See who's talking so near to me.

ASTAPHIUM (*to* PHRONESIUM): It's your soldier Stratophanes approaching, my dear Phronesium. Now you must pretend to be a sick woman.

PHRONESIUM: Hush! Would you surpass me in cunning, when I've been your instructress in cunning so far?

STRATOPHANES: She's already had the child, I suppose.

ASTAPHIUM (*to* PHRONESIUM): You wish me to go up to him?

PHRONESIUM: Please do.

STRATOPHANES (*as she approaches*): Fine! Astaphium is coming to meet me.

ASTAPHIUM: Goodness, I'm glad to see you, Stratophanes. You've had a safe—

STRATOPHANES (*impatiently*): I know. Tell me, has Phronesium had her baby?

ASTAPHIUM: Yes. A fine, bouncing baby boy.

STRATOPHANES: Aha! Does he take after me at all?

ASTAPHIUM: You ask? Why, the minute he was born he asked for a sword and a shield.

STRATOPHANES (*delighted*): He's my son. Such evidence convinces me.

ASTAPHIUM: He's really the very image of you.

STRATOPHANES: Hoho! So big already? Has he joined the army yet? Brought back any spoils?

ASTAPHIUM: Now, now! He was born only five days ago.

STRATOPHANES: What of it? After so many days he should have done something worthwhile, damn it! What business had he to leave the womb before he could go forth to battle?

ASTAPHIUM: Follow me and greet her and congratulate her.

STRATOPHANES: Right with you. (*They approach* PHRONESIUM.)

PHRONESIUM (*in a faint voice*): Oh! Oh! Where is the girl that left me and went away? Where is she?

ASTAPHIUM: Here I am, ma'am, and I'm bringing Stratophanes, whom you long for.

PHRONESIUM: Where is he, I beg of you?

STRATOPHANES (*going to* PHRONESIUM'S *couch*): Mars greets his wife Neriene on his arrival from abroad. Congratulations on coming through it well and being blest with offspring; you've given birth to great glory for me and for yourself.

PHRONESIUM (*sullenly*): Welcome to you, who almost deprived me of life and the light of day by burying great anguish in my body for your own gratification; and even now I'm racked with pain.

STRATOPHANES: Hush, my dear! This labour will prove to your advantage; you've borne a son who will fill your house with booty.

PHRONESIUM: Oh, dear! There's much more need of having our storerooms filled with grain, so that we won't die of hunger before he gets the spoils.

STRATOPHANES: Come, cheer up.

PHRONESIUM (*sadly*): Kiss me, please, here. Ah! I can't lift my head, it pains me so, and I haven't yet the strength to walk by myself.

STRATOPHANES (*kissing her*): Mighty Mars! If you asked me to cross the sea to get a kiss of yours, I'd do it gladly, honey mine. You've learned that this was so; and now, dear Phronesium, you'll learn the extent of my love. Look, I've brought you two Syrian maids as a present. (*To his orderly*) Bring the girls here. (*As* PHRONESIUM *shows no interest*) But these girls were both princesses in their own country, and their native land I laid waste with my own hand. They're a present for you.

PHRONESIUM (*still indifferent*): Aren't you sorry for me that I have so many maids to feed now, without bringing me another group to eat up all my food?

STRATOPHANES (*aside*): Confound it! This gift isn't very welcome. (*To his orderly*) Boy, hand me that bag. (*To* PHRONESIUM, *as he takes out a cloak*) Look, darling, here's a cloak I brought you from Phrygia. Take it, it's yours. (*Placing it on the couch.*)

PHRONESIUM: Such a little gift for all those terrible labour pains?

STRATOPHANES (*aside*): God help me, I'm ruined! That son of mine is already costing me his weight in gold. The purple cloak doesn't make any impression either. (*To* PHRONESIUM) And I've brought you incense from Arabia, balsam from Pontus. They're all yours, darling. (*Displaying the gifts.*)

PHRONESIUM: They're accepted. (*To* ASTAPHIUM) Take these Syrian girls in out of my sight. (ASTAPHIUM *obeys and returns.*)

STRATOPHANES (*plaintively*): Don't you love me at all?

PHRONESIUM: Gracious, no! You don't deserve it.

STRATOPHANES (*aside*): Doesn't anything satisfy her? She hasn't had a single kind word for me. Why, those gifts I just gave her could sell for twenty minae, I'm sure. She's awfully mad at me now, I can see that plain enough. Well, I'd better go. (*To* PHRONESIUM) Tell me, darling, you don't mind if I go off to accept a dinner invitation, do you? I'll be back later to sleep here. Why are you silent? (*Aside*) Damn it! I'm completely done for! (*Looking down the street*) But what's this strange sight? Who's this fellow heading such a parade? I'd better watch where they're taking the stuff. They're bringing it to her, I do believe. Anyway, I'll soon know for sure. (STRATOPHANES *and his orderly stand at a distance from the house.*)

Act Two. Scene VII

(*Enter* CYAMUS, *followed with several slaves laden with provisions.*)

CYAMUS (*to the slaves*): Come along with you, this way, you wreck-
ers for wenches, you cleaner-outers, you property-movers! (*To the
audience, in disgust*) Can't a person in love keep from being good for
nothing and robbing himself in the most shameful fashion. Just to
keep any of you from asking me how I know this, there's a lover at
home who's acting just shamefully; he treats his property like dung and
orders it swept outside; he's afraid of the public officers, and, being
a clean sort of fellow, wants his house spotless; so everything he has
in it is tossed *dehors*. Since he's so anxious to ruin himself, I'll give him
a little aid on the sly, by Jove, and with my help he'll make the swift-
est possible progress to— (*grinning*) his destruction. Why, from this
one mina for provisions, I just got a ten drachma discount; I deducted
for myself the tenth due to Hercules. It's really just like a fellow divert-
ing some water from a river to his own use; if it wasn't diverted, all
the water would run into the sea. (*Looking at the provisions*) Well, all
this stuff is running into the sea, and it's being utterly wasted to no
good purpose whatsoever. When I see these things going on, I take to
pilfering and plundering and looting the loot. It seems to me that a
harlot is just like the sea: she swallows up everything you give her, but
she never overflows from the gifts. This much is true, at least; she
keeps the gifts and no one sees where they are; give as much as you
will, it's nowhere visible to giver or acceptress. Take this harlot, for
instance; her blandishments have almost impoverished my poor master;
she'll deprive him of fortune, life, honour, and friends. (*Catching sight
of* PHRONESIUM) Ow! There she is nearby. She heard what I said, I'll
bet. She's pale too, from having had a baby. I'll speak to her as though
ignorant. (*To* PHRONESIUM *and* ASTAPHIUM) My best greetings to
you both.

PHRONESIUM: And ours to you, Thracian; how are you? How are you
feeling?

CYAMUS: Quite well, thanks, and I come to one who's not so well and
bring her something to make her better. My master, the apple of your
eye, ordered me to bring you the gifts you see these fellows carrying,
and these five minae of silver. (*Handing her the purse.*)

PHRONESIUM (*loud enough for* STRATOPHANES *to hear*): Goodness! It's
well worth while for me to love him so.

CYAMUS: He urged me to ask you to be pleased with these gifts.

PHRONESIUM: Heavens! I am pleased, and I accept them gladly. Have the vessels taken off inside, Cyamus.

ASTAPHIUM (*sharply, as* CYAMUS *hesitates*): Don't you hear her orders?

CYAMUS: I don't want any vessels taken off; just have them emptied out. (*The slaves take the gifts inside, returning later.*)

ASTAPHIUM: Gracious me, you're impudent, Cyamus.

CYAMUS: I?

ASTAPHIUM: You.

CYAMUS: Oh, really? You say I'm impudent, when you're a hotbed of iniquity yourself?

PHRONESIUM: Tell me, please, where is Diniarchus?

CYAMUS: At home.

PHRONESIUM (*in a loud voice*): Tell him that for the gifts he sent me I love him more than any man on earth and that I honour him more than any man, and that I'm anxious to have him come to see me.

CYAMUS: I'll do so. (*Noticing* STRATOPHANES) But who in the world is that man eating himself up, and looking so glum and ferocious? Jove! He's low in his mind, whoever he is.

PHRONESIUM: My goodness! He deserves to be, the good-for-nothing! I say, don't you know the soldier that used to live with me? He's the father of my child. He cast his eye upon me, he came to see me, he remained; now he's listening and watching to see what lover I ruin.

CYAMUS: I know the worthless wretch. Is that the fellow?

PHRONESIUM: That's the one.

CYAMUS: He groans as he looks at me; he heaved a sigh from the bottom of his belly. Just look at that! He's gnashing his teeth and smacking his thigh. He isn't a frenzied soothsayer, is he, to beat himself that way?

STRATOPHANES (*coming up to* CYAMUS): Now I shall bring forth from my breast the full force of my raging temper and my wrath. Speak! Where do you come from? Who do you belong to? How did you dare speak so rudely to me?

CYAMUS: I wanted to.

STRATOPHANES: Don't you talk that way to me.

CYAMUS: This way, then. I don't give a damn for you.

STRATOPHANES (*turning to* PHRONESIUM): And what about you? How did you dare to say you loved another man?

PHRONESIUM (*very indifferent*): I wanted to.

STRATOPHANES: You say so, eh? I'll just see about that first. Do you, for the sake of a piddling little gift of vegetables, fodder, and vinegar-water, bestow your love upon an adulterous, effeminate, frizzle-pated, drum-drubbing debauchee of a good-for-nothing?

CYAMUS: What goes on here? You rascal, do you dare to abuse my master, you fount of vice and perjury?

STRATOPHANES (*his hand on his sword*): You add just one more word, and damned if I won't take this sword and hew you to splinters!

CYAMUS (*his hand on his knife*): You just touch me, and I'll make a lamb of you and de-sever you right through the middle. You may be famous as a warrior in the army, but that's what I am in the kitchen.

PHRONESIUM (*to* STRATOPHANES): If you had any decency, you wouldn't abuse my visitors who bring me gifts I like to receive, quite different from the unwelcome stuff you gave me.

STRATOPHANES (*in despair*): Oh, God! I've lost my gifts and I'm lost as well.

PHRONESIUM: That's the fact of the matter.

CYAMUS (*to* STRATOPHANES): Why do you stay here and annoy us, then, since you're such a complete wreck?

STRATOPHANES (*to* PHRONESIUM): I'll die this very day, by Jupiter, if I don't drive this fellow from you.

CYAMUS (*drawing his knife*): You just come here, you just step here!

STRATOPHANES: Threatening me, eh, you villain? Why, this very minute I'll rend you to splinters! What business have you coming here? What business have you approaching her? What business, I say, have you to be acquainted with my mistress? (*Drawing his sword*) You'll die instantly, unless you defeat me at arms.

CYAMUS (*eyeing the sword*): What! Defeat you at arms? (*Backing away.*)

STRATOPHANES: Do as I ordered. Stop! Now I shall hew you to splinters. A splintery death is quite satisfactory. (*Advancing.*)

CYAMUS (*retreating*): There's a catch here; that sword of yours is longer than my knife. Just let me go and get my spit. If I have to wage war with you, you warrior, I'll go home and get myself the right sort of referee. (*Aside*) I'd better make a quick exit, while I can get away with my belly intact. (CYAMUS *departs, followed by the slaves.*)

Act Two.   Scene VIII

PHRONESIUM (*calling to her maids within*): Bring me my sandals, please. (*The maids obey, and* PHRONESIUM *rises from her couch*) Now, take me inside at once. My poor head! It aches so from all this wind.

STRATOPHANES: What about me and the ache I get from the two maids I gave to you? (*As* PHRONESIUM *and the maids go into the house*) Gone in, have you? (*He kicks the door*) There, take that! (*To himself*) How could I be more shut out than I am right now, I'd like to know? A fine way to trifle with me! Well, all right. It wouldn't take much now to persuade me to smash the ankles of this whole house. How women's ways can change so! What airs she put on after the baby was born! Now she as good as tells me, "I neither ask you nor forbid you to come into the house." I don't want to go in, I won't go in; I'll make her say a few days from now that I'm a man of iron. (*To his orderly*) Follow me this way. Enough said! (*They depart.*)

Act Three.   Scene I

(*Enter* STRABAX *from the country.*)

STRABAX (*to himself*): Father sent me off to the country earlier this morning to give a meal of nuts to the cattle. After I got there, a man arrived at the farmhouse who owed my father some money, thank the gods! He had bought some Tarentine sheep from father. He asks for father; I say he's in the city, and ask what he wants of him. . . .[10] The fellow unslings a sack of money from his neck and gives me twenty minae. I take it gladly and put it in a sack. Off he went. So I hurried back here to the city with twenty minae of sheep in my purse. Gad, but Mars was angry at my father, for these sheep of his are getting pretty close to the wolves.[11] (*Approaching* PHRONESIUM'S *house*) With one stroke of this purse I'll smite those citified, dandified lovers, and throw them out on their ears. I'm determined to wreck my father first, root and branch, and after that my mother. Now I'll take this money to the girl that I love more than my own mother. (*Knocking*) Ho, there! Anyone in? Anyone there to open the door?

(*Enter* ASTAPHIUM *into the doorway.*)

ASTAPHIUM: What's this? (*Observing the purse*) Why, my dear Strabax, are you a stranger, that you don't come in at once?

STRABAX (*timidly*): Should I have?

ASTAPHIUM: Why, of course; you're one of the family.

STRABAX: I'll go in then, so you won't think I'm slow.

ASTAPHIUM: That's nice of you. (STRABAX *goes inside.*)

Act Three.   Scene II

(*Enter* TRUCULENTUS *from the house of the father of* STRABAX.)

TRUCULENTUS (*to himself*): It seems awful strange to me that young master Strabax hasn't returned from the country; unless maybe he's sneaked into this here den of depravity and destruction.

ASTAPHIUM (*aside*): Gracious, but he'll be roaring at me, if he sees me.

TRUCULENTUS (*sees her and approaches*): I'm much less savage than I was, Astaphium. I'm not the least bit truculent now; don't be afraid. (*Leering*) What d'ye say?

ASTAPHIUM (*sweetly*): What do you wish?

TRUCULENTUS: Well, I'd like you to show a little kissability. Talk to me, command me to do whatever you please, anything you wish. I got all new manners now; I chucked the old ones away. I can make love or have a harlot now.

ASTAPHIUM: Gracious! What welcome news! But tell me, do you have—

TRUCULENTUS (*holding up a purse*): This grub-bag you mean, perhaps?

ASTAPHIUM: You understand my meaning perfectly.

TRUCULENTUS: Lookit, you! Now that I keep coming to the city so often, I've become witty, I have. I'm getting to be a fine juster now.

ASTAPHIUM: Dear me, what's that? You mean telling funny stories, jesting, I suppose.

TRUCULENTUS: Sure; that's not much different from justing.

ASTAPHIUM: Please come on in now, my darling.

TRUCULENTUS (*giving her some money*): Here, take this. It's my posit, so you can spend the night with me.

ASTAPHIUM (*aside, taking the money*): "Posit," eh? What kind of strange beast is this? (*Aloud*) Why don't you say "deposit"?

TRUCULENTUS: I'm saving a syllable, just as they do in Praeneste, when they say "nary" for "canary."[12]

ASTAPHIUM: Well, come in, please.

TRUCULENTUS (*suddenly shy*): I'd better wait here for Strabax to come from the farm.

ASTAPHIUM: Why, Strabax is already in the house; he just came from the country.

TRUCULENTUS: Before going to see his mother? God! The worthless so-and-so!

ASTAPHIUM (*soothing him*): Now, now! Back to your old ways?

TRUCULENTUS (*subsiding*): Now, I ain't saying a word.

ASTAPHIUM (*leading him to the door*): Come in, dear. Give me your hand.

TRUCULENTUS: Here it is. (*Aside*) Now for the tavern where I'll get bad treatment for my money. (*They go into* PHRONESIUM's *house.*)

Act Four. Scene I

(*Enter* DINIARCHUS, *in high spirits.*)

DINIARCHUS (*to himself*): There isn't a person born and there won't be a person born that I'd want better praised or better treated than Venus. O mighty gods, how happy I am, how bursting with joy! Such glorious tidings that Cyamus brought me today! Phronesium's glad to get my gifts and thinks they're wonderful. I just love this, but it's even more honey-sweet that the soldier's presents are unwelcome and displeasing. I'm all enraptured! The game's mine. If the soldier's sent away, the girl's to be with me. (*Reflecting*) I'm saved, because I'm lost; if I weren't lost, I'd be completely ruined. (*Eyeing* PHRONESIUM's *house*) Now I'll keep watch on activities there; I want to see who goes in and who comes out. I'll take my stand here at a distance and find out what my fate will be. Now that I've brought everything here, I don't have a cent; I'll have to plead for her favour.

Act Four.   Scene II

(*Enter* ASTAPHIUM *from* PHRONESIUM's *house*.)

ASTAPHIUM (*to* PHRONESIUM *within*): I'll tend to my job cleverly enough out here; be sure that you do yours as well inside. Love your own interest, that's what you should do; desiccate the fellow. Now's the favourable time for it, while he's got the desire and got the cash. Display your charms to your lover, so that he'll be happy to be ruined. Meanwhile, I'll be a loiteress and stay on guard out here while his export business is proving profitable for you; I won't let a single soul come in to annoy you. So play your game as it pleases you.

DINIARCHUS (*advancing*): Tell me, Astaphium, who's on the road to ruin now?

ASTAPHIUM: Good Lord! Are you here?

DINIARCHUS: I'm not unwelcome, am I?

ASTAPHIUM: Yes, more than you were before. Whenever any profit comes our way, you get in our way. But listen, please; here's something I want to tell you.

DINIARCHUS (*eagerly*): Well, what is it? Does it concern me at all?

ASTAPHIUM: I won't keep quiet about it. The hauls that she's making inside!

DINIARCHUS: What? Some new lover?

ASTAPHIUM: She's found an untouched treasure, a huge one.

DINIARCHUS: Who is he?

ASTAPHIUM: I'll tell you, but you keep it secret. You know Strabax here? (*Pointing to his father's house.*)

DINIARCHUS: Of course.

ASTAPHIUM: He rules the roost in our house now, all alone; he's our new bit of real estate. The good nature with which he takes bad treatment!

DINIARCHUS: He's done for, all right. (*Bitterly*) And so am I; I got a bad return for the good money I wasted, for I'm shut out of your house.

ASTAPHIUM: You're a fool, if you expect to undo with words what's been done. Even Thetis finally stopped mourning for her son.

DINIARCHUS: You won't let me into your house now?

ASTAPHIUM: Why you more than the soldier?

DINIARCHUS: Because I gave her more.

ASTAPHIUM: Well, we let you in more, while you did the giving. Now, in turn, let those who give profit by what they give. You've learned your letters; now that you know them, let others learn.

DINIARCHUS: Let them have their lessons, provided that I can have a review session to keep me from forgetting mine.

ASTAPHIUM: But what about the teacher, while you repeat your lesson? She wants a bit of repetition, too.

DINIARCHUS: How's that?

ASTAPHIUM: Payment for tuition from time to time.

DINIARCHUS: I certainly paid mine today. I had five minae of silver brought to her, besides a mina's worth of provisions.

ASTAPHIUM: All of which arrived, I know. We're having a nice time now, thanks to you.

DINIARCHUS: Oh, oh! Are my enemies devouring my property in there? Damn me! I'd rather be dead than endure this!

ASTAPHIUM (*not unkindly*): You're a poor fool.

DINIARCHUS: How's that? Explain. What now, Astaphium?

ASTAPHIUM: Because I'd certainly rather have my enemies envy me than me my enemies. It's misery to envy another for being well off, when you're bad off. The envious ones are in need, the ones who are envied are the prosperous ones.

DINIARCHUS (*pitifully*): Can't I have a share in half of the provisions?

ASTAPHIUM: If you wanted a share in them, you should have taken half home. We keep an account of the receipts here in our house, just as they do in Hades. We take in the receipts; and once they're entered, they can't be taken out again. (*Turning away*) Good-bye.

DINIARCHUS (*seizing her*): Stop!

ASTAPHIUM: Let me go.

DINIARCHUS: Let me go in, then.

ASTAPHIUM: Yes, in your own house.

DINIARCHUS: No, I want to go into your house here.

ASTAPHIUM: You can't do it, you're too demanding.

DINIARCHUS: Give me a trial—

ASTAPHIUM (*breaking away*): No, wait a while. This trial of yours is downright force.

DINIARCHUS: Tell her I'm here.

ASTAPHIUM: Oh, get out; she's busy. And that's true, don't fool yourself about it. (*She goes to the door.*)

DINIARCHUS: Are you going to come back or not?

ASTAPHIUM (*pretending to hear* PHRONESIUM *calling*): I'm being called by a person who has more power over me than you possess.

DINIARCHUS: Just one word—

ASTAPHIUM: Say it.

DINIARCHUS: You'll let me in?

ASTAPHIUM: You're a liar. Off with you. "One word," you said; you've spoken four, and they're all lies. (*She goes into the house.*)

DINIARCHUS (*to himself*): She's gone inside, she's shut me out! Am I to put up with treatment like this? (*Shouting to* PHRONESIUM *inside*) Damn it, you seductress, I'll yell out and ridicule you right here in the street, the way you take money illegally from man after man! Lord, if I don't have your name brought before the new police commissioners and make you pay fourfold damages, you sorceress, you child kid-napperess! I'll disclose all your disgraceful doings, by gad! There's nothing to stop me; I've lost every cent I had. I'm shameless now, and I don't give a damn what sort of shoes I wear.[13] (*To himself*) But what am I shouting here for? What if she did tell them to let me in? I'd swear solemnly to be quiet, if she wanted me to. If you beat a stick with your fists, it's your hands that suffer most. There's no point in being angry at nothing, when a girl doesn't care a straw for you. (*Looking down the street*) But what's this? Immortal gods! I see old Callicles, my prospective father-in-law, bringing along two maid servants in bonds. One is Phronesium's hairdresser, the other's a slave girl of his own. I'm scared, all right; here I was all wretched with one worry, and now I'm afraid that all my former sins have been discovered! (*He withdraws.*)

Act Four.   Scene III

(*Enter* CALLICLES, *followed by slaves in charge of his own* MAID *and* SURA.)

CALLICLES (*to his* MAID): Am I a person to abuse you? Or to show favour to you rather than (*to* SURA) to you? You've both found pretty well from experience what a gentle and easygoing man I am. I questioned you both when you were being strung up and flogged. My memory's good, I recall each point of your confession; now I want to know if you'll make the same confession without punishment. You're a snaky-minded couple, I know, so I warn you first not to try your double tongues on me, or I'll slaughter you both, double tongues and all—unless you prefer to be led off to the tinkle tankle torturers.[14]

MAID: We're forced to confess the truth, the bonds bruise our arms so.

CALLICLES: Well, if you do confess the truth, you'll be freed of your bonds.

DINIARCHUS (*aside*): Even now I'm confused and uncertain as to what goes on here. The one thing I'm sure about is my fright, because I know I've sinned.

CALLICLES: First of all, you two girls separate. (*They obey*) There, that's right. That's the way I want you. I'll be a wall between you, so that you can't signal to each other. (*To his* MAID) Talk, you.

MAID: Talk about what, sir?

CALLICLES: What became of the boy that my daughter bore, my own grandson? Give me the main points of the matter.

MAID: I gave it to this woman (*indicating* SURA).

CALLICLES: You keep quiet, now. (*To* SURA) Did you receive the boy from her?

SURA: I did, sir.

CALLICLES: Quiet! I don't want any more. You've confessed enough.

SURA: I don't deny it.

CALLICLES: And that's enough to make your shoulder blades a darker shade. (*Aside*) The statements of both agree so far.

DINIARCHUS (*aside*): Oh, I'm a miserable wretch! The deeds that I hoped to keep hidden are being found out.

CALLICLES (*to his* MAID): Speak up, you. Who told you to give her the baby?

MAID: My elder mistress.

CALLICLES (*to* SURA): And now you; why did you receive him?

SURA: My younger mistress told me to; she wanted the child brought to her and everything kept secret.

CALLICLES: Well, tell me. What did you do with the child?

SURA: I took it to my mistress.

CALLICLES: What did she do with the child?

SURA: Gave it to my mistress at once.

CALLICLES: Damn it! What mistress are you talking about?

MAID (*helpfully*): She has two mistresses.

CALLICLES (*to his* MAID): Don't you say a word except what I ask you. (*To* SURA) It's you I'm questioning.

SURA: The mother gave the baby as a gift to the daughter, I say.

CALLICLES: You're telling more than you did a while ago.

SURA: Well, you're asking more.

CALLICLES: Tell me quickly; the girl that received the baby, what did she do?

SURA: Palmed it off.

CALLICLES: On whom?

SURA: On herself.

CALLICLES: As her own child?

SURA: Yes, as her own.

CALLICLES: The gods protect us! How much easier it is for one woman to give birth to the same child than for another! This woman produced a baby without any pain, through another's labour. A lucky child! He has two mothers and two grandmothers. How many fathers he had, that's what bothers me. Look at it, the fine way women act!

MAID (*catching sight of* DINIARCHUS): Goodness me! You must blame men rather than women for this wrongdoing. It's a man that made her pregnant, not a woman.

CALLICLES (*sharply*): You don't have to tell me that. And a fine guardian for the girl you were!

MAID: "The greater the strength, the greater the power." He was a man, he had greater strength; he overpowered her and got what he wanted.

CALLICLES: He got you in plenty of trouble, too, by Jove!

MAID: I know that from what I've been through, without your telling me.

CALLICLES: I haven't been able so far today to make you tell who the man was.

MAID: I've kept silent so far. But I won't keep silent now, for the man is present and doesn't reveal himself.

DINIARCHUS (*aside*): I'm petrified! I don't dare to move an inch. The whole secret's out, and now they're holding court there with my life at stake. It's my own fault, my own stupidity. I dread to think how soon my name will be mentioned. (*Tries to hide.*)

CALLICLES: Tell me who it was that raped my innocent daughter.

MAID (*to* DINIARCHUS): I see you there, trying to prop up the wall because of your sins.

DINIARCHUS (*aside, against the wall*): I'm neither living nor dead! I don't know what to do now; I don't know how to get away from here or how to face him! I'm scared senseless!

CALLICLES: Will you name him or not?

MAID: It's Diniarchus, the man you had betrothed your daughter to.

CALLICLES: Where is the man you name? (*Looking around.*)

DINIARCHUS (*coming forward*): Here I am, Callicles. (*Falling on the ground before* CALLICLES) By your knees I beseech you, bear with wisdom what was done in folly, and forgive me for the sin I committed when wine overpowered my senses.

CALLICLES: I don't like this. You're putting the blame on an accomplice that can't speak. If wine were able to talk, it would defend itself. Wine's not in the habit of controlling men, but men wine, that is, if they're any good. A man who's no good is just naturally no good, whether he drinks wine or abstains from it.

DINIARCHUS: I realise, because of my guilt, that I must listen to many unwelcome words. I admit that I'm to blame, and I'm in your power.

MAID: Callicles, make sure you're not being terribly unfair here; the defendant's free as he pleads his case, while you've got the witnesses bound up.

CALLICLES (*to the slaves*): Set the girls free. (*To the girls, as the slaves obey*) Off with you, now. (*To his* MAID) You go on home, and (*to* SURA) you, too! Just tell your mistress this: she's to return the child when someone comes for him. (*To* DINIARCHUS, *as the girls depart*) Come, let's go to court.

DINIARCHUS: Why do you want me to go to court? You're my judge. I beg you, Callicles, let me marry your daughter.

CALLICLES: Let you marry her? Damn it! I think you decided that point long ago. You didn't wait for me to let you have her; you took her for yourself. Now that you've got her, keep her. But I'll penalise you with this big fine; I'll deduct six talents from her dowry because of this stupid act of yours.

DINIARCHUS: That's fair treatment.

CALLICLES: You'd better get your son back from that place (*indicating* PHRONESIUM's *house*). And take your wife away from my house as soon as possible. I'm going now. I must send a message at once to that connection of mine and tell him to find another match for his son. (CALLICLES *departs.*)

DINIARCHUS (*to himself, turning towards* PHRONESIUM'S *door*): I'll ask her for the child right now, lest later on she deny everything. (*Reflecting*) But she can't do that, for she's the one that revealed the whole story to me. Gad, how fortunate! Here she is just coming out. (*Stepping back*) Ah, what a long sting the woman has! Even from that distance she's puncturing my heart.

Act Four. Scene IV

(*Enter* PHRONESIUM *and* ASTAPHIUM.)

PHRONESIUM: A courtesan's a silly little slut, if she can't drink wine and still look after her own interests; the rest of her can be soused, but her head must be clear, at least. I'm really grieved that my hairdresser has been so badly treated. She told me that the child has been discovered to be the son of Diniarchus.

DINIARCHUS (*aside*): I see her, I hear her; she's the one that's got a grip on my property and my children. (*He approaches her.*)

PHRONESIUM (*aside*): Why, here's the lover that made me guardian of all his goods.

DINIARCHUS: Woman, I was coming in to see you.

PHRONESIUM (*sweetly*): How's everything, my darling?

DINIARCHUS: Don't you "darling" me! No nonsense, now! I'm through with that sort of thing.

PHRONESIUM: Gracious me! I know what you want and what you expect and what you're coming for; you want to see me, you expect me to love you, you're coming for your child.

DINIARCHUS (*aside*): Ye immortal gods! How plain-spoken she is! How quickly she hit the nail on the head!

PHRONESIUM: And I know, of course, that you have a fiancée and a son by your fiancée, and that you must marry her now, and that your thoughts are now elsewhere. You're going to leave me, a poor, forlorn girl. (*Seductively*) Just think of the tiny mouse and what a wise little animal he is; he never entrusts his life to just one cubbyhole, but has another refuge ready, if one hole is blocked up.

DINIARCHUS (*weakening slightly*): I'll talk this matter over with you more fully when I have time. Now, return the child.

PHRONESIUM: Oh, please let him stay with me for the next few days,

DINIARCHUS: Certainly not.

PHRONESIUM (*fondling him*): Please, for my sake.

DINIARCHUS: What's the reason for it?

PHRONESIUM: It'll help me a lot. Just let me have him for the next three days, anyway, while the soldier's being swindled. If I get anything from him, you'll profit by it too; but if you take the child away, all my hopes will breathe their last, as far as the soldier is concerned.

DINIARCHUS (*giving in*): All right, I'm willing, for even if I wished to do it later, I wouldn't have the chance. Use the child now, and provide for him, since you have money for provisions.

PHRONESIUM: Goodness me, how much I love you for your kindness! When you're scared of a scolding at home, just take refuge here with me. We'll have a profitable friendship, I assure you.

DINIARCHUS (*turning away*): Good-bye, Phronesium.

PHRONESIUM (*plaintively*): Won't you call me "apple of your eye"?

DINIARCHUS: There'll be a chance for that on the sly from time to time. Nothing more you wish, is there?

PHRONESIUM: Take good care of yourself.

DINIARCHUS: I'll come to see you, when I have the opportunity. (*He departs.*)

PHRONESIUM: Well, he's gone and departed. Now I can say what I wish. It's a true proverb that they quote: "Where your friends are, there your wealth is." Thanks to him, I still have hopes of tricking the soldier today. I love that soldier better than my own soul—while I get what I want from him. But even after we girls get a lot, there isn't much to show for what's been given. Such are the glories of harlot-hood!

ASTAPHIUM (*looking down the street*): Aha! Hush, please!

PHRONESIUM: Heavens! What's the matter?

ASTAPHIUM: Here comes the father of the child.

PHRONESIUM: Let him come here. Let him, if it's only he.

ASTAPHIUM: It certainly is.

PHRONESIUM: Let him come to me, as he wishes.

ASTAPHIUM: He's headed straight for us.

PHRONESIUM: He'll be finished off in cunning fashion today.[4]

Act Five

(*Enter* STRATOPHANES.)

STRATOPHANES (*to himself*): I'm bringing a mina of gold as a necessary offering to my mistress. To make my earlier extravagance acceptable to her, I'll add this as well. (*Noticing the girls*) What's this I see? Mistress and maid in front of their house. I must approach them. (*Addressing them*) What are you two doing here?

PHRONESIUM (*turning away*): Don't speak to me.

STRATOPHANES (*trying to soothe her*): You're too cross.

PHRONESIUM: Can't you stop bothering me?

STRATOPHANES: What's the quarrel about, Astaphium?

ASTAPHIUM: Goodness me! She's right in being angry at you.

PHRONESIUM (*to* ASTAPHIUM): I certainly am; I treat him far too well.

STRATOPHANES: Look, darling; even if I did offend you before, I'm bringing you a present of a mina of gold. Just look, if you don't believe me. (*He holds out the purse.*)

PHRONESIUM: My hand forbids me to believe anything that's not inside it. We need food for the baby, and for the woman who bathes it, too. In order to have milk, the nurse needs to drink lots of old wine day and night. We need wood, we need coal, we need baby clothes, pillows, cradle, cradle bedding. We need oil, we need flour; the child eats the entire day. We can never satisfy the needs of this one day without more needs popping up. Sons of military men can't be raised like birds,[15] you know.

STRATOPHANES (*holding the purse*): Please look at me, then. Take this to satisfy those needs.

PHRONESIUM (*turning and taking the purse*): Give it to me, but it isn't enough.

STRATOPHANES: I'll add another mina to it later.[1]

PHRONESIUM: It still isn't enough.

STRATOPHANES: I'll give you what you want, whenever you desire it. (*Embracing her*) Now give me a nice kiss.

PHRONESIUM (*pushing him away*): Let go of me, I say! You tire me out.

STRATOPHANES (*aside*): It's no use, she doesn't love me, the day's being wasted. Little by little here I've let more than ten pounds—of love go oozing out of me.

PHRONESIUM (*to* ASTAPHIUM): Take the money and carry it inside. (ASTAPHIUM *goes into the house with the purse.*)

(*Enter* STRABAX *from* PHRONESIUM'S *house.*)

STRABAX (*to himself*): Where in the world is my sweetheart? I don't get anything done in the country, or here either. I'm all spoiled and mouldy, I'm all numb, drat it, lying here waiting on the couch! (*Seeing* PHRONESIUM) Ah, there she is! Hey, sweetheart, what are you doing?

STRATOPHANES: Who in the devil is that?

PHRONESIUM (*sweetly*): The man I love far more than you.

STRATOPHANES: Than me?

PHRONESIUM: Yes, than you.

STRATOPHANES: How's it possible?

PHRONESIUM: Possibly so that you won't bother me. (*Turning away.*)

STRATOPHANES: Are you going now, after taking my money?

PHRONESIUM: What you gave me is stored away inside.

STRABAX (*impatiently*): Come here, sweetheart; I'm calling you.

(*Enter* ASTAPHIUM, *who stands in the doorway and enjoys the situa tion.*)

PHRONESIUM (*to* STRABAX): You dear sweet thing, I was just coming to you.

STRABAX: Seriously now, by Jove! No matter how silly I seem to you, I still want to have some fun. You may be pretty, but you'll suffer for it, if I don't have some fun.

PHRONESIUM: Do you want me to hug you and give you a nice long kiss?

STRABAX: Do anything you like, so I can have some fun. (*She kisses him.*)

STRATOPHANES (*aside, in anger*): Am I to let her hug other men before my very eyes? Damn it, I'd rather die this very day. (*Aloud, drawing his sword*) Take your hands off him, woman, unless you both want to die by my hand on this blade of mine.

PHRONESIUM: You'd better stop threatening,[4] soldier, if you expect to be loved. It's gold, not iron, Stratophanes, that'll keep me from loving him. (*She caresses* STRABAX.)

STRATOPHANES: How the devil can a pretty and clever girl like you love a man like that?

PHRONESIUM: Don't you recall what an actor once said in the theatre? "All people are insensitive or squeamish according to the profits involved."

STRATOPHANES: How can you embrace such a fellow, a man so unkempt and so filthy?

PHRONESIUM: He may be filthy, he may be unkempt, but he's clever and handsome to me.

STRATOPHANES: Didn't I give money—

PHRONESIUM: To me? You gave it to provide food for your son. If you want this lady for yourself, another mina of gold is now needed.

STRABAX (*to* STRATOPHANES, *insolently*): You're headed for hell in a great hurry; you'd better keep your money to pay your fare.

STRATOPHANES (*to* PHRONESIUM): What d'ye owe this fellow?

PHRONESIUM: Three things.

STRATOPHANES: What three things?

PHRONESIUM: Perfume, kisses, a night together.

STRATOPHANES (*aside*): That's tit for tat. (*Aloud*) But now at least, even if you do love him, won't you give me just a few of your choice endearments?

PHRONESIUM: What is it I'm to give you, my dear man? Say. . . .¹
(*She again embraces* STRABAX; STRATOPHANES *grows more furious*)
Take care you don't bite yourself with those iron teeth of yours.

STRATOPHANES (*in disgust*): She keeps open house for everyone, all
sorts of people. (*To* STRABAX) Take your hands off her.

STRABAX: Oh, go to hell! Give yourself a good thrashing, my brave hero!

STRATOPHANES: But I gave her gold.

STRABAX: And I gave her silver.

STRATOPHANES: And I gave her maids and incense and a purple cloak.¹⁶

STRABAX: And I gave her sheep and wool, and I'll give her many other
things she asks for. It'd be much better for you to compete with minae
instead of menaces.

PHRONESIUM: Lord love me! You're a charming creature, my dear
Strabax. Just keep at him, please.

ASTAPHIUM (*aside*): A fool and a madman competing for their own
ruin! It's fine for us.

STRATOPHANES: Come, you squander first.

STRABAX: No, you squander first, and to the devil with you!

STRATOPHANES (*to* PHRONESIUM, *wildly tearing off his money-belt*):
There's a silver talent for you. It's good coin. Take it! Keep it!

PHRONESIUM (*taking the money*): That's much better. Now you're one
of the family—but provide your own food.

STRATOPHANES (*to* STRABAX): Where's your gift, now? Come on, chal-
lenger, produce your money-belt. What are you afraid of?

STRABAX: You're a foreigner. I live here, and I don't go walking around
with a money-belt on. I bring her flocks, I do, tied up in this sack on
my neck. (*To* PHRONESIUM) What a gift! How I stripped the fellow!

STRATOPHANES: No, I did it; I'm the one that made the gift.

PHRONESIUM (*to* STRABAX): Go on in, dear; you can be with me. (*To*
STRATOPHANES) Then you too can be with me.

STRATOPHANES (*horrified*): What's this? What do you say? He can
be with you? And I play second fiddle, after that gift I made?

PHRONESIUM: You've made your gift; he hasn't, yet. I've got yours (*indicating the belt*), I'm waiting for his. But I'll please both of you to your heart's content.

STRATOPHANES (*giving in*): Well, so be it! As I view the situation, I must take what's offered me.

STRABAX (*to* STRATOPHANES, *as they enter the house*): There's one thing certain, I won't let you have my bed.

PHRONESIUM (*to the audience*): Gracious! What happy hunting I've had, quite to my liking. And now that my own affairs are in such good shape, I'll be glad to help you with yours. If anyone wishes to have a good time, just let me know. For the sake of Venus, give your applause; this play is under her care. Farewell, spectators; applaud and arise.

1. The text of this sentence is corrupt.

2. The text of the last two lines of the Prologue is hopelessly corrupt.

3. The text is corrupt here; the conjecture of Buecheler, *supplicia danda,* has been adopted.

4. The text of this sentence is corrupt in part.

5. Lindsay brackets this verse as spurious.

6. The emendation of Bugge and Buecheler, *ne ut iusta utamur,* has been adopted here.

7. In the original, *comprime eiram,* "restrain your wrath," is taken by Truculentus as *comprime eram,* "have intercourse with your mistress."

8. The significance of this is not clear; things human and divine may be meant.

9. This is explained as referring to some wretched imitator of Homer.

10. There is a short lacuna here.

11. *Lupae* in Latin means both "she-wolves" and "harlots."

12. Literally, *ciconia,* a stork, which people in Praeneste called *conia.*

13. In other words, "I don't care how I act."

14. Plautus calls the torturers or executioners *tintinnaculi,* probably from the sound of the fetters put on the prisoners.

15. The text is uncertain here; *ut avis,* the conjecture of Schoell, has been adopted.

16. The text here is corrupt; Schoell's conjecture, *at ego ancillas tura purpuram,* has been adopted.

THE PLAYS OF
TERENCE

I
THE WOMAN OF ANDROS

Characters in the Play

SIMO, *an old gentleman of Athens*
SOSIA, SIMO'S *freedman*
DAVUS, *slave of* SIMO *and* PAMPHILUS
MYSIS, *maid of* GLYCERIUM
PAMPHILUS, *son of* SIMO, *in love with* GLYCERIUM
CHARINUS, *friend of* PAMPHILUS, *in love with* PHILUMENA
BYRRIA, *slave of* CHARINUS
LESBIA, *a midwife*
GLYCERIUM, *the woman of Andros*
CHREMES, *father of* PHILUMENA *and* GLYCERIUM
CRITO, *an old gentleman of Andros*
DROMO, *slave of* SIMO

Didascalia [1]

The Woman of Andros by Terence. Acted at the Megalensian Games [2] during the curule aedileship of Marcus Fulvius and Manius Glabrio. The chief parts were taken by Lucius Ambivius Turpio and Lucius Atilius Praenestinus. It was set to music by Flaccus, the slave of Claudius, for flutes of equal size, right- and left-handed. It was taken entirely from the Greek, and was produced in the consulship of Marcus Marcellus and Gaius Sulpicius. [3]

Summary [4]

Pamphilus seduces Glycerium, wrongly supposed to be the sister of a courtesan from Andros; when she becomes pregnant, he gives his word that he will marry her. His father has arranged for him to marry the daughter of Chremes, and when he discovers the intrigue he pretends that the marriage is about to take place, desiring in this way to learn what his son's real intentions are. Pamphilus follows the advice of Davus and does not object. But Chremes discovers that Glycerium has given birth to a child; he breaks off the match and refuses Pamphilus as a son-in-law. He later learns to his surprise that Glycerium is his own daughter; he gives her in marriage to Pamphilus, and his other daughter he gives to Charinus.

INTRODUCTION

The Woman of Andros (the *Andria*) was Terence's first play and was produced in 166 B.C. The youthful dramatist states in his prologue that the comedy was adapted from two plays by Menander, *The Lady of Andros* and *The Lady of Perinthos,* and he justifies the combination of two Greek originals into one Latin play by appealing to the procedure of his predecessors, Naevius, Plautus, and Ennius.

Terence's first comedy displays the characteristics for which the dramatist is noted. The language is natural and refined and the humour is subtle. The action is close-knit and there are no digressions. The play as comedy is far more serious than most of Plautus' work, and lacks the robust humour, the jests and witticisms, the slapstick farce, and the exaggerated and often grotesque characterisations to be found in the plays of the older dramatist. While it is generally believed that Terence in tone and style stands much closer to his Greek originals than does Plautus, he is not lacking in originality or in creative power. One of the most characteristic features of his plays is the double plot; *The Woman of Andros* shows his first attempt at this structural device which was handled later with far greater skill, particularly in the *Phormio* and *The Brothers.*

Pamphilus is deeply in love with Glycerium, a girl from Andros, and has promised to marry her, but his father, Simo, wishes him to marry Philumena, the daughter of Chremes. Charinus, a young friend of Pamphilus, is in love with Philumena. Chremes learns of Pamphilus' love affair and refuses to allow his daughter to marry. Simo, in order to test the depth of his son's feelings, pretends that the marriage is about to take place, and the resulting complications, which are increased when Glycerium gives birth to a child, lead both Charinus and Pamphilus to the depths of despair. The discovery that Glycerium too is the daughter of Chremes solves the problems of the two young men. Pamphilus' difficulty and its solution recall the similar situation of Alcesimarchus in Plautus' *The Casket,* also based upon a Menandrian original.

Terence's handling of the double plot in this play has been criticised, and Charinus, the second lover, has been called structurally useless; that is, the two love affairs parallel but hardly affect each other. It is true that Charinus' difficulty is clearly of secondary interest, as is Pistoclerus' love affair in Plautus' *The Two Bacchides*. But the problems of the two young men are amusingly combined, since Pamphilus doesn't want to marry the very girl that Charinus is so eager to marry, and the difficulties of both are brought to an end by one and the same discovery. Gilbert Norwood suggests that the reason for the addition of Charinus to the plot is to provide a husband for Philumena; Charinus has an excuse for his presence, but does not actually help the action.

The plot of *The Woman of Andros* is not in itself strikingly original. Like most plays of Terence and many of Plautus, the comedy is one of mistaken identity and recognition. Terence has introduced into the play, however, some refreshingly new variations of old themes which add delightful humour to many of the situations. The better acquainted one is with the stock situations and characters of Roman comedy, the more amusing these innovations are. The following are worth noting. (1) It is the father, Simo, who attempts to trick his son and the slave by means of the pretended wedding; usually the father is the butt of the trickery. (2) The plans and suggestions of Davus, the slave, merely get Pamphilus into greater trouble; Davus is far different from such a clever slave as Chrysalus in Plautus' *The Two Bacchides* or Palaestrio in *The Braggart Warrior*. (3) Simo, in Act Three, Scenes I and II, deceives himself by refusing to accept the truth; Terence here makes an amusing use of the convention of characters speaking to those inside. Again, in Act Five, Scene II, Simo deceives himself and punishes Davus for telling the truth. The role of Davus, which has been criticised as useless, provides much humour, for he aids constantly in the self-deception of Simo who is always expecting trickery at the wrong moment. (4) The arrival of Crito and the recognition of Glycerium are unexpected. The possibility of Glycerium's being a freeborn Athenian had earlier been rejected by Davus as nonsense. This is far different from the foreshadowing of the recognition so frequently found in Plautus. (5) W. Beare points out that Charinus' love for Philumena is the first instance in ancient comedy of a young man pining for a marriageable young Athenian woman of good family. In other plays the young women are foreigners, courtesans, or girls brought up in humble homes. Beare sees here something approaching a modern attitude in love and sex. In the light of Terence's procedure in this, his first play, it seems clear that he was striving to present the usual comic plot with new and interesting variations.

The Woman of Andros was adapted by Baron in his *L'Andrienne* (1703), by Steele in *The Conscious Lovers* (1722), and by Bellamy in *The Perjured Devotee* (1739). Terence's comedy was the inspiration of Thornton Wilder's novel, *The Woman of Andros* (1930).

THE WOMAN OF ANDROS

(SCENE:—*A street in Athens in front of the houses of* SIMO *and* GLYCERIUM.)

Prologue[5]

WHEN our poet first turned his mind to playwriting, he imagined that his sole concern was to see that the plays which he wrote should please the people; but he finds that the reality is very different, and he has to waste his labour in writing prologues, not thereby to explain the plot of the play, but to answer the slanders of a certain spiteful old poet.[6] Now, I beg you, give your attention to the matter for which they blame our poet. Menander wrote *The Andrian* and *The Perinthian*. If you know one of these plays well, you know them both; for they are not unlike in plot, although very different in language and style. The poet admits that he has transferred such passages as suited him from *The Perinthian* to *The Andrian,* and used them both as his own. His enemies blame him for having done this, and maintain that it is wrong to mix plays together. Does not this affectation of learning show that they know nothing about the matter? When they blame him, they are blaming Naevius, Plautus, and Ennius, whom our poet can appeal to as having done the same thing. He wishes rather to rival their fine carelessness than the obscure and minute pedantry of his detractors; and what is more, I warn them to hold their peace for the future, and leave off abusing him, or they will find their own misdeeds published. Favour us with silence; listen impartially and weigh the facts of the case, that you may thoroughly examine if any hope remains: whether you mean to listen to the new plays which I may hereafter write, or to damn them without hearing them.

Act One.   Scene I

(Enter SIMO *and* SOSIA, *followed by slaves carrying provisions.)*

SIMO *(to the servants)*: You carry all that into the house, and be off with you. *(The servants enter* SIMO's *house)* Sosia, stay awhile; I want to say a few words to you.

SOSIA: Account them said. You mean, I suppose, that all this must be cooked properly.

SIMO: No, I mean something else.

SOSIA: What is there besides this that my skill can do for you?

SIMO: I want none of that skill of yours for the matter which I am planning. I want the qualities which I have always found in you—loyalty and silence.

SOSIA: I'm all attention to know what you want.

SIMO: You know that, ever since I bought you as a little boy, you have always been justly and kindly treated while serving me. I have promoted you from being my slave to be my freedman, because you served me faithfully as a slave. I have given you the highest reward that it was in my power to give you.

SOSIA: I haven't forgotten it.

SIMO: I'm not sorry for what I have done.

SOSIA: I am glad of having done, or if I can now do, anything that pleases you, Simo; and I am thankful for your gratitude. But this is distasteful to me, for counting up of benefits conferred seems like reproaching me with forgetfulness of them. Just tell me in one word what you want with me.

SIMO: I will do so. The first thing that I will tell you in this matter is this: this is not a real marriage, as you think.

SOSIA: Then why do you make this pretence?

SIMO: You shall hear the whole story from the beginning; by that means you will understand both my son's way of life, and my plans, and what I want you to do in this matter. When he reached man's estate, Sosia, he became more his own master; before that, how could one know what his true character was, when youth, and fear, and his schoolmaster prevented his showing it?

SOSIA: True.

SIMO: Nearly all young men take up some particular line, either keeping horses, or hounds, or frequenting the philosophers' schools. He didn't devote himself to any one of these pursuits more than another, yet he practised them all in moderation. I was delighted.

SOSIA: And you had good cause to be, for I think this "golden mean" to be the most valuable rule for a man's life.

SIMO: This was his life: he bore and forbore good-naturedly with all men; he made himself agreeable to any society into which he was thrown; he accommodated himself to his friends' wishes; he quarrelled with no man, and never put himself before others; that is the easiest way to win praise without jealousy and gain friends.

SOSIA: He ordered his life wisely, for in these days friends are won by humouring, while truthfulness begets hatred.

SIMO: Meanwhile, some three years ago a lady from Andros came to live in this neighbourhood, driven here by poverty and the neglect of her relatives. She was very beautiful, and still young.

SOSIA: Dear me, I fear some mischief may come of this Andrian.

SIMO: At first she lived a virtuous, frugal, hardworking life, eking out her living by her spinning-wheel and her loom; but when first one lover and then another came with offers of money, why then, as human nature always shuns labour and inclines to pleasure, she accepted their terms, and became a professional courtesan. Now it so happened that her lovers took my son to her house with them for company. I said to myself straightway, "He's caught, for sure; he's hit." I used to watch in the morning for the slave-boys belonging to the others as they came or went away. I used to say, "My boy, tell me, if you please, who had Chrysis last night?" For that was the name of the lady from Andros.

SOSIA: I know.

SIMO: They used to say, "Phaedrus," or "Clinias," or "Nicaretus," for all these three were then her lovers. "Ah, but what of Pamphilus?" "Oh, he paid his shot and ate his dinner." I was delighted. I made enquiries on another day; I learned that Pamphilus was in no way concerned. Well, I thought that he had been sufficiently proved, and was a shining example of self-restraint; for when a man encounters characters of that sort, and yet his heart is not moved by them, you may be sure that he is already capable of self-control. This pleased me, and at the same time everybody with one voice kept praising him to me and congratulating me on my good fortune in having a son of such a character. Why say more about it? Encouraged by this report, Chremes came to me of his own accord and offered to give his only daughter to my son to wife, with a handsome dowry. I agreed; I betrothed him to her; today was fixed upon for the wedding.

SOSIA: And what hindrance is there to the wedding taking place?

SIMO: You shall hear. A few days after this took place, my neighbour Chrysis died.

SOSIA: Oh, what a good thing! I'm delighted to hear it; I was afraid that Chrysis might do him harm.

SIMO: Hereupon my son, together with those who had been Chrysis' lovers, was much at her house, and took part with them in settling about the funeral; meanwhile he was gloomy, and sometimes in tears. At the time I was pleased at this, for I thought to myself, "How deeply he takes her death to heart, and yet he had but little to do with her! What would he have done had he been her lover? What would he feel for me, his father?" I went on thinking that all these were signs of a kindly temper and a good heart. Why make a long story of it? I myself, for his sake, went to the funeral, and even then didn't suspect anything wrong.

SOSIA: Ah! and what—

SIMO: You shall hear. The body was carried out of the house. We started. Meanwhile, among the women who were present I espied one young girl, whose face—

SOSIA: Was beautiful, perhaps?

SIMO: It was, Sosia, and her looks were as modest and charming as they could be. As she seemed to me to mourn more deeply than the other women, and because she was far more beautiful and ladylike than they, I went up to the followers, and asked who she was. They told me that she was Chrysis' sister. Straightway the thought struck me, "Why, that is the meaning of it. That is what these tears, this sorrow was about."

SOSIA: I am terribly afraid of what the outcome of this will be.

SIMO: Meanwhile the funeral procession went on; we followed; we came to the grave; the body was put on the burning pyre; we wept. Meanwhile, this sister of whom I spoke went imprudently near the fire, and was in considerable danger. Hereupon Pamphilus became scared, and betrayed the love which he had so well concealed. He ran up to her, seized her by the waist, and said, "Dear Glycerium, what are you about? Why are you going to destroy yourself?" She then flung herself into his arms, and wept as if most intimate with him, so that you could easily see that they had long been lovers.

SOSIA: What's this you say?

SIMO: I came home angry and vexed, and yet without any sufficient grounds for scolding him. He would have said, "What have I done, father? Of what crime am I guilty? How have I sinned? I held her back when she would have cast herself into the fire, and saved her life!" It would have been a reasonable excuse.

SOSIA: You are right; for if you scold one who saved life, what would you do to one who did hurt or mischief?

SIMO: On the morrow Chremes came to me in a great stew. "Most disgraceful," he declared; "I have learned that Pamphilus is living with this foreign woman as his wife." I positively denied this; he insisted that it was true; and finally, I left him in no humour to give his daughter to my son.

SOSIA: Didn't you even then attack your son?

SIMO: Not even this was a sufficient reason for scolding him.

SOSIA: Pray why not?

SIMO: His answer would have been: "You yourself, father, have ordained the limits of my liberty; the time will soon come when I shall have to live to please someone else; in the meantime, let me live in my own way."

SOSIA: Then what have you left to scold him about?

SIMO: If he won't marry because of this amour, that will at least be a punishable offence on his part; and now I am trying, by this false pretence of marriage, to get some real ground for scolding him if he refuses it. Besides, if that scoundrel Davus has any plan in his head, I want him to carry it out now when his tricks will be harmless; and I believe that he will work tooth and nail; more, however, to spite me than to please my son.

SOSIA: Why should he?

SIMO: Why? Bad thoughts, bad intentions. If I only catch him— But what's the use of talking? If it turns out, as I trust it will, that Pamphilus makes no objection, then I still have Chremes to win over; and I hope that it will come off. Now what you have to do is to make a good pretence of belief in this wedding; to frighten Davus, and to watch my son, and see what he does and what plot he concocts with Davus.

SOSIA: Enough; I'll attend to it: now let us go indoors.

SIMO: You go first. (SOSIA *goes into* SIMO's *house*.)[7]

Act One.   Scene II

SIMO (*to himself*): There can be no doubt that my son is unwilling to marry, for I saw how frightened Davus was just now, when he heard that the wedding was to take place. But here he himself is coming out of the house.

(*Enter* DAVUS.)

DAVUS (*to himself*): I wondered whether it would pass off so, and I always feared what would come of master's easygoing ways. When he heard that his son's bride was going to be refused to him, he never said a word about it to any of us, or made a fuss about it.

SIMO (*aside, overhearing him*): But he will now, and it will be very much the worse for you, I reckon, when he does.

DAVUS: What he meant was, that we should be lulled into security by a false dream of hope, and that, when we thought we had nothing to fear, he would then catch us unawares, and give me no time to plot anything to upset the marriage. Cunning old fox!

SIMO (*aloud*): What's that scoundrel saying?

DAVUS (*aside*): The master, and I didn't see him!

SIMO: Davus!

DAVUS: Eh, what's that!

SIMO: Here, come to me!

DAVUS (*aside*): What does he want?

SIMO: What do you say?

DAVUS: About what?

SIMO: About what, indeed! They say that my son has a mistress.

DAVUS (*aside*): Of course, that's common talk.

SIMO: Are you listening to me or not?

DAVUS: I am.

SIMO: But I have no right, as his father, to go into that matter, for I have no concern with what he may have done up to this present time. While he was of an age for it, I let him have his fling; now the time has come for him to lead a different life, and he is expected to behave differently. Now, therefore, I ask you, or even entreat you, Davus, that he may return to respectability.

DAVUS: What does all this mean?[8]

SIMO: All lovers are much grieved at being made to marry someone else.

DAVUS: So people say.

SIMO: And if the lover has taken to himself an evil counsellor, he generally gives his lovesick mind a twist the wrong way.

DAVUS: I don't understand you at all.

SIMO: You don't, eh?

DAVUS: No, I don't. I'm Davus, not Oedipus.[9]

SIMO: Why, do you want me to tell you plainly what I have still to say?

DAVUS: By all means.

SIMO: Well, then, Davus, in the matter of this marriage, if I find you this day attempting any trick to prevent its coming off, or wanting to show your cleverness in connection with it, I'll have you flogged and make you grind flour in the mill till you die of it, on this condition and with the solemn assurance that, if ever I take you out, I will go and grind flour in your stead. There! Do you understand that? Or don't you comprehend even yet?

DAVUS: Nay, I understand it perfectly; you have gone so straight to the point, without any beating about the bush.

SIMO: I would let you cheat me in any matter rather than in this.

DAVUS: Hush, I pray!

SIMO: What! Are you laughing at me? You don't deceive me. I give you notice not to play the fool. And you won't be able to plead that you haven't had fair warning. So look out. (SIMO *departs.*)

Act One. Scene III

DAVUS (*to himself*): Indeed, Davus, there is no time for idling or laziness, from what I have just heard of the old gentleman's ideas about this marriage. If they are not cleverly looked after, they will ruin me or my master. I am not quite certain what to do, whether to help Pamphilus or to obey the old gentleman. If I desert Pamphilus, I fear for his life; if I help him, I fear Simo's threats; and it is not easy to humbug Simo, for, in the first place, he knows of this amour; he is angry with me, and watches me jealously, for fear I should play any trick about this wedding. If he finds me doing so, I am lost; or if he pleases, he will at once seize upon some excuse to cast me headlong into the mill, right or wrong. Then, besides all these mischiefs, there is another; this Andrian, whether she be Pamphilus' wife or mistress, is pregnant by him. And just listen to their assurance; it is a plan fit for lunatics rather than for lovers; they have made up their minds to acknowledge the child when it is born, whether it is a boy or a girl. They are making up some story between them about her being a citizen of Athens. "Once upon a time there was an old man, a trader, whose ship was wrecked upon the isle of Andros. The old man died, and then the father of this woman Chrysis adopted his destitute orphan daughter, who was then a little girl." Rubbish! It doesn't sound probable to me, though the tale meets with their approval. But here's Mysis coming out from her house. Well, I'll be off to the market place and meet Pamphilus, for fear his father should take him unawares. (DAVUS *departs*.)

Act One. Scene IV

(*Enter* MYSIS *from the house of* GLYCERIUM.)

MYSIS (*to* ARCHILIS, *within*): Yes, Archilis, you told me so long ago; you bid me fetch Lesbia. (*To herself*) The real truth is, she's a drunken, careless woman, and not fit to manage anyone's first childbirth. And yet I must bring her. Just see how obstinate the old beldam is, just because the other gets drunk with her. O ye Gods! I pray you grant that my mistress may bear her child easily, and Lesbia may blunder with somebody else. (*Looking down the street*) But why is Pamphilus looking so downcast? I hope there is nothing wrong. I'll wait to find out whether this distress of his means any trouble for us.

Act One.   Scene V

(*Enter* PAMPHILUS.)

PAMPHILUS (*to himself*): Is this well done or like a man? Is this how a father ought to behave?

MYSIS (*aside*): What's all this?

PAMPHILUS: By heaven, it's a mere outrage! He had made up his mind that I should be married today, had he? Ought I not to have known it before; ought I not to have some previous notice of it?

MYSIS (*aside*): Oh, dear me! What do I hear?

PAMPHILUS: Well, and Chremes, who declared that he wouldn't give me his daughter to wife, has he changed his mind, because he saw that I didn't change mine? Is the old gentleman so determined to separate me from Glycerium? If he does, it's all over with me. Was ever any man so unlucky in love, so unhappy as I? Great heavens! Are there no means by which I can escape from this connection with Chremes? I've been rebuffed and flouted in every way; the whole business was at an end, when, lo and behold! I, the rejected, am sought for again. What is the reason of this? I can't tell, unless it be, as I suspect, that they have got some frightful monster hidden away, and come to me because they can't put her off upon anyone else.

MYSIS (*aside*): This talk of his frightens me to death.

PAMPHILUS: What am I to say of my father's conduct? Really, to manage such an important matter in such an offhand manner! Just now he met me in the market place and said as he passed, "You've got to be married today, Pamphilus, so go home and get ready." It was just as if he had said to me, "Go home and hang yourself." I was dumbfounded; do you think I could say a single word or make a single excuse, even a silly, false, or wicked one? No, I was mute. Suppose anyone were to ask me what I should have done if I had known this before; well, I would have done anything to avoid doing this; but now, what course am I to take? I have so many troubles drawing me in different ways—my love and pity for Glycerium here; then all the pressure put upon me to marry, and also my respect for my father, who has hitherto so good-naturedly let me do whatever I pleased. How can I oppose him? O Lord! I don't know what to do.

MYSIS (*aside*): Oh, dear me! I dread what this uncertainty of his may end in. But now, if ever, he must either speak to her or I must speak to him on her behalf. While the mind is not made up, it does not take much to sway it one way or the other.

PAMPHILUS: Who is that talking? Oh, good day, Mysis.

MYSIS: Good day to you, Pamphilus.

PAMPHILUS: How is she?

MYSIS: Can you ask? She is in the pains of labour, and besides that, she is anxious, poor thing, because this was long ago fixed for your wedding day, and she dreads that you will desert her.

PAMPHILUS: Now, can I attempt this great wickedness? Shall I let this poor girl be deceived through me, after she has given her heart and her whole life into my keeping? After I have treated her as my dearly loved wife? Shall I let her, well brought up and modest as she is, be driven to evil courses by want? I will not.

MYSIS: I should have no fear if it depended upon you alone, but can you hold out against pressure?

PAMPHILUS: Do you think me so mean, so wanting in gratitude, or so brutal a savage, that our long intimacy, our love, and mere shame cannot move me, or remind me to be true to her?

MYSIS: I only know that she does not deserve that you should forget her.

PAMPHILUS: Forget her? O Mysis, Mysis, Chrysis' last words about Glycerium are still written on my heart. When she was on her deathbed she called me to her. I went; all of you left the room; we were alone. She began, "Dear Pamphilus, you see how pretty and how young she is; and you know how little these qualities will avail to help her to keep her virtue or position. Now I entreat you, by this your right hand, by your guardian angel, by your honour and by her desolate state, do not separate her from you nor abandon her. As I have esteemed you like my own brother, and as she has always loved you, and you only, with all her heart, and has done your pleasure in all things, I do now constitute you her husband, her friend, her father, and her guardian. I hand over and bequeath to your care all my property and hers." She gave her to me, and died. I undertook the trust, and I will be faithful to it.

MYSIS: I sincerely hope you will.

PAMPHILUS: But why are you leaving her?

MYSIS: I am going to fetch the midwife.

PAMPHILUS: Make haste; and, hark! Not a word about my marriage, to add to the trouble she has already.

MYSIS: I understand. (MYSIS *departs;* PAMPHILUS *enters his father's house.*)

Act Two. Scene I

(*Enter* CHARINUS *and* BYRRIA.)

CHARINUS: What do you say, Byrria? Is she to be married to Pamphilus this day?

BYRRIA: That's right.

CHARINUS: How do you know?

BYRRIA: I heard it just now in the market place from Davus.

CHARINUS: Ah, me! My heart has hitherto been on the stretch between hope and fear, but, now that hope is taken away, weary with anxiety, it feels only dull despair.

BYRRIA: Since you can't get what you want, Charinus, you had better want something that you can get.

CHARINUS: I don't want anything except Philumena.

BYRRIA: Bah! How much better it would be to give your mind to forgetting this love of yours, than to talk in a way which only kindles your hopeless passion.

CHARINUS: When we are well, we all find it easy to give good advice to sick people. If you were in my place, you'd see things in a different light.

BYRRIA: Well, well, have it your own way.

(*Enter* PAMPHILUS.)

CHARINUS: But there's Pamphilus; I am determined to leave nothing untried before I am utterly lost.

BYRRIA (*aside*): What's he up to?

CHARINUS: I will implore Pamphilus himself, I will entreat him, I will tell him how I love her. I think I shall at any rate get him to put off the wedding for a few days; in the meantime, I hope something may be done.

BYRRIA (*aside*): That "something" is nothing at all.

CHARINUS: What do you think, Byrria? Shall I accost him?

BYRRIA: Why shouldn't you? Even if you don't gain anything, still you can let him think that you are ready to be his wife's lover, if he marries her.

CHARINUS: Go to the devil with your base suspicions, you scoundrel!

PAMPHILUS (*approaching*): Why, here's Charinus; good day to you.

CHARINUS: Greetings to you, Pamphilus! I come to you begging you to give me hope, to save me, to advise me, to help me.

PAMPHILUS: I have no time to give you advice, and no means to help you with. But pray what is the matter?

CHARINUS: Are you to be married today?

PAMPHILUS: So they say.

CHARINUS: Pamphilus, if you do this, you see me now for the last time.

PAMPHILUS: Why so?

CHARINUS: Oh, dear! I don't like to say why. Pray tell him, Byrria.

BYRRIA: I will tell him.

PAMPHILUS: What is it?

BYRRIA: He's in love with your bride.

PAMPHILUS: Then his feelings are not the same as mine. I say, Charinus, did anything further ever pass between you and her?

CHARINUS: Oh, for shame, Pamphilus! Nothing.

PAMPHILUS: How I wish there had.

CHARINUS: Now I beg you, in the name of our friendship and of my love, in the first place, not to marry her.

PAMPHILUS: I will do my best not to do so.

CHARINUS: But if this may not be, and if you have set your heart on this marriage—

PAMPHILUS: My heart?

CHARINUS: At least put it off for the next few days, till I can set out on a journey to some place, and avoid seeing it.

PAMPHILUS: Now listen to me, Charinus. I don't think that a gentleman ought to ask for gratitude for doing what deserves none. I am more eager to avoid this marriage than you are to contract it.

CHARINUS: You have made a new man of me.

PAMPHILUS: Now if you or Byrria here can do anything, pray set to work, invent some plot, manage to get her married to you. I will do my best to prevent her being married to me.

CHARINUS: Say no more.

PAMPHILUS: Just in the nick of time I see Davus, on whose advice I rely.

CHARINUS (*to* BYRRIA): Now, *you* never tell me anything except what is not worth knowing; be off with you.

BYRRIA: With all the pleasure in the world. (BYRRIA *departs.*)

Act Two.   Scene II

(*Enter* DAVUS *from the forum.*)

DAVUS (*to himself*): Great heavens! What good news I bring! But where shall I find Pamphilus, that I may take away the fear which now oppresses him and surfeit his soul with joy?

CHARINUS (*to* PAMPHILUS): He's pleased about something or other.

PAMPHILUS (*to* CHARINUS): There's nothing for him to be pleased at; he hasn't yet learned my misfortunes.

DAVUS (*to himself*): I suppose that, if he heard that his marriage had been arranged, he would—

CHARINUS (*to* PAMPHILUS): Do you hear what he is saying?

DAVUS: Be running wild all over the town looking for me. But where shall I seek him, or which way shall I go first?

CHARINUS (*to* PAMPHILUS): Why don't you speak to him?

DAVUS: I know; I'm off. (*Starting off at a run.*)

PAMPHILUS: Davus, come here, stay.

DAVUS: Who's that calling me back? O Pamphilus, you are the very man I am looking for. Bravo! Charinus; well met, both of you; I have something to say to you.

PAMPHILUS: Davus, I'm ruined.

DAVUS: But just you listen to this.

PAMPHILUS: I'm a lost man.

DAVUS: I know what you're afraid of.

CHARINUS: Indeed, my life is at stake.

DAVUS (*to* CHARINUS): And I know what *you* are afraid of too.

PAMPHILUS: My marriage—

DAVUS: But suppose I know all about it.

PAMPHILUS: This day—

DAVUS: You keep dinning your marriage into my ears; but suppose I understand all about it. You (*to* PAMPHILUS) are afraid of being married to her. You (*to* CHARINUS) are afraid of *not* being married to her.

CHARINUS: You know the whole story.

PAMPHILUS: That's the case exactly.

DAVUS: And yet there's no fear of any marriage at all. Trust to me.

PAMPHILUS: I implore you, set me free as soon as you can from this fear.

DAVUS: I will—I do. Chremes is not now going to give you his daughter in marriage.

PAMPHILUS: How do you know?

DAVUS: I know. A little while ago your father laid hold of me and said that you were to be married today, and a lot more that I have no time to tell you now. Straightway I ran hurriedly off to the market place to tell you this. Not finding you there, I went up to a high place and looked round; nowhere could I see you; but I chanced to see Byrria, this gentleman's servant. I enquired of him; he said that he hadn't seen you. I was vexed, and considered what I had better do. As I was going home the circumstances made me suspicious. I said to myself: "There is very little for dinner at home; the old gentleman is in low spirits; this marriage is a very sudden affair; things don't tally."

PAMPHILUS: What are you driving at?

DAVUS: I took myself off straightway to Chremes's house. When I came there, I found nothing stirring before the front door. I was delighted.

CHARINUS: Good!

PAMPHILUS: Go on.

DAVUS: I waited there. While I waited, I saw no one going into the house, no one coming out; no married lady[10] indoors, no dressing, no fussing. I went up to the house and peeped in.

PAMPHILUS: I understand; this seems a strong proof.

DAVUS: Does all this agree with the story of the marriage?

PAMPHILUS: I don't think it does, Davus.

DAVUS: "Think," do you say? You don't grasp the situation. It's quite certain; besides, as I was coming away, I met Chremes' lad carrying home a few pennies' worth of salad and sprats for the old gentleman's supper.

CHARINUS: Davus, you have saved me this day.

DAVUS: No, not at all.

CHARINUS: How's that? He certainly won't give his daughter to Pamphilus.

DAVUS: Goose! As if it was certain that you would marry her, even if she were not married to Pamphilus! You will never get her unless you look out, unless you beg the old gentleman's friends to help you, unless you win their favour.

CHARINUS: You give good advice. I'll go, although I have often been disappointed in this hope. Farewell. (CHARINUS *departs*.)

Act Two.   Scene III

PAMPHILUS: Well, now, what does my father mean? Why is he making this pretence?

DAVUS: I'll tell you. If he were angry with Chremes for not giving you his daughter, before he knew your mind about the marriage, he would

feel, and rightly feel, that he was himself in the wrong. But if you refuse to marry her, then he'll shift all the blame on to your shoulders.
Then the row will start.

PAMPHILUS: I'll endure anything.

DAVUS: He is your father, Pamphilus; it is hard for you to thwart him;
and this is a lone woman; no sooner said than done; he'll find some
excuse for turning her out of the place altogether.

PAMPHILUS: Turn her out?

DAVUS: Directly.

PAMPHILUS: Then pray, Davus, what am I to do?

DAVUS: Say that you'll be married.

PAMPHILUS: What?

DAVUS: What's the matter?

PAMPHILUS: I! Say that I'll be married?

DAVUS: Why not?

PAMPHILUS: I'll never do that.

DAVUS: Don't say "no."

PAMPHILUS: Don't try to persuade me.

DAVUS: See what will happen if you do.

PAMPHILUS: What will happen will be, that I shall be shut out from
Glycerium, and shut up with Philumena.

DAVUS: Not so; I expect this will be the way of it: your father will say,
"I want you to be married today." You reply, "I will." Tell me, what
fault can he find with you then? You will thereby upset all his plans
without any danger, for there can be no doubt that Chremes will not
give you his daughter. But don't you alter your present conduct, for
fear lest, if you do, Chremes may change his mind. Tell your father that
you are willing to be married, so that he cannot reasonably be angry
with you even if he wishes it. As to that hope of yours: "I can easily
repel a wife with this character of mine; no one will give his daughter
to me"; your father will find a dowerless girl for you rather than let
you go to the bad. But if he finds that you take it coolly, you will make
him careless: he will take his time about finding another wife for you;
in the meantime something good may turn up.

PAMPHILUS: Do you really think so?

DAVUS: There can't be any doubt about that.

PAMPHILUS: See what you are committing me to.

DAVUS: Hold your tongue.

PAMPHILUS: I will say it; but we must take care that he doesn't find out that there's a child coming, for I have promised to acknowledge it.

DAVUS: What a reckless thing to do!

PAMPHILUS: She begged me to give her my word of honour to do this, as a proof that I should never desert her.

DAVUS: I'll see about it; but here comes your father. Mind that he doesn't notice your low spirits.

Act Two.   Scene IV

(Enter SIMO *from the forum.)*

SIMO *(to himself)*: I'll have another look at what they are doing, and what plans they are meditating.

DAVUS *(aside to* PAMPHILUS*)*: Now he is quite sure that you will refuse to be married; he has come from some quiet place where he has been thinking it over, and he hopes that he has found some argument to worry you with; so mind you keep your wits about you.

PAMPHILUS: I will if I can, Davus.

DAVUS: And believe me, Pamphilus, your father won't say a single cross word to you this day, if you say that you'll be married.

Act Two.   Scene V

(Enter BYRRIA.*)*

BYRRIA *(aside)*: My master bade me leave my work and watch Pamphilus today, to see what he does about his marriage (that is why I am following him here). And there he stands, I see, and Davus with him. I'm all attention.

SIMO (*aside*): There they both are.

DAVUS (*aside to* PAMPHILUS): Now, remember.

SIMO (*aloud*): Pamphilus.

DAVUS (*aside to* PAMPHILUS): Look round at him as if you were taken unawares.

PAMPHILUS (*affecting to start*): What! My father!

DAVUS (*aside to* PAMPHILUS): Well done!

SIMO: As I said before, I intend you to be married today.

BYRRIA (*aside*): Now I'm afraid, for our side, what answer he will give.

PAMPHILUS: I shall always obey your commands in this and in everything else.

BYRRIA: H'm!

DAVUS (*aside to* PAMPHILUS): There, you see, he's dumbfounded.

BYRRIA (*aside*): What did he say?

SIMO: You behave as becomes you, when you grant my requests with a good grace.

DAVUS: Am I a true prophet?

BYRRIA (*aside*): My master has lost his wife, by what I hear.

SIMO (*to* PAMPHILUS): Well now, go indoors that you may not keep us waiting when you're wanted.

PAMPHILUS: I am going. (*He enters his father's house.*)

BYRRIA (*aside*): Well, you can't trust anybody in anything. The proverb is quite true, that everyone thinks of himself first. I have seen the girl, and remember that she is handsome; so I can the more readily excuse Pamphilus if he prefers sleeping with her in his arms to letting my master do so. I'll go and tell him what I have learned, and then he'll whack me for my bad news. (BYRRIA *departs*.)

Act Two.   Scene VI

DAVUS (*aside*): Now Simo thinks that I am bringing some trick to play upon him, and that that's why I am staying here.

SIMO: What is Davus saying?

DAVUS: Just as much as I said before.

SIMO: What? Nothing? H'm!

DAVUS: Nothing at all.

SIMO: And yet I expected something.

DAVUS (*aside*): He's disappointed; I can see that; it nettles him.

SIMO: Are you capable of telling me the truth?

DAVUS: Nothing easier.

SIMO: Is this marriage at all distasteful to Pamphilus because of his connection with that foreigner?

DAVUS: Not a bit of it; or, if he does worry about it, it will only be for two or three days at the outside, you know, and then it will be over. Indeed, he has been thinking the matter over in its true light.

SIMO: I am glad of that.

DAVUS: While he was allowed by you, and as long as his youth prompted it, he kept a mistress, but it was under the rose. Like a man of spirit, he took care that his amour should never be a disgrace to him. Now he ought to marry, and he has made up his mind to take a wife.

SIMO: He struck me as being rather out of spirits.

DAVUS: Yes, but not on account of that affair; he is displeased with you.

SIMO: Why, what's the matter?

DAVUS: Oh! A mere trifle.

SIMO: But what is it?

DAVUS: Nothing.

SIMO: Won't you tell me what it is?

DAVUS: He says you are not spending your money liberally enough on the occasion.

SIMO: What! I?

DAVUS: Yes; you. Says he: "My father has hardly spent ten drachmae on the feast; it doesn't seem as if he was having his son married." "Whom of my friends," says he, "had I better invite to my wedding-dinner?" And, be it said between ourselves here, you really are too stingy about it. I don't like that.

SIMO (*angrily*): Be quiet.

DAVUS (*aside*): I've stung him.

SIMO: I will see that these things are managed properly. (*Aside*) What's the meaning of this? What is this old fox driving at? For if there is any mischief afoot, there's the man who set it going.

Act Three. Scene I

(*Enter* MYSIS *and* LESBIA.)

MYSIS: Indeed, Lesbia, what you said is quite true, you can hardly find a man who will be faithful to a woman.

SIMO (*aside to* DAVUS): This servant comes from the Andrian.

DAVUS (*aside to* SIMO): Nonsense!

SIMO (*aside to* DAVUS): It's true.

MYSIS: But this Pamphilus—

SIMO (*aside*): What's that she is saying?

MYSIS: Has pledged himself to her—

SIMO: Hah!

DAVUS (*aside*): Would to heaven that he were deaf or she were dumb.

MYSIS: For he has given orders that her child shall be brought up.

SIMO (*aside*): O Jupiter! What do I hear? All's lost, if that woman speaks the truth.

LESBIA: A noble young gentleman, by what you tell me.

MYSIS: Excellent! But come indoors with me, so that we don't keep her waiting.

LESBIA: I am coming. (LESBIA *and* MYSIS *enter the house of* GLYCERIUM.)

DAVUS (*aside*): What can I invent to repair this mischief?

SIMO: What's this? Can he be so mad? His child by a foreigner? Ah! Now I see it. I was such a fool; I didn't understand till just now.

DAVUS (*aside*): What's this that he says he understands?

SIMO (*aside*): This is the first of Davus' tricks played upon me. They are pretending that she is in childbirth, to frighten Chremes out of giving his daughter to Pamphilus.

GLYCERIUM (*within*): Juno, goddess of childbirth, help me, save me, I beseech thee!

SIMO (*aside*): What, so soon? How absurd! As soon as she heard that I was standing in front of her door, she makes haste to be in labour. (*Turning to* DAVUS) You haven't timed the incidents of this scene well, Master Davus.

DAVUS: What, I?

SIMO: Or is it that your pupils have forgotten their lesson?

DAVUS: I don't know what you are talking about.

SIMO (*aside*): If Davus had caught me today off my guard in the midst of a real wedding, what game he would have made of me! But now the danger is his, and I am sailing in quiet waters.

Act Three.   Scene II

(*Enter* LESBIA *from the house of* GLYCERIUM.)

LESBIA (*speaking to* ARCHILIS *within*): Well, Archilis, so far I see all the usual signs of a healthy confinement. Now, first of all, see that she is washed, then let her have what I ordered her to drink, and no more than I told you. I shall be back directly. (*To herself*) Gracious me, Pamphilus has got a bouncing boy. I hope to heaven that the child will live, for his father is a good young man, and wouldn't wrong this dear young lady. (LESBIA *departs.*)

SIMO (*to* DAVUS): Anybody who knew you might be sure that you were at the bottom of this.

DAVUS: Of what?

SIMO: She didn't give her orders to the servant face to face about what was to be done to the mother but waited till she was out of the house, and then bawled from the middle of the street to the women within. O Davus, do you despise me as much as this? Or do you think me so fit a subject for you to try to cheat me by such obvious tricks? At least you might have laid your plot carefully, so as to look as if you were afraid of me if I found it out.

DAVUS (*aside*): Indeed, he's deceiving himself now, I'm not deceiving him.

SIMO: I gave you notice, I charged you with threats not to do this. Did you fear me? What good has it been? Now, am I to believe this story of yours, that this woman has had a child by Pamphilus?

DAVUS: I see his mistake, and I know what I'll do.

SIMO: Why don't you answer?

DAVUS: Are you to believe? Why, weren't you told that this would happen?

SIMO: No; who told me?

DAVUS: Why, did you find out for yourself that this was all a pretence?

SIMO: You're laughing at me.

DAVUS: You must have been told, for how else should you have conceived this suspicion?

SIMO: How? Because I knew you.

DAVUS: That's as much as to say that all this was planned by me.

SIMO: I'm quite sure it was.

DAVUS: You don't yet understand my real character, Simo.

SIMO: I not know you?

DAVUS: But, whenever I begin to tell you anything, you straightway think that you are being cheated, so that I don't dare whisper a single word.

SIMO: I am sure of this much, that no one has borne a child in this house.

DAVUS: You've hit it. But, for all that, they will presently bring out the baby and lay it on your doorstep here. I tell you now beforehand, master, that this will be done, that you may understand, and may not hereafter say that it was done by Davus' advice, or to carry out his tricks. I want to do away altogether with the opinion that you have of me.

SIMO: How do you know this?

DAVUS: I have heard, and I am sure of it; besides, many circumstances combine to make me guess it. First of all, this woman declared that she was in the family way by Pamphilus; that was proved to be untrue. Now, as soon as she sees preparations being made for a wedding at your house, a servant is straightway sent to fetch the midwife to her, and to bring a child at the same time, for they think that, unless they do this, unless you see the child, they cannot upset the marriage.

SIMO: What's that you say? When you understood that they were planning this, why didn't you tell Pamphilus about it?

DAVUS: Why, who but I got him away from her? For all of us know how deeply he was in love with her. Now he begs to be given a wife. So just leave this business in my hands, and do you, nevertheless, go on as you are, making preparations for this marriage; and may the gods assist you!

SIMO: Nay; get you gone into the house. Wait for me there, and prepare whatever wants preparing. (*To himself, as* DAVUS *enters* SIMO'S *house*) He hasn't quite made me believe this; and yet I don't know but what all that he has said may be true. But I care little whether it is or no; the most important point of all is that my son has given me his promise. Now I'll see Chremes; I'll beg his daughter for my son. If I can gain his consent, why shouldn't the wedding come off today? My son has promised, and it is clear that, if he refuses, I shall be within my rights in making him keep his promise. And see, just in the nick of time, there comes Chremes.

Act Three.   Scene III

(*Enter* CHREMES.)

SIMO: Good day, Chremes!

CHREMES: Oh, you're the very man I was looking for!

SIMO: So was I looking for you.

CHREMES: Well met. People have been coming to me and saying that you told them my daughter was this day to be married to your son; so I want to know whether you are mad or they are.

SIMO: Listen to me for awhile, and I will tell you what I want of you and what you want to know.

CHREMES: I am listening; say what you will.

SIMO: I implore you, Chremes, in the name of heaven and of our friendship, which began when we were children and has grown with our growth, and in the name of your only daughter and of my son, whom you now have the best of opportunities to reclaim, help me in this business, and let the marriage take place as it was arranged that it should.

CHREMES: Oh, don't implore me. As if you needed to entreat me to grant you this! Do you suppose that I have changed since I offered her to you before? If it is for their good, then send for the bride; but if it is likely to do each of them more harm than good, then I beg you to take the whole matter into consideration, just as though she were your daughter and I Pamphilus' father.

SIMO: Nay, I wish it to be, and that is why I ask you to let it take place, Chremes. I should not ask this of you if circumstances did not call for it.

CHREMES: What circumstances?

SIMO: My son and Glycerium have quarrelled.

CHREMES: Indeed?

SIMO: So seriously, that I hope he may be separated from her.

CHREMES: Nonsense.

SIMO: It is really the case.

CHREMES: Ay, indeed, thus: lovers' quarrels do but renew their love.

SIMO: Oh, but I beseech you, let us forestall them while we have time, and while his passion has been quenched by her reproaches. Let us give him a wife before the tricks of these bad women and their artificial tears have softened his lovesick mind into pitying them. I hope, Chremes, that when he gets used to living in honourable wedlock he will easily free himself from these entanglements.

CHREMES: That is your view of the matter; but I don't believe that he will remain faithful to my daughter, nor can I permit anything else.

SIMO: How can you be sure of that unless you risk it?

CHREMES: But it is a serious risk to expose one's daughter to.

SIMO: Well, the worst that can come of the affair is separation, if that should come to pass, and may heaven forbid it. But if it reforms him, see how much good would come of it. In the first place, you will have brought your friend's son back to him, you will win for yourself a worthy son-in-law and a husband for your daughter.

CHREMES: Well, well, if you have made up your mind that it would be of use, I don't like to stand in your way.

SIMO: I always thought a great deal of you, Chremes, and I was right.

CHREMES: But, one moment!

SIMO: What?

CHREMES: How do you know that they have disagreed?

SIMO: It was Davus, who knows all their secrets, who told me, and he advises me to hurry on the wedding as soon as possible. Now, do you think that he would do that, unless he knew that my son wished it? You yourself shall hear what he says. (*Calling into the house*) Ho, there, send Davus out here to me! And there he is; I see the very man coming out of the door.

Act Three.   Scene IV

(*Enter* DAVUS *from the house.*)

DAVUS: I was coming to you.

SIMO: Why, what's the matter?

DAVUS: Why don't you send for the bride? Here, it's getting late in the day.

SIMO (*to* CHREMES): Do you hear him? (*To* DAVUS) I have long been afraid of you, Davus, that you would play me some such trick as most slaves do their masters, because my son has a mistress.

DAVUS: I do such a thing!

SIMO: I believed you would, and so, out of fear, I have kept secret from you two what I'm now going to tell you.

DAVUS: What?

SIMO: You shall know; for I have almost come to trust you.

DAVUS: Have you at last learned what sort of man I am?

SIMO: This marriage was not going to take place.

DAVUS: What? Not take place?

SIMO: But I pretended that it was, in order to try you and Pamphilus.

DAVUS: What's this you tell me?

SIMO: The truth.

DAVUS: There now! I never could have understood that. Oh, what a clever idea!

SIMO: Now listen to me; just as I ordered you into the house, Chremes here fortunately met me.

DAVUS (*aside*): What? Are we lost?

SIMO: I am telling Chremes what you just now told me.

DAVUS (*aside*): What do I hear?

SIMO: I begged him to give Pamphilus his daughter in marriage, and with difficulty I won his consent.

DAVUS (*aside*): The devil!

SIMO: Eh, what did you say?

DAVUS: I say, a devilish good thing!

SIMO: Now he'll be no hindrance to the marriage.

CHREMES: I'll go home now, and order all preparations to be made; then I'll come back and report progress. (CHREMES *departs*.)

SIMO: I beg you, Davus, since you alone have brought about this marriage for me—

DAVUS: I have, alone.

SIMO: Do try, now, to reform my son.

DAVUS: I will do my best.

SIMO: You can do so now, when his mind is irritated against her.

DAVUS: Make yourself easy.

SIMO: Come then, where is he now?

DAVUS: I am much mistaken if he isn't at home.

SIMO: I'll go to him and tell him over again what I have told you. (SIMO *enters his house*.)

DAVUS (*to himself*): I am lost. What is to keep me from going straight to prison? I have made it impossible for anyone to say a word on my behalf. I have upset everything. I've deceived my master; I've cast my master's son into matrimony; I have brought about the wedding this day, beyond Simo's hopes and against Pamphilus' will. There's fine plotting for you! If I had only kept quiet, no harm would have come of it. But there I see Pamphilus himself. O heavens! Would that there were some pit handy for me to throw myself into it.

Act Three.   Scene V

(*Enter* PAMPHILUS.)

PAMPHILUS: Where is he? The scoundrel who ruined me today?

DAVUS (*aside*): I'm lost.

PAMPHILUS: And yet I admit that it serves me right, for being so lazy, so helpless. To think that I should have entrusted my fortunes to a slave who can't keep a secret! I certainly have been rewarded according to my folly. But he won't get off scot-free after doing this.

DAVUS (*aside*): If I get out of this scrape, I have no fear of anything else that can befall me.

PAMPHILUS: What am I to say to my father? Am I to say that I won't marry the girl whom I just now promised to marry? How can I have the impudence to do that? I don't know what will become of me.

DAVUS (*aside*): Neither do I, although I am thinking hard about it. I will say that I'll invent something, so as to put off my fate for a little while, at any rate.

PAMPHILUS (*seeing* DAVUS): Aha!

DAVUS (*aside*): He sees me.

PAMPHILUS: Now then, my good man, what do you say to this? Don't you see that I've ruined and entangled myself by following your advice?

DAVUS: But I'll soon disentangle you.

PAMPHILUS: You will?

DAVUS: Of course I will, Pamphilus.

PAMPHILUS: Yes; as well as you did just now, I suppose.

DAVUS: Nay; better, I hope.

PAMPHILUS: As if I should trust you, you scoundrel! As if you could put straight a tangled and ruined cause! See! There's the man whom I trusted, who this day has brought me out of peace and happiness and cast me into—marriage! Didn't I tell you what would come of it?

DAVUS: Yes, you did.

PAMPHILUS: Then what do you deserve?

DAVUS: The gallows. But give me a little time to pull myself together; I'll soon contrive something.

PAMPHILUS: I am sorry that I haven't the leisure to punish you as I should like, for time only permits me to look out for myself, not to revenge myself upon you.

Act Four. Scene I

(Enter CHARINUS, *not seeing them.)*

CHARINUS *(to himself)*: Would it be believed, is it conceivable that anyone's heart could be so unreasonably spiteful that he should take a delight in the sufferings of others and reap advantage from their misfortunes? Is this fair? The worst sort of men are those who feel modesty about saying "no"; then when the time is come for them to perform their promise, they are forced to show their true character and are afraid; and yet they are obliged to refuse. Then they talk in the most shameless fashion: "Who are you?" "What have I to do with you?" "Why am I to help you before myself?" "Look you, charity begins at home." But when you ask them, "How about your word of honour that you gave?" they have no shame when they ought to feel shame; it's when there is no need for it that they are afraid to say "no." But what shall I do? Shall I go to him and reproach him with the wrong he has done me? Abuse him thoroughly? You may say, "That will do you no good." Yes, it will, a great deal. I shall at least annoy him and indulge my resentment.

PAMPHILUS *(seeing him)*: Charinus, unless the gods help us, I have unintentionally ruined both myself and you.

CHARINUS: Unintentionally, indeed? So you've found an excuse at last. How nicely you have kept your word!

PAMPHILUS: What do you mean by "at last"?

CHARINUS: Do you expect to take me in a second time with words like that?

PAMPHILUS: What is the matter?

CHARINUS: As soon as I told you that I was in love with her she began to have charms for you. Unlucky man that I was, I judged of your heart from my own.

PAMPHILUS: You are mistaken.

CHARINUS: Didn't your joy seem complete enough without making a fool of me when I was in love, and deluding me with false hope? Well, take her.

PAMPHILUS: I take her? Oh, you know not the troubles that poor I am struggling with, and what embarrassments that scoundrel of mine has brought upon me by his advice.

CHARINUS: One needn't be surprised at that, if he takes you for a pattern.

PAMPHILUS: You wouldn't say that if you knew me or my love.

CHARINUS (*ironically*): I understand; you have just had a quarrel with your father, and therefore, I suppose, he is angry with you, and could not force you into marrying her today.

PAMPHILUS: Nay, to show how little you know about my sorrows, this marriage was not arranged for me, and till just now no one wanted to give me a wife.

CHARINUS: I understand; you were forced into it of your own free will.

PAMPHILUS: Stay, you don't yet understand.

CHARINUS: At any rate, I understand that you are going to marry her.

PAMPHILUS: Why do you keep on pestering me? Listen: he never ceased urging me to tell my father that I was prepared to marry, and begged and prayed until at last he drove me to do it.

CHARINUS: Who did this?

PAMPHILUS: Davus.

CHARINUS: Why?

PAMPHILUS: I don't know; all that I know is that it must have been the wrath of heaven that made me listen to his advice.

CHARINUS: Is this the truth, Davus?

DAVUS: It is.

CHARINUS: Eh, what d'you say, you villain? May the gods destroy you as your sins deserve! Just tell me this: if all Pamphilus' enemies had wanted to drive him into marriage, what advice but this could they have given him?

DAVUS: I am at fault, but not tired out.

CHARINUS: I understand.

DAVUS: We have failed on this line; we must try some other, unless you think that this mischief can never now be put right, because our first attempt did not succeed.

PAMPHILUS: No, I don't think so; I am pretty sure that, if you give your mind to it, you will get me married twice instead of once.

DAVUS: Pamphilus, my duty towards you as your slave is to strive to help you tooth and nail, by night and by day, and even at the risk of my life. It is for you to make allowances for me in case my plan does not succeed as I hope. My present manoeuvre has failed; but I am doing my best for you. If you're not satisfied, find out a better plan yourself, and dismiss me.

PAMPHILUS: I should like to; just put me back where you found me.

DAVUS: I will.

PAMPHILUS: But you must do it now.

DAVUS: Hush! Stay! Glycerium's door is opening.

PAMPHILUS: That's nothing to you.

DAVUS: I'm thinking.

PAMPHILUS: What! At last?

DAVUS: I'll soon tell you my idea.

Act Four. Scene II

(Enter MYSIS *from the house of* GLYCERIUM.*)*

MYSIS *(to* GLYCERIUM *within)*: Wherever your Pamphilus may be, I will be sure and find him and bring him to you; only don't you fret, my love.

PAMPHILUS: Mysis!

MYSIS: Who's that? O Pamphilus, well met!

PAMPHILUS: What's the matter?

MYSIS: My mistress bade me pray you, if you love her, to come to her directly. She says she wants to see you.

PAMPHILUS: Oh, good gracious! Here's this trouble breaking out afresh. *(To* DAVUS) See how sadly she and I are being worried through what you have done; for the reason why she sends for me is that she has heard of this marriage being arranged for me.

CHARINUS: And how quiet everything might have been, had that fellow been quiet!

DAVUS *(to* CHARINUS): That's right, egg him on, as if he was not wild enough of himself!

MYSIS: Indeed, that is the reason; poor thing, that's what she is now grieving about.

PAMPHILUS: Mysis, I declare to you in the name of all the gods, that I never will desert her, not if I have to make enemies of all mankind. I chose her for my own; I won her; we suit one another; away with those who seek to part us; nought but death shall take her from me.

CHARINUS: I breathe again.

PAMPHILUS: Apollo's oracle is not more true than what I say. If it could be managed, I shouldn't like my father to think that it was I who broke off the marriage, but if it can't be managed, I'll do what I can to make him think that it was I. What think you of me?

CHARINUS: A miserable man, even as I myself.

DAVUS: I am trying to find a plan.

CHARINUS: Wonderful fellow!

PAMPHILUS: I know what you are trying to do.

DAVUS: I'll carry it through for you.

PAMPHILUS: But I want it now.

DAVUS: Well, I've got it ready now.

CHARINUS: What is it?

DAVUS: It's for Pamphilus, not for you; don't you make any mistake.

CHARINUS: I am satisfied.

PAMPHILUS: What are you going to do? Tell me.

DAVUS: I am afraid that this day will scarcely be long enough to carry it out; don't suppose that I have any leisure to tell it to you. So take yourselves off, for you are hindering me.

PAMPHILUS: I shall go and see her. (*He enters* GLYCERIUM's *house.*)

DAVUS (*to* CHARINUS): And what about you? Where are you going to?

CHARINUS: Do you want me to tell you the truth?

DAVUS: Oh! Now I'm in for a long yarn.

CHARINUS: What is to become of me?

DAVUS: Why, you shameless fellow, aren't you satisfied that all the time I can defer Pamphilus' marriage is a respite for you?

CHARINUS: Yes, but Davus—

DAVUS: But what?

CHARINUS: Help me to marry her.

DAVUS: Nonsense!

CHARINUS: Mind you come to me there (*pointing in the direction of his house*), if you can do anything for me.

DAVUS: Why should I come? I have nothing to help you with.

CHARINUS: Still, if you should have.

DAVUS: Very well, I'll come.

CHARINUS: If you should, I'll be at home. (CHARINUS *departs.*)

DAVUS (*preparing to go into* GLYCERIUM's *house*): Mysis, do you wait here for a few minutes till I come out again.

MYSIS: Why?

DAVUS: It will have to be so.

MYSIS: Well, make haste then.

DAVUS: I tell you, I'll be back directly. (*He goes into* GLYCERIUM'S *house.*)

Act Four.   Scene III

MYSIS (*to herself*): Is there nothing we can call our own? Good heavens! I thought that this Pamphilus was the greatest of blessings to my mistress—a friend, a lover, and a husband ready to stand by her on every occasion; and now see what trouble he is giving the poor thing. The misery of this far outweighs her former pleasure. But here's Davus coming out of the house.
(*Re-enter* DAVUS *carrying the baby.*)
My good man, pray what is the meaning of this? Where are you taking the child?

DAVUS: Now, Mysis, I need your ready cunning and skill in this business.

MYSIS: Why, what are you going to do?

DAVUS: Take this child from me directly, and lay him in front of our door.

MYSIS: Oh! But not on the ground.

DAVUS: Take some verbena from the altar here and lay it under him.

MYSIS: Why don't you do this yourself?

DAVUS: Because I want to be able to answer my master with a clear conscience if he asks me on my oath whether I put it there.

MYSIS: I understand, but it is something new for you to have any scruples about perjury.

DAVUS: Be quick about it; I want to tell you what's to be done next. (*Starting*) By Jupiter!

MYSIS (*laying the child at* SIMO'S *door*): What's the matter?

DAVUS: Here comes the bride's father. I give up my first plan.

MYSUS: I don't know what you are talking about.

DAVUS: Now, I'll pretend to have just come from the street here on the right hand; do you mind and help out my talk with a word thrown in whenever it is wanted. (*He departs in the direction of the forum.*)

MYSIS: I don't understand in the least what you're doing; but whatever it may be that you want me for, as you know best, I'll wait here, so as not to hinder your plans.

Act Four.   Scene IV

(*Enter* CHREMES.)

CHREMES (*to himself*): I have got everything ready for my daughter's marriage, and now I have come back to tell them to fetch her. (*Sees the child*) But what's this? Why, it's a baby-boy. Woman, did you put it here?

MYSIS (*aside*): Where's Davus?

CHREMES: Won't you answer me?

MYSIS (*aside*): I don't see him anywhere; unlucky woman that I am; the fellow has made off and left me in the lurch.

(*Re-enter* DAVUS *from the direction of the forum.*)

DAVUS (*to himself*): Good gracious! Such crowds in the market place! Such a lot of lawsuits going on! And corn such a price! (*Aside*) I don't know anything more to say.

MYSIS (*to* DAVUS): Pray, why did you leave me here alone?

DAVUS: Eh, what's all this story? Why, Mysis, where does this child come from? Who brought him here?

MYSIS: Are you in your right mind to ask me such a question?

DAVUS: Whom am I to ask, then, for I see no one else here?

CHREMES (*aside*): I wonder where the child did come from.

DAVUS: Are you going to answer my question?

MYSIS: Oh!

DAVUS (*aside to* MYSIS): Come over here to the right.

MYSIS: You are mad—didn't you yourself—

DAVUS (*aside to* MYSIS): I'll do you a mischief if you say a single word more than I ask you. (*Aloud*) None of your abuse. Where does the child come from? Tell me distinctly.

MYSIS: From our house.

DAVUS: Aha! It's an audacious thing, if the courtesan has done it.

CHREMES (*aside*): This maidservant, as I understand, comes from the Andrian woman.

DAVUS (*to* MYSIS): Do you think us fit subjects for you to play such tricks upon?

CHREMES (*aside*): I came just in good time.

DAVUS (*to* MYSIS): Now be quick and take that child away from the door. (*Aside to* MYSIS) Mind you, don't stir from where you stand.

MYSIS: The gods confound you; you do so frighten poor me!

DAVUS (*to* MYSIS): Did I give you that order or no?

MYSIS: What's your will?

DAVUS: What! Do you still keep asking me? Tell me, whose child is it that you have put here?

MYSIS: Don't you know?

DAVUS (*aside to* MYSIS): Never mind what I know; answer my question.

MYSIS: Yours.

DAVUS: Ours? Whose?

MYSIS: Pamphilus'.

CHREMES (*aside*): Ha!

DAVUS: What? Pamphilus'?

MYSIS: Why, isn't it?

CHREMES (*aside*): I was quite right in always objecting to this marriage.

DAVUS (*shouting*): O monstrous impudence!

MYSIS: What are you bawling about?

DAVUS: Do you mean the child that I saw carried into your house yesterday evening?

MYSIS: O you shameless liar!

DAVUS: It's true; I saw Canthara with a bundle under her cloak.

MYSIS: Thank heaven there were several freeborn women present at her confinement.

DAVUS: She doesn't know the man for whom she's trying that game. She thinks, "If Chremes sees the child lying at the doorstep, he will not give his daughter to Pamphilus"; but, by Jove! He'll give her all the more willingly.

CHREMES (*aside*): By Jove, he won't!

DAVUS (*to* MYSIS): Now then, I give you fair warning, if you don't take up that child, I'll throw it away into the middle of the road, and throw you into the mud after it.

MYSIS: Man, you're drunk!

DAVUS: One trick follows another. Now I hear a rumour about her being a citizen of Athens.

CHREMES (*aside*): Indeed!

DAVUS: He's to be legally compelled to marry her.[11]

MYSIS: Well, pray, isn't she a citizen?

CHREMES (*aside*): A ludicrous scrape I had almost fallen into in my ignorance!

DAVUS: Who is speaking there? (*Pretending to see* CHREMES *for the first time*) Oh, Chremes! You have come just in time. Listen!

CHREMES: I have already heard all.

DAVUS: Do you mean to say that you have heard all that story?

CHREMES: I tell you I have heard it all from the beginning.

DAVUS: Have you heard it? What rascality! This woman ought to be put on the rack straightway. (*To* MYSIS) This is Chremes himself; don't suppose that it was Davus you imposed upon.

MYSIS: Unhappy woman that I am! My good old gentleman, I have not told any lies.

CHREMES: I understand the whole affair. Is Simo at home?

DAVUS: He is. (CHREMES *enters* SIMO'S *house.*)

MYSIS (*to* DAVUS): Keep off me, you villain! If I don't tell Glycerium all!

DAVUS: Why, you fool, don't you know what you've done?

MYSIS: How should I know?

DAVUS: This is the bride's father; there was no other way of telling him what we want him to know.

MYSIS: You should have explained that to me beforehand.

DAVUS: Don't you know what a difference it makes whether you do a thing naturally from the heart or merely repeat a lesson?

Act Four.   Scene V

(*Enter* CRITO *from the harbour.*)

CRITO (*to himself*): This is the street where they say Chrysis used to live. She preferred to gain wealth here by her shame to living in honest poverty in her own country. By her death all her property comes to me. But I see some people there of whom I can enquire. (*To* MYSIS *and* DAVUS) Good day to you.

MYSIS: Goodness, who's this? Is not this Crito, Chrysis' own first cousin?

CRITO: I'm glad to see you, Mysis.

MYSIS: And I you, Crito.

CRITO: So then Chrysis, eh?

MYSIS: Yes, she left us poor souls in distress.

CRITO: And how are you getting on here? All right, eh?

MYSIS: We? Oh, we do the best we can, as the saying is, since we can't do what we should like.

CRITO: What about Glycerium, has she found her parents here yet?

MYSIS: I wish she had.

CRITO: What! Not yet? I haven't come here at a lucky moment. By heaven, had I known that, I never would have set my foot ashore here. She was always called and passed for Chrysis' sister; she now owns what property Chrysis had. Now I am warned by what has befallen others, how difficult and useless it is for a foreigner to engage in a lawsuit at Athens; besides, I expect that she has already got some friend and protector, for she was quite a big girl when she left Andros. They would cry shame on me for a swindler, a beggarly legacy-hunter; and then, too, I don't want to leave her destitute.

MYSIS: Excellent man; still the same good old Crito.

CRITO: Take me to her, that I may see her, now that I have come here.

MYSIS: Certainly.

DAVUS: I'll go after them; I don't want the old gentleman to see me just now. (*They enter the house of* GLYCERIUM.)

Act Five.   Scene I

(*Enter* CHREMES *and* SIMO *from the latter's house.*)

CHREMES: Simo, my friendship for you has been sufficiently, quite sufficiently proved already. I have very nearly got into serious trouble; don't ask it of me any more. I have all but wrecked my daughter's happiness through trying to comply with your wishes.

SIMO: Why, I now more than ever pray and beseech you, Chremes, to confirm by deeds the kindness which you used to profess in words.

CHREMES: See how unreasonable your eagerness makes you; so long as you can get what you want, you don't set any bounds to my compliance, nor reflect what it is that you ask of me; for if you did reflect, you would leave off loading me with wrongs.

SIMO: What wrongs?

CHREMES: You ask? Why, you have driven me into giving my daughter to a young fellow who is in love with someone else and loathes the idea of marriage, to undergo domestic unhappiness, and perhaps to be repudiated, in order that by her sufferings and sorrows I might bring your son to his senses. Well, you have gained your wish; I worked for it while it was possible; now it is impossible; you must bear it. They say that Glycerium is an Athenian citizen; a boy has been born; let us go.

SIMO: In the name of the gods, I beg you not to permit yourself to believe what they say; it is their interest to make him out to be as bad as he can be. All this has been invented and got up to stop his marriage; when the reason for doing so has been removed, they will drop it.

CHREMES: You are mistaken; I saw Davus with my own eyes quarrelling with the maidservant.

SIMO: Of course you did (*ironically*).

CHREMES: Ah, but it was in real earnest, when neither of them knew that I was there.

SIMO: I believe it, and Davus prophesied to me some time ago that they would do that; I don't know how it is that I forgot to tell you today as I meant to do.

Act Five.   Scene II

(*Re-enter* DAVUS *from* GLYCERIUM'S *house.*)

DAVUS (*to someone within*): So now I bid you set your mind at rest.

CHREMES (*to* SIMO): There's Davus for you.

SIMO: Out of which house did he come?

DAVUS (*to someone within*): By my assistance and that of the stranger.

SIMO: What mischief is this?

DAVUS (*to himself*): I never saw man, time, and arrival fall out more handily.

SIMO: The villain! Who is this whom he is praising?

DAVUS (*to himself*): The whole business is in smooth water now.

SIMO: Why don't I speak to him?

DAVUS (*to himself*): It's master; what shall I do?

SIMO: Good day to you, you man of worth.

DAVUS: What, Simo! And our good master Chremes! All's now in readiness in the house.

SIMO: You have seen to that excellently well.

DAVUS: You may send for the bride when you please.

SIMO: Excellent, that indeed is all that is wanting now. Will you also tell me what you have been doing in that house?

DAVUS: What I've been doing?

SIMO: Yes.

DAVUS: I?

SIMO: You.

DAVUS: I only just went in.

SIMO: As if I asked you how long ago you went in!

DAVUS: Together with your son.

SIMO: Why, is Pamphilus in there? O misery! You scoundrel, didn't you tell me that they were at variance?

DAVUS: So they are.

SIMO: Then why is he there?

CHREMES (*with sarcasm*): What do you reckon? He's quarrelling with her.

DAVUS: No, Chremes, I'll tell you of a shameful plot. Just now some old man or other arrived—a man like this, bold and shrewd; when you look at his face you see that he's a man of worth; there is a sour honesty in his look and truth in his words.

SIMO: What's this you're bringing in?

DAVUS: I'm not bringing in anything except what I heard him say.

SIMO: Well, what does he say?

DAVUS: He says that he knows Glycerium to be an Athenian citizen.

SIMO (*calling at his door*): Here, Dromo! Dromo!

DAVUS: What's the matter?

SIMO: Dromo.

DAVUS: But listen—

SIMO: If you say another word— Dromo.

DAVUS: Pray listen to me.

(*Enter* DROMO.)

DROMO: What do you want?

SIMO: Truss up that fellow and carry him into the house as quick as you can.

DROMO: Which fellow?

SIMO: Davus.

DAVUS: What for?

SIMO: Because I choose. Off with him, I say.

DAVUS: What have I done?

SIMO: Off with him.

DAVUS: If you find that I have told a single lie, kill me.

SIMO: I'm not listening to what you say. I'll make you stir yourself presently.

DAVUS: Even if my story is true?

SIMO: Even then. Put him in chains, and, hark ye, fasten him hand and foot. Away with him! If I live, I'll show you this day the danger of deceiving your master, and that fellow the danger of deceiving his father. (DROMO *drags* DAVUS *inside.*)

CHREMES: Oh, don't put yourself into such a passion.

SIMO: Oh, Chremes, this is how my son treats me! Don't you pity me? To think that I should take so much trouble for the sake of such a son! Now then, Pamphilus, Pamphilus, come out of that; have you no shame?

Act Five.   Scene III

(*Enter* PAMPHILUS *from* GLYCERIUM'S *house.*)

PAMPHILUS: Who wants me? Good gracious! It's my father.

SIMO: What do you say, you most—

CHREMES: Hush! Better say what you want, and don't abuse him.

SIMO: As if one could say anything harder of him than he deserves. Tell me now, is Glycerium a citizen of Athens?

PAMPHILUS: So they say.

SIMO: "So they say," indeed. What monstrous impudence! Does he think what he says? Is he ashamed of what he has done? Look, does his face show any trace of a blush? To think that he should be so weak as to want to keep this woman, against the law and the usage of citizens of Athens, and against his own father's wishes, to his own utter shame!

PAMPHILUS: Oh, unhappy me!

SIMO: Ah, have you only just found that out, Pamphilus? It was long ago that that word really applied to you, when you first made up your mind to get what you wanted by fair means or foul. But why do I speak? Why do I torment myself? Why do I fret? Why do I make my old age miserable because of his folly? Is it that I may pay the penalty of his sins? Nay, let him take her; let him live with her and make the best of her.

PAMPHILUS: Father.

SIMO: What do you say "father" for? As if you wanted me for your father! You have provided yourself with a house, a wife, and child against your father's will; you have suborned witnesses to swear that she's a citizen. You have won the day.

PAMPHILUS: Father, mayn't I say a few words?

SIMO: What have you to say to me?

CHREMES: But hear him, Simo.

SIMO: I hear him! What shall I hear, Chremes?

CHREMES: Still, let him speak.

SIMO: Well, I let him speak.

PAMPHILUS: I admit that I love her; if it be a sin, I admit it, nevertheless. Father, I place myself in your hands; lay what burden you please upon me; give your orders. Do you wish me to marry? To put away Glycerium? I will bear it as well as I can. Only, I beseech you, do not suppose that this old man was suborned by me. Let me clear myself of that suspicion, and bring him hither into your presence.

SIMO: Into my presence?

PAMPHILUS: Let me, father.

CHREMES: He only asks what is fair; let him.

PAMPHILUS: Grant me this favour.

SIMO: I give in. (PAMPHILUS *goes into* GLYCERIUM'S *house*) I am willing to do anything, provided I don't find myself cheated by him, Chremes.

CHREMES (*aside*): In the case of a father a little punishment is enough for a great fault.

Act Five.   Scene IV

(*Re-enter* PAMPHILUS *with* CRITO.)

CRITO (*to* PAMPHILUS): You need not entreat me. I would do it for any one of the following reasons: either because of you, or because it is true, or because I am Glycerium's friend.

CHREMES: Is it Crito of Andros that I see? 'Tis he, for certain.

CRITO: How do you do, Chremes.

CHREMES: What brings you to Athens? You seldom come here.

CRITO: Oh, circumstances! But is this Simo?

CHREMES: It is.

CRITO: Simo, are you asking for me?

SIMO: Perhaps you say that Glycerium is a citizen of this city.

CRITO: Do you say that she is not?

SIMO: Oh, are you come prepared?

CRITO: Prepared for what?

SIMO: For what, indeed! Do you suppose that you can do this without being punished for it? Do you suppose that young gentlemen, liberally educated, knowing nothing of business, are to be led into mischief by you? That you are going to lead them by the nose with your fine words and promises?

CRITO: Are you in your right mind?

SIMO: And patch up marriages with whores?

PAMPHILUS (*aside*): O Lord, I fear the stranger will give way before all this abuse.

CHREMES: Simo, if you knew this man properly, you would not think so of him; he is an honest man.

SIMO: He an honest man? That turns up just in the nick of time on the wedding-day, though he never came here before! Am I to believe this man, Chremes?

PAMPHILUS (*aside*): If I did not fear my father, I could give him a very good reason for that.

SIMO (*to* CRITO): You thief!

CRITO: What's that you say?

CHREMES: Never mind him, Crito, that's his way.

CRITO: He had better take care; if he goes on calling me what he pleases, he will hear something that won't please him. Did I take any part in this business? Have I any interest in it? Man, bear your misfortunes coolly. As for whether what you have heard me say is true or false, that can soon be proved. Some time ago, an Athenian was shipwrecked on the coast of Andros, and she with him; she was then a little girl. In his poverty he first betook himself to Chrysis' father.

SIMO: He's beginning his yarn.

CHREMES: Let the man speak.

CRITO: Is he going to interrupt me like that?

CHREMES: Proceed.

CRITO: Now he who took him in was a relative of mine, it was in his house that I learned that he was a citizen of Athens. He died there.

CHREMES: His name?

CRITO: What a hurry you are in for his name.

PAMPHILUS: Phania.

CHREMES (*aside*): Oh, I'm lost![12]

CRITO: Well, now, I think his name was Phania; but I'm quite sure that he said he belonged to the deme of Rhamnus.

CHREMES (*aside*): O Jupiter!

CRITO: Many people in Andros besides me, Chremes, have heard this same story.

CHREMES (*aside*): May it be as I hope. (*Aloud*) Tell me, what about the girl then? Did he call her his own child?

CRITO: No.

CHREMES: Whose child, then?

CRITO: His brother's daughter.

CHREMES: She's mine, for certain.

CRITO: What do you say?

SIMO: Yes, what's that you say?

PAMPHILUS (*aside*): Prick up your ears, Pamphilus.

SIMO: What makes you believe this?

CHREMES: This Phania was my brother.

SIMO: I knew him, and that's true.

CHREMES: Wishing to avoid the war here, he set out to follow me into Asia Minor, and he didn't want to leave her behind him here. I now hear for the first time what became of him.

PAMPHILUS: I am almost beside myself, my mind is so excited with fear, hopes and joy, and with surprise at this unlooked-for blessing.

SIMO (*to* CHREMES): Indeed, I am greatly delighted at her being proved to be your daughter.

PAMPHILUS: I believe you, father.

CHREMES: But there's just one small point left that troubles me.

PAMPHILUS: Drat you and your scruples; you are only looking for knots in a bulrush.

CRITO: What is this point?

CHREMES: The name does not agree with that of my daughter.

CRITO: Indeed, she had another when she was little.

CHREMES: What was it, Crito? Can you remember?

CRITO: I am trying to remember it.

PAMPHILUS: Am I going to let this man's memory stand in the way of my happiness, when I can help myself in this business? Not I. I say, Chremes, Pasibula is the name that you want.

CHREMES: The very name.

CRITO: That's it.

PAMPHILUS: I have heard her say it a thousand times.

SIMO: I believe, Chremes, you understand that we all congratulate you.

CHREMES: So help me heaven, I do believe it.

PAMPHILUS: Father, what remains to be done?

SIMO: Nay, circumstances have long ago reconciled me to it.

PAMPHILUS: Oh, there's a charming father! Does Chremes change his mind about my wife, now that I am already in possession of her?

CHREMES: No, for very good reasons, unless your father says anything different.

PAMPHILUS: Yes, just so.

SIMO: Of course.

CHREMES: Pamphilus, her dowry is ten talents.[13]

PAMPHILUS: I accept it.

CHREMES: I am in a hurry to see my daughter. Come with me, Crito, for I don't suppose that she knows me. (*They enter* GLYCERIUM's *house.*)

SIMO (*to* PAMPHILUS): Why not have her brought across to our house?

PAMPHILUS: Well said; I will entrust that job to Davus.

SIMO: He can't do it.

PAMPHILUS: Why not?

SIMO: Because he has got another bigger job, that has more to do with himself.

PAMPHILUS: What is it?

SIMO: He's in chains.

PAMPHILUS: Father, he is not rightly chained.[14]

SIMO: Isn't he? I ordered him to be.

PAMPHILUS: Pray order him to be set free.

SIMO: Well, it shall be done.

PAMPHILUS: But quickly.

SIMO: I am going indoors. (*He goes into his house.*)

PAMPHILUS: O lucky, happy day!

Act Five. Scene V

(*Enter* CHARINUS.)

CHARINUS (*to himself*): I am on the lookout for what Pamphilus is doing; and there he is.

PAMPHILUS (*to himself*): One might think, perhaps, that I do not think this true; but I like to think that it is true. I think that is the reason why the life of the gods is eternal, because their pleasures are their own; for I have won immortality if no trouble comes to spoil my joy. Now, whom should I like best to meet with, to tell him this story?

CHARINUS (*aside*): What's this joy that he's talking about?

PAMPHILUS: There's Davus: rather him than anyone else; for I know that he will truly be pleased at my good fortune.

Act Five. Scene VI

(*Enter* DAVUS.)

DAVUS: Wherever is Pamphilus?

PAMPHILUS: Davus.

DAVUS: Who's that?

PAMPHILUS: It is I.

DAVUS: O Pamphilus!

PAMPHILUS: You don't know what has befallen me.

DAVUS: No, I don't; but I do know what has befallen me.

PAMPHILUS: So do I.

DAVUS: It's the way of the world, that you should hear of my ill luck before I hear of your good luck.

PAMPHILUS: My Glycerium has found her parents.

DAVUS: That's a good thing.

CHARINUS (*aside*): What's this?

PAMPHILUS: Her father is our greatest friend.

DAVUS: Who is he?

PAMPHILUS: Chremes.

DAVUS: Capital!

PAMPHILUS: And I'm to marry her as soon as may be.

CHARINUS (*aside*): Is he dreaming of what he would like to happen when he is awake?

PAMPHILUS: And then the boy, Davus.

DAVUS: Tell me no more. He is heaven's own favourite.

CHARINUS (*aside*): If this is true I am saved. I will address him.

PAMPHILUS: Who's this? Oh, Charinus, you are well met.

CHARINUS: All's right.

PAMPHILUS: You have heard—

CHARINUS: All. Come, now that you are prosperous, think of me. Chremes is now in your hands. I am sure he will do whatever you wish.

PAMPHILUS: I will remember; but it would be a long time for us to wait till he comes out. You, Charinus, follow me in here to Glycerium; Davus, go home, make haste, and bring a procession to fetch home the bride. Why do you stand still? Why don't you bestir yourself? (PAMPHI-LUS *and* CHARINUS *go into* GLYCERIUM'S *house.*)

DAVUS (*to the audience*): Don't wait till they come out; Pamphilus will plight his troth indoors; and all that remains to be done will be done indoors. Give us your applause.

The Second Ending[15]

(*Enter* CHREMES.)

PAMPHILUS (*to* CHREMES): I was waiting for you. I want to discuss with you a matter that concerns you. I don't want you to say that I've forgotten your other daughter. I think that I've found a husband that will meet with your approval, and hers too.

CHARINUS (*aside*): I'm done for, Davus; my love and my life are now at stake.

CHREMES: This is no new proposal to me, Pamphilus, if I had liked it.

CHARINUS: Davus, I'm ruined!

DAVUS: Just wait a minute.

CHARINUS: I'm dead!

CHREMES (*to* PAMPHILUS): I'll tell you why I didn't wish it. Not that I didn't want the young man for a relative—

CHARINUS (*aside*): Hm-m!

DAVUS: Hush!

CHREMES: But I was anxious that the friendship which Simo and I inherited from our fathers should be handed down to our children unimpaired, and even increased. And now, since I have the means and opportunity of pleasing both of you, I'll consent.

PAMPHILUS: Excellent!

DAVUS (*to* CHARINUS): Go up and thank the man.

CHARINUS (*coming forward*): Greetings to you, Chremes, the best friend of all my friends. Well, it is no less a pleasure to find out how you felt toward me formerly, than it is to gain my present request.

CHREMES: No matter what direction you turn your mind, Charinus, you must judge for yourself of the resulting enthusiasm.

PAMPHILUS: I can see from my own case that this is true.

CHARINUS: Though not related to you I knew the kind of man you were.

CHREMES: The matter stands this way: I betroth my daughter Philumena to you and promise a dowry of six talents.

1. The *didascalia,* or official notice of the production, is lacking for this play, but has been restored from the commentary of Donatus.

2. The Megalensian Games were celebrated in April in honour of Cybele, the Great Goddess.

3. Marcellus and Sulpicius were consuls in 166 B.C.

4. The summaries of the comedies of Terence are ascribed to Gaius Sulpicius Apollinaris, a critic of the second century A.D.

5. The prologues of Terence's plays differ from those of Plautus in that they give no account of the plot of the play, but are devoted chiefly to a defence of the poet's literary position and to a criticism of his rivals and detractors.

6. This dramatist was Luscius Lanuvinus, one of Terence's chief rivals.

7. Sosia does not appear again; he is a *protatic* character, one who is brought in at the opening of the play to make possible the expository dialogue.

8. Kauer and Lindsay assign this speech also to Simo.

9. Davus means that he is no guesser of riddles. It was Oedipus who solved the riddle of the Sphinx.

10. This refers to the *pronuba,* a married woman who attended the bride at the time of the wedding.

11. An Athenian was obliged to marry a free woman if he seduced her.

12. Kauer and Lindsay assign these two speeches to Crito also. The anonymous translator omits the first speech and assigns the second to Pamphilus. The arrangement of Bentley and Fleckeisen has been adopted.

13. This is a large dowry, almost $11,000, with a purchasing power many times greater.

14. There is a play here upon *recte,* which means both "justly" and "securely."

15. The second ending which is supposed to begin after verse 976 was perhaps added later to provide more satisfactorily for the future of Charinus.

II
THE SELF-TORMENTOR

CHARACTERS IN THE PLAY

CHREMES, *an old gentleman of Attica*
MENEDEMUS, *neighbour of* CHREMES
CLITIPHO, *son of* CHREMES, *in love with* BACCHIS
CLINIA, *son of* MENEDEMUS, *in love with* ANTIPHILA
SYRUS, *slave of* CHREMES
DROMO, *slave of* CLINIA
BACCHIS, *a courtesan*
ANTIPHILA, *sweetheart of* CLINIA
SOSTRATA, *wife of* CHREMES
NURSE *of* ANTIPHILA
PHRYGIA, *maid of* BACCHIS

DIDASCALIA

The Self-Tormentor of Terence. Acted at the Megalensian Games during the curule aedileship of Lucius Cornelius Lentulus and Lucius Valerius Flaccus. The chief parts were taken by Lucius Ambivius Turpio and Lucius Atilius Praenestinus. It was set to music by Flaccus, the slave of Claudius. It was acted, at its first representation, with unequal flutes, afterwards with two right-handed flutes. Adapted from the Greek of Menander. The poet's third play, presented during the consulship of Manius Juventius and Tiberius Sempronius.[1]

SUMMARY

A severe father compels his son Clinia, in love with Antiphila, to go abroad to the wars. Afterwards the father repents of what he has done and torments himself with regret. The son on his return stays at the house of Clitipho without his father's knowledge. Clitipho is in love with Bacchis, a courtesan. When Clinia sends for his beloved Antiphila, Bacchis comes and pretends to be his sweetheart, and Antiphila wears the garb of her servant. The purpose of this was to conceal Clitipho's love affair from his father. By the tricks of Syrus Clitipho gets ten minae from the old man for the courtesan. Antiphila is discovered to be the sister of Clitipho. Clinia marries her and Clitipho marries another girl.

INTRODUCTION

The Self-Tormentor (the *Heauton Timorumenos*), based upon Menander's comedy of the same title, marks a definite advance in Terence's skill as a dramatist. Again the plot is double, and the love affairs of the two young men, Clinia and Clitipho, are much more closely interwoven than those of Pamphilus and Charinus in *The Woman of Andros*. The action is based upon both trickery and recognition, as in many of Plautus' comedies, but Terence introduces a new feature by having the recognition in the middle of the play and using it to complicate the situation rather than to bring about the usual solution. Few plays in Roman comedy have a more complicated deception, and it seems doubtful if the average Roman spectator could have followed it with ease. Even the trickery in Plautus' *Epidicus,* which has often been criticised for its complexity, seems relatively simple by comparison.

Menedemus, the father of Clinia, regrets that he has been so severe to his son, who had been keeping a mistress, and resolves to punish himself by hard work during his son's absence. Chremes, the father of Clitipho, disapproves of Menedemus' present way of life; returning home, he finds that Clinia has come back and is visiting his son. Clinia's sweetheart, Antiphila, arrives, accompanied by Bacchis, the courtesan whom Clitipho loves. To keep Clitipho's love affair from being known, Bacchis poses as Clinia's sweetheart, thereby creating a situation which is extremely difficult for Clitipho, who almost gives himself away. Menedemus wants his son to have money, but not wishing to appear too generous, is willing to be cheated out of the money. Chremes, believing Bacchis is the mistress of his son's friend, urges Syrus, his slave, to cheat Menedemus, little realising that he himself is to be the object of the deception. Antiphila, meanwhile, proves to be Chremes' own daughter, and the recognition almost brings the pretended love affair of Clinia and Bacchis to an end. But Clinia consents to keep up the pretence and moves Bacchis and her belongings to the home of Menedemus, his father.

Syrus' deception, on which he prides himself, is very unlike those of the intriguing slaves in Plautus; "I shall deceive them both," he says, "by telling them the truth." Menedemus is told that Bacchis is really

Clitipho's mistress and that Clinia wants to marry Antiphila; Chremes thinks that this is the expected trick by which Clinia will get money from his father. In the meantime, he himself pays to Syrus the money which Antiphila is supposed to owe Bacchis, but which Syrus is actually getting for Clitipho to give to Bacchis. The weakness of the deception is that it leads nowhere, and the money transaction depends entirely on the recognition; without the discovery of Antiphila's parentage, Chremes would not have paid her supposed debt. The cleverness with which Syrus confuses Chremes obscures this weakness. When Clinia fails to ask Menedemus for money and persists in his desire to marry Antiphila, the truth comes out, and Chremes' rage knows no bounds. He, the father who favoured frank confidences between father and son, has been deceived by his own son, whose escapades are far more serious than those of Menedemus' son.

The contrast between the two fathers is not stressed as in *The Brothers*, but there is a striking similarity to the later play, particularly in the way both sons disregard their fathers' wishes. The delineation of the characters in general is far inferior to that of Terence's masterpiece, but the characters are clearly drawn and have their effect upon the plot structure. Gilbert Norwood states, "(Chremes) explains to Menedemus that he has not revealed to Clinia the change in his father's attitude, lest this knowledge should corrupt the youth; this leads to the singular scheme whereby Menedemus arranges to be swindled. Theories of education have often led to wild results, but rarely to so quaint an outcome as this."

THE SELF-TORMENTOR

(SCENE:—*A country road in Attica in front of the houses and lands of*
MENEDEMUS *and* CHREMES.)

Prologue

THAT you may not wonder why the playwright has assigned to an old
man like me[2] the post of Prologue, which is generally given to a young
man, I will first explain this to you, and then tell you why I have
come here.

I am going today to act *The Self-Tormentor,* a new play, taken from
a new Greek one. The original had only a single plot; this is a play of
two plots. I have now explained that it is a new play, and what it is;
now, unless I thought that almost all of you knew, I would tell you
who wrote it, and what Greek play it was taken from. Now I will tell
you briefly why I undertook this part. The playwright wanted me to be
an advocate, not to speak a prologue. He leaves it to you to pronounce
your verdict, and has chosen me to plead before you; though in this
case the pleader's eloquence will be measured by the power of the
writer who composed the address which I am about to deliver. As for
the charge put about by his enemies, that he has combined many Greek
plays to make a few Latin ones out of them, he does not deny having
done so, and declares that he is not ashamed of having done so, and
means to do it again. He has before him the example of good writers,[3]
and thinks that he may be allowed to do what they did. As for the
reproach so often cast in his teeth by that spiteful old poet,[4] that he
has suddenly betaken himself to the profession of a poet, relying for
success, not upon his own ability, but on the genius of his friends,[5] your
opinion and judgment will settle that matter; wherefore, I entreat all
of you not to let wrong prevail against right. Be impartial; give writers
a chance of making their way when they give you the opportunity of
seeing new plays, without faults. When I say this, I don't wish the
playwright, who lately made the people make way for a slave running
along the street, to suppose that I am speaking for him; why be enslaved to a madman? The playwright will say something more about
that writer's mistakes when he produces new plays, unless he leaves off
his evil speaking. Listen now without prejudice, and give me a chance

to play a quiet comedy in silence, that I may not always have to play
the parts of a bustling slave, an angry old gentleman, a hungry parasite,
an impudent flatterer, or a greedy slave-dealer, at the top of my voice,
to my great distress. For my sake, make up your minds that the cause
which I plead is a just one, that some part of my labour may be lightened. For the people who write new plays nowadays show no mercy
to an old actor. If their play is a heavy job, they come to me to act
it, but if it goes smoothly, they take it to some other company. Now,
in this play the style is pure; so try what my talents are worth in both
characters. [If I never greedily put too high a price upon my art, but
always reckoned it the greatest gain, to do all in my power to entertain
you,]⁶ make me an example, so that our young men may try to please
you rather than themselves.

Act One.   Scene I

(MENEDEMUS *is working on his land. Enter* CHREMES *from his house.*)

CHREMES: Although our acquaintance is but of recent date, having only
begun when you bought this farm next to mine, and although we have
had scarcely any other business with one another, nevertheless, either
your goodness, or our being neighbours, which I think is the next thing
to being friends, makes me deal with you boldly and familiarly, and
warn you that you seem to me to be working too much for a man of
your age, and harder than your circumstances require you to do. Good
gracious! What do you mean? What do you want? You are sixty years
old, or more, I should think; no one in these parts has a better or more
valuable estate; you have many slaves; and yet you strive to do all
their work yourself, just as if you hadn't a single one. I never come out
of my house so early or go home so late that I don't see you at work
on your farm, digging or ploughing or carrying something; in a word,
you never take any rest or any care of yourself. Now I am pretty sure
that you can't be doing this for pleasure; but perhaps you will say, "I
am not satisfied with the amount of work done here." Why, you would
do more good if the time which you waste in labouring with your own
hands was spent in keeping your slaves hard at work.

MENEDEMUS: Chremes, does your own business afford you so much
leisure that you can attend to other people's, with which you have
nothing to do?

CHREMES: I am a human being; I am interested in everything human.[7] You may take it that I am giving you this advice, or asking you the question: if it is right to do so, then I will do so myself; but if it is wrong, then let me dissuade you from it.

MENEDEMUS: I must do so; you may do what you please.

CHREMES: Must any man torment himself?

MENEDEMUS: I must.

CHREMES: If it were merely a question of work, I would say no more, but pray what is this trouble of yours? What have you done to deserve such punishment?

MENEDEMUS: Alas!

CHREMES: Don't weep. Just let me know what the trouble is. Put aside reserve; don't be afraid to tell it; trust me, I say. I will help you, either with consolation, or advice, or money.

MENEDEMUS: Do you want to know this?

CHREMES: I do, for the reason I gave you.

MENEDEMUS: Then I'll tell you.

CHREMES: But in the meantime, lay down those rakes; don't work.

MENEDEMUS: Oh, I must.

CHREMES: What is the matter with you?

MENEDEMUS: Let me give myself no moment free from labour.

CHREMES: I will not, I tell you. (*Takes the rakes from him.*)

MENEDEMUS: Oh, you're not doing right.

CHREMES (*feeling the weight of the rakes*): Gracious! Why such heavy ones, pray?

MENEDEMUS: I deserve them to be heavy.

CHREMES: Now tell me your story.

MENEDEMUS: I have an only son, a youth. Ah! Why did I say "I have"? Nay, I had a son, Chremes. Whether I have one now or not, I don't know.

CHREMES: How is that?

MENEDEMUS: I'll tell you. There is here in Athens a poor old stranger woman from Corinth. My son fell desperately in love with her daughter, so as to treat her almost as his wife. All this was done without my knowledge. When I learned about this, I did not go to work in a kindly fashion, or treat the lovesick youth as I should have done, but I behaved brutally, like a regular father of the old school. I used to reproach him every day, saying, "Pray do you suppose that while I, your father, am still alive, you will be allowed to go on any longer like this, keeping a mistress almost upon the same footing as a wife? You are mistaken if you think so, Clinia, and you don't know your father. I am willing that you should be called my son, as long as you behave as becomes you; but if you do not, I shall find out the proper course to be taken with you. All this comes of your not having enough to do. When I was your age I didn't give myself up to amours, but through poverty I went over to Asia, and there gained both money and glory in the wars." At last it came to this: the youth heard the same thing said so often and so solemnly, that he gave way; he thought that with my age and wisdom I understood his true interests better than he did himself, and, O Chremes! He has gone to Asia to serve the King of Persia.

CHREMES: What's this you say?

MENEDEMUS: He set out, without telling me, and has been gone three months.

CHREMES: Both of you are to be blamed; but still this adventure of his shows him to be of a modest, and yet not unmanly character.

MENEDEMUS: When I learned what he had done from those who shared his secret, I went sadly home, terribly upset, and almost beside myself with grief. I sat down; slaves came running and took off my shoes. I saw others bustling about, laying the cloth and cooking my dinner, each one doing all that he could to assuage my misery. When I saw this, I began to think thus in my own mind: "See here, shall all these people be kept on the alert to minister to my single needs? Shall so many slave-women spin clothes for me? Shall I incur so much expense at home, while as for my only son, who ought to have enjoyed all these things as much as I, or even more, since his age was better fitted to enjoy them,—poor boy, I have driven him from his home by my injustice? I should deserve the worst that could befall me if I did that. As long as he lives a life of hardship, driven into exile by my wrongdoing, so long will I do penance for him, by toiling, striving, sparing, and working for him." No sooner said than done. I left nothing in the house, neither pot nor rag; I made a clean sweep of everything. I sold all my slaves, both men and women, except such as could easily pay for their keep by working in the fields. I wrote "For sale" on my house, scraped together some fifteen talents, bought this farm, and here I work. I have got it into my head, Chremes, that I am not wronging my son so much while I am miserable myself; and, indeed, it is not right that I should have any pleasure here until he comes back hither, safe and sound, to share it with me.

CHREMES: I think that you are a kindly father, and that your son would have obeyed you if he had been properly managed; but you didn't know him well enough, nor did he know you. When people don't live openly with one another, this always happens. You never showed him how dearly you loved him, and he didn't dare to trust his father as he should have done. Had you both acted thus, this would never have happened.

MENEDEMUS: That's true, I admit; I have done very wrong.

CHREMES: But, Menedemus, I have good hope for the future, and that ere long he will be safe at home again.

MENEDEMUS: Please heaven he may!

CHREMES: It will please heaven. Now, if it would be agreeable to you, today is the festival of Dionysus, I wish you would spend it at my house.

MENEDEMUS: I cannot.

CHREMES: Why not? I entreat you, give yourself just a little rest; your absent son would wish you to do so too.

MENEDEMUS: It isn't right that I, who have driven him from his home to hardship, should now shun it myself.

CHREMES: Is that your determination?

MENEDEMUS: It is.

CHREMES: Then farewell.

MENEDEMUS: And fare you well also. (*He goes into his house.*)

CHREMES (*to himself*): He has moved me to tears, and I am grieved for him; but seeing what time of day it is, it is time for me to remind my neighbour Phania here to come to dine with me; I will go and see whether he is at home. (CHREMES *departs, but returns at once*) Oh, he wanted no reminder; they tell me that he has long been ready at my house; it is I that am keeping my guests waiting, so I'll go into the house. But why this creaking of my door? Who is coming out? I'll withdraw. (*Retires.*)

Act One.   Scene II

(Enter CLITIPHO *from his father's house.)*

CLITIPHO (*speaking to* CLINIA *within*): There's nothing to be afraid of yet, Clinia; they are not at all behind their time, and I'm sure that she will be here to meet you as soon as the messenger, so put aside that unfounded anxiety that is worrying you.

CHREMES (*aside*): With whom is my son talking?

CLITIPHO (*aside*): Here is my father, whom I wanted to meet; I will go to him. (*Aloud*) Father, well met!

CHREMES: What is the matter?

CLITIPHO: Do you know this Menedemus our neighbour?

CHREMES: Yes, I know him well.

CLITIPHO: Do you know that he has a son?

CHREMES: I have heard that he has a son; he is in Asia.

CLITIPHO: No, father, he is at our house.

CHREMES: What's that you say?

CLITIPHO: I found him just arrived and disembarking, and straightway brought him off with me to dine with us, for we have always been great friends from childhood.

CHREMES: I'm very pleased to hear it. How I wish I had been more pressing when I invited Menedemus to dine with us, that I might be the first to give him this unexpected pleasure in my house! And there is still time to do so.

CLITIPHO: Pray don't do it, father; better not.

CHREMES: Why?

CLITIPHO: Because Clinia has not yet decided what he is going to do with himself. He has only just returned; he fears his father's anger, and fears his mistress may have changed her mind. He is passionately in love with her; indeed, it was about her that all this trouble and his leaving the country came about.

CHREMES: I know that.

CLITIPHO: Now he has sent a slave boy into Athens to her, and I have sent our slave Syrus with him.

CHREMES: What does Clinia say?

CLITIPHO: What does he say? He says that he is unhappy.

CHREMES: Unhappy! The last person you ought to think so. What more could he have of what men call this world's goods? He has parents, a free country, friends, good family, relatives, riches. Yet all these vary according to their owner's character; they are good things to him who knows how to use them, but they are evils to him who uses them ill.

CLITIPHO: Nay; the old man was always scolding him, and now I am afraid that in his anger he may do something outrageous to him, father.

CHREMES: He? (*Aside*) But I will restrain myself, for it is as well that the son should be alarmed.

CLITIPHO: What are you saying to yourself?

CHREMES: I'll tell you. Whatever treatment he may have received, still it was his duty to stay at home. Perhaps his father was somewhat unjust in crossing his wishes; well, he should have borne with him; whom should he bear with if not with his own father? Which was right? That the father should live as his son chose, or that the son should live as his father chose? And as for the harshness which he hints at, it isn't really harshness, for the reproaches of parents, if they are reasonable at all, are nearly all of the same kind; they don't like their sons to visit courtesans often, or to give wine-parties often, and they are sparing in granting allowances; yet all this makes their sons better men; for the fact is, Clitipho, that when once the mind has become the slave of evil habits, it must follow evil counsels. It is wise for you to learn from the misfortunes of others what is useful for you to know.

CLITIPHO: So I believe.

CHREMES: I'll go into the house here and see what there is for dinner. As it is so late, pray don't you stray far away. (CHREMES *goes into his house.*)

Act Two.   Scene I

CLITIPHO (*to himself*): How unjustly all fathers judge young men; they think that when we cease to be boys we ought straightway to turn into old men, and have nothing to do with the pleasures youth brings with it. They govern us according to what their own desires are now, not according to what they used to be. If ever I have a son, he will indeed find me an easygoing father, for I shall find means to learn what he does wrong and to forgive him for doing so. I shall not be like my father, who shows me what he thinks I ought to do by his talk about someone else. Dear me! When he has had a drop or two more than usual, what escapades of his own he tells me about. Now he says, "Gain experience which will be valuable to yourself at the expense of others." How clever of him! He little knows how deaf are the ears to which he is talking. I pay much more attention to my mistress's words. She says "Give me this," and "Bring me that," and I can make no answer; I am the most miserable of men. Now this Clinia, though he too has his hands full of trouble, nevertheless has a mistress who has been well and modestly brought up, and who knows nothing of the trade of a courtesan. Mine is imperious, forward, grand in her ideas, extravagant, notorious. As for what I am to give her, "All right," I say, for I am ashamed to tell her that I have nothing. I have only lately discovered this, and my father hasn't yet found it out.

Act Two.   Scene II

(*Enter* CLINIA *from* CHREMES' *house.*)

CLINIA (*to himself*): If I were fortunate in my love affairs, I am sure they would have been here long ago, but I fear that while I have been away she may have gone to the bad. Many things combine to make me think so, her opportunities, the place where she lives, her age, and the mother under whose rule she is, a wicked woman who cares for nothing but money.

CLITIPHO: Clinia.

CLINIA: Ah, poor me!

CLITIPHO: Take care, too, that no one coming out of your father's house may see you.

CLINIA: I will take care, but I have a presentiment of evil in my mind.

CLITIPHO: And are you going to decide that it is so without waiting to learn the truth?

CLINIA: They would have been here by now if there hadn't been something wrong.

CLITIPHO: They will be here presently.

CLINIA: And when will that "presently" be?

CLITIPHO: You don't remember that it is a goodish way from here, and besides, you know women's ways; one has to wait a twelvemonth while they are making ready and getting under way.

CLINIA: Oh, I am afraid.

CLITIPHO: Fear no more, I see Dromo there, together with Syrus; there you have them.

Act Two.   Scene III

(Enter SYRUS *and* DROMO *conversing.)*

SYRUS: You really mean it?

DROMO: That's so.

SYRUS: But while we are gossiping we have left the ladies behind.

CLITIPHO (*to* CLINIA): There, do you hear, Clinia? Your ladylove is here.

CLINIA: Yes, now at last I do hear and see, and I'm well again, Clitipho.

DROMO: No wonder they're behind, with such a caravan as theirs; they are bringing a troop of maidservants with them.

CLINIA (*to* CLITIPHO): Good gracious, how should she get maidservants?

CLITIPHO: Do you ask me?

SYRUS: They ought not to have been left behind; look what they have to carry.

CLINIA: Oh, dear!

SYRUS: Jewelry and clothes; and it is getting dusk, too, and they don't know the way. We have behaved like fools. Dromo, you run back to meet them. Off with you; why do you stand still?

CLINIA: Oh, unhappy me, how disappointed I am!

CLITIPHO: What's the matter? What's worrying you?

CLINIA: Do you ask me what is the matter? See here. How do you think that she can have got maidservants, jewels, and clothes, when I left her here with one little slave-girl?

CLITIPHO: Ah, now at last I understand.

SYRUS: Good heavens, what a mob! Our house will scarce take them in, I am sure. How much they will eat and drink! Who will be so wretched as our old gentleman? But there, I see the people that I wanted. (*Seeing* CLITIPHO *and* CLINIA.)

CLINIA: O Jupiter! Where may loyalty be found? While I, like a fool, was wandering in exile for your sake, Antiphila, you have been enriching yourself, and have abandoned me in this my misery. It was on your account that I have got into this deep disgrace and have been disobedient to my father. Now I am ashamed to meet him, and am sorry for him. He was always telling me how such women behave, and warned me in vain, for he never could tear me away from her. But now I'll break with her; I wouldn't do this when I might have got credit for doing it. Oh, no man is more wretched than I!

SYRUS: The young gentleman seems to have misunderstood our talk. Clinia, you misjudge your love, for her way of life is the same as ever, and her regard for you is the same, as far as we could guess from what we saw.

CLINIA: What was that, pray? For nothing in the world would please me more than to find that my suspicions are unfounded.

SYRUS: First of all, that you may know the whole story, the old woman who used to be called her mother was not her mother, and she is dead. I chanced to hear her telling this to the other lady on the way.

CLITIPHO: Who on earth is the other lady?

SYRUS: Be patient. Let me tell first what I have begun to tell, Clitipho, and I will come to that afterwards.

CLITIPHO: Well, make haste.

SYRUS: First of all, when we came to the house, Dromo knocked at the door. An old woman appeared: as soon as she opened the door Dromo straightway rushed in, and I followed. The old woman bolted the door, and went back to her spinning. Here, if anywhere, Clinia, we could tell what sort of life Antiphila had been living in your absence, when we suddenly broke in upon her, for this gave us an opportunity of guessing the fashion of her daily life, a thing which above all else shows a person's character. We found her diligently weaving at her loom. She was dressed shabbily, in a sad-coloured dress (mourning, I fancy, for the old woman who is dead). She wore no jewelry; and she was dressed as women are who dress only to please themselves, without any women's toilet trumpery. Her hair hung loosely down, and was carelessly flung back round her head—enough.

CLINIA: My dear Syrus, I beg you, don't make me happy without cause.

SYRUS: The old woman was spinning the thread for the loom. Besides them there was one slave-girl, who was helping them to weave; she was in rags, shabby and dirty.

CLITIPHO: If this be the truth, Clinia, as I believe it to be, who is luckier than you? You know this girl that he tells us was ill-clad and in wretched plight; well, it is a great proof of the mistress's innocence when those who run her errands are so ill-cared for; for it is the regular practice of those who are laying siege to the mistress to begin by bribing the maids.

CLINIA: Go on, I beg you, and mind you don't try to please me by a false tale. What did she say when you mentioned me?

SYRUS: When we said that you had come back again and wanted her to come to you, the lady left her loom, and straightway her face was flooded with tears, which it was easy to see were shed through love of you.

CLINIA: I declare to heaven I am beside myself with delight. I was so afraid.

CLITIPHO: Well, I knew that your fears were vain, Clinia. Come, now's my turn, Syrus; tell me, who is that "other lady"?

SYRUS: We are bringing your mistress, Bacchis.

CLITIPHO: Eh? What? Bacchis! Tell me, you villain, to what place are you bringing her?

SYRUS: To what place am I bringing her? Why, to our house, of course.

CLITIPHO: To my father?

SYRUS: To his very self.

CLITIPHO: Oh, the shameless impudence of the man!

SYRUS: Look here, master! You can't carry out a great and glorious adventure without risk.

CLITIPHO: But consider, you scoundrel, you are trying to win credit for yourself at the risk of my life, for if you make the very slightest mistake, I'm lost. (*To* CLINIA) What would you do with him?

SYRUS: But—

CLITIPHO: But what?

SYRUS: Let me speak.

CLINIA: Let him.

CLITIPHO: Well, I give him leave.

SYRUS: You see this here business is like as if—

CLITIPHO: Drat you, what rigmarole is this that you are telling me?

CLINIA: Syrus, Clitipho is right; never mind all that, come to the point.

SYRUS: Indeed, I can't restrain myself; you are atrociously rude, Clitipho, and unbearable.

CLINIA: Damn it! Clitipho, we must hear what he has to say, so hold your tongue.

SYRUS: You want your mistress, you want to possess her; you want to get money to give her; you want to enjoy all this without any risk to yourself. That's very clever of you, if it be cleverness to want what you cannot have. You must take the pleasure with the risk, or do without them both. Now just make up your mind which of these alternatives you choose. However, I am sure that the plan that I have formed is a sound and safe one. You may enjoy your mistress' society in your father's house without fear; and then, as to the money that you have promised her, that you have almost deafened me by worrying me to find for you, I'll get that by the same means. What more do you want?

CLITIPHO: Nothing more, provided that your plan succeeds.

SYRUS: Succeeds! You will find that when you try it.

CLITIPHO: Come, come, let me know this plan of yours; what is it?

SYRUS: We will pretend that your mistress is Clinia's mistress.

CLITIPHO: A pretty plan; and pray what is he to do with his own? Is she also to be called his mistress, as if one was not disgrace enough?

SYRUS: No; she shall be taken to your mother.

CLITIPHO: Why there?

SYRUS: It would take a long time, Clitipho, if I were to tell you why I do this; but I have a good reason for it.

CLITIPHO: Nonsense! I don't see any sufficiently solid reason to make it worth my while to run this risk.

SYRUS: Stay; if you are afraid of this plan, I have another which both of you will admit is free from danger.

CLITIPHO: Oh, pray invent some plan of that sort!

SYRUS: Certainly. I'll go to meet Bacchis, and bid her go home again.

CLITIPHO: Eh? What's that you say?

SYRUS: I will set you free from all fear, so that you may sleep at your ease on whichever side you choose.

CLITIPHO (*to* CLINIA): What am I to do now?

CLINIA: What are you to do? Whatever best suits—

CLITIPHO: Syrus, do just speak the truth.

SYRUS: Come, say yes; you will regret it today, if you don't.

CLINIA: You've got your chance; enjoy it while you can, for you can't tell—

CLITIPHO: But I say, Syrus.

SYRUS: Say what you will, I shall go and do it all the same.

CLINIA: Whether you will ever be able to enjoy her again.

CLITIPHO: Heavens! that's true. (*To* SYRUS, *who is going*) Syrus! Syrus, I say! Here! Here, Syrus!

SYRUS (*aside*): The man has got excited. (*To* CLITIPHO) What do you want?

CLITIPHO: Come back! Come back!

SYRUS: Here I am; what do you want, sir? Presently you will say that you don't approve of this plan either.

CLITIPHO: Nay, Syrus, I place both myself, my amour, and my reputation in your hands. You are the judge; take care that you don't deserve to be judged yourself.

SYRUS: It's absurd for you to warn me of that, Clitipho, as though I had a lesser stake in the business than you. If anything goes wrong with our plot, you will get a lecture, but I shall get a licking; so I can nowise afford to be careless about it. But you beg Clinia there to pretend that she is his mistress.

CLINIA: Of course I shall pretend, for matters have come to such a pass that I have no choice.

CLITIPHO: You're an excellent fellow, Clinia.

CLINIA: But take care that she doesn't make any mistake.

SYRUS: She has been thoroughly schooled.

CLITIPHO: But I'm surprised at your having been able to prevail on her so easily, seeing what she is, and what rich men she is wont to disdain.

SYRUS: I came to her in the nick of time, which is the most important point of all; I found a military man abjectly begging for a night with her; she was handling him so cleverly as to kindle his desire all the more by her refusals, and at the same time to ingratiate herself as much as possible with you. But now look here, mind you don't unwittingly fall into some blunder. You know how sharp-sighted your father is in these things, and I know how little you are able to control yourself. Now drop your innuendoes, your sidelong glances, your hems and haws, and coughs and grins.

CLITIPHO: You shall approve my conduct.

SYRUS: Pray mind that I do.

CLITIPHO: You yourself will be surprised at me.

SYRUS: Why, how quickly the ladies have followed us!

CLITIPHO: Where are they? Why do you hold me back? (*As* SYRUS *catches him by the arm.*)

SYRUS: She is not yours for the present.

CLITIPHO: I know, not in my father's house, but now, here, in the meantime.

SYRUS: None the more here.

CLITIPHO: Just allow me.

SYRUS: I won't, I say.

CLITIPHO: Pray, just for a moment.

SYRUS: I forbid it.

CLITIPHO: Just to ask her how she is.

SYRUS: Go away, if you are a sensible man.

CLITIPHO: I am going. How about Clinia?

SYRUS: He shall stay.

CLITIPHO: Happy man!

SYRUS: Be off. (CLITIPHO *goes into his father's house.*)

Act Two.   Scene IV

(*Enter* BACCHIS *and* ANTIPHILA, *followed by servants with luggage; they do not at first see* CLINIA.)

BACCHIS: Indeed, my dear Antiphila, I commend you and think you a lucky woman for having kept your morals as good as your looks. So help me heaven, I don't wonder a bit at all the men running after you; for your talk has shown me your true character, and when I think of your way of life, and the life of all women of your sort, who keep themselves to themselves, I see that it is not surprising that you should be like that, and that we should not, for it is your interest to be good; but the men that we have to deal with won't let us be so. Our lovers pay their court to us because they are enamoured of our beauty; when we lose it, they transfer their affections elsewhere. Unless we have looked after our interests in the meantime, we are left forlorn. But you modest women, when once you have decided to pass your whole life with a man whose character is as like your own as possible, find your husbands devoted to you, and your mutual love attaches you so closely to one another, that no disaster can sunder you.

ANTIPHILA: I don't know about other women, but I know that I have always made a point of thinking his interests to be my interests.

CLINIA (*aside*): And therefore, dear Antiphila, it is you alone that have brought me back to my country, for while I was absent from you, all the troubles which I underwent were easy to bear, except my having to do without you.

SYRUS (*to* CLINIA): I believe you.

CLINIA (*to* SYRUS): Syrus, I can hardly bear it. That I, unhappy man that I am, should not be allowed to indulge my love for so noble a girl as this!

SYRUS: Why, from what I have seen of your father's temper, he will give you trouble for a long time yet.

BACCHIS (*seeing* CLINIA): Who, pray, is this young man who is looking at us?

ANTIPHILA: Oh! Hold me, I beg you.

BACCHIS: Why, what is the matter with you?

ANTIPHILA: Oh, unhappy me! Oh, I am undone!

BACCHIS: What has made you lose your wits?

CLINIA (*advancing*): Antiphila![8]

ANTIPHILA: Do I see Clinia or do I not?

BACCHIS: Who is it that you see?

CLINIA: Welcome, my love!

ANTIPHILA: Oh, my darling Clinia!

CLINIA: How fares it with you?

ANTIPHILA: I am rejoiced at your return.

CLINIA: Do I hold you in my arms, my Antiphila, for whom I have longed above all else?

SYRUS: Go into the house, for the old gentleman has long been expecting you. (*All go into* CHREMES' *house. A night is supposed to elapse before the next Act.*)

Act Three. Scene I

(Enter CHREMES from his house.)

CHREMES *(to himself)*: It is just getting light; why don't I knock at
my neighbour's door, that I may be the first to tell him of his son's
return? I know the youth himself doesn't wish me to do this, but when
I see this poor man suffering such agonies at his absence, am I to hide
such an unexpected joy from him, especially when telling the news can
do the son no harm? I will not hide it. As far as I can, I'll help the old
man; for it is right for us old men to help one another, just as I see my
son helping the friend of his own age, and forwarding his interests.

(Enter MENEDEMUS from his house.)

MENEDEMUS *(to himself)*: Either I have been specially formed by nature
for misery, or else there is no truth in the common saying, that time
takes away sorrow; for my sorrow for my son increases day by day,
and the longer he is absent the more I wish and long for him.

CHREMES *(aside)*: Why, there I see him out of doors. I will go to him
and speak to him. *(Aloud)* Good morning, Menedemus; I bring you
news which I particularly wish you to hear.

MENEDEMUS: You haven't heard anything about my son, Chremes?

CHREMES: He is alive and well.

MENEDEMUS: But where is he, pray?

CHREMES: At my house.

MENEDEMUS: What! My son?

CHREMES: That's the truth.

MENEDEMUS: He has come?

CHREMES: Yes, he has.

MENEDEMUS: My Clinia has come?

CHREMES: I told you so before.

MENEDEMUS: Let us go; take me to him, I entreat you.

CHREMES: He doesn't wish you to know just yet that he has come back,
and he shrinks from coming into your presence. This fear of his is due

to his offence, and he is afraid that your former harshness may have grown even greater than before.

MENEDEMUS: Didn't you tell him of my state of mind?

CHREMES: No.

MENEDEMUS: Why not, Chremes?

CHREMES: Because you would do the very worst thing possible both for him and for yourself by showing yourself to be so mild and so easily persuaded.

MENEDEMUS: I can't do this. I have long, too long, played the part of the stern father.

CHREMES: Ah, Menedemus, you go too far both in the one direction and in the other, both in excessive extravagance and in stinginess; you will come to the same harm by this course as by that. Formerly, at the outset, you scared your son into flying the country rather than let him visit this girl, who was then contented with a little and easily satisfied. Afterwards, she was driven against her will to gain her living as a courtesan. Now, when she cannot be kept without very great expense, you are ready to give anything. Just to let you know what a thorough-paced instrument of ruin she is, first of all she has already brought with her more than ten maidservants, loaded with fine clothes and jewelry. If a Persian satrap were her lover, he never could bear her expenses, let alone you.

MENEDEMUS: Is she in your house?

CHREMES: I should just think she was. I have felt her presence, for I have given one dinner to her and her crew. It would be all over with me if I had to give another. Why, not to mention anything else, what a lot of wine she wasted just by tasting, saying "This is only so-so," and "This is too sharp-tasted, governor; be so good as to find something softer to the palate." I broke the seal of every jar, every cask in the house. She kept all my household on the run; and that was for one night only. What do you suppose will become of you, when they are eating you out of house and home every day? May the gods be gracious to me, Menedemus, but I am sorry for your estate.

MENEDEMUS: Let him do what he pleases; let him take my fortune and squander it or lose it; I have made up my mind to put up with everything, so long as I can have him with me.

CHREMES: If you have determined to act thus, I think it a matter of very great importance that he should not know that you give it him knowingly.

MENEDEMUS: What am I to do?

CHREMES: Anything rather than what you think of doing. Give him money through some third person; let yourself be cheated by plots by your slave; although, by the way, I have a suspicion that this is what they are at, they're hatching something in secret. Syrus keeps whispering to that slave of yours, and then they lay their plans before the young gentlemen. Now, it's better for you to lose a talent in this way than a mina in that other way. This is not a question of money, but of how we can give the young man the same with the least risk; for if he once learns what your state of mind is, that you would lose your life and your entire fortune rather than be deprived of your son, why, good heavens! what a wide door you will have thrown open to profligacy; and, besides, how miserable your own life will be, for licence spoils all men's characters! They long for whatever fancy comes into their heads, and never think whether it be right or wrong. You will not be able to let him throw away your fortune and his own life; suppose you refuse him supplies, then he will straightway use the argument which he will know to be all-powerful with you—he will threaten to go away at once and leave you.

MENEDEMUS: You seem to speak truly and according to the facts of the case.

CHREMES: Confound it! I haven't closed my eyes all night for thinking how to bring your son back to you.

MENEDEMUS: Give me your hand. I beg, Chremes, that you will go on doing as you have begun.

CHREMES: I am prepared so to do.

MENEDEMUS: Now, do you know what I want you to do?

CHREMES: Tell me.

MENEDEMUS: That plot which you have noticed that they are hatching against me, make them bring it to a head soon. I long to give him what he wants; I long to see him.

CHREMES: I will see to it; but a little matter of business stands in my way. Our neighbours Simus and Crito are at variance about the boundary of their estates, and have chosen me to arbitrate between them. I'll go and tell them that I can't attend to them today as I said I would, and then I'll come back directly.

MENEDEMUS: Pray do so. (*To himself, as* CHREMES *departs*) Great heaven! How strangely all men are formed by nature, that they can take so much clearer views and be so much better judges of other men's affairs than of their own! Perhaps this is owing to our judgment in our own affairs being obscured by excess of joy or grief. See how much wiser this man is for me than I am for myself!

(*Re-enter* CHREMES.)

CHREMES: I have excused myself, so that I can put myself entirely at your disposal. I must get hold of Syrus and give him some hints. Here is somebody coming out of my house; go away home, that they won't know that you and I are of one mind. (MENEDEMUS *goes into his house.*)

Act Three. Scene II

(*Enter* SYRUS *from* CHREMES' *house.*)

SYRUS (*to himself*): Bustle about all over the place; the money must be found. Some dodge must be devised to cheat the old gentleman out of it.

CHREMES (*aside*): There; didn't I know that they were concocting a plot? I suppose it is because that slave of Clinia's is rather a slow-poke, that this task has been handed over to our man.

SYRUS: Who is speaking here? Good Lord! I wonder whether he heard me.

CHREMES: Syrus.

SYRUS: Hem!

CHREMES: What are you doing there?

SYRUS: Oh, I'm doing well, but I wonder at you, Chremes, being out so early, after drinking so much wine last night.

CHREMES: None too much.

SYRUS: None too much! Why, your old age seems lusty as an eagle's, as the saying is.

CHREMES: Aha!

SYRUS: A pleasant and amusing woman, this courtesan.

CHREMES: Yes.

SYRUS: Ah, you think so, too; and, my master, very good looking, too.

CHREMES: Fairly good.

SYRUS: Not so handsome as she has been, but very well, even at this day. I'm not at all surprised at Clinia's passion for her. But he has a stingy wretch of a father, this old hunks our neighbour; do you know him? Why, his son ran away for sheer want, just as if he wasn't rolling in riches. You know that what I say is true?

CHREMES: Of course I know it. That fellow deserved the treadmill.

SYRUS: What fellow?

CHREMES: I mean, that slave-boy of the young gentleman's—

SYRUS (*aside*): Syrus, I was afraid for you.

CHREMES: —who allowed it to happen.

SYRUS: What could he have done?

CHREMES: Done? He should have invented something, hatched some plot to get the youth some money to give his mistress, and been the saving of the cross old man against his will.

SYRUS: Nonsense!

CHREMES: That's what he should have done, Syrus.

SYRUS: Pray, then, do you approve of slaves who cheat their masters?

CHREMES: I do indeed, when they cheat in due season.

SYRUS: You are quite right.

CHREMES: Why, doing this often saves men from great troubles; for instance, if it had been done, this man's only son would have stayed at home.

SYRUS (*aside*): Whether he's saying this in jest or earnest I cannot tell; but, beyond that, it encourages me all the more to work with a will.

CHREMES: And now, Syrus, what is this slave waiting for? Is he going to wait until the youth has to go on his travels a second time, when he can no longer bear the cost of a mistress? Isn't he laying some plot against the old man?

SYRUS: He's a stupid fellow.

CHREMES: But you ought to help him, for the youth's sake.

SYRUS: I could easily do that, if you give me the order, for I know perfectly how such things are managed.

CHREMES: Then you are so much the better man to manage it.

SYRUS: Oh, it's not my way to tell lies.

CHREMES: Then do it.

SYRUS: But I say, mind you don't forget this, in case it should happen, seeing what human nature is, that your son should do anything of this sort.

CHREMES: I hope I shall not have occasion.

SYRUS: Indeed, I hope so too; and I don't say this because I have any suspicion of him; but if he does, don't you fly out. Consider how young he is. And upon my word, Chremes, if occasion offered, I could handle you in fine fashion.

CHREMES: When the occasion comes, we'll see what will have to be done; now attend to this business. (CHREMES *goes into his house.*)

SYRUS (*to himself*): I never have heard a master talk more accommodatingly, and never believed that I should have such a chance of swindling with impunity. But who is this coming out of our house?

Act Three. Scene III

(*Re-enter* CHREMES *with* CLITIPHO.)

CHREMES: What sort of conduct is this, pray? What a way to act, Clitipho! Is this proper behaviour?

CLITIPHO: What have I done?

CHREMES: Didn't I see you just now putting your hand into this girl's bosom?

SYRUS (*aside*): All's lost, I am a ruined man!

CLITIPHO: Me?

CHREMES: I saw you with these eyes, so don't deny it. You are wronging your friend shamefully by not keeping your hands off her; it is a shocking action to invite a friend to your house and then to insult his mistress. And yesterday, over the wine, how badly you behaved!

SYRUS (*aside*): He did, too.

CHREMES: How troublesome you were! So help me heaven, I was afraid some harm would come of it! I know what lovers are, they take offence at things you wouldn't expect them to mind.

CLITIPHO: But, father, I am upon my honour with Clinia not to do anything of the kind.

CHREMES: So be it. But you certainly had better remove yourself for a while out of their sight. Love prompts them to much which your presence forbids them to do. I guess this from myself. Clitipho, there is no friend of mine before whom I would display all my secret thoughts; before one I should be restrained by my self-respect, before another I should be ashamed to show my love, for fear he should think me silly or wanton. Now bear in mind that this is Clinia's case; but it is our duty to understand this, and always and everywhere to consult their convenience.

SYRUS (*to* CLITIPHO): What is this story that he is telling?

CLITIPHO: All's lost.

SYRUS: Clitipho, is this the advice that I gave you? Have you behaved like a man of decency and self-restraint?

CLITIPHO: For God's sake, hold your tongue!

SYRUS: What I say is quite true.

CHREMES: I am ashamed of him.

SYRUS: No wonder, and you have a right to be. Why, I am vexed at it myself.

CLITIPHO: Is that how you are going on?

SYRUS: No, I am saying what I think.

CLITIPHO: And am I not to go near them?

CHREMES: What! Is there only one way of going near them?

SYRUS (*aside*): All's lost; he will betray himself before I get the money. (*Aloud*) Chremes, will you take the advice of a fool like me?

CHREMES: What do you advise?

SYRUS: Bid him take himself off somewhere.

CLITIPHO: Where am I to go to?

SYRUS: Wherever you please; make way for them; go and take a walk.

CLITIPHO: Where am I to walk to?

SYRUS: Nonsense, as if there were not plenty of places. Go this way, or that way, wherever you please.

CHREMES: Good advice! I think you ought to do so.

CLITIPHO (*aside to* SYRUS): May the gods confound you for driving me away, Syrus.

SYRUS: And mind that henceforth you keep those hands of yours to yourself. (CLITIPHO *departs*) Well, I never! What do you think he will do, Chremes, unless you, with heaven's leave, keep him within bounds, punish him, and warn him?

CHREMES: I'll see to that.

SYRUS: But, master, now is the time that he needs your care.

CHREMES: He shall have it.

SYRUS: If you are wise he will, for he minds me less every day.

CHREMES: And what have you been doing, Syrus? Have you done anything about that plan that I spoke of to you? Have you invented a plot that you approve of, or not?

SYRUS: The swindling, do you mean? Yes, I've just now thought of a plan.

CHREMES: You're a good fellow; tell me what it is.

SYRUS: Well, I'll tell you; but, somehow, one thing leads to another.

CHREMES: How so, Syrus?

SYRUS: This courtesan is a most abominable woman.

CHREMES: That's what I think.

SYRUS: Nay, if you knew all. Just hear what a plot she is hatching. There was an old woman from Corinth to whom she lent a thousand drachmas.

CHREMES: What then?

SYRUS: The old woman is dead; she left a daughter, a young girl. This girl was left in Bacchis' hands as security for the money.

CHREMES: I understand.

SYRUS: Now Bacchis has brought this girl with her to our house; it is she who is now with your wife.

CHREMES: Well, what then?

SYRUS: Now she wants Clinia to pay her the money, and then she will hand over the girl to him; she demands the thousand drachmas.

CHREMES: Does she?

SYRUS: Why, can there be any doubt about it? That's the way I understood it.

CHREMES. What are you thinking of doing now?

SYRUS: What, I? I shall go to Menedemus, and tell him that this girl was carried off from Caria, that she is rich and of noble birth; that, if he redeems her from slavery, he will get great profits out of the transaction.

CHREMES: You're mistaken.

SYRUS: How so?

CHREMES: I now take it upon myself to answer for Menedemus, and I say, "I won't buy her." What are you going to do then?

SYRUS: You give just the answer I wish for.

CHREMES: How?

SYRUS: It's not worth while to explain how.

CHREMES (*bewildered*): Not worth while?

SYRUS: No, indeed.

CHREMES: How is that? I don't understand.

SYRUS: You'll know before long.

CHREMES: Wait a minute. Why is our door opening with all that noise?

Act Four. Scene I

(*Enter* SOSTRATA *and the* NURSE *from* CHREMES' *house.*)

SOSTRATA (*to the* NURSE): Unless my wishes deceive me, this is indeed the ring which I believe it to be, the ring wherewith my daughter was exposed.

CHREMES (*aside to* SYRUS): Syrus, what is the meaning of this?

SOSTRATA (*to the* NURSE): Tell me, don't you think that it is the same?

NURSE: Indeed, when you showed it to me I said directly that it was.

SOSTRATA: But, nurse dear, have you looked at it carefully enough?

NURSE: I have.

SOSTRATA: Then go into the house, and if she has finished her bath, tell her to come to me. Meanwhile, I will wait here for my husband. (*The* NURSE *goes into the house.*)

SYRUS (*to* CHREMES): She wants you; you had better see what the matter is; she is in trouble about something, and something of importance; I am alarmed about it.

CHREMES: Why, what should it be? She has always been in the habit of making mountains out of molehills.

SOSTRATA (*seeing* CHREMES): Good day, husband.

CHREMES: Good day, wife.

SOSTRATA: I was looking for you.

CHREMES: Tell me what you want.

SOSTRATA: First of all, I beseech you, believe that I have never dared to do anything contrary to your orders.

CHREMES (*aside*): Do you wish me to believe that, a thing I can't possibly do? (*Aloud*) Well, I believe it.

SYRUS (*aside*): This justification implies some wrongdoing.

SOSTRATA: Do you remember when I was in the family way, and you solemnly declared to me that if it should be a girl, you would put it away?

CHREMES: I know what you have done, you didn't put it away.

SYRUS (*aside*): That's true; so I've gained another mistress and my master has gained a loss.

SOSTRATA: Nay, but there was a very decent old woman here, a Corinthian; I gave the child to her to put away.

CHREMES: O Jupiter, that you should have been such a fool!

SOSTRATA: Dear me, what harm did I do?

CHREMES: Do you ask me?

SOSTRATA: If I did wrong, Chremes dear, I did it in ignorance.

CHREMES: Whether you say so or no, I am quite sure of this one thing— everything you say and do is said and done in ignorance and foolishness. What a number of things you prove yourself to have done wrong in this business! First of all, if you had chosen to carry out my order, the child ought to have been made away with; you ought not to have pretended that it was dead, and really given it a chance to live. But I will let that pass; it was done out of tender-heartedness; a mother's feelings—I forgive you that. But just consider how well you laid your plan to carry out your wish. You just simply gave your daughter to that old woman for her ruin, and did all that you could to get her either sent on to the streets or sold as a slave. I suppose you thought, "Anything is better than that the child should die." What is one to do with creatures who have no sense of right and wrong, who care nothing whether they help or hinder, whether they do good or harm, provided they get what they want?

SOSTRATA: My dear Chremes, I confess that I have done wrong; what you say is true; now I beg you, since your character is naturally calmer and more inclined to forgiveness, let your justice be a protection to my folly.

CHREMES: Of course I will pardon this act of yours, but indeed, Sostrata, my easygoing kindness leads you into evil ways. However, tell me now why you began this story.

SOSTRATA: As all we poor silly women are full of superstition, I pulled a ring from my finger when I gave her to the woman to be exposed, and told her to expose the ring together with the child, so that, if she died, she might nevertheless not be quite disinherited.

CHREMES: Therein you did right; you have saved the child and your own conscience.

SOSTRATA: This is the ring.

CHREMES: Whence did you get it?

SOSTRATA: The girl that Bacchis brought with her—

SYRUS (*aside*): Eh? What's that she says?

SOSTRATA: When she went to take a bath she gave it to me to keep for her. I didn't notice it at first; but when I looked at it, I straightway recognised it, and rushed out to you.

CHREMES: What do you suspect, or what have you made out about this girl?

SOSTRATA: I don't know, beyond that you had better ask her yourself where she got it from, if it can be found out.

SYRUS (*aside*): Damn it! This business is more hopeful than I want it to be. If this be true, she is our master's daughter.

CHREMES: Is the old woman to whom you gave the ring alive?

SOSTRATA: I don't know.

CHREMES: What did she tell you at the time?

SOSTRATA: That she had done what I bade her do.

CHREMES: Tell me what the woman's name was, that we may search for her.

SOSTRATA: Philtera.

SYRUS (*aside*): Her very name. For certain, she is saved and I am lost.

CHREMES: Sostrata, come this way with me into the house.

SOSTRATA: Better than I could have hoped! I was dreadfully afraid, Chremes, that you would be as harsh now as you were then about having the child exposed.

CHREMES: A man often can't do what he would, if his means do not permit him. Now the time has come when I should like to have a daughter; formerly I didn't want one at all. (CHREMES *and* SOSTRATA *go into their house.*)

Act Four. Scene II

SYRUS (*to himself*): If I am not mistaken, I shall get into trouble before long; this discovery has driven all my forces into a corner; that is, unless I can find some way of preventing the old gentleman finding out that Bacchis is his son's mistress. As for my hope of the money, or for supposing that I can cheat them out of it, that is all gone; I shall come off with flying colours if I can save my skin. I *am* vexed at such a nice titbit being so suddenly taken out of my mouth. What shall I do? Or what shall I devise? I must begin my plans all over again. There's nothing so hard that one can't find it out by patient search. (*Reflecting*) Suppose I were to set about it so? No, that's no good. Or so? That's no better. But that way I think I might manage it. No, I could not. Nay, but I could most excellently. Hurrah! I have a capital plan. I do really believe that I shall bring back that runaway money to me.

Act Four. Scene III

(*Enter* CLINIA *from* CHREMES' *house.*)

CLINIA (*to himself*): Hereafter, no misfortune great enough to cause me any sorrow can happen to me, such joy has come into my life. I will now straightway put myself into my father's hands, and live even more steadily than he wants me to live.

SYRUS (*aside*): I was right in my guess: the girl has been recognised, from what I hear him say. (*To* CLINIA) I am glad the matter has ended to your satisfaction.

CLINIA: Oh, my dear Syrus, pray have you heard?

SYRUS: Why, of course I have, seeing that I was here all the while.

CLINIA: Did you ever hear of anybody having such a stroke of luck?

SYRUS: Never.

CLINIA: And I declare to heaven it is not so much on my own account that I am overjoyed, as on hers; she is, I know, worthy of any honour that can befall her.

SYRUS: So I understand; but now come, Clinia, let me have your help in my turn, for we must see about arranging your friend's business safely, that the old gentleman may not get wind of his mistress.

CLINIA: O Jupiter!

SYRUS: Be quiet.

CLINIA: My Antiphila is going to marry me.

SYRUS: What a way to interrupt one!

CLINIA: What else can I do? Syrus, my good fellow, I am delighted; bear with me.

SYRUS: Well, I bear with you.

CLINIA: We have gained Paradise.

SYRUS: It seems to me that I am wasting my time.

CLINIA: Speak; I am listening.

SYRUS: Even now you're not paying attention to me.

CLINIA: I'll pay attention.

SYRUS: I repeat, Clinia, that we must see about arranging your friend's business safely. For if you leave us now, and leave Bacchis here, the old gentleman will straightway see that she is Clitipho's mistress; but if you take her with you, the intrigue will be hidden just as it has been hitherto.

CLINIA: But then, Syrus, nothing can be more likely than that to break off my marriage, for with what face can I meet my father? Do you see anything that I can say?

SYRUS: Why not?

CLINIA: What am I to say? What reason can I give?

SYRUS: Well, I don't want you to tell a lie. Tell him the whole story openly.

CLINIA: What?

SYRUS: That's what I bid you do. Tell him that you love Antiphila, and want to marry her, and that this woman here belongs to Clitipho.

CLINIA: This is indeed a good and righteous deed that you bid me do, and one easy to accomplish. And I suppose presently you will want me to beg my father to keep it secret from your old gentleman?

SYRUS: Not at all; bid him tell him the whole story straightway.

CLINIA: Good gracious! Are you sane? Are you sober? You will ruin Clitipho utterly. Tell me how he can possibly be saved.

SYRUS: This is the plan to which I give the prize; upon this I greatly pride myself, since I have so much depth and power of scheming that I shall deceive them both by telling the truth; so that when your old gentleman tells our old gentleman that she is his son's mistress, he won't believe it for all that.

CLINIA: But then by this plot you take away again all hopes of my marriage; for he will never entrust me with his daughter as long as he thinks that Bacchis is my mistress. I suppose you care nothing about what becomes of me, provided you can do Clitipho a service.

SYRUS: What the devil! Do you suppose that I want to keep up the deception for an age? I only need one day, time to get the money, and then hush! All's over.

CLINIA: Do you think that enough? And pray what will happen should Clitipho's father learn the truth?

SYRUS: Supposing I repeat the proverb, "What if the sky should fall?"

CLINIA: I am anxious about what I ought to do.

SYRUS: Anxious? As if you didn't have it always in your power to reveal the whole truth, whenever you want to prove yourself blameless!

CLINIA: Well, well, bring Bacchis over.

SYRUS: And by good luck there she herself comes out of our door.

Act Four.   Scene IV

(*Enter* BACCHIS *with* PHRYGIA.)

BACCHIS (*to herself*): This is a pretty fool's errand that Syrus' promises have brought me on to this place, promising me ten minae.[9] If he has played me false now, he may often come begging me to meet his master, but he will come in vain; or else, after I have promised to meet his master and arranged a rendezvous, then, when Clitipho shall have been told so for certain, and when his heart's in a flutter, I'll play him a trick and won't come. Then I shall have my revenge on Syrus' back.

CLINIA (*aside to* SYRUS): She is making nice promises for you.

SYRUS (*aside to* CLINIA): Yes, and do you suppose that she is joking? She'll carry them out unless I take care.

BACCHIS (*to* PHRYGIA, *catching sight of the men*): They are asleep. Heavens! I'll wake them up. (*Louder*) My Phrygia, did you hear just now which country-house it was which that fellow told us was Charinus'?

PHRYGIA: Yes, I did.

BACCHIS: The next one to this farm on the right-hand side of the way.

PHRYGIA: I remember.

BACCHIS: Hurry there as fast as you can; my captain is spending the Dionysia there.

SYRUS (*aside*): What is she going to do?

BACCHIS: Tell him that I am here quite against my will, and am re-tained by force, but that somehow or other I will outwit these people here and will come to him.

SYRUS (*aside*): I am utterly undone. (*Aloud*) Bacchis, Bacchis, stay; pray, whither are you sending that girl? Bid her remain here.

BACCHIS (*to* PHRYGIA): Be off with you.

SYRUS: But the money is ready.

BACCHIS: Then I stay. (PHRYGIA *comes back.*)

SYRUS: Indeed it shall be given you at once.

BACCHIS: As you please. I don't press for it, do I?

SYRUS: But pray now, do you know what you must do?

BACCHIS: What?

SYRUS: You must transfer yourself to Menedemus' house, and all your train must be taken over there.

BACCHIS: What are you at, villain?

SYRUS: I? I'm forging the money that I am to give to you.

BACCHIS: Do you think me a proper subject for your insults?

SYRUS: Why, I'm in earnest.

BACCHIS: Must I go on dealing with you this way?

SYRUS: Not a bit. I only give you what is your own.

BACCHIS: Then let us go.

SYRUS: Come this way. (*Knocking at* MENEDEMUS' *door*) Hi! Dromo!

(*Enter* DROMO.)

DROMO: Who wants me?

SYRUS: Syrus wants you.

DROMO: What's the matter?

SYRUS: Take all Bacchis' maidservants across to your house as fast as you can.

DROMO: What for?

SYRUS: Don't you ask "what for." Let them take with them all the baggage that they brought here. Chremes will hope that this departure will lighten his expenses, but he little knows how much loss this small gain will cause him. As for you, Dromo, if you are wise, you will know nothing at all.

DROMO: You may call me dumb. (DROMO *goes into* CHREMES' *house*; CLINIA, BACCHIS, *and* PHRYGIA *into the house of* MENEDEMUS.)

Act Four.   Scene V

(*Enter* CHREMES *from his house.*)

CHREMES (*to himself*): So help me heaven, I am now really sorry for Menedemus, that so great a disaster should have befallen him, as having to keep that woman there with all her servants, though I know that he won't feel it for the first few days, he was so eager to get his son back. But when he sees such extravagance going on every day in his house, and no bounds to it, he'll want his son to go away again. There's Syrus, just the man I wanted to see.

SYRUS (*aside*): I'll tackle him straightway.

CHREMES: Syrus.

SYRUS: Yes.

CHREMES: What is going on?

SYRUS: I have long been wanting to meet you.

CHREMES: It seems that you have already done something with the old gentleman.

SYRUS: About what we spoke of some time ago? It was word and deed with me.

CHREMES: 'Pon your honour, now?

SYRUS: Upon my honour, by Jove!

CHREMES: I can't help patting you on the head; come here, Syrus, I will do something good to you for this, and with all my heart.

SYRUS: Ah, but if you only knew how neatly it came into my head.

CHREMES: What, are you taking to yourself the credit of your plot having turned out as you wished?

SYRUS: No, indeed, I only speak the truth.

CHREMES: Tell it me.

SYRUS: Clinia has told Menedemus that this Bacchis is your son Clitipho's mistress, and that he has taken her over with him that you might not find it out.

CHREMES: Capital!

SYRUS: What d'ye think of that, pray?

CHREMES: Very clever indeed.

SYRUS (*aside*): If you did but know! (*Aloud*) But now hear the rest of the plot. He will say that he has seen your daughter, that he admires her, and wishes to marry her.

CHREMES: What, the daughter whom I have just found?

SYRUS: The same; and he will bid his father demand her formally.

CHREMES: What will he do that for, Syrus? For I can't understand it at all.

SYRUS: Oh, you're dull.

CHREMES: I may be.

SYRUS: He must be given money to spend on his marriage, money with which jewelry and new clothes—don't you understand?

CHREMES: For him to buy them with?

SYRUS: Exactly.

CHREMES: But I shall not give him my daughter, neither will I betroth her to him.

SYRUS: No? Why not?

CHREMES: Why not? Do you ask me why not? Give my daughter to a man who—

SYRUS: Just as you please. I never said that you were to give her to him for good, but that you should only pretend to do so.

CHREMES: I am not given to pretending. Concoct your plots how you please, but don't mix me up with them. Do you suppose that I should betroth my daughter to a man whom I wouldn't let her marry?

SYRUS: I thought that you would.

CHREMES: Certainly not.

SYRUS: It might have been very neatly managed, and I began it this way because you so strongly advised me to do so before.

CHREMES: I daresay.

SYRUS: However, Chremes, I bear you no malice for all that.

CHREMES: Indeed, I most particularly wish you to manage it, but by some other way.

SYRUS: I'll manage it, I'll invent something; but as for what I told you of just now, the money which this girl owes to Bacchis, that will now have to be repaid to her. You can't get out of it by the excuses, "What has that to do with me?" "Was the money lent to me?" "Did I tell her to lend it?" or, "Could she pledge my daughter for it against my will?" Indeed, Chremes, what they say is true, the letter of the law is often the height of injustice.

CHREMES: I won't do it.

SYRUS: No, sir; others might act thus, but you can't, for all men think that you are a man of wealth and substance.

CHREMES: Well, then, I'll take it to her myself directly.

SYRUS: No, it would be better to tell your son to take it.

CHREMES: Why?

SYRUS: Because we have made him suspected of being her lover.

CHREMES: What then?

SYRUS: Because it will look more natural for him to give it to her, and at the same time I shall manage what I want more easily so. (*Looking down the street*) Why, there he is; go into the house and bring out the money.

CHREMES: I'll bring it. (CHREMES *goes into his house.*)

Act Four.　Scene VI

(*Enter* CLITIPHO.)

CLITIPHO (*to himself*): There is nothing so easy to do that it does not weary you when you have to do it against your will. Why, even this walk of mine, though far from a hard one, has quite tired me; and I fear nothing so much as being turned out of the house a second time, so that I may not get near Bacchis. (*Seeing* SYRUS) May all the gods and goddesses in heaven confound you, Syrus, with your devices and your plots; you are always inventing something of this sort to torment me with.

SYRUS: Go to the place you deserve. How near your petulance has been to ruining me!

CLITIPHO: I wish it had, with all my heart, for it is what you deserve.

SYRUS: What I deserve? How so? Indeed, I am pleased to hear this from you before you have got the money that I am going to give you presently.

CLITIPHO: Why, what do you want me to say to you? You went there. You brought my mistress to me, and now I am not allowed to touch her.

SYRUS: I am not angry with you now; but do you know where your Bacchis is now?

CLITIPHO: In our house.

SYRUS: No.

CLITIPHO: Where then?

SYRUS: At Clinia's.

CLITIPHO: All's over with me.

SYRUS: Keep your spirits up; you shall presently take her the money that you promised her.

CLITIPHO: Nonsense! Where am I to get it?

SYRUS: From your father.

CLITIPHO: Are you making fun of me?

SYRUS: The event will show you.

CLITIPHO: Why, then, I am a lucky man indeed. Syrus, I'm your friend forever.

SYRUS: But here comes your father out of the house; now mind you, don't show any surprise about why he does this; fall in with his humour judiciously; do what he bids you; say little.

Act Four.   Scene VII

(*Re-enter* CHREMES *from his house.*)

CHREMES: Now, where is Clitipho?

SYRUS (*aside to* CLITIPHO): Say "Here I am."

CLITIPHO: Here I am, father.

CHREMES (*to* SYRUS): Have you told him what the matter is?

SYRUS: I have told him pretty nearly the whole story.

CHREMES (*to* CLITIPHO): Take that money and carry it over to her.

SYRUS (*aside to* CLITIPHO): Go on; what are you standing still for, blockhead? Why don't you take it?

CLITIPHO: Give it me, then.

SYRUS (*to* CLITIPHO): Follow me this way quickly. (*To* CHREMES) You will wait here for us until we come out again, for there is nothing to keep us there long. (SYRUS *and* CLITIPHO *go into the house of* MENEDEMUS.)

CHREMES (*to himself*): So; my daughter has had ten minae out of me, which I reckon as payment for her board and lodging. Next there will come a second ten for a wedding outfit; and then all this will want two talents for her dowry. How we are governed by fashion, whether it be right or wrong! Now I must put business aside and look out for some one on whom to bestow my hard-earned wealth.

Act Four.   Scene VIII

(Enter MENEDEMUS *from his house.)*

MENEDEMUS *(speaking to* CLINIA *within)*: I consider that I have been made the most fortunate of men, my son, now that I understand that you have come to your right mind.

CHREMES *(aside)*: How mistaken he is!

MENEDEMUS *(seeing him)*: You're the very man I was looking for, Chremes. Do what you can to save me, my son, and my whole house.

CHREMES: Pray what do you want me to do?

MENEDEMUS: You have today found a daughter.

CHREMES: What then?

MENEDEMUS: Clinia wants her for his wife.

CHREMES: Pray what sort of a man are you?

MENEDEMUS: What's the matter?

CHREMES: Have you already forgotten what we said to one another about the trick, that this was how the money was to be got out of you?

MENEDEMUS: I know.

CHREMES: Well, that's the very thing that is now being done.

MENEDEMUS: What are you talking about, Chremes? No, the lady who is in my house is Clitipho's mistress; they say that she is.

CHREMES: And do you believe what they say?

MENEDEMUS: Every word.

CHREMES: And they say that Clinia wants a wife, that, when I have betrothed my daughter to him, you may give him money to buy jewelry and clothes and whatever else is wanted.

MENEDEMUS: Just so; then he will give that money to his mistress.

CHREMES: Of course he will.

MENEDEMUS: Oh, dear me! I was wrong to feel glad; yet I prefer anything now to losing him. What answer shall I take him from you, Chremes, that he may not understand that I see through his plot, and be vexed?

CHREMES: Vexed, indeed! Menedemus, you indulge him over much.

MENEDEMUS: Suffer me to do so. I have begun it; continue to help me, Chremes.

CHREMES: Say that we are agreed, and that you have arranged about the marriage.

MENEDEMUS: I'll say so; what next?

CHREMES: Say that I will do all that is needful; that I approve of him as a son-in-law; say, indeed, if you like, that I have betrothed her to him.

MENEDEMUS: That was what I wanted to hear.

CHREMES: What? That he may ask you for the money all the sooner, and you may give it him all the sooner, as you desire.

MENEDEMUS: That's what I want.

CHREMES: Upon my word, from my point of view, you will soon be sick of him; but however that may be, you will give him money cautiously and little at a time, if you are a wise man.

MENEDEMUS: I will.

CHREMES: Go into your house and hear how much he asks for. I shall be at home, in case you should want me.

MENEDEMUS: Indeed, I do want you, for whatever I may do, I shall do nothing without letting you know it. (*Each goes into his own house. A short time is supposed to elapse before the next Act.*)

Act Five.   Scene I

(*Enter* MENEDEMUS *from his house.*)

MENEDEMUS (*to himself*): I am quite aware that I am not so very clever, so very clearheaded; but this Chremes, my helper and monitor and guide, goes beyond me. All the common names that are given to a fool, blockhead, stock, donkey, stupid, may apply to me, but there is no word for him; his folly transcends everything.

(*Enter* CHREMES *from his house.*)

CHREMES (*speaking to his wife within*): Oh, wife, leave off deafening the gods with your thanksgivings on having found your daughter, unless you judge of their intelligence by your own, and think that they can't understand unless they hear the same thing a hundred times repeated. (*To himself*) But in the meantime, why does my son dawdle there with Syrus so long?

MENEDEMUS: Who do you say are dawdling, Chremes?

CHREMES: O Menedemus, have you come? Tell me, did you tell Clinia what I said?

MENEDEMUS: Yes, all that you said.

CHREMES: And what does he say?

MENEDEMUS: He began straightway to be pleased, as men are when they want to marry.

CHREMES: Ha, ha, ha!

MENEDEMUS: What are you laughing at?

CHREMES: I was thinking of the devices of my slave Syrus.

MENEDEMUS: Indeed?

CHREMES: That scoundrel can mould men's very faces according to his wish.

MENEDEMUS: Do you mean that my son is only pretending to be pleased?

CHREMES: I do.

MENEDEMUS: That is just the very thing that I was thinking.

CHREMES: Old fox!

MENEDEMUS: If you knew more about it, you'd be more inclined to believe it to be true.

CHREMES: What's that you say?

MENEDEMUS: Why, just you listen.

CHREMES: Wait a moment, I want first to know how much money you've lost, for as soon as you told him that my daughter was betrothed to him, of course Dromo dropped a hint to you that the bride would need dresses and jewels and maidservants, to get you to give him the money for them.

MENEDEMUS: No, he didn't.

CHREMES: What, he didn't?

MENEDEMUS: He didn't, I assure you.

CHREMES: Nor your son himself?

MENEDEMUS: Nothing of the kind, Chremes. The one matter that he did become more eager about was, that the marriage should be celebrated this day.

CHREMES: This is a strange story. What did my Syrus do? Didn't he ask for any money?

MENEDEMUS: He asked for nothing.

CHREMES: I am sure I don't know why he didn't.

MENEDEMUS: I am surprised at your not knowing, seeing that you understand everything else so well. But that Syrus has wondrously well schooled your son, so that no one would ever suspect Bacchis of being Clinia's mistress.

CHREMES: What's that you say?

MENEDEMUS: I pass over their kissing and hugging one another, for I don't think anything of that.

CHREMES: How much further does this pretence go?

MENEDEMUS: Bah!

CHREMES: What do you mean?

MENEDEMUS: Listen to me. At the end of my house there is a room that stands back. A bed was brought into this room; then the bed had bedclothes put upon it.

CHREMES: What happened after that?

MENEDEMUS: Straightway Clitipho went into the room.

CHREMES: Alone?

MENEDEMUS: Alone.

CHREMES: I am getting afraid.

MENEDEMUS: Immediately afterwards Bacchis followed him.

CHREMES: Alone?

MENEDEMUS: Alone.

CHREMES: Oh, good heavens!

MENEDEMUS: When they were inside, they locked the door.

CHREMES: Well, and did Clinia see this done?

MENEDEMUS: Of course he did; I was there with him.

CHREMES: Bacchis is my son's mistress! Menedemus, I am a ruined man!

MENEDEMUS: Why ruined?

CHREMES: I have scarce enough to keep me for ten days.

MENEDEMUS: What, are you alarmed at his standing by his friend?

CHREMES: His lady friend.

MENEDEMUS: If he really does.

CHREMES: Why, can you have any doubt about it? Do you think that anybody could be so obliging or so easygoing, as to let his mistress, before his face—

MENEDEMUS: Why not? The easier to swindle me.

CHREMES: You have a right to laugh at me; I am now angry with myself. What a number of hints they have let fall which I might have taken if I had not been an oaf! What things I have seen them do! Oh, unhappy man that I am! But, by heaven, they shall not carry it off with impunity if I live, for I'll—

MENEDEMUS: Won't you restrain yourself? Won't you show respect to yourself? Am I not a sufficient warning to you?

CHREMES: Menedemus, I am beside myself with rage.

MENEDEMUS: That you should talk like that! Is it not a shame that you should give advice to others? That you should be wise abroad, and unable to help yourself at home?

CHREMES: What am I to do?

MENEDEMUS: Do what you said I failed to do. Make him feel that you are his father; make him dare to confide all his wants to you, and ask you to supply them, lest he should find some other source of supply and desert you.

CHREMES: No, I'd rather have him go away to any place in the world rather than stay here and ruin his father by his crimes. If I go on supplying him with means to carry out his extravagance, Menedemus, I shall have to take to working with your rakes.

MENEDEMUS: Unless you're careful, a great deal of unpleasantness will arise out of this affair: you will show yourself harsh, and then afterwards you will pardon him, and with a bad grace.

CHREMES: You don't know how hurt I am.

MENEDEMUS: Well, do as you please. What about my request that your daughter should marry my son? Unless you would prefer something else.

CHREMES: No, both the son-in-law and the family please me.

MENEDEMUS: How much dowry shall I tell my son that you will give? Why are you silent?

CHREMES: Dowry?

MENEDEMUS: That is what I said.

CHREMES: Oh, dear me!

MENEDEMUS: Chremes, pray don't feel any shame if it is rather a small dowry that you offer; it is not the dowry which influences us.

CHREMES: I had decided that a dowry of two talents would be sufficient, considering our position; but if you would save me and my son, I want you to say that I have made over all my property to her as dowry.

MENEDEMUS: What are you at?

CHREMES: Pretend that you are surprised at this, and ask him at the same time why I am doing it.

MENEDEMUS: But I really don't know why you are doing it.

CHREMES: Why? That I may break his spirit, which now revels in luxury and debauchery, and may bring him down so low that he won't know which way to turn.

MENEDEMUS: Oh, what are you doing?

CHREMES: Never mind; let me have my own way in this business.

MENEDEMUS: I do let you. Shall our contract stand?

CHREMES: Yes.

MENEDEMUS: So be it.

CHREMES: Then let him get ready to fetch home his bride; I will lecture this son of mine, as a child should be. But as for Syrus—

MENEDEMUS: What will you do to him?

CHREMES: What will I do? If I live, I'll give him such a dressing, such a curry-combing, that he'll never forget me as long as he lives. (*To himself, as* MENEDEMUS *goes inside*) He thought that he could play with me and make game of me, did he? So help me heaven, he wouldn't have dared to play such tricks upon a lone woman as he has upon me.

Act Five. Scene II

(*Re-enter* MENEDEMUS *with* CLITIPHO *and* SYRUS.)

CLITIPHO: Is it really true, Menedemus, that my father has in so short a time lost all fatherly feeling for me? Why is this? What is this dreadful crime which I have committed? It's a thing everybody does.

MENEDEMUS: I know that this must press much more hardly and grievously upon you, who are the victim of it, than upon anyone else; but I am no less grieved at it. I don't know the reason of it, and can't see the sense of it; all I know is that I wish you well.

CLITIPHO: I think you said that my father was near this place.

MENEDEMUS: There he is. (MENEDEMUS *returns to his house.*)

CHREMES (*advancing*): Why do you blame me, Clitipho? Whatever I have done in this matter has been out of consideration for your interests and your folly. When I saw that you were heedless, and considered present enjoyment as the chief thing, and could not look forward to the future, I adopted a plan whereby you might never want, and yet might never squander your inheritance. Since I cannot, through your fault, give it to you, who are the person who ought to receive it, I have applied to your nearest connection; I have placed it all in his hands as trustee. There you will always be defended against your own folly, Clitipho; you will get fed and clothed, and have a roof to shelter you.

CLITIPHO: Damnation!

CHREMES: This is much better than that you should really be heir, and that Bacchis should get all this property of mine.

SYRUS (*aside*): Good heavens! What a storm I have unwittingly raised!

CLITIPHO: I wish I were dead!

CHREMES: First learn how to live, if you please; when you have learned, then, if life does not please you, try the other thing.

SYRUS: Master, may I speak?

CHREMES: Speak.

SYRUS: Yes, but safely?

CHREMES: Speak.

SYRUS: What madness or wickedness this is, that he should be punished for my wrongdoing.

CHREMES: Go; don't you meddle; no one accuses you, Syrus; you need not get an altar to take sanctuary at, or an intercessor to plead your cause.

SYRUS: What is it that you're doing?

CHREMES: I feel no anger against either you or him; and you have no right to be angry with me for what I am doing. (CHREMES *goes into his house.*)

SYRUS: He's gone. Dear me! I wish I had asked him.

CLITIPHO: What?

SYRUS: Where I'm to go for my meals; he has completely cast us off; you will always have a knife and fork at your sister's table, I understand.

CLITIPHO: To think that things should have come to such a pass, Syrus, that I should actually be in danger of being starved.

SYRUS: While there's life there's hope that—

CLITIPHO: That what?

SYRUS: That we shall both be hungry enough.

CLITIPHO: Do you laugh at me when I am in such a serious scrape, instead of helping me with any advice?

SYRUS: Indeed, that is just what I am now trying to do, and I have been trying for some time, while your father was talking; and, as far as I can understand—

CLITIPHO: What?

SYRUS: I can't keep it back any longer. (*Thinking*.)

CLITIPHO: Keep back what?

SYRUS: It must be so. I believe that you are not these people's child.

CLITIPHO: Why do you think that, Syrus? Are you in your right mind?

SYRUS: I will tell you what my thoughts are; do you give judgment. As long as you were their only one, as long as they had no darling nearer to them, they indulged you and gave you money; now, since they have found a real daughter, they have found a reason for turning you out of doors.

CLITIPHO: It does seem likely.

SYRUS: Do you suppose that he's angry with you because of your fault?

CLITIPHO: I don't think so.

SYRUS: Now, consider another point: all mothers help their sons when they are in disgrace, and protect them against their father's violence; now yours does not do so.

CLITIPHO: What you say is true, Syrus; so what shall I do now?

SYRUS: Ask them whether there are any grounds for this suspicion of yours; sift the whole matter publicly. If the notion is not a true one, you will soon melt both their hearts, or else you will know whose son you are.

CLITIPHO: You give me good advice, that's what I'll do. (CLITIPHO *goes into his father's house*.)

SYRUS (*to himself*): That was well thought of; for, the more he finds this fancy to be groundless, the more easily he'll make his peace with his father on his own terms; I don't know whether he won't even marry and settle—and no thanks to Syrus. But what's this? Our old gentleman is coming out; I'm off. I wonder he hasn't had me put in irons straightway for what I've done already. I'll go to this Menedemus, and get him to plead my cause; I don't trust our old gentleman a bit. (SYRUS *goes into the house of* MENEDEMUS.)

Act Five.   Scene III

(Enter SOSTRATA *and* CHREMES.)

SOSTRATA: Man, if you're not careful, you'll do our son some mischief; and I am surprised, husband, at how such a silly idea could have got into your head.

CHREMES: Oh, go on behaving like a woman. Am I never in my life, Sostrata, to form a wish without your trying to thwart me? But if I were to ask wherein I am wrong, or what reasons I have for doing this, why, then, you goose, you don't know, and yet you oppose me so confidently in this matter.

SOSTRATA: As if I didn't know.

CHREMES: Oh, well then, you do know; anything rather than that you should begin your cackle all over again.

SOSTRATA: Oh, but you are wrong to bid me hold my tongue about so serious a matter.

CHREMES: I don't bid you now; talk as much as you please; but I shall do it all the same.

SOSTRATA: You will?

CHREMES: In truth I will.

SOSTRATA: Don't you see how much trouble you'll cause thereby? He suspects that he is a supposititious child.

CHREMES: Supposititious, do you say?

SOSTRATA: That's what he'll think, my husband.

CHREMES: So you confess it.

SOSTRATA: Oh, I pray you, let our enemies confess such things. Am I to say that he isn't my own son, when he is?

CHREMES: What, are you afraid that you can't prove him to be your son whenever you please?

SOSTRATA: Because my daughter has been found?

CHREMES: No, but a much stronger proof than that; because his character is so like yours that you could easily prove him to be your son; for he is the image of you. He hasn't a single fault which you haven't got too. Besides, no one but you could have borne such a son. But here he comes in person; how serious he looks! (*Ironically*) You'd think so, if you knew the truth.

Act Five.   Scene IV

(*Enter* CLITIPHO *from his father's house.*)

CLITIPHO: Mother, if ever there was a time when you had any pleasure in me, and when you were pleased that I should be called your son, by the memory of that time I implore you to pity me now in my misery, and grant my request, to tell me who my parents are.

SOSTRATA: Pray, my son, do not get it into your head that you are not our son.

CLITIPHO: I am not.

SOSTRATA: Oh, dear! Oh, dear! Can you, pray, ask me such a question? As I hope that you will outlive me and my husband, so true it is that you are my son and his; and hereafter, if you love me, mind that you never let me hear a word about that from you.

CHREMES: And I say to you, hereafter, if you fear me, mind that you never let me find such qualities in you as before.

CLITIPHO: What qualities?

CHREMES: If you want to know, I will tell you. A do-nothing idler, a cheat, a glutton, a debauchee, a spendthrift. Think thus, and think yourself our son.

CLITIPHO: This is not how a father speaks.

CHREMES: Clitipho, if you had been born out of my own head, as they say Minerva was out of Jove's, even then I would not suffer you to disgrace me by your infamous behaviour.

SOSTRATA: The gods forbid that he should.

CHREMES: I don't know about the gods; I will take care to do what I can myself. You are seeking for what you have got, parents; you do not seek for what you haven't got, the will to obey your father and the power to keep what his labour has won. To bring under false pretences, before my very eyes, a— I am ashamed to utter the shocking word before your mother, but you were not ashamed to do it.

CLITIPHO (*aside*): Oh, dear, how utterly displeased I am with myself and ashamed of myself; and I don't see how to begin to make my peace.

Act Five.   Scene V

(*Enter* MENEDEMUS *from his house.*)

MENEDEMUS (*to himself*): Upon my word, Chremes is far too hard upon the youth, and shows no mercy; so I am come out to reconcile them; and there, most luckily, I see them.

CHREMES: Well, Menedemus, why don't you bid them send for my daughter, and settle what I said about her dowry?

SOSTRATA: Husband, I beg you not to do so.

CLITIPHO: Father, I beg you to pardon me.

MENEDEMUS: Pardon him, Chremes, let him persuade you.

CHREMES: What, give my property to Bacchis with my eyes open? I won't do such a thing.

MENEDEMUS: But we won't allow that.

CLITIPHO: Father, if you wish me to live, pardon me.

SOSTRATA: Come, my dear Chremes.

MENEDEMUS: Come, Chremes, don't be so obstinate.

CHREMES: Well, well. I see that I can't carry this matter through as I intended.

MENEDEMUS: Now you are behaving as becomes you.

CHREMES: I will pardon him on condition that he does what I think right.

CLITIPHO: Father, I will do anything; command me.

CHREMES: Take a wife.

CLITIPHO: Oh, but, father—

CHREMES: I won't listen to any objections.

SOSTRATA: I take upon myself to promise for him; he shall do it.

CHREMES: I haven't yet heard him say anything.

CLITIPHO: Good heavens!

SOSTRATA: Clitipho, do you hesitate?

CHREMES: Well, he can take his choice.

SOSTRATA: He will do anything.

MENEDEMUS (*to* CLITIPHO): It's hard at first, when you don't understand it, but when you learn how to manage, it's easy enough to endure.

CLITIPHO: Father, I will do it.

SOSTRATA: My son, I declare I'll get you that nice girl, whom you will easily learn to love, our friend Phanocrates' daughter.

CLITIPHO: What, that red-haired girl with cat's eyes, a spotty face and turned-up nose? Father, I can't marry her.

CHREMES: Dear me, how particular he is! You would think that he had given his mind to the matter.

SOSTRATA: I will get you another.

CLITIPHO: No, if I must marry, I know pretty well the girl that I should like.

SOSTRATA: That's speaking like a good boy.

CLITIPHO: Archonides' daughter here.

SOSTRATA: She will do very well.

CLITIPHO: Father, there still remains one thing to be done.

CHREMES: What?

CLITIPHO: I want you to forgive Syrus for what he did for me.

CHREMES: I will. (*To the audience*) Farewell, and give us your applause.

1. *The Self-Tormentor* was presented in April, 163 B.C. It was Terence's third play. The second play, *The Mother-in-law*, first presented in 165, failed at its first two productions, and was finally favourably received in 160 B.C.

2. The speaker of this prologue was probably the veteran actor, Lucius Ambivius Turpio.

3. The writers referred to are Naevius, Plautus, and Ennius.

4. This is a reference to Terence's rival, Luscius Lanuvinus.

5. The friends of Terence were Scipio, Laelius, and other young men of the Scipionic circle.

6. Kauer and Lindsay bracket this passage as an interpolation; it occurs also in *The Mother-in-law*, lines 49-51.

7. This verse became famous and was often cited by later Roman writers as expressing the sentiment of the common brotherhood of man.

8. Kauer and Lindsay follow the Mss. in assigning this speech to Bacchis. It was assigned to Clinia by Bergk.

9. Ten minae was the equivalent of a thousand drachmae; cf. Syrus' yarn in Act Three, Scene III about Bacchis' demand for a thousand drachmae.

III
THE EUNUCH

CHARACTERS IN THE PLAY

PHAEDRIA, *a young Athenian, in love with* THAIS
PARMENO, *slave of* PHAEDRIA
THAIS, *a courtesan*
GNATHO, *a parasite*
CHAEREA, *younger brother of* PHAEDRIA, *in love with* PAMPHILA
THRASO, *a soldier, rival of* PHAEDRIA
PYTHIAS, *maid of* THAIS
CHREMES, *brother of* PAMPHILA
ANTIPHO, *friend of* CHAEREA
DORIAS, *maid of* THAIS
DORUS, *a eunuch*
SANGA, *one of* THRASO'S *subalterns*
SOPHRONA, *nurse of* PAMPHILA
LACHES, *father of* PHAEDRIA *and* CHAEREA[1]

DIDASCALIA

The Eunuch of Terence. Acted at the Megalensian Games during the curule aedileship of Lucius Postumius Albinus and Lucius Cornelius Merula. The chief parts were taken by Lucius Ambivius Turpio and Lucius Atilius Praenestinus. It was set to music by Flaccus, the slave of Claudius, for two right-handed flutes. It is from the Greek of Menander. It was performed twice,[2] during the consulship of Marcus Valerius and Gaius Fannius.[3]

SUMMARY

The soldier Thraso brought from abroad a girl who was wrongly considered the sister of Thais; in ignorance of the supposed relationship he gave her to Thais. The girl was an Attic citizen. Phaedria, a lover of Thais, had purchased a eunuch; he ordered the eunuch to be sent to her and he himself went away to the country, since Thais had requested him to give up two days to Thraso. Phaedria's young brother fell madly in love with the young girl who had been presented to Thais and he dressed up as the eunuch at the suggestion of Parmeno. He entered the house and raped the maiden. Her brother is revealed as an Attic citizen and betroths to the youth the girl who has been wronged. Thraso arranges terms with Phaedria.

INTRODUCTION

TERENCE's third play, *The Eunuch,* produced in 161 B.C., marks something of a departure from his earlier comedies. He again shows his fondness for dualism in his plot construction by weaving together the love affairs of two young brothers, Phaedria and Chaerea. Phaedria is in love with a courtesan Thais, and Chaerea is smitten by the charms of a young girl who is believed to be the sister of Thais but who is actually an Attic citizen, as is revealed during the course of the play. In addition to this double plot dealing with the fortunes of the two couples there is a more farcical underplot in which appear two stock characters, the boastful soldier Thraso and the parasite Gnatho. The prologue states that Terence has introduced these characters into his play from a second Menandrian original. The soldier and his parasite in their relations with the main characters provide scenes rich in humour, especially in the attack of Thraso and his "army" on Thais' house, but their presence in the action does not upon analysis seem strictly necessary, and Terence has been charged here of attempting to imitate Plautus without success. Gilbert Norwood writes, *"The Eunuch* is a strange medley of qualities. Dull and brilliant, immoral and edifying, abjectly Plautine and splendidly Terentian—it is all these by turns."

The comedy takes its name from the younger brother in the role he assumed to get into Thais' house. Phaedria had purchased a eunuch as a present for Thais; Chaerea disguises himself as Dorus, the eunuch, and is admitted to the house where he can be near the girl he loves. The results are unexpected and serious. In one of the most suggestive scenes in Roman comedy, Chaerea himself describes the seduction of the young girl who had just been brought to Thais' house and whose real identity Thais was trying to discover. Terence treats the subject with delicacy and there is no indecency in his description. The indecency resides in Terence's portrayal of the effect which the picture of Jupiter and Danae has upon Chaerea's emotions and in the generally sympathetic treatment of sexual misconduct. Likewise objectionable is the closing scene with its arrangement between Phaedria and the soldier. Phaedria will take advantage of his rival's infatuation for Thais and get from him funds to satisfy the needs of Thais. The method is highly improper even if Thais is to have only Phaedria as her lover, and is somewhat reminiscent of Phronesium's acceptance of two lovers in the conclusion of the *Truculentus*. As a character, however, Thais is on a far higher level than Phronesium and many other courtesans in Roman comedy. She is wise, generous, and sympathetic, truly in love with Phaedria, and interested in the welfare and happiness of the girl in her charge; altogether she is a charming forerunner of Bacchis, the noble courtesan of *The Mother-in-law*. Perhaps the greatest tribute to Thais is the attitude of Phaedria's father. Won over by her charm, Laches agrees to be her patron and consents to her living with Phaedria.

Although *The Eunuch* is in many respects the most Plautine of Terence's comedies, it reveals the dramatist's eagerness to achieve new effects and to depart from some of the usual comic conventions. Parmeno is no rascally intriguing slave. The impersonation of the eunuch was his suggestion, but he spoke in jest and later endeavoured to dissuade Chaerea from carrying out the idea. Parmeno was himself later deceived by Pythias' fiction concerning the punishment to be meted out to Chaerea and so revealed the whole truth to his aged master—not the conventional thing for a slave to do. Thraso differs in many respects from the soldier as portrayed by Plautus. Although he is amusingly stupid and conceited, he does not boast of his military exploits; he prides himself upon his wit, and his victories are those of the word rather than of the sword. Terence has endeavoured to make Gnatho an unconventional parasite. Instead of telling jokes like a Gelasimus (in Plautus' *Stichus*) he earns his livelihood by flattering people and laughing at them. He even considers founding a new school of parasites to be called "Gnathonians." But Gnatho is less original than he implies. Any parasite of a conceited soldier is apt to be a flatterer, and Gnatho's praise of Thraso's witticisms is not unlike Artotrogus' comments on Pyrgopolynices' impossible exploits in Plautus' *The Braggart Warrior*. He runs true to type also in his interest in food, recalling Peniculus' "When do we eat?" in Plautus' *The Twin Menaechmi*.

The Eunuch in antiquity was one of Terence's most popular plays. The ancient *Life of Terence* states that it was produced twice in one day, and there can be no doubt that it had a far greater appeal for the Roman audience than Terence's more serious comedies. Several modern dramatists have been influenced by the play, e.g. Baif in *L'Eunuque*, Larivey in *Les Jaloux*, Wycherley in *The Country Wife*, Sedley in *Bellamira, or The Mistress*, and Cooke in *The Eunuch, or The Darby Captain*. Udall's *Ralph Roister Doister* was modelled partly on *The Eunuch*, partly on Plautus' *The Braggart Warrior*. Ariosto's *I Suppositi*, and imitations such as Gascoigne's *Supposes* are indebted to *The Eunuch* and to Plautus' *The Captives*.

THE EUNUCH

(SCENE:—*A street in Athens in front of the houses of* THAIS *and* LACHES.)

Prologue

OUR poet wishes his name to be enrolled among those writers who make it their object to please as many good people and hurt the feelings of as few as possible. If any writer[4] thinks that he has been harshly spoken of by our poet, he ought to consider that the words were an answer to him, not an attack upon him, because he began the strife. It is he who by translating well but writing badly has made feeble Latin plays out of good Greek ones. Of late he has put upon the stage Menander's *The Phantom,* and in *The Treasure* makes the defendant who has got the money show cause why it should be his own, before the claimant has set forth why it belongs to him, and how it found its way into his father's tomb. Now, for the future, that he may not deceive himself, or think "I have got rid of him, there is nothing that he can say to me," I warn him to behave himself and plague me no more. I have many more things to tell about him, which I will spare him now, but which shall be brought out hereafter if he goes on attacking me as he has begun to do.

As for the play which we are now about to act, Menander's *The Eunuch,* after the aediles had bought it, he got permission to read it. When it was being rehearsed in the presence of the magistrates, he cried out, "It is a thief, not a poet, that has written this play, but he has not deceived me for all that." He said that there was an old play, *The Flatterer,* by Naevius and Plautus,[5] and that the characters of the parasite and the soldier were borrowed from it. If this is a crime, it was committed by the poet unwittingly, not because he intended to plagiarise. You may prove the truth of this for yourselves. *The Flatterer* is a play of Menander's; in it there is a flattering parasite and a swaggering soldier; he does not deny that he transferred these characters into his *The Eunuch* from the Greek play; but he utterly denies that, to his knowledge, they ever appeared before this day in Latin plays. If he may not use these characters, why should he be any more allowed to describe a slave running, or to put on the stage virtuous matrons, vicious courtesans, hungry parasites, swaggering soldiers, babies substituted, old

254

gentlemen tricked by their slaves, love, hatred or suspicion? In short, nothing is said now that has not been said before; you ought to reflect upon this, and pardon us new writers if we practise the same tricks as the old ones. Now pray make up your minds to listen in silence, that you may learn the meaning of *The Eunuch*.

Act One.   Scene I

(*Enter* PHAEDRIA *and* PARMENO.)

PHAEDRIA: What shall I do, then? Shall I not go? Not even now, when she specially sends for me? Or shall I rather make up my mind not to stand the insolent airs of courtesans? She once closed her door against me; now she calls me back; shall I return to her? No, not if she were to beg me on her knees.

PARMENO: If you can do it, there is no better or manlier course; but if you begin it and don't go through with it to the end; if, when you can bear it no longer, you go back to her of your own accord, when nobody asks you, without having made up your quarrel, showing that you love her and can't do without her; why then all's lost; you're done for and ruined; she'll laugh at you when she sees that you're her own. So, master, while you have time, think of this over and over again; you cannot manage according to rule a thing that has no rule or bounds. Love carries with it reproaches, suspicions, quarrels, truces, war, and then peace again; you can no more manage such an uncertain business on any fixed plan than you can give your mind to going mad according to regular rules. And as for what you are thinking about now in your anger, "I go to her who has preferred him?—who has turned me out, who has not let me in? Not I; I would die rather; she shall see what sort of a man I am"—well, with one little bit of a tear that she will scarce be able to squeeze out of her eyes, she will quench all this fine talk, and reproach you, and you'll be at her mercy.

PHAEDRIA: Oh, shame! Now I see how wicked she is, and how wretched I am, and I am disgusted; and yet I love her dearly, and am rushing on my fate with my eyes open, and all my wits about me, but yet I don't know what to do.

PARMENO: What to do? What but redeem yourself from captivity for as small a ransom as possible? If you can't do it cheaply, then do it at what price you can, and don't trouble yourself.

PHAEDRIA: Is that your advice?

PARMENO: If you are wise, you won't bring any troubles upon yourself beyond those that necessarily accompany love, and those you'll bear in a proper spirit. But see, here she comes herself, the ruin of my estate, for she intercepts the revenue which ought to come to us.

Act One. Scene II

(Enter THAIS *from her house.)*

THAIS *(to herself)*: Unhappy that I am; I fear Phaedria may have taken too much to heart his being shut out yesterday, and put a wrong meaning on my action.

PHAEDRIA *(aside to* PARMENO*)*: Parmeno, I am all quivering and shaking at the sight of her.

PARMENO *(aside to* PHAEDRIA*)*: Never fear; go near this fire, and you will soon be warmer than you need to be.

THAIS: Who's that talking? Oh, are you here, my dear Phaedria? Why did you stand here? Why didn't you come straight into the house?

PARMENO *(aside to* PHAEDRIA*)*: But not a word about shutting her door against you.

THAIS: Why don't you speak?

PHAEDRIA *(ironically)*: Oh, because of course this door is always open to me, and I am your favoured lover.

THAIS: Oh, never mind that.

PHAEDRIA: Never mind! Ah, Thais, Thais! Would that my share of love was the same as yours, that it was equally divided between us, so that either you might be as deeply hurt by this as I am, or else that I might care as little as you do about what you have done.

THAIS: My love, my Phaedria, pray don't worry yourself. I assure you I didn't do it because I love anyone more than yourself, but as the case stood, it had to be done.

PARMENO *(ironically)*: I suppose, as usual, it was because you were so deeply in love with him that you shut him out of doors.

THAIS: Is this the way you deal with me, Parmeno? (*To* PHAEDRIA) But come, listen to why I had you sent for.

PHAEDRIA: Very well.

THAIS: First of all, tell me, can this fellow hold his tongue?

PARMENO: What, I? Excellently well. But mark you, I give you my word to keep your secret on one condition only: I keep silence capitally about everything I hear that is true; but as for what is false, unreal, or made up, that must come out straightway. I am full of leaks, I overflow in every direction. So if you want silence to be kept, tell the truth.

THAIS: My mother was a Samian; she dwelt at Rhodes.

PARMENO: I can hold my tongue about that.

THAIS: At Rhodes a slave-dealer made her a present of a little girl who had been kidnapped from Athens here.

PHAEDRIA: A citizen?

THAIS: I imagine so. We don't know for certain. She told us the names of her father and mother, but as to her country, or any other tokens, she knew nothing, nor could she by reason of her age. The slave-dealer added, that he had been told by the pirates from whom he bought her, that she had been carried off from Sunium.[6] My mother, when she received her, straightway took pains to teach her and bring her up just as though she had been her own daughter; most people believed that she was my sister. Now I came off to this place with the stranger who was then my only lover, who left me all the property that I have.

PARMENO: Both of these stories are false; it will leak out.

THAIS: Why so?

PARMENO: Because you were not satisfied with one lover, and he did not give you all your property, for Phaedria here has given you a good big share of it.

THAIS: True; but let me bring my story to the point that I wish. The officer, my lover, went to Caria; during his absence, I made your acquaintance. You yourself know how dear a friend you have been to me since then, and how I confide all my plans to you.

PHAEDRIA: Parmeno won't keep this secret either.

PARMENO: Oh! Can there be any doubt about that?

THAIS: Now attend, please. My mother has lately died at Rhodes; her brother is rather greedier of gain than he ought to be. When he saw how nice-looking the girl was, and how well she could play the lute, thinking to make money out of her, he straightway sent her to the slave-market and sold her. By great good luck, this friend of mine was there; he bought her as a present for me, knowing nothing whatever about this story. He came back. Then, since he has found out that I was carrying on with you as well as himself, he keeps on making excuses for not giving her to me. He says that he would give her to me if he felt certain that I should prefer him to you, and did not fear that, when I got her, I should throw him over; but that this is what he fears. However, what I suspect is, that he himself has taken a fancy to the girl.

PHAEDRIA: Has it gone any further?

THAIS: No, for I have made enquiries. Now, my dear Phaedria, I have many reasons for wishing to get her away from him. First of all, because she used to pass for my sister, and then because I want to restore and give her back to her own people. I am a lone woman; I have neither friend nor kinsman here; so, Phaedria, I want to win some friends for myself by doing them a good turn. Now, I beg you, help me to accomplish this more easily. Let the captain be first in favour with me for the next few days. What! No answer?

PHAEDRIA: Wretch! What answer can I give, when you behave as you are doing?

PARMENO: Well done our side! I approve. He's been roused at last. (*To* PHAEDRIA) You're a man.

PHAEDRIA: I didn't know what you were driving at. "A little girl was stolen from Attica; your mother brought her up as her own child; she was called your sister; you want to get her away from him to give her back to her people." Well, the long and the short of all this story is, that I am shut out and he is let in. Why? The only answer is, because you love him better than you love me, and you are afraid of this girl that he has brought, lest she should rob you of such a lover.

THAIS: I afraid of that?

PHAEDRIA: Why, what else should you be anxious about? Answer me that. Is he the only one who makes you presents? Have you ever found me stingy to you? When you said that you wanted a slave-girl from Ethiopia, did I not neglect everything else to find one for you? Then you said that you wanted a eunuch, because only princesses were served by them; well, I've found one; I paid twenty minae yesterday for the pair of them. I didn't forget, in spite of your ill-usage of me, and now that I have done this you flout me.

THAIS: Well, well, Phaedria, although I do want to get her away from him, and think that this is the best way to manage it; still, rather than quarrel with you, I will do as you bid me.

PHAEDRIA: Oh, I would that you spoke from your heart and truly when you said, "rather than quarrel with you"; if I could believe that you were sincere in saying so, I could endure anything.

PARMENO (*aside*): How soon he gives in; one word's enough to conquer him.

THAIS: Unhappy that I am, as if I was not sincere! What did you ever ask of me, even in jest, without getting it? And can I not win this favour from you, that you should grant me just these two days?

PHAEDRIA: If it were two days only; but I am afraid it may be twenty days.

THAIS: Really not more than two days, or—

PHAEDRIA: I've nothing to do with "or."

THAIS: It shan't be more; only give me your consent to this.

PHAEDRIA: I suppose I must do what you want.

THAIS: You deserve my love; you are behaving well.

PHAEDRIA: I'll go into the country, and there do penance for two days. I am determined; Thais must be humoured. Parmeno, see that those slaves are brought here to her.

PARMENO: Very well. (PARMENO *goes into* LACHES' *house.*)

PHAEDRIA: Farewell, my Thais, for these next two days.

THAIS: And you too, my Phaedria, fare you well. Have you anything else to say to me?

PHAEDRIA: Anything else to say to you? Yes; mind that when with the captain in body, you be absent from him in spirit; that both by day and by night you love me, long for me, dream of me, wait for me, think of me, hope for me, have all your pleasure in me, be altogether mine; in short, give me all your heart, as mine is all yours. (PHAEDRIA *embraces her and goes into his father's house.*)

THAIS (*to herself*): Unhappy that I am, I suppose he doesn't put much faith in me, and judges of me from other women; but from my conscience I can truly say that I have told Phaedria no falsehood, and that there is no man dearer to my heart than he. Whatever I have done has been done for this girl's sake; for I hope that I have all but found her brother, a youth of very noble family; he has made an appointment to call on me this day. I'll go into the house and wait till he comes. (*She goes inside.*)

Act Two.   Scene I

(*Enter* PHAEDRIA *from his father's house, accompanied by* PARMENO.)

PHAEDRIA: Mind you see about taking these two slaves to her, as I have ordered you.

PARMENO: Yes, sir.

PHAEDRIA: And be careful how you do it.

PARMENO: Yes, sir.

PHAEDRIA: And do it quickly.

PARMENO: Yes, sir.

PHAEDRIA: Now, do you think that what I have ordered you to do is enough?

PARMENO: What a question! As if there were any difficulty about doing it. Oh, Phaedria, I wish you could earn something as easily as you will throw away this present!

PHAEDRIA: Well, I am throwing away myself with them, which I value more. Don't fret about that.

PARMENO: Not at all; I'll carry out your orders. Have you any further commands?

PHAEDRIA: Yes; set off my present with the prettiest speeches that you can muster, and do your best to drive away my rival from her.

PARMENO: Oh, I can remember that, whether you remind me or not.

PHAEDRIA: I'm going into the country, and there I will remain.

PARMENO: I should advise you to do so.

PHAEDRIA: But I say!

PARMENO: What do you want?

PHAEDRIA: Do you think I can endure and hold out without coming back during that time?

PARMENO: You? No, by heavens, I don't believe that you can, for you will either come back as soon as you get there, or else a sleepless night will soon drive you back.

PHAEDRIA: I'll do hard work, and make myself so tired that I shan't be able to help sleeping.

PARMENO: You'll lie awake tired; that's all you'll gain.

PHAEDRIA: Oh, you're wrong, Parmeno. I must conquer this weakness of mind; I indulge myself too much. As if I couldn't do without her, if need be, even for three whole days?

PARMENO: What! Three whole days? Take care what you are doing.

PHAEDRIA: My mind is made up. (PHAEDRIA *departs*.)

PARMENO (*to himself*): Good heavens, what a distemper this is! To think that men should be so altered by love that you wouldn't know them for the same! Why, once he was the least foolish, the most austere and continent of men. (*Looking down the street*) But who's this côming this way? Why, it's Gnatho, the officer's toady. He's bringing the girl with him for a present to her. By Jove, she's a beauty! I shall be much surprised if I don't cut a sorry figure today with this broken-down eunuch of mine. This girl surpasses Thais herself in beauty.

Act Two. Scene II

(*Enter* GNATHO *with* PAMPHILA *and a maid*.)

GNATHO (*to himself*): Immortal gods, how superior one man is to another! What a difference there is between a wise man and a fool! This thought came into my mind because, as I was coming here, I met a man of my own station in life, a very decent fellow, who had run through his inheritance, like myself. I saw him looking untidy, shabby, sickly, ragged, and aged. "What sort of a get-up do you call that?" said I. He answered, "See to what I have come, poor devil that I am; all my friends and acquaintances have deserted me, because I have lost all my property." Hearing this, I scorned him, comparing him with myself. "What," says I, "you helpless creature, have you wrecked yourself so utterly, that you have no resources left in yourself? Have you lost your wits as well as your property? Look at me; I started from the same condition as you. See how rosy I am, how smart, well-dressed and in good condition! I own nothing, yet I have everything; I am a pauper, and yet want for nothing." "But," says he, "I cannot play the fool, or stand being knocked about." "What!" says I, "do you think that is how it is done? You are altogether mistaken. In the days of old one could make a living in that fashion, but the modern method is different; I, indeed, was its inventor. There is a class of men who want to be first in every walk of life, but who are not. These are the people to whom I attach myself. I don't lay myself out to make them laugh at me, but I am the first to laugh at them, and express my admiration of their wit. Whatever they say, I applaud; if afterwards they say the exact opposite, I applaud that too. If the man says 'no,' I say 'no'; if he says 'yes,' I say 'yes'—in short, I have made it my rule to agree with whatever he says, and I make a very profitable business of it."

PARMENO (*aside*): A smart fellow, by Jove! He would turn mere fools into utter madmen.

GNATHO: While talking thus, we came to where the shops are. All the confectioners ran delightedly to meet me, and all the fishmongers, butchers, cooks, sausage-makers, and fishermen, whom I had been of use to, both when I had my own property and after I had lost it. I often do them a good turn now. They all wished me good day, asked me to dinner, and said how pleased they were at my coming. When that poor starveling saw the respect with which I was treated, how easily I gained my living, he began to entreat me to let him learn this profession from me. I bade him follow me. It may be that parasites will henceforth be called Gnathonians, just as the disciples of philosophers are called after the names of their masters.

PARMENO (*aside*): See what effect ease and eating other people's dinners have upon a man!

GNATHO: But I must take this girl over to Thais and ask her to come to dinner. Oh, here's Parmeno, our rival's slave, at Thais' door; he looks down in the mouth; that's all right; I expect these people are left out in the cold. Now I mean to amuse myself with this scoundrel.

PARMENO (*aside*): They think to make Thais their own with this present of theirs.

GNATHO: Gnatho's best compliments to his good friend Parmeno; what are you about?

PARMENO: I'm standing still.

GNATHO: So I perceive. Pray do you see anything that you don't like?

PARMENO: Yes, I see you.

GNATHO: I believe it; but isn't there anything else?

PARMENO: Why should there be?

GNATHO: Because you look glum.

PARMENO: Oh, it's nothing.

GNATHO: Well, don't be so. What do you think of this piece of goods? (*Pointing to* PAMPHILA.)

PARMENO: Pretty well, confound it!

GNATHO (*aside*): I'm stirring his bile.

PARMENO (*aside*): How mistaken he is!

GNATHO: How do you think Thais will like this present?

PARMENO: What you mean is, that this door is now closed against us; well, it's a long lane that has no turning.[7]

GNATHO: Parmeno, I'll give you a rest for the next six months; you'll have no running backwards and forwards, and sitting up waiting till daylight. Isn't that a blessing for me to bestow upon you?

PARMENO: On me? Wonderful!

GNATHO: That's the way I always treat my friends.

PARMENO: It's very good of you.

GNATHO: I'm detaining you; perhaps you were going somewhere else?

PARMENO: No.

GNATHO: Then do me a trifling service; gain me admittance to the lady.

PARMENO: Go on with you; her door is open to you now, because you are bringing her this girl.

GNATHO: There isn't anybody that you would like me to call out of the house to you? (GNATHO *takes* PAMPHILA *and the maid into* THAIS' *house.*)

PARMENO: Wait another two days, and I'll make you kick for hours at this door in vain, though you are now in luck, and can open it with your little finger.

(*Re-enter* GNATHO.)

GNATHO: What, still here, Parmeno? Pray have you been left on guard to see that no messenger pass on the sly between her and the captain?

PARMENO: How witty! (*To himself, as* GNATHO *departs*) It's a wonder what the officer can see in him. But I see my master's younger son coming this way. I wonder how he has got away from Piraeus, for he is on guard there now.[8] There's something important the matter, and he's coming in haste; and he's looking round him for something or other.

Act Two.　Scene III

(*Enter* CHAEREA *in great haste.*)

CHAEREA (*to himself*): Confusion! the girl's nowhere, and I'm nowhere, now that I've let her out of my sight. I don't know where I shall seek her, where I shall search for her, whom I shall ask about her, which way I shall go. I have this one hope, that, wherever she is, she cannot long remain hid. Oh, what a beautiful face! From henceforth I wipe all other women out of my memory. I am weary of your commonplace beauties.

PARMENO (*aside*): Why, there's the other of them talking some nonsense about love. Poor old gentleman! If this one once begins, you'll call his brother's doings mere child's play compared with what he will do in his madness.

CHAEREA: May all the gods and goddesses confound the dotard who hindered me today, and me too for stopping for him; especially as I don't care a straw about him. But there's Parmeno. Good day, Parmeno.

PARMENO: Why so troubled and excited? Where do you come from?

CHAEREA: I? Oh, I don't know either where I'm coming from or where I am going, I have so utterly forgotten myself.

PARMENO: Why, pray?

CHAEREA: I'm in love.

PARMENO: H'm!

CHAEREA: Now, Parmeno, is the time for you to prove your worth. You know you often promised me, "Chaerea, find out something to set your heart on; then I'll show you how useful I can be to you." That was when I used to carry all my father's larder into your cell on the sly.

PARMENO: Go away, you silly!

CHAEREA: You did, by Jove! Now, pray, fulfil your promise, if you think it a worthy subject for you to employ all your strength upon. This girl isn't like our girls, whose mothers try to make them sloping-shouldered, and tight-laced, that they may look slender. If a girl is a trifle plump, they say that she's a prize-fighter, and put her on short rations. However well nature may have shaped them, by this treatment their mothers make them like laths; and that's why people fall in love with them.

PARMENO: And what's this girl of yours like?

CHAEREA: Oh, quite a new style of face.

PARMENO: Amazing!

CHAEREA: Natural complexion, strong and healthy.

PARMENO: What age?

CHAEREA: Age? Sixteen.

PARMENO: The very flower of youth.

CHAEREA: Now you must either by force or fraud or entreaty make her mine; I don't care a straw how, so long as I have her.

PARMENO: Well, whom does this girl belong to?

CHAEREA: Indeed, I don't know.

PARMENO: Where does she come from?

CHAEREA: That I don't know.

PARMENO: Where does she live?

CHAEREA: Nor that either.

PARMENO: Where did you see her?

CHAEREA: In the street.

PARMENO: How did you lose her?

CHAEREA: That's what I was cursing myself about as I came along just now; and I don't believe there's such another unlucky fellow in all the world. Oh, what a misfortune! I'm undone.

PARMENO: What happened?

CHAEREA: Do you ask? You know my father's relative and crony, Archidemides?

PARMENO: Of course I do.

CHAEREA: While I was following the girl he met me.

PARMENO: Very inconvenient, certainly.

CHAEREA: Nay, disastrous, Parmeno; inconvenient is no word for it. I am prepared to swear that I haven't seen him for the last six months, except today, just when I wanted it least and had least need of him. Tell me, isn't it something monstrous; what do you say?

PARMENO: Certainly.

CHAEREA: Straightway he runs up to me, but so slowly, bent double, shaky, loose-lipped, and groaning. "Here, here," says he, "Chaerea, it's you I'm speaking to." I stopped. "Do you know what I wanted you for?" says he. "No," says I, "tell me." "I've got a trial on tomorrow," says he. "What then?" says I. "Mind and tell your father not to forget to come early as a witness on my side." While he was saying this, a whole hour passed. I asked him if that was all. "All right," says he. Off I go. When I look this way after the girl, she in the meantime had just turned quietly down here into our street.

PARMENO (*aside*): It's a wonder if he doesn't mean the girl who has just been presented to Thais.

CHAEREA: When I get here, no signs of her.

PARMENO: I suppose the girl had some attendants with her?

CHAEREA: True; a parasite and a maidservant.

PARMENO: The very one. No more; leave off; all's over.

CHAEREA: You are talking about something else.

PARMENO: Nay, I'm talking about this very thing.

CHAEREA: Do you know who she is? Tell me. Have you seen her?

PARMENO: I have seen her; I know her; I know where she's been taken.

CHAEREA: What, my dear Parmeno, you know her, and know where she is?

PARMENO: She was brought to this house, to Thais, the courtesan; she was given her for a present.

CHAEREA: Who is so important a person as to be able to give such presents?

PARMENO: Thraso the soldier, Phaedria's rival.

CHAEREA: It will be hard for my brother to hold his own against him, to judge from what you say.

PARMENO: Well, if you knew what present Phaedria sends to compare with this one, you'd be more inclined to say so.

CHAEREA: And what in the world is it?

PARMENO: A eunuch.

CHAEREA: What, that ugly old thing of no sex that he bought yesterday?

PARMENO: The very one.

CHAEREA: He'll certainly be kicked out of doors, present and all. But I didn't know that Thais was our neighbour.

PARMENO: She hasn't been so long.

CHAEREA: Gracious, to think that I've never even seen her! Tell me, now, is she as good-looking as they say?

PARMENO: Oh, yes.

CHAEREA: But nothing to my girl here.

PARMENO: That's another matter.

CHAEREA: Parmeno, I pray and beseech you, help me to possess her.

PARMENO: I'll do my utmost, I'll put my mind to it, and help you. Have you any other commands?

CHAEREA: Where are you going now?

PARMENO: Home; to take these slaves to Thais, as your brother ordered me.

CHAEREA: O lucky eunuch, whose lot it is to be given to this house!

PARMENO: Why so?

CHAEREA: Don't you know why? He will continually see the beauty, his fellow slave, in this house; he will speak to her, be under one roof with her; sometimes he will take his meals with her; sometimes he will sleep near her.

PARMENO: What if you yourself became that fortunate being?

CHAEREA: How, Parmeno? Tell me.

PARMENO: You might take his dress.

CHAEREA: His dress; and what then?

PARMENO: I will take you there instead of him.

CHAEREA: I hear.

PARMENO: I'll say that you are he.

CHAEREA: I understand.

PARMENO: You may enjoy those advantages of which you spoke just now; you may eat with her, be with her, touch her, toy with her, sleep near her, seeing that none of these women know you by sight or have heard who you are. Besides, you are just of the very look and age to pass easily for a eunuch.

CHAEREA: A splendid scheme! I never had better advice given me. Come, let's go indoors straight. Dress me up and take me over as soon as you can.

PARMENO: What are you doing? I was only joking.

CHAEREA: Nonsense! (*He pushes* PARMENO *towards the door.*)

PARMENO (*aside*): I'm lost! What have I done, unhappy wretch that I am? (*To* CHAEREA) Where are you shoving me to? You'll throw me down. Stop, I tell you!

CHAEREA: Come along!

PARMENO: Are you going to do it?

CHAEREA: I'm determined.

PARMENO: But just consider whether it isn't too mad a prank.

CHAEREA: No, it isn't at all; let me do it.

PARMENO: But the punishment of it will fall on me.[9]

CHAEREA: Will it?

PARMENO: What we are doing is an outrage.

CHAEREA: Is it an outrage for me to be taken into a courtesan's house? To pay out those pests who despise us and our youth, and always plague us in every way? For me to cheat them, even as they cheat us? Do you think that it's more proper for me to play tricks upon my father? Everybody who heard of my doing that would blame me; but everybody would say that I had served the woman right.

PARMENO: Well, well, if you are determined to do it, you must; but don't lay the blame on me afterwards.

CHAEREA: I won't.

PARMENO: Well, do you bid me do it?

CHAEREA: Bid you? I compel and command you. I will never shirk the responsibility.

PARMENO: Follow me, and may heaven get us well out of this adventure. (*They go into* LACHES' *house. A few minutes are supposed to elapse before the next Act.*)

Act Three.   Scene I

(*Enter* THRASO *and* GNATHO.)

THRASO: Did you say that Thais was much obliged to me?

GNATHO: Enormously.

THRASO: Say, was she pleased?

GNATHO: Yes; not so much at the present as at *your* having given it to her; that is a real triumph for her.

(*Enter* PARMENO *from* LACHES' *house, unseen by the others.*)

PARMENO (*to himself*): I'm here on the lookout for a good opportunity to take them over; but here's the captain.

THRASO: I have this especial gift—that everything that I do wins favour for me.

GNATHO: Indeed, I have observed that.

THRASO: Even the king always thanked me heartily for whatever I did; he didn't do that to anyone else.

GNATHO: A clever man like you can often appropriate to himself by speech the glory which others have won by laborious action.

THRASO: You have hit it.

GNATHO: So the king, I suppose, always kept you—

THRASO: Of course.

GNATHO: Before his eyes.

THRASO: I should think so; he entrusted his entire army to me, and all his plans.

GNATHO: Wonderful!

THRASO: Then, whenever he became sick of men or weary of business of State; when he wanted a holiday, don't you know—

GNATHO: I understand; when he wanted, as it were, to cast away all his cares.

THRASO: Exactly; then he used to take me with him as his only guest.

GNATHO: Dear me! By your account, the king must be a man of taste.

THRASO: That's the sort of man that he is; he doesn't care for much company.

GNATHO (*aside*): Not for any at all, I should think, if he lived with you.

THRASO: All were jealous of me and secretly carped at me; I didn't care a straw. They were all wretchedly jealous; but one of them in particular, he who had charge of the Indian elephants. When he made himself unusually offensive, I said to him, "Pray, Strato, are you fierce because you are keeper of the wild beasts?"

GNATHO: Gad, a clever and a wise saying—wonderful! You shut him up. What did he say?

THRASO: He was struck dumb.

GNATHO: Of course, he would be.

PARMENO (*aside*): Good heavens! What a wretched, hopeless brute; and what a scoundrel the other is, too!

THRASO: But, Gnatho, the way that I scored off that Rhodian[10] at the wine party! Didn't I ever tell you?

GNATHO: Never; but pray tell it me. (*Aside*) I have heard it a thousand times.

THRASO: Once, at a party, I met this young man from Rhodes that I told you of. I happened to have a harlot with me; he began to make allusions and chaff me. "Look here," says I, "you impudence! Do you go hunting for game, when you're a hare yourself?" [11]

GNATHO: Ha, ha, ha!

THRASO: What's the matter?

GNATHO: Very clever, very neat, capital, quite unsurpassed! May I ask, was that joke your own? I thought it was an old one.

THRASO: Why, had you heard it before?

GNATHO: Often, and it was thought a most excellent one.

THRASO: It's my own.

GNATHO: But I'm rather sorry that you said that to an innocent young gentleman.

PARMENO (*aside*): You be damned!

GNATHO: Pray, what did he do?

THRASO: He was struck all of a heap; all the company were in fits of laughter; and the end of it was that they all were afraid of me.

GNATHO: No wonder.

THRASO: But come, now, am I to prove myself innocent to Thais about that girl, because she suspects me of being in love with her?

GNATHO: Not at all; rather make her suspect you more.

THRASO: Why?

GNATHO: Do you ask why? Don't you know how she makes you suffer whenever she mentions Phaedria, or praises him?

THRASO: I do feel it.

GNATHO: Well, this is your only remedy for that. When she names Phaedria, you straightway speak of Pamphila. If she says, "Let's ask Phaedria to dine with us," say, "Let's send for Pamphila to sing to us"; if she praises his looks, you praise hers; in fact, give her tit for tat, and make her jealous in her turn.

THRASO: That would do well if she were in love with me, Gnatho.

GNATHO: Since she looks out for and loves the presents that you make her, she has long been in love with you; you have long been easily able to vex her, for she is always afraid that you may in a passion transfer to some one else what she now reaps the benefit of.

THRASO: Well argued; now I had never thought of that!

GNATHO: Nonsense! You never thought about it! But how much better you would have put it if you had, Thraso!

Act Three.   Scene II

(*Enter* THAIS *and* PYTHIAS *from the former's house.*)

THAIS: I thought just now that I heard the captain's voice. And there he is. Welcome, my dear Thraso!

THRASO: Ah! My Thais, my sweet, how goes it? Were you pleased with me for giving you that lute-player?

PARMENO (*aside*): What manners! To talk of his present as soon as he arrives!

THAIS: Many thanks to you.

GNATHO: Then let's to dinner; why do you stand still?

PARMENO (*aside*): And there's the other one. Would you call him human?

THRASO: When you please, I am ready.

PARMENO (*aside*): I'll go to them and pretend that I have only just come out. (*Aloud*) Are you going anywhere, Thais?

THAIS: Oh, Parmeno! I'm glad to see you. I was just going—

PARMENO: Where?

THAIS (*aside*): What! Don't you see him there?

PARMENO (*aside*): Yes, I see him, and he disgusts me. Phaedria's presents are ready for you whenever you please.

THRASO: What are we stopping here for? Why don't we go away?

PARMENO: By your leave, I beg permission to give Thais the presents we have for her, and to have a few minutes' conversation with her.

THRASO (*with sarcasm*): I warrant they are mighty fine presents, doubtless as good as mine.

PARMENO: The event will show. Ho, there! (*To slaves within*) Bid those that I ordered to come out of the house straightway. (*Enter a black maidservant and* CHAEREA *in disguise*) Come this way, lassie. This girl comes all the way from Aethiopia.

THRASO: Three minae for that lot.

GNATHO: Scarce that.

PARMENO (*to* CHAEREA): Where are you, Dorus? Come here. There's a eunuch for you! See how good-looking, how young he is!

THAIS: Upon my word, he is handsome.

PARMENO: What say you, Gnatho? Have you any fault to find with him? What say you, Thraso? They say nothing; that is great praise. (*To* THAIS) Examine him in literature, in gymnastics, in music; I'll warrant him well skilled in all that a well-born young gentleman ought to know.

THRASO (*aside to* GNATHO): I could fancy that eunuch, even when I was sober.

PARMENO: And he who sent them does not expect you to live only for himself, and to shut your doors against everybody else to please him. He doesn't bore you with his battles or show you his scars, or hinder you, as a certain person does; but he is satisfied to be admitted when he is not in your way, when you wish for him, when you have time to spare for him.

THRASO: This slave seems to belong to a poor and shabby master.

GNATHO: Yes, by Jove! I am quite sure that nobody who could afford to buy another one would put up with him.

PARMENO (*to* GNATHO): Hold your tongue! I count you lower than the lowest of mankind; for if you can bring yourself to be this fellow's toady, I believe that you would be capable of snatching food from funeral pyres.

THRASO: Isn't it time for us to be going?

THAIS: I want to take these people into the house first, and at the same time I'll give some orders; I'll come out directly after that. (THAIS *goes into her house with* PYTHIAS, CHAEREA, *and the black maidservant.*)

THRASO (*to* GNATHO): I'm going; you wait here for her.

PARMENO: It is not seemly for a field-marshal to walk along the street with his mistress.

THRASO: Why should I waste words on you? You're just like your master. (PARMENO *departs.*)

GNATHO: Ha, ha, ha!

THRASO: What are you laughing at?

GNATHO: At what you said just now; and when that story about the Rhodian comes into my head. But here is Thais coming out.

(*Enter* THAIS *with* PYTHIAS *and attendants.*)

THRASO: Go on ahead, and see that all is ready at home.

GNATHO: I will. (GNATHO *departs.*)

THAIS: Now, Pythias, if Chremes should come here, mind you beg him to wait; if that doesn't suit him, ask him to call again if possible; if he can't wait, bring him to me.

PYTHIAS: I will.

THAIS: Well, and what else was there that I wanted to say to you? Oh, yes; take good care of that young lady, and mind you all stay at home. (PYTHIAS *goes inside.*)

THRASO: Let's be going.

THAIS (*to her maids*): Follow me. (THAIS *departs with* THRASO; *her maids follow.*)

Act Three.   Scene III

(*Enter* CHREMES.)

CHREMES (*to himself*): Indeed, the more I keep on thinking of it, the more convinced I am this Thais will do me some great mischief; I see that she's been cleverly plotting my ruin from the very first time she sent for me. If anybody should ask me, "What have you to do with her?" why, I didn't even know her. When I came to see her, she found an excuse for detaining me. She said she had been sacrificing, and that she wanted to talk to me on serious business; even then I suspected that she was doing all this with some evil purpose. She sat down at table with me, made herself agreeable to me, tried to get up a conversation. When it began to flag, she came to asking me how long my father and mother had been dead. I told her, "ever so long." She asked whether I had a farm at Sunium, and how far it was from the sea. I believe that she has taken a fancy to it, and hopes to get it out of me. And last of all, she asked whether a little sister of mine had been lost from there; whether anyone was with her; what she had about her when she was lost; whether anybody could recognise her. What did she ask all these questions for? Unless, indeed, she means that she herself is the little girl who was lost. It would be like her audacity to say so; but the girl, if she lives, cannot be more than sixteen; whereas Thais is a bit older than I am. Now she has sent, earnestly inviting me to call again. She must either tell me what she wants, or leave off bothering me. I certainly won't come a third time. Here! Hi! (*Knocking*) Is anybody at home? I am Chremes.

(*Enter* PYTHIAS *from* THAIS' *house.*)

PYTHIAS: Oh, ducky! Just the man that we wanted.

CHREMES (*aside*): I said that they were laying a plot against me.

PYTHIAS: Thais begs you most earnestly to call tomorrow.

CHREMES: I am going out of town.

PYTHIAS: Oh, pray come.

CHREMES: Can't, I tell you.

PYTHIAS: Then wait in our house here until she comes back.

CHREMES: Certainly not.

PYTHIAS: Why not, Chremes dear?

CHREMES: Go to the devil with you.

PYTHIAS: Well, if you are determined not to wait, please come over to where she is.

CHREMES: I'll go there.

PYTHIAS (*to* DORIAS, *who now comes out of the house*): Off with you, Dorias, and lead the gentleman quickly to the captain's. (CHREMES *and* DORIAS *depart;* PYTHIAS *goes back into the house.*)

Act Three.   Scene IV

(Enter ANTIPHO *from the harbour.)*

ANTIPHO (*to himself*): Some of us young fellows met yesterday in Piraeus and arranged to club together for a dinner today. We appointed Chaerea to manage the business; our rings[12] were all given to him; the time and place agreed upon. Now the time is past, and nothing is ready at the appointed place. He himself is nowhere to be found, and I don't know what to say or what to guess. The others have given me the job of finding him, so I'll go and see whether he is at home. (*As* CHAEREA *appears in* THAIS' *door*) Who's this coming out of Thais' house? Is it he or is it not? The man himself. What sort of creature is this? What a dress! What the devil! I'm astounded; I can't guess what it's all about. But whatever it is, I'll stand here just at first, a little way off, and try to find out the meaning of it.

Act Three.   Scene V

(Enter CHAEREA, *peering about anxiously.)*

CHAEREA (*to himself*): Anyone here? Nobody! Anyone following me? Not a soul. May I now let my joy have vent? By Jupiter, I could let myself be put to death, for fear that some trouble in life should spoil this bliss. But why doesn't some inquisitive fellow meet me now, follow me wherever I go, and pester me and bore me with questions as to why I am in these transports, what I am pleased at, where I am going, where I come from, where I got this dress, what I am after, whether I'm in my right senses or no?

ANTIPHO (*aside*): I'll accost him, and do him the favour which I see he wants. (*Aloud*) Chaerea, what are you so overjoyed about? What's the meaning of this dress? Why so delighted? What's your game? Are you in your senses? Why do you stare at me? Why don't you speak?

CHAEREA: O day of joy! Welcome, my friend, there is no one whom I had rather see than you.

ANTIPHO: Please tell me what it's all about.

CHAEREA: Why, I beg you to listen to my tale. Do you know my brother's mistress, who lives here?

ANTIPHO: Yes; I suppose you mean Thais.

CHAEREA: Herself.

ANTIPHO: I thought it was.

CHAEREA: She has had a girl given her today as a present. I need not now tell you of her looks or praise them, Antipho; you know how critical I am on the subject of beauty. She made a conquest of me.

ANTIPHO: What's that you say?

CHAEREA: If you saw her, you'd say she was the loveliest of women. Well, in short, I fell in love with her. By great good luck there was a eunuch in our house whom my brother had bought as a present for Thais, but who hadn't yet been taken over to her. Parmeno, our slave, then dropped a hint, at which I caught.

ANTIPHO: What was it?

CHAEREA: You'll hear it quicker if you hold your tongue. It was that I should change clothes with the eunuch and bid Parmeno take me over there, instead of him.

ANTIPHO: Instead of the eunuch?

CHAEREA: Exactly.

ANTIPHO: And pray what were you to gain by that?

CHAEREA: What? Why, Antipho, I should see, hear, and be in the company of my love. Was that a slight reason or a bad argument for doing it? I was presented to the lady, who, directly she got me, took me gladly into her house and entrusted the girl to my care.

ANTIPHO: What? To your care?

CHAEREA: Yes; to mine.

ANTIPHO: To safe keeping, eh?

CHAEREA: She gave orders that no man should come near her and forbade me to leave her, but stay alone with her by ourselves in the inner part of the house. I said that I would, with eyes modestly cast down.

ANTIPHO (*sarcastically*): Poor wretch!

CHAEREA: Says she, "I'm going out to dinner"; she took her maids with her; a few raw slave girls stayed behind to wait on her, and straightway prepared her for a bath. I told them to be quick about it. While they were getting it ready, the girl sat in the room, looking up at a picture which showed how Jupiter came down into Danae's lap in a shower of gold. I too began to look at the picture, and was highly delighted at the thought of his once having played the same game, at the god having changed himself into a man and come down on to another man's tiles in a shower by stealth, to make a fool of a woman. And which of the gods did this? Why, he that rends the heavens with his thunder. And might not a mere mortal such as I do what he did? Nay, I did it, and with all my heart. While I was turning this over in my mind the girl was fetched away for her bath; she went, bathed, and came back, then the girls laid her on a sofa. As I stood waiting for orders, one of them came and said, "Here, Dorus, take this fan and fan her like this, while we go and bathe; when we have done you can bathe if you like." I took the fan sullenly.

ANTIPHO: Oh! I should have liked to have seen your impudent face and the figure you cut, as you stood holding the fan and looking such an ass.

CHAEREA: She had scarcely finished saying this, when they all ran out of the room to bathe, chattering, as servants do when their master is away. Meanwhile, the girl fell asleep. I kept peeping at her sidelong through the fan, like that; and at the same time I looked around to see if the coast was clear. I saw that it was, so I bolted the door.

ANTIPHO: And what then?

CHAEREA: What? What then? What a silly question!

ANTIPHO: It is.

CHAEREA: Was I going to lose such a chance, so brief, so eagerly longed for, so unhoped for, when it was offered? If I had, I should indeed have been what I pretended that I was.

ANTIPHO: True! But in the meantime, what has been done about our club dinner?

CHAEREA: All's ready.

ANTIPHO: Good man! Where, at your house?

CHAEREA: No, at the house of our freedman Discus.

ANTIPHO: It's a deuce of a way off.

CHAEREA: We'll walk all the faster.[13]

ANTIPHO: Then change your dress.

CHAEREA: Where can I change? Plague take it! I can't go home now, for I am afraid my brother may be in the house, or that my father may be back from the farm by now.

ANTIPHO: Come to my house, that's the nearest place where you can change.

CHAEREA: A good suggestion; let's go. And I should like to have your advice about how I am to get hold of that girl.

ANTIPHO: All right. (ANTIPHO *and* CHAEREA *depart.*)

Act Four. Scene I

(*Enter* DORIAS.)

DORIAS (*to herself*): Gracious heavens! From what I've seen of him, I'm dreadfully afraid that that madman will either make a riot or do Thais some hurt. When that young fellow Chremes, the girl's brother, came there, she asked the officer to invite him in; the officer straight-way became angry, and yet didn't dare to say "no." Then Thais kept on pressing him to ask the man in. She did this in order to keep him near her; for it was not yet a fitting time to tell him all that she wanted about his sister. Thraso invited him with a gloomy air; he stayed. Thais began to talk to him directly; then the officer thought that a rival had been brought before his very face, and tried to be dis-agreeable in his turn. "Boy," cries he, "fetch Pamphila here to play to us." Thais exclaimed, "Never! To think of bringing her to a wine party." The officer insisted, and then they quarrelled. Meanwhile, she quietly slipped off her jewelry and gave it to me to take home; which means, I know, that she herself will get away as soon as she can.

Act Four. Scene II

(*Enter* PHAEDRIA *from the country.*)

PHAEDRIA (*to himself*): On my way to our country seat I began, as people do who have any trouble on their minds, to meditate first on one thing and then on another, taking the worst view of all of them. Well, while thinking over this, I went past the farm without noticing it. I was a long way off when I found what I had done, and walked back discontented. When I came to the turning up to it, I stood still, and began to consider. "Now I've got to stay here two days without her. Well, what then? That's nothing. What? Nothing? Why, if I mayn't touch her, is that any reason I shouldn't see her? If I mayn't do the one, surely I may do the other. It is something to be one of her lovers, even as a rank outsider." I went past the farm on purpose. But what's the matter? Why is Pythias bouncing out like that in a fright?

Act Four.   Scene III

(*Enter* PYTHIAS *from the house, not seeing the others.*)

PYTHIAS: Unhappy me, where shall I find the wicked villain? Where shall I look for him? To think of his daring to commit such an audacious crime!

PHAEDRIA (*aside*): Good gracious! I dread what this news may be.

PYTHIAS: And to add insult to injury, the scoundrel, after ravishing the maid, has torn the poor thing's dress to pieces and pulled out her hair.

PHAEDRIA (*aside*): What's that?

PYTHIAS: I wish I'd got him now, I'd scratch the scamp's eyes out with my nails.

PHAEDRIA (*aside*): Something has certainly gone wrong in the house while I have been away. I'll go to her. (*Aloud*) What's the matter, Pythias, why are you hurrying? Whom are you looking for?

PYTHIAS: Ha, Phaedria! Whom am I looking for? Go to the devil where you deserve, you and your fine presents!

PHAEDRIA: What's the matter?

PYTHIAS: What's the matter? Why, see what a row the eunuch that you gave us has kicked up; he's raped the girl that the captain presented to my mistress.

PHAEDRIA: What do you say?

PYTHIAS: And I'm a lost woman. (*Sobs.*)

PHAEDRIA: You're drunk.

PYTHIAS: I wish my enemies were drunk in the same way.

DORIAS: Oh, gracious me! My dear Pythias, what's this monstrous thing?

PHAEDRIA: You're crazy; how could a eunuch do this?

PYTHIAS: I don't know who did it, the facts show what he has done; the girl is crying and is ashamed to say what's the matter when you ask her; our fine fellow is nowhere to be found, and to my sorrow I suspect he's taken something out of the house with him.

PHAEDRIA: Never was so surprised in my life! This dastard cannot have gone any distance off, except home. Perhaps he has gone back to us.

PYTHIAS: Pray see whether he has.

PHAEDRIA: I'll let you know directly. (*He goes into his father's house.*)

DORIAS: Good gracious! My dear, I never even heard of such a shocking thing.

PYTHIAS: My word, I've heard tell that they were excessively fond of women, but couldn't do anything. To my sorrow I never gave it a thought, or I'd have locked him up somewhere and not have given him the maid to take care of.

Act Four.   Scene IV

(*Re-enter* PHAEDRIA, *dragging* DORUS *in* CHAEREA'S *clothing.*)

PHAEDRIA (*to* DORUS): Come out, you scoundrel! What, won't you go, gallows bird? Forth with you, you bad bargain! (*Beats him.*)

DORUS: Oh, please don't.

PHAEDRIA: Just look what faces the murderer is making! What do you mean by coming back here? Why did you change your clothes? What have you got to say for yourself? If I had been a little later, Pythias, I shouldn't have found him in the house; he was just preparing to run away.

PYTHIAS: Pray, have you got the man?

PHAEDRIA: Of course I've got him.

PYTHIAS: That's fine.

DORIAS: A good job, indeed.

PYTHIAS: Where is he?

PHAEDRIA: Where is he? Why, can't you see him?

PYTHIAS: See! See whom?

PHAEDRIA: This fellow, of course.

PYTHIAS: Who's this?

PHAEDRIA: The man who was brought to you today.

PYTHIAS: Phaedria, none of us has ever set eyes on this man.

PHAEDRIA: No?

PYTHIAS: Why, did you believe that he had been brought over to us?

PHAEDRIA: Yes, for I had nobody else.

PYTHIAS: Oh, he's not to be compared to the other one; the other was handsome and gentlemanlike.

PHAEDRIA: He looked so before, because he was wearing gay clothing; now he looks ugly because he hasn't got it on.

PYTHIAS: Please be quiet; as if that were all the difference between them! A young man was brought to us this day, Phaedria, who was a pleasure to look upon; this is a withered, worn-out, flabby old man, with the complexion of a weasel.

PHAEDRIA: What tale is this? You're bringing me to such a pass that I don't myself know what I have done. Say, you fellow, didn't I buy you?

DORUS: You did.

PYTHIAS: Now bid him answer *me*.

PHAEDRIA: Put your question.

PYTHIAS (*to* DORUS): Did you come to our house today? (DORUS *shakes his head*) He says "no." But that other one came; he was about sixteen years old. Parmeno brought him.

PHAEDRIA (*to* DORUS): Now come, first of all, where did you get those clothes? No answer? You monster of iniquity, won't you tell me?

DORUS: Chaerea came.

PHAEDRIA: What, my brother?

DORUS: Yes.

PHAEDRIA: When?

DORUS: Today.

PHAEDRIA: How long ago?

DORUS: Just now.

PHAEDRIA: With whom?

DORUS: With Parmeno.

PHAEDRIA: Did you know him previously?

DORUS: No; nor had I ever heard anyone say who he was.

PHAEDRIA: Then how did you know that he was my brother?

DORUS: Parmeno said he was; he gave me these clothes.

PHAEDRIA: Oh, Lord!

DORUS: He put on mine; then they both went out together.

PYTHIAS: Now are you convinced that I'm not drunk, and that I've told you no lies? Are you convinced now that the girl has been raped?

PHAEDRIA: Come, come, you bitch; do you believe what this fellow says?

PYTHIAS: Why should I believe him? The thing speaks for itself.

PHAEDRIA (*to* DORUS): Come a little this way, do you hear? A little further; that will do. Now tell me again, did Chaerea take off your clothes?

DORUS: Yes.

PHAEDRIA: And put them on?

DORUS: Yes.

PHAEDRIA: And was brought here instead of you?

DORUS: Just so.

PHAEDRIA: Great Jove, what a daring scoundrel!

PYTHIAS: Oh, dear! Won't you even now believe that we have been shamefully insulted?

PHAEDRIA: No wonder that you believe what the fellow says. (*Aside*) I don't know what to do. (*Aside to* DORUS) Now, then, deny it all again. (*Aloud*) Can't I wring the truth out of you today? Did you see my brother Chaerea?

DORUS: No.

PHAEDRIA (*pretends to beat him*): I see; he won't tell the truth without being beaten. (*Aside to* DORUS) Follow me this way. (*Aloud*) First he says "yes," and then he says "no." (*Aside to* DORUS) Beg me to leave off.

DORUS: I entreat you, Phaedria!

PHAEDRIA (*kicking him*): Get you gone into the house.

DORUS: Ouch! (DORUS *goes into the house.*)

PHAEDRIA (*aside*): How else I'm to get creditably out of this I don't know. (*Aloud*) All's up if you too, you villain, play the fool with me here. (*Follows* DORUS *into the house.*)

PYTHIAS: As sure as I'm alive, this is some trick of Parmeno's.

DORIAS: That's it.

PYTHIAS: Upon my word, I'll find some way to pay him out for this today. But what do you think we had better do now, Dorias?

DORIAS: Do you mean about that girl?

PYTHIAS: Yes; should I tell the tale or hold my tongue?

DORIAS: If you are sensible, you won't know anything about it, either about the eunuch or about the girl being raped. In that way, you'll keep yourself clear of any bother, and you'll be doing her a service. Say merely that Dorus has gone.

PYTHIAS: That's what I'll do.

DORIAS: But isn't that Chremes? Thais will be here soon.

PYTHIAS: Why?

DORIAS: Because, when I was leaving, they had already begun to quarrel.

PYTHIAS: Take away this jewelry; I'll find out from him what's going on. (DORIAS *goes into* THAIS' *house.*)

Act Four.   Scene V

(Enter CHREMES, *somewhat tipsy.)*

CHREMES *(to himself)*: I say, they've made a fool of me; the wine that I've drunk has gone to my head. As long as I was at table, I thought I was as sober as a judge; since I've been on my legs, neither my feet nor my wits work properly.

PYTHIAS: Chremes!

CHREMES: Who's that? What, Pythias! Dear me, how much prettier you look now than you did before.

PYTHIAS: There's no mistake about your being much merrier than you were before.

CHREMES: The proverb's quite true, "Venus is a poor thing without Ceres and Bacchus." But did Thais get here much before me?

PYTHIAS: Has she already left the captain?

CHREMES: Long ago, an age ago. They quarrelled most bitterly.

PYTHIAS: Did she say anything about your following her?

CHREMES: Nothing more than a nod to me as she went away.

PYTHIAS: Well, wasn't that sufficient?

CHREMES: Why, I didn't know that was what she meant, until the captain supplied my want of wits by turning me out of the house. But there she is; I wonder how it was that I got here before her.

Act Four.   Scene VI

(Enter THAIS *with her maids.)*

THAIS *(to herself)*: I expect he will be here directly, to try to take her away from me; let him come. If he lays but one finger upon her, we'll scratch his eyes out straightway. I can stand his folly and his boastful talk as long as they are only words; but if they come to deeds, I'll make him smart for it.

CHREMES: Thais, I've been here ever so long.

THAIS: Oh, my dear Chremes, the very man that I was expecting. Do you know that all this quarrel has arisen about you? And that you are the mainspring of the whole of this business?

CHREMES: I am? Pray how's that?

THAIS: Because I have suffered this violence, and much more of the same sort, while striving to restore your sister to you.

CHREMES: Where's she?

THAIS: In my house at home.

CHREMES: Ho!

THAIS: What's the matter? She has been brought up as becomes both you and her.

CHREMES: What do you say?

THAIS: The truth. I give her to you, and I ask no money for her.

CHREMES: I thank you, Thais, and you shall be rewarded as you deserve.

THAIS: But now, Chremes, mind you don't lose her before you've got her from me, for it is she whom the captain is now coming to take away from me. Pythias, go and bring out the little box with the tokens.

CHREMES: Do you see the captain, Thais?

PYTHIAS: Where is the little box?

THAIS: In the chest; what are you loitering for, you hussy? (PYTHIAS *goes into the house.*)

CHREMES (*looking down the street*): What a large force he is bringing against you. Goodness me!

THAIS: My good man, do you feel at all frightened?

CHREMES: Go along with you! I frightened? No man living less so.

THAIS: That's the sort of man we want.

CHREMES: Why, I'm afraid you think me a coward.

THAIS: Why no, bear this in mind, the man we have to do with is a foreigner, less influential than you, less known, and has fewer friends here.

CHREMES: I know that, but it is silly to risk a danger that you can guard against. I had rather prevent his doing me an injury than have to revenge one upon him. You go into the house and lock the door, while I run over to the market place. I should like to have witnesses on our side in this fray.

THAIS: Stay here.

CHREMES: Mine's the better plan.

THAIS: Stay here.

CHREMES: Let me go, I'll be back directly.

THAIS: We don't want your friends, Chremes. All you have to say is that she is your sister, that you lost her as a little girl and now recognise her. (*Re-enter* PYTHIAS *with the tokens.*) (*To* PYTHIAS) Show him the proofs.

PYTHIAS: There they are.

THAIS: Take them. If he offers any violence, have the law on him; do you understand?

CHREMES: Quite.

THAIS: Now mind you keep your wits about you when you say this.

CHREMES: I will.

THAIS: Tuck up your cloak. (*Aside*) Oh, dear me! The man that I've put up to defend me needs somebody to defend him. (*All go into* THAIS' *house.*)

Act Four.   Scene VII

(*Enter* THRASO, *followed by* GNATHO, SANGA, *and other slaves, armed with household implements.*)

THRASO: That I should be so signally insulted, Gnatho! I'd rather die. Simalio, Donax, Syriscus, follow me. First I'll storm the house.

GNATHO: That's right.

THRASO: I'll carry off the maiden.

GNATHO: Admirable!

THRASO: I'll punish Thais severely.

GNATHO: Capital!

THRASO: Donax, the battering-ram party here, in the centre; Simalio, to the left wing; Syriscus, to the right. Bring on the rest; where's my lieutenant Sanga and his platoon of pickpockets?

SANGA: Here, sir. (*Holding up a sponge.*)

THRASO: What, lubber! Do you think you are going to fight with sponges, that you bring that thing with you?

SANGA: I? Why, I know the valour of my chief, and the might of his soldiers; I know that this affair must cost blood; what am I to staunch the wounds with?

THRASO: Where are the rest?

SANGA: What the deuce do you mean by "the rest"? Sannio's left at home alone.

THRASO (*to* GNATHO): Draw up these men in order of battle; I will take my post behind the front line, and issue orders to all from there.

GNATHO: That's true wisdom. (*Aside*) He's drawn these men up in front, and got a safe place for himself behind.

THRASO: This is how Pyrrhus[14] used to form his line.

(CHREMES *and* THAIS *appear at an upper window.*)

CHREMES: Do you see, Thais, what he's doing? I think I was right about locking the door.

THAIS: My good sir, this that you take for a brave man is a great coward; you needn't be afraid of him.

THRASO (to GNATHO): What do you think?

GNATHO: I wish you had a sling, that you might attack them from a distance in ambush; they'd be put to flight.

THRASO: But there I see Thais herself.

GNATHO: When shall we charge?

THRASO: Halt! A wise commander should try every expedient before coming to blows. How do you know that they won't do what I bid them without an appeal to arms?

GNATHO: Great heaven! What a thing it is to be so clever; I never come near you without going away a wiser man.

THRASO: First of all, Thais, answer me this. When I gave you that girl, didn't you say that you were to be mine for these next few days?

THAIS: Well, what then?

THRASO: What then? Why, you have paraded your lover before my very face.

THAIS (*to* CHREMES): What can you do with a fellow like that?

THRASO: And stole away from me with him.

THAIS: I chose to do so.

THRASO: Then give Pamphila back to me, unless you prefer to have her taken from you by force.

CHREMES: As if she would give Pamphila back to you, or you lay a finger upon her, you utter—

GNATHO: Oh, hush! What are you doing?

THRASO: What do you want? Am I not to touch my own property?

CHREMES: Your property, you convict?

GNATHO: Take care; you don't know what a man you are abusing.

CHREMES: Just you take yourself off. (*To* THRASO) Do you understand? If you make any disturbance here today, I'll make you remember me and this place as long as you live.

GNATHO: I pity you for making so great a man your enemy.

CHREMES: I'll break your head presently, if you're not off.

GNATHO: What, puppy, is this how you treat him?

THRASO: Who are you? What do you mean? What have you to do with her?

CHREMES: I'll tell you. In the first place, I declare that she is a freewoman.

THRASO: Eh!

CHREMES: A citizen of Athens.

THRASO: Bah!

CHREMES: And my own sister.

THRASO: Brazen liar!

CHREMES: So now, master captain, I warn you to do her no violence. Thais, I'm going to Sophrona, her nurse, to bring her here and show her these proofs.

THRASO: Are you going to prevent my laying hands upon my own slave?

CHREMES: Yes, I am, I say.

GNATHO: Do you hear that? He's accessory to a theft; that's enough for you.

THRASO: And do you say the same, Thais?

THAIS: Find someone to answer you. (THAIS *and* CHREMES *leave the window.*)

THRASO (*to* GNATHO): What are we to do now?

GNATHO: Go home again; she will soon come of her own accord and beg your pardon.

THRASO: Do you think so?

GNATHO: Why, I'm quite certain; I know the ways of women; they won't when you want them, when you don't want them they're eager for it.

THRASO: You're quite right.

GNATHO: Shall I dismiss the army?

THRASO: Whenever you like.

GNATHO: Sanga, like brave soldiers, think of your hearths and homes again.

SANGA: My mind has long been among the stewpans.

GNATHO: A worthy man.

THRASO (*at the head of his troops*): Follow me this way. (*All depart.*)

Act Five.   Scene I

(Enter THAIS *from her house with* PYTHIAS.)

THAIS: Vile woman, why do you prevaricate so with me? "I know," "I don't know," "He is gone away," "I heard of it," "I wasn't there." Won't you tell me openly what is the matter? The girl's clothes are torn; she cries, and won't say a word; the eunuch is gone. Well, what is she crying about? What has happened? Won't you speak?

PYTHIAS: Oh, dear me, what am I to say? They say that he wasn't a eunuch.

THAIS: Who was he, then?

PYTHIAS: That Chaerea.

THAIS: What Chaerea?

PYTHIAS: The youth, Phaedria's brother.

THAIS: What do you say, viper?

PYTHIAS: Why, I know for sure.

THAIS: What had he to do with us? Why was he brought here?

PYTHIAS: I don't know; except, I believe, he was in love with Pamphila.

THAIS: Oh, dear, all's over with me. Unhappy woman that I am, if what you say is true. Is that what the girl is crying about?

PYTHIAS: I believe it is.

THAIS: What do you say, you blasphemer? Didn't I give you strict orders about this as I left the house?

PYTHIAS: What was I to do? I gave her into his sole charge, as you bade me.

THAIS: Wicked woman that you are, you have set the wolf to guard the sheep. I am terribly ashamed of having been made such a fool of. What sort of man is that?

PYTHIAS: Hush, mistress, hush, I pray you; all's right. Here we have the man himself.

THAIS: Where is he?

PYTHIAS: See, there, to the left.

THAIS: I see him.

PYTHIAS: Order him to be taken into custody as quick as may be.

THAIS: What shall we do with him, simpleton?

PYTHIAS: What shall we do with him? Pray look at him; doesn't his face look impudent? And just think of the boldness of this fellow!

Act Five.   Scene II

(*Enter* CHAEREA *in* DORUS' *dress*.)

CHAEREA (*to himself*): At Antipho's, both his father and mother made a point of being at home, so I couldn't manage anyhow to get into the house without their seeing me. While I was standing outside the door, an acquaintance of mine came up. When I saw him, I took to my heels as fast as I could and ran up a deserted street, out of that into another, and then into another. I've had an awful time, running about to prevent people recognising me. But isn't this Thais whom I see? It's she. I'm not certain what to do. After all, what do I care? What can she do?

THAIS (*to* PYTHIAS): Let's go and speak to him. (*To* CHAEREA) Good day to you, friend Dorus. Tell me, have you been running away?

CHAEREA: Yes, ma'am.

THAIS: Not satisfied with your place?

CHAEREA: No.

THAIS: Do you suppose you won't be punished for this?

CHAEREA: Forgive me this one offence; kill me if I ever commit another.

THAIS: Are you afraid of my cruelty?

CHAEREA: No.

THAIS: What of, then?

CHAEREA (*pointing to* PYTHIAS): I am afraid of her; she may have slandered me to you.

THAIS: What had you done?

CHAEREA: Nothing to speak of.

THAIS: "Nothing," d'ye say, shameless fellow? Do you count it nothing to rape a maid that is a citizen of Athens?

CHAEREA: I thought she was my fellow-servant.

PYTHIAS: Fellow-servant, indeed! I can hardly keep myself from pulling the brute's hair! Has he come to us to add insult to injury?

THAIS: Get along, madwoman!

PYTHIAS: Why madwoman? If I had pulled his hair, I should have very little to answer for to that scoundrel, especially when he owns himself your slave.

THAIS: No more of this. Chaerea, you have acted unworthily of yourself; for though I may be a very fit subject for this insult, still it was ungentlemanly of you to put it upon me. Gracious! I don't know now what I am to do about this girl; you have so upset all my plans, that now I can't hand her over to her friends, as it was right that I should, and as I had intended to do, Chaerea, in order to win some solid advantage for myself thereby.

CHAEREA: But now, Thais, I hope that we shall hereafter always be on the best of terms; great friendships have often sprung out of something not altogether right in the beginning, like this. What if some god ordained it all?

THAIS: I am prepared to take that view of it, and willingly.

CHAEREA: Why, that's what I beg you to do. Understand this, that I did it out of love, not to insult you.

THAIS: I am sure you did; and, indeed, that's why I am more ready to pardon you. I am not so uncouth, nor so inexperienced, Chaerea, as not to know the power of love.

CHAEREA: So help me heaven, Thais, I'm in love with you too, now.

PYTHIAS: Then, mistress, you had better be on your guard against him.

CHAEREA: Oh, I shouldn't dare.

PYTHIAS: I don't trust you a bit.

THAIS: Hold your tongue.

CHAEREA: Now I beg you to help me in this matter. I entrust myself to you and confide in your honour. I take you for my patroness, Thais; I entreat you. I shall die if I don't make her my wife.

THAIS: But if your father—

CHAEREA: Oh, I'm sure he will approve, provided only that she is a citizen.

THAIS: If you can wait for a short time, the girl's brother will be here; he's gone to fetch her nurse, who suckled her when she was a child. You yourself, Chaerea, shall be present at the recognition.

CHAEREA: I will wait.

THAIS: Don't you think that until he comes we had better wait in the house rather than here, outside the street-door?

CHAEREA: Why, I should like it much better.

PYTHIAS (*to* THAIS): What are you going to do?

THAIS: What's the matter with you?

PYTHIAS: What? Why, do you mean to receive him in the house?

THAIS: Why shouldn't I?

PYTHIAS: I assure you on my honour he'll kick up some fresh row.

THAIS: Oh, pray be quiet.

PYTHIAS: You don't seem to have fathomed his audacity.

CHAEREA: I won't do anything, Pythias.

PYTHIAS: I'll not believe it till I see it, Chaerea.

CHAEREA: Well, Pythias, you must be my keeper.

PYTHIAS: I shouldn't venture to entrust anything to your keeping, nor to keep you myself. Get along with you.

THAIS: By good luck, here comes her brother himself.

CHAEREA: Good gracious! Pray let's go into the house, Thais; I don't want him to see me in the street in this dress.

THAIS: And why, pray? Are you ashamed of it?

CHAEREA: Yes.

PYTHIAS: "Yes," says he; and how about the maid?

THAIS: Go in, I will follow. Pythias, stay here and show Chremes in. (THAIS *and* CHAEREA *go inside*.)

Act Five. Scene III

(*Enter* CHREMES *with* SOPHRONA.)

PYTHIAS (*to herself*): Now what in the world can I think of, what can I devise to pay out the scoundrel who sent this young gentleman to us under false colours?

CHREMES: Do move along a little faster, nurse.

SOPHRONA: I am moving.

CHREMES: So I see, but not forward.

PYTHIAS: Have you shown the tokens to the nurse?

CHREMES: Yes, all of them.

PYTHIAS: And what does she say, pray? Does she recognise them?

CHREMES: Yes, she remembers them all.

PYTHIAS: Goodness, but I'm glad to hear it, for I like that girl. Come indoors, both of you; my mistress has long been waiting for you in the house. (CHREMES *and* SOPHRONA *go into* THAIS' *house*) There, I see that nice man, Parmeno, coming. Heavens! What a leisurely swagger! I hope I've got the means of tormenting him to my heart's content. First, I'll go in to learn the truth about the recognition, and then I'll come out again and frighten that rascal out of his wits. (PYTHIAS *goes inside*.)

Act Five. Scene IV

(*Enter* PARMENO.)

PARMENO (*to himself*): I'm come to see how Chaerea is getting on. If he has managed the business cleverly, how much and how rightly Parmeno will be praised; for, not to mention that without trouble, expense, or payment I've managed a most difficult intrigue for him, and one which would have cost him very dear, getting him the girl that he wanted from a grasping courtesan; the next point, and that which I think the finest of my devices is, that, as a mere lad, he has had a chance of learning the characters and ways of courtesans, so that, having thoroughly learned them, he may for ever loathe them. When they are out of doors, they look as clean, neat, and smart as possible, and when they sup with their lover they are dainty about their food; but to see how nasty, dirty, and untidy they are at home, and how greedy, how ravenously they swallow black bread dipped in stale broth—it's the salvation of a young man to know all this.

(*Re-enter* PYTHIAS.)

PYTHIAS (*aside*): You villain, I'll have my revenge on you for what you've said and what you've done; you shan't make game of us with impunity. (*Aloud*) Good gods, what a shocking thing! Poor young gentleman! Oh, what a villain that Parmeno was that brought him here!

PARMENO (*aside*): What's this?

PYTHIAS: I do pity him, and so I've run out of doors here that I mightn't see the shameful example they talk of making of him.

PARMENO (*aside*): Oh, Jupiter, what's all this row about? Am I a ruined man? I'll speak to her. (*Aloud*) What's that, Pythias? What are you talking about? Who is to be made an example of?

PYTHIAS: Who? You impudent villain! You've been the ruin of the young gentleman you brought to us for a eunuch, thinking to make fools of us.

PARMENO: How so? What's happened? Tell me.

PYTHIAS: I'll tell you. That girl who was presented to Thais this day, do you know that she is a citizen of this city, and that her brother is one of our chief nobles?

PARMENO: No.

PYTHIAS: Well, that's what she turns out to be; and he, poor fellow, has raped her. Now, when her brother learned this, as he is a very passionate man—

PARMENO: Whatever did he do?

PYTHIAS: He first of all tied him up barbarously.

PARMENO: Tied him up?

PYTHIAS: Yes, in spite of Thais' entreaties not to do it.

PARMENO: What?

PYTHIAS: And now he threatens to treat him like those caught in adul-tery.[15] I never have seen that done, and I never want to.

PARMENO: How dares he venture to commit such a great crime?

PYTHIAS: Why such a great crime?

PARMENO: Isn't this the greatest of crimes? Who ever saw anyone taken up for adultery in a brothel?

PYTHIAS: I don't know.

PARMENO: But know this, Pythias, and the rest of you: I tell you, I proclaim to you, that this is my master's son.

PYTHIAS: Is he really, now?

PARMENO: And mind that Thais doesn't permit any violence to be done to him. And, indeed, why don't I myself go into the house?

PYTHIAS: Take care, Parmeno, what you do, or you may do him no good and lose your own life; for they think that you are at the bottom of the whole business.

PARMENO: Then what am I to do, wretch that I am? Where am I to begin? (*Looking down the street*) There I see our old gentleman coming back from his country-place. Shall I tell him or not? Yes, I'll tell him, though I know that I shall get a big beating; but I must help Chaerea.

PYTHIAS: You're wise. I'm going into the house. Tell him the whole story from beginning to end. (PYTHIAS *goes inside.*)

Act Five.   Scene V

(*Enter* LACHES *from the country.*)

LACHES (*to himself*): There's this advantage in my farm being so close to Athens, that I never get weary of either country or town; whenever I've had enough of one, I change my abode. But is not this our Parmeno? His very self. Whom are you waiting for, Parmeno, before the door here?

PARMENO (*pretending not to see him*): Who's there? (*Turning*) Oh, master, I am glad to see you well.

LACHES: Whom are you waiting for?

PARMENO: Good heavens! My tongue sticks fast through fear.

LACHES: Eh, what are you afraid of? Is all right? Tell me.

PARMENO: Master, first of all I want you to believe the truth. Whatever has happened was through no fault of mine.

LACHES: What?

PARMENO: You are right to ask me. I ought to have told you the story first. Phaedria bought a eunuch for a present for her.

LACHES: For whom?

PARMENO: For Thais.

LACHES: Bought him? Good gracious! How much did he pay for him?

PARMENO: Twenty minae.

LACHES: Ruined!

PARMENO: And Chaerea's in love with a music girl here.

LACHES: Eh, what? In love? Does he know already what a courtesan is? Has he come into town? We've one trouble on the top of another.

PARMENO: Master, don't glare at me. I didn't put him up to doing it.

LACHES: Leave off talking about yourself. If I live, you scoundrel, I'll— (*Restraining his anger*) But tell me first what this business is.

PARMENO: He was taken over to Thais', passing for the eunuch.

LACHES: Passing for the eunuch?

PARMENO: Yes. Now they've caught him in the house and bound him as an adulterer.

LACHES: Damnation!

PARMENO: To think of the impudence of these courtesans!

LACHES: Is there any evil or misfortune left that you haven't told me about?

PARMENO: That's all.

LACHES: Then why don't I burst into the house? (LACHES *rushes inside.*)

PARMENO: (*to himself*): There's no doubt but what I shall pay heavily for this; but I couldn't help doing it. I am glad that these women will get into trouble, for I know that the old gentleman has long been trying to find some excuse for making an example of them. Now he has found one.

Act Five. Scene VI

(*Re-enter* PYTHIAS *from the house.*)

PYTHIAS (*to herself*): Never, I vow, for a long time, has anything happened to me that pleased me more than this old gentleman's coming in just now under a mistake. I was the only one who enjoyed the joke, because I knew what he was afraid of.

PARMENO (*aside*): Why, what does this mean?

PYTHIAS: Now, I've come out to talk to Parmeno about it. But wherever is he?

PARMENO (*aside*): She's looking for me.

PYTHIAS: And there I see him. I'll go and talk to him.

PARMENO: What's the matter, idiot? What do you mean? What are you laughing at? Stop it.

PYTHIAS: Oh, dear! My sides ache with laughing at you.

PARMENO: Why?

PYTHIAS: Why? Oh, I never have seen, and I never shall see, a bigger fool than you! I can't tell you what sport you made for us in the house. Why, at first I took you for a smart, clever man. To think of your believing what I told you right off! Weren't you satisfied with the crime which you had made the young gentleman commit, without betraying the poor boy to his father as well? What do you suppose his feelings must have been when his father saw him in that dress? And I suppose you know it's all up with you?

PARMENO: Eh? What's that you say, vilest of women? Have you been lying to me? Do you actually laugh at me? Do you think it such fun, you brute, to make fools of us?

PYTHIAS: Quite too funny!

PARMENO: If you can do it with impunity.

PYTHIAS: Certainly.

PARMENO: Jove! I'll make you pay.

PYTHIAS: I verily believe you; but what you threaten me with is a long way off, Parmeno. You'll be at the whipping post before long, first for making a silly young gentleman conspicuous for disgraceful conduct and then informing upon him; both he and his father will make an example of you.

PARMENO: I'm a lost man!

PYTHIAS: This is given you by way of reward for the present you sent us. I'm off. (*She goes into the house.*)

PARMENO: Ruined like a rat, betrayed by my own squeak!

Act Five. Scene VII

(*Enter* GNATHO *and* THRASO.)

GNATHO: What now? With what hope or plan do we come here? What are you trying for, Thraso?

THRASO: Trying for? Why, to surrender to Thais and do whatever she bids me.

GNATHO: What's the meaning of that?

THRASO: Why should I not be her slave? Hercules was Omphale's slave.

GNATHO: A good precedent! (*Aside*) I should like to see her pounding your head with her slipper. (*Aloud*) But her door is opening.

THRASO: Oh, dear! What mischief is this? Here's another fellow that I never saw before; why does he bounce out in such a hurry?

Act Five. Scene VIII

(*Enter* CHAEREA *from* THAIS' *house.*)

CHAEREA: Oh, my countrymen, who in the world is more lucky than I? No one, by Jove; for the gods have clearly shown forth all their power in me, so many blessings have of a sudden been heaped upon me.

PARMENO (*aside*): What's he pleased about? (*Approaches him.*)

CHAEREA: Oh, Parmeno, the contriver, beginner, and accomplisher of all my joys, do you know what delights I am enjoying? Do you know that my Pamphila has turned out to be a citizen of Athens?

PARMENO: I have heard it.

CHAEREA: Do you know that she's betrothed to me?

PARMENO: Capital, upon my word.

GNATHO (*aside to* THRASO): Do you hear what the man says?

CHAEREA: Then I'm pleased to say that my brother Phaedria's love affairs are all in smooth water; the two houses are as one. Thais has taken my father for her patron, and arranged to live as our client under our protection.

PARMENO: Then Thais is your brother's very own.

CHAEREA: Of course.

PARMENO: Then there's another thing to be glad of; the captain will be driven from her house.

CHAEREA: Mind, let my brother know this as soon as may be, wherever he is.

PARMENO: I will look for him at home. (*He goes into* LACHES' *house*.)

THRASO (*to* GNATHO): Well, Gnatho, have you any doubt about my being utterly undone?

GNATHO: Certainly I think you are.

CHAEREA (*to himself*): What shall I talk of first, or praise most, him for having advised me to do this, or myself for daring to follow his advice? Or shall I praise Fortune for having guided the whole affair, and for having so happily accomplished so many great things all on one day? Or my father for his kindness and good nature? O Jupiter! Preserve these blessings to our use, I beseech thee.

Act Five.   Scene IX

(*Enter* PHAEDRIA *from* LACHES' *house*.)

PHAEDRIA: Good heavens! Parmeno's story is too good to be true. Now, where is my brother?

CHAEREA: Here he is.

PHAEDRIA: I congratulate you.

CHAEREA: I am sure you do. Brother, there is no one more lovable than this Thais of yours; she has done good to all our family.

PHAEDRIA: You need not praise her to me.

THRASO (*aside to* GNATHO): Dear me! The less hope I have, the more I love her. Gnatho, help, I implore you; all my hope is in you.

GNATHO (*aside to* THRASO): What do you want me to do?

THRASO: Manage either by entreaties or bribes to let me retain some small share in Thais.

GNATHO: That's a hard matter.

THRASO: If you want to do a thing, I know you will do it. Now if you can manage this, ask any reward you like of me, and you shall have your wish.

GNATHO: Really?

THRASO: So it shall be.

GNATHO: If I succeed, I ask that your house be always open to me, whether you are at home or not; that I may always have a place at your table with or without invitation.

THRASO: I give you my word of honour that you shall.

GNATHO: Then I'll set about it.

PHAEDRIA: Whom do I hear talking? (*Turning round*) What, Thraso!

THRASO: Good day to both of you.

PHAEDRIA (*to* THRASO): Perhaps you don't know what has happened here today.

THRASO: Yes, I do.

PHAEDRIA: Then how is it that I see you in these parts?

THRASO: Trusting to you.

PHAEDRIA: I'll show you how much you ought to trust to me, captain. If ever I find you in this street again, even if you say, "I'm looking for someone; I was passing this way," I'll be the death of you.

GNATHO: Oh, that's not the way you ought to talk.

PHAEDRIA: I have spoken.

GNATHO: It's not like you to give yourself such airs.

PHAEDRIA: You'll find it my way.

GNATHO: Both of you listen first to a few words that I have to say; when I have spoken, if you like my advice, take it.

CHAEREA: Let's listen.

GNATHO: Thraso, go a little off that way. (*To* PHAEDRIA *and* CHAEREA, *as* THRASO *moves away*) In the first place, I especially want you to believe that what I am doing in this matter I do chiefly for my own sake; but yet it would be folly on your part not to do it, if your interests agree with mine.

PHAEDRIA: What is it?

GNATHO: I advise you to admit the captain as your rival.

PHAEDRIA: What, admit him?

GNATHO: Just reflect, Phaedria. At the rate that you live with Thais (for you're very extravagant), what you can give her is very little; now Thais must have a large income. Now there's nobody handier or more fitted to supply all the necessaries for your love affair, without any cost to you, than the captain. In the first place he has money, and nobody spends it more freely. He is a fool, he is silly and dull-witted; he is asleep all day and all night. No fear of any woman falling in love with him; besides, you can easily kick him out whenever you please.

CHAEREA: What shall we do?

GNATHO: And moreover—which I think the most important matter of all—no one certainly gives better or more liberal dinners.

CHAEREA: I think we are sure to find a man like that useful.

PHAEDRIA: I think so too.

GNATHO: You are right. I have one more request to make, that you will receive me into your company. I have been rolling that stone uphill long enough.[16]

PHAEDRIA: We receive you.

CHAEREA: With pleasure.

GNATHO: Now, in gratitude for that, Phaedria, and you, Chaerea, I give you Thraso to eat and drink him dry, and make game of him.

CHAEREA: I agree.

PHAEDRIA: He deserves it.

GNATHO: Thraso, come this way if you please. (THRASO *rejoins them.*)

THRASO: Pray tell me how we stand.

GNATHO: How! Oh, these gentlemen didn't know you; when I told them what your real character was, and praised you as your achievements and qualities deserve, I won their consent.

THRASO (*to* GNATHO): You have done good service. (*To* PHAEDRIA *and* CHAEREA) I am greatly obliged. I have always been most popular in society wherever I have been.

GNATHO: Didn't I tell you that he had the true Attic wit?

PHAEDRIA: He's all that you promised he would be. Let us go this way. (*To the audience*) Farewell, and give us your applause.

NOTES

1. The name of the father of Phaedria and Chaerea is also given as Demea.

2. The text is uncertain here. Some editors read *facta III,* which would mean the third play in order of production.

3. Valerius and Fannius were consuls in 161 B.C.

4. This refers to Luscius Lanuvinus, Terence's rival.

5. *The Flatterer* of Naevius was apparently revised and brought out by Plautus.

6. Sunium was a promontory of Attica.

7. The literal meaning is, "there comes a change in everyone's fortune."

8. The Athenian youths took turns doing patrol duty at Piraeus, the port of Athens.

9. Literally, "this bean will be cracked upon my head." The origin of the phrase is not known.

10. The Rhodians were famous for their wit.

11. In other words, "do you want a mistress, when you're no better than a woman yourself?"

12. The rings were to serve as security for their share of the expenses.

13. Kauer and Lindsay assign this speech to Antipho.

14. This refers to Pyrrhus, the famous king of Epirus, who invaded Italy in the early part of the third century B.C.

15. The punishment for adultery was mutilation; cf. Plautus, *The Braggart Warrior,* Act Five.

16. This is an allusion to the punishment of Sisyphus.

IV
PHORMIO

COPYRIGHT, 1915, BY SAMUEL FRENCH

This play may be produced by amateurs without the payment of a royalty fee. For other rights of every kind, application must be made to Samuel French, 25 West 45th Street, New York City.

Characters in the Play

DAVUS, *a slave*

GETA, *slave of* DEMIPHO

ANTIPHO, *a young man, son of* DEMIPHO

PHAEDRIA, *a young man, son of* CHREMES

DEMIPHO, *an aged Athenian*

PHORMIO, *a parasite*

HEGIO

CRATINUS *legal advisers of* DEMIPHO

CRITO

DORIO, *a pimp*

CHREMES, *an old man, brother of* DEMIPHO

SOPHRONA, *a nurse*

NAUSISTRATA, *wife of* CHREMES

Didascalia

The *Phormio* of Terence. Acted at the Roman Games during the curule aedileship of Lucius Postumius Albinus and Lucius Cornelius Merula. The chief parts were taken by Lucius Ambivius Turpio and Lucius Atilius Praenestinus. Set to music by Flaccus, the slave of Claudius, for flutes of unequal length. The play was taken entirely from *The Claimant,* a Greek comedy by Apollodorus. The poet's fourth comedy.[1] Produced in the consulship of Gaius Fannius and Marcus Valerius.[2]

Summary

Demipho, the brother of Chremes, went abroad and left his son Antipho at Athens. Chremes had a wife and a daughter secretly at Lemnos, and at Athens he had another wife and a son devoted to a music girl. The Lemnian wife came to Athens and died there; the girl arranged for the funeral, Chremes being away. Antipho saw the girl at the funeral, fell in love with her, and with the aid of a parasite made her his wife. His father and Chremes returned and were angry. Then they gave thirty minae to the parasite so that he would marry the girl himself. The music girl was bought with this money. Antipho kept his wife when she had been recognised by Chremes as his daughter.

INTRODUCTION

THE *Phormio* is one of Terence's two most successful comedies. It lacks the more serious content and the psychological interest of *The Brothers* but it is fully its equal in brilliance of dialogue and neatness of construction. The liveliness of the play and the presence of the parasite Phormio and the pimp Dorio make the comedy rather more Plautine than Terence's other works, with the exception of *The Eunuch*. Phormio is not the typical hungry parasite of Plautus, however; he is an impudent rogue who engineers the trickery and whose cleverness solves the difficulties of the play. He has been called "one of the most engaging scoundrels in the rich annals of the stage."

Phaedria, son of Chremes, is in love with a music girl, Pamphila, but has no money to buy her from Dorio. Antipho, son of Chremes' brother Demipho, falls in love with Phanium, a poor but respectable girl. Here again we have the dual structure of which Terence is so fond; in the solution of the two difficulties both deception and recognition have their place. During the absence of the fathers Phormio arranges a scheme whereby Antipho shall be legally compelled to marry. Since Phanium's mother is dead, Phormio brings suit against Antipho claiming that the youth is the girl's nearest relative and according to the law should therefore marry her. Antipho purposely loses the suit and makes Phanium his wife. The problems of the two young men are thus very different: Phaedria fears he will be unable to possess Pamphila, and Antipho dreads the possibility that he may be forced to give up Phanium. This is the situation when Demipho and Chremes, the two fathers, return. Demipho is angry and in spite of the so-called lawsuit wants Antipho to give up his wife. Terence's use of the double plot at this point is particularly skilful; he employs one difficulty to solve the other. Phormio pretends to be willing to marry Phanium upon payment of thirty minae—the very sum needed by Phaedria to get the music girl from Dorio.

Chremes, who had a second wife and a daughter in Lemnos, was trying to locate his daughter and was eager for her to marry Antipho. The revelation that Phanium is his daughter, like the recognition of Antiphila in *The Self-Tormentor*, complicates the situation, for Demipho at that very moment is arranging with Phormio to have the parasite take Phanium off Antipho's hands. Chremes' desire to have Antipho's marriage stand and his attempts to reveal the truth to Demipho without letting his own wife find it out are highly amusing. Geta, Demipho's slave who has been assisting Phormio in his schemes, learns of Chremes' double life and reveals it to Phormio. The secret which brings a happy solution to Antipho's problem is now used by Phormio to confirm Phaedria in his possession of Pamphila. Here again is unusual skill in the handling of the double plot.

Structurally the *Phormio* is one of Terence's finest plays. The situation is complex but not puzzling, and the plot develops naturally from one stage to the next. The spectator is kept in suspense, for the dramatist seeks to achieve his effects by uncertainty and surprise. The revelation of Chremes' secret life comes as a complete surprise, as does that of Phanium's identity. This type of suspense is characteristic of Terence and is best illustrated in *The Mother-in-law,* where the secret is withheld from the audience until the very end. Another interesting feature of the plot is the manner in which Phormio's fiction concerning the relationship of Antipho and Phanium proves to be true. This is not unlike Milphio's second trick in *The Carthaginian* of Plautus, which makes Hanno the father of the Carthaginian maidens as he proves to be in reality.

There are numerous scenes in the *Phormio* full of irony and humour. Antipho's cowardice and his inability to face his father, his misunderstanding of Phormio's second trick which appears to oppose the continuance of his marriage, the not too helpful advice of Demipho's three friends, Chremes' attempt to conceal his secret from his wife, the impudence and ingenuity of Phormio throughout and especially in the final scene when he reveals the truth to Chremes' wife—all these make the play one of the most amusing and delightful in Roman comedy.

The best-known adaptation of the *Phormio* in modern times is Molière's *Les Fourberies de Scapin* (1671). Later plays, such as Otway's *The Cheats of Scapin* (1677) and Ravenscroft's *Scaramouch a Philosopher* (1677) are related to Terence through their imitation of Molière. Colman's *The Man of Business* (1774) combined elements from Terence's *Phormio* and Plautus' *The Three Penny Day.*

PHORMIO

(SCENE:—*A street in Athens in front of the houses of* DEMIPHO, CHREMES, *and* DORIO.)

Prologue

SINCE the old poet[3] can't divert our poet from his profession and take away his occupation, he's using abuse to scare him from writing plays. He keeps saying that the plays which our poet has written are weak in dialogue and commonplace in style, and that's because our poet has never portrayed a crazy young man seeing a doe running with hounds after her, and the beast weeping and crying for help. If the old playwright had known that the success of his play, when it was put on the stage, was due more to the skill of the actor than to that of the author, he wouldn't be so bold in his attacks.

If there is anyone here who speaks and thinks as follows, "If the old poet hadn't abused him first, this young poet couldn't have written a prologue at all, having no one to attack," that man shall receive this answer: all literary men have an equal right to win success if they can. The old poet has tried to drive our poet from his work and make him starve. Our poet wished to answer him, not to attack him. If he had carried on his rivalry in pleasant terms, he would have received pleasant terms in reply; as it is, he must realise that he is only getting back what he gave. I shall stop talking about him now, although he for his part does not stop his wrongdoing.

Please give me your attention. I bring you a new comedy, called *The Claimant* in Greek but *Phormio* in Latin, because the actor who takes the leading part is Phormio the parasite, and he will carry on the main part of the plot, if you grant your favour to the poet. Therefore give us your attention, and listen in fairness and silence, that we may not suffer the misfortune we did when our company was driven from the stage by a riot.[4] The excellence of our chief actor, supported by your kindness and good will, has enabled us to return again to the stage.

Act One.   Scene I

(Enter DAVUS, *carrying a bag of money.)*

DAVUS *(to himself)*: My good friend and fellow-townsman Geta came
to me yesterday, and asked me to get hold of a little money I'd been
owing him. Well, I've got it and here I am. I understand his master's
son's just married, and I'll wager this money goes for a present to his
wife. The woman will take all the earnings of a miserable man, who's
saved up little by little, cheating himself of the bare necessities of life;
and she won't give a thought to how much trouble it took to get that
present. Poor Geta'll be stuck again for another present when a child is
born; for another when its birthday comes around. The mother takes
it all; the child is only the excuse for the presents. Is that Geta there?

Act One.   Scene II

(Enter GETA *from* DEMIPHO'S *house.)*

GETA *(speaking to someone within)*: Now, if a red-headed fellow asks
for me—

DAVUS: He's here already; sh-h!

GETA: Oh, Davus, I was looking for you.

DAVUS: Well, here you are. *(Hands him the bag of money)* It's counted
out; you'll find the amount correct.

GETA: My best thanks.

DAVUS: I tell you, in these times if anybody pays his debts, you should
be glad. What makes you so melancholy?

GETA: I'm frightened out of my wits. Don't you know what's happened?

DAVUS: No.

GETA: I'll tell you, if you'll keep still.

DAVUS: Go on, you fool! Are you afraid to trust me with words when
you've already trusted me with money? What's the use of cheating you,
anyway?

GETA: Listen, then.

DAVUS: Proceed.

GETA: Do you know Chremes, my master's elder brother?

DAVUS: Certainly.

GETA: And Phaedria, his son?

DAVUS: As well as I know you.

GETA: Well, it happened that my master was forced to make a journey to Cilicia, to visit a friend who sent letters to the old man and tempted him with mountains of gold.

DAVUS: Didn't he have enough already?

GETA: Keep still; this is the way it happened.

DAVUS: I wish I had been a rich man!

GETA: When Chremes went away to Lemnos at the same time, both the old men left me as a sort of tutor to their sons, Phaedria and Antipho.

DAVUS: Geta, you had your hands full!

GETA: I found that out soon enough. Luck left me then and there. First, I opposed them; no use; so long as I was faithful to the old men, my only reward was beatings.

DAVUS: The old proverb occurs to me: "It's folly to kick against the pricks."

GETA: Then I decided to reverse myself, so I did everything I could for the young fellows.

DAVUS: That was sensible.

GETA: Antipho didn't do anything bad for a while; but Phaedria at once found a little harp-player and fell desperately in love with her. She was a slave—her master a villainous trader. The old men didn't leave the young fellows much extra cash, so Phaedria could do no more than feast his eyes on her. He accompanied her back and forth to school; that was all. Having nothing in particular to do, we turned our attention to the young man. Right across from the music school there's a barber shop. He used to wait there every day and go home with her. One day when we were there, a young man came in weeping. We were dumb-founded and asked him what the matter was. "Never," said he, "has poverty seemed to terrible or so great a burden. Just now I saw a girl who lives nearby, mourning her dead mother; there wasn't a single friend around, except one old woman who helped the girl with the funeral arrangements. I was sorry for her. She was good looking, too." In short, he moved us all to tears. Then Antipho said, "Let's go and see her." We went and saw her, and she certainly was handsome; hair loose, feet bare, and dress shabby. She would have been disgusting in these circumstances, had she not been so beautiful. Phaedria said, "Oh, she's well enough, I suppose"—but Antipho—

DAVUS: Fell in love!

GETA: Right. But listen to the sequel. The next day he went straight to the old woman and begged her to let him see the girl; but she wouldn't listen to him, and told him he was not acting honourably; that she was an Athenian citizen, born of good parents, and that if he wished to make the girl his wife, he might do so according to law; otherwise, she would have nothing to do with him. He didn't know what to do. He wanted to marry the girl, but he was afraid of his father.

DAVUS: Wouldn't his father give him permission when he returned?

GETA: Do you think he'd let his son marry a girl without a dowry? Never in the world.

DAVUS: What happened then?

GETA: There is a certain fellow named Phormio, a parasite—confound him!

DAVUS: What did he do?

GETA: He advised Antipho in this fashion: "There is a law that orphans are compelled to marry their nearest relatives; I will say that you are the girl's nearest relative, and bring suit against you; I'll make believe I'm a friend of the girl's father. We'll come before the judges. I'll arrange to supply a father and a mother, and tell how she's related to you. Now, *you* won't deny anything, then *I'll* win my case; you see? Your father'll come home, and I'll have a fight with him; what's the difference? We'll have the girl."

DAVUS: Ha! That's funny. He's courageous enough!

GETA: Antipho agreed; Phormio won, and the young fellow is married.

DAVUS: What do you say?

GETA: Just what I've told you.

DAVUS: Oh, Geta, what'll happen to you?

GETA: Well, I don't know about that; but I *do* know that whatever happens, I'll bear it bravely.

DAVUS: That's right; and spoken like a man!

GETA: My only hope lies in myself.

DAVUS: Excellent!

GETA: I'll go for a pleader, who'll plead for me in this wise: "Forgive him this time; if he ever does anything wrong after this, I'll not plead for him." Just so he doesn't add: "And when I go, kill him, for all I care!"

DAVUS: What about the little harpist's attendant? How's he?

GETA: None too well.

DAVUS: He hasn't much to give, has he?

GETA: He has nothing but hope.

DAVUS: Has his father returned yet?

GETA: No.

DAVUS: Tell me, when do you think your master will arrive home?

GETA: I don't exactly know—but I hear a letter has come from him. It's at the post-office now. I'm going to get it.

DAVUS: Do you need me any longer, Geta?

GETA: No. Good-bye. (DAVUS *departs.* GETA *calls to slave within*) What ho, boy!—Nobody there? (*Enter slave.* GETA *gives him the bag of money*) Here, take this in and give it to Dorcium. (GETA *departs towards the harbour.*)

Act Two.   Scene I

(*Enter* ANTIPHO *and* PHAEDRIA *from* CHREMES' *house.*)

ANTIPHO: Think of it! That matters should come to this pass! That I should fear my father, who is always planning what is best for me, whenever I think of his return! If I hadn't been so impetuous I might have welcomed him as became a dutiful son.

PHAEDRIA: Why, what's the matter?

ANTIPHO: Do you ask? You who know of my foolish deed? I wish Phormio had never thought of persuading me to do this, eager as I was! Oh, that was the beginning of all my troubles. Then I shouldn't have got her; for a few days I might have suffered; but this daily distraction would not have tortured my conscience as it has.

PHAEDRIA: I see.

ANTIPHO: And now I await the person who is to break off my union with Phanium.

PHAEDRIA: Others grieve because they cannot have those whom they desire; you're sad because you enjoy the object of your love. You have too much; you are overwhelmed with love, Antipho. You live an enviable life. The gods bless me—if I could have the woman I love, I would willingly die! See here now: you have a cultured and well-bred girl of good principles. You couldn't wish for more. Why, you would be completely happy if you had only the courage to bear misfortune. If you had to deal with that slave-trader, as I do, then you'd know what it is to have troubles.

ANTIPHO: But you are fortunate, Phaedria; you can do whatever you please: keep the girl, or let her go. But I, unhappy man, haven't the right either to keep my beloved or to let her go. But what's this? Is that Geta running here? I'm afraid I know what ill news he brings.

Act Two.   Scene II

(*Enter* GETA, *running.*)

GETA (*to himself, not seeing* ANTIPHO *and* PHAEDRIA): Geta, you must devise at once some plan of escape. Great dangers are threatening you, and you can't avoid them. How shall I get out of this scrape? I can't keep the secret dark any longer.

ANTIPHO (*aside to* PHAEDRIA): I wonder why he's so upset?

GETA: I have only a second to make my plans; my master'll be here any minute.

ANTIPHO (*aside to* PHAEDRIA): What's this?

GETA: When he hears what's happened, what shall I do? Shall I speak? I'll only make him angry. Shall I keep still? That'll arouse him. Clear myself? No use at all; I might as well try to wash the colour out of a brick. This is terrible. I'm afraid on my own account—and Antipho drives me to distraction. If it weren't for him, I should have been revenged on the old men long ago, and run away immediately.

ANTIPHO (*aside to* PHAEDRIA): What's that he says about running away?

GETA: Where can I find Antipho?

PHAEDRIA (*aside to* ANTIPHO): Aha! He's talking about you.

ANTIPHO (*aside to* PHAEDRIA): I'm afraid he has bad news for me.

GETA: I'm going to his home; he's usually to be found there.

ANTIPHO (*to* GETA, *as he is making for the house*): Stop, there!

GETA (*without looking back*): You order me about familiarly enough, whoever you are.

ANTIPHO: Geta!

GETA (*turning around*): Why, it's the very man I'm looking for.

ANTIPHO: Quick now, what's the news? Tell me in one word.

GETA: I'll do it.

ANTIPHO: Speak, then.

GETA: Just now, at the harbour——

ANTIPHO: My—?

GETA: You're right.

ANTIPHO: I'm dead and buried.

PHAEDRIA: Is it possible!

ANTIPHO: Wh-wh-what'll I do?

PHAEDRIA (*to* GETA): What do you say?

GETA: That I saw his father, your uncle.

ANTIPHO: How can I bear up under this disaster? Oh, Phanium, if Fortune decrees that I be torn from your arms, life will mean nothing for me.

GETA: Antipho, you must be careful; Fortune favours the brave, you know.

ANTIPHO: I'm not myself at all.

GETA: But now, of all times, you must be, Antipho. If your father should see that you're afraid, he'd think you were in the wrong.

PHAEDRIA: That's true enough.

ANTIPHO: I can't change my nature.

GETA: Well, what would you do if you had something worse on your hands?

ANTIPHO: Since I can't do this, I'd be still less able to do that.

GETA (*to* PHAEDRIA, *with a wink*): This is nothing, Phaedria. Come along. Why should we waste our time here? I'm going.

PHAEDRIA: So am I. (GETA *and* PHAEDRIA *turn to go away.*)

ANTIPHO: Please stay! What if I should bluster it through? Put on a brave front? (*Looking brave*) How's this?

GETA (*not looking at him*): Nonsense.

ANTIPHO: Look at my expression. Hm! Br-r! Is this all right?

GETA (*turning around and looking at him*): No.

ANTIPHO: Is this?

GETA: Better. Try again.

ANTIPHO: How about this?

GETA: That's all right; now, hold that expression. Answer him word for word, argument for argument, and don't let him scare you with big talk.

ANTIPHO: I see—I—I see.

GETA: Tell him you were forced to marry unwillingly.

PHAEDRIA: By the law and by the judge.

GETA: Understand? (*He sees* DEMIPHO *at a distance*) Who's that old man I see at the end of the street? It's he, indeed.

ANTIPHO: I *can't* stay. (*Going.*)

GETA: What are you going to do? Where are you going, Antipho? Stay here, I tell you.

ANTIPHO: I'm too conscious of my crimes. I entrust Phanium and my life to your charge! (*He runs off.*)

PHAEDRIA: Geta, what now?

GETA: Now you'll hear some accusations. I'll be beaten, hung up by the wrists, if I'm not very much mistaken. By the way, do you remember what you said to me once, when we were embarking on this enterprise? To defend ourselves from trouble we should say that our cause was right, just, and honourable?

PHAEDRIA: Yes, I do.

GETA: Well, we have need of those arguments, or even better ones, if we can find them.

PHAEDRIA: I'll do my best.

GETA: You greet him first, and I'll wait here in ambush, as a reserve force, in case you have to retreat.

PHAEDRIA: Very well, then. (*They withdraw.*)

Act Two.   Scene III[5]

(*Enter* DEMIPHO *from the harbour.*)

DEMIPHO (*to himself*): So Antipho has married without my consent, has he? To think that he should have no regard for my authority—or fear of my anger! Isn't he ashamed of himself? Geta, Geta, wily counsellor!

GETA (*aside*): At last!

DEMIPHO: What can they say to me, what excuse can they find for their conduct?

GETA (*aside*): Oh, I've found an excuse; think of something harder!

DEMIPHO: Perhaps he'll say: "I did it unwillingly; the law forced me to." Very well—I don't deny it.

GETA (*aside*): Good! Excellent!

DEMIPHO: To give up the case to the prosecutors, without saying a word —did the law compel him to do that?

GETA (*aside*): That *is* more difficult!⁶ But I'll think up a good answer to that.

DEMIPHO: I don't know what to do, this is so unexpected. I am so angry I can't think. I hold that when any man's affairs are in good order, he ought to consider how he should bear adversity: dangers of every kind, lawsuits, exile, and the like; and returning from travel he should always imagine that his son is in a bad scrape, his wife dead, and his daughter ill. These accidents are common to all humanity. He should let nothing upset him. Whatever comes out better than was expected, he should consider as so much to the good.

GETA (*aside to* PHAEDRIA): Oh, Phaedria, it's wonderful how much more I know than my master! I have considered long ago everything that might happen to me in case my master should return. I must grind away at the mill, be beaten, put in chains, and labour and sweat in the fields. Nothing unexpected is possible. Whatever comes out better than I thought is so much to the good. Why don't you go up to him and begin to explain your case?

DEMIPHO: Oho! I see Phaedria. (PHAEDRIA *goes towards* DEMIPHO.)

PHAEDRIA: Welcome, uncle.

DEMIPHO: Welcome to you; but where's Antipho?

PHAEDRIA: I'm glad you have re—

DEMIPHO (*interrupting*): That's all very well, but tell me this—

PHAEDRIA: He is in good health. Is everything well with you, sir?

DEMIPHO: I wish it were.

PHAEDRIA: What is the trouble?

DEMIPHO: Do you ask, Phaedria? You have allowed a fine marriage to take place while I was away.

PHAEDRIA: Oh, you are annoyed with him on that account?

GETA (*aside*): Cunning dog!

DEMIPHO: Why shouldn't I be? Ah, I'm just waiting for him to cross my path, so that he may see how by his fault I have been changed from a most indulgent to a most severe father.

PHAEDRIA: But he's done nothing, uncle, deserving of blame.

DEMIPHO: Nonsense—you are birds of a feather; know one and you know all.

PHAEDRIA: That's not so.

DEMIPHO: If one's in trouble, the other's ready to plead his cause: turn and turn about.

GETA (*aside*): There he's right.

DEMIPHO: If that weren't true you would not have upheld his case.

PHAEDRIA: At any rate, if Antipho has been a little neglectful of his reputation, I'm not trying to excuse him or find reasons why he shouldn't get what he deserves. But if by chance someone lays a snare for our tender years and catches us, is it our fault, or that of the judges? And anyway, the judges are often spiteful; they take away from the rich and then out of pity give it to the poor.

GETA (*aside*): If I didn't know the facts about the trial, I'd think he was telling the truth.

DEMIPHO: What judge could possibly know your rights, when you didn't say a word in your defence? That's what happened with him.

PHAEDRIA: He did just as any other young man would do: when he came before the judges, he couldn't say what he had planned to say— he was too upset.

GETA (*advancing to* DEMIPHO): Well, master, I'm glad to see you home again!

DEMIPHO: Oh, most excellent guardian, welcome! Mainstay of the family, protector and adviser of my son!

GETA: For some time I have heard you blaming us all, and wrongly, *me* most of all! What would you have had me do in this case? The law doesn't allow a slave to plead or to give testimony.

DEMIPHO: Very true. I'll grant he might have been nervous, and that you as a slave could do nothing in court; but if the woman were related so closely, he did not have to marry her; he should have given her a dowry, according to law, and let her find another husband. On what account did he marry a girl without a thing?

GETA: On no account: he needed the cash.

DEMIPHO: He might have borrowed it from someone.

GETA: Easier said than done!

DEMIPHO: If the worst had come to the worst, he might have borrowed it at interest.

GETA: Fine words! As if anybody would trust him, with you still alive!

DEMIPHO: No, no, it can't be; it isn't possible. Am I to allow her to be his wife? She deserves no pity. I'd like that fellow pointed out to me; where does he live?

GETA: You mean Phormio?

DEMIPHO: Yes, the fellow who pleaded for her.

GETA: I'll see that he comes at once.

DEMIPHO: Where is Antipho now?

GETA: Off somewhere.

DEMIPHO: Phaedria, bring him here, please.

PHAEDRIA: Very well, I'll go by the shortest road. (*He goes into* DORIO'S *house.*)

GETA (*aside*): To Pamphila! (GETA *departs.*)

DEMIPHO (*to himself*): I'll go into the house, and render offerings to the gods; then I'll go to the forum, and call my friends together to help me in the matter, so that I shan't be unprepared when Phormio comes. (*He goes into his own house. A short time is supposed to elapse before the next Act.*)

Act Three.   Scene I

(*Enter* PHORMIO *and* GETA.)

PHORMIO: You say he ran off because he was afraid of his father?

GETA: Yes.

PHORMIO: And Phanium is left alone?

GETA: Yes.

PHORMIO: And the old man is angry?

GETA: Very.

PHORMIO (*aside*): The whole thing rests on you alone, Phormio; you've got us into the trouble and you must get us out.—Well, to work now!

GETA: Please—

PHORMIO (*to himself, not listening to* GETA): If he asks—

GETA: You are my only hope.

PHORMIO (*as before*): Well, now, what if he should—?

GETA: You are the one who urged us on. Please help us.

PHORMIO (*to* GETA): Let him come! All my plans are made.

GETA: What'll you do?

PHORMIO: Phanium stays with Antipho; I clear him of blame, and bring down on my own head all the anger of the old man!

GETA: You're a brave man and a true friend. Indeed, I've often feared that that bravery would some day land you in jail.

PHORMIO: Not so; the danger's begun, and I've mapped out my course. How many people do you suppose I've beaten to death already? As my technique improves, my practice increases! Come now, did you ever hear of anyone bringing a suit for damages against me?

GETA: Why is that?

PHORMIO: Because a net isn't spread for a hawk or a kite, birds that do us harm; it's spread for harmless birds, for there's some profit in them; it's labour wasted to catch the others. The men from whom some profit can be squeezed are the ones in danger. They know I haven't a thing to lose. You'll say they might bring me home as a slave after condemning me. But they don't want to feed a man with my appetite; and I think they're wise, because they don't wish to return good for evil.

GETA: Wonderful! How grateful he ought to be to you!

PHORMIO: You take your place at the table, free from cares, while I am burdened with your troubles and my own. While you have whatever you want, I am worried; you laugh gaily, are the first to drink, take the place of honour at table, and have doubtful viands placed before you. Then you have—

GETA: What do you mean by "doubtful viands"?

PHORMIO: I mean that when you look at the various delicacies, you are in doubt as to which one to begin with.

GETA (*seeing* DEMIPHO *approach*): The old man's coming. See what he's doing. The first encounter is the worst. If you survive that, you may do what you please afterward. (*They retire.*)

Act Three.　Scene II

(*Enter* DEMIPHO, HEGIO, CRATINUS, *and* CRITO.)

DEMIPHO: Have you ever heard of anything more ridiculous than what has happened to me? I implore you to help me.

GETA (*aside to* PHORMIO): He's getting angry.

PHORMIO (*aside to* GETA): Now, pay attention; I'm going to stir him up. (*Speaking aloud*) By the immortal gods, does Demipho say that Phanium is not his relative? Does he?

GETA: He does.

PHORMIO: Does he deny that he knows who her father was?

GETA: He denies it.

DEMIPHO (*turning to his friends*): I believe this is the fellow I was talking about. Follow me.

PHORMIO: And that he knows who Stilpo was?

GETA: Absolutely.

PHORMIO: And why? Because the miserable creature was left in poverty, her father ignored, she herself neglected. See what avarice will do to a man!

GETA: If you accuse my master of any wrong, you'll hear something you won't like!

DEMIPHO: The idea! Does he come here on purpose to accuse me?

PHORMIO: I have no reason to be angry at the youth if he didn't know my friend. He was old and poor and generally worked hard in the country; he rented some land there from my father. But the old man often told me how his relative neglected him. And what a fine man he was, too, the best I've ever seen!

GETA (*with sarcasm*): And you're the same sort of fellow, I suppose.

PHORMIO: Oh, go to the devil! If I hadn't thought so highly of him, I wouldn't have been so bitter against your family. And it's on account of his daughter, whom your master now rejects, like the cad he is.

GETA: Be careful what you say!

PHORMIO: Doesn't he deserve it?

GETA: Is that so, you rascal?

DEMIPHO: Geta!

GETA (*to* PHORMIO, *pretending not to hear* DEMIPHO): You cheat the citizens and twist the laws up into knots.

DEMIPHO: Geta!

PHORMIO (*aside to* GETA): Answer him.

GETA (*turning around*): Who is it? Well?

DEMIPHO (*to* GETA): Sh-h!

GETA: He never stopped abusing you while you were away.

DEMIPHO: Stop it! (*To* PHORMIO) Young fellow, with your very kind permission, if you will be good enough to answer me, tell me what friend of yours you just mentioned, and in what manner he claims I am related to him?

PHORMIO: There now, you're trying to pump me. As if you didn't know!

DEMIPHO: *I* know?

PHORMIO: Certainly you know.

DEMIPHO: But I say I don't; tell me about it; *you* seem to know.

PHORMIO: Well, well, don't you know your own first cousin?

DEMIPHO: You're joking! What's the name?

PHORMIO: The name? The name—indeed—

DEMIPHO: Why don't you tell me?

PHORMIO (*aside*): I'm dead: I've forgotten the name.

DEMIPHO: What do you say?

PHORMIO (*aside to* GETA): Geta, if you remember that name I told you just now, help me out. (*To* DEMIPHO) Well, I won't tell you; as if you didn't know! You came here to get me to tell you.

DEMIPHO: I get you to tell me!

GETA (*aside to* PHORMIO): Stilpo.

PHORMIO: Well, what's the difference? Stilpo is the name.

DEMIPHO: What?

PHORMIO: Stilpo, I say; you know him.

DEMIPHO: I never heard of him before. Related to me?

PHORMIO: Aren't you ashamed? If he'd left you ten talents—

DEMIPHO: Go to the devil!

PHORMIO: You would be the first to trace your ancestors back even as far as your great-grandfather.

DEMIPHO: That may be, but if I had begun, I should have stated what relation she was to me. Come now, what relation is she to me?

GETA (*to* DEMIPHO): That's right, master. (*To* PHORMIO) Look out, now.

PHORMIO: I have explained my case clearly to the judge, as was my duty. Besides, if this were wrong, why didn't your son deny it?

DEMIPHO: Don't mention his name to me.

PHORMIO: Oh, most wise of men, go to a magistrate, and have him give you another decision on the same case, since you are the only man who can get two decisions!

DEMIPHO: I'll do what the law advises, rather than listen to you or involve myself in lawsuits. Give her a dowry! Take her away! Take the five minae!

PHORMIO: Ha, ha, ha, what a dear fellow!

DEMIPHO: What's that? Don't I ask what's right? Can't I even have common justice?

PHORMIO: I ask you, is that the law? Does it say you can treat her as a courtesan and then pay her and send her away? Doesn't the law say that no citizen is to be driven to shame because of her poverty? That's why she's ordered to marry her next of kin and live her life with him. And that's just what you forbid.

DEMIPHO: Surely, to her next of kin; but how does that concern us?

PHORMIO: My good sir, don't try a case that's been tried already, as they say.

DEMIPHO: I shan't stop until I have established my rights.

PHORMIO: Nonsense.

DEMIPHO: Leave that to me!

PHORMIO: Well, I'll have nothing to do with it, Demipho, nor with you. *Your* son is the one who is in trouble.

DEMIPHO: I'll shut him out of the house at once, and his wife with him.

PHORMIO: You wouldn't do that!

DEMIPHO: Rascal, are you always troubling me for the amusement you get out of it?

PHORMIO (*aside to* GETA): He's afraid of us, but he's trying to conceal it.

GETA (*aside to* PHORMIO): You've made a good beginning.

PHORMIO (*to* DEMIPHO): If you'll do the right thing, we'll remain on good terms.

DEMIPHO: Do you think I want your friendship, or wish to hear or see you?

PHORMIO: If you can get on well with her, you'll have her to cheer your old age; you're getting on in years.

DEMIPHO: Let her cheer you up; you may have her.

PHORMIO: There, there, keep cool!

DEMIPHO: You've said enough. Unless you take that woman away, I'll send her packing. Phormio, I have spoken.

PHORMIO: If you lay hands on her in any other way than befits a free woman, I'll bring suit against you. I have spoken, Demipho. (*Aside to* GETA) If you want me, I'll be home.

GETA (*aside to* PHORMIO): Yes, I know. (PHORMIO *goes out.*)

Act Three. Scene III

DEMIPHO: What troubles and cares does my son heap on my poor old back! And this marriage! Oh! Why doesn't he come, and try at least to explain the matter to me? (*To* GETA) Go and see whether he's home yet.

GETA: Very well. (*He goes into* DEMIPHO's *house.*)

DEMIPHO: You see how matters stand? What shall I do? Tell me, Hegio.

HEGIO: I? I think that Cratinus ought to give his opinion, if you have no objection.

DEMIPHO: Tell me, Cratinus.

CRATINUS: Do you wish *me* to speak?

DEMIPHO: Yes, you.

CRATINUS: Well, I think you should do what is best; what this son of yours has done in your absence should be undone. In that way you will secure justice. That is my opinion.

DEMIPHO: Now you, Hegio.

HEGIO: I believe that Cratinus has spoken with good sense. But it's a fact that "So many men, so many opinions": each man after his own fashion. Now, it doesn't seem to me that what has been done by law can be undone; and it's wrong to try to change it.

DEMIPHO: It's your turn now, Crito.

CRITO: I think we should consider the matter more fully. It's an important affair.

HEGIO: Anything else?

DEMIPHO: No, you have done very well. (HEGIO, CRATINUS, *and* CRITO *go out*) Now I'm more uncertain what to do than I was before.

(*Enter* GETA *from* DEMIPHO's *house.*)

GETA: They say he hasn't come back yet.

DEMIPHO: I'll wait for my brother, and do what he advises. I'll go down to the harbour now and find out when he is expected to return. (*He goes out.*)

GETA (*to himself*): I'll go and find Antipho and tell him what's just happened. But I see him coming. He's just in the nick of time.

Act Three. Scene IV⁷

(*Enter* ANTIPHO.)

ANTIPHO (*to himself*): Oh, Antipho, you are to blame for the way you feel; to think that I ran away and left my life and safety in the hands of others! Did you believe that they would take care of your interests better than you could yourself? No matter how the other things were, you should have thought of the girl you had at home, that she might not suffer through her trust in you. All her hopes are placed in you alone.

GETA (*advancing to* ANTIPHO): Well, master, we've been angry with you for some time, because you ran off.

ANTIPHO: I was looking for you.

GETA: But we weren't any the less careful on your behalf.

ANTIPHO: Tell me, please, how are my affairs proceeding? Does my father suspect anything yet?

GETA: Not a thing.

ANTIPHO: Is there any hope?

GETA: I don't know.

ANTIPHO (*disappointed*): Oh—

GETA: But Phaedria has never ceased helping you.

ANTIPHO: That's nothing new; he always helps me.

GETA: Then Phormio once again proved himself an enormously clever fellow, in this as in other matters.

ANTIPHO: What did he do?

GETA: He pacified the old man, who was very angry.

ANTIPHO: Oh, my dear Phormio.

GETA: And—I myself did what I could.

ANTIPHO: Oh, Geta, you are all my friends.

GETA: So far, so good. Your father is waiting for your uncle to arrive.

ANTIPHO: Why?

GETA: Because he said he wanted to do as his brother advised.

ANTIPHO: Oh, Geta, how I dread to see my uncle arrive here safe and sound! For by his sentence alone, as I hear, I am to live or die.

GETA: Here's Phaedria.

ANTIPHO: Where?

GETA: See, he's coming out of his training-school.

Act Three.   Scene V

(*Enter* DORIO *from his house, followed by* PHAEDRIA.)

PHAEDRIA: Dorio, please listen to me.

DORIO: I won't.

PHAEDRIA: Only a minute.

DORIO: Leave me alone.

PHAEDRIA: Listen to what I have to tell you.

DORIO: I'm tired of hearing the same thing a thousand times over.

PHAEDRIA: But now I'm going to tell you something you'll be glad to hear.

DORIO: Speak; I'll listen.

PHAEDRIA: Can't I persuade you to wait for three days? (DORIO *turns away*) Where are you going?

DORIO: I thought you were going to offer me something different.

ANTIPHO (*aside to* GETA): I'm afraid this slave-trader—

GETA (*aside to* ANTIPHO): —won't be safe?

PHAEDRIA: Don't you believe me?

DORIO: I don't.

PHAEDRIA: But if I promise?

DORIO: Nonsense.

PHAEDRIA: You'll be well paid for your trouble.

DORIO: No.

PHAEDRIA: Take my word for it; you'll be satisfied.

DORIO: You're dreaming.

PHAEDRIA: Just try. I don't ask you to wait long.

DORIO: Same old story.

PHAEDRIA: You'll be a second father to me, my best friend, my—

DORIO: Nonsense.

PHAEDRIA: How can you be so hard-hearted? Won't you be softened by pity or prayers?

DORIO: And to think that you, Phaedria, are so impudent and foolish as to think you could deceive me with your fine talk, and have for nothing what belongs to me!

ANTIPHO (*aside to* GETA): Poor fellow!

PHAEDRIA (*aside to himself*): True enough.

GETA (*aside to* ANTIPHO): See how each one acts his part.

PHAEDRIA (*to himself*): I wish this hadn't happened to me now that Antipho's in trouble.

ANTIPHO (*advancing*): What's all this trouble about, Phaedria?

PHAEDRIA: Oh, lucky Antipho.

ANTIPHO: What, I?

PHAEDRIA: Yes, you, who have your loved one at home.

ANTIPHO: Yes, indeed, but I've a wolf by the ears, as they say. I don't see how I can let her go, nor how to keep her.

DORIO: That's just the way with me.

ANTIPHO (*to* DORIO): Then be a real slave-trader, if you're going to be one at all. (*To* PHAEDRIA) Now, what's he done?

PHAEDRIA: What has he done? The villain has sold my Pamphila.

ANTIPHO: What? Sold her?

GETA: Do you mean to say he sold her?

PHAEDRIA: Yes, sold her.

DORIO: Why, what a wicked crime! To sell a girl whom I bought with my own money!

PHAEDRIA: I can't make him wait three days for me, and put off that man who wants to buy her, till I get the money my friends have promised me. And then, I told him, if I don't give him the money he needn't wait a minute longer.

DORIO: Talk away!

ANTIPHO (*to* DORIO): He doesn't ask you to wait long, Dorio. If you'll do this, he'll give you twice as much.

DORIO: Words, words.

ANTIPHO: How could you allow Pamphila to be taken away from the city? Would you allow their love to be destroyed?

DORIO: It's no affair of yours or mine; it's Phaedria's.

PHAEDRIA: May all the gods give you what you deserve!

DORIO: I have suffered your delays and insults against my will for a long time; always weeping and promising, and not giving me a thing; but now I've found a man who pays and isn't always whimpering. Give way to your betters!

ANTIPHO: Now, if I remember well, a day was agreed on when you should pay him.

PHAEDRIA: That's true.

DORIO: Well, what of it?

ANTIPHO: Has that day passed?

DORIO: No, but this has come before!

ANTIPHO: Aren't you ashamed of your trickery?

DORIO: Not in the least, especially when it's to my interest.

GETA: Rascal!

PHAEDRIA: Dorio, do you think you're acting rightly in this matter?

DORIO: That's my way of doing business; if you want me, use me.

ANTIPHO: Don't trifle with him.

DORIO: Antipho, he's trifled with me, rather; he knew I was this kind of man, but I thought *he* was very different. He's the one who's fooled me;

I've not acted differently. However, I'll do this. The captain who wants to buy the girl said he'd bring the money tomorrow morning; now, Phaedria, if you bring me the money before then, I'll act according to my motto: "First come, first served." I bid you good-bye. (*He goes into his house.*)

Act Three. Scene VI

PHAEDRIA: What shall I do now? Where can I get the money at once? I, who have less than nothing? If he had only been willing to wait three days—the money was promised at that time.

ANTIPHO: Geta, shall we let this poor fellow waste away in misery? He who helped me just now, as I told you? Come, now, shouldn't we try to return good for good, when there's such need for help?

GETA: I think it only fair we should.

ANTIPHO: You're the one man who can help him.

GETA: What can I do?

ANTIPHO: Get the money.

GETA: I'd like to; but tell me where.

ANTIPHO: My father has just returned.

GETA: Yes, I know, but what then?

ANTIPHO: A word to the wise—

GETA: What? That?

ANTIPHO: That's what I mean.

GETA: Well, you do give me fine advice indeed. Go on with you! Shouldn't I be satisfied at avoiding trouble from your marriage, without your urging me to risk my life for Phaedria's sake?

ANTIPHO (*to* PHAEDRIA): There's truth in what he says.

PHAEDRIA: What, Geta? Am I a stranger to you?

GETA: Come now, is it so small a thing that the old man is angry with us all? Should we make him angrier, so that he may never forgive us?

PHAEDRIA: And shall another take her away to a foreign land, before my very eyes? Oh, Antipho, speak to me, while I am here; look at me!

ANTIPHO: What are you going to do? Tell me.

PHAEDRIA: Wherever she is taken, I am determined to follow her, or perish in the attempt.

GETA: May the gods help you! I implore you, be careful.

ANTIPHO: See if you can help him in some way.

GETA: In what way?

ANTIPHO: Try, please; let him do nothing we may be sorry for.

GETA: Wait a minute—I think he's safe; but I fear harm.

ANTIPHO: Never fear; with you (*to* PHAEDRIA) we share good and ill fortune.

GETA (*to* PHAEDRIA): Now, tell me how much you need.

PHAEDRIA: Only thirty minae.

GETA: Only thirty! By the gods, she's expensive, Phaedria.

PHAEDRIA: Oh, that's very cheap.

GETA: Well, well, I'll get them for you. (ANTIPHO *and* PHAEDRIA *embrace him*) Away with you.

PHAEDRIA: I need it right away, remember.

GETA: At once I'll bring you the money. But I need Phormio to help me in this affair.

PHAEDRIA: He's ready; place any load on him and he'll carry it. He's a real friend.

GETA: Let's go to him now.

ANTIPHO: Will you need my help?

GETA: No; you'd better go home and comfort that poor girl. She is almost dead from fear, I'm thinking. Why do you hesitate?

ANTIPHO: Oh, there's nothing I would more willingly do! (*He goes hastily into* DEMIPHO'S *house.*)

PHAEDRIA: How'll you do this?

GETA: I'll tell you on the way; come along. (*They depart in the direction of the forum.*)

Act Four. Scene I

(*Enter* DEMIPHO *and* CHREMES *from the harbour.*)

DEMIPHO: Well, Chremes, have you brought back your daughter, for whom you went to Lemnos?

CHREMES: No, I have not.

DEMIPHO: And why not?

CHREMES: Mother and child couldn't wait for me, because of the girl's age; they told me that she and the whole family had set out to find me.

DEMIPHO: Well, when you heard this, why did you remain so long?

CHREMES: I was detained by sickness.

DEMIPHO: What sickness?

CHREMES: You ask what sickness? Why, old age itself is a sickness. But I heard the captain who brought them over say that they arrived here safe and sound.

DEMIPHO: Chremes, have you heard what's happened? About my son, when I was away?

CHREMES: That's what has made me so uncertain about my plans; because if I offer my daughter in marriage to a stranger, he must know where and how I got her. I always knew I could depend on you as upon myself. Now if a stranger should wish to marry my daughter, he'll keep still so long as we're friends; but if he takes a dislike to me, he'll learn more than he ought to know. I'm afraid, too, that my wife might find out about this some way. If she does, I must be off in a hurry. I'm the only one I can count on at home.

DEMIPHO: I know that; and that's what's troubling me. But I shan't stop till I've carried out my promise to you.

Act Four. Scene II

(*Enter* GETA.)

GETA (*to himself*): I never saw such a clever fellow in all my life as that Phormio. I come up to him, tell him we need money, and explain how to get it. I'd scarcely told him half, and he knew all about it. He was very glad, and complimented me, then asked where the old man was. He thanked the gods that he was given a chance to show that he was just as good a friend to Phaedria as he was to Antipho. I told him to wait for me at the forum, till I brought the old man. Well, here he is himself. Who's the other? Oh, Phaedria, *your* father's come back, too? Coward, what am I afraid of, anyway? Simply because I have two men to fool instead of one? It's better to have a double hope, I'm thinking. I'll go attack the first one now; if he gives me the money, that'll be enough. If I can't get anything out of him, I'll try the other.

Act Four. Scene III

(*Enter* ANTIPHO *from* DEMIPHO'S *house, unseen.*)

ANTIPHO (*to himself*): Geta will be here any time now. Ha, my uncle and my father together! I'm afraid he'll influence my father against me.

GETA (*to himself*): I'll speak to them. (*Advancing to* CHREMES) Welcome, Chremes.

CHREMES: Welcome, Geta.

GETA: I'm glad to see you've arrived safe at home.

CHREMES: Thanks.

GETA: How are things with you? Many changes since you went away?

CHREMES: Yes, a great many.

GETA: Indeed? And you have heard what has happened to Antipho?

CHREMES: Yes, everything.

GETA (*to* DEMIPHO): Did you tell him? Well, well, Chremes, and you believed it?

CHREMES: I was just now talking about it with him.

GETA: Now, after thinking over the case, I believe I've found a remedy.

CHREMES: What do you say, Geta?

DEMIPHO: What remedy?

GETA: Just after I left you, I met Phormio.

CHREMES: Who is Phormio?

DEMIPHO: The man who acted as the girl's patron.

CHREMES: Oh, yes, I know.

GETA: Well, it seemed best to find out what he thought; so I took him off alone and said to him: "Phormio, why not arrange the matter peaceably, rather than quarrel over it? My master's reasonable, and doesn't want to go to law; but all his friends have advised him to turn the poor girl out."

ANTIPHO (*aside, to himself*): What's he talking about, anyway?

GETA: "He'll have to pay the penalty by law provided, if he throws her out, you say? Oh, he's found out about that already; I tell you, you'll have your hands full if you do business with that fellow; why, he'll make you believe anything, he's such a glib talker. For the sake of argument, suppose he gets beaten; they only take his money, not his life." When I saw he was affected by what I told him, I reminded him that we were alone, and asked him how much cash he'd take to stop the suit at once and let the girl go.

ANTIPHO (*aside to himself*): Why, the fellow's crazy!

GETA: Then I said: "I'm positive that if you propose anything that's fair and square—because he's a fair man—you won't have to wait a second."

DEMIPHO: Who told you to talk that way?

CHREMES (*to* DEMIPHO): Why, he couldn't have done more to accomplish the very thing we are wishing for.

ANTIPHO (*aside*): Good-bye for me now.

CHREMES: Go on, Geta.

GETA: At first he raved like a madman.

CHREMES: Come, come, how much did he ask?

GETA: Oh, a great deal too much.

CHREMES: *How* much? Tell me, now.

GETA: Well—what if he should have asked a great talent?

DEMIPHO: The devil! Wasn't he ashamed of himself?

GETA: That's just what I told him—in these very words: "What if he were disposing of his only daughter in marriage, and giving her a dowry? What's the difference if he has one or not, when someone else is ready to ask for the fortune?" Well, to make a long story short, this was what he answered: "I've wanted all the time to marry my friend's daughter, as I ought; for I knew very well there'd be trouble if a poor wife married into a rich family. Now, to tell the truth, I needed a wife to pay off my debts; even now, indeed, I don't know of anyone I'd rather marry, if Demipho will give as much as I get from the one I'm engaged to now."

ANTIPHO (*aside*): Is he a fool, or is he deceiving me?

DEMIPHO: What if he's head over heels in debt?

GETA: He said his land's mortgaged for ten minae.

DEMIPHO: Well, let him marry her; I'll give the ten minae.

GETA: Then, his house is mortgaged for another ten.

DEMIPHO: Here, here, hold on; that's too much!

CHREMES (*to* DEMIPHO): Say no more about it; I'll pay that ten.

GETA: Now, his wife must have a waiting-maid; then, they've got to have a little more for odds and ends, and wedding expenses. He said that ten minae would cover these items.

DEMIPHO (*enraged*): He may bring a thousand suits against me for all I care! I won't give anything! The scoundrel's making game of me!

CHREMES: Please keep calm; I'll give the money, I tell you; you just bring along your son and we'll marry him off.

ANTIPHO (*aside*): Geta, Geta, you've completely ruined me by your falsehoods!

CHREMES: She's turned out because of me, and it's only right that I should make amends for it.

GETA: Then he said to me: "Let me know as soon as you can, if he'll let me marry her, so that I can let the other one go, and be sure how I stand. The other party'll pay me spot cash, you know."

CHREMES: Let him have her and marry her. Break off the other engagement; quick, now.

DEMIPHO: Yes, do! Curse him!

CHREMES: I'm glad I had some cash with me. I have the rent payments from my wife's farm at Lemnos. (CHREMES *and* DEMIPHO *go into* CHREMES' *house.*)

Act Four.   Scene IV

ANTIPHO (*advancing*): Geta!

GETA: Yes.

ANTIPHO: What have you done?

GETA: Cleaned the old men out of their money.

ANTIPHO: Is that so?

GETA: I did what I was ordered to do.

ANTIPHO: Do you give me an answer when I don't ask?

GETA: Well, what *did* you ask me to do?

ANTIPHO: What? Through your fault matters have come to such a state that I had better go and hang myself. May all the gods and goddesses, below and above, curse you! I see now, if you want anything done, let the man do it who will take you out of calm smooth water to a sharp and dangerous rock! Why should you now touch my wound, by mentioning my wife? My father has great hopes that he can get rid of her. See here, now: what if Phormio should accept the dowry? He'd have to marry her. What then?

GETA: But he's not going to marry her.

ANTIPHO: I know it. But when they ask for the dowry back again, Phormio will of course, out of consideration for us, march right off to jail!

GETA: Antipho, there is nothing that can't be made worse in the telling. You tell the worst side, and leave out all that's good. Now listen to what I've to say on the other side of the question: if he should take the money, he must, as you say, marry her. I'll grant that. Yet, some time is necessary to prepare for the ceremony, invite the guests, and for the sacrifices. Now, during this interval Phormio's friends will give the money they've promised.

ANTIPHO: But what friends? On what grounds? What'll he say?

GETA: What? "How many extraordinary things have happened to me! A strange dog came into my house; a serpent entered the skylight from the roof, and—a hen crowed! The soothsayer prevented it, the fortune-teller forbade it; it's impossible to begin any new business before the shortest day of winter!" And that's the best excuse of all. You see?

ANTIPHO: I wish it would happen that way.

GETA: It will; just trust me. Here comes your father; go and tell Phaedria that I've got the money. (ANTIPHO *departs hurriedly*.)

Act Four. Scene V

(*Enter* DEMIPHO *and* CHREMES *from* CHREMES' *house*.)

DEMIPHO: Silence, I tell you! I'll see that he plays no tricks on me. I won't pay any money till I have witnesses. I'll have it set down to whom and for what I give it.

GETA (*aside*): How careful he is!

CHREMES: You're perfectly right; and you should do it at once while you're in the mood. Now if the other woman insists a little more than ours does, he may give us the slip.

GETA (*aloud*): There, sir, you are right.

DEMIPHO (*to* GETA): Take me to him.

GETA: At once, sir.

CHREMES (*to* DEMIPHO): Go to my wife when you're done, so she may visit Phanium before she leaves. Let her tell her that we are going to marry her off to Phormio, to prevent her being angry with us; say that he's better suited to her, because he knows her; that we've done our best, and that the dowry is as large as he asked for.

DEMIPHO: What the deuce do you care?

CHREMES: I care a great deal, Demipho. It's not sufficient for a man to do his duty—people must know all about it. I wish this to be done as she wants it done, that she may not say she was turned out.

DEMIPHO: Why, I myself can do that.

CHREMES: It's better for a woman to do it.

DEMIPHO: I'll go and ask for her. (DEMIPHO *and* GETA *go out towards the forum.*)

CHREMES (*to himself*): I wonder where my wife and daughter can be?

Act Four.   Scene VI[8]

(*Enter* SOPHRONA *from* DEMIPHO'S *house.*)

SOPHRONA (*to herself, not seeing* CHREMES): What *shall* I do? I'm so miserable, I haven't a friend in the world! Where shall I get advice or help? I'm so afraid that my dear mistress may get into trouble through my negligence. She does not deserve it at all. I hear that the young man's father is very angry at what's been done.

CHREMES (*aside*): Who's this old woman, I wonder, coming out of my brother's house? She seems very much upset.

SOPHRONA (*still not seeing* CHREMES): Poverty forced me to do it, even though I knew the marriage wasn't strictly legal; but I had to find some way to keep her alive.

CHREMES (*aside*): Why, she's my daughter's nurse, if I'm not mistaken.

SOPHRONA (*as before*): And we can't find—

CHREMES (*aside*): What shall I do?

SOPHRONA (*as before*): —her father anywhere.

CHREMES (*aside*): There's no mistake about it. I'll speak to her.

SOPHRONA: Who's that talking?

CHREMES (*advancing*): Sophrona!

SOPHRONA: He knows my name!

CHREMES: Look at me; turn round.

SOPHRONA (*turning around, and with great surprise*): Heavens! Aren't you Stilpo?

CHREMES: No.

SOPHRONA: Do you deny it?

CHREMES (*lowering his voice, and glancing suspiciously towards the house*): Just come away from the door a few steps, please. Now, don't call me Stilpo any more.

SOPHRONA: Why not? Didn't you always tell me you were called Stilpo?

CHREMES: Sh-h-h—(*Looking again at the house.*)

SOPHRONA: Why are you so afraid of that door?

CHREMES: I've a fiery-tempered wife caged up there. I changed my name to Stilpo so that you wouldn't tell it to anybody; my wife might learn the truth.

SOPHRONA: Yes, and that's just why we could never find you.

CHREMES: Tell me, what have you to do with that family in there? Where are the women?

SOPHRONA: Oh, I'm so miserable!

CHREMES: What's the matter? Are they—still living?

SOPHRONA: The daughter is; but her mother, poor creature, died of grief.

CHREMES: Well, well, that's very sad, very sad, indeed.

SOPHRONA: And I, an old woman, lonely, poor and without friends, did what I could to marry the girl to the young man who lives there— (*Pointing to* ANTIPHO'S *house*).

CHREMES: What's that? To Antipho?

SOPHRONA: Yes; he's the one.

CHREMES: Do you mean to tell me he has two wives?

SOPHRONA: Not at all. This is the only one.

CHREMES: Well, what about that girl they say is his relative?

SOPHRONA: This is the one.

CHREMES: Why—why—how?

SOPHRONA: It was done on purpose, in order that he might marry her without a dowry.

CHREMES: Blessed be the gods, by whose aid things happen that we wouldn't even dare hope for! Here I am returning to find my daughter about to marry the very man I wished her to. The very thing we were trying so hard to bring about he has arranged by his own efforts.

SOPHRONA: Now let's see what is to be done. His father has just returned, and they say he's very angry.

CHREMES: There's no danger, however. By gods and men, I beg you not to let anyone know she's my daughter!

SOPHRONA: Never fear: no one shall know it from me.

CHREMES: Follow me, please. I'll tell you the rest inside. (*They go into* DEMIPHO'S *house.*)

Act Five.   Scene I

(*Enter* DEMIPHO *and* GETA, *from the forum.*)

DEMIPHO: Well, it's our own fault that it's better to be dishonest; and yet we want to be called honest and honourable! I suppose it wasn't enough to be injured by him, but he must go and get my money, and live on that while he's planning how to fleece someone else.

GETA: Perfectly right.

DEMIPHO: People nowadays get the best of it who don't recognise the difference between right and wrong.

GETA: Certainly.

DEMIPHO: We were fools to do business with him as we did.

GETA: I only hope we can manage to have him marry her this way.

DEMIPHO: Is there any doubt about that?

GETA: Now, considering what sort of fellow he is, he might perhaps change his mind.

DEMIPHO: Change his mind?

GETA: I'm not sure. I said "Perhaps."

DEMIPHO: I'll do what my brother told me to do: I'll bring his wife and have her talk with her. You go ahead, Geta; tell her Nausistrata is going to call on her. (DEMIPHO *goes into* CHREMES' *house.*)

GETA (*to himself*): I must get that money for Phaedria; the lawsuit business is out of the way, and she is going to remain where she is now. Well, what then? I'm still sticking in the mud; I'm only borrowing money to pay off a debt. Clouds are gathering round me, and I'd better be on the lookout. Well, I'll go home now, and tell Phanium not to be afraid of Phormio, and not to fear Nausistrata's words. (*He goes into* DEMIPHO's *house.*)

Act Five.   Scene II

(*Enter* DEMIPHO *and* NAUSISTRATA *from* CHREMES' *house.*)

DEMIPHO: Come, Nausistrata, cheer her up, as you always do, and make her do what must be done.

NAUSISTRATA: Willingly.

DEMIPHO: Do you know you're a great help to me, Nausistrata?

NAUSISTRATA: Not so much as I should wish to be, because of that husband of mine.

DEMIPHO: How's that?

NAUSISTRATA: He's so careless with that farm my father left him; why, my father used to get two talents a year from the products. Just see how much one man surpasses another!

DEMIPHO: Two talents, you say?

NAUSISTRATA: Yes, and that much even when times were worse.

DEMIPHO (*in astonishment*): Whew!

NAUSISTRATA: Are you surprised?

DEMIPHO: Of course.

NAUSISTRATA: *I* should have been a man; I'd have shown them what—

DEMIPHO: Undoubtedly.

NAUSISTRATA: How I—

DEMIPHO: Stop, please, so that you can talk with her. She's a young girl and may tire you out.

NAUSISTRATA: Very well. There's my husband.

(*Enter* CHREMES, *running from* DEMIPHO'S *house.*)

CHREMES (*not seeing* NAUSISTRATA): Demipho, Demipho, have you paid him yet?

DEMIPHO: Yes—just a few minutes ago.

CHREMES: Well, I wish you hadn't. (*Aside, as he sees* NAUSISTRATA) Aha, my wife! I almost said too much.

DEMIPHO: How's that, Chremes?

CHREMES: Never mind; everything's all right.

DEMIPHO: What? Did you let her know why we're bringing her? (*Points to* NAUSISTRATA.)

CHREMES: I've arranged everything.

DEMIPHO: What does she say?

CHREMES: She won't leave.

DEMIPHO: Why is that?

CHREMES: They love each other.

DEMIPHO: What's the difference?

CHREMES: A great deal. (*Aside*) Then, I just found out she's a relative of yours.

DEMIPHO (*aside*): You're crazy!

CHREMES (*aside*): I tell you, she is.

DEMIPHO (*aside*): She isn't.

CHREMES (*aside*): Her father took another name, and that threw us off the scent.

DEMIPHO (*aside*): Didn't she know her own father?

CHREMES (*aside*): Of course.

DEMIPHO (*aside*): Then why did she call him by another name?

CHREMES (*aside*): Don't you understand, or won't you?

DEMIPHO (*aside*): But if you don't—?

CHREMES (*aside*): Do you still wish to keep it up?

NAUSISTRATA: What's all this fuss about?

DEMIPHO: I'm sure I don't know.

CHREMES (*whispering to* DEMIPHO): Do you really want to know? Well, I swear by Jupiter, she's our closest relative.

DEMIPHO: By all the gods, let's go to her; I must know all about this. (*Turning to leave.*)

CHREMES (*stopping him*): Here, stop!

DEMIPHO: What's the matter?

CHREMES (*reproachfully*): Don't you believe me?

DEMIPHO: You want me to believe you? Very well, then. But—what shall we do about—our friend's— (*With a significant wink at* CHREMES) —daughter?

CHREMES: She's all right.

DEMIPHO: Shall we let her go?

CHREMES: Why not?

DEMIPHO: And allow the other to stay?

CHREMES: Yes.

DEMIPHO: We don't need you any longer, Nausistrata.

NAUSISTRATA: I think it's better for us all that she stay here. She seemed very nice when I saw her. (NAUSISTRATA *goes into* CHREMES' *house.*)

DEMIPHO: How about this, Chremes?

CHREMES (*looking anxiously at the door of his house*): Is the door closed?

DEMIPHO: Yes.

CHREMES: Oh, Jupiter, we're fortunate! I've found that my daughter has married your son!

DEMIPHO: Is it possible! How did it happen?

CHREMES: This isn't the place to tell you.

DEMIPHO: Let's go inside.

CHREMES: Listen; I don't want our sons to know anything about this business. (DEMIPHO *and* CHREMES *go into* DEMIPHO'S *house.*)

Act Five.   Scene III

(*Enter* ANTIPHO *from the forum.*)

ANTIPHO (*to himself*): Well, I'm delighted that my cousin's affairs are going so well, no matter how mine are going. How wise it is to have only such longings as can be easily satisfied when things go wrong! He has plenty of money and no cares; now, I can't possibly get out of my troubles; if it's kept secret, I'm afraid—if it's known, I'm disgraced. I shouldn't go home now, if I didn't think that in some way I could keep her. Where is Geta? I want to find out where I may safely meet my father.

Act Five.   Scene IV

(*Enter* PHORMIO *from the forum.*)

PHORMIO (*aside to himself, not seeing* ANTIPHO): I got the money, gave it to the slave-trader, took the girl and gave her to Phaedria. There's just one more thing to be done—get the old men to let me have time for a grand night of it!

ANTIPHO: Aha, Phormio! (*Advancing*) Well, what have you to say?

PHORMIO: What's that?

ANTIPHO: What is Phaedria going to do?

PHORMIO: Just what you did.

ANTIPHO: And what is that?

PHORMIO: Run away from his father; and he asks you to make his excuses. He's going to have a grand time of it at my house. I'll tell the old men I'm going to the fair at Sunium to buy the lady's maid that Geta told them about just now. I don't want them to think I'm wasting their money when they find I've gone. But I hear your door creaking.

ANTIPHO: See who's coming out.

PHORMIO: It's Geta.

Act Five. Scene V

(*Enter* GETA *from* DEMIPHO'S *house.*)

GETA (*to himself*): Oh! Goddess of Good Fortune, how great and manifold are the blessings thou hast heaped upon Antipho!

ANTIPHO (*to* PHORMIO): What's he talking about?

GETA (*as before*): And freed us, his friends, from all our fears. But I'd better hurry up and find him.

ANTIPHO (*aside to* PHORMIO): Can you make out what he's talking about?

PHORMIO (*aside to* ANTIPHO): Can *you*?

ANTIPHO (*aside to* PHORMIO): Not a word.

PHORMIO (*aside to* ANTIPHO): Neither can I.

GETA (*as before*): Well, I'll hurry to the slave-trader's; that's where they are. (*Turns and starts away.*)

ANTIPHO: Oh, Geta!

GETA (*not turning*): That's nothing new!

ANTIPHO: Geta, Geta!

GETA (*still farther away*): Keep it up! That's right!

ANTIPHO (*running out after* GETA): We'll see about this!

GETA: You'll get whipped, if you don't take care.

ANTIPHO: You villain, you're the one who'll get the whipping.

GETA: Must be someone I know, if *he'll* beat me. (GETA *turns around and is surprised*) The very man!

ANTIPHO: Well, what is it?

GETA: You're the happiest man alive, Antipho.

ANTIPHO: I wish it with all my heart; but tell me why. Don't keep me waiting.

PHORMIO: Hurry up and tell us, won't you?

GETA (*seeing* PHORMIO): Oh, you are here, too?

PHORMIO: Yes, but go on.

GETA: Listen to me. Just after we gave you the money, we went to Chremes; in the meanwhile, my master sent me to get your wife.

ANTIPHO: Why did he do that?

GETA: Never mind, Antipho. Just as I was going to the room where the ladies were, the boy ran up and stopped me. He said no one was allowed to see his mistress, and that Sophrona was talking with Chremes. Then I listened at the door and heard what they said.

ANTIPHO: Good! Go on.

GETA: I heard a fine piece of news. I almost shouted for joy.

ANTIPHO: What was it? Quick!

GETA: What do you think?

ANTIPHO: I don't know.

GETA: Most wonderful! Your uncle is your wife Phanium's father!

ANTIPHO (*excitedly*): *What!*

GETA: He had a secret love affair with her mother long ago in Lemnos.

PHORMIO: You're dreaming. How did it happen that she didn't know her own father?

GETA: I know there's some good reason. Besides, I couldn't hear everything.

ANTIPHO: Now, I've heard that same story before.

GETA: Yes, and I'll tell you one reason for believing it: your uncle came out and went away. Then he came back with your father, and they both agreed to let you marry her. They sent me to find you and bring you where they are.

ANTIPHO: Well, why don't you take me at once? Hurry.

GETA: By all means.

ANTIPHO: Good-bye, dear Phormio.

PHORMIO: Good-bye, Antipho. (*To himself, as* ANTIPHO *and* GETA *go into* DEMIPHO's *house*) This is lucky, and I'm glad of it. Here's my chance to outwit the old fellows, and fix Phaedria in a comfortable way. The money has been given to Phaedria and he shall keep it, whether they wish it or not. I've found the means now to force their hand. I must assume a different air and expression. I'll hide in this alley and wait for them. I shan't go on that business journey that I pretended a while ago.[9] (*He retires into the alley.*)

Act Five. Scene VI

(*Enter* DEMIPHO *and* CHREMES *from* DEMIPHO'S *house.*)

DEMIPHO: The gods be thanked, brother, for this good fortune! We'd better find Phormio before he spends the money, and get it back from him.

PHORMIO (*advancing from the alley*): I'll go and see whether Demipho's home, and—

DEMIPHO: Phormio, we were looking for you.

PHORMIO: For the same reason, I suppose?

DEMIPHO: That's right.

PHORMIO: Certainly; but why were you coming to me?

DEMIPHO: Don't waste time.

PHORMIO: Do you think I shan't do what I undertook? No matter how poor I am, I've always kept my word. And I come to you now, Demipho, to tell you that I am ready. Give me the girl, if you please; I understand that you desire it with all your heart.

DEMIPHO: But this man has persuaded me not to let you have her. He said, "What will people say if you do this? A while ago, when she might have been honourably married off, no one wanted her. Now, it's wrong to turn her out." He told me almost the same things you told me not long ago.

PHORMIO: You are certainly very impudent.

DEMIPHO: How is that?

PHORMIO: Don't you see that I can't marry the other one now, after I've let her go?

CHREMES (*aside to* DEMIPHO): "Then I see Antipho won't let his wife go." Tell him that.

DEMIPHO: Then I see Antipho—a—a won't let his wife go. But please come over to the forum, and give me back my money.

PHORMIO: I can't; I've just paid off my debts.

DEMIPHO: What of it?

PHORMIO: If you wish to let me have the girl you promised me, I'll marry her. But if you want her to remain with you, the dowry remains here, Demipho. It isn't right for me to lose out on your account; it was for your sake that I broke my engagement with the other girl, who was to bring me just as large a dowry.

DEMIPHO: Do you think we don't know all about your trickery, you villain?

PHORMIO: Don't make me too angry, now.

DEMIPHO: Would you marry the girl?

PHORMIO: Just try and see.

DEMIPHO: Come along with the money.

PHORMIO: Come along and give me the girl.

DEMIPHO (*seizing him*): Come to court at once—

PHORMIO: Take care, or I'll—

DEMIPHO: What'll you do?

PHORMIO: What? Oh, I do more than protect girls without dowries.

CHREMES: What do we care?

PHORMIO: Oh, nothing. But I heard of a woman here whose husband—

CHREMES (*startled*): Oh!

DEMIPHO: What's the matter, Chremes?

PHORMIO: Had another wife at Lemnos.

CHREMES (*aside*): I'm dead!

PHORMIO: He had a daughter by her, and brought her up secretly.

CHREMES (*aside*): I'm buried!

PHORMIO: I'm going to tell her about this at once. (*Starts towards* CHREMES' *house.*)

CHREMES: Don't, don't. (*Catching him.*)

PHORMIO: Perhaps you were that man?

DEMIPHO: He's making fun of us.

CHREMES: We'll let it drop, Phormio.

PHORMIO: Nonsense!

CHREMES: What more do you want? We'll let you have the money, too.

PHORMIO: Very well; but why do you pester me with your childish actions? "I will, I won't. Give me this, keep it."

CHREMES (*aside to* DEMIPHO): How did he find out about this?

DEMIPHO (*aside to* CHREMES): I don't know. I haven't told anyone.

PHORMIO (*aside*): I've got them this time.

DEMIPHO (*aside to* CHREMES): Shall I let him carry off so much money? I'd rather die. You see, this little indiscretion of yours is well known, and you can't conceal it any longer from your wife. I think you'd better tell her yourself before she hears it from anybody else; then we can get even with this Phormio fellow.

PHORMIO (*aside*): Oho! I'd better look out now or I'll get caught. They're ganging up against me.

CHREMES (*to* DEMIPHO): I'm afraid she'll never forgive me.

DEMIPHO (*to* CHREMES): Cheer up. I'll restore you to her favour, Chremes, with the argument that the girl's mother has died.

PHORMIO (*as they approach nearer*): So this is how you treat me, is it? Very well. Demipho, you've made me angry now, and it won't do Chremes any particular good, I can tell you. (*To* CHREMES) So you thought you could amuse yourself abroad and neglect your wife here and wrong her in this way, eh? And then you'll come whining to her for forgiveness? Well, I'll make her so blazing angry that you can't quench her fury even if you dissolve in tears.

DEMIPHO: Damn this fellow! That anyone should have such impudence! He ought to be dumped on some desert island at the public expense.

CHREMES (*aside*): Now I *am* in trouble.

DEMIPHO: I've an idea. Let's go to court.

PHORMIO: To court? No, no, here. (*Pointing to* CHREMES' *house, and trying to go in that direction.*)

DEMIPHO (*to* CHREMES): Hold him till I fetch servants.

CHREMES (*trying to hold* PHORMIO): I can't do it alone; you help me. (*They both hold him and begin to drag him towards the forum.*)

PHORMIO: Oho, I see I must use my lungs. Nausistrata, Nausistrata, come here!

CHREMES (*to* DEMIPHO): Stop his mouth.

DEMIPHO: He's too strong.

PHORMIO: Nausistrata!

CHREMES: Keep still, won't you!

PHORMIO: Keep still?

DEMIPHO (*to* CHREMES): Strike him hard, if he won't come.

PHORMIO: Yes, or put out an eye. But I'll have my revenge.

Act Five.   Scene VII

(*Enter* NAUSISTRATA *from her house.*)

NAUSISTRATA: Who's calling me?

CHREMES: Oh!

NAUSISTRATA: Husband, what does this mean?

PHORMIO (*to* CHREMES): Why don't you tell her?

NAUSISTRATA: Who is this man? Answer me.

PHORMIO (*to* NAUSISTRATA): He doesn't know where he is.

CHREMES (*to* NAUSISTRATA): Don't believe him, I beg you.

PHORMIO (*to* NAUSISTRATA): Look at him; scared to death!

CHREMES: I'm not.

NAUSISTRATA: What's he talking about, then?

PHORMIO: Listen, and I'll tell you.

CHREMES (*to* NAUSISTRATA): Will you believe him?

NAUSISTRATA: He hasn't told me anything yet. You're frightened.

CHREMES: I?

PHORMIO (*to* CHREMES): Well, since this is nothing and you're not frightened, you tell her.

NAUSISTRATA: Please tell me, Chremes.

CHREMES: But I—

NAUSISTRATA: But what?

CHREMES: What's the use anyway?

PHORMIO: No use—for you. But she ought to know all about it. In Lemnos—

DEMIPHO: What are you doing?

CHREMES (*to* PHORMIO): Keep still, I tell you!

PHORMIO (*to* NAUSISTRATA): You didn't know it—

CHREMES: Stop!

PHORMIO: He married another woman!

NAUSISTRATA: It can't be!

PHORMIO: It is.

NAUSISTRATA: How wretched I am!

PHORMIO: And he had a daughter by her.

NAUSISTRATA: What a wicked deed!

DEMIPHO (*aside to* CHREMES): You're done for!

NAUSISTRATA: Oh, what wickedness! (*To* DEMIPHO) Demipho, I appeal to you, for it makes me sick to speak to him. So this was the meaning of the many voyages and the long stays in Lemnos! This was the low prices that brought down our rents!

DEMIPHO: Nausistrata, of course he is somewhat to blame, but might he not be forgiven?

PHORMIO: He's speaking for a corpse.

DEMIPHO: It wasn't that he was tired of you or disliked you. Fifteen years ago he seduced the girl's mother when he was drunk. He had no intercourse with her after that. She's dead now and the difficulty's vanished. So just be patient.

NAUSISTRATA: Patient? How do I know he won't do the same thing again?

PHORMIO (*loudly*): All who wish to attend the funeral of Chremes, this way, please! I've had my revenge. Make it up with him, Nausistrata. Now, you've got something to pester him with for the rest of your life.

NAUSISTRATA (*ironically*): I suppose this was my fault. Why should I tell him now, Demipho, how devoted I've been to him?

DEMIPHO: I know this as well as you do.

NAUSISTRATA: Have I deserved such treatment, then?

DEMIPHO: Of course not. But he begs you to forgive him—he confesses his fault. What more can you ask?

PHORMIO (*to* NAUSISTRATA): Just a minute, Nausistrata; listen to me before you answer him.

NAUSISTRATA: What is it?

PHORMIO: I got thirty minae out of him, which I gave to your son, who purchased his wife from the slave-trader.

CHREMES: What's that?

NAUSISTRATA: Do you think it's so disgraceful for your son, a young man, to have one mistress, when you have two wives? Aren't you ashamed of yourself? How will you have the face to scold him? Tell me that.

PHORMIO: He'll do as you wish.

NAUSISTRATA: I won't say anything till I see my son. I'll do just as he advises.

DEMIPHO: That's right, Nausistrata.

NAUSISTRATA: Are you satisfied, Chremes?

CHREMES: Yes—(*aside*) and more than satisfied.

NAUSISTRATA (*to* PHORMIO): What is your name, please?

PHORMIO: Phormio, a good friend to your son, Phaedria.

NAUSISTRATA: Phormio, I shall do for you what I can.

PHORMIO: Many thanks. First, will you do something to make your husband angry?

NAUSISTRATA: Gladly. What is it?

PHORMIO: Invite me to dinner.

NAUSISTRATA: Very well; I invite you.

DEMIPHO: Come, let's go in.

CHREMES: Yes, but where is Phaedria?

PHORMIO: He'll be here in a minute. (*Turning to the audience*) Farewell—and give us your applause.

THE TRANSLATION of the *Phormio* by Barrett H. Clark was an acting version and several passages of the original were omitted or abridged. The editor has added or revised the following lines: 1-34 (the prologue), 77-78, 276-278, 330-333, 361-371, 412-419, 428-429, 545, 708-710, 760-761, 794, 821-822, 838-840, 873, 888-890, 893, 927-929, 963-979, 1011-1020, 1031-1033, 1040-1042.

1. This disregards the unsuccessful performance of *The Mother-in-law* in 165 B.C.

2. The *Phormio* was produced in the year 161 B.C. at the *ludi Romani,* or Roman Games, given in honour of Jupiter.

3. This is a reference to Terence's rival, Luscius Lanuvinus.

4. This apparently refers to the failure of *The Mother-in-law* at its first production.

5. The translator's division into acts has been adopted. Kauer and Lindsay begin Act Two at this point.

6. This sentence is assigned to Phaedria by Kauer and Lindsay.

7. Kauer and Lindsay begin Act Three here.

8. Kauer and Lindsay begin Act Five here.

9. Phormio's soliloquy forms a separate scene in most editions.

V
THE MOTHER-IN-LAW

Characters in the Play

PHILOTIS, *a courtesan*
SYRA, *an old bawd*
PARMENO, *slave of* LACHES *and* PAMPHILUS
LACHES, *an old man, father of* PAMPHILUS
SOSTRATA, *wife of* LACHES
PHIDIPPUS, *neighbour of* LACHES
PAMPHILUS, *son of* LACHES *and* SOSTRATA
SOSIA, *slave of* PAMPHILUS
MYRRINA, *wife of* PHIDIPPUS
BACCHIS, *a courtesan, former mistress of* PAMPHILUS

DIDASCALIA

The Mother-in-law of Terence. Acted at the Megalensian Games during the curule aedileship of Sextus Julius Caesar and Gnaeus Cornelius Dolabella. It was not acted through. It was set to music by Flaccus, slave of Claudius, to the accompaniment of equal flutes. It is entirely taken from the Greek of Menander.[1] It was acted for the first time without a prologue; [it was given for the second time][2] during the consulship of Gnaeus Octavius and Titus Manlius. It was tried again at the Funeral Games in honour of Lucius Aemilius Paulus.[3] It did not meet with approval. It was brought on again for the third time during the curule aedileship of Quintus Fulvius and Lucius Marcius. Under the management of Lucius Ambivius and Lucius Sergius Turpio, it met with a favourable reception.[4]

SUMMARY

Pamphilus has married Philumena, whom he had earlier wronged without knowing who she was; a ring, which he had forcibly snatched from her, he gave to his mistress, the courtesan Bacchis. Then he set out to Imbros without having touched his bride. Since she was pregnant, her mother took her to her own house under the pretence of illness, so that her mother-in-law wouldn't know about it. Pamphilus returns, discovers that she has had a child, and keeps it secret, but he refuses to take her back as his wife. His father accuses him of being in love with Bacchis. While Bacchis is clearing herself, Myrrina, the mother of the outraged girl, happens to recognise the ring. Pamphilus takes back his wife together with their son.

INTRODUCTION

The Mother-in-law is the most serious comedy to be found among the plays of Plautus and Terence. Terence here adapted to the Roman stage a Greek original by Apollodorus which in turn had been strongly influenced by Menander's *The Arbitration*. The comedy by Apollodorus is lost, but the greater part of Menander's play survives. There is a basic similarity of theme, in spite of numerous differences of detail. Terence, like Menander, starts at the point where ancient comedy usually ended —the marriage of the youth and the maiden. Both *The Arbitration* and *The Mother-in-law* deal in a serious way with a married couple, the complications which bring about a separation, and the misunderstandings which develop before a reconciliation can be effected. The reasons for the separation and the discovery that leads to the reconciliation are similar in both plays.

The Mother-in-law tells the story of Pamphilus and his wife Philumena. Pamphilus had been in love with a courtesan Bacchis and had married against his will. He had no intercourse with Philumena, but her sweetness and patience won his love. Then he was compelled to go abroad on business. He returns to find that his wife has been unable to live with her mother-in-law and has returned to her parents. His discovery of the real reason—that she has given birth to a child—makes the situation more difficult. The fathers of the young couple believe that the child should unite husband and wife. Pamphilus knows that the child is not his; his wife had been ravished by an unknown stranger before her marriage, and he is all the more determined not to take her back and accept another man's child as his own. The misconceptions of the others concerning both Philumena's actions and Pamphilus' attitude lead to excellent irony; the separation which had originally been blamed on Sostrata, Philumena's mother-in-law, is now attributed to Pamphilus' love for Bacchis. The intervention of Bacchis brings about a new discovery—an occurrence which had been known neither to the characters of the play nor to the audience. The revelation of this fact brings the series of complications to a happy conclusion.

The comedy contains many stock themes such as the violation of a maiden and the use of a ring to bring about a recognition. Its unusual features, however, are even more numerous and striking and deserve further comment. (1) The play gives a serious portrayal of married life, as has been pointed out. (2) The spectators are kept in ignorance of the true facts of the situation until the very end. Terence in most of his plays refrained from foreshadowing the later action, but in no other comedy has he so eliminated anticipation and used the elements of uncertainty and surprise. This more modern conception of suspense is believed by Tenney Frank and others to constitute Terence's great contribution to ancient dramatic technique. (3) The play is essentially a woman's play and contains two of Terence's most brilliant creations. Pamphilus, his father, and his father-in-law are well portrayed; Pamphilus loves his wife, but adheres to a double standard of morality in his attitude towards her; of the two old men Laches is firmer and more hot-tempered, Phidippus better-natured and weaker. These characters are respectable and sensible, but they are drawn with less care than the two outstanding women characters, Bacchis and Sostrata. Bacchis is the most attractive courtesan in Roman comedy, dignified, kind-hearted, and generous. Her actions in the play are the result of her character, and she is happy to be the means of reconciling Pamphilus and his wife. Sostrata, the mother-in-law, is everything that a mother-in-law is supposed not to be; she is tender and patient and self-sacrificing; devoted to her son Pamphilus and believing herself the innocent cause of Philumena's departure, she is eager to leave the city rather than stand in the way of her son's happiness. There is nothing conventional in Terence's delineation of these two characters. (4) The comedy is the only one of Terence's plays in which he does not use the double plot of two young men whose love affairs are more or less tightly interwoven. Although attempts have been made to find a dual structure in the plot of *The Mother-in-law* by arguing that there are two difficulties which concern the same man and woman, it can hardly be claimed with success that the play is similar in this respect to the other five comedies. (5) While there is considerable irony in the wrong conclusions which Laches, Phidippus, and others draw in trying to solve Pamphilus' marital difficulties, the play has very little humour. Parmeno is the exact opposite of the knavish slave. He adds an occasional touch of comedy to the play but in an unconventional manner. He is funny when he is prevented from being funny. He is constantly being shoved off the stage on one pretext or another, and even at the end, when he is the bearer of good tidings to Pamphilus, he has no knowledge of the significance of the message. No other slave in Roman comedy is ever kept so completely in the dark. His final speech sounds the keynote of Terence's treatment, "I've done more good today unknowingly than I ever did knowingly before."

The Mother-in-law is one of Terence's best plays, but its unconventionality of theme, character, and treatment was apparently too great for the theatre audiences of the second century B.C. The play failed twice and only at its third production did it gain a successful hearing. In modern times also the comedy has been grossly underrated; e.g. S. G. Ashmore says that it has the "least merit" of Terence's work, and M. S. Dimsdale considers it "hardly a comedy at all." Gilbert Norwood rightly condemns such unfavourable criticism. He himself believes that in *The Mother-in-law* "we find the purest and most perfect example of classical high comedy, strictly so called, which dramatic literature can offer from any age or any nation." This praise is undoubtedly excessive, and most scholars and readers will prefer to look upon *The Brothers* as Terence's masterpiece. Yet *The Mother-in-law* must be considered as Terence's most courageous undertaking, as a play which reveals his ability to rise far above the conventional technique of his day and to write more serious drama with vigour and originality.

THE MOTHER-IN-LAW

(SCENE:—*A street in Athens in front of the houses of* LACHES, PHIDIP-
PUS, *and* BACCHIS.)

First Prologue[5]

THE NAME of this play is *The Mother-in-Law*. When it was first put on
the stage a strange misfortune befell it, so that it could neither be seen,
nor heard, so full were the silly people's heads of a rope-dancer. So now
it is quite as good as new, for the writer would not bring it on the stage
a second time that day, that he might be able to sell it to the aediles a
second time. You have heard other plays by the writer; now pray hear
this one.

Second Prologue[6]

I come to you really as a pleader, though dressed as one who speaks
a prologue. Let me win my cause, and let me now, that I am old, succeed as I used to do when I was a younger man, in giving new life to
plays which have failed, so that they have a long run on the stage, and
the poet and his writings may not perish together.

When first I began to act Caecilius'[7] plays, when they were new to
the stage, some of them were damned and some I just carried through.
Now, as I know how uncertain are the fortunes of plays, I undertook
an undoubted labour with but doubtful hope of success; I proceeded to
act them that he might give me new plays to act, and I took pains that
I might not drive him to give up playwriting. I succeeded in getting a
hearing for them, and when they became known they were approved.
Thus did I reinstate as a playwright one who had almost been driven
from his profession, his work, and from poetry itself, by the malice of
his enemies. Now if I had scoffed at his works at first and chosen to
give my mind to scare him into idleness, I could easily have stopped his
writing any more plays.

Now, for my sake, hear with forbearance what I beg of you. I bring
back again *The Mother-in-law,* a play which I have never been allowed
to act in peace; it was ruined by ill-luck. This ill-luck will now be
dispelled if your good taste will second our efforts. When first I began

366

to act it, the excitement of boxing-matches, added to the expectation
of rope-dancing, the throngs of great men's retainers, the bustle, and
the squalls of women drove me from the stage before the play was at an
end.

I meant to deal with this new play according to my old rule, and
give it a fair trial, so I began it a second time. In the first act I was
successful; but then a rumour spread through the audience that a show
of gladiators was going to be exhibited, whereupon, rioting, shouting,
and fighting for places, the populace hurried off together, and I could
not hold my own. There is no disturbance now; all is peace and quiet.
I have a chance to act the play; you have an opportunity of doing
honour to the theatre by your patronage. Do not, by your fault, let the
art of playwriting fall into the hands of a small clique; let your influence help and back up mine. I have never charged unconscionable
prices for my services, and have always thought it my highest reward
to please you to the best of my ability; wherefore, grant me what I ask.
Do not let the author, who has entrusted his work to me, and himself
to your honour, be undeservedly discomfited and put to shame by his
enemies. Listen to this plea for my sake, and grant me silence, that other
authors may be encouraged to write for the stage, and it may be worth
my while to bring out new plays hereafter at my own expense.

Act One. Scene I

(*Enter* PHILOTIS *and* SYRA *from* BACCHIS' *house*.)

PHILOTIS: Gracious me, Syra, how few lovers you can find who prove
faithful to courtesans. Look at Pamphilus; how often did he swear to
Bacchis so solemnly that anyone might have believed him, that while
she lived he never would marry. Well, now he is married.

SYRA: This is why I am always counselling you and urging you never
to show mercy to anyone, but to strip, maim and rend to pieces every
man you get hold of.

PHILOTIS: Am I to spare no one?

SYRA: No one; for you may be sure that everyone who visits you does
his best to coax you into letting him have his will as cheaply as possible; and, pray, are you not to lay traps for fellows of this kind?

PHILOTIS: Still, it is wrong to treat them all alike.

SYRA: Is it wrong to revenge yourselves on your foes, or to take them in just as they take you in? Oh, dear me! Why am I not as young and as pretty as you, or why can't you have sense like me?

Act One.   Scene II

(Enter PARMENO *from* LACHES' *house.)*

PARMENO (*to* SCIRTUS, *behind the scenes*): If the old gentleman asks for me, tell him that I've just gone down to the harbour to enquire when Pamphilus will return. You hear what I say, Scirtus? Tell him this tale if he asks for me, but don't say a word of it if he doesn't ask, so that I may have this story fresh for use another time. (*Turning round*) But isn't this little Philotis whom I see? Where does she come from? My best respects, Philotis.

PHILOTIS: Good day, Parmeno.

SYRA: Good day to you, Parmeno.

PARMENO: Same to you, Syra. Tell me, Philotis, where you have been amusing yourself for all this long time.

PHILOTIS: Very little amusement I've had; for I went off from here to Corinth with a great brute of a soldier, and endured his company there for two mortal years.

PARMENO: Gad, Philotis mine, I expect you often sighed for Athens, and repented of your bargain.

PHILOTIS: No tongue can tell how eager I was to get home again, to get away from the soldier, and to see all of you here, and spend a merry life in freedom as I used to do, for with him one had to speak by rule, and say only what he liked.

PARMENO: It was awkward for you that the soldier tied your tongue.

PHILOTIS: Now what is this business that Bacchis has just been telling me about in the house here? I never thought that this would happen, that Pamphilus would ever make up his mind to marry while Bacchis was alive.

PARMENO: Marry?

PHILOTIS: Why, isn't he married?

PARMENO: Well, yes, he is; but I am afraid the marriage isn't going to last.

PHILOTIS: Please heaven it may not, if it be to Bacchis' advantage that it should not; but what reason is there for thinking so? Tell me, Parmeno.

PARMENO: The reason is best kept secret; don't question me about it.

PHILOTIS: What, for fear that I should tell the secret? So help me heaven, I am not asking you this with a view to telling it, but for my own private gratification.

PARMENO: Your pretty speeches will never bring me to trust my back to your word.

PHILOTIS: Oh, don't talk like that, Parmeno; as if you weren't far more eager to tell me this story than I am to hear the answer to my question!

PARMENO (*aside*): She's right, that's my greatest fault. (*Aloud*) If you give me your word of honour that you will hold your tongue, I'll tell you.

PHILOTIS: That's more like you. I give you my promise; now tell me.

PARMENO: Listen.

PHILOTIS: 1 am listening.

PARMENO: Pamphilus was as much in love with Bacchis as he could be, when his father began to beg him to marry, using all the commonplace arguments which fathers usually do, that he was an old man, and Pamphilus was his only son, and that he wanted grandchildren to protect him in his old age. At first Pamphilus refused; but when his father pressed the matter more eagerly, he became troubled in his mind, not knowing whether he ought to obey love or duty. At last, by hammering and pestering, the old man got his own way, and engaged him to the daughter of our next-door neighbour here. So far Pamphilus had not taken the matter seriously; but when the wedding-day approached, and he saw that all was prepared and that he would be given no respite, but must marry her, he took it so much to heart that I believe Bacchis her very self would have pitied him had she been there. Whenever he got any time to himself, so that he could talk to me, he would say, "Parmeno, I'm ruined! What have I done? What misery have I brought upon myself? I can't bear it, Parmeno! It's all over with me!"

PHILOTIS: Now may the gods and goddesses confound you, Laches, for pestering him into it!

PARMENO: In short, he brought home his bride. On the first night he didn't have intercourse with her, nor yet on the following night.

PHILOTIS: What's this you tell me? That he, a young man, after drinking more than usual, lay with a maid, and yet had self-control enough to refrain from her? That isn't likely, and I don't believe it.

PARMENO: That is how it would seem to you, for no one visits you unless he wants you; but he had married her against his will.

PHILOTIS: What happened next?

PARMENO: A few days afterwards Pamphilus took me aside out of the house and told me that the girl was still a virgin, and that he had hoped before he brought her home as his wife that he might be able to put up with this marriage. "Now that I have made up my mind, Parmeno," said he, "that I can't keep her any longer, it would not be honourable in me, and it would ruin the girl's prospects to make a scandal about her, and not to give her back to her people just as I received her from them."

PHILOTIS: A right-thinking modest youth is Pamphilus, from what you say.

PARMENO: "I don't think it would be right," he went on, "to make this public, for to send a girl back to her father without having any fault to find with her is an outrage; but I hope that she will go away of her own accord when she understands that I can't live with her."

PHILOTIS: Well, while all this was going on, did he visit Bacchis?

PARMENO: Every day. But as you might expect, when she saw that he was another's, she straightway became much more disagreeable and more mercenary.

PHILOTIS: Gracious, I'm not surprised at that.

PARMENO: And what estranged him from Bacchis most of all was the contrast between their two characters, when he once came to have a thorough knowledge of himself, of Bacchis, and of his wife at home; for she, as became her breeding, was modest and retiring, endured all the wrongs and slights which she received from her husband, and tried to conceal his affronts to her. Thus, partly won by pity for his wife, and partly sickened by Bacchis' insults, his heart by degrees slipped out of her keeping, and he gave it to his wife, finding her to be a character worthy of himself. Meanwhile, there died at Imbros an old man, a relation of these folk, and his inheritance fell to them by law; so Pamphilus' father sent him off there, against his will, for he was in love. He left his wife here with his mother, for the old gentleman has buried himself in the country, and seldom comes to town.

PHILOTIS: Then what further question is there about the marriage holding good?

PARMENO: I'll tell you. For the first few days or so the women agreed very well together; but presently the bride took a strange dislike to Sostrata. They never quarrelled, there was no wrangling between them.

PHILOTIS: What did she do then?

PARMENO: Whenever Sostrata went to talk to her, she straightway ran out of her sight; she wouldn't see her; at last, when she could bear it no longer, she pretended that she had been sent for to join her mother for some religious service, and off she went. After she had been there (*pointing to the house of* PHIDIPPUS) for some days, Sostrata had her sent for; they put her off with some excuse. She sent again, but the girl didn't return; after she had sent for her several times, they pretended that she was ill. Our mistress straightway went to see her; no admittance. When the old gentleman heard this, he came up here from the country last night to see about it, and the first thing he did was to have a talk with Philumena's father. What they settled between them I don't know as yet, but I'm anxious to know what the end of this will be. Now you know the whole story, and I'll proceed on my errand.

PHILOTIS: And so will I, for I have made an appointment with a stranger.

PARMENO: Good luck to you.

PHILOTIS: Farewell.

PARMENO: And fare you well also, my Philotis. (PARMENO *departs in the direction of the harbour;* PHILOTIS *and* SYRA *in the direction of the forum.*)[8]

Act Two.   Scene I

(*Enter* LACHES *and* SOSTRATA *from their house.*)

LACHES: Gods and men! What a set women are! How they all conspire together! How exactly the same all their likes and dislikes are, and you never find one of them differing the least in character from the rest.

For instance, all mothers-in-law are of one mind in hating their daughters-in-law. All of them take the same pains and show the same energy in thwarting their husbands' wishes. It seems to me as if they've all been taught in the same school of mischief. If there be such a school, for sure this wife of mine must be the school-mistress.

SOSTRATA: Oh, dear, I am sure I don't know what I am being blamed for.

LACHES: You don't know?

SOSTRATA: No, my Laches, so help me heaven, as I hope we may live long together, I don't know.

LACHES: God forbid!

SOSTRATA: And I know that after a while you will see that you have blamed me unjustly.

LACHES: Unjustly! Can one find any words fit to tell what you have done? You have brought disgrace upon me and on yourself and on our family; you are preparing sorrow for your son when he returns; and, besides this, you have made enemies instead of friends of our kinsfolk here, who thought our son worthy to be their daughter's husband. You alone have sprung up and upset all our plans with your shameful behaviour.

SOSTRATA: What, I?

LACHES: Yes, you, I say, woman. Do you take me for a stock or a stone, and not a man? Because I live much in the country, do you suppose that I don't know how each of you here passes her life? Why, I know what is going on here much better than I do what goes on where I live, for this reason, that my reputation abroad depends upon your behaviour at home. Indeed, I heard long ago that Philumena had taken a dislike to you, and no wonder if she did; I should have wondered more if she had not. But I didn't believe that she hated the whole house. Had I known, she should rather have stayed here, and you should have been turned out of doors. Now just consider, Sostrata, how little I deserve that you should have brought this trouble upon me. I went away to live in the country out of consideration for you, and for the good of our property, so that our income might suffice for your expenses and keep you in idleness. I don't spare my labour, although I work more than reason or my age requires. In return for this, you didn't try to save me any vexation!

SOSTRATA (*weeping*): Oh, dear, this didn't happen through any act or fault of mine.

LACHES: Why, it's your fault entirely; you were here alone; yours is the whole blame, Sostrata. You should have managed matters properly here, seeing that I keep you free from other troubles. Isn't it a shame for an old woman like you to have quarrelled with a young girl? I suppose you will say that that was her fault.

SOSTRATA: My dear Laches, I don't say that.

LACHES: I am glad of that, for my son's sake, for as for you, your evil deeds can do no harm.

SOSTRATA: But husband, how do you know but what she may have pretended to dislike me, that she might spend more time with her mother?

LACHES: What's this? Why, isn't it proof enough that yesterday, when you went to visit her, you were denied admittance?

SOSTRATA: Well, they said that she was very tired, and that's why I wasn't allowed to see her.

LACHES: I expect it is your ways more than anything else that has made her sick. You deserve it, too, for every one of you women wants her son to marry; then they make a match to please you, and after you have driven them into wedlock, you then want them to turn their wives out of doors.

Act Two.   Scene II

(Enter PHIDIPPUS *from his house.)*

PHIDIPPUS *(to his daughter within)*: Now, Philumena, I know that I have the right to force you to do my bidding, but out of fatherly love I'll yield to you and won't oppose your wishes.

LACHES: And there I see Phidippus, just when I wanted him; he'll tell me what is really the matter. Phidippus, I'm aware that I am extremely accommodating to all my family, but I don't go so far as to let my good nature spoil them. It would be more to your advantage, and to ours, if you were to do likewise; but I see that you are under their thumb.

PHIDIPPUS: Too true!

LACHES: I called upon you yesterday to talk about your daughter, and you sent me away knowing no more than when I came. If you wish our connexion to endure, you ought not to bear these concealed grudges. If we have done you any wrong, out with it, and let us set it right, either by proving our innocence or by making amends. You shall yourself be judge. If your reason for keeping her in your house is that she is ill, then I think that you do me wrong, Phidippus, if you think that in my house she would not be well cared for. Why, although you are her father, yet, so help me heaven, I don't think that her health can be dearer to you than to me; my interest is for my son's sake, for I see that he thinks as much of her as he does of himself, and I know well how grievously vexed he would be to hear of this. So I want her to come home again before his return.

PHIDIPPUS: Laches, I know your affection and goodness, and I have made up my mind that all is as you say. Now I want you too to believe me, when I tell you that I wish her to return to you, if I can by any means make her do so.

LACHES: What prevents your doing it? Tell me, does she throw any blame upon her husband?

PHIDIPPUS: Not at all; for when I became more earnest with her and was going to make her go back by force, she declared by all that is holy that she couldn't endure to live in your house while Pamphilus was away. Every man has his own weakness; for my part, I have an easy disposition, and I can't go against my family.

LACHES: There, Sostrata!

SOSTRATA: Unhappy woman that I am!

LACHES: Well, is that settled?

PHIDIPPUS: It seems so, for the present; but have you any further commands? For I have business now which I must tend to in the marketplace.

LACHES: I'll go with you. (LACHES *and* PHIDIPPUS *depart*.)

Act Two.　Scene III

SOSTRATA (*to herself*): Dear me, it's a shame for husbands to blame all wives alike, because of a few who make us all seem to deserve blame. So help me heaven! I am quite innocent of what my husband accuses me, but it isn't easy to clear myself; they have got it so firmly into their heads that all mothers-in-law treat their daughters-in-law unfairly. I am sure I do not, for I have always treated her as if she were my own daughter. I don't know what will be the end of this, I only know how anxious I am to have my son come home. (*She goes into her house.*)

Act Three.　Scene I

(*Enter* PAMPHILUS *and* PARMENO *from the harbour.*)

PAMPHILUS: I think no man ever was so unfortunate in love as I. Wretched man that I am, why was I so anxious to save my life? Was this why I was so eager to return home? Ah, me! How much better it would have been for me to live anywhere else in the world, than to come back here and learn to my sorrow what has happened. Indeed, when any of us is doomed to misfortune, all the time before we hear of it is so much clear gain.

PARMENO: But as it is, you will sooner find a way out of all these troubles; if you hadn't returned, these quarrels would have grown far more bitter. As it is, I know, Pamphilus, that both your mother and your wife will stand in awe of you now that you have come home. You will sift the whole matter, quell their anger, and reconcile them once more. These things that you've convinced yourself are so important are really trifles.

PAMPHILUS: Why try to console me? Was ever any man in the world so unlucky? Before I married this wife of mine, I had bestowed my affections elsewhere, but I hadn't the face to refuse the wife that my father forced upon me. To say nothing of other matters, anyone can easily understand how unhappy this made me. Scarce had I torn myself away from my old love, got free from Bacchis, and transferred my affection to my wife, when, lo and behold! this new trouble crops up, which will separate me from her too. Besides, I suppose that this quarrel has come about either by my mother's fault or my wife's, and if I find it to be so, what is there before me but misery? As a son, it is my duty to endure wrongs that my mother does me, and I am under obligations to my wife for bearing with me so nobly and never making known to anyone the many wrongs that I did her. But something very serious must have been done to cause a quarrel between them that has lasted so long.

PARMENO: Or perhaps something very trifling, if you take the trouble to find out the real beginning of it. Frequently, it is not the greatest injuries that cause the greatest quarrels; something which would not ruffle another man's temper will often make a hasty man your bitterest foe. See what trifles cause quarrels among children, because the mind that governs them is weak; and most of these women are quite as silly as children. So, I dare say, master, you will find that it was just one word that led to all this quarrel between them.

PAMPHILUS: Go into the house, Parmeno, and announce my return. (*A noise is heard from* PHIDIPPUS' *house.*)

PARMENO: Why, what's this?

PAMPHILUS: Hush! I hear a bustle in the house and running to and fro.

PARMENO: Come on, I am going nearer to the door. There, didn't you hear it?

PAMPHILUS: Don't talk. By Jupiter! I heard a scream.

PARMENO: You forbid me to talk, and then you talk yourself.

MYRRINA (*within the house*): Hush, my daughter, please!

PAMPHILUS: I think that is the voice of Philumena's mother. I am a lost man!

PARMENO: What for?

PAMPHILUS: Oh, I'm ruined!

PARMENO: Why?

PAMPHILUS: Parmeno, I am certain that you are hiding some great trouble from me.

PARMENO: They said that your wife Philumena had a shivering fit; I don't know whether that's what is the matter with her.

PAMPHILUS: Death! Why didn't you tell me?

PARMENO: Because I couldn't tell you everything at once.

PAMPHILUS: What is the matter with her?

PARMENO: I don't know.

PAMPHILUS: What, has no one been for the doctor?

PARMENO: I don't know.

PAMPHILUS: Why don't I go into the house, and learn for certain what's the matter as soon as possible? In what state shall I find thee, my Philumena? If thou art in any danger, I shall die with thee. (PAMPHILUS *goes into* PHIDIPPUS' *house.*)

PARMENO: There's nothing to be gained by my going in after him, for I know they hate us all there; yesterday they wouldn't let Sostrata into the house. If the illness were to take a turn for the worse, which, for my master's sake above all, I hope that it will not, they would say directly that Sostrata's slave went into the house, and would pretend that he brought in some pestilence to assail their persons and lives, and made Philumena's sickness worse. My mistress will get blamed, and I shall get into terrible trouble.

Act Three.   Scene II

(Enter SOSTRATA *from her house.)*

SOSTRATA *(to herself)*: Unhappy me! For some time I seem to have heard a bustle going on here about something. I am sadly afraid that Philumena is worse. *(Reverently)* I pray thee, Æsculapius, and thee, Hygeia,[9] that it be not so.

PARMENO: Ho there, Sostrata!

SOSTRATA: Eh! What!

PARMENO: You'll be denied admittance a second time.

SOSTRATA: Oh, Parmeno, are you here? Oh, dear me, it's dreadful! What am I to do? Am I not to visit Pamphilus' wife, when she lies sick next door?

PARMENO: Don't visit her, and don't so much as send anyone to see her; for I count him doubly a fool who loves those that hate him; he wastes his own labour and displeases the other. Besides, your son went in there as soon as he returned to see how she was.

SOSTRATA: What do you say? Has Pamphilus returned?

PARMENO: He has.

SOSTRATA: Thanks to heaven! Oh, that news has brought back my courage and driven sorrow from my heart.

PARMENO: That's the very reason that I don't want you to go in there now, for if Philumena's pain grows any easier, I am sure that she will tell him the whole story quite privately, what it was that came between you, and how this quarrel arose. And see, there he is himself coming out of the house! How sad he is!

(*Enter* PAMPHILUS.)

SOSTRATA: Oh, my son!

PAMPHILUS: Mother, I greet you.

SOSTRATA: I am glad that you have come home safe. Is Philumena well?

PAMPHILUS (*sadly*): A little better.

SOSTRATA: May heaven keep her so! But why in tears? Why are you so unhappy?

PAMPHILUS: I'm all right, mother.

SOSTRATA: What was all the bustle about? Tell me. Did pain come upon her suddenly?

PAMPHILUS: That's what happened.

SOSTRATA: What is the matter with her?

PAMPHILUS: Fever.

SOSTRATA: Quotidian?

PAMPHILUS: So they say. Please, mother, go into the house, and I'll follow presently.

SOSTRATA: I'll do so. (SOSTRATA *goes inside.*)

PAMPHILUS: Parmeno, you run and meet my servants, and help them with their loads.

PARMENO: What, don't they know their way home?

PAMPHILUS: Get out, won't you? (PARMENO *departs.*)

Act Three.   Scene III

PAMPHILUS (*to himself*): I can't find any proper starting-point, I can't begin to tell of the troubles into which I have unexpectedly fallen. Some of them I've seen with my eyes, others I've heard with my ears, and this is why I have hurried out, beside myself. I went in there just now in fear, expecting to find my wife suffering from some very different disease from what I saw it was. Ah me! As soon as the maid servants saw that I was come they all straightway cried out with delight, "He's come," just because they had suddenly set eyes on me. But then straightway I saw all their countenances fall because chance had brought me home at such an inconvenient time. Meanwhile one of them ran fast before me bearing the news that I was come, and I, eager to see my wife, followed straight after her. When I came in, wretch that I am, I saw directly what was the matter with her, for there had been no time given them to hide it, and she couldn't help crying out as the pains of labour forced her to do. When I saw this I exclaimed, "Shame!" and straightway ran off in tears, quite upset at such a shocking and incredible state of things. Her mother ran after me, and just as I was passing the threshold, fell at my knees in tears, poor thing. I felt sorry for her; I suppose it is the way of mankind to be haughty or gentle according to one's own circumstances. She began to address me thus: "Oh, my Pamphilus, you see the reason why she left your house; indeed, the maid was done violence to by some unknown scoundrel long ago. Now she has fled here for refuge, to hide her delivery from you and from the world." But I can't but weep, unhappy that I am, when I think of her entreaties. "Whatever fortune it was," said she, "that brought you to us this day, we both of us beseech you by it, if righteousness and duty permit, to let her misfortune be hidden from all men as far as you are able. If ever, my Pamphilus, you have felt that she loved you, she begs you now to do her this easy kindness in return. As for taking her back again, you must please yourself; but you alone know that she is in labour, and that you are not the father; for I believe she did not go with you till two months afterwards; yes, this is the seventh month since she was taken to your house. All circumstances prove that you know this. Now, Pamphilus, if it be possible, I wish above all, and am doing my best, to keep her delivery a secret from her father, and so from all the world; but if we cannot avoid suspicion, I will say that it was a miscarriage; I am sure it never will occur to anyone to doubt that you are the father. The child shall be exposed straightway; you shall have no trouble from us in the matter, and you will hide the wrong that my poor girl has sustained." I gave her my promise, and I am determined to keep my word; but as for taking her back, that I cannot think would be honourable, and I won't do it, although love and companionship make me strongly attached to her. I weep when I think of the loneliness of the life that is before me. O Fortune, how shortlived is thy kindness! But my former love affair has put me into training for this; I reasoned myself out of that, and I'll try to do the same for this. (*Looking down the street*) Here comes Parmeno with the servants; he is the last person who ought to be here, for to him alone did I confide my having abstained from her at the beginning, when she first was married to me. I am afraid that if he hears much of her cries he will perceive that she is in labour. I must send the fellow off somewhere out of the way while Philumena is being delivered.

Act Three.　Scene IV

(*Enter* PARMENO *with* SOSIA *and other slaves carrying luggage.*)

PARMENO: Do you say that your voyage turned out an unpleasant one?

SOSIA: Parmeno, words can't express how unpleasant a sea-voyage actually is.

PARMENO: Is that so?

SOSIA: Lucky fellow! You don't realise what misery you've escaped in having never been to sea. Not to mention other troubles, consider this one alone. I was on board ship more than thirty days. And all that time, poor wretch that I was, I expected to be drowned any minute. We had such devilish weather!

PARMENO: How horrid!

SOSIA: I know it. Damn it! I'd run away rather than go back, if I knew that I had to endure it all again.

PARMENO: A very little would once have made you do what you now threaten to do, Sosia. But I see Pamphilus himself standing at the door. Go indoors; I will go to him and see if he wants me for anything. (SOSIA *and the other slaves go into* LACHES' *house*) Well, master, are you still standing here?

PAMPHILUS: I'm waiting for you.

PARMENO: What for?

PAMPHILUS: You must run over to the acropolis.

PARMENO: Who must?

PAMPHILUS: You must.

PARMENO: To the acropolis? Why there?

PAMPHILUS: Meet my friend Callidemides of Myconos, who came in the same ship with me.

PARMENO (*aside*): Damnation! It looks as if he must have made a vow to kill me with walking, in case he ever got home safe.

PAMPHILUS: Why don't you go?

PARMENO: What do you want me to say to him? Or am I only to meet him?

PAMPHILUS: No, you're to say that I can't keep the appointment which I made to meet him today, and that he's not to waste his time waiting for me; now, off you go.

PARMENO: But I don't know the man by sight.

PAMPHILUS: Then I'll make you know him: he's a big man, with a red face, curly hair, fat, with cat's eyes and cadaverous complexion.

PARMENO: The gods confound him! Suppose he doesn't come, am I to wait till evening?

PAMPHILUS: Yes, wait. Now run.

PARMENO: I can't run, I'm so tired. (PARMENO *departs*.)

PAMPHILUS (*to himself*): Well, he's gone. Now what am I to do? Unhappy man that I am! I am sure I don't know how I'm to keep this secret which Myrrina implored me to do—her daughter's being in childbed. I am sorry for Myrrina, and will do what I can, consistently with my duty to my father, for I ought to obey my father before my love. Why, there I see Phidippus himself and my father; they are coming this way. I am at my wits' end what to say to them.

Act Three.   Scene V

(*Enter* LACHES *and* PHIDIPPUS.)

LACHES: Didn't you say that she declared she was only waiting for my son's return?

PHIDIPPUS: Yes.

LACHES: They say that he's returned, so let her come back.

PAMPHILUS (*aside*): I don't know what reason I can give my father for not taking her back.

LACHES: Whom do I hear speaking here?

PAMPHILUS (*aside*): I am determined to persist in carrying out what I have resolved to do.

LACHES: The very man I was telling you about.

PAMPHILUS: Good day, Father.

LACHES: Welcome, my son.

PHIDIPPUS: It is well that you have returned, Pamphilus, and what is best of all, safe and sound.

PAMPHILUS: I believe you.

LACHES: Have you just returned?

PAMPHILUS: Just now.

LACHES: Pray how much did our kinsman Phania leave?

PAMPHILUS: Well, the fact is, Phania was fond of pleasure during his life, and men who live like that are not of much use to their heirs, though they gain for themselves the glorious epitaph, "He lived well while he lived."

LACHES: Then is that one sentiment all that you have brought back?

PAMPHILUS: Well, we shall be glad for what little he did leave.

LACHES: Why, no, I shall be sorry for it, for I would rathr er have had him alive and well.

PAMPHILUS (*aside*): Yes, you may safely wish that, for he will never come to life again; but for all that, I know which you prefer.

LACHES: Phidippus here ordered Philumena taken to his house yes-terday. (*Aside to* PHIDIPPUS, *digging him in the ribs*) Say that you ordered it.

PHIDIPPUS (*aside to* LACHES): Don't dig me. (*Aloud*) Yes, I did.

LACHES: But he will send her right back again.

PHIDIPPUS: Of course.

PAMPHILUS: I know how the whole affair happened. I have just heard it on my arrival.

LACHES: The gods confound those spiteful creatures who enjoy telling such news!

PAMPHILUS: I am sure that I have been careful not to deserve any re-proach from your family, and if I chose to tell you now how faithful, kind, and gentle I have been to her, I could do so with truth; but I had rather you should learn this from her own lips, for it will make you more inclined to think well of me if she who now wrongs me says any good of me. I call heaven to witness that this disagreement of ours has not been brought about by any fault of mine; but since she scorns to make allowances for my mother, and to bear with her ways in a proper spirit, and the quarrel between them cannot otherwise be made up, why then, Phidippus, I must either part with my mother or with Philumena. So my filial respect bids me take my mother's side rather than my wife's.

LACHES: Pamphilus, I am not displeased at hearing your words, when I learn from them that you value your mother above everything else; but take care that your anger doesn't lead you too far.

PAMPHILUS: Pray, how should anger make me treat her ill, father, when I know that she has never done anything to me that I could wish undone, and has often done me good? I love her, I admire her, and greatly long for her, for she has dealt nobly with me, and my prayer is that she may pass the rest of her life with a luckier husband than I, since it is fated that I must leave her.

PHIDIPPUS: It lies in your power to prevent this.

LACHES: If you're in your right mind, bid her come back.

PAMPHILUS: That is not my intention, father; I will respect my mother's wishes.

LACHES: Where are you going to? Stop, stop, I say! Where are you off to? (PAMPHILUS *goes into* LACHES' *house.*)

PHIDIPPUS (*aside*): How obstinate he is!

LACHES: Didn't I tell you, Phidippus, that he would be put out at this business? That's why I implored you to send your daughter back.

PHIDIPPUS: Confound it! I never thought that he could be so discourteous. So now he expects me to go on my knees to him, does he? Nay; if he chooses to take his wife back, let him; if he has changed his mind, let him repay me her dowry and go his way.

LACHES: There now, you too have got into a rage about nothing.

PHIDIPPUS: Oh, Pamphilus, you have come home to us in a very stubborn state of mind!

LACHES: His anger will pass away, although he has had enough to make him angry.

PHIDIPPUS: You are all so proud because you've come into a little money.

LACHES: Do you want to pick a quarrel with me too?

PHIDIPPUS: Let him think the matter over, and let me know this day whether he wants her or no, that I may get her another husband if this one won't have her. (*He goes into his house.*)

LACHES (*calling after him*): Phidippus, come here; listen to me for a moment. (*To himself*) He is gone. Well, what's that to me? After all, let them manage it between them, however they please, since neither he nor my son shows any consideration for me, or takes any heed of what I say. I'll take this quarrel to my wife, who was the cause of all the trouble, and discharge my ill-temper upon her. (*He goes into his house.*)

Act Four. Scene I

(*Enter* MYRRINA *from her house.*)

MYRRINA (*to herself*): Oh, dear, what shall I do? Where shall I turn? Unhappy woman that I am, what shall I say to my husband? He seems to have heard the baby crying, so suddenly and silently he went off to his daughter. If he finds out that she has borne a child, I am sure I don't know what reason I can give for having concealed it from him. But the door rattles. I expect he's coming out; I am lost!

(*Enter* PHIDIPPUS.)

PHIDIPPUS: As soon as my wife saw me go to her daughter, she went out of doors, and there she is. What do you say, Myrrina? Here! It is you I am speaking to.

MYRRINA: Me, husband?

PHIDIPPUS: Am I your husband? Do you really think that I am your husband, or that I am anybody at all? Why, woman, if you had ever thought so of me, you would not have made such a laughingstock of me by your actions.

MYRRINA: What actions?

PHIDIPPUS: Do you ask what? Has my daughter had a child? There, you're silent! Who is the father?

MYRRINA (*aside*): Her father has a right to ask that question. I am a lost woman. (*Aloud*) Gracious, who but her husband do you suppose is the father of her child?

PHIDIPPUS: I do suppose that he is, and it's not for her father to suppose anything else; but I wonder what your reason could have been for taking such pains to try to conceal her confinement from all of us, especially since she has borne her child properly and at the right time. Oh, that you should be so perverse as to wish the baby to die, when you knew that he would be a pledge of the closer alliance of the two families, rather than let your daughter marry a man whom you did not fancy. And I, too, believed that it was they that were to blame, whereas it was you.

MYRRINA: I am an unhappy woman.

PHIDIPPUS: I wish that I knew you spoke the truth; but I now remember what you said about this matter long ago, when we chose him for a son-in-law. You said that you couldn't bear your daughter to marry a man who kept a mistress, a man who didn't sleep at home.

MYRRINA (*aside*): I prefer him to suspect any reason rather than the real one.

PHIDIPPUS: Myrrina, I knew that he had a mistress long before you did, but I never counted that a fault in a young man, for it is their nature; but the time will soon come when he will be ashamed of himself. But you have never to this day ceased trying to carry out what you said then was your set purpose, to get your daughter away from him, and upset the arrangement which I had made. What has happened is a plain proof of what you wanted.

MYRRINA: Do you think me so obstinate as to deal so with my own daughter, if I thought that this marriage was to our advantage?

PHIDIPPUS: As if you could provide for her, or had sense enough to know what is to our advantage! I suppose somebody told you that he had seen her husband coming out of his mistress' house or going into it. Well, what of it? If he did so quietly and not too often, wouldn't it have been more reasonable to pretend that you didn't know about it, than to take pains to find out and so make him hate us for knowing? Indeed, if he could all of a sudden break off with the woman with whom he had consorted for so many years, I should not consider him a man, nor likely to be a trustworthy husband for my daughter.

MYRRINA: Never mind the young man, I beseech you, and the wrong which you say I have done. Go and talk to him alone, without any one else. Ask him whether he wants his wife or not. If he says that he does, send her back to him; if he doesn't want her, then I have done well for my daughter.

PHIDIPPUS: Even supposing that he doesn't want her, and that you, Myrrina, knew of his wrongdoing, I was here, and it was your duty to have taken my advice. That's what makes me so furious, that you should have dared to do all this without consulting me. Now I forbid you to take this child anywhere out of the house. (*Aside*) But I am a greater fool than she, to expect her to obey me. I'll go into the house and give warning to the slaves not to allow the child to be carried anywhere out of doors. (PHIDIPPUS *goes inside.*)

MYRRINA (*to herself*): I think that I am the most wretched woman alive, for I can see plainly how furious he will be when he learns the whole story, since he has got into such a rage at this, which is a trifle compared to it. Nor do I see any way of making him change his mind. This was the only addition possible to my many misfortunes, that he should force me to acknowledge this baby, when we don't know who his father is. When my daughter was outraged, she couldn't make out his face in the dark, nor could she take anything from him by which she could learn who he might be; but he, as he left her, pulled off a ring which she was wearing on her finger. And then, too, I fear that Pamphilus will be too angry to keep our secret any longer, when he hears that another man's child is acknowledged as his. (*She goes into the house.*)

Act Four.   Scene II

(Enter SOSTRATA *and* PAMPHILUS *from their house.)*

SOSTRATA: My son, I am well aware that you fancy your wife went away from this house because of my disagreeable ways, although you take care to hide your thoughts. But, as I hope for the love of heaven, as I trust to receive your affection, believe me, I never knowingly did anything that would have set her against me. I always thought that you loved me, and now you have proved it, for your father just now told me how you preferred me to your ladylove. Now I have made up my mind to repay you for this, that you may know how I value such a good son. Pamphilus, this is what I think is the best thing for you and for my good name. I have positively determined to go away into the country with your father, so that my presence here may be no hindrance, and that nothing may be left to prevent your Philumena coming back to you.

PAMPHILUS: Pray what sort of plan is this? Are you going to let her folly drive you out of town to live in the country? Mother, you shall not; and I will not suffer our enemies to say, as they will, that this removal was due to my wrongheadedness, not to your kindness. I don't wish you to leave your friends and kinsfolk and festivals on my account.

SOSTRATA: These things give me no pleasure now. When I was young I enjoyed them thoroughly, but now I am tired of such amusements. All that I care for now is, that my old age may not be a hindrance to my daughter-in-law, and that she may not wish for my death. Here I see that I am disliked for no fault of mine; it is time for me to go. By going, I think that I shall most effectually remove all grounds of complaint against me, clear myself from this suspicion, and please our neighbours. Pray let me escape the common reproach of my sex.

PAMPHILUS: How fortunate I would be in having so good a mother and so good a wife, if it were not for this one thing.

SOSTRATA: I entreat you, my Pamphilus, won't you make up your mind to put up with this inconvenience, whatever it may be, if everything else is as you wish it and as I believe it to be? Then, my son, be ruled by me, and take her back again.

PAMPHILUS: Oh, I'm so miserable!

SOSTRATA: And I too, for I suffer from this misunderstanding no less than you, my son.

Act Four. Scene III

(Enter LACHES *from his doorway.)*

LACHES: Wife, I have heard your talk with Pamphilus from where I stood aside. There is good sense in accommodating yourself to circumstances, and doing at the present time what you may have to do in the future.

SOSTRATA: Heaven help us.

LACHES: So come away to the country; there you and I will put up with one another.

SOSTRATA: I hope we may, I'm sure.

LACHES: Then go into the house and pack up what is to go with you; that is all I have to say.

SOSTRATA: I'll do as you bid me. (SOSTRATA *goes inside.*)

PAMPHILUS: Father.

LACHES: What do you want, Pamphilus?

PAMPHILUS: My mother leave this house? Certainly not.

LACHES: Why do you oppose it?

PAMPHILUS: Because I haven't yet decided what I mean to do about my wife.

LACHES: What! Why, what can you want to do, except to take her back?

PAMPHILUS: I should like it, and can scarce refrain from doing so, but I will not change my determination; I will do what is expedient. I think that there will be peace between them if I don't take her back.

LACHES: You don't know that; but what they do doesn't concern you at all, after she is gone. People of our age are hateful to the young; it is time for us to go, Pamphilus. We old folk are even as a tale that is told: "Old man and old woman." But I see Phidippus coming out just in the nick of time; let us go to him.

Act Four.   Scene IV

(Enter PHIDIPPUS *from his house.)*

PHIDIPPUS *(to* PHILUMENA *within)*: And indeed, Philumena, I am extremely angry with you, too, for by Jove, you have behaved shamefully. However, you have some excuse for what you did, it was at your mother's instigation; but she has no excuse.

LACHES: Phidippus, you appear before me just when I wanted you.

PHIDIPPUS: What is the matter?

PAMPHILUS *(aside)*: What am I to say to them? How shall I explain my attitude?

LACHES: Tell your daughter that Sostrata is going to leave this house and retire to the country, that Philumena may be less unwilling to return home.

PHIDIPPUS: Oh, but your wife is not at all to blame for all this business; all the trouble comes from my wife, Myrrina.

PAMPHILUS *(aside)*: This is a change of front.

PHIDIPPUS: It is she that is the cause of our troubles, Laches.

PAMPHILUS *(aside)*: So long as I don't have to take her back, they may squabble as much as they please.

PHIDIPPUS: For my part, Pamphilus, I should be glad for our relationship to endure for ever, if possible; but if you do not agree to this, you will, I hope, take the child.

PAMPHILUS *(aside)*: He know of the birth? I'm done for!

LACHES: Child? What child?

PHIDIPPUS: We have got a grandson; for my daughter was in the family way when she left you, though I never knew that she was so before this day.

LACHES: God bless my soul! You bring me good news. I am glad that the child has been born, and that the mother is doing well. But whatever kind of a woman is your wife, and what strange ways she must have, to have kept it a secret from us for so long? I can't tell you how wrongly I think she has behaved about it.

PHIDIPPUS: Her conduct doesn't please me any more than it does you, Laches.

PAMPHILUS (*aside*): If I ever had any doubt about taking her back, I have none now, when she would bring somebody else's brat with her.

LACHES: There's no further room for hesitation, Pamphilus.

PAMPHILUS (*aside*): Damnation!

LACHES: We have often longed to see this day, when you would have someone to call you "father," and now it has come, thanks be to heaven.

PAMPHILUS (*aside*): It's all over with me.

LACHES: Now, take your wife back, and don't thwart my wishes.

PAMPHILUS: Father, I am sure that she would not have kept her secret as she has, if she had wanted to have children by me or to be my wife. Why should I take her back now, when I feel that she is estranged from me, and I don't suppose that we shall ever make it up?

LACHES: She was young, and did what her mother advised; why be surprised at that? Do you suppose that you can find any woman who is faultless? Why, can you find any men who never do anything wrong?

PHIDIPPUS: Now then, you two, Laches and Pamphilus, must decide whether you want to send her away or take her home again. I shall raise no difficulties in either case, though I can't answer for what my wife may do. But what are we to do with the child?

ˉACHES: What an absurd question! Whatever comes of it, you must give Pamphilus his son for us to bring up as one of our family.

PAMPHILUS (*aside*): When his own father abandoned the child, am I to bring it up?

LACHES (*overhearing the last words*): What do you say, Pamphilus? Shall we not bring it up? Pray, are we to expose it? What madness is this? I really can't keep silence any longer, for you make me say what I don't like to say before Phidippus. Do you suppose that I don't know what you are crying for, or what it is that you are so troubled about? The first reason you gave was, that you couldn't have this wife of yours in the house because of your mother; well, your mother has promised to leave the house; now since you have been deprived of this reason you find another one, because this child has been born without your knowledge. You're mistaken if you think that I don't know what's in your head. But just reflect what a long time I have allowed you to enjoy your mistress' society, how patient I have been over the money you spent upon her. I begged and prayed you to take a wife; I said it was time you were married, and at my instance you did marry, and your obedience did you credit. But now your love has gone back to your mistress, with whom you are intriguing, and greatly wronging your wife, for I see that you have fallen back again into your old way of life.

PAMPHILUS: What? I?

LACHES: Yes, you! And you are behaving wrongly; you are trumping up untrue grounds of quarrel with your wife that you may live with your mistress, as soon as you have got this witness out of your way. It is clear that your wife saw this, for what other reason could she have had for leaving you?

PHIDIPPUS: The man's a perfect conjuror. Why, of course, that's the reason.

PAMPHILUS: I'll take my oath that I have no such motive.

LACHES: Then take back your wife, or else tell us why you don't want to take her back.

PAMPHILUS: I have no time now.

LACHES: You will acknowledge the child, I suppose, for he at any rate is innocent; I will see about his mother afterwards.

PAMPHILUS (*aside*): I'm so wretched in every way, and I don't know what to do; my father drives me into a corner with so many arguments. I'll go away, for I gain little by being here. I don't suppose that they will acknowledge the child without my consent, especially since my mother-in-law is on my side in wishing to make away with it. (PAMPHILUS *departs*.)

LACHES (*to* PAMPHILUS): What, are you running away? And won't you give me a plain answer? (*To* PHIDIPPUS) Do you think that he is in his right mind? Come, Phidippus, give me the child, I will bring it up.

PHIDIPPUS: By all means. I am not surprised at my wife's anger about it, for women are bitterly jealous, and can't put up with infidelities. This is what the quarrel is about; she told me so herself. I didn't want to tell you so before him, and at first I didn't believe it of him, but now it is clearly true, for I see that his mind is quite set against marrying.

LACHES: Then, Phidippus, what am I to do? What do you advise?

PHIDIPPUS: What are you to do? Why, I think we had better see this courtesan first; let us entreat her, and charge her with it, and finally threaten her with serious consequences if she has anything to do with him hereafter.

LACHES: I'll do as you suggest. (*Calling a slave from his house*) Here, boy, run over to our neighbour Bacchis, and ask her to come here, with my compliments. (*To* PHIDIPPUS, *as the slave goes into* BACCHIS' *house*) Now, I beg you, stand by me in this matter.

PHIDIPPUS: Oh, I said long ago, Laches, and I say now, that I wish this alliance between us to continue, if it can anyhow be managed, and I hope that it can. But would you like me to be with you when you meet her?

LACHES: No, you had better leave me, and get some woman to nurse the child. (PHIDIPPUS *departs*.)

Act Five.   Scene I

(*Enter* BACCHIS *with two slave girls*.)

BACCHIS (*to herself*): It must be something serious that Laches wants to meet me about, and I am pretty sure that I know what he wants.

LACHES (*aside*): I must be on my guard, so that my anger against that woman won't prevent my getting less out of her than I want, and that I won't do something that I shall be sorry for afterwards. Well, I'll tackle her. (*Aloud*) Good day, Bacchis.

BACCHIS: Good day, Laches.

LACHES: I believe, Bacchis, that you are somewhat in doubt about the reason why I had my servant call you out here.

BACCHIS: I also, when I remember what I am, feel afraid that the name of my profession may stand in my way; as for my conduct, I can easily defend that.

LACHES: If what you say is true, you have nothing to fear from me, for I have come to a time of life when I can't expect my mistakes to be pardoned, and so I'm careful in all my actions to do nothing rashly. If you are behaving or are going to behave like a good woman, it would be wrong for me in my ignorance to do you any harm when you don't deserve it.

BACCHIS: I am sure I am much obliged to you for that, for it is not of much use to apologise to me for an injury after you have done it. But what is the matter?

LACHES: You are receiving the visits of my son, Pamphilus.

BACCHIS: Oh!

LACHES: Let me speak. Before his marriage I winked at his connection with you. (*As* BACCHIS *tries to interrupt*) Stop! I have not yet said what I want to say. He is now a married man. Find some more lasting lover for yourself now, while you still have a chance to find one, for Pamphilus will not always be your lover, and you will not always be as young as you are.

BACCHIS: Who says that he is my lover?

LACHES: His mother-in-law.

BACCHIS: My lover?

LACHES: Yes, yours, and she has taken away her daughter from him, and wants to make away secretly with the boy who has been born to him.

BACCHIS: If I knew anything more sacred than an oath to make you believe me, I would use it, Laches, to affirm to you that I have had no dealings with Pamphilus since his marriage.

LACHES: I am charmed with you; but do you know I want you to do something better than this?

BACCHIS: What? Tell me.

LACHES: I want you to go to the women within here, and assure them what you have assured me. Set their minds at rest, and clear yourself from this accusation.

BACCHIS: I'll do it; though I am sure there is not another woman of my trade that would appear before a married woman about such a matter. But I don't wish your son to be falsely suspected, or that you, who have no right to do so, should think ill of him unjustly; for at my hands he deserves all the good that I can do him.

LACHES: Your words have quieted my fears and made me your friend. Indeed, it was not only the women who thought it was so: I believed it myself. Now that I have found you to be a better woman than we thought you, mind that you keep the character you have won; make what use you please of my good will. If you don't behave yourself—

well, I will hold my tongue, for fear you should hear something unpleasant. But I give you this one piece of advice, to find out what I am and what I can do as a friend rather than as an enemy.

Act Five. Scene II

(*Enter* PHIDIPPUS *with a nurse.*)

PHIDIPPUS (*speaking to the nurse*): I won't let you want for anything in my house, but when you are full of meat and drink, make the child full too. (*The nurse goes into his house.*)

LACHES (*to* BACCHIS): Here, I see, comes our father-in-law; he is bringing a nurse for the child. (*To* PHIDIPPUS) Phidippus, Bacchis swears by all that is holy.

PHIDIPPUS: Is this she?

LACHES: It is.

PHIDIPPUS: Women of that class don't fear the gods, and I don't believe that the gods take any heed of them.

BACCHIS: I offer you my slave-girls; question them under what tortures you please, as far as I am concerned. What I have said is true. Now I must get Pamphilus' wife to go back to him; if I can bring that about, I shall not heed the reproach that I have done what every other courtesan tries not to do.

LACHES: Phidippus, the facts of the case prove that we were wrong in suspecting our wives; now let us try what Bacchis can do. If your wife understands that she has given ear to a false charge she will put away her anger; if, as is the case, my son is angry because his wife concealed the birth of her child from him, that's a trifle, his anger at that will soon pass away. Really there is nothing in all this business which is worth separating about.

PHIDIPPUS: I wish there wasn't.

LACHES: Ask her! Here she is; she herself will do all that is needful.

PHIDIPPUS: Why do you talk like that to me? Have I not told you long ago what I think about this business, Laches? Only set their minds at rest.

LACHES: I beg you now, Bacchis, to perform the promise that you made me.

BACCHIS: Then do you wish me to go into the house and explain that matter?

LACHES: Go, set their minds at rest; make them believe you.

BACCHIS: I'll go, though I know well that the sight of me will be hateful to them today, for a courtesan is an enemy to a married woman who is separated from her husband.

LACHES: Why, they will be your friends when they know why you've come.

PHIDIPPUS: Oh, I warrant you they will be your friends when they learn the truth, for you will free them from their mistake, and free yourself from suspicion at the same time.

BACCHIS: Dear me! I am ashamed of meeting Philumena. (*To her maids*) Follow me this way, both of you. (BACCHIS *and her maids accompany* PHIDIPPUS *into his house.*)

LACHES (*to himself*): There's nothing which I would rather have had happen than that she should have had this opportunity of winning favour and of helping me at no cost to herself. If it is really true that she has broken off her connection with Pamphilus, she knows that thereby she has gained credit, fortune, and respect; she will repay him for what he has done for her, and at the same time will make us her friends. (*He goes into his house. A short time is supposed to elapse before the next Scene.*)

Act Five. Scene III

(*Enter* PARMENO.)

PARMENO (*to himself*): Confound it! My master can't set much value on my time, for he sent me on a fool's errand to a place where I have wasted the whole day, waiting in the acropolis for his friend Callidemides of Myconos. So there I sat, idiot that I was, and whenever anyone came I went up to him and said, "Pray, young gentleman, are you from Myconos?" "No," was the answer. "But your name is Callidemides?" "No, it isn't." "Have you a friend named Pamphilus?" Everybody said "No," and I don't believe there's any such person. At last I got quite ashamed, and went away. But how is it that I see Bacchis coming out of our father-in-law's house? What is she doing here?

(*Enter* BACCHIS *from* PHIDIPPUS' *house.*)

BACCHIS: Parmeno, it's lucky that you are here; run straightway to Pamphilus.

PARMENO: Why to Pamphilus?

BACCHIS: Tell him that I beg him to come.

PARMENO: To you?

BACCHIS: No, to Philumena.

PARMENO: What's the matter?

BACCHIS: Don't ask questions about what doesn't concern you.

PARMENO: Am I to say nothing but this?

BACCHIS: Yes, something more: tell him that Myrrina has recognised the ring which he gave to me some time ago as having belonged to her daughter.

PARMENO: I know the ring. Is that all?

BACCHIS: That's all; he will come at once when you tell him that. Why are you dawdling?

PARMENO: I'm not dawdling, but I haven't any strength to move faster; I've spent the whole of this day running and walking about. (PARMENO *departs.*)

BACCHIS (*to herself*): What joy have I brought to Pamphilus today by my visit! How many blessings have I bestowed upon him, from how many cares have I set him free! I restore to him his son, whom he and these women were just about to make away with; I bring back to him the wife who he never thought would be his again, and I prove him innocent of what his father and Phidippus suspected. Now it was this ring of mine that put me in the way of finding out all these things. I remember how, about ten months ago, he ran breathless into my house, early in the night, unaccompanied, far gone in drink, and with this ring in his hands; I was frightened. I said, "Pamphilus dear, please tell me why you are so out of breath, I beg you, and where you found this ring?" He pretended that he didn't hear what I said. When I saw that I guessed that there was something; I began to press him all the more to tell me what it was. He then confessed that he had raped some girl in the street, and said that in the struggle he had pulled this ring off her finger. This was the ring which Myrrina recognised on my hand just now. She asked me how I came by it; I told her all this, and then at last it came out that it was Pamphilus who had raped Philumena, and that he was the father of her child. Now I am well pleased at my having brought him all this good fortune, although it is not what other courtesans would do, for it is not at all good for our trade that any of our lovers should be happily married; but, good gracious, I'll never behave badly for the sake of gain. While our connection was permitted, I found him kind, charming, and affectionate. I was put out at his marrying, I can't deny that, but I really don't think that it was through any fault of mine that he did it. I have got many advantages from him; it is only fair that I should put up with the disadvantages.

Act Five.   Scene IV

(*Enter* PAMPHILUS *and* PARMENO.)

PAMPHILUS: My good Parmeno, pray think once more whether this story that you have brought me is clear and certain? Don't let me enjoy this news and then find that it is untrue.

PARMENO: It's certain.

PAMPHILUS: Are you sure?

PARMENO: Sure.

PAMPHILUS: If it's true, I am a god, not a man.

PARMENO: You'll find that it is true.

PAMPHILUS: Wait a bit, if you please; I am afraid that you are telling one story and I am believing another.

PARMENO: Well, I am waiting.

PAMPHILUS: This, I think, was what you said: that Myrrina found that Bacchis had her ring.

PARMENO: That was so.

PAMPHILUS: The ring which I gave her some time ago? And Bacchis told you to bring this news to me? Is that what happened?

PARMENO: Yes.

PAMPHILUS: Then I am the luckiest and happiest man alive! What shall I give you for bringing me this good news? What? What? I don't know.

PARMENO: But I know what you will give me.

PAMPHILUS: What?

PARMENO: Nothing at all! For neither I nor the news has done you any good.

PAMPHILUS: What! When you have brought me back from the shadow of death to the light of day, shall I let you leave me without a reward? No; you wrong me by thinking me so ungrateful. But there I see Bacchis standing at the door; I suppose she is waiting for me. I'll go to her.

BACCHIS: Good day, Pamphilus.

PAMPHILUS: O Bacchis, my Bacchis, my preserver!

BACCHIS: All's well, and I'm delighted.

PAMPHILUS: Your acts make me believe your words, and you still retain your old charm, so that to meet you anywhere, to hear you talk, to see you arrive, is a pleasure.

BACCHIS: And bless me! You still keep your old ways and disposition, and are still the most engaging man in all the world.

PAMPHILUS: Ha, ha, ha! You to say that of me!

BACCHIS: You are quite right, Pamphilus, in being in love with your wife. I never set eyes on her, to my knowledge, before this day. I thought her very gracious.

PAMPHILUS: Speak the truth.

BACCHIS: I am speaking the truth, Pamphilus, so help me heaven.

PAMPHILUS: I say, have you told my father anything about these matters?

BACCHIS: Not a word.

PAMPHILUS: There's no need for him to hear so much as a whisper. I don't wish this to be done as they do in the stage plays, where everybody learns everything at the end. Here those who ought to know the truth know it; those who ought not to know it don't know it, and shall never learn it.

BACCHIS: Well, I'll even make it easier for you to conceal it: Myrrina said to Phidippus that she believed my oath, and held your innocence to be proved.

PAMPHILUS: Excellent! I hope matters will turn out as I wish.

PARMENO: Master, mayn't I be told today what that good thing is that I have done, or what it is that you and Bacchis are talking about?

PAMPHILUS: No, you mayn't.

PARMENO: Still, I can guess. Brought you back from the shadow of death! How was that?

PAMPHILUS: Parmeno, you don't know how useful you have proved to me this day, and from what misery you have rescued me.

PARMENO: Oh, but I do know, and I did it on purpose.

PAMPHILUS: I am sure you did.

BACCHIS: Is it likely that Parmeno would miss doing anything that wanted doing?[10]

PAMPHILUS: Follow me into the house, Parmeno.

PARMENO: I'm coming. (*To the audience*) Well, I've done more good today unknowingly than I ever did knowingly before. Now give us your applause.

1. This is inaccurate. The Greek original of *The Mother-in-law* was written by Apollodorus, as Donatus states.

2. This is deleted by editors, as Octavius and Manlius were consuls in 165 B.C., the date of the first presentation of *The Mother-in-law*.

3. The funeral games in honour of Paulus were in 160 B.C. *The Brothers* was presented at these same games.

4. The third presentation of the play was also in 160 B.C., probably at the *ludi Romani* in September.

5. This prologue seems to have been written for the second presentation of the play.

6. The second prologue, written for the third presentation of *The Mother-in-law,* was spoken by the manager-actor, Lucius Ambivius Turpio.

7. Caecilius Statius was a writer of comedy who flourished between the time of Plautus and Terence.

8. Philotis and Syra do not appear again; they are *protatic* characters, introduced for the purpose of providing Parmeno with an audience on the stage.

9. Literally, *Salus,* "Health," the daughter of Aesculapius, god of healing.

10. Bentley, following Donatus, assigned this speech to Bacchis.

VI
THE BROTHERS

CHARACTERS IN THE PLAY

MICIO, *an aged Athenian*
DEMEA, *his brother, father of* AESCHINUS *and* CTESIPHO
SANNIO, *a pimp*
AESCHINUS, *son of* DEMEA, *adopted by* MICIO
SYRUS, *slave of* MICIO *and* AESCHINUS
CTESIPHO, *son of* DEMEA
SOSTRATA, *an Athenian lady*
CANTHARA, *an old woman, servant of* SOSTRATA
GETA, *slave of* SOSTRATA
HEGIO, *an old man of Athens*
PAMPHILA, *daughter of* SOSTRATA
DROMO, *slave of* MICIO

DIDASCALIA

The Brothers of Terence. Acted at the Funeral Games in honour of Lucius Aemilius Paulus which were given by Quintus Fabius Maximus and Publius Cornelius Africanus. The chief actors were Lucius Ambivius Turpio and Lucius Atilius Praenestinus. It was set to music by Flaccus, slave of Claudius, to the accompaniment of Tyrian flutes. It is from the Greek of Menander and is the poet's sixth play. It was presented during the consulship of Marcus Cornelius Cethegus and Lucius Anicius Gallus.[1]

SUMMARY

Since Demea has two sons, he permits his brother Micio to adopt Aeschinus but he himself keeps Ctesipho. Demea was a harsh and strict father and when Ctesipho fell in love with a music girl his brother Aeschinus concealed it and took on himself the blame for the love affair; finally he took the music girl away from the pimp. Aeschinus had already seduced an impoverished Athenian girl and had promised to marry her. Demea upbraids him and is greatly vexed. Later, when the truth is revealed, Aeschinus marries the girl he has wronged and Ctesipho retains possession of the music girl.

INTRODUCTION

The Brothers, based on Menander's comedy of the same title, was presented in 160 B.C. It is a thoroughly delightful comedy and deserves to rank as Terence's masterpiece. The play is primarily a study of human nature, and the amusing complications and misunderstandings in the plot are not the result of trickery or coincidence, as is so often the case, but are the logical outcome of the virtues and the weaknesses of the characters themselves. More than any other play in Roman comedy, *The Brothers* may be called a play with a purpose. As M. S. Dimsdale says, "The interest is educational and ethical as much as dramatic." Terence here presents a definite problem—the problem of education. Two opposing systems of education are set forth and the results of each method are clearly shown.

Micio, a genial bachelor, adopts Aeschinus, his brother's son, and rears him with kindness and generosity; he believes it a father's duty to train his son to do right from choice rather than from fear of punishment. Demea, his brother, uses a very different method in the training of Ctesipho—the method of harshness and restraint. Neither son lives up to the expectations of the two older men, and it is the love affairs of Aeschinus and Ctesipho which form the basis of the plot. Here again, as in all Terence's plays except *The Mother-in-law,* we find the double plot, but in this play the two love affairs do not constitute the main interest. The fundamental question deals with the relations of father and son, and the main conflict of the drama is the clash between the educational policies of the two older men.

Demea is shocked at the news that Aeschinus has openly and forcibly taken a music girl from the pimp Sannio. Micio too is grieved but is less bitter about the affair and is not long kept in ignorance of the truth— that the girl is really Ctesipho's mistress. Ctesipho is weak and timid and in general a far less attractive youth than Aeschinus, who has generously taken on himself the blame for the entire incident. The scenes with Sannio, which the prologue says are taken from a second original, serve to bring out the characters of both Aeschinus and Ctesipho. It will be noted that Sannio eventually receives fair treatment at the hands of Aeschinus—one of the few cases in Roman comedy where a pimp is not mercilessly cheated. Although Aeschinus is merely the agent in the abduction, his own life has not been blameless. He has seduced Sostrata's daughter Pamphila and promised to marry her, but he fears to confess his wrongdoing to his adoptive father. Micio's educational system has been no more successful in creating frankness between father and son than has Demea's sterner treatment of Ctesipho.

Of the two pairs of men Micio and Aeschinus are portrayed with the greater sympathy. Micio's tolerance and wisdom, his understanding of human nature, make him Terence's most attractive male character. One of the best scenes in the play is his meeting with Aeschinus after his discovery of the latter's secret love affair (Act Four, Scene V). Micio wishes to draw a frank confession from Aeschinus and to force him into action; he describes the arrival of a purely imaginary person who, as next of kin to Pamphila, will marry her and take her away. Aeschinus is terrified; he tries to argue against the supposed match without revealing his own concern in the affair. When he finally breaks down, Micio knows that he need go no farther; he pardons the youth with kindly words and at the same time reproaches him for his inaction and lack of candour. His speech is severe, but he closes with the permission that Aeschinus may marry Pamphila. The young man is overjoyed and promises that Micio will never again have cause to criticise his conduct.

Soon after this Micio meets Demea, who has finally learned of Ctesipho's escapade, and persuades the outraged father to accept the situation calmly. He points out to Demea that both young men have basically sound characters; if they are extravagant, age will take care of that, for the one vice of old age is to be "keener after money-making than we ought to be." If the play had ended with this scene (Act Five, Scene III), Micio's system would undoubtedly have scored a victory. Demea's anger at Aeschinus' supposed villainies has made him a laughable figure and he has been the butt of Syrus' ridicule. But it is not Terence's purpose to have Micio remain the most sympathetic character to the end or to have his generous theories win out. They too have their element of weakness, and Terence makes this clear in a clever and surprising conclusion. Demea realises that his way of life has been wrong, so he determines to gain the love and esteem of his sons by being generous and indulgent.

The closing scenes of the play contain excellent humour but underneath it lies a note of seriousness; Terence clearly believes that the proper course is a wise and sympathetic treatment of youth which avoids the weaknesses of either extreme. Demea's astonishing *volte-face* is, according to J. W. Duff, "the drollest thing in Terence." He gains the popularity he desires and makes everyone else happy—Aeschinus, Ctesipho, Hegio, Syrus and his wife—at the expense of Micio. Demea reminds Micio that the fault of men is "that of being too keen after money when we are old." Micio tries to resist, but he is unable to refuse Aeschinus' requests; his power to refuse has been undermined by his own methods. Gilbert Norwood says, "This final scene is the legitimate fruit of the whole play, the perfectly sound result of that collision between Micio and Demea which has created and sustained the whole wonderful drama."

The Brothers has been one of the most popular of Terence's comedies, as is shown by the number of modern plays influenced by it wholly or in part. The more important of these are Cecchi's *I Dissimili,* Marston's *The Parasitaster or The Fawn* (1606), Beaumont and Fletcher's *The Scornful Lady* (c. 1609), Molière's *L'Ecole des Maris* (1661), Shadwell's *The Squire of Alsatia* (1688), Baron's *L'Ecole des Pères,* Steele's *The Tender Husband* (1705), Garrick's *The Guardian,* Diderot's *Le Père de Famille* (1758), Colman's *The Jealous Wife* (1761), Cumberland's *The Choleric Man* (1774), and Fielding's *The Fathers* (1778).

THE BROTHERS

(SCENE:—*A street in Athens in front of the houses of* MICIO *and* SOSTRATA. *The time is early morning.*)

Prologue

WHEN the poet found that his writings were likely to be attacked by malicious critics, and that his adversaries did all in their power to discredit the play we are now going to act, he resolved to give evidence regarding himself, and leave it to your judgment, whether what they reproach him with is worthy of praise or blame.

The *Synapothnescontes* is a comedy written by Diphilus. Plautus has rendered it into Latin, and called it *Commorientes*.[2] In the Greek of Diphilus there is a youth, who, in the beginning of the play, takes a girl by force from a pimp. This Plautus has left untouched, and our poet has transferred it word for word into his *Brothers*, a new play that we are this day to act before you. Judge, therefore, whether this ought to be called a theft, or if it is not rather recovering what another's negligence has overlooked. For as to what these envious men allege, that some of our great men assist him, and are constantly writing with him; this, which they look upon as a mighty reproach, he regards as his greatest merit, that he has it in his power to please those, with whom you, and the whole people of Rome, are so much pleased; and whose services in war, in peace, and even in your private affairs, each one of you has used unreservedly, according to his need. As to what remains, do not expect now to hear from me the subject of the play; the two old men, who come on first, will partly explain it, and the rest will gradually appear in the representation. Do you, by a candid and impartial attention, encourage the poet to industry in writing.

Act One.   Scene I

(Enter MICIO *from his house.)*

MICIO *(calling within)*: Storax! *(To himself, as there is no answer)* Well, Aeschinus didn't return last night from supper, nor any of the servants who went to meet him. It is, indeed, a true saying: if you are absent anywhere, or chance to stay longer than ordinary, better those things happen to you, which your wife says, or fancies in her resentment, than what indulgent parents are apt to suspect. Your wife, if you are out late, fancies you have picked up a girl, or a girl you, or that you are at the tavern, or amusing yourself somewhere, and that you make yourself quite happy, while she is uneasy and pines at home. But for me now, what apprehensions am I under, because my son has not returned; how anxious, lest he may have caught cold, or had a fall, or broken some limb! Good gods! That a man should set his mind so much upon anything, as to allow it to become dearer to him than he is to himself! Nor is this boy, indeed, my son, but my brother's, one who is of a temperament very different from mine. Even from my youth, I have courted ease, and the quiet enjoyments of a town life, and, what men of pleasure count a happiness, have always lived single. He again is quite the reverse of all this. He has lived in the country, being always sparing and laborious; he married, and had two sons. Of these, I have adopted the elder; bred him up from a child, kept him with me, and loved him as my own; he is now my whole delight, and what alone I hold dear; and I do all I can, too, that I may be equally dear to him. I give, I overlook things, I don't think it necessary to exert my authority on every occasion. In short, I have accustomed my son not to conceal from me those little extravagances natural to youth, which others are at so much pains to hide from their parents. For he who is accustomed to lie to, or deceive his father, will be more likely to cheat others. And I think it more prudent, to hold children to their duty by the ties of kindness and honour, than by the restraints of fear. In this my brother and I differ widely, nor is he at all pleased with my manner. He often comes to me, loudly exclaiming, "What are you about, Micio? Why do you thus ruin the youth? Why does he drink? And why do you supply him with funds for all those extravagances? You indulge him too much in fine dress; you are quite silly in doing so." Why truly, he himself is much too severe, beyond what is either just or reasonable. And, in my judgment, he deceives himself greatly, to imagine that an authority established by force will be more lasting, or of greater weight, than one which is founded on friendship. For in this manner do I reason, and thus persuade myself to believe. He that

does his duty from mere motives of fear, will be upon his guard no
longer than while he thinks there is danger of his being discovered, but
if he can hope to escape notice, he returns to his natural bent; but
where one is won over by kindness, he acts from inclination, strives
to make a due return, and, present or absent, will be the same. This,
indeed, is the part of a father, to accustom his son to do what is right,
more from his own choice, than any fear of another; and here chiefly
lies the difference between a father and a master. He who can't do this
should admit that he doesn't know how to train up children. But isn't
this the very man of whom I was speaking? 'Tis the same; he seems
vexed too, I can't think why. I believe, as usual, we shall have a quarrel.
Demea, I am glad to see you so well.

Act One.　Scene II

(Enter DEMEA *from the country.)*

DEMEA: H'm! Just in time. You're the very man I was looking for.

MICIO: What makes you look so vexed?

DEMEA: Can you ask why? Do you know where our son Aeschinus is?
Do you know now why I am vexed?

MICIO *(aside)*: Didn't I say it would be so? *(To* DEMEA) What has he
done?

DEMEA: What has he done? He is ashamed of nothing and afraid of
nobody and thinks no law binding upon him. I pass over his former
escapades; what an outrage he has just now perpetrated!

MICIO: Why, what has he done?

DEMEA: He has broken open a street-door and made his way into a
strange house, has beaten the master of the house and all his people
nearly to death, and carried away a woman he's in love with. Everybody declares that it is a most shameful thing. As I was coming here,
Micio, you don't know how many people told me this story; all Athens
is full of it. If the boy needs an example, doesn't he see his brother
working away in the country thriftily and soberly? He does nothing
of this sort. Now Micio, when I say this to him, I say it to you, for you
are letting him go to the bad.

MICIO: There never is anything so unfair as an ignorant man, who
thinks that nothing can be right except what he does himself.

DEMEA: What do you mean by that?

MICIO: I mean, Demea, that you take a wrong view of this. Believe me, it is not a monstrous crime for a young man to indulge in wine and women; it isn't, really; nor yet to break open street-doors. If neither you nor I did such things, it was because poverty did not permit us to do them; you now are taking credit to yourself for not having done what you could not afford to do. This is quite wrong, for had we had the means, we should have done these things; and if you were a sensible man, you would let that son of yours do so now, while he is of an age for such follies, rather than that he should do them all the same when he ought to be too old for them, when at last he has had the pleasure of putting you underground.

DEMEA: By Jupiter, you make me wild! Not a monstrous crime for a young man to do so?

MICIO: Listen, and don't din this into my ears. You have given me your son to be mine by adoption; he has become my son. Now, Demea, if he does wrong, that is my affair; I shall have to bear most of the expenses. Suppose that he makes love, drinks wine, perfumes himself: I shall pay for it. Suppose he keeps a mistress: well, as long as I find it convenient, I shall let him have money for her; if I don't find it convenient, perhaps he will find her door shut against him. Now, if he has broken open a street-door, it will have to be mended; if he has torn any clothes, they must be sewn up again; and, thanks be to the gods, I can afford to have these things done, and thus far they do not weigh heavily upon me. The long and the short of it is, either leave off interfering, or choose someone to arbitrate between us. I can show that you are more to blame than I.

DEMEA: Oh, dear me! Learn to be a father from those who really know what it is!

MICIO: You are his father according to nature; but in care for him, I am.

DEMEA: As if you cared at all for him!

MICIO: If you go on talking like that, I shall go away.

DEMEA: That you should act thus!

MICIO: How many times over am I to hear the same thing?

DEMEA: It is a matter of interest to me.

MICIO: So it is to me; but let us each look after our own part: you see to one brother, Demea, and I will see to the other; for if you look after both of them, it is much the same thing as asking back the son you gave to me.

DEMEA: Oh, Micio!

MICIO: That's my view of the matter.

DEMEA: Well, well, if you like it, let him squander, waste, and go to the devil; it's nothing to me. And if I ever hear another word—

MICIO: Why, Demea, are you getting into a passion again?

DEMEA: Don't you believe me? Do I ask you to give me back the son I gave you? I own it is hard; I am not a stranger to him; it would not be surprising if I were to interfere—well, I leave off interfering. You wish me to look after one of my sons; very good, I am looking after him, and I am thankful to heaven that he is such a son as I should wish. That one of yours will find out some day how wrong he has been. I do not want to say anything worse about him. (DEMEA *departs*.)

MICIO (*to himself*): What he says is not all true, yet there is some truth in it, and I myself am vexed at it somewhat, though I wouldn't show him that I was sorry for it; for he is the sort of man that, to try to appease him I must be careful to oppose and thwart him, and even then he does not take it kindly; but if I were to increase his anger or add fuel to it, why I should be as mad as he is. Yet, for all that, Aeschinus has not treated me quite properly by doing this. What courtesan is there in all Athens whom he has not been in love with, or to whom he has not made a present? Last of all, the other day, sick of them all, I believe, he said that he should like to marry. I hoped that he had sown his wild oats, and was glad of it; now, behold, he has begun afresh. But whatever it is that he has done, I should like to know about it and have a talk with him, if he's in the market place. (MICIO *departs towards the forum. A short time is supposed to elapse before the next Act.*)

Act Two.   Scene I

(*Enter* AESCHINUS *with a music girl;* PARMENO *and other slaves attend him.* SANNIO *follows.*)

SANNIO: My countrymen, I beseech you, help an injured and innocent man. Assist one who is helpless.

AESCHINUS (*to the girl*): Take it easy, stand still here now. Why do you look behind you? There's no danger; he will never lay a finger on you while I'm here.

SANNIO: I'll get her back, in spite of all of you.

AESCHINUS (*to the girl*): Scoundrel as he is, he won't risk getting another thrashing today!

SANNIO: Aeschinus, listen to me, that you mayn't say you didn't know my ways. I am a slave-dealer.

AESCHINUS: I know that you are.

SANNIO: But the most honourable in my business that there ever was. Now I don't care a straw for what you will plead in your defence —that you are sorry for having committed this outrage upon me. Mark me, I'll stand out for my lawful rights, and it will not be by words alone that you will pay for the harm you have done me by deeds. I know your excuses—"Sorry it was done; will make an affidavit that you didn't deserve such ill-treatment," after I have been so shamefully misused!

AESCHINUS (*to the slaves*): Go on ahead quickly and open the door.

SANNIO: Then don't you pay any attention to what I say?

AESCHINUS (*to the girl*): Go into the house straightway.

SANNIO: But I won't let her go into the house.

AESCHINUS: Close up on that side, Parmeno; you are too far away; stand here close to him; there, that's where I want you to be. Now, mind you never take your eyes off mine, so that you may lose no time, when I give you the wink, in bringing your fist down on his jaw.

SANNIO: I should like him to try. (*Lays hold of the girl.*)

AESCHINUS: Here, mind what you're about. Let the girl go. (PARMENO *hits* SANNIO *in the face.*)

SANNIO: Oh, shame!

AESCHINUS (*to* SANNIO): He'll do it again, if you don't take care. (PARMENO *hits* SANNIO *again.*)

SANNIO: Oh, dear me!

AESCHINUS: I didn't wink to you to do it again; still, it's a fault on the right side. Now be off! (PARMENO *takes the girl into* MICIO's *house.*)

SANNIO: What's all this mean? Are you king in these parts, Aeschinus?

AESCHINUS: If I were, you would meet your deserts.

SANNIO: What have you to do with me?

AESCHINUS: Nothing.

SANNIO: What? Do you know who I am?

AESCHINUS: I don't want to know.

SANNIO: Have I meddled with any of your property?

AESCHINUS: It would have been the worse for you if you had.

SANNIO: Why should you have my slave, that I bought and paid for? Answer me.

AESCHINUS: You had better not abuse me in front of my own house; for if you go on making yourself a nuisance, I'll have you taken into the house and flogged there within an inch of your life.

SANNIO: Flog me, a free man!

AESCHINUS: That's what will be done.

SANNIO: O villain; and this is the place where they say that all men are free alike!

AESCHINUS: Now then, master slave-dealer, if you have quite done storming, be good enough to listen to me.

SANNIO: Have I been storming against you, or you against me?

AESCHINUS: Never mind that, come to the point.

SANNIO: What point? Where am I to come to?

AESCHINUS: Are you ready for me to tell you about your concern in this matter?

SANNIO: I am willing, provided that I get some of my rights.

AESCHINUS: Ho! Ho! Here's a slave-dealer bids me talk righteously!

SANNIO: I am a slave-dealer, I confess it, the ruin of all young men; I am a liar and a scoundrel; but still I have never done you any wrong.

AESCHINUS: No, that's the one thing that's left for you to do.

SANNIO: Pray, Aeschinus, return to what you began about.

AESCHINUS: You bought this girl for twenty minae; you shall be paid the same sum, and much good may it do you.

SANNIO: What if I refuse to sell her to you? Will you make me?

AESCHINUS: Not at all.

SANNIO: I was afraid that you would.

AESCHINUS: I don't believe that she is saleable, for I claim her as a free woman as the law directs in such cases. Now make your choice, whether you will take the money or think what defence you can make. I leave you to your reflections here, master slave-dealer, until I return. (AESCHINUS *goes into the house*.)

SANNIO (*to himself*): Almighty Jove! I don't wonder at men being driven mad by outrage. He has dragged me out of my house, beaten me, and carried off my slave-girl against my will; he has bestowed more than five hundred blows upon me; and now, as the reward of his crimes, he expects to get her for no more than I gave for her. (*Ironically*) Well, since he has treated me so well, so be it; he has a right, no doubt. Why, I'm quite willing, provided he pays me the money for her. But I'm talking nonsense. When I say that I gave so much for her, he will straightway have witnesses ready to prove that I have sold her to him, and the money will be all moonshine. He'll say, "Call again tomorrow." Well, I could put up with that, too, if only he would pay, in spite of the injustice of it. But I know how things are: if you ply my trade, you must submit to outrages from young gentlemen and hold your tongue. I shall never be paid; it's no use for me to make these calculations.

Act Two.   Scene II

(*Enter* SYRUS *from* MICIO'S *house*.)

SYRUS (*to his master within*): Say no more; I'll see the man myself; I'll make him glad to take the money, and declare that he has been well treated. (*To* SANNIO) What's this I hear, Sannio, about your having been fighting with my master?

SANNIO: I never saw a more one-sided fight than that between him and me today, for I got beaten, and he beat me till we were both tired out.

SYRUS: Well, it was all your fault.

SANNIO: What ought I to have done?

SYRUS: You ought to have made allowances for the young gentleman.

SANNIO: What more could I have done; haven't I allowed him to hit me in the face?

SYRUS: Come, you understand what I mean. Sometimes the most profitable thing we can do is not to be overkeen after one's money.

SANNIO: The deuce it is![3]

SYRUS: You great goose, if you don't insist upon your rights just now, and let the young gentleman have his way, you surely cannot fear that you will not profit by so doing in the long run?

SANNIO: A bird in the hand is worth two in the bush.[4]

SYRUS: You will never make a fortune; get along with you, Sannio, you don't understand how to entice men on.

SANNIO: I believe that is the best way, but I never was so cunning as not to prefer to get what I could in ready money.

SYRUS: Come, I know what you're thinking of; as if twenty minae made any difference to you, in comparison with doing my master a favour. Besides, they say you are on the point of setting sail for Cyprus.

SANNIO (*aside*): The devil!

SYRUS: That you have bought up a large cargo for that place, and hired a ship. Come, I know you're in two minds about it; when you return, I hope, you can still settle this affair.

SANNIO: I'm not going to stir from this place. (*Aside*) Confound it! This was what they were relying upon when they began.

SYRUS (*aside*): He's afraid. I've put a spoke in his wheel.

SANNIO (*aside*): What villainy! See how he has caught me just in the very nick of time. I've bought lots of slave-girls, and other merchandise besides, which I am going to take to Cyprus. Unless I get them there in time for the fair, it will be a dead loss. But if 1 drop this business now, and begin it again when I return from Cyprus, all's lost; the whole thing will have blown over. They will say, "Why didn't you come into court before? Why did you let him do it? Where were you?" So it is better to lose the money than either to wait here so long or to try to get it when I come back.

SYRUS: Well, have you finished reckoning up what you expect to make by your voyage?

SANNIO: Is this the way that Aeschinus ought to behave? To think that he should try to do such a thing; to expect to take this girl from me by main force.

SYRUS (*aside*): He is giving way. (*Aloud*) Now, Sannio, I've only one proposal to make; see whether it suits you. Rather than risk winning or losing it all, split the difference. He'll scrape up ten minae somehow.

SANNIO: Confound it, am I now to lose the principal as well as the interest? Has he no shame? He has loosened all my teeth; besides, my head is all bumps with his knocks; and is he going to cheat me as well? I won't leave this place.

SYRUS: Please yourself. Anything else before I go?

SANNIO: Yes, damn it! I beg you, Syrus, no matter what has been done, rather than go to law about it, let me have the bare price that I gave for the girl, anyway, my good Syrus. I know that you have not as yet profited by my friendship, but hereafter you will find me mindful of your kindness, and grateful.

SYRUS: I'll do my best. But I see Ctesipho there; he's pleased at getting his mistress.

SANNIO: What are you going to do about my request?

SYRUS: Wait a bit.

Act Two.   Scene III

(*Enter* CTESIPHO, *overjoyed.*)

CTESIPHO (*to himself*): One is always pleased to be done a good turn in time of need, by anybody; much more pleasant is it when one whose duty it is does one good. My dear brother, what need is there for me to praise you now? I am quite sure that, however grandly I spoke of you, it would fall short of your real merit. I think that I have this great advantage over everybody else, that no one has so noble a gentleman for a brother.

SYRUS: Good day, Ctesipho.

CTESIPHO: Oh, Syrus, where is Aeschinus?

SYRUS (*pointing to the house*): There he is; he's waiting for you in the house.

CTESIPHO: Aha!

SYRUS: What is the matter?

CTESIPHO: The matter! Why, Syrus, I owe him my life for what he has done, the delightful fellow, who has thought nothing of his own disgrace compared with my interests. He has taken upon his own shoulders all the scandal, reproach, intrigue, and blame that belongs to me. He could do nothing more. What's that noise at the door?

SYRUS: Wait; he himself is coming out.

Act Two.   Scene IV

(*Enter* AESCHINUS *from* MICIO's *house.*)

AESCHINUS: Where's that scoundrel?

SANNIO (*aside*): He is seeking me; is he bringing any money out with him? Confusion! I don't see any.

AESCHINUS: Oh, well met, Ctesipho; the very man I was looking for! How goes it? All is safely finished, so lay aside your gloom.

CTESIPHO: I do indeed lay it aside, because I have you for my brother. Oh, Aeschinus, my own brother, I am ashamed to praise you more to your face, for fear you should think I do it to flatter rather than because I am grateful to you.

AESCHINUS: Go on, goose; as if we didn't understand each other, Ctesipho. What I am sorry for is that we very nearly learned it too late, and that matters very nearly went so far that all the people in the world could not have helped you, if they had wanted.

CTESIPHO: I was ashamed to tell you.

AESCHINUS: That is folly, not shame. That you should have been on the point of leaving your native land all because of a trifle of money like that! Disgraceful! May heaven save us from such a fate!

CTESIPHO: I was wrong.

AESCHINUS (*to* SYRUS): And, pray, what terms does Sannio propose to us now?

SYRUS: He is quite reasonable now.

AESCHINUS: I'll go to the market place and pay him. Ctesipho, you go into the house to the girl.

SANNIO: Syrus, help me.

SYRUS (*to Aeschinus*): Let us be going, for this man is in a hurry to go to Cyprus.

SANNIO: Yes; but not so much of a hurry as you wish. I have plenty of time to wait here.

SYRUS: You shall be paid, never fear.

SANNIO: But see that he pays me in full.

SYRUS: He will pay you in full; only hold your tongue and follow me this way.

SANNIO: I am following you. (AESCHINUS *and* SANNIO *depart.* SYRUS *is detained by* CTESIPHO.)

CTESIPHO: I say, Syrus.

SYRUS: What is it?

CTESIPHO: I entreat you, close your account with that loathsome villain as soon as may be, for fear that if he be made angrier than he is, my father may somehow get wind of this and I be ruined for ever.

SYRUS: You won't be, be of good cheer; go into the house and take your pleasure with her in the meantime, and tell them to lay the table for us and get things ready for dinner; as soon as I have transacted the business I will come home again with something to cook.

CTESIPHO: Do so, I pray you; after our success we will have a jolly day. (CTESIPHO *goes into* MICIO'S *house;* SYRUS *hurries after* AESCHINUS.)

Act Three.   Scene I

(*Enter* SOSTRATA *from her house, followed by* CANTHARA.)

SOSTRATA: Pray, my dear nurse, what will happen now?

CANTHARA: What will happen, do you ask? All will go right, I hope.

SOSTRATA: My dear, her pains are just beginning to come upon her.

CANTHARA: You are as much afraid as if you had never seen a child born, never borne a child yourself.

SOSTRATA: Wretched woman that I am, I have no one, we are all alone, and Geta is not here. No one to send to the midwife, or to fetch Aeschinus.

CANTHARA: Heavens, he will be here soon, for he never misses a day without calling.

SOSTRATA: He is my only protection against my miseries.

CANTHARA: Mistress, after what has happened, things could not have turned out better than they have; since the girl has been violated, it is well that her seducer is such a fine young man, such a fine character and spirit, and belonging to so noble a family.

SOSTRATA: What you say is true; may the gods preserve him for us.

Act Three.   Scene II

(Enter GETA, *hurrying in great excitement.)*

GETA *(to himself)*: Now this is a matter in which, if all mankind gave all the advice they could, and tried to find a remedy for this misfortune which has befallen me and my mistress and my daughter, they could give us no help. Oh, dear me! So many things suddenly threaten us on every side, from which there is no escape: violence, poverty, injustice, loneliness, disgrace. What a time we live in! What crimes are committed! What a vile race it is! What a wicked man he is!

SOSTRATA *(aside to* CANTHARA): Oh, dear me, why do I see Geta frightened and hurrying like this?

GETA: Neither honour, nor his plighted word, nor pity could hold him back or turn him from his purpose, nor yet the thought that the girl whom he had outraged was about to become a mother.

SOSTRATA *(aside to* CANTHARA): I don't quite understand what he's saying.

CANTHARA: Pray, Sostrata, let us go nearer to him. *(They approach.)*

GETA: Oh, dear! I am so hot with anger that I am scarcely in my right mind. I should like nothing better than to meet the whole of that household, that I might vent my rage upon them now, while the pain is fresh.

I should not care how much I was punished if only I could take a thorough revenge upon them. First of all, I would choke the life out of the old man who begat the monster; then Syrus, the instigator of his wickedness! Oh, how I would mangle him! First, I would take him by the middle, hoist him up aloft, and bring his head down on to the ground, so that his brains bespattered the road. As for the young man himself, I would first tear his eyes out, and then fling him down a cliff headfirst. The rest I would fall upon, beat them, dash them down, smash them, overthrow them. But why don't I tell my mistress this bad news straightway?

SOSTRATA (*to* CANTHARA): Let us call him back. Geta!

GETA: Now, whoever you are, let me go my way.

SOSTRATA: It is I, Sostrata.

GETA (*turning round*): Where is she? It is you yourself that I am seeking, my mistress, it is you that I want; indeed, it's fortunate that you have fallen in with me.

SOSTRATA: What is it? Why are you in a flutter?

GETA: Oh, dear!

CANTHARA: Why are you in such a hurry, my good Geta? Wait and get your breath.

GETA: We are utterly—

SOSTRATA: What does that "utterly" mean?

GETA: Ruined. All's over with us.

SOSTRATA: Tell me, I beseech you, what the matter is?

GETA: By this time—

SOSTRATA: What is "by this time," Geta?

GETA: Aeschinus—

SOSTRATA: Well, what of him?

GETA: Is a stranger to our family.

SOSTRATA: What? Good gracious! Why so?

GETA: He has begun an amour with another woman.

SOSTRATA: Oh, miserable woman that I am!

GETA: And he makes no secret of it, but has carried her off from the slave-dealer in the sight of all men.

SOSTRATA: Is this proved to be true?

GETA: True! I saw it, Sostrata, with these very eyes.

SOSTRATA: Oh, poor wretch that I am! What is one now to believe, or whom should one believe? That our Aeschinus should have done this! He that was our very life, our only hope and help; he who used to swear that without her he could not live for one day; who used to say that he would set her child in his father's lap, and entreat him to let him marry her.

GETA: Mistress, dry your tears, and consider what we ought to do in this case. Are we to put up with his conduct, or shall we tell some one about it?

CANTHARA: Good gracious, man, are you in your right mind? Do you think that ours is a tale for anyone to hear?

GETA: I myself am against telling it. In the first place, what he has done shows that he doesn't care for us, and now, if we publish our story, I am quite sure he will contradict it, and then you will risk your good name and your daughter's prospects in life. Secondly, even if he admits the truth of our story, there's no point to letting him marry your daughter, since he loves another woman. So, in either case, you must hold your tongue.

SOSTRATA: Ah, but I won't; not a bit.

GETA: What will you do?

SOSTRATA: Publish the whole story.

CANTHARA: But, my dear Sostrata, just think what you are doing.

SOSTRATA: Matters can't be worse for us than they are; first of all she has no dowry, and then, too, her honour, her second dowry, is lost. I can't give her to anyone as a maid. If he disowns her, all that I shall have left to prove my story is the ring that he lost, which I have. Finally, as I am aware in my own mind that there has been nothing to blame in my conduct, Geta, that she has not received any money or anything else as compensation, and that neither of us has acted dishonourably, I'll try what the law will do for us.

GETA: Well, well, I agree; your suggestion is better.

SOSTRATA: Run as fast as you can and tell the whole story from the very beginning to Hegio, who was my Simulus' greatest friend, and was very fond of us.

GETA: Indeed, no one besides him takes any notice of us now. (GETA *departs.*)

SOSTRATA: My good Canthara, do you haste to bring a midwife, so that she may be at hand when we want her. (CANTHARA *departs;* SOSTRATA *goes into her house.*)

Act Three.　Scene III

(*Enter* DEMEA, *much troubled.*)

DEMEA (*to himself*): Confusion! I have heard that my son Ctesipho took part with Aeschinus in this abduction. It would, indeed, be the last straw for me, if he is able to seduce the son, who really is good for something, into mischief. Where am I to look for him? I suppose he has been carried off into some low dive; that profligate has led him away, I'm sure. Why, there I see Syrus going along. I will soon make out from him where he is. And yet Syrus is one of that gang; if he sees that I am looking for Ctesipho, the scoundrel will never tell me where he is. I won't let him see that I want to know.

(*Enter* SYRUS *with a basket of provisions.*)

SYRUS (*to himself*): We told the old gentleman the whole story just as it happened from the outset. I never saw anyone better pleased.

DEMEA (*aside*): Great Jupiter, that the man should be such a fool!

SYRUS: He highly commended his son, and thanked me for having suggested the plan to him.

DEMEA (*aside*): I'm fit to burst with anger.

SYRUS: He counted out the money then and there, and gave us half a mina besides for our expenses. That has been laid out according to my ideas.

DEMEA (*aside*): Oh, yes, this is the man to entrust your business to, if you want it looked after properly! (*Advancing.*)

SYRUS: Why, Demea, I didn't see you; how goes it?

DEMEA: How goes it! I am astounded at your proceedings.

SYRUS: Silly enough they are; to speak plainly, ridiculous. (*He goes to the door and hands his basket to the cooks within*) Dromo, clean the fish all but that big eel; let him play in the water a little while; he shall be boned when I come back, but I don't want him killed till then.

DEMEA: Such atrocities as these!

SYRUS: Indeed, I don't approve of them myself, and I often cry out. (*To the cooks within*) Stephanio, mind you soak that salt fish thoroughly.

DEMEA: Good heavens! Is it his object to ruin his son, or does he think that it would be to his credit? Oh, dear me, I already seem to see the day when he will run away somewhere and enlist.

SYRUS: Indeed, Demea, this is true wisdom, not to see only what stares you in the face, but also what is to come.

DEMEA: Now then, is that music girl in your house now?

SYRUS: Yes, she's within.

DEMEA: Pray, is he going to keep her in his own house?

SYRUS: I believe he is; he's crazy enough to do it.

DEMEA: That such things should be done!

SYRUS: All the fault lies with his father's silly good-nature and criminal weakness.

DEMEA: I am ashamed of my brother and grieve for him.

SYRUS: Demea, I say this before your face as I would say it behind your back; there is too much, far too much difference between you and your brother. What a man you are, every inch a sage! He's a stupid fool! Would you have let your son do this?

DEMEA: Would I have let him? Wouldn't I have smelt a rat six months before he set about doing anything!

SYRUS: You need not tell me how sharp-sighted you are.

DEMEA: I hope I shall always be as sharp as I am now.

SYRUS: Each son is as his father would have him be.

DEMEA: What of mine? Have you seen him today?

SYRUS: Your son? (*Aside*) I'll send this old man off to the country. (*Aloud*) I think he's been working on your farm in the country for some time now.

DEMEA: Are you quite sure that he is there?

SYRUS: Why, I myself saw him off.

DEMEA: Capital! I was afraid he might be hanging about here.

SYRUS: And a fine rage he was in.

DEMEA: What about?

SYRUS: He quarrelled with his brother in the market place about this music girl.

DEMEA: Indeed?

SYRUS: Yes, he didn't mince matters; he came upon us all of a sudden when the money was being paid, and began to cry out, "Oh, Aeschinus, that you should behave so scandalously! That you should disgrace our family by such escapades!"

DEMEA: Oh, I weep with joy.

SYRUS: "It is not only this money," said he, "but your life that you are throwing away."

DEMEA: Long may he live; he, I hope, is a chip off the old block.

SYRUS: Quite.

DEMEA: Syrus, he's full of those wise saws.

SYRUS: Right. He had some one at home to learn them from.

DEMEA: I took care of that: I never lose an opportunity of instruction; I accustom him to virtue; in fact, I bid him look into all men's lives as into a mirror, and make others serve as examples to himself. I say to him, "Practise this."

SYRUS: Excellent!

DEMEA: "Avoid that."

SYRUS: A wise education!

DEMEA: I say, "Men praise this."

SYRUS: That's the way to teach.

DEMEA: "They disapprove of that."

SYRUS: You couldn't do better.

DEMEA: And moreover—

SYRUS (*interrupting*): Indeed, I have no leisure now to listen to you any longer, Demea. I have got some fish after my own heart; I must take care that they're not spoiled; for with us, Demea, this is as great a crime as it is with you, not to practise those noble precepts which you have just told us of, and I do my best to give my fellow-servants instruction after the same fashion, saying, "This is too salt"; "this is over-cooked"; "this is not properly cleaned"; "this is as it should be"; "bear this in mind another time." In fact, I bid them look into the dishes, Demea, as into a mirror, and tell them what they ought to do. I am aware that you think these pursuits of ours silly; but what are you to do? You must deal with a man according to his character. Have you anything further for me?

DEMEA: Only to pray that heaven may give you all better sense.

SYRUS: Are you going to the country?

DEMEA: Straightway.

SYRUS: Yes, indeed, what should you do here, where, if you did give good advice, no one would follow it? (SYRUS *goes into the house.*)

DEMEA (*to himself*): Now I'm off to the country, because the boy I came here about has himself gone there: he is my only care; he belongs to me. As my brother wishes to have it so, he may look after the other one himself. (*Looking down the street*) But who is that I see in the distance? Is it not my fellow-tribesman, Hegio? If my eyes don't deceive me, it is he, indeed. Now there's a man who has been my friend from his youth up. Good heavens! We are not rich in citizens of his sort; he is of the good and honourable old school. It will be long ere the state suffers any injury from him. How pleased I am; I find life worth living even at the present day, when I see some remnants of that race still surviving. I'll wait for him here, that I may greet him and talk with him.

Act Three.   Scene IV

(Enter HEGIO *and* GETA *conversing.)*

HEGIO: By the immortal gods, this is a disgraceful action! What is it that you tell me?

GETA: The truth.

HEGIO: That such an ungentlemanly act should come from one of that family! By Jove, Aeschinus, you have shown little of your father's character in this!

DEMEA *(aside)*: Of course, he must have heard about this music girl; the thing grieves him, though he is a stranger; but his father thinks nothing of it. Oh, dear! I wish he were somewhere close by here, and could hear this.

HEGIO: Unless they behave properly, they shall not get away with it.

GETA: Hegio, our only hope is in you; we have no one beside you; you are our patron, our father. The old man, on his deathbed, entrusted us to your care. If you forsake us, we're lost.

HEGIO: Don't speak of such a thing. I won't desert you, nor could I, without disloyalty to my friend.

DEMEA *(aside)*: I'll accost him. *(Aloud)* Hegio, my very best respects.

HEGIO: Well, you're the very man I was seeking; good day, Demea.

DEMEA: What is the matter?

HEGIO: That elder son of yours, Aeschinus, whom your brother adopted, has not behaved like a good man or like a gentleman.

DEMEA: What has he done?

HEGIO: You know my friend Simulus; he was about our own age?

DEMEA: Of course I knew him.

HEGIO: He has seduced his daughter.

DEMEA: Gracious heavens!

HEGIO: Wait, Demea, you haven't yet heard the worst part of it.

DEMEA: Why, is there anything worse?

HEGIO: Worse, indeed; for this might have been excused somehow; he was excited by the darkness, by passion, by wine, by youth; it is human nature. Now when he learned what he had done, he went of his own accord to the maiden's mother; he wept, prayed, and implored her, giving his word of honour and swearing that he would make her his wife. He was pardoned, the affair was hushed up, his word was believed. The girl became pregnant through his violence; this is the tenth month. Now, if you please, my young gentleman has carried off this music girl to live with him, and has deserted the other.

DEMEA: Are you sure of the truth of what you say?

HEGIO: There is the girl's mother, the girl herself, the thing itself; besides, here is Geta, not a bad slave as slaves go, and a hard-working one; he supports them, he alone maintains the whole household. Take him, put him in chains, and enquire into the matter.

GETA: Nay, put me to the torture if that isn't the truth, Demea. Moreover, he won't deny it; bring him into my presence.

DEMEA (*aside*): I am ashamed. I don't know what to do, or what answer to give to him.

PAMPHILA (*within* SOSTRATA'S *house*): Oh, dear me! I am in agonies. Juno, thou that bringest babes to light, save me, I beseech thee!

HEGIO: What's that? Can she be in labour?

GETA: She is indeed, Hegio.

HEGIO: Well, Demea, she now appeals to you to do of your own free will what the law can make you do. I hope that you will behave as becomes you in this matter; but, Demea, if you do not choose to do so, I will fight as hard as I can to protect her, and him who is gone. He was my kinsman; we were always together, both at home and in the wars; we endured bitter poverty together, and therefore I will struggle, and strive, and go to law, and lay down my very life sooner than desert his family.

DEMEA: I will talk to my brother, Hegio.

HEGIO: But, Demea, mind that you consider this point. You and your brother are powerful, rich, prosperous, and noble; but in proportion as life is easy to you, all the more ought you to judge things rightly and act righteously, if you wish to be esteemed honourable men. (*He turns towards* SOSTRATA'S *door.*)

DEMEA: Come back, come back; whatever is right shall be done.

HEGIO: That's what you ought to do. Geta, take me into the house to Sostrata. (HEGIO *and* GETA *go inside.*)

DEMEA (*to himself*): These things have not come to pass for want of my warnings. Please heaven, this may be the end of it all! But this excessive indulgence will certainly lead to some terrible mischief in the end. I will go and look for my brother, and pour all this into his ears. (DEMEA *departs towards the forum.*)

Act Three. Scene V

(*Re-enter* HEGIO.)

HEGIO (*to* SOSTRATA *within*): Be of good cheer, Sostrata, and console the girl as well as you can. I will see Micio, if he's in the market place, and tell him the whole story, from beginning to end; then, if he is inclined to do his duty, he may do it; but if not, he shall give me his answer, and then I'll know without delay what steps I am to take. (HEGIO *departs towards the forum.*)

Act Four. Scene I

(*Enter* CTESIPHO *and* SYRUS *from* MICIO's *house.*)

CTESIPHO: Did you say that my father went off to the country?

SYRUS: Long ago.

CTESIPHO: Pray tell me about it.

SYRUS: He is at his farm, and just about now, I fancy, he's engaged on some piece of work.

CTESIPHO: I trust so. I hope that, without doing himself any serious harm, he may so tire himself out that he won't be able to get out of bed for the whole of these next three days.

SYRUS: So be it; and better than that, if possible.

CTESIPHO: Yes; for I am desperately eager to pass all this day as I have begun it, in enjoyment; and the reason why I dislike this farm so much is that it is so near Athens. Now, if it had been further off, night would have overtaken him before he could have returned here.

As it is, when he doesn't see me there, he will run back here, I am quite sure; he'll ask me where I have been; he'll say, "I haven't seen you the whole of this day." What answer am I to make?

SYRUS: Doesn't anything come into your head?

CTESIPHO: Nothing whatever.

SYRUS: So much the worse for you. Have you no dependent, no friend, no guest from abroad?

CTESIPHO: Yes, I have; what then?

SYRUS: Can't you say that you were attending to them?

CTESIPHO: When I wasn't attending to them? No, that won't do.

SYRUS: Yes, it will.

CTESIPHO: In the daytime, I grant you; but, Syrus, if I pass the night here, what reason can I give?

SYRUS: Dear me! How I wish it was the fashion to attend to one's friends by night as well as by day! But don't you trouble yourself, I know his ways perfectly; when he is at his angriest I can make him as quiet as a lamb.

CTESIPHO: How do you manage it?

SYRUS: He likes to hear your praises; I make a regular god of you in his mind. I tell him about your virtues.

CTESIPHO: My virtues?

SYRUS: Yes, yours; and straightway the tears roll down his cheeks for joy, as if he was a child. But look out!

CTESIPHO: What is it?

SYRUS: Talk of the devil![5]

CTESIPHO: Is it my father?

SYRUS: His very self!

CTESIPHO: O Syrus! What are we to do?

SYRUS: Run indoors directly, and I will see after him.

CTESIPHO: If he asks you, mind, you haven't seen me anywhere; do you hear?

SYRUS: Can't you hold your tongue? (CTESIPHO *goes inside.*)

Act Four. Scene II

(*Enter* DEMEA.)

DEMEA (*to himself*): Indeed I am an unlucky man; first of all I can't find my brother anywhere in the world, and besides that, while I was looking for my son, I saw a labourer from my farm who says that my son is not in the country. I don't know what to do.

CTESIPHO (*aside to* SYRUS *from the house*): Syrus!

SYRUS (*aside to* CTESIPHO): What's the matter?

CTESIPHO (*aside to* SYRUS): Is he after me?

SYRUS (*aside to* CTESIPHO): Yes.

CTESIPHO (*aside to* SYRUS): I am lost!

SYRUS (*aside to* CTESIPHO): No, keep your heart up.

DEMEA: What a mass of disaster this is! I can't get a right understanding of it, except on the supposition that I was born for nothing else but to endure miseries. I am the first to become aware of the misfortunes of the family: I learn the truth of them first; then, too, I am the first to bring the bad news to Micio; and I suffer alone for all that is done.

SYRUS (*aside*): He makes me laugh, saying that he was the first to know, when he's the only man who knows nothing about it.

DEMEA: Now I've come back, I'll see whether my brother has come home.

CTESIPHO (*aside to* SYRUS *from the house*): Syrus, pray take care he does not blunder straight in here.

SYRUS (*aside to* CTESIPHO): Can't you be quiet. I'll take care.

CTESIPHO (*aside to* SYRUS): I won't ever trust you to do that today; I'll lock myself in some room with the girl, that'll be the safest thing to do.

SYRUS (*aside to* CTESIPHO): Come, I'll send him away.

DEMEA: Why, there's that scoundrel Syrus.

SYRUS (*pretending not to see* DEMEA): No, by heaven! If this sort of thing goes on, nobody can stay in this house. I should like to know how many masters I have; what misery this is!

DEMEA: What's he babbling about? What does he want? What are you saying, my good man? Is my brother at home?

SYRUS: What the devil do you mean by your "good man"? I am done for!

DEMEA: What's the matter with you?

SYRUS: The matter! Why, Ctesipho has thrashed me and that music girl almost to death.

DEMEA: Eh! What's that you tell me?

SYRUS: Why, see how he has split open my lip.

DEMEA: What did he do it for?

SYRUS: He says that it was by my advice that she was bought.

DEMEA: Didn't you say just now that you had seen him off to the country?

SYRUS: So I did, but after that he came back raving mad, and had no pity. He should have been ashamed to beat an old man like me; why, I carried him in my arms when he was only so big.

DEMEA: Well done, Ctesipho, you take after your father. Come, I count you a man.

SYRUS: What, do you praise him for it? Nay, if he is wise, he'll keep his fists to himself for the future.

DEMEA: He did bravely.

SYRUS: Oh, very bravely, to beat a wretched girl, and me, a slave, who dared not hit him back. Mighty bravely, indeed!

DEMEA: He could not have done better; like me, he saw that you were at the bottom of all this business. But is my brother at home?

SYRUS: No, he isn't.

DEMEA: I wonder where I can find him.

SYRUS: I know where he is, but I'll never tell you the place today.

DEMEA: Eh, what's that you say?

SYRUS: Just that.

DEMEA: You will have your head broken in a minute.

SYRUS: Well, I don't know the man's name, but I know where the place is.

DEMEA: Then tell me where the place is.

SYRUS: Do you know that colonnade at the butcher's shop down the street?

DEMEA: Of course I do.

SYRUS: When you've passed that, go straight up the street; when you've come there, there's a hill leading downwards; down that you go, and then there is a chapel on this side (*pointing*); close by that there is a lane.

DEMEA (*looking*): Where?

SYRUS (*pointing*): There, where the great wild fig-tree stands.

DEMEA: I know.

SYRUS: Go that way.

DEMEA: But that lane is no thoroughfare.

SYRUS: True, by Jove! Why, what a fool I must be! I have made a mistake. You must come back to the colonnade again; indeed, this is a much shorter way, and less chance of your missing it. Do you know that house there, that belongs to the rich Cratinus?

DEMEA: Yes, I know it.

SYRUS: When you have passed it, turn to the left, go straight on that way till you come to Diana's temple, then to the right. Before you come to the city gate, just by the pond, there's a pounding-mill, and opposite a carpenter's shop; that's where he is.

DEMEA: What is he doing there?

SYRUS: He has ordered some benches to be made with oak legs, to stand the sun.

DEMEA (*sneering*): For you to lie upon and drink. Very well; I had better be off to him. (DEMEA *departs*.)

SYRUS: Off with you, in heaven's name! I'll work you today as you deserve, you old fossil! (*Reflecting*) It's very wrong of Aeschinus not to come; our dinner is being spoiled. Ctesipho is thinking of nothing but his love; I must look out for myself. I'll go in and pick out the choicest morsel of all for myself, and then I'll linger over my wine for the rest of the day. (*He goes into the house.*)

Act Four.   Scene III

(*Enter* MICIO *and* HEGIO, *conversing.*)

MICIO: Hegio, I don't see anything in this for which I deserve such high praise. I am only doing my duty; I am repairing the fault which we have committed; unless you used to reckon me among those who think that you are doing them an injury and abuse you if you complain of the wrong they have done you. Do you thank me because I don't act thus?

HEGIO: Oh, not at all; I never thought of you otherwise than as you are. But, Micio, I pray you, come with me to the girl's mother, and tell her yourself what you have told me, that all this suspicion arose on account of Aeschinus' brother and his music girl—

MICIO: Well, if you think it right, or that it needs doing, let us go.

HEGIO: You are right, for you will cheer up the woman, who is wasting away with sorrow and wretchedness, and you will have done your duty; still, if you don't wish to, I myself will tell her what you said.

MICIO: No, I'll go.

HEGIO: You are right. Somehow all those who are unsuccessful in life are prone to suspicion; they take everything as an insult, and believe that they are being slighted because they are helpless; so you are more likely to win their pardon if you defend yourself in person before them.

MICIO: What you say is true and proper.

HEGIO: Then come this way after me into the house.

MICIO: With all my heart. (*They go into* SOSTRATA'S *house.*)

Act Four.　Scene IV

(Enter AESCHINUS, *much troubled.)*

AESCHINUS *(to himself)*: I am in terrible distress; so much trouble has come upon me all of a sudden that I don't know what to do with myself or how to act. My limbs quake with fear; my mind is stupefied with dread; my heart can form no plan. Heavens! How can I get myself out of this mess? I have become gravely suspected, and on very good grounds. Sostrata believes that I have bought this music girl for myself. The old woman told me this; she was going to fetch a midwife when I saw her. I straightway went to her and asked her how Pamphila was, whether her confinement was at hand and that was why she was fetching the midwife. She cried out, "Be off with you, Aeschinus; you have fooled us long enough; you have deceived us long enough with your fine professions." "Eh," says I, "pray what is all this?" "Good-bye," says she; "keep the girl you like best." I saw straightway what the women suspected, but still I restrained myself, for fear of telling that old chatterbox anything about my brother, and letting out the whole story. Now, what am I to do? Shall I tell them that the girl is my brother's mistress? That secret must not be breathed to anyone. And never mind that, for I think the secret may be kept; but I fear they would not believe the truth; so many circumstances point to the other as the real story. I myself carried off the girl; I paid the money for her; she was brought home to my house. I admit that I was wrong in that matter, not to have told my father the whole story of my love, and wrung permission from him to marry her. Hitherto I have been idling; now then, Aeschinus, my man, wake up. Now, first of all, I will go to the women and clear my character. Let me go up to the door. Oh, dear! I am always in a fright when I begin to knock at this door. *(Knocking)* Ho, there! It is Aeschinus. Open the door quick, somebody. Here is somebody coming out; I will stand aside here.

Act Four.   Scene V

(Enter MICIO *from* SOSTRATA's *house.)*

MICIO (*to* SOSTRATA *within*): Do as I tell you, Sostrata; I will see Aeschinus, that he may know what has been done. But who is that who knocked?

AESCHINUS (*aside*): Heavens, it's my father! Confusion!

MICIO: Aeschinus!

AESCHINUS (*aside*): What is he doing here?

MICIO: Was it you who knocked at this door? (*Aside*) He doesn't answer. Why shouldn't I play with him for a while? It's right, seeing that he never chose to tell me anything about this. (*Aloud*) Do you give me no answer?

AESCHINUS: It wasn't that door, as far as I know.

MICIO: Indeed! I was wondering what business you could have here. (*Aside*) He blushes; all is well.

AESCHINUS: Tell me, pray, father, what business you have there.

MICIO: I have none. A friend just now brought me away from the market place as a witness.

AESCHINUS: What for?

MICIO: I'll tell you. Some poverty-stricken women live here; I don't suppose that you know them, indeed, I am quite sure you don't, for they have only lately moved into this house.

AESCHINUS: Well, what then?

MICIO: There is a young girl and her mother.

AESCHINUS: Yes, go on.

MICIO: The young girl has lost her father. This friend of mine is her next of kin, and is compelled by the law to marry her.[6]

AESCHINUS (*aside*): The devil!

MICIO (*overhearing*): What's the matter?

AESCHINUS: Oh, nothing. I am all right. Go on.

MICIO: He is come to take her away with him, for he lives at Miletus.

AESCHINUS: What? To take the girl away with him?

MICIO: Yes.

AESCHINUS: What? All the way to Miletus?

MICIO: Just so.

AESCHINUS (*aside*): I feel as if I should faint. (*To* MICIO) And what of the women? What do they say?

MICIO: What do you suppose they would say? Nothing at all. The mother did, indeed, make up a story that the girl had had a child by somebody else, some man or other, she didn't tell his name, and said that he came first, and that the girl ought not to marry my friend.

AESCHINUS: Well, don't you think that she was right to ask this?

MICIO: No.

AESCHINUS: What? "No?" And, father, is this man going to take her away?

MICIO: Why shouldn't he take her away?

AESCHINUS: Father, you have acted harshly and pitilessly, and even, to be plain, ungentlemanly.

MICIO: Why?

AESCHINUS: Do you ask me why? What do you suppose must be the feelings of that poor fellow, her former lover, who, unhappy man, perhaps is still desperately fond of her, when he has to stand by and see her carried off before his face and taken out of his sight? Father, it is a shameful thing to do.

MICIO: On what grounds do you say that? Who betrothed her to him? Who gave her to him? When was she married? Whom did she marry? Who gave his consent to these proceedings? Why did the man marry a girl who belonged to another?

AESCHINUS: Why, was such a great girl to sit at home waiting till her relative came to Athens from all that way off? That was what you should have urged, father, and pleaded.

MICIO: Absurd! Was I to plead against the interest of the man whom I had come to help as a witness? But what have we to do with this, Aeschinus, or what are these women to us? Let us be going. (*As*

AESCHINUS *breaks down and weeps*) What's the matter? Why are you in tears?

AESCHINUS: I beseech you, father, listen to me.

MICIO: I have heard all, Aeschinus, and I know all; I love you, and so I take all the more interest in your doings.

AESCHINUS: As I hope, father, that I shall deserve your love as long as I live, so I declare that I am deeply grieved at having committed this fault, and I am ashamed of myself in your sight.

MICIO: I verily believe you, for I know your honourable character; but I fear you are too remiss in this matter. In what city do you suppose that you are living? Here you have seduced a young lady whom you had no right to touch. This was your first sin, and a great one; a great sin, but after all, human nature. Many good men have done the same. But after that, pray did you ever think the matter over, or look forward on your own account to what would have to be done? If you were ashamed to tell me this story yourself, how was I to learn it? While you were hesitating, ten months have slipped away. You have, as far as in you lay, betrayed yourself and this poor girl and the child. What! Did you suppose that the gods would manage this business for you while you lay asleep, and that she would be brought home to you and installed in your bedroom without your taking any trouble about it? I hope you won't manage other business so negligently. Now be of good cheer, she shall be your wife.

AESCHINUS: What?

MICIO: Be of good cheer, I say.

AESCHINUS: Father, I beseech you, are you mocking me?

MICIO: Mocking you? Why should I?

AESCHINUS: I don't know; but I am so terribly anxious that this should be true, that I am all the more inclined to doubt it.

MICIO: Go home, and pray to the gods that you may bring home your bride; off with you!

AESCHINUS: What? My bride already?

MICIO: Already.

AESCHINUS: What? Now?

MICIO: As soon as may be.

AESCHINUS: Father, may all the gods abhor me if I don't love you better than my own eyes.

MICIO: What? Better than her?

AESCHINUS: Just as much.

MICIO (*smiling*): That's very kind of you.

AESCHINUS: I say, where's that man from Miletus?

MICIO: He's gone; he's gone on board ship. But why do you linger here?

AESCHINUS: Father, you go and pray to the gods, rather than I, for I am quite sure that they will be more likely to hear your prayers, as you are a far better man than I.

MICIO: I'll go into the house to make what preparations are necessary; you, if you are wise, do as I have said. (MICIO *goes inside.*)

AESCHINUS (*to himself*): What's this? Is this to be a father or to be a son? What more could he do for me if he were my brother or my bosom friend? Is he not a man to be loved? To be carried next one's heart? His kindness, however, has made me very anxious, for fear that through carelessness I may do something that will displease him. I must be on my guard. But why don't I go into the house, that I may not myself delay my own marriage? (AESCHINUS *goes inside.*)

Act Four.   Scene VI

(*Enter* DEMEA *wearily.*)

DEMEA (*to himself*): I have walked till I'm dead tired. Syrus, may great Jove confound you with your directions. I have crawled about all over the town—to the gate, to the pond; where haven't I been? There was no carpenter's shop there, and not a soul said he had seen my brother. Now I've made up my mind to wait for him in his house till he returns.

Act Four.   Scene VII

(*Enter* MICIO *from his house.*)

MICIO (*to* AESCHINUS *within*): I'll go and tell them that there shall be no delay on our part.

DEMEA: Why, there's the man himself. I have long been seeking you, Micio.

MICIO: What for?

DEMEA: I bring you news of more outrageous wickedness done by that nice young man.

MICIO: More, eh?

DEMEA: Hanging matters.

MICIO: Oh, nonsense.

DEMEA: You don't know what sort of a man he is.

MICIO: Yes, I do.

DEMEA: Fool, you are mooning, thinking that I mean the affair of the music girl; but this is a rape committed on a young lady, a citizen of Athens.

MICIO: Yes, I know.

DEMEA: What? You know of it and you endure it?

MICIO: Why shouldn't I endure it?

DEMEA: Tell me, don't you cry out at it? Doesn't it drive you mad?

MICIO: No, it does not. I might have preferred—

DEMEA: There is a baby boy born.

MICIO: Heaven bless him!

DEMEA: The girl hasn't a penny.

MICIO: So I have heard.

DEMEA: And she is to be married without a dowry.

MICIO: Of course.

DEMEA: What's to be done now?

MICIO: What the occasion requires; the girl must be brought over from that house to this.

DEMEA: O Jupiter! Is that the way that you ought to take it?

MICIO: What more can I do?

DEMEA: What can you do? Why, if you are not really put out at this, at any rate it would be your duty to pretend that you are.

MICIO: Why, I have betrothed the girl to him; the whole affair is set-tled; the wedding is just going to take place. I have set them free from all fear; this was much more my duty.

DEMEA: But, Micio, do you approve of what he has done?

MICIO: No, not if I could alter it; but since I can't, I make the best of it. The life of man is like playing with dice: if you don't throw ex-actly what you want, you must use your wits to make shift with what you have thrown.

DEMEA: Make shift, indeed! By this use of your wits you have lost twenty minae for that music girl, whom you must now dispose of for nothing, if you can't sell her.

MICIO: I shall not; nor do I want to sell her.

DEMEA: Then what will you do with her?

MICIO: She will live with us.

DEMEA: Heavens and earth! A mistress and a wife in the same house-hold?

MICIO: Why not?

DEMEA: Do you think you're in your right mind?

MICIO: I believe so.

DEMEA: So help me heaven, when I consider what a fool you are, I believe that you mean to keep her to give you music lessons!

MICIO: Why shouldn't she?

DEMEA: And will she give the bride music lessons too?

MICIO: Of course she will.

DEMEA: And you will dance "the ladies' chain" between them, I sup-pose?

MICIO: Very well.

DEMEA: Very well?

MICIO: Yes; and you shall join us, if need be.

DEMEA: Damn it! Aren't you ashamed of this?

MICIO: Now, Demea, just put away this ill temper of yours, and be merry and good-humoured, as you ought to be, on your son's wedding-day. I'll go and see the ladies, and then I'll come back here again. (MICIO *goes into* SOSTRATA'S *house.*)

DEMEA (*to himself*): Oh, Jupiter, what a life! What morals! What folly! A bride without a dowry is to be brought home; there's a music girl in the house; an extravagant establishment; a youth given over to debauchery, an old dotard. Why, the goddess of Salvation could not save this household, even if she wanted to.

Act Five.   Scene I

(*Enter* SYRUS *from the house.*)

SYRUS (*drunk, talking to himself*): Faith, Syry, my boy, you've done finely for yourself and managed your part of the business sumptuously. Well, now that I've had a bellyful of all sorts of good things indoors, I've taken a fancy to a stroll out in front of the house here.

DEMEA: See, there's an instance of the way the household is kept in order.

SYRUS: Why, here's our old gentleman. How goes it? What are you so gloomy about?

DEMEA: Oh, you scoundrel!

SYRUS: Shut up! None of your jaw here, old wiseacre!

DEMEA: If you were my slave—

SYRUS: You'd have been a rich man, Demea, and have made your fortune.

DEMEA: I'd see that you were made a warning to all men.

SYRUS: What for? What harm have I done?

DEMEA: Do you ask me? Why, just at the very crisis, and after the worst of wrongdoing, you get drunk, you scoundrel, before things have even been quieted down, just as if you had done some good action.

SYRUS (*aside*): Oh, hell! I wish I'd stayed indoors.

Act Five.   Scene II

(DROMO appears in the doorway.)

DROMO: Here, Syrus, Ctesipho wants you to come back.

SYRUS: Get along with you! *(DROMO disappears.)*

DEMEA: Ctesipho here! What's that he says?

SYRUS: Nothing.

DEMEA: Is Ctesipho here, scoundrel?

SYRUS: No.

DEMEA: Then why did he mention his name?

SYRUS: It's another man, a little parasite chap. Don't you know him?

DEMEA: I will directly. *(He approaches the door.)*

SYRUS: What are you doing? Where are you going to? *(Catching hold of DEMEA.)*

DEMEA: Let me go! *(Threatens him.)*

SYRUS: I say, don't.

DEMEA: Will you take your hands off me, you villain, or do you prefer to have your brains knocked out here? *(DEMEA dashes into the house.)*

SYRUS: He's gone. A damned unwelcome addition to their wine party, especially to Ctesipho. What am I to do now? Better get out of the way somewhere into a corner, and sleep off this drop of wine, until all these rows quiet down; that's what I'll do. *(SYRUS goes inside unsteadily.)*

Act Five.   Scene III

(Enter MICIO from SOSTRATA's house.)

MICIO *(to SOSTRATA within)*: We have everything ready, as I told you, Sostrata; so when you like— Why, who is that knocking so loud at my door?

(Re-enter DEMEA from MICIO's house.)

DEMEA (*to himself*): Oh, dear me! What shall I do? What's to be done? How can I cry aloud and lament enough? O heavens, earth and seas!

MICIO (*aside*): There you are! He has found out the whole story; you may be sure that that's what he's crying out about. There'll be a row. I must try to help.

DEMEA: See, there he is, the debaucher of both our sons!

MICIO: Pray restrain your passion and calm yourself.

DEMEA: I have restrained it. I am calm. I don't say another word of abuse. Let us look at the facts. Was it not arranged between us (you started the arrangement) that you were not to meddle with my son, and I was not to meddle with yours? Answer me.

MICIO: It was, I don't deny it.

DEMEA: Then why is he now drinking in your house? Why do you harbour my boy, Micio? Why do you buy a mistress for him? Isn't it fair that I should have as much rights over my son as you have over yours? Since I don't look after your son, don't you look after mine.

MICIO: What you say is not fair; no, it isn't; for it is an old proverb that friends have all things in common.

DEMEA: How clever! But this suggestion is a little late, isn't it?

MICIO: If you don't mind, Demea, listen while I say a few words. First of all, if you are vexed at the extravagance of your sons, pray bear these facts in mind. You, in the beginning, were going to bring up both your sons as your means permitted, because you supposed that your fortune would be enough for both of them, and of course you thought at that time that I should marry. Well, you keep on in that same old style now: pinch, scrape, and be stingy. Take care to leave them as large a fortune as ever you can, and glory in doing so. But let them use my fortune, which is available for them contrary to their expectations. Your property will not suffer thereby. What you get from me you may count as clear gain. If you would think these things over impartially, Demea, you would save both me and yourself and the boys much unpleasantness.

DEMEA: I pass over the expense; but their morals—

MICIO: Stay. I know; I was coming to that. There are many signs in people's characters whereby you may easily guess, when two of them are doing the same thing, how it will affect them, so that you can often say: "It will do this one no harm, it will do that one harm"; not because the thing that they are doing is different, but because their characters are different. Now by what I see of them, I am confident that they will turn out as we wish. I see that they are sensible, intelligent, high-minded, and fond of one another. You can see that they are gentlemen in thought and disposition; you can pull them in any day you please. Perhaps you are afraid that they are rather neglectful of business. Oh, my dear Demea, as we grow older we grow wiser about everything else, but the one vice which age brings to us, is that of being keener after money-making than we ought to be. Time will make them sharp enough at that.

DEMEA: Always provided, Micio, that your specious reasoning and easy good nature does not do them too much harm.

MICIO: Hush, I shall not do that. Now let us say no more about this business; be my guest today and clear your brow.

DEMEA: Well, it seems to be the fashion; I must do so; but at break of day I am off to the country with my son.

MICIO: Oh, tonight, for all I care; only do be cheerful today.

DEMEA: And I'll take that music girl away with me.

MICIO: Then you will have won your battle. By so doing you will quite gain your son's heart; only mind you keep her.

DEMEA: I will see to that: at the farm I'll make her cook and grind corn till she's all over ashes and smoke and flour; besides, I'll make her go gleaning under the noonday sun; I'll burn her as black as a coal.

MICIO: Right; now you seem to me to be showing good sense; and there I'd make him sleep with her, even if he doesn't want to.

DEMEA: Are you laughing at me? Well, you are lucky to be able to take it so. I feel—

MICIO: Now, no more of that.

DEMEA: Well, I'm just leaving off.

MICIO: Then come into the house, and let us spend this day as we ought. (*They go into* MICIO'*s house. A short time is supposed to elapse before the next Scene.*)

Act Five.   Scene IV

(Enter DEMEA *from* MICIO'S *house.)*

DEMEA *(to himself)*: No man ever lived in so well-regulated a fashion but what circumstances, years, and experience must continually present something new to him, and suggest something to him; so that you don't know what you once thought you knew, and cast away what you once supposed to be of the first importance. That is what's happened to me, for now, when my time is almost spent, I renounce the severe life that I have hitherto lived. Why do I do that? Because I have been taught by circumstances that nothing suits a man better than easygoing good nature. Anybody could tell this easily by comparing me and my brother. He has always spent his life at leisure, and in entertainments, in good humour, with unruffled temper, giving no man a harsh word, with a smile for everyone: he has lived to please himself, and has spent money on himself alone; well, all men speak well of him and love him. I, the countryman, rude, harsh, stingy, ill-tempered and self-willed—I married, and what wretchedness I went through. Sons were born: more trouble; and then, why, dear me! in trying to do the best I can for them, I have wasted all my life and manhood. Now, at the end of my days, what is my reward at their hands? Dislike; while that brother of mine has all a father's pleasures without the trouble. They are fond of him, and they run away from me. They tell him all their secrets, they love him, they are both at his house, and I am left alone. They hope that he will live, while of course they look forward to my death. Thus, for a small outlay, he has made them into his own sons, after I had brought them up with enormous trouble. I get all the pain, and he enjoys all the pleasure. Come, come now, let us try the other tack; let me see whether I can speak gently or behave kindly, since my brother challenges me to do so. I also demand to be loved and thought much of by my people; if that can be got by giving them presents and humouring their whim, I will not be behindhand. There will be a deficit in my exchequer, but that won't matter to me, seeing that I am the elder brother.

Act Five.   Scene V

(*Enter* SYRUS *from* MICIO'S *house.*)

SYRUS: Demea, your brother begs you to keep near the house.

DEMEA: Who's there? Oh, my good Syrus! How goes it? How's all with you?

SYRUS: Very well.

DEMEA (*aside*): I'm getting on capitally. There, for the first time in my life I have forced myself, against my true character, to add these three sayings, "My good," "how goes it?" and "how's all with you?" (*Aloud*) You are not a badly behaved slave, and I should be glad to do you some service.

SYRUS: Much obliged.

DEMEA: Indeed, Syrus, this is true, and facts will prove it to you before long.

Act Five.   Scene VI

(*Enter* GETA *from* SOSTRATA'S *house.*)

GETA (*to* SOSTRATA *within*): I'm going across to our neighbours', ma'am, to see when they will be ready to fetch the young lady. (*Looking round*) Why, there is Demea! Good day, sir.

DEMEA: Oh, what's your name?

GETA: Geta.

DEMEA: Geta, I have today made up my mind that you are an invaluable fellow, for I think that the worth of a slave is thoroughly proved when he is zealous for his owner, as I have noticed you are, Geta, and for that I shall be pleased to be of service to you whenever I have an opportunity. (*Aside*) I am studying how to be amiable, and really making progress.

GETA: You are very good to think so.

DEMEA (*aside*): I am beginning with the mob and gradually winning their affections.

Act Five.   Scene VII

(Enter AESCHINUS *from* MICIO'S *house.)*

AESCHINUS *(to himself)*: They plague me to death, wanting to make such an ultra-solemn wedding of it; they are wasting the whole day with their preparations.

DEMEA: How goes it, Aeschinus?

AESCHINUS: Why, father, are you here?

DEMEA: Yes, your father both in will and in deed, who loves you more than his own eyes. Why don't you bring home your bride?

AESCHINUS: I want to, but I am waiting for flute-players and people to sing the wedding hymn.

DEMEA: Now, will you take the advice of an old man like me?

AESCHINUS: What do you advise?

DEMEA: Get rid of the wedding procession, hymns, torches, flute-players and all, and order this party-wall in the garden to be pulled down as soon as may be. Bring your bride through that way; throw the two houses into one. Bring her mother and all her household over to us.

AESCHINUS: Well said, my most charming father.

DEMEA *(aside)*: Capital! I'm called charming already. My brother's house will become a thoroughfare; he will take a host of people into it, he will spend much money in entertaining them, there will be lots of expenses—well! what do I care? I am charming, and making myself popular. *(To* AESCHINUS*)* Here, order old Croesus to pay you twenty minae straightway. Syrus, why don't you go and do what you are ordered?

SYRUS: What am I to do?

DEMEA: Pull down the wall. *(To* GETA, *as* SYRUS *goes inside)* You go and bring the ladies through the garden.

GETA: May the gods bless you, Demea, for I see that you are a true well-wisher to our family.

DEMEA: I think that they deserve it. *(To* AESCHINUS, *as* GETA *goes into* SOSTRATA'S *house)* What do you say?

AESCHINUS: I quite agree.

DEMEA: It is much more proper than that she should be brought here along the public road, being ill and weak after childbirth.

AESCHINUS: Father, I never saw anything better arranged.

DEMEA: That's the way I always do arrange things; but see, here's Micio coming out of his house.

Act Five. Scene VIII

(*Enter* MICIO, *somewhat upset.*)

MICIO (*to the men within who are pulling down the wall*): My brother's orders, d'ye say? Where is my brother? (*Seeing him*) Are these your orders, Demea?

DEMEA: My orders are both in this and all other matters to make one household of it as far as may be, to cherish, help, and unite them.

AESCHINUS: Do so, father, I pray you.

MICIO: I think that we ought.

DEMEA: Nay, it's our duty so to do. In the first place, this bride has a mother.

MICIO: She has; what then?

DEMEA: An honest and discreet lady.

MICIO: So they say.

DEMEA: She's a trifle elderly.

MICIO: I know that she is.

DEMEA: She has long been too old to bear children, and she has no one to take care of her, a lone woman.

MICIO (*aside*): What is he driving at?

DEMEA (*to* MICIO): It is your duty to marry her, and (*to* AESCHINUS) yours to see that he does so.

MICIO: Me marry!

DEMEA: Yes, you.

MICIO: Me?

DEMEA: Yes, you, I say.

MICIO: Nonsense.

DEMEA (*to* AESCHINUS): If you're a man, he'll do it.

AESCHINUS: Father, dear.

MICIO: What, you young donkey, are you giving ear to his proposals?

DEMEA: It is no use, you cannot help doing it.

MICIO: You're out of your mind.

AESCHINUS: Let me win your consent, father.

MICIO: You're mad; be off with you.

DEMEA: Come, do your son this favour.

MICIO: Are you in your right senses? Am I, in my sixty-fifth year, to become a bridegroom for the first time, and marry a decrepit old woman? Is that what you seriously propose that I should do?

AESCHINUS: Do it, father; I have promised them that you will.

MICIO: Promised, have you! Promise what is your own to give, my boy.

DEMEA: Come! Suppose he were to ask some greater favour of you.

MICIO: As if this wasn't the greatest of all!

DEMEA: Grant it.

AESCHINUS: Don't be cross.

DEMEA: Do it; promise you will do it.

MICIO: Leave me alone, can't you?

DEMEA: I won't, till you give your consent.

MICIO: This is assault and battery.

DEMEA: Behave generously, Micio.

MICIO: Although this marriage seems to me to be a mistaken, absurd, foolish proceeding, yet if you are so eager for it, let it take place.

AESCHINUS: You are right.

DEMEA: You deserve my affection: but—

MICIO: But what?

DEMEA: Now that I have got my wish, I will tell you.

MICIO: What next? What more am I to do?

DEMEA: The next of kin to these ladies, who is now a connection of ours, is Hegio, a poor man; it is our duty to do something for him.

MICIO: What are we to do?

DEMEA: There is a small piece of land here just outside the city, which you let out on hire. Let us give him the use of it.

MICIO: A small piece, d'ye call it?

DEMEA: If it were a big one, still you ought to do it; he has been like a father to her, he is a good man, and one of ourselves now; it is right to give it to him. Besides, I am now myself putting into practice the maxim which you, Micio, enunciated so wisely and so well a short time ago: "A vice common to all mankind is that of being too keen after money when we are old." It is our duty to put away this reproach from us; your maxim is a true one, and should be acted upon.

AESCHINUS: Dear father.

MICIO: Well, well, he shall have it, since Aeschinus so wishes it.

AESCHINUS: I am delighted.

DEMEA: Now you are truly my brother alike in body and in soul. (*Aside*) I am cutting his throat with his own sword.

Act Five.   Scene IX

(*Enter* SYRUS.)

SYRUS: I have done what you ordered, Demea.

DEMEA: You're an honest fellow; and now my opinion is that this day Syrus ought to be made a free man.

MICIO: Him a free man? Why, what for?

DEMEA: For many things.

SYRUS: Oh, dear Demea, you are indeed a good man. I have watched over both your sons for you ever since they were boys with the greatest care; I have taught them and admonished them, and always given them the best advice that I could.

DEMEA: The facts prove that you did; moreover, you can be trusted to buy fish for dinner, you can bring a courtesan into the house, and you can prepare a feast in the middle of the day. It requires no ordinary man to do this.

SYRUS: What a pleasant old gentleman!

DEMEA: Moreover, he helped today to buy the music girl. He managed the business, and he ought to be repaid for his trouble. The other slaves will be all the better for the example; besides, Aeschinus wishes it.

MICIO (*to* AESCHINUS): Do you wish it?

AESCHINUS: I do.

MICIO: Well, if you wish it (*to* SYRUS) Syrus, come here to me. (*Strikes him with a stick*) Be a free man.

SYRUS: 'Tis generously done: I return my thanks to you all; and to you in particular, Demea.

DEMEA: I rejoice at it.

AESCHINUS: And I too.

SYRUS: I believe it. I wish this my joy were complete, and that I might see my wife Phrygia free too.

DEMEA: An excellent woman, truly!

SYRUS: And the first that suckled my young master's son, your grandson today.

DEMEA: Indeed? Why, if she really was the first that suckled him, without any question she ought to be made free.

MICIO: What, for that?

DEMEA: For that: in fine, you shall have the price of her freedom from me.

SYRUS: May the gods ever grant you all your desires, Demea!

MICIO: Syrus, you've done nicely for yourself today.

DEMEA: Moreover, brother, if you'll do your duty, and let him have a little ready money to begin with, he'll soon repay it.

MICIO: Not this much. (*Snapping his fingers.*)

AESCHINUS: He's an industrious honest fellow.

SYRUS: I'll return it, indeed; only let me have it.

AESCHINUS: Do, father.

MICIO: I'll consider it.

DEMEA: He'll do it.

SYRUS: O excellent man!

AESCHINUS: O delightful father!

MICIO: What means all this, brother? Whence this sudden change in your temper? What is this whim? What a hasty fit of prodigality!

DEMEA: I'll tell you, in order to make you realise that your passing for an easy agreeable man is not genuine, or founded on equity and good sense, but is due to your overlooking things, your indulgence, and giving them whatever they want. Now, Aeschinus, if I am, therefore, odious to you, because I don't wholly humour you in everything right or wrong, I'll concern myself with you no farther; squander, buy, do whatever you have a mind to. But if you had rather that I check and restrain you in pursuits, which, by reason of your youth, you are not aware of the consequences of, when passion misleads you or prompts you too far, and that I direct you, as occasion offers: behold me ready to do you that service.

AESCHINUS: Father, we submit to you entirely: you best know what is fit and proper. But how will you do with my brother?

DEMEA: I consent that he may have his girl, provided his follies end there.

AESCHINUS: That's well. (*To the spectators*) Give us your applause.

1. *The Brothers* was presented in 160 B.C.

2. Both the Greek title and that of Plautus' adaptation mean "Comrades in Death."

3. This exclamation (*hui*) is assigned to Syrus by Kauer and Lindsay.

4. The literal meaning is, "I don't pay cash for expectations."

5. The corresponding phrase in the original is, "The wolf in the fable."

6. This law is the basis of the first trick in Terence's *Phormio*, whereby Phormio makes it possible for Antipho to marry Phanium.

THE PLAYS OF
SENECA

I
MAD HERCULES

Characters in the Play

JUNO, *sister and wife of Jupiter, and queen of heaven*
CHORUS OF THEBANS
AMPHITRYON, *husband of* ALCMENA
MEGARA, *wife of* HERCULES *and daughter of Creon*
LYCUS, *the usurping king of Thebes*
HERCULES, *son of Jupiter and* ALCMENA, *reputed son of* AMPHITRYON
THESEUS, *king of Athens and friend of* HERCULES

INTRODUCTION

THE *Mad Hercules* is based upon Euripides' *Heracles* and well illustrates Seneca's characteristic handling of the themes of his Greek models. The main outline of the story is the same in both plays. During the absence of Hercules, Lycus kills Creon, king of Thebes, and usurps the royal power. Hercules returns in time to rescue his wife Megara, his children, and his reputed father Amphitryon. He slays Lycus and then, at the moment of victory, he falls victim to a tragic madness sent by Juno and in his frenzy kills both wife and children. Recovering from his madness he contemplates suicide but is dissuaded; he agrees to accept refuge in Athens where his friend Theseus is king.

The Euripidean version contains two reversals—the change from sorrow to joy when Hercules returns and kills Lycus, and the sudden reversal that comes with the madness of Hercules and the slaughter of his loved ones. The tragic outcome is unexpected in Euripides' play, for it is not until after the death of Lycus that the supernatural messengers of Juno appear and bring madness upon the hero. The structure of the Greek play is such that the full impact of the tragedy comes with stunning swiftness. On the other hand, the play appears to fall into two parts that are somewhat loosely joined. Seneca, in his handling of the theme, endeavoured to simplify and unify his material. He gave far greater unity and coherence to the drama by assigning the opening speech to Juno, Hercules' bitter enemy. The goddess describes her hatred of Hercules, threatens him with madness, and speaks in veiled terms of the horrible crime that he will commit:

> "Now I pray that he may come
> To earth again, and see his sons unharmed;
> May he return with all his old-time strength. . . .
> I'll stand by him
> And nicely poise his hand, that so his darts
> May with more deadly aim be hurled. I'll guide
> The madman's arms."

The Senecan prologue thus foreshadows the action of the second part of the play and subordinates the slaying of Lycus. The madness with its tragic results provides the main theme of interest from the opening of the play, for the reader is fully aware that the death of Lycus will bring only temporary relief for the family of Hercules.

Many other changes were made by Seneca in his version of the play. Lycus, who in Euripides was eager to destroy the hated race of Hercules, offers to marry Megara since he wishes to strengthen his power by union with royal blood; when repulsed with scorn he determines to destroy her and her children. The decision which Megara must make in the Senecan drama is thus very different from her plight in the Greek play. Euripides has Theseus enter suddenly late in the action, while Seneca brings him on the stage with Hercules. During the slaying of Lycus off-stage the Senecan Theseus tells of Hercules' trip to the Underworld and his capture of Cerberus—a lengthy description which, however effective as narrative, lacks dramatic vigour and slows up the action of the play. When the madness descends upon Hercules, he labours under the delusion that he is killing Juno and the sons of Lycus; this serves to give a more realistic motivation to the killing of Megara than appeared in Euripides' play, where Megara was slain accidentally as she was trying to protect one of the children. In the Euripidean version, moreover, Hercules thought that he was destroying the children of Eurystheus, the man who had been responsible for his many labours. By making Hercules think that the children were the sons of Lycus, Seneca again unifies the play and links together the story of Lycus and the main theme of the drama. Another effective innovation occurs when Hercules awakens from the deep sleep that follows the madness. Instead of being told of the murders, as in the Euripidean play, he realises from the blood on his arrows that the crime is his.

The full force of the tragedy is felt in the final Act with Hercules' struggle against himself. He wishes to commit suicide:

> "I have lost my all: my balanced mind,
> My arms, my reputation, children, wife,
> The glory of my strength—my madness too.
> There is no remedy for tainted souls;
> But death alone can cure me of my sin."

His resolve to live on and to face the responsibility for his deeds lacks the rational basis of the Greek Heracles; it is rather on the emotional level that Seneca's Hercules makes his decision, for he wishes to prevent the threatened suicide of Amphitryon. Hercules as a tragic character does not have the grandeur of the Euripidean hero, but the Roman play is nevertheless one of Seneca's most successful dramas, and reveals not only his desire for structural unity but also his interest in psychological realism.

MAD HERCULES

(SCENE:—*Before the palace of* HERCULES *at Thebes.*)

Act One.   Scene I

(*Enter* JUNO.)

JUNO (*to herself*): Lo I, the sister of the Thunderer
        (For, save this name alone, I've nothing more),
        Have left my lord, so often false to me,
        Have left, in widowhood, the realms of heaven,
        And, banished from the sky, have given place
        Unto my hated rivals. Now must earth
        Be my abode, while they in heaven reign.
        Behold, the Bear, far in the frozen north,
        Is set on high to guide the Argive ships;
        Behold, in southern skies, where days grow long
        Beneath the warmth of spring, the Bull shines bright,
        Who once the Tyrian Europa bore.
        There gleam the wandering Atlantides,
        A fearful band for ships and sea alike;
        And yonder fierce Orion with his sword
        The very gods affrights; his stars, as well,
        The golden Perseus boasts; while Leda's sons[1]
        With shining banners glitter in the sky;
        And they, Latona's children,[2] for whose birth
        The floating land stood firm. And not alone
        Have Bacchus and his mother gained the heavens;
        But, that the infamy may be complete,
        The skies must needs the Cretan maiden's[3] crown
        Endure. But these are ancient wrongs I tell:
        One wild and baneful land alone is full
        Of shameless mistresses—the Theban land,
        Which all too oft has me a stepdame made.

And though Alcmena scale the heights of heaven,
And hold my place, victorious over me;
And though her son his promised star obtain
(Whose hateful getting cost the world a day,
Since Phoebus, bidden to hold his shining car
In Ocean hid, with tardy light shone forth
From eastern seas); still ever in my heart
Shall hate relentless dwell. Undying wrath
My outraged soul shall kindle; and my grief,
All hope of truce denying, endless wars
Shall fiercely wage. But what avail my wars?
Whatever savage things the hurtful earth,
The sea or air produce, terrific shapes,
Fierce, pestilential, horrible, and dire,
The power of all is broken and subdued.
Alcides towers above and thrives on woe;
My wrath is his delight, and to his praise
He turns my deadly hate. While I, too stern,
Impose his dreadful tasks, I do but prove
His origin, and opportunity
For glorious achievement render him.
Where Phoebus with his neighbouring torch illumes
The east and western shores of Aethiop's land,
Alcides' dauntless courage is adored;
While all the world considers him a god.
And now have I no monsters more to send;
And less his toil to do the tasks I bid,
Than mine to set them. Joyfully he hears
My several commands. But what dire tasks
The tyrant may conceive can harm that youth
Impetuous? His very arms, forsooth,
Are torn from monsters which he feared—and slew;
With spoils of lion and of hydra armed,
He walks abroad. Nor are the lands of earth
Enough for him: behold, the doors of Dis
Are burst, and to the upper world he brings
The booty taken from the vanquished king.
'Tis not enough that he returns alive:
The law that binds the shades is set at naught.
Myself I saw him, when he had o'ercome
The king of Hades and escaped the night
Of that deep underworld, display to Jove
The spoils of Dis. But why does he not lead,

Oppressed and overcome, the king himself
Who gained by lot an equal realm with Jove?
Why rules he not in conquered Erebus?
Why bares he not the Styx? His upward way
From deepest hell to earth he has retraced,
And all the sacred mysteries of death
Lie open to the world. Not yet content,
And proud that he has burst the bars of night,
He triumphs over me, and, insolent,
He leads through all the cities of the land
That gruesome dog of hell. I saw, myself,
The daylight pale at sight of Cerberus,
The sun start in affright. Nay, even I
Was struck with terror; and, as I beheld
That triple-headed beast in bondage led,
I trembled at the thought that 'twas my will.
But all too trivial ills do I lament;
My fears must be aroused for heaven itself,
Lest he who overcame the lowest depths
Should scale the very skies, and from his sire
His sceptre snatch away. Nor to the stars
Will he, like Bacchus, by an easy path
Ascend; through ruin would he make his way,
And wish to rule an empty universe.
He is inflamed with pride of tested strength;
But he has learned by bearing up the heavens,
That by his power the heavens can be subdued.
Upon his head he bore the universe,
Nor did his shoulders bend beneath the weight
Of that stupendous mass; the vault of heaven
Upon his neck was poised, and steadily
He bore the expanse of sky, the shining stars;
And even me, down pressing, he endured.
He seeks a place among the immortal gods.
Then up, arouse thee to destructive wrath,
Destroy him meditating plans so great.
Meet him in single strife; with thine own hands
Asunder rend him. Why thy mighty hate
Dost thou consign to others to appease?
Enough of monsters; let Eurystheus rest,
All weary with imposing thy commands.
Though thou shouldst open wide Sicilia's vaults,
And free the Titans who essayed to wrench

The sceptre from the hand of mighty Jove;
Though the Doric isle, which trembles with affright
Whene'er the heaving giant turns himself,
Should ease her weight upon the monster's head;
Though in the moon another race of beasts
Should be conceived; yet all of these, I know
Alcides conquered and will conquer still.
Seek'st thou his match? There is none save himself.
Then set him on to war against himself;
Let Furies from the lowest depths of hell
Be roused and come to aid, their flaming locks
Aglow with maddening fire, their savage hands
The horrid snaky scourges brandishing.
Go now, thou proud one, seek the seats of heaven,
And scorn the lot of men. And dost thou think,
O hero brave, that thou hast fled the Styx
And gloomy shades? Here will I show thee hell;
Here will I summon up the goddess dire
Of Discord, deep in darkness thick confined
Far down below the abode of guilty souls.
A cavern huge within a mountain's hold
Is her dark prison. Her will I call forth,
And from the deepest realms of Dis bring up
Whate'er thou hast escaped: base Crime shall come;
Impiety that fiercely stains its hands
In kindred blood; the shape of Error too,
And Fury ever armed against itself.
This, this assistance shall my grief employ.
Come then, ye ever-faithful slaves of Dis,
Begin your task. Shake high the blazing torch;
And let Megaera lead her dreadful band
Of sisters viperous. With deadly hand
Let her from off the blazing funeral pyre
A burning brand snatch up. Now to your task;
Thus seek revenge for violated Styx:
Distract his heart with madness; let his soul
More fiercely burn than that hot fire which glows
On Aetna's forge. But first, that Hercules
May be to madness driven, smitten through
With mighty passion, I must be insane.
Why rav'st thou not, O Juno? Me, oh, me,
Ye sisters, first of sanity deprive,
That something worthy of a stepdame's wrath

I may prepare. Let all my hate be changed
To favour. Now I pray that he may come
To earth again, and see his sons unharmed;
May he return with all his old-time strength.
Now have I found a day when Hercules
May help me with his strength that I deplore.
Now let him equally o'ercome himself
And me; and let him, late escaped from death,
Desire to die. Now let it profit me
That he is born of Jove. I'll stand by him
And nicely poise his hand, that so his darts
May with more deadly aim be hurled. I'll guide
The madman's arms. And so at last I help
Alcides in his wars. The crime complete,
Then let his father to the heavens admit
Those guilty hands. Now must the attack begin.
The day is breaking, and with saffron light
The rising sun dispels the gloom of night.
(JUNO *departs*.)

Act One.   Scene II

(*Enter* CHORUS OF THEBANS.)

CHORUS: Now scattered and with paling light
The stars gleam in the sinking west;
Now vanquished night collects her fires,
Whose shining band at the day's return
The star of morning drives away.
High up in the frozen northern sky,
The Arcadian Bears with their sevenfold stars,
Their course completed, hail the dawn.
Now borne along by his azure steeds
The sun looks forth from Oeta's ridge;
With whose light suffused, the clustering grapes
In the vineyards to Theban Bacchus dear
Flush rosy red. The waning moon
Fades out of sight, to return again.
Hard Toil awakens, at whose knock
The doors of men are opened wide,
And daily cares resumed.

The shepherd sends his flock afield,
And plucks, himself, the tender grass
Still sparkling with the frosty rime.
The young bull sports among the fields
At liberty; the dams refill
Their empty udders; sportive kids
Leap lightly o'er the tender grass
In aimless course. On the topmost branch
The Thracian Philomela sings
Her strident song, and near her nest
Of chattering young she spreads her wings
To the morning sun; while all around
The throng of birds with united songs
Announce the day.
The daring sailor spreads his sails
To the freshening wind, as the breezes fill
Their flapping folds. From wave-worn rocks
The fisher leans and baits anew
His cunning hook; he feels his line
A-tremble with the struggling fish,
Or weighs his prize with practiced hand
And eager eye.
Such are the joys of him who lives
In tranquil and unworried peace;
Whose pleasure is a humble house,
His own, though small; whose simple hopes
Are in the open fields.
But worried hopes in cities dwell,
And trembling fears. There some would haunt
The rich man's haughty vestibules,
Wait at their proud, unfeeling doors,
Forego their sleep. Some heap up wealth,
Though blest with boundless wealth, and gaze
In admiration at their heaps;
And yet, with all their gold, are poor.
Some strain for the applause of men,
The vulgar throng, whose fickle will
Is shifting as the sea, and swell
With empty pride. The noisy mart
Still others claim, who meanly deal
In quarrelsome suits, and profit make
Of wrath and empty words.
Few know untroubled peace, the men

Who, heeding time's swift flight, hold fast
The years that never will return.
While fate permits, live happily;
For life runs on with rapid pace,
And with headlong speed the year's swift wheel
With wingéd hours is turned.
The cruel sisters urge their task,
Nor backward turn the threads of life.
But the race of men is hurried on
To meet the quick approaching fates,
Uncertain of their own.
Of our own will we haste to cross
The Stygian waves. Thou, Hercules,
With heart too brave, before thy time
Didst see the grieving shades. The fates
In pre-established order come;
And none may stay when they command,
None may put off the appointed day.
The swiftly whirling urn of fate
Contains all mortal men.
Let glory then to many lands
Proclaim some names, and chattering fame
Through every city sing their praise,
And raise them to the stars. Sublime
In triumph let another ride.
Me let my native land conceal
Within a safe and humble home.
'Tis unambitious souls who come
To hoary-headed age at last.
If humble, still the lot is sure
Of lowly homes. Souls lifted high,
For this to greater depths must fall.
But see, sad Megara comes with flowing hair,
Her little children closely pressing round;
And with her, with the tardy step of age,
The sire of Hercules, Amphitryon.

Act Two.   Scene I

(Enter from the palace MEGARA *with her children, and* AMPHITRYON.*)*

AMPHITRYON: O mighty ruler of Olympus' heights,
Thou judge of all the world, now set at length
A limit to my cares, and make an end
Of my disasters. No untroubled day
Doth dawn for me; but one misfortune's end
Marks but the starting-point of future woes.
Fresh foes are ready for my Hercules
Straightway on his return; ere he can reach
His happy home, another warfare bids
That he set forth again. No time for rest
Is given, save while he waits a fresh command.
'Twas ever thus: from earliest infancy
Unfriendly Juno follows on his track.
Was e'en his cradle free from her assaults?
He conquered monsters ere he learned to know
What monsters were. Two crested serpents huge
Against him reared their heads; the dauntless child
Crawled forth to meet them, and, with placid gaze
Intently fixed upon their fiery eyes,
With fearless look he raised their close-coiled folds,
And crushed their swollen necks with tender hand.[4]
And thus he practiced for the hydra's death.
He caught the nimble stag of Maenalus,
Its beauteous head adorned with horns of gold.
The lion, terror of Nemean woods,
Groaned out his life beneath the mighty arms
Of Hercules. Why should I call to mind
The stables dire of that Bistonian herd,
And the king[5] as food to his own horses given?
The rough Maenalian boar, which, from his lair
On Erymanthus' thickly wooded heights,
Filled all the groves of Arcady with dread?
Or that fell Cretan bull whose terror filled
A hundred towns? Among his herds remote,
The three-formed shepherd by Tartessus' shore
Was slain, and from the farthest west his herds
Were driven as booty. Now Cithaeron feeds
The cattle once to Ocean known. Again,

When bidden to penetrate the sultry zone
Of summer's burning sun, those scorchéd realms
Which midday parches with its piercing rays,
He clove the ponderous mountain barriers,
And made a pathway for the rushing sea.
He next assailed the rich Hesperides,
And bore therefrom the watchful dragon's spoil
Of golden fruit. Then Lerna's savage beast,
An evil creature constantly renewed,
Did he not overcome by fire at last,
And teach it how to die? Did he not seek
Within the clouds the dire Stymphalian birds,
Whose spreading wings were wont to obscure the day?
He was not conquered by the maiden queen
Who ruled the Amazons and ever kept
Her couch in virgin state. Nor did his hands,
Courageous to attempt all glorious deeds,
Disdain to cleanse the vile Augean stalls.
But what avail these toils? For he alone
Cannot enjoy the world he saved. And now
The world perceives the giver of its peace
Is absent from its sight. Now prosperous crime
Is called by virtue's name; good men obey
The guilty, might is counted right, and fear
O'ershadows law. Before my eyes I saw
The sons who dared defend their father's throne
Fall dead beneath the tyrant's murderous hand;
I saw King Creon's self by death o'ercome,
The latest son of Cadmus' noble line;
And with his head the royal diadem
Was reft away. Who now could weep enough
For Thebes? Proud land and mother of the gods,
What master fears she now, she, from whose fields
And fertile bosom sprang that band of youth
With swords all ready drawn; whose mighty walls
Amphion, son of Jove, once built, its stones
Compelling by the magic of his lyre;
Down to whose citadel not once alone
The father of the gods from heaven came?
This royal city which the immortals oft
Has entertained, which has divinities
Produced, and (heaven forgive the boastful word)
Perchance will yet produce, is now oppressed

Beneath a shameful yoke. O royal race
Of Cadmus, noble state Amphion ruled,
Low hast thou fallen indeed! Dost thou obey
A low-born exile, driven from his land
And yet oppressing ours? And now, alas,
He, who on land and sea doth punish crime,
Who breaks all cruel rule with righteous hand,
Far off obeys another, and himself
Endures those ills from which he others saved;
And Lycus rules the Thebes of Hercules!
But not for long; he soon will come again,
And punish all the wrongs; he suddenly
Will to the upper world emerge; a way
He'll find—or make. Oh, come unharmed, I pray;
As victor come at last unto thy home
Which now in ruins lies.

MEGARA: O husband, come,
With thy strong hand break through the shades of hell
And if no way is open, if the road
Is closely barred, then rend the earth and come;
And all that lies in keep of dismal night
Bring forth with thee. As once, through riven hills
A passage seeking for a headlong stream,
Thou stood'st, and, with thy strength gigantic cleft,
The vale of Tempe opened wide; as then,
Impelled by might of thy resistless breast,
The mountains fell away from either side,
And through the broken masses poured the stream
Of Thessaly along a channel new:
So now to parents, children, native land,
A passage burst. And bring away with thee
The shapes of death, and all that greedy time
Through countless rounds of years has hidden away;
Those nations who have drunk forgetfulness,
Drive out before thee, fearful of the light.
The spoils are all unworthy of thy fame,
If thou shouldst bring from Hades only that
Which was commanded. But too bold my words,
And thoughtless of my present lot I speak.
Oh, when will come at last that day for me
When I shall clasp my husband once again,
And weep no more his long-delayed return,

His long forgetfulness of me? To thee,
O ruler of the gods, a hundred bulls
Shall bleed; to thee, thou goddess of the fruits,
Thy secret rites I'll pay: for thee shall blaze
Upon Eleusin's shrine the sacred torch
In celebration of thy mysteries.
Then shall I think my brothers' lives restored,
My father once again upon his throne.
But if some power more potent than thine own
Holds thee in durance, we shall come to thee.
Return in safety and protect us all,
Or drag us down with thee. This wilt thou do;
No god will e'er our broken fortunes mend.

AMPHITRYON: O ally of my house, with wifely faith
Preserving for the great-souled Hercules
His couch and children, be of better mind.
Take heart again, for surely he will come,
Increased in fame by this, as is his wont
By other tasks.

MEGARA: What wretched men desire
They readily believe.

AMPHITRYON: Nay, what they fear
They think can never be escaped or borne.
For fear is prone to see the darker side.

MEGARA: Submerged, deep buried, crushed beneath the world,
What chance has he to reach the upper realms?

AMPHITRYON: The same he had, when, through the arid plain,
And sands that billowed like the stormy sea,
Those twice receding, twice returning gulfs,
He made his way; when on the dangerous shoals
Of Syrtes he was wrecked, he left his ship
A helpless hulk and crossed the sea on foot.

MEGARA: Unjust is fortune, rarely does she spare
The bravest souls. No one with safety long
Can brave so frequent perils; he who oft
Has shunned misfortune meets at last his fate.
But see, with threatening looks fierce Lycus comes,
His hateful soul in hateful bearing shown,
And bears the stolen sceptre in his hand.

Act Two.   Scene II

(Enter LYCUS.)

LYCUS: The rich domain of this proud town of Thebes,
With all the fertile soil which Phocis bounds
Within its winding borders, all the land
Ismenus waters; all Cithaeron sees
From his high top; the narrow Isthmus, too,
Two seas asunder cleaving: all I own,
Not by prerogative of long descent,
A worthless heir. No noble ancestors,
Nor family adorned with lofty names
Have I; but splendid valour. He who boasts
His noble ancestry exalts a thing
Which is not his to boast. But power usurped
Is held with anxious hands; the sword alone
Can guard it. All thou hold'st against the will
Of citizens the sword must hold for thee.
No kingdom built upon a foreign soil
Is safe for long. One thing alone I see
Which can our power establish—Megara,
By ties of royal marriage bound to me.
From her illustrious line my humble blood
Shall a richer hue derive. Nor do I think
That she will scorn me and refuse my suit.
But should she with a blind and stubborn soul
Refuse my proffered hand, my mind is fixed
To give to utter ruin all the house
Of Hercules. Will such a deed arouse
A storm of scandal and the people's hate?
The art of ruling chiefly lies in this:
The power to bear the people's hate unmoved.
Let me make trial then. Occasion smiles,
For she herself. in mourning vestments clad,
Stands by the altars of her guardian gods,
While near at hand Alcides' father waits.

MEGARA *(seeing* LYCUS, *aside)*: What new outrage does yonder wretch
            prepare,
The pestilent destroyer of our race?

LYCUS:

O thou, who bear'st a name illustrious
From royal stock, with patient ear awhile
Receive my words. If everlasting hate
The hearts of men should feel, if fury dire,
Once in the heart conceived, should never cease;
If prosperous men must ever fight to rule,
And those who fail obey because they must:
Then never-ending wars would nothing leave,
And all the fields would be a barren waste;
Homes would be burned, and 'neath their ashes deep
All nations of the earth would be o'erwhelmed.
The victor's profit is in peace restored,
But for the vanquished 'tis their direful need.
Come, share my throne; let us unite our wills.
And, as my pledge of faith, receive my hand.
But why dost thou in scornful silence wait?

MEGARA:

And dost thou think that I would touch the hand
That is besprinkled with my father's gore,
And my two brothers' blood? Oh, sooner far
Shall day's last beams go out in eastern skies,
And dawn break in the west; sooner shall peace
Be made 'twixt snow and flame, and Scylla join
Sicilia's shores with those of Italy;
And sooner shall Euripus' rushing waves
Lap peacefully upon Euboea's shores.
My father and my brothers hast thou slain,
My kingdom ruined, home and native land.
What still is left? One thing remains to me,
That's dearer than my father, brother, home,
And kingdom: 'tis my deadly hate of thee.
That I must share this with the land at large
Is grief to me. For in their cause for hate
How small a share have I? Thou, swollen with pride
Rule on, and let thy soul exalt itself;
But know that evermore the avenging god
Pursues the proud of heart. Well do I know
The history of Thebes. Why need I tell
Of matrons who have dared and suffered wrong?
Why name the double crime, the mingled names
Of husband, father, son,[6] the opposing camps
Of brothers?[7] Why describe the funeral pyres?
The haughty mother,[8] child of Tantalus,

Still sits in stony grief; the mourning rock
On Phrygian Sipylus still drips with tears.
Nay, Cadmus' self, in form of serpent, still
Flees through Illyria's realm with crested head,
And leaves behind his dragging body's trail.
Such fates admonish thee. Rule as thou wilt:
But may the accustomed doom of Thebes be thine.

LYCUS: Come then, have done with this wild talk of thine,
And learn from Hercules to obey the will
Of kings. Although by right of victory
I wield this sceptre, though I reign supreme
Without the fear of laws which arms annul,
Still will I briefly speak in my defence.
And did thy father fall in bloody war?
Thy brothers too? But arms no limit know,
Cannot be checked with ease, nor can the sword,
Once drawn, restrain its wrath. War will have blood.
But (you will say), he fought to save his state,
While I was prompted by the lust of power.
Still we should look, not at the cause of war,
But at its outcome. Now let memory
Of all the former wrongs pass from thy heart.
When the victor lays aside his arms, 'tis meet
The vanquished should abandon hatred too.
I ask thee not upon thy bended knees
To acknowledge me as king; for it is well
That thou shouldst meet thy ruin dauntlessly.
Lo, thou art worthy of a royal mate:
Be then my wife and not my enemy.

MEGARA: Cold horror creeps throughout my lifeless limbs.
What shameful proposition do I hear?
I did not shrink when loud alarms of war
Rang round our city's walls; and all my woes
I've bravely borne. But marriage—and with him!
Now do I think myself indeed a slave.
Load down my tender frame with heavy chains;
Be lingering death by long starvation sought;
Still shall no power o'ercome my wifely faith.
I shall be thine, Alcides, to the death.

LYCUS: Such spirit does a buried husband give?

MEGARA: He went below that he might reach the heavens.

LYCUS: The boundless weight of earth oppresses him.

MEGARA: No weight of earth can overwhelm the man
              Who bore the heavens up.

LYCUS: Thou shalt be forced.

MEGARA: He can be forced who knows not how to die.

LYCUS: Tell me what gift I could bestow more rich
              Than royal wedlock?

MEGARA: Grant thy death, or mine.

LYCUS: Then die, thou fool.

MEGARA: 'Tis thus I'll meet my lord.

LYCUS: Is that slave more to thee than I, a king?

MEGARA: How many kings has that slave given to death!

LYCUS: Why does he serve a king, and bear the yoke?

MEGARA: Remove hard tasks, and where would valour be?

LYCUS: To conquer monsters call'st thou valour then?

MEGARA: 'Tis valour to subdue what all men fear.

LYCUS: The shades of Hades hold that boaster fast.

MEGARA: No easy way leads from the earth to heaven.

LYCUS: Who is his father, that he hopes for heaven?

AMPHITRYON: Unhappy wife of mighty Hercules,
              Be silent now, for 'tis my part to tell
              Alcides' parentage. After his deeds,
              So many and so great; after the world,
              From rising unto setting of the sun,
              Has been subdued, so many monsters tamed;
              After the giants' impious blood was spilled
              In Phlegra's vale, and gods were reinforced,
              What need we yet to prove his parentage?
              Do we make false pretense of Jupiter?
              Then Juno's hate believe.

LYCUS: Why blaspheme Jove?
              The race of mortals cannot mate with gods.

AMPHITRYON: Such is the origin of many gods.

LYCUS: But were they slaves before their heaven was gained?

AMPHITRYON: The Delian at Pherae kept the flocks.

LYCUS: But he did not in exile roam the world.

AMPHITRYON: His mother bore him in a roaming land,
Herself a fugitive.

LYCUS: Did Phoebus fear
Wild beasts and monsters?

AMPHITRYON: Yes, in dragon's blood
His earliest shafts were stained.

LYCUS: Thou knowest not
What heavy ills the young Alcides bore.

AMPHITRYON: But Bacchus by a thunderbolt was ripped
From out his mother's womb; and yet he stood
In after time beside the Thunderer,
His sire. Nay, Jove himself, who rules the stars
And drives the clouds, did he not lie concealed,
In helpless infancy in Ida's cave?
A heavy price must so high lineage pay,
And suffering is the birthright of a god.

LYCUS: Whoe'er is wretched, thou wouldst mortal know.

AMPHITRYON: Whoe'er is brave, thou wouldst not wretched call.

LYCUS: But is he brave, from whose broad shoulders fell
The lion's skin and club, that they might be
A maiden's plaything? Who himself shone bright
In Tyrian vestments? Should we call him brave,
Whose bristling locks were wet with fragrant nard,
Whose famous hands in woman's wise essayed
To play the tambour; on whose frowning brow
The Phrygian turban shamelessly was worn?

AMPHITRYON: But youthful Bacchus did not blush to wear
His locks in flowing ringlets, in his hand
The thyrsus light to brandish, as he walked
With steps unsteady, clad in trailing robes
Bright with barbaric gold. 'Tis virtue's right
In foolishness to ease the strain of toil.

LYCUS: 'Twas for this cause the house of Eurytus
          Was overthrown, and troops of maidens slain
          Like helpless sheep! No Juno ordered this,
          Nor yet Eurystheus: these his works alone.

AMPHITRYON: Thou know'st not all his deeds: it was his work
          That Eryx fell, by his own gauntlets slain;
          That in his death Antaeus, too, was joined;
          That those foul altars, dripping with the blood
          Of hapless strangers, drank the blood at last
          Of murderous Busiris. 'Twas his work
          That Cycnus, proof against the sword, was slain,
          Though still unwounded; by his hand alone
          The threefold Geryon fell. And thou shalt be
          As one of these, though they ne'er basely sinned
          Against the rites of marriage.

LYCUS: What to Jove
          Is lawful, is my kingly right as well.
          A wife thou gav'st to him; so for thy king
          Shalt thou a mate provide. Now Megara
          From thine example shall the lesson learn,
          Not new, that wives may yield to better men,
          When husbands give consent. But if, self-willed,
          She still refuse to take me for her lord,
          I'll force her will to bear me noble seed.

MEGARA: Ye shades of Creon, and ye household gods
          Of Labdacus, ye impious nuptial fires
          Of Oedipus, your wonted fortune give
          To this our union! O ye savage wives[9]
          Of king Aegyptus' sons, be present now,
          With blood-stained hands. Your count is incomplete.
          I gladly will that impious number fill.

LYCUS: Since thou dost stubbornly refuse my suit,
          And striv'st to fright the king, now shalt thou feel
          The strength of royal power. Cling as thou mayst
          To altar horns: no god shall save thee now
          From me; not though the earth itself be rent,
          And Hercules victorious come again
          Unto the upper world.
                    (*To slaves*)
                              Heap high the logs,

And let the sacred temple blazing fall
Upon its suppliants. Now let the wife
And all her brood upon the funeral pyre
Be burned to ashes in the kindling flames.
(MEGARA *departs with her children.*)

AMPHITRYON: This boon Alcides' father asks of thee,
Which fits me well, that I be first to die.

LYCUS: Who bids all men meet punishment with death
Knows not the ruler's art. Seek varied pains;
Forbid the wretch to die, the happy slay.
Now, while the pyre is growing for the flames,
I'll pay my vows unto the ocean's god.
(LYCUS *departs.*)

AMPHITRYON: O god of gods, O ruler of the skies,
Whose hurtling bolts make mortals quake with fear,
Check thou the impious hand of this dire king.
Why do I vainly importune the gods?
Where'er thou art, hear thou and answer, son.
But why this sudden rocking of the shrine?
Why groans the earth? Far in her lowest hold
A crashing deep resounds. Our prayer is heard!
It is, it is the step of Hercules!

Act Two. Scene III

CHORUS: O Fortune, envious of the brave,
Unjustly are thy prizes given!
Behold Eurystheus reigns at ease,
While our Alcmena's noble son,
With hands which could the heavens uplift,
Must endless wars with monsters wage;
Must sever the hydra's teeming necks,
And from the cheated sisters bear
The apples, when the dragon huge,
The guardian of the golden fruit,
Had given to sleep his watchful eyes.
To the wandering homes of Scythia,
Where tribes in their ancestral seats
As strangers dwell, he made his way.

He trod the frozen ocean's crust,
A still sea hemmed by silent shores;
There no waves beat on the rigid plains,
And where but now full-swelling sails
Had sped their barks, a path is worn
By the long-haired Sarmatae.
There the waters change with the changing year,
Now ships, now horses bearing up.
From the queen who rules o'er virgin tribes,
With golden girdles on their loins,
He took her body's noble spoil,
Her shield and her snowy bosom's guard.
On bended knee she acknowledged him victor.
With what hope, driven to the depths of hell,
Bold to tread irretraceable ways,
Didst thou behold the dusky realms
Of Proserpine of Sicily?
There Notus and Favonius lash
No seas to rage with swelling floods;
There do no frightened vessels find
Help from the twin Tyndaridae.
Those waters lie in stagnant pools
And black; and when, with greedy teeth,
Pale Death bears off uncounted tribes
Unto the shades, one oarsman grim
Bears all across their gloomy depths.
Oh, that the laws of cruel Styx
Thou mightst annul, and the distaff break,
Relentless, of the fates. And lo,
Thou canst avail, for he who rules
O'er many nations once with thee
His deadly hands in battle joined,
When thou didst wage 'gainst Nestor's land
A mighty war. A three-pronged spear
He bore; but soon, by but a wound
O'ercome, he fled. He feared to die,
Though lord of death. Burst with thy hands
The bonds of fate. To those sad souls
In hell let in the light of day,
And to the upper world reveal
An easy path. Once, by his songs
And suppliant prayers, did Orpheus bend
The stubborn lords of hell, when he

His lost Eurydice would seek.
That art which drew the forest trees,
Which held the birds and rocks enthralled,
Which stopped the river's headlong race,
And tamed the hearts of savage beasts,
Soothed with its strains ne'er heard before
Those darksome realms, and clear and fine
Resounded through that silent land.
Eurydice the Thracian dames
Bewailed; Eurydice, the gods,
Who ne'er had wept before; and they
Who with forbidding, awful brows,
In judgment sit and hear the crimes
Long since committed, unconfessed,
They sat and wept Eurydice,
Until the lord of death exclaimed:
"We grant thy prayer. Away to earth;
But on this sole condition go:
Do thou behind thy husband fare;
And look thou not upon thy wife,
Until the light of day thou see,
And Spartan Taenarus appear."
Love hates delay, nor suffers it:
He hasted to behold his wife—
And she again was lost to him.
So, then, the fortress that could yield to song,
Be sure that fortress shall to strength belong.

Act Three. Scene I

(*Enter* HERCULES, *just returned from the lower world, accompanied by* THESEUS.)

HERCULES:　O kindly lord of light, heaven's ornament,
Who circlest all the spaces of the sky
With thy flame-bearing car, and thy bright head
Dost lift to glad a new-awakened earth:
Thy pardon, O Apollo, do I crave,
If aught unlawful thou dost see in me;
For by another's will have I revealed
The hidden things of earth. Thou lord of heaven,

And sire, behind thy flaming thunderbolt
Conceal thy face; and thou who rul'st the seas
By second lot, seek thou their lowest depths.
Whoever from on high beholds the earth,
And would not by strange sights be vision-stained,
To heaven look and so these portents shun.
Two only may behold this horrid sight:
The one who brought and she who ordered it.
To work my punishment and fated toils
The earth was not enough. Through Juno's hate
Have I seen regions unapproachable,
Unknown to Phoebus' rays; yea, I have seen
Those gloomy spaces which the nether pole
Has yielded to the dusky Jove's domain.
And had the regions of the final lot
Been pleasing, there could I myself have reigned.
That seething chaos of eternal night,
And, what is worse than night, the gloomy gods,
And fates I conquered; and in scorn of death
I have come back again. What else remains?
I've seen and shown the lower world to men.
If aught beyond is left to do, command.
Why dost thou for so long allow these hands,
O Juno, to remain in idleness?
What conquest still dost thou command? But why
Do soldiers hold the temple walls in siege,
And fear of arms beset their sacred doors?

AMPHITRYON: Now do my fervent hopes deceive my sight,
Or is this he, the tamer of the world,
The pride of Greece, from that sad, silent land
Returned? Is this my son? My agéd limbs
Give way through utter joy. O son, of Thebes
The sure though long-delayed preserver thou!
And do I hold thee sent to earth again,
Or does some empty shadow mock my joy?
And art thou he indeed? I recognise
Thy arms and shoulders and the mighty club
Within thy hands renowned.

HERCULES: .   O father, whence
These marks of grief, and why do I behold
My wife in dusky mourning garments clad,

My children garbed in these vile signs of woe?
What fell disaster hath o'erwhelmed my house?

AMPHITRYON: Thy father-in-law is slain, his kingdom gone,
For Lycus hath usurped it; now he seeks
Thy children, father, wife, to bring to death.

HERCULES: Ungrateful land! Did no one come to aid
The home of Hercules? Did all the world,
Defended by my arm, look on this deed
And suffer it? But why waste time in grief?
My enemy must die.

THESEUS (*seeking to detain him*):   O Hercules,
Let not thy mighty courage bear this stain,
And such a foe as Lycus be thy last.
I go myself to drink his hateful blood.[10]

HERCULES: My Theseus, stay thou here, lest violence
From some new source arise. This war is mine.
Let thy embraces wait awhile, my sire,
And thine, my wife. Let Lycus first announce
To Dis that I have safe returned to earth.
                    (HERCULES *departs*.)

THESEUS: Now let thy face give o'er its grief, my queen;
And thou, O father, check thy falling tears,
Since this thy son is safe returned to thee.
If I know Hercules, for Creon's death
This Lycus soon shall pay the penalty.
"Shall pay" is slow; he pays; nay more, has paid.

AMPHITRYON: Now may some favouring god our prayers fulfil,
And help us in our need. O trusty friend
Of our great son, his deeds in order tell:
How long the way that leads to the sorrowing shades;
How bore the dog of hell his heavy chains.

THESEUS: Thou bid'st me call to memory such deeds
As e'en in safety make me tremble still.
For I can scarce believe that even yet
I breathe the vital air. My eye's clear sight
Is blinded, and, by that thick darkness dimmed,
Can scarce endure the unaccustomed light.

AMPHITRYON: But conquer thou the fear that still remains
Deep in thy heart; and do not rob thyself

Of the best fruit of toil. For what was hard
To bear becomes most sweet in memory.
Go on, and tell us all thy sufferings.

THESEUS: O god of heaven, and thou who holdest sway
In that deep, all-embracing realm of death,
And thou whose mother sought thee (but in vain)
Through all the world: your powers I supplicate
That I may speak with boldness of the things
Concealed and buried in the hold of earth.
The Spartan land lifts high a famous cliff
Where Taenarus juts out upon the sea,
Dense wooded. Here the realm of hated Dis
Opes wide its mouth; the high cliff spreads apart,
And in a mighty cavern yawns a pit
With jaws portentous, huge, precipitous;
And for all nations ample passage gives.
The way begins, not dark with heavy shades.
A watery gleam of daylight follows in,
And doubtful light, as of the sun eclipsed,
Falls there and mocks the eye. Such light the day,
While mingled still with night, at early dawn
Or in its waning hour, is wont to give.
The way then broadens into spaces vast
And empty, where the human race entire
Might plunge and perish. 'Tis no labour here
To travel, for the road itself draws down.
As often whirlpools suck unwilling ships,
So does the air, down streaming, urge us on,
And hungry chaos. Here the clutching shades
Permit no backward step. Deep in the abyss,
With peaceful shallows gentle Lethe glides,
And by its draughts removes all mortal care
And, that no backward way may be allowed,
With many folds it wraps the stream of death;
Just as the wandering Maeander sports
With waves uncertain, now upon itself
Retreats, now halts in hesitation slow,
Whether it shall its fountain seek again,
Or journey to the sea. Here lies the marsh
Of sluggish, vile Cocytus; here, behold,
The vulture, there the doleful owl laments,
And through the air the fearsome screech-owl sends

Its sad, foreboding cry. There stands the yew,
Its black leaves shuddering on the gloomy boughs;
And 'neath its shelter hover sluggish Sleep,
And mournful Famine with her wasting jaws,
And Shame, at last her guilty face concealed.
Here quaking Fear, and Murder, desperate Grief,
Black Mourning, tottering Disease, and War
With weapons girded on, lie hid; and last
Comes feeble Age upon his staff upheld.

AMPHITRYON: Are there no fruitful fields of corn or wine?

THESEUS: Not so; no joyful fields with verdure shine,
No ripening grain waves gently in the breeze,
No stately trees bear apple-laden boughs;
But sterile wastes defile those lonely depths,
And in eternal sloth the foul earth lies.
Here lie the lonesome remnants of the world.
The air hangs motionless; and thick night broods
Upon a sluggish, horror-stricken land.
The place of death is worse than death itself.

AMPHITRYON: And what of him who rules those dusky realms?
Where sits he as he rules his shadowy folk?

THESEUS: There is a place in an obscure recess
Of Tartarus, which, with its heavy shades,
Dense vapour shrouds. Hence, from a single source,
Two different rivers flow: with silent stream
One bears along the sacred Stygian waves
On which the gods take oath; with mighty roar
The other fiercely rolls the rocks along
Within its flood, the raging Acheron,
Which may not be recrossed. Set opposite,
By these two streams encircled, stands the hall
Of royal Dis; and by a shading grove
The mighty house is hid. A spacious cave
Of overhanging rock the threshold forms.
This is the path of souls; here is the door
Of Pluto's realm; and, round about, there spreads
The plain wherein the frowning monarch sits
And new-come souls reviews. Of lowering brow
And awful majesty the god appears;
Yet in his face his brother's likeness bears,

And proves his noble birth. Jove's face is his,
But thundering Jove's. And of that savage realm
The master's self makes up the largest part,
For every fearful thing holds him in fear.

AMPHITRYON: And is the story true that down below
Stern justice is at last administered,
And guilty souls, who have their crimes forgot,
At last atone for sin? Who is he, then,
Who searches out the truth, and justice gives?

THESEUS: There is not one inquisitor alone
Who sits in judgment on the lofty seat,
And tries the trembling culprits: in that hall
Sit Cretan Minos, Rhadamanthus too,
And Aeacus. Each for his sins of earth
Must suffer here; the crime returns to him
Who did it, and the guilty soul is crushed
By its own precedents. There, deep immured
In prison, bloody leaders have I seen,
And bleeding backs of heartless tyrants, scourged
By base plebeian hands. Who mildly reigns,
And, though the lord of life, restrains his hands;
Who mercifully rules a bloodless realm,
And spares the lives of men: he shall enjoy
Long years of happy life, and, at the end,
Attain to heaven, or to those regions blest
Of the Elysian fields, himself a judge.
Refrain from human blood, all ye who rule;
Your sins with heavier judgment shall be judged.

AMPHITRYON: Does any certain place enclose the lost,
And do, as rumour says, the impious
Sharp punishments in endless chains endure?

THESEUS: On swiftly flying wheel Ixion turns;
And on the neck of Sisyphus a stone
Weighs heavily. There stands in middle stream,
With throat thirst-parched, the poor old man, and seeks
To catch the cooling waves which wash his chin.
He, oft deceived, hopes now at last to drink;
As often fails the water at his lips.
So also do the fruits his hunger fail.
There Tityus eternal banquets gives

Unto the greedy vulture; and in vain
Do Danaus' daughters bear their brimming urns.
There wander, raging still, the Cadmeids;
And greedy birds still fright old Phineus.

AMPHITRYON: Now tell the noble struggle of my son.
Does he bring back his uncle's willing gift,
Or does he lead the dog as spoil of war?

THESEUS: A gloomy cliff o'erhangs the sluggish shoals,
Whose waves are dead, and waters motionless.
This stream is guarded by a grim old man,
Of squalid garb and aspect hideous,
Who carries o'er the pool the quaking shades.
His long beard hangs unkempt; his shapeless robe
Is knotted into place; his fierce eyes gleam
From sunken cheeks; and he, as ferryman,
With his long pole propels his bark across.
He now his empty boat unto the shore
Was turning to receive the waiting souls,
When Hercules requested to be borne
Across the stream. The throng of shades give way;
But fiercely Charon cries: "Whither so bold
Dost thou haste on? Stay there thy hurrying steps."
Alcmena's son would no delay endure,
But with the pole itself the boatman tamed,
And climbed aboard the boat. The roomy craft,
For nations ample, groaned beneath his weight;
And as he sat, the heavy-weighted skiff
With rocking sides drank in the Lethe stream.
Then quaked the conquered monsters at the sight:
The Centaurs, fierce and wild, the Lapithae,
Inflamed to strife by copious draughts of wine;
And, seeking out the farthest pools of Styx,
The beast of Lerna hid his fertile heads.
Soon there appeared the home of greedy Dis,
Where the fierce Stygian dog affrights the shades,
Who, tossing back and forth his triple heads,
With mighty bayings watches o'er the realm.
Around his head with damp corruption foul,
Writhe deadly serpents, and his shaggy mane
With vipers bristles; while a twisting snake
Forms his long, hissing tail. His wrath and form
Are both alike terrific. When he heard

The sound of coming feet, straightway he raised
His hackles, bristling with their darting snakes,
And with erected ears caught at the sound
(For even noiseless spirits can he hear).
When Jove's son nearer came, within his cave
The dog stood hesitant, and nameless fear
Each of the other felt. Then suddenly
The silence shudders with his bayings deep,
And threatening snakes along his shoulders hiss.
The clamour of his dreadful voice, sent forth
Three-throated, even happy shades dismayed.
Then did the hero from his left arm loose
The lion's skin with head and grinning jaws,
And 'neath this mighty shield opposed the dog.
Then in his right all conquering, he raised
His mighty club, and with a rain of blows,
Now here, now there, he drove the frightened beast.
The conquered dog at last gave o'er his threats,
And, spent with fighting, lowered all his heads,
And left the entrance free. Then did the king
And queen of hell sit trembling on their thrones,
And bade the dog be led away. Me, too,
Did Dis at Hercules' request release,
A royal gift. Then with his soothing hand
Alcides stroked the monster's massive necks,
And bound him with an adamantine chain.
The watchful guardian of the dusky world
Forgot his wonted fierceness, and his ears
Drooped timidly. He let himself be led,
Confessed his master, and, with muzzle low,
Submissively he went, his snaky tail
Beating his sides the while. But when he came
To Taenarus, and in his eyes there smote
The gleam of unknown light, though strongly bound,
His courage he regained and madly shook
His mighty chains. Even his conqueror
Was backward borne and forced to yield his stand.
Then even my aid did the hero seek;
And with united strength we dragged the dog,
Still mad with rage, attempting fruitless war,
Into the upper world. But when he saw
The gleaming spaces of the shining sky,
The light of day, thick darkness blinded him;

He turned his gaze to earth, and closed his eyes,
Expelled the hated light, looked backward, sought
With all his necks the sheltering earth; and last,
He hid his head within Alcides' shade.
But see, a mighty throng with shouts of joy
Comes yonder, wearing laurel on their brows,
Who chant the well-earned praise of Hercules.

Act Three.   Scene II

CHORUS:
Eurystheus, brought untimely forth,
Had bidden Hercules to pierce
The depths of earth. This task alone
Of all his labours yet remained—
To rob the dusky king of hell.
He dared to enter that dark way
Which to the distant manes leads,
Dismal, with gloomy forests set,
Yet crowded with the thronging souls.
As when the eager people haste
Throughout the city to behold
The play in some new theatre;
As when they crowd the Pisan fields
When the fifth summer brings again
The Elean Thunderer's sacred games; [11]
As, when the lengthening nights return,
And the balanced Scales the sun's bright car
Detain, to gentle sleep inclined,
The people throng the mysteries
Of Ceres, while the Attic priests
Lead through the fields with hurried steps
The worshippers: such thronging hordes
Are driven through those silent plains.
A part goes slow with steps of age,
Sadly, and sated with the years;
Some, in the earlier flush of life,
Advance with the sprightly step of youth,
Young maids not yet in wedlock joined,
And boys with flowing ringlets, babes,
Who have not yet learned to repeat
Their mother's name. To these alone

'Tis given to dispel the night
With torches, and their fears relieve.
The rest in utter darkness fare,
And sadness. So our spirits mourn,
When each one, grieving o'er his fate,
Feels crushed in darkness 'neath the weight
Of all the world. There chaos reigns,
Repulsive glooms, the hateful dark
Of night, the empty veil of clouds,
The weary inactivity
Of that still, empty universe.
Oh, may the time far distant be
When old age bears us to that land.
None come too late, and ne'er can he,
Who once has come, return again.
What need to hasten cruel fate?
For all the wandering tribes of earth
Shall surely seek the land of shades,
And on the still Cocytus spread
Their sails; all things the sun beholds,
In rising and in setting, grow
But to decay. Then spare, O death,
Those who are doomed to come to thee.
Life is but practicing for death;
Though thou be slow in coming, still
We hasten of ourselves. The hour
Which gave us life begins our death.
The joyful day of Thebes is here;
Now at the altars sacrifice,
And let the choicest victims fall.
Ye maids and men, in mingled bands
Begin the stately choral dance;
And let the cattle of the fields
Put off their yokes and be glad today;
For by the hand of Hercules
Has peace from east to west been won,
And in that land where the sun rides high
In middle heaven, and the shadows fail.
Whatever region Tethys laves
In her long reach has been o'ercome
By great Alcides' toils. Borne now
Across the shoals of Tartarus,
With hell subdued, he comes again.

No room is left for fear; for what
Beyond the world of death remains?
And now ye priests, adorn your bristling hair
With poplar which Alcides loves to wear.

Act Four. Scene I

(*Enter* HERCULES, *fresh from the slaying of* LYCUS, *intending to offer
sacrifices to the gods.*)

HERCULES: By my avenging hand lies Lycus slain;
And all, who in his life the tyrant claimed
As comrades, now by death are comrades still
In punishment. Now will I offerings pay
Unto my father and the gods of heaven
For victory, and heap the altars high
With bleeding victims to their kindness due.
Thee, thee, O friend and helper in my toils,
O warlike Pallas, unto thee I pray,
Upon whose left the petrifying shield
Makes direful threats. And be thou here I pray,
Thou tamer of Lycurgus,[12] who didst cross
The ruddy sea, who in thy hand dost bear
The thyrsus, ivy-wreathed; and ye twin gods,
Apollo and Diana, hear my prayer.
(Her hand the bow adorns, but his, the lyre.)
Ye, too, I worship, all ye brothers mine,
Who dwell in heaven; but not my stepdame's sons.
    (*To his attendants*)
And do ye hither drive my richest flocks;
Whatever fragrant spices India bears
And far Arabia, to the altars bring,
And let the savoury smoke of sacrifice
To heaven ascend. Now let us crown our locks
With wreaths of poplar; but the olive leaves,
Thy nation's symbol, should adorn thy head,
O Theseus. Now in prayer we lift our hands
To Jove the Thunderer: do thou protect
The founders of our state, the wooded caves
Of savage Zethus, Dirce's famous fount,

And the Tyrian lares of our pilgrim king.
(*To the attendants*)
Now throw the fragrant incense on the flames.

AMPHITRYON: O son, thy hands, all dripping with the blood
Of thy slain foe, thou first shouldst purify.

HERCULES: Would that his hateful blood I might pour out
Unto the gods; for no libation poured
Could stain the altars more acceptably.
No ampler, richer victim could be paid
To mighty Jove, than this unrighteous king.

AMPHITRYON: Beseech thy father that he end thy tasks;
Pray that at last he give surcease of toil,
And to the wearied rest.

HERCULES: I shall myself
Frame prayers more worthy Jupiter and me:
May heaven, earth, and air their order keep,
And the everlasting stars wheel on their way,
Unchanged; may peace profound brood o'er the world;
May iron be used for harmless toil alone,
And deadly weapons vanish from the earth;
May no unbridled tempest lash the sea;
May angry Jove send forth no lightning bolts;
And may no river, fed by winter's snows,
O'erflow the troubled fields; may venom fail;
And may no noxious herb its fruitage bear;
May fierce and cruel tyrants rule no more.
If the pregnant earth still foster any crime,
Let her make haste to bring it to the light;
And if she still another monster bear,
Let it be mine to meet.
(*The madness planned by* JUNO *begins to come upon him*)
                                        But what is this?
The day's bright noon is by dark shadows dimmed,
And, though the sky be cloudless, Phoebus fares
With face obscured. Who puts the day to flight,
And drives it back to seek the dawn again?
Whence rears unheard-of night its gloomy head?
Why do so many stars the heavens fill
In daylight hours? See where the Lion fierce,
My earliest labour, glitters in the sky,

Inflamed with wrath, and threatens with his fangs.
Now, surely, will he some bright star devour.
With gaping jaws and menacing he stands;
He breathes out fire, and on his flaming neck
His mane he tosses. Soon will he o'erleap
With one huge bound the fruitful autumn's stars,
And those which frozen winter brings to view,
And slay with savage lunge the vernal Bull.

AMPHITRYON: What sudden ill is this? Why dost thou turn
Now here now there thy burning eyes? And why
Dost thou so falsely see the heavens?

HERCULES: Now is the whole round earth at last subdued;
The swollen seas give place, and e'en the realms
Infernal have our toils heroic known.
The heavens alone remain untried, a task
Well worth the struggles of a Hercules.
Now shall I soar aloft to those far heights,
And seek the heavenly spaces; for a star
Has Jupiter, my father, promised me.
What if he should refuse? Nay, but the earth
No longer can Alcides hold, and now
Returns him to the heavens whence he came.
Behold, the whole assembly of the gods
Invite me to their midst, and open wide
The doors of heaven—with one dissenting voice.
                    (*To* JUNO, *in apostrophe*)
And wilt thou not receive me into heaven?
Wilt not unbar the gates? Wouldst have me rend
The portals of the stubborn sky away?
And dost doubt thou my power? Nay, Saturn's chains
Will I unbind, and loose my grandsire's might
Against his impious son's unbridled sway.
I'll stir the Titans up to war again,
And lead them on; great rocks and trees I'll bring,
And with my strong right hand I'll snatch and hurl
The ridges where the Centaurs have their home.
Two mountains, one on other, will I pile
And so construct a highway to the skies.
Then shall old Chiron see Mount Ossa placed
Upon his Pelion; and if to heaven
Olympus reach not, third in order set,
I'll hurl it there.

AMPHITRYON: Such thought be far from thee!
Check this mad impulse of a heart insane,
Though great.

HERCULES: But what is this? With dire intent
The giants are in arms. Great Tityus
Has fled the shades, and, towering aloft
With torn and empty breast, has almost gained
The heavens. Cithaeron totters to his base,
Pallene trembles, Tempe faints in fear.
One has Mount Pindus snatched away, and one
Mount Oeta. Mimas rages horribly.
Now comes Erinnys with her flaming torch,
And shakes her hissing scourge; my face she seeks
Nearer and nearer with ill-omened brands
On funeral pyres enkindled. There I see
Tisiphone with snake-encircled head;
With brandished torch she guards the gate of hell,
Now that their watchdog has been stolen away.
                    (*He catches sight of his children*)
But see where lurk the children of the king,
The impious spawn of Lycus whom I hate.
To your detested sire I'll send you now.
Let darting arrows from my bowstring fly;
Such errands fit my noble weapons well.
                    (*He aims an arrow at one of the children.*)

AMPHITRYON: What will he do in his blind passion's rage?
Now he has bent his mighty bow, and now
His quiver loosed. The hissing dart is sped.
Straight through the neck it flies, and leaves the wound.

HERCULES: The rest will I hunt out, yea, all that lurk
Within this city's walls, without delay.
A greater war against Mycenae waits,
That by my hands those Cyclopean walls
May be o'erthrown; and that the royal hall,
Its high walls shattered, noble roof in-fall'n,
Doors burst, may be to utter ruin brought,
And all its royal secrets be revealed.
                    (*He sees his second son hiding*)
Ah, here I see another hiding son
Of that most wicked sire.
          (*He seizes the child and drags him from the scene.*)

AMPHITRYON (*standing where he can see what is being done within
            the palace*): Behold the child,
            His coaxing hands stretched out to clasp the knees
            Of his mad father, begs with piteous tones.
            Oh, crime unspeakable, pathetic, grim:
            For by his pleading hand the child is caught,
            And, madly whirled again and yet again,
            Sent headlong through the air. A sickening sound—
            And with his scattered brains the roof is wet.
            But wretched Megara, her little son
            Protecting in her arms, flees madly forth.

HERCULES (*behind the scenes, to* MEGARA *also behind the scenes*):
            Though thou shouldst hide thee in the Thunderer's arms,
            This hand of mine will seek and snatch thee forth.

AMPHITRYON (*standing throughout this scene as above*): Oh, whither,
            wretched woman, dost thou flee?
            What flight, what hiding-places dost thou seek?
            No place is safe from angry Hercules.
            Embrace his knees the rather, and with prayer
            Attempt to soothe his wrath.

THE VOICE OF MEGARA: O husband, spare;
            Thy Megara behold and recognise;
            This son of thine thy face and manner bears.
            See how he stretches out his hands to thee.

THE VOICE OF HERCULES: At last I have thee, stepdame, in my power.
            Come thou with me, and pay full penalty
            For all my wrongs; free thy poor, troubled lord
            From his base yoke. But ere the mother dies,
            This little monster must be put to death.

THE VOICE OF MEGARA: What wouldst thou, madman? Shed thine in-
            fant's blood?

AMPHITRYON: The child, in terror of his father's face,
            Died ere he felt the blow. 'Twas fear that snatched
            His spirit forth. Now 'gainst his trembling wife,
            His mighty club is raised—her bones are crushed,
            Her head is stricken from the mangled trunk
            And may no more be seen.
                                (*To himself*)
                                O stubborn age,

Too long enduring, canst thou bide this sight?
But if thy grief is irksome, death is near.
                    (*To* HERCULES)
Impale me on thy darts; that club of thine,
With blood of monsters smeared, raise to my death.
Come, slay me who am falsely called thy sire,
And so remove this blot upon thy name,
That I no longer may thy fame obscure.

CHORUS: Why shouldst thou wantonly provoke thy death,
Old man? Why this mad haste to die? Away,
And hide. From this one crime spare Hercules.

                    (*Enter* HERCULES.)

HERCULES: 'Tis well; the household of the shameless king
Is utterly destroyed. To thee, O wife
Of mighty Jove, this promised sacrifice
Have I performed; my vows I've gladly paid;
And other victims shall thine Argos give.

AMPHITRYON: Thou hast not yet enough atonement made,
O son. Complete the sacrifice. Behold,
A victim at the altar stands, and waits,
With willing neck, thy hand. I offer here
My life, and eagerly; I seek to die.
Slay me.
                    (HERCULES *appears to be fainting*)
                    But what is this? His eye's keen glance
Cannot maintain its gaze; grief dims his sight;
And do I see the hands of Hercules
A-tremble? Now his eyelids fall in sleep,
His head sinks down upon his weary breast,
His knees give way, and down upon the earth
His whole great body falls; as when some ash
Is felled in forest glades, or when some cliff
Falls down and makes a harbour in the sea.
                    (*To* HERCULES)
Dost thou yet live? Or has thy furious rage,
Which sent thy friends to death, slain thee as well?
                    (*He examines the prostrate body*)
He slumbers; this his measured breathing proves.
Let him have time for rest, that heavy sleep
May break his madness' force, and so relieve

His troubled heart.
(*To attendants*)
Ye slaves, his arms remove,
Lest, waking, he again his madness prove.

Act Four.   Scene II

CHORUS: Let heaven and heaven's creator mourn,
The fertile earth, the wandering wave
Upon the restless sea. And thou,
Who over lands and ocean's plains
Dost shed thy light, whose beauteous face
Drives night away, O glowing Sun,
Grieve more than all. For equally
Thy risings had Alcides seen,
And eke thy settings; both thy homes
Were known to him. His spirit loose
From monstrous madness; loose him, ye
Who rule above. His mind restore
To sanity again. And thou,
O Sleep, subduer of our ills,
The spirit's rest, thou better part
Of human life, swift-wingéd one,
Astraea's child, of cruel Death
The sluggish brother, mixing false
With true, prescient of future things,
But oftenest of misery;
O sire of all things, gate of life,
Day's respite and the comrade true
Of night, who com'st impartially
To king and slaves, with gentle hand
The wearied spirit comforting;
Thou who dost force the race of men
Who quail at mortal doom, to gain
A foretaste of the sleep of death:
Subdue and overwhelm him quite
With heavy stupor; let his limbs,
Unconquered hitherto, be held
Fast bound in chains of deepest sleep;
Take not the spell from his fierce heart,
Until his former mind return

To its accustomed course.
But see, prone on the ground he lies,
His savage dreams in his fierce heart
Still hold their sway. Not yet, alas,
Is his dire madness overcome.
Accustomed to recline his head
Upon his heavy club, see now,
He feels about with empty hand
To find the ponderous trunk, his arms
With fruitless motion tossed. Not yet
Has all the fever from his veins
Been driven out, but rages on;
As waves, by mighty tempests vexed,
Toss wildly on and swell with rage,
Although the winds have ceased to blow.
Oh, calm this tempest in his soul;
Let piety and manly strength
Return; or, rather, let his mind
Be still by mad impulses stirred,
And his blind error go the way
It has begun. For madness now
Alone can make him innocent.
To have the hands unstained by guilt
Is best, but next to this is sin
Done in unconsciousness.
Now let thy breast resound with blows,
And let those arms which once have borne
The heavens up be smitten now
By thy victorious hands; thy cries
Be heard throughout the realms of air,
By her who rules the world of night,
And Cerberus crouching in his cave,
His neck still burdened with thy chains.
Let Chaos with the dolorous sound
Re-echo, and the widespread waves
Of ocean, and the air above
Which had thy darts in better use
Beheld. Thy breast, with ills beset
So mighty, must with no light blow
Be smitten. With one great sound of grief
Let heaven, sea, and hell be filled.
And thou, brave shaft, above his neck
So long suspended, armament

And weapon too, thou quiver huge,
Smite heavily his savage back.
Thou sturdy club of oak, come beat
His mighty shoulders, and oppress
His breast with thy hard-knotted stock.
Let all his weapons worthily
Of so great grief lament with him.

(*To the dead children*)

But you, who in your father's praise
Can never share, who ne'er from kings
Have taken deadly recompense,
Who never in the Argive games
Have learned to bend your youthful limbs,
In wrestling and in boxing strong
To strive; who have but dared as yet
To poise the slender Scythian dart
With steady hand, and pierce the stag
Who safety seeks in flight, but not
The lion fierce with tawny mane:
Go to your Stygian refuge, go,
Ye guiltless shades, who on life's verge
Have by your father's mad assault
Been overwhelmed. Poor children, born
Of an ill-omened, luckless race,
Fare on along your father's toilsome path,
To where the gloomy monarchs sit in wrath!

Act Five

HERCULES (*waking up in his right mind*): What place is this? What
        quarter of the world?
Where am I? 'Neath the rising sun, or where
The frozen Bear wheels slowly overhead?
Or in that farthest land whose shores are washed
By the Hesperian sea? What air is this
I breathe? What soil supports my weary frame?
For surely have I come again to earth.

(*His eyes fall on his murdered children*)

Whence came those bloody corpses in my house?
Do I behold them, or not even yet
Have those infernal visions left my mind?

Even on earth the ghostly shapes of death
Still flit before mine eyes. I speak with shame:
I am afraid. Some great calamity,
Some hidden ill my prescient soul forebodes.
Where is my father? Where my faithful wife,
Proud of that troop of children at her side?
Why does my left side miss the lion's skin,
My shield in danger and my couch in sleep?
Where is my bow, my darts? Who, while I live,
Has dared remove my arms? Who so great spoils
Has gained? Who then so bold as not to fear
The very slumber of a Hercules?
'Twould please me well to see my victor—well.
Arise, thou victor, whom my sire begot,
A later wonder, leaving heaven behind;
At whose begetting, longer than at mine,
The night stood waiting.
      (He recognises his dead wife and children)
                    Oh, what sight is this?
My sons lie murdered, weltering in their blood;
My wife is slain. What Lycus rules the land?
Who could have dared to do such things in Thebes,
And Hercules returned? Whoever dwells
Along Ismenus' stream, in Attic plains,
Or in the land Dardanian Pelops rules,
By two seas lapped, come to my aid, and tell
The name of him who has this murder done.
If not, my wrath will turn against you all;
For he's my foe who shows me not my foe.
Why dost thou hide, Alcides' vanquisher?
I care not whether thou dost vengeance seek
For those wild horses of the Thracian king,[5]
Or Geryon's flock, or Libya's vanquished lords;
I do not shun the fight; see, here I stand,
Defenceless, even though with my own arms
Thou com'st against me, armourless. But why
Do Theseus and my father shun my glance?
Why do they turn away? Postpone your tears,
And tell me who has given my loved ones all
To death. What, father, art thou silent still?
Then do thou tell me, Theseus, faithful friend.
Each turns away in silence, and his face,
As if in shame, conceals; while down his cheeks

The tears flow stealthily. In so great ills
What cause for shame can be? Is this the work
Of him who ruthlessly at Argos rules?
Has dying Lycus' hostile soldiery
With such disaster overwhelmed our house?
O father, by the praises of my deeds,
By thine own name which ever was to me
Propitious, tell, I pray thee, who it is
Who hath o'erthrown my house. Whose prey am I?

AMPHITRYON: Let ills like these in silence pass away.

HERCULES: And I be unavenged?

AMPHITRYON: But vengeance hurts.

HERCULES: Who has, inactive, ever borne such wrongs?

AMPHITRYON: He who feared greater wrongs.

HERCULES: Than these my wrongs
Can any greater, heavier be feared?

AMPHITRYON: The part thou knowest of thy woes is least.

HERCULES: Have pity. See, I stretch my suppliant hands.
But what is this? He will not touch my hands.
In these must be the sin.
But whence this blood?
Why is that shaft, once dipped in Hydra's gall,
Now wet with infant gore? They are my own,
These arrows that I see; the guilty hand
I need no longer seek; for who but me
Could bend that mighty bow, or whose right hand
Could draw the string that scarcely yields to me?
(*To* AMPHITRYON *and* THESEUS)
To you I turn again. O father, tell:
Is this my deed?
(*Both men hesitate in silence*)
They hesitate—'tis mine.

AMPHITRYON: Thine is the grief; thy stepdame's is the crime.
From fault of thine this sad mischance is free.

HERCULES: Now hurl thy wrathful bolts from all the heavens,
O sire, who hast forgotten me, thy son;
Avenge at least, though with a tardy hand,

Thy grandsons. Let the star-set heavens resound,
And darting lightnings leap from pole to pole.
Let me be bound upon the Caspian rocks,
And let the birds of prey devour my flesh.
Why lacks Prometheus' cliff a prisoner?
Prepare for me the bare, steep mountain side
Of Caucasus, that, on his towering peak,
The birds and beasts of prey may feed on me.
Or let the blue Symplegades, which hedge
The Scythian deep, stretch out my fettered hands
This way and that; and, when with rhythmic change
The rocks together clash, which fling to heaven
The sea that lies between the rushing cliffs,
May I lie there, the mountains' restless check.
Or why not heap a mighty pyre of wood,
And burn my body stained with impious blood?
Thus, thus it must be done; so Hercules
Shall to the lower world return again.

AMPHITRYON: Not yet has madness ceased to vex his heart.
But now his wrath has changed, and, fury's sign,
He rages 'gainst himself.

HERCULES: Ye dire abodes
Of fiends, ye prison-house of damnéd shades,
Ye regions set apart for guilty throngs,
If any place of exile lie beyond
Deep Erebus, unknown to Cerberus
And me, there hide ye me. I'll go and dwell
Upon the farthest bound of Tartarus.
O heart, too hard! Who worthily will weep
For you, my children, scattered through my house?
This face, woe-hardened, knows not how to weep.
Bring me my sword, and give me here my darts,
My mighty club.
          (*He addresses the four corpses in order*)
                    For thee, poor murdered boy,
I'll break my shafts; for thee my mighty bow
Shall be asunder riven; to thy shades
My heavy club shall burn; and on thy pyre
My quiver, full of venomed darts, shall lie.
My arms shall pay their penalty for sin.
You, too, my guilty hands, with these shall burn,
Too prompt to work a cruel stepdame's will.

THESEUS: Who ever called an act of madness crime?

HERCULES: Unbridled madness often ends in crime.

AMPHITRYON: Now is there need of Hercules to bear
This greatest weight of woe.

HERCULES: Not yet is shame
So utterly extinguished in my heart,
That I can bear to see all people flee
My impious presence. Arms, my Theseus, arms!
I pray you give them quickly back to me.
If I am sane, trust weapons to my hands;
If madness still remains, O father, fly;
For I shall quickly find the road to death.

AMPHITRYON: By holy ties of birth, and by the name
That makes us one, be it of father true,
Or foster-father; by these hoary locks
Which pious souls revere: I pray thee spare
My lonely age and my enfeebled years.
Spare thou thyself to me, the only prop
Of this my falling house, the only light
That's left to cheer my woeful heart. No fruit
Of all thy toils have I as yet enjoyed;
But ever either stormy seas I've feared,
Or monsters. Every savage king who raves
In all the world, for impious altars famed,
Is cause of dread to me. Thy father longs
For joy of thee, to feel and see thee near.

HERCULES: Why I should longer keep my soul in life,
And linger on the earth, there is no cause;
For I have lost my all: my balanced mind,
My arms, my reputation, children, wife,
The glory of my strength—my madness too.
There is no remedy for tainted souls;
But death alone can cure me of my sin.

AMPHITRYON: And wilt thou slay thy father?

HERCULES: Lest I do,
I'll kill myself.

AMPHITRYON: Before thy father's face?

HERCULES: Such impious sights I've taught him to behold.

AMPHITRYON: Nay, rather think upon thy worthy deeds,
            And grant thyself remission of one sin.

HERCULES: Shall he give absolution to himself,
            Who granted none to other men? My deeds
            Which have deserved the praise of men, I did
            Because another bade. This is my own.
            Then help me, father, whether piety
            Or my sad fortune move thee to my aid,
            Or the glory of my manhood, now profaned.
            Give me my arms again, that my right hand
            May vanquish fate.

THESEUS: Thy father's prayers, indeed,
            Are strong enough; but by my pleadings, too,
            Be moved. Rise up, and meet adversity
            With thine accustomed force. Thy strength of mind
            Recall, which no misfortune ever yet
            Has daunted. Now must thou with all thy might
            Contend, and curb the wrath of Hercules.

HERCULES: If yet I live, I have committed wrong;
            But if I die, then have I suffered it.
            I haste to purge the earth of such as I.
            Now long enough has there been hovering
            Before my eyes that monstrous shape of sin,
            So impious, savage, merciless, and wild.
            Then come, my hand, attempt this mighty task,
            Far greater than the last. Dost hesitate
            Through cowardice? Or art thou brave alone
            'Gainst boys and trembling mothers?
                                              Give my arms,
            Or else I shall from Thracian Pindus strip
            The woods, the groves of Bacchus, and shall burn
            Cithaeron's ridgy heights along with me.
            The homes of Thebes together with their lords,
            The temples with their gods, will I o'erthrow,
            And 'neath a ruined city will I lie.
            And if this weight of walls should prove too light
            For these strong shoulders, and the seven gates
            Be not enough to crush me to the earth,
            The mighty mass of earth which separates
            The upper from the nether skies I'll take,
            And hurl its crushing weight upon my head.

AMPHITRYON: Lo, I return thine arms.

HERCULES: Now are thy words
More worthy of the sire of Hercules.
See, by this arrow pierced, my child was slain.

AMPHITRYON: 'Tis true, but Juno shot it by thy hand.

HERCULES: Then I myself shall use it now.

AMPHITRYON: Behold,
How throbs my heart within my anxious breast!

HERCULES: The shaft is ready.

AMPHITRYON: Ah, now wilt thou sin,
Of thine own will and with full consciousness.
Have then thy will; we make no further prayer.
For now my grief has gained a safe retreat.
Thou only canst preserve my son to me;
Thou canst not take him from me. For my fear
I've sounded to the depths and feel no more.
Thou canst no longer give me any pain,
Though happy thou canst make me even yet.
Decide then as thou wilt decide: but know
That here thy cause and reputation stand
In doubtful balance. Either thou dost live,
Or thou dost kill thy sire. This fleeting soul,
Now worn with age and shattered by its grief,
Is trembling on my lips in act to go.
Art thou so slow to grant thy father life?
I can no longer brook delay, nor wait
To thrust the fatal sword into my breast.
And this shall be a sane Alcides' crime.

HERCULES: Now stay, my father, stay; withhold thy hand.
Yield thee, my manhood; do a father's will.
Add this task also to thy former toils—
And live! Lift up my father's fainting form,
O Theseus, friend; for these my guilty hands
That pious duty shun.

AMPHITRYON: But I with joy
Will clasp this hand, with its support I'll walk,
And to my aching heart I'll clasp it close,
And banish all my woes.

HERCULES: Where shall I flee?
Where hide myself? What land shall bury me
From human sight? What Tanais or Nile,
What Tigris, with the waves of Persia mad,
What warlike Rhine, or Tagus, flowing full
And turgid with Iberia's golden sands,
Can ever cleanse this right hand of its stains?
Though chill Maeotis pour its icy floods
Upon me; though the boundless sea should pour
Its waters o'er my hands; still would they be
Deep dyed with crime. Where wilt thou take thyself,
Thou murderer? Wilt flee to east, or west?
Known everywhere, I have no place of flight.
The whole world shrinks from sight of me; the stars
Avert their courses from me, and the sun
Saw even Cerberus with milder face.
O Theseus, faithful friend, seek out a place,
Far off from here, where I may hide myself.
Since thou a lenient judge of others' sins
Hast ever been, grant mercy now to me.
Restore me to the infernal shades, I beg,
And load me with the chains thou once didst wear.
That place will hide me—but it knows me too!

THESEUS: My land awaits thy coming; there once Mars
Washed clean his hands, and gave them back to war.[1]
That land, O Hercules, now calls to thee,
Which even gods from sin is wont to free.

1. The sons of Jupiter and Leda were Castor and Pollux.

2. The children of Jupiter and Latona were Apollo and Diana.

3. The Cretan maiden is Ariadne, who was loved by Bacchus after she was abandoned on the island of Naxos by Theseus. Her bridal wreath was hung in the heavens as the constellation Corona.

4. This episode is treated by Plautus in the *Amphitryon,* Act Five, Scene I.

5. This is a reference to Diomedes, king of the Thracian Bistones, who fed his captives to his man-eating horses.

6. This refers to Oedipus who by his marriage to Jocasta became his mother's husband. Both the Sophoclean and Senecan tragedies on the story of Oedipus are extant.

7. The brothers were Eteocles and Polynices, sons of Oedipus and Jocasta; cf. Seneca's *The Phoenician Women.*

8. This refers to Niobe, whose seven sons and seven daughters were slain by Apollo.

9. This is a reference to the fifty daughters of Danaus (the Danaides), forty-nine of whom slew their husbands on their wedding night.

10. This speech is assigned to Hercules in many editions.

11. The Olympian games were held every four years in honour of Zeus (Jupiter).

12. This refers to Bacchus who punished Lycurgus, king of the Thracian Edoni, for expelling him from his kingdom.

13. The translation of this verse has been revised by the editor.

II
THE TROJAN WOMEN

CHARACTERS IN THE PLAY

HECUBA, *widow of Priam, one of the Trojan captives*
CHORUS OF TROJAN WOMEN
TALTHYBIUS, *a Greek messenger*
PYRRHUS, *son of Achilles, one of the active Greek leaders*
AGAMEMNON, *commander-in-chief of the Greek forces*
CALCHAS, *a priest and prophet among the Greeks*
ANDROMACHE, *widow of Hector, and one of the Trojan captives*
AN OLD MAN, *faithful to* ANDROMACHE
ULYSSES, *king of Ithaca, the most crafty of the Greek leaders*
ASTYANAX, *little son of Hector and* ANDROMACHE
HELEN, *wife of Menelaus, king of Sparta, and afterward of Paris, a
      prince of Troy; the exciting cause of the Trojan war.*
POLYXENA, *daughter of* HECUBA *and Priam*

INTRODUCTION

The Trojan Women portrays the plight of the captive women after the destruction of Troy. This theme had been treated by earlier dramatists, both Greek and Roman. Sophocles had written *Polyxena* and *The Captive Women,* Ennius *Andromacha* and *Hecuba,* and Accius *Astyanax* and *The Trojan Women,* but the loss of these tragedies makes it impossible to estimate the extent of their influence upon Seneca. Euripides' *Hecuba* and *The Trojan Women* are extant, however, and there seems little doubt that Seneca was indebted to both these plays. The sacrifice of Polyxena, which the ghost of Achilles demands before the Greeks sail home, is found in the *Hecuba,* and the execution of the youthful Astyanax, son of Hector and Andromache, occurs in Euripides' *The Trojan Women.* Seneca has apparently taken these two incidents and combined them in one tragedy.

The Roman play thus has a double interest, but Seneca has carefully avoided a division of the action into two parts. Acts Two and Four are concerned with the sacrifice of Polyxena, and the long third Act depicts Andromache's futile attempt to conceal Astyanax from Ulysses. The tragedy cannot be said to have a double plot, for the two events are really two aspects of the same theme—the sufferings and hardships which the conquered must endure in time of war. Hecuba, widowed queen of Troy, is prominent in both Acts One and Five. When the messenger appears with the news of the courageous deaths of the two Trojans, Hecuba says:

> "Weep whosesoe'er thou wilt—thou weepest mine.
> While others bow beneath their single cares,
> I feel the weight of all. All die to me;
> Whatever grief there is, is Hecuba's."

As mother and grandmother of the two victims, her sorrow gives unity to the play as a whole. Like Euripides' *The Trojan Women* which was written soon after the siege and capture of Melos by the Athenians, the Senecan tragedy is a strong indictment of the cruelty and futility of war. The bitter irony of Hecuba's final speech could hardly be surpassed:

"Now go, ye Greeks, and seek your homes in peace.
With spreading sails your fleet in safety now
May cleave the welcome sea; the maid and boy
Are slain, the war is done."

The Trojan Women is beyond doubt Seneca's finest tragedy. In no other play, as J. W. Duff asserts, does he so hold his own in rivalry with his Greek sources. H. E. Butler, no admirer of Seneca as a dramatist, admits that in *The Trojan Women* and the *Phaedra* the declamatory rhetoric rises above mere declamation to something akin to real poetry. An excellent feature is Seneca's skilful portrayal of the characters. The contrast between Agamemnon and Pyrrhus is well handled: Agamemnon, saddened by the destruction that the Greeks have caused, opposes the sacrifice of Polyxena; Pyrrhus is cruel and unbending, far different from the honest youth in Sophocles' *Philoctetes,* and resembles more closely the Pyrrhus of Book II of Vergil's *Aeneid,* who kills the aged Priam at the altar without compassion. The conflict between the two men leads to typically Senecan stichomythia—line by line dialogue filled with epigrammatic statements—but the stichomythia is particularly striking here, and instead of obscuring the characters of the speakers, as is sometimes the case, it serves to strengthen the delineation of the two men. The finest scene in the play is that of Andromache and Ulysses—perhaps the most successful scene in all Seneca's tragedies. In order to save Astyanax from the Greeks the mother conceals him in the tomb of his father Hector. Ulysses, refusing to believe her tale of the child's death, threatens to destroy Hector's tomb. The brutality of Ulysses' demands, the dilemma in which the mother is placed, and the final surrender of the child to certain death make this scene one of great tragic power.

The Trojan women—Hecuba, Andromache, Polyxena—have dignity and courage in the face of disaster. Seneca has given them a Stoic attitude towards life and death, but the Stoicism here seems far more natural than in many other of his plays. Hecuba laments that death comes to others and avoids her, Andromache would have joined Hector in death had not her care for Astyanax held her back, Polyxena goes bravely to her death, preferring it to marriage with Pyrrhus, a fate which Helen had pretended was in store for her. To these women death is something not to be feared but to be welcomed, and it is appropriate that one of the choral lyrics deals with the theme of Death as utter annihilation.

With the exception of the third choral ode which is merely a catalogue of places to which the Trojan captives may be taken, the lyric songs have unusual beauty and pathos. Perhaps the finest passage of all is the conclusion of the fourth ode which describes the departure of the Trojans from their native land; as the land sinks from sight, a mother will say, as she points

> "Where Ilium's smouldering ruins lie
> Far off beneath the eastern sky:
> 'See there, my child, our Trojan ashes glow,
> Where wreathing smoke in murky clouds
> The distant, dim horizon shrouds.'
> And by that sign alone our land we know."

THE TROJAN WOMEN

(SCENE:—*The seashore, with the smouldering ruins of Troy in the background.*)

Act One.   Scene I

(*Enter* HECUBA, *attended by the* CHORUS OF TROJAN WOMEN.)

HECUBA: Whoe'er in royal power has put his trust,
And proudly lords it in his princely halls;
Who fears no shifting of the winds of fate,
But fondly gives his soul to present joys:
Let him my lot and thine, O Troy, behold.
For of a truth did fortune never show
In plainer wise the frailty of the prop
That doth support a king; since by her hand
Brought low, behold, proud Asia's capitol,
The work of heavenly hands, lies desolate.
From many lands the warring princes came
To aid her cause: from where the Tanais
His frigid waves in sevenfold channel pours;[1]
And that far land which greets the newborn day,
Where Tigris mingles with the ruddy sea
His tepid waves;[2] and where the Amazon,
Within the view of wandering Scythia
Arrays her virgin ranks by Pontus' shores.
Yet here, o'erthrown, our ancient city lies,
Herself upon herself in ruins laid;
Her once proud walls in smouldering heaps recline,
Mingling their ashes with our fallen homes.
The palace flames on high, while far and near
The stately city of Assaracus
Is wrapped in gloomy smoke. Yet e'en the flames
Keep not the victor's greedy hands from spoil;

And Troy, though in the grasp of fiery death,
Is pillaged still. The face of heaven is hid
By that dense, wreathing smoke; the shining day,
As if o'erspread by some thick, lowering cloud,
Grows black and foul beneath the ashy storm.
The victor stands with still unsated wrath,
Eyeing that stubborn town of Ilium,
And scarce at last forgives those ten long years
Of bloody strife. Anon, as he beholds
That mighty city, though in ruins laid,
He starts with fear; and though he plainly sees
His foe o'ercome, he scarce can comprehend
That she could be o'ercome. The Dardan spoil
Is heaped on high, a booty vast, which Greece,
In all her thousand ships, can scarce bestow.
  Now witness, ye divinities whose face
Was set against our state, my fatherland
In ashes laid; and thou, proud king of Troy,
Who in thy city's overthrow hast found
A fitting tomb; thou shade of mighty Hector,
In whose proud strength abiding, Ilium stood;
Likewise ye thronging ghosts, my children all,
But lesser shades: whatever ill has come;
Whatever Phoebus' bride[3] with frenzied speech,
Though all discredited, hath prophesied;
I, Hecuba, myself foresaw, what time,
With unborn child o'erweighed, I dreamed a dream
That I had borne a flaming brand. And though,
Cassandra-like, I told my fears, my warnings,
Like our Cassandra's words in after time,
Were all in vain. 'Tis not the Ithacan,[4]
Nor yet his trusty comrade of the night,
Nor that false traitor, Sinon, who has cast
The flaming brands that wrought our overthrow:
Mine is the fire—'tis by my brands ye burn.
But why dost thou bewail the city's fall,
With ancient gossip's prattle? Turn thy mind,
Unhappy one, to nearer woes than these.
Troy's fall, though sad, is ancient story now.
I saw the horrid slaughter of the king,
Defiling the holy altar with its stain,
When bold Aeacides,[5] with savage hand
Entwined in helpless Priam's hoary locks,

Drew back his sacred head, and thrust the sword
Hilt-buried in his unresisting side.
And when he plucked the deep-driven weapon back,
So weak and bloodless was our agéd king,
The deadly blade came almost stainless forth.
Whose thirst for blood had not been satisfied
By that old man just slipping o'er the verge
Of life? Whom would not heavenly witnesses
Restrain from crime? Who would not stay his hand
Before the sacred altar, last resort
Of fallen thrones? Yet he, our noble Priam,
The king, and father of so many kings,
Lies like the merest peasant unentombed;
And, though all Troy's aflame, there's not a brand
To light his pyre and give him sepulture.
And still the heavenly powers are not appeased.
Behold the urn; and, subject to its lot,
The maids and matrons of our princely line,
Who wait their future lords. To whom shall I,
An agéd and unprized allotment, fall?
One Grecian lord has fixed his longing eyes
On Hector's queen; another prays the lot
To grant to him the bride of Helenus;
Antenor's spouse is object of desire,
And e'en thy hand, Cassandra, hath its suitor:
My lot alone they deprecate and fear.
And can ye cease your plaints? O captive throng,
Come beat upon your breasts, and let the sound
Of your loud lamentations rise anew,
The while we celebrate in fitting wise
Troy's funeral; let fatal Ida, seat
Of that ill-omened judgment, straight resound
With echoes of our pitiful refrain.

Act One.   Scene II

CHORUS: Not an untrained band, to tears unknown,
                      Thou callest to grief, for our tears have rained
                      In streams unending through the years,
                      Since the time when the Phrygian guest arrived
                      At the friendly court of Tyndarus,

Sailing the sea in his vessel framed
From the sacred pines of Cybele.
Ten winters have whitened Ida's slopes,
So often stripped for our funeral pyres;
Ten years have ripened the waving grain
Which the trembling reaper has garnered in
From wide Sigean harvest-fields:
But never a day was without its grief,
Never a night but renewed our woe.
Then on with the wailing and on with the blows;
And thou, poor fate-smitten queen, be our guide,
Our mistress in mourning; we'll obey thy commands,
Well trained in the wild liturgy of despair.

HECUBA: Then, trusty comrades of our fate,
Unbind your tresses and let them flow
Over your shoulders bent with grief,
The while with Troy's slow-cooling dust
Ye sprinkle them. Lay bare your arms,
Strip from your breasts their covering;
Why veil your beauty? Shame itself
Is held in captive bonds. And now
Let your hands wave free to the quickening blows
That resound to your wailings. So, now are ye ready,
And thus it is well. I behold once more
My old-time Trojan band. Now stoop
And fill your hands; 'tis right to take
Her dust at least from fallen Troy.
Now let the long-pent grief leap forth,
And surpass your accustomed bounds of woe.
Oh, weep for Hector, wail and weep.

CHORUS: Our hair, in many a funeral torn,
We loose; and o'er our streaming locks
Troy's glowing ashes lie bestrewn.
From our shoulders the veiling garments fall,
And our breasts invite the smiting hands.
Now, now, O grief, put forth thy strength.
Let the distant shores resound with our mourning,
And let Echo who dwells in the slopes of the moun·
    tains
Repeat all our wailings, not, after her wont,
With curt iteration returning the end.
Let earth hear and heed; let the sea and the sky

Record all our grief. Then smite, O ye hands,
With the strength of frenzy batter and bruise.
With crying and blows and the pain of the smiting—
Oh, weep for Hector, wail and weep.

HECUBA:

Our hero, for thee the blows are descending,
On arms and shoulders that stream with our blood;
For thee our brows endure rough strokes,
And our breasts are mangled with pitiless hands.
Now flow the old wounds, reopened anew,
That bled at thy death, the chief cause of our sorrow.
O prop of our country, delayer of fate,
Our Ilium's bulwark, our mighty defender,
Our strong tower wast thou; secure on thy shoulders,
Our city stood leaning through ten weary years.
By thy power supported, with thee has she fallen,
Our country and Hector united in doom.
Now turn to another the tide of your mourning;
Let Priam receive his due meed of your tears.

CHORUS:

Receive our lamentings, O Phrygia's ruler;
We weep for thy death, who wast twice overcome.
Naught once did Troy suffer while thou didst rule
    o'er her:
Twice fell her proud walls from the blows of the
    Grecians,
And twice was she pierced by great Hercules' darts.[6]
Now all of our Hecuba's offspring have perished,
And the proud band of kings who came to our aid;
Thy death is the last—our father, our ruler—
Struck down as a victim to Jove the Almighty,
All helpless and lone, a mute corpse on the ground.

HECUBA:

Nay, give to another your tears and your mourning,
And weep not the death of Priam our king.
But call ye him blessed the rather; for free,
To the deep world of shadows he travels, and never
Upon his bowed neck the base yoke shall he bear.
No proud sons of Atreus shall call him their captive,
No crafty Ulysses his eyes shall behold;
As boast of their triumphs he shall not bear onward
In humble submission their prizes of war.
Those free, royal hands to the sceptre accustomed,
Shall never be bound at his back like a slave,

As he follows the car of the triumphing chieftain,
A king led in fetters, the gaze of the town.

CHORUS: Hail! Priam the blessed we all do proclaim him;
For himself and his kingdom he rules yet below;
Now through the still depths of Elysium's shadows
'Midst calm, happy spirits he seeks the great Hector.
Then hail, happy Priam! Hail all who in battle
Have lost life and country, but liberty gained.

Act Two.   Scene I

(*Enter* TALTHYBIUS.)

TALTHYBIUS: Alas, 'tis thus the Greeks are ever doomed
To lie impatient of the winds' delay,
Whether on war or homeward journey bent.

CHORUS: Tell thou the cause of this the Greeks' delay.
What god obstructs the homeward-leading paths?

TALTHYBIUS: My soul doth quake, and all my limbs with fear
Do tremble. Scarce is credence given to tales
That do transcend the truth. And yet I swear,
With my own eyes I saw what I relate.
Now with his level rays the morning sun
Just grazed the summits of the hills, and day
Had vanquished night; when suddenly the earth,
'Mid rumblings hidden deep and terrible,
To her profoundest depths convulsive rocked.
The tree-tops trembled, and the lofty groves
Gave forth a thunderous sound of crashing boughs;
While down from Ida's rent and rugged slopes
The loosened bowlders rolled. And not alone
The earth did quake: behold, the swelling sea
Perceived its own Achilles[7] drawing near,
And spread its waves abroad. Then did the ground
Asunder yawn, revealing mighty caves,
And gave a path from Erebus to earth.
And then the high-heaped sepulchre was rent,
From which there sprang Achilles' mighty shade,
In guise as when, in practice for thy fates,

O Troy, he prostrate laid the Thracian arms,[8]
Or slew the son of Neptune,[9] doomed to wear
The swan's white plumes; or when, amidst the ranks
In furious battle raging, he the streams
Did choke with corpses of the slain, and Xanthus
Crept sluggishly along with bloody waves;
Or when he stood as victor in his car,
Plying the reins and dragging in the dust
Great Hector's body and the Trojan state.
So there he stood and filled the spreading shore
With wrathful words: "Go, get you gone, ye race
Of weaklings, bear away the honours due
My manes; loose your thankless ships, and sail
Across my seas. By no slight offering
Did ye aforetime stay Achilles' wrath;
And now a greater shall ye pay. Behold,
Polyxena, once pledged to me in life,
Must by the hand of Pyrrhus to my shade
Be led, and with her blood my tomb bedew."
So spake Achilles and the realms of day
He left for night profound, reseeking Dis;
And as he plunged within the depths of earth,
The yawning chasm closed and left no trace.
The sea lies tranquil, motionless; the wind
Its boisterous threats abates, and where but now
The storm-tossed waters raged in angry mood,
The gentle waves lap harmless on the shore;
While from afar the band of Tritons sounds
The marriage chorus of their kindred lord.

(TALTHYBIUS *departs.*)

Act Two.   Scene II

(*Enter* PYRRHUS *and* AGAMEMNON.)

PYRRHUS: Now that you homeward fare, and on the sea
Your joyful sails would spread, my noble sire
Is quite forgot, though by his single hand
Was mighty Troy o'erthrown; for, though his death
Some respite granted to the stricken town,
She stood but as some sorely smitten tree,

That sways uncertain, choosing where to fall.
Though even now ye seek to make amends
For your neglect, and haste to grant the thing
He asks, 'tis but a tardy recompense.
Long since, the other chieftains of the Greeks
Have gained their just reward. What lesser prize
Should his great valour claim? Or is it naught
That, though his mother bade him shun the war,
And spend his life in long, inglorious ease,
Surpassing even Pylian Nestor's years,
He cast his mother's shamming garments off,
Confessing him the hero that he was?
When Telephus, in pride of royal power,
Forbade our progress through his kingdom's bounds,
He stained with royal blood the untried hand
That young Achilles raised. Yet once again
He felt that selfsame hand in mercy laid
Upon his wound to heal him of its smart.
Then did Eetion, smitten sore, behold
His city taken and his realm o'erthrown;
By equal fortune fell Lyrnessus' walls,
For safety perched upon a ridgy height,
Whence came that captive maid, Briseis fair;
And Chrysa, too, lies low, the destined cause
Of royal strife; and Tenedos, and the land
Which on its spreading pastures feeds the flocks
Of Thracian shepherds, Scyros; Lesbos too,
Upon whose rocky shore the sea in twain
Is cleft; and Cilla, which Apollo loved.
All these my father took, and eke the towns
Whose walls Caycus with his vernal flood
Doth wash against. This widespread overthrow
Of tribes, this fearful and destructive scourge,
That swept through many towns with whirlwind power—
This had been glory and the height of fame
For other chiefs; 'twas but an incident
In great Achilles' journey to the war.
So came my father and such wars he waged
While but preparing war. And though I pass
In silence all his other merits, still
Would mighty Hector's death be praise enough.
My father conquered Troy; the lesser task
Of pillage and destruction is your own.

'Tis pleasant thus to laud my noble sire
And all his glorious deeds pass in review:
Before his father's eyes did Hector lie,
Of life despoiled; and Memnon, swarthy son
Of bright Aurora, goddess of the dawn,
For whose untimely death his mother's face
Was sicklied o'er with grief, while day was veiled
In darkness. When the heaven-born Memnon fell,
Achilles trembled at his victory;
For in that fall he learned the bitter truth
That even sons of goddesses may die.
Then, 'mongst our latest foes, the Amazons,
Fierce maidens, felt my father's deadly power.
So, if thou rightly estimate his deeds,
Thou ow'st Achilles all that he can ask,
E'en though he seek from Argos or Mycenae
Some highborn maid. And dost thou hesitate
And haggle now, inventing scruples new,
And deem it barbarous to sacrifice
This captive maid of Troy to Peleus' son?
But yet for Helen's sake didst thou devote
Thy daughter to the sacrificial knife.[10]
I make in this no new or strange request,
But only urge a customary rite.

AGAMEMNON: 'Tis the common fault of youth to have no check
On passion's force; while others feel alone
The sweeping rush of this first fire of youth,
His father's spirit urges Pyrrhus on.
I once endured unmoved the blustering threats
Of proud Achilles, swoll'n with power; and now,
My patience is sufficient still to bear
His son's abuse. Why do you seek to smirch
With cruel murder the illustrious shade
Of that famed chief? 'Tis fitting first to learn
Within what bounds the victor may command,
The vanquished suffer. Never has for long
Unbridled power been able to endure,
But lasting sway the self-controlled enjoy.
The higher fortune raises human hopes,
The more should fortune's favourite control
His vaulting pride, and tremble as he views
The changing fates of life, and fear the gods

Who have uplifted him above his mates.
By my own course of conquest have I learned
That mighty kings can straightway come to naught.
Should Troy o'erthrown exalt us overmuch?
Behold, we stand today whence she has fallen.
I own that in the past too haughtily
Have I my sway o'er fallen chieftains borne;
But thought of fortune's gift has checked my pride,
Since she unto another might have given
These selfsame gifts. O fallen king of Troy,
Thou mak'st me proud of conquest over thee,
Thou mak'st me fear that I may share thy fate.
Why should I count the sceptre anything
But empty honour and a tinsel show?
This sceptre one short hour can take away,
Without the aid, perchance, of countless ships
And ten long years of war. The steps of fate
Do not for all advance with pace so slow.
For me, I will confess ('tis with thy grace,
O land of Greece, I speak) I have desired
To see the pride and power of Troy brought low;
But that her walls and homes should be o'erthrown
In utter ruin have I never wished.
But a wrathful foe, by greedy passion driven,
And heated by the glow of victory,
Within the shrouding darkness of the night,
Cannot be held in check. If any act
Upon that fatal night unworthy seemed
Or cruel, 'twas the deed of heedless wrath,
And darkness which is ever fury's spur,
And the victorious sword, whose lust for blood,
When once in blood imbued, is limitless.
Since Troy has lost her all, seek not to grasp
The last poor fragments that remain. Enough,
And more has she endured of punishment.
But that a maid of royal birth should fall
An offering upon Achilles' tomb,
Bedewing his harsh ashes with her blood,
While that foul murder gains the honoured name
Of wedlock, I shall not permit. On me
The blame of all will come; for he who sin
Forbids not when he can, commits the sin.

PYRRHUS: Shall no reward Achilles' shade obtain?

AGAMEMNON: Yea, truly; all the Greeks shall sing his praise,
                And unknown lands shall hear his mighty name.
                But if his shade demand a sacrifice
                Of out-poured blood, go take our richest flocks,
                And shed their blood upon thy father's tomb;
                But let no mother's tears pollute the rite.
                What barbarous custom this, that living man
                Should to the dead be slain in sacrifice?
                Then spare thy father's name the hate and scorn
                Which by such cruel worship it must gain.

PYRRHUS: Thou, swoll'n with pride so long as happy fate
                Uplifts thy soul, but weak and spent with fear
                When fortune frowns; O hateful king of kings,
                Is now thy heart once more with sudden love
                Of this new maid inflamed? Shalt thou alone
                So often bear away my father's spoils?
                By this right hand he shall receive his own.
                And if thou dost refuse, and keep the maid,
                A greater victim will I slay, and one
                More worthy Pyrrhus' gift; for all too long
                From royal slaughter hath my hand been free,
                And Priam asks an equal sacrifice.

AGAMEMNON: Far be it from my wish to dim the praise
                That thou dost claim for this most glorious deed—
                Old Priam slain by thy barbaric sword,
                Thy father's suppliant.[11]

PYRRHUS: I know full well
                My father's suppliants—and well I know
                His enemies. Yet royal Priam came,
                And made his plea before my father's face;
                But thou, o'ercome with fear, not brave enough
                Thyself to make request, within thy tent
                Didst trembling hide, and thy desires consign
                To braver men, that they might plead for thee.[12]

AGAMEMNON: But, of a truth, no fear thy father felt;
                But while our Greece lay bleeding, and her ships
                With hostile fire were threatened, there he lay
                Supine and thoughtless of his warlike arms,
                And idly strumming on his tuneful lyre.

PYRRHUS: Then mighty Hector, scornful of thy arms,
               Yet felt such wholesome fear of that same lyre,
               That our Thessalian ships were left in peace.

AGAMEMNON: An equal peace did Hector's father find
               When he betook him to Achilles' ships.

PYRRHUS: 'Tis regal thus to spare a kingly life.

AGAMEMNON: Why then didst thou a kingly life despoil?

PYRRHUS: But mercy oft doth offer death for life.

AGAMEMNON: Doth mercy now demand a maiden's blood?

PYRRHUS: Canst *thou* proclaim such sacrifice a sin?

AGAMEMNON: A king must love his country more than child.

PYRRHUS: No law the wretched captive's life doth spare.

AGAMEMNON: What law forbids not, this let shame forbid.

PYRRHUS: 'Tis victor's right to do whate'er he will.

AGAMEMNON: Then should he will the least who most can do.

PYRRHUS: Dost thou boast thus, from whose tyrannic reign
               Of ten long years but now the Greeks I freed?

AGAMEMNON: Such airs from Scyros!

PYRRHUS: Thence no brother's blood.[13]

AGAMEMNON: Hemmed by the sea!

PYRRHUS: Yet that same sea is ours.
               But as for Pelops' house, I know it well.

AGAMEMNON: Thou baseborn son of maiden's secret sin,
               And young Achilles, scarce of man's estate—

PYRRHUS: Yea, that Achilles who, by right of birth,
               Claims equal sovereignty of triple realms:
               His mother rules the sea, to Aeacus
               The shades submit, to mighty Jove the heavens.

AGAMEMNON: Yet that Achilles lies by Paris slain!

PYRRHUS: But by Apollo's aid, who aimed the dart;
               For no god dared to meet him face to face.

AGAMEMNON: I could have checked thy words, and curbed thy tongue,
Too bold in evil speech; but this my sword
Knows how to spare. But rather let them call
The prophet Calchas, who the will of heaven
Can tell. If fate demands the maid, I yield.
          (*Enter* CALCHAS.)
Thou who from bonds didst loose the Grecian ships,
And bring to end the slow delays of war;
Who by thy mystic art canst open heaven,
And read with vision clear the awful truths
Which sacrificial viscera proclaim;
To whom the thunder's roll, the long, bright trail
Of stars that flash across the sky, reveal
The hidden things of fate; whose every word
Is uttered at a heavy cost to me:
What is the will of heaven, O Calchas; speak,
And rule us with the mastery of fate.

CALCHAS: The Greeks must pay th' accustomed price to death,
Ere on the homeward seas they take their way.
The maiden must be slaughtered on the tomb
Of great Achilles. Thus the rite perform:
As Grecian maidens are in marriage led
By other hands unto the bridegroom's home,
So Pyrrhus to his father's shade must lead
His promised bride.
                    But not this cause alone
Delays our ships: a nobler blood than thine,
Polyxena, is due unto the fates;
For from yon lofty tower must Hector's son,
Astyanax, be hurled to certain death.
Then shall our vessels hasten to the sea,
And fill the waters with their thousand sails.
(CALCHAS, AGAMEMNON, *and* PYRRHUS *depart.*)

Act Two.   Scene III

CHORUS: When in the tomb the dead is laid,
When the last rites of love are paid;
When eyes no more behold the light,
Closed in the sleep of endless night;
Survives there aught, can we believe?

Or does an idle tale deceive?
What boots it, then, to yield the breath
A willing sacrifice to death,
If still we gain no dreamless peace,
And find from living no release?
Say, do we, dying, end all pain?
Does no least part of us remain?
When from this perishable clay
The flitting breath has sped away;
Does then the soul that dissolution share
And vanish into elemental air?
Whate'er the morning sunbeam knows,
Whate'er his setting rays disclose;
Whate'er is bathed by Ocean wide,
In ebbing or in flowing tide:
Time all shall snatch with hungry greed,
With mythic Pegasean speed.
Swift is the course of stars in flight,
Swiftly the moon repairs her light;
Swiftly the changing seasons go,
While time speeds on with endless flow:
But than all these, with speed more swift,
Towards fated nothingness we drift.
For when within the tomb we're laid,
No soul remains, no hov'ring shade.
Like curling smoke, like clouds before the blast,
This animating spirit soon has passed.
Since naught remains, and death is naught
But life's last goal, so swiftly sought;
Let those who cling to life abate
Their fond desires, and yield to fate;
And those who fear death's fabled gloom,
Bury their cares within the tomb.
Soon shall grim time and yawning night
In their vast depths engulf us quite;
Impartial death demands the whole—
The body slays nor spares the soul.
Dark Taenara and Pluto fell,
And Cerberus, grim guard of hell—
All these but empty rumours seem,
The pictures of a troubled dream.
Where then will the departed spirit dwell?
Let those who never came to being tell.

Act Three.   Scene I

(*Enter* ANDROMACHE, *leading the little* ASTYANAX, *and accompanied by an* OLD MAN.)

ANDROMACHE: What do ye here, sad throng of Phrygian dames?
Why tear your hair and beat your wretched breasts?
Why stream your cheeks with tears? Our ills are light
If we endure a grief that tears can soothe.
You mourn a Troy whose walls but now have fall'n;
Troy fell for me long since, when that dread car
Of Peleus' son, urged on at cruel speed,
With doleful groanings 'neath his massive weight,
Dragged round the walls my Hector's mangled corse.
Since then, o'erwhelmed and utterly undone,
With stony resignation do I bear
Whatever ills may come. But for this child,
Long since would I have saved me from the Greeks
And followed my dear lord; but thought of him
Doth check my purpose and forbid my death.
For his dear sake there still remaineth cause
To supplicate the gods, an added care.
Through him the richest fruit of woe is lost—
The fear of naught; and now all hope of rest
From further ills is gone, for cruel fate
Hath still an entrance to my grieving heart.
Most sad his fear, who fears in hopelessness.

OLD MAN: What sudden cause of fear hath moved thee so?

ANDROMACHE: Some greater ill from mighty ills doth rise.
The fate of fallen Troy is not yet stayed.

OLD MAN: What new disasters can the fates invent?

ANDROMACHE: The gates of deepest Styx, those darksome realms
(Lest fear be wanting to our overthrow),
Are opened wide, and forth from lowest Dis
The spirit of our buried foeman comes.
(May Greeks alone retrace their steps to earth?
For death at least doth come to all alike.)
That terror doth invade the hearts of all;
But what I now relate is mine alone—
A terrifying vision of the night.

OLD MAN: What was this vision? Speak, and share thy fears.

ANDROMACHE: Now kindly night had passed her middle goal,
            And their bright zenith had the Bears o'ercome.
            Then came to my afflicted soul a calm
            Long since unknown, and o'er my weary eyes, `
            For one brief hour did drowsy slumber steal,
            If that be sleep—the stupor of a soul
            Forespent with ills: when suddenly I saw
            Before mine eyes the shade of Hector stand;
            Not in such guise as when, with blazing torch,
            He strove in war against the Grecian ships,
            Nor when, all stained with blood, in battle fierce
            Against the Danai, he gained true spoil
            From that feigned Peleus' son;[14] not such his face,
            All flaming with the eager battle light;
            But weary, downcast, tear-stained, like my own,
            All covered o'er with tangled, bloody locks.
            Still did my joy leap up at sight of him;
            And then he sadly shook his head and said:
            "Awake from sleep and save our son from death,
            O faithful wife. In hiding let him lie;
            Thus only can he life and safety find.
            Away with tears—why dost thou mourning make
            For fallen Troy? I would that all had fall'n.
            Then haste thee, and to safety bear our son,
            The stripling hope of this our vanquished home,
            Wherever safety lies."
                                    So did he speak,
            And chilling terror roused me from my sleep.
            Now here, now there I turned my fearful eyes.
            Forgetful of my son, I sought the arms
            Of Hector, there to lay my grief. In vain:
            For that elusive shade, though closely pressed,
            Did ever mock my clinging, fond embrace.
            O son, true offspring of thy mighty sire,
            Sole hope of Troy, sole comfort of our house,
            Child of a stock of too illustrious blood,
            Too like thy father, thou: such countenance
            My Hector had, with such a tread he walked,
            With such a motion did he lift his hands,
            Thus stood he straight with shoulders proudly set,
            And thus he oft from that high, noble brow

Would backward toss his flowing locks.—But thou,
O son, who cam'st too late for Phrygia's help,
Too soon for me, will that time ever come,
That happy day, when thou, the sole defense,
And sole avenger of our conquered Troy,
Shalt raise again her fallen citadel,
Recall her scattered citizens from flight,
And give to fatherland and Phrygians
Their name and fame again?—Alas, my son,
Such hopes consort not with our present state.
Let the humble captive's fitter prayer be mine—
The prayer for life.
                 Ah me, what spot remote
Can hold thee safe? In what dark lurking-place
Can I bestow thee and abate my fears?
Our city, once in pride of wealth secure,
And stayed on walls the gods themselves had built,
Well known of all, the envy of the world,
Now deep in ashes lies, by flames laid low;
And from her vast extent of temples, walls
And towers, no part, no lurking-place remains,
Wherein a child might hide. Where shall I choose
A covert safe? Behold the mighty tomb
Wherein his father's sacred ashes lie,
Whose massive pile the enemy has spared.
This did old Priam rear in days of power,
Whose grief no stinted sepulture bestowed.
Then to his father let me trust the child.—
But at the very thought a chilling sweat
Invades my trembling limbs, for much I fear
The gruesome omen of the place of death.

OLD MAN: In danger, haste to shelter where ye may;
In safety, choose.

ANDROMACHE: What hiding-place is safe
From traitor's eyes?

OLD MAN: All witnesses remove.

ANDROMACHE: What if the foe inquire?

OLD MAN: Then answer thus:
"He perished in the city's overthrow."
This cause alone ere now hath safety found

For many from the stroke of death—belief
That they have died.

ANDROMACHE: But scanty hope is left;
Too huge a weight of race doth press him down.
Besides, what can it profit him to hide
Who must his shelter leave and face the foe?

OLD MAN: The victor's deadliest purposes are first.

ANDROMACHE: What trackless region, what obscure retreat
Shall hold thee safe? Oh, who will bring us aid
In our distress and doubt? Who will defend?
O thou, who always didst protect thine own,
My Hector, guard us still. Accept the trust
Which I in pious confidence impose;
And in the faithful keeping of thy dust
May he in safety dwell, to live again.
Then son, betake thee hither to the tomb.
Why backward strain, and shun that safe retreat?
I read thy nature right: thou scornest fear.
But curb thy native pride, thy dauntless soul,
And bear thee as thine altered fates direct.
For see what feeble forces now are left:
A sepulchre, a boy, a captive band.
We cannot choose but yield us to our woes.
Then come, make bold to enter the abode,
The sacred dwelling of thy buried sire.
If fate assist us in our wretchedness,
'Twill be to thee a safe retreat; if life
The fates deny, thou hast a sepulchre.

(The boy enters the tomb, and the gates are closed and barred behind him.)

OLD MAN: Now do the bolted gates protect their charge.
But thou, lest any sign of fear proclaim
Where thou hast hid the boy, come far away.

ANDROMACHE: Who fears from near at hand, hath less of fear;
But, if thou wilt, take we our steps away.

(ULYSSES *is seen approaching.*)

OLD MAN: Now check thy words awhile, thy mourning cease;
For hither bends the Ithacan his course.
(The OLD MAN *departs.)*

ANDROMACHE (*with a final appealing look towards the tomb*): Yawn
        deep, O earth, and thou, my husband, rend
    To even greater depths thy tomb's deep cave,
    And hide the sacred trust I gave to thee
    Within the very bosom of the pit.
    Now comes Ulysses, grave and slow of tread;
    Methinks he plotteth mischief in his heart.

Act Three.   Scene II

(*Enter* ULYSSES, *accompanied by attendants.*)

ULYSSES: As harsh fate's minister, I first implore
    That, though the words are uttered by my lips,
    Thou count them not my own. They are the voice
    Of all the Grecian chiefs, whom Hector's son
    Doth still prohibit from that homeward voyage
    So long delayed. And him the fates demand.
    A peace secure the Greeks can never feel,
    And ever will the backward-glancing fear
    Compel them on defensive arms to lean,
    While on thy living son, Andromache,
    The conquered Phrygians shall rest their hopes.
    So doth the augur, Calchas, prophesy.
    Yet, even if our Calchas spake no word,
    Thy Hector once declared it, and I fear
    Lest in his son a second Hector dwell;
    For ever doth a noble scion grow
    Into the stature of his noble sire.
    Behold the little comrade of the herd,
    His budding horns still hidden from the sight:
    Full soon with arching neck and lofty front,
    He doth command and lead his father's flock.
    The slender twig, just lopped from parent bough,
    Its mother's height and girth surpasses soon,
    And casts its shade abroad to earth and sky.
    So doth a spark within the ashes left,
    Leap into flame again before the wind.
    Thy grief, I know, must partial judgment give;
    Still, if thou weigh the matter, thou wilt grant

That after ten long years of grievous war,
A veteran soldier doeth well to fear
Still other years of slaughter, and thy Troy,
Still unsubdued. This fear one cause alone
Doth raise—another Hector. Free the Greeks
From dread of war. For this and this alone
Our idle ships still wait along the shore.
And let me not seem cruel in thy sight,
For that, compelled of fate, I seek thy son:
I should have sought our chieftain's son as well.
Then gently suffer what the victor bore.[15]

ANDROMACHE: Oh, that thou wert within my power to give,
My son, and that I knew what cruel fate
Doth hold thee now, snatched from my eager arms—
Where thou dost lie; then, though my breast were
    pierced
With hostile spears, and though my hands with chains
Were bound, and scorching flames begirt my sides,
Thy mother's faith would ne'er betray her child.
O son, what place, what lot doth hold thee now?
Dost thou with wandering footsteps roam the fields?
Wast thou consumed amid the raging flames?
Hath some rude victor reveled in thy blood?
Or, by some ravening beast hast thou been slain,
And liest now a prey for savage birds?

ULYSSES: Away with feignéd speech; no easy task
For thee to catch Ulysses: 'tis my boast
That mother's snares, and even goddesses'
I have o'ercome.[16] Have done with vain deceit.
Where is thy son?

ANDROMACHE: And where is Hector too?
Where agéd Priam and the Phrygians?
Thou seekest one; *my* quest includes them all.

ULYSSES: By stern necessity thou soon shalt speak
What thy free will withholds.

ANDROMACHE: But safe is she,
Who can face death, who ought and longs to die.

ULYSSES: But death brought near would still thy haughty words.

ANDROMACHE: If 'tis thy will, Ulysses, to inspire
              Andromache with fear, then threaten life;
              For death has long been object of my prayer.

ULYSSES: With stripes, with flames, with lingering pains of death
              Shalt thou be forced to speak, against thy will,
              What now thou dost conceal, and from thy heart
              Its inmost secrets bring. Necessity
              Doth often prove more strong than piety.

ANDROMACHE: Prepare thy flames, thy blows, and all the arts
              Devised for cruel punishment: dire thirst,
              Starvation, every form of suffering;
              Come, rend my vitals with the sword's deep thrust;
              In dungeon, foul and dark, immure; do all
              A victor, full of wrath and fear, can do
              Or dare; still will my mother heart, inspired
              With high and dauntless courage, scorn thy threats.

ULYSSES: This very love of thine, which makes thee bold,
              Doth warn the Greeks to counsel for their sons.
              This strife, from home remote, these ten long years
              Of war, and all the ills which Calchas dreads,
              Would slight appear to me, if for myself
              I feared: but thou dost threat Telemachus.

ANDROMACHE: Unwillingly, Ulysses, do I give
              To thee, or any Grecian, cause of joy;
              Yet must I give it, and speak out the woe,
              The secret grief that doth oppress my soul.
              Rejoice, O sons of Atreus, and do thou,
              According to thy wont, glad tidings bear
              To thy companions: *Hector's son is dead.*

ULYSSES: What proof have we that this thy word is true?

ANDROMACHE: May thy proud victor's strongest threat befall,
              And bring my death with quick and easy stroke;
              May I be buried in my native soil,
              May earth press lightly on my Hector's bones:
              According as my son, deprived of light,
              Amidst the dead doth lie, and, to the tomb
              Consigned, hath known the funeral honours due
              To those who live no more.[17]

ULYSSES (*joyfully*):   Then are the fates
Indeed fulfilled, since Hector's son is dead,
And I with joy unto the Greeks will go,
With grateful tale of peace at last secure.
                    (*Aside*)
But stay, Ulysses, this rash joy of thine!
The Greeks will readily believe *thy* word;
But what dost thou believe?—his mother's oath.
Would then a mother feign her offspring's death,
And fear no baleful omens of that word?
They omens fear who have no greater dread.
Her truth hath she upheld by straightest oath.
If that she perjured be, what greater fear
Doth vex her soul? Now have I urgent need
Of all my skill and cunning, all my arts,
By which so oft Ulysses hath prevailed;
For truth, though long concealed, can never die.
Now watch the mother; note her grief, her tears,
Her sighs; with restless step, now here, now there,
She wanders, and she strains her anxious ears
To catch some whispered word. 'Tis evident,
She more by present fear than grief is swayed.
So must I ply her with the subtlest art.
                (*To* ANDROMACHE)
When others mourn, 'tis fit in sympathy
To speak with kindred grief; but thou, poor soul,
I bid rejoice that thou hast lost thy son,
Whom cruel fate awaited; for 'twas willed
That from the lofty tower that doth remain
Alone of Troy's proud walls, he should be dashed,
And headlong fall to quick and certain death.

ANDROMACHE (*aside*): My soul is faint within me, and my limbs
Do quake; while chilling fear congeals my blood.

ULYSSES (*aside*): She trembles; here must I pursue my quest.
Her fear betrayeth her; wherefore this fear
Will I redouble.—
                (*To attendants*)
                        Go in haste, my men,
And find this foe of Greece, the last defence
Of Troy, who by his mother's cunning hand
Is safe bestowed, and set him in our midst.
(*Pretending that the boy is discovered*)

'Tis well! He's found. Now bring him here with haste.
  (*To* ANDROMACHE)
Why dost thou start, and tremble? Of a truth
Thy son is dead, for so hast thou declared.

ANDROMACHE: Oh, that I had just cause of dread. But now,
  My old habitual fear instinctive starts;
  The mind cannot forget a well-conned woe.

ULYSSES: Now since thy boy hath shunned the sacrifice
  That to the walls was due, and hath escaped
  By grace of better fate, our priest declares
  That only can our homeward way be won
  If Hector's ashes, scattered o'er the waves,
  Appease the sea, and this his sepulchre
  Be leveled with the ground. Since Hector's son
  Has failed to pay the debt he owed to fate,
  Then Hector's sacred dust must be despoiled.

ANDROMACHE (*aside*): Ah me, a double fear distracts my soul!
  Here calls my son, and here my husband's dust.
  Which shall prevail? Attest, ye heartless gods,
  And ye, my husband's shades, true deities:
  Naught else, O Hector, pleased me in my son,
  Save only thee; then may he still survive
  To bring thine image back to life and me.—
  Shall then my husband's ashes be defiled?
  Shall I permit his bones to be the sport
  Of waves, and lie unburied in the sea?
  Oh, rather, let my only son be slain!—
  And canst thou, mother, see thy helpless child
  To awful death given up? Canst thou behold
  His body whirling from the battlements?
  I can, I shall endure and suffer this,
  Provided only, by his death appeased,
  The victor's hand shall spare my Hector's bones.—
  But he can suffer yet, while kindly fate
  Hath placed his sire beyond the reach of harm.
  Why dost thou hesitate? Thou must decide
  Whom thou wilt designate for punishment.
  What doubts harass thy troubled soul? No more
  Is Hector here.—Oh, say not so; I feel
  He is both here and there. But sure am I
  That this my child is still in life, perchance

          To be the avenger of his father's death.
          But both I cannot spare. What then? O soul,
          Save of the two, whom most the Greeks do fear.

ULYSSES: I must fulfill the oracle. From its base
          Will I this tomb destroy.

ANDROMACHE: The tomb of him
          Whose body thou didst ransom for a price?

ULYSSES: I will destroy it, and the sepulchre
          From its high mound will utterly remove.

ANDROMACHE: The sacred faith of heaven do I invoke,
          And just Achilles' plighted word: do thou,
          O Pyrrhus, keep thy father's sacred oath.

ULYSSES: This tomb shall soon lie level with the plain.

ANDROMACHE: Such sacrilege the Greeks, though impious,
          Have never dared. 'Tis true the sacred fanes,
          E'en of your favouring gods, ye have defiled;
          But still your wildest rage hath spared our tombs.
          I will resist, and match your warriors' arms
          With my weak woman's hands. Despairing wrath
          Will nerve my arm. Like that fierce Amazon,
          Who wrought dire havoc in the Grecian ranks;
          Or some wild Maenad by the god o'ercome,
          Who, thrysus-armed, doth roam the trackless glades
          With frenzied step, and, clean of sense bereft,
          Strikes deadly blows but feels no counter-stroke:
          So will I rush against ye in defense
          Of Hector's tomb, and perish, if I must,
          An ally of his shade.

ULYSSES (*to attendants*):   Do ye delay,
          And do a woman's tears and empty threats
          And outcry move you? Speed the task I bid.

ANDROMACHE (*struggling with attendants*): Destroy me first! Oh, take
                my life instead!
          (*The attendants roughly thrust her away*)
          Alas, they thrust me back! O Hector, come,
          Break through the bands of fate, upheave the earth,
          That thou mayst stay Ulysses' lawless hand.
          Thy spirit will suffice.—Behold he comes!

His arms he brandishes, and firebrands hurls.
Ye Greeks, do ye behold him, or do I,
With solitary sight, alone behold?

ULYSSES: This tomb and all it holds will I destroy.

ANDROMACHE (*aside, while the attendants begin to demolish the tomb*):
Ah me, can I permit the son and sire
To be in common ruin overwhelmed?
Perchance I may prevail upon the Greeks
By prayer.—But even now those massive stones
Will crush my hidden child.—Oh, let him die,
In any other way, and anywhere,
If only father crush not son, and son
No desecration bring to father's dust.
(*Casts herself at the feet of* ULYSSES)
A humble suppliant at thy knees I fall,
Ulysses; I, who never yet to man
Have bent the knee in prayer, thy feet embrace.
By all the gods, have pity on my woes,
And with a calm and patient heart receive
My pious prayers. And as the heavenly powers
Have high exalted thee in pride and might,
The greater mercy show thy fallen foes.
Whate'er is given to wretched suppliant
Is loaned to fate. So mayst thou see again
Thy faithful wife; so may Laertes live
To greet thee yet again; so may thy son
Behold thy face, and, more than that thou canst pray,
Excel his father's valour and the years
Of old Laertes. Pity my distress:
The only comfort left me in my woe,
Is this my son.

ULYSSES: Produce the boy—and pray.

ANDROMACHE (*goes to the tomb and calls to* ASTYANAX): Come forth,
my son, from the place of thy hiding
Where thy mother bestowed thee with weeping and fear.

(ASTYANAX *appears from the tomb.* ANDROMACHE *presents him to*
ULYSSES)
Here, here is the lad, Ulysses, behold him;
The fear of thy armies, the dread of thy fleet!
(*To* ASTYANAX)

My son, thy suppliant hands upraise,
And at the feet of this proud lord,
Bend low in prayer, nor think it base
To suffer the lot which our fortune appoints.
Put out of mind thy regal birth,
Thy agéd grandsire's glorious rule
Of wide domain; and think no more
Of Hector, thy illustrious sire.
Be captive alone—bend the suppliant knee;
And if thine own fate move thee not,
Then weep by thy mother's woe inspired.
                    (*To* ULYSSES)
That older Troy beheld the tears
Of its youthful king, and those tears prevailed
To stay the fierce threats of the victor's wrath,
The mighty Hercules. Yea he,
To whose vast strength all monsters had yielded,
Who burst the stubborn gates of hell,
And o'er that murky way returned,
Even he was o'ercome by the tears of a boy.
"Take the reins of the state," to the prince he said;
"Reign thou on thy father's lofty throne,
But reign with the sceptre of power—and truth."
Thus did that hero subdue his foes.
And thus do thou temper thy wrath with forbearance.
And let not the power of great Hercules, only,
Be model to thee. Behold at thy feet,
As noble a prince as Priam of old
Pleads only for life! The kingdom of Troy
Let fortune bestow where she will.

ULYSSES (*aside*): This woe-struck mother's grief doth move me sore;
          But still the Grecian dames must more prevail,
          Unto whose grief this lad is growing up.

ANDROMACHE (*hearing him*): What? These vast ruins of our fallen town,
          To very ashes brought, shall he uprear?
          Shall these poor boyish hands build Troy again?
          No hopes indeed hath Troy, if such her hopes.
          So low the Trojans lie, there's none so weak
          That he need fear our power. Doth lofty thought

Of mighty Hector nerve his boyish heart?
What valour can a fallen Hector stir?
When this our Troy was lost, his father's self
Would then have bowed his lofty spirit's pride;
For woe can bend and break the proudest soul.
If punishment be sought, some heavier fate
Let him endure; upon his royal neck
Let him support the yoke of servitude.
Must princes sue in vain for this poor boon?

ULYSSES: Not I, but Calchas doth refuse thy prayer.

ANDROMACHE: O man of lies, artificer of crime,
By whom in open fight no foe is slain,
But by whose tricks and cunning, evil mind
The very chiefs of Greece are overthrown,
Dost thou now seek to hide thy dark intent
Behind a priest and guiltless gods? Nay, nay:
This deed within thy sinful heart was born.
Thou midnight prowler, brave to work the death
Of this poor boy, dost dare at length alone
To do a deed, and that in open day?

ULYSSES: Ulysses' valour do the Grecians know
Full well, and all too well the Phrygians.
But we are wasting time with empty words.
The impatient ships are tugging at their chains.

ANDROMACHE: But grant a brief delay, while to my son
I pay the rites of woe, and sate my grief
With tears and last embrace.

ULYSSES: I would 'twere mine
To spare thy tears; but what alone I may,
I'll give thee respite and a time for grief.
Then weep thy fill, for tears do soften woe.

ANDROMACHE (*to* ASTYANAX): O darling pledge of love, thou only stay
Of our poor fallen house, last pang of Troy;
O thou whom Grecians fear, O mother's hope,
Alas too vain, for whom, with folly blind,
I prayed the war-earned praises of his sire,
His royal grandsire's prime of years and strength:
But God hath scorned my prayers.

Thou shalt not **live**
To wield the sceptre in the royal courts
Of ancient Troy, to make thy people's laws,
And send beneath thy yoke the conquered tribes;
Thou shalt not fiercely slay the fleeing Greeks,
Nor from thy car in retribution drag
Achilles' son; the dart from thy small hand
Thou ne'er shalt hurl, nor boldly press the chase
Of scattered beasts throughout the forest glades;
And when the sacred lustral day is come,
Troy's yearly ritual of festal games,
The charging squadrons of the noble youth
Thou shalt not lead, thyself the noblest born;
Nor yet among the blazing altar fires,
With nimble feet the ancient sacred dance
At some barbaric temple celebrate,
While horns swell forth swift-moving melodies.
Oh, mode of death, far worse than bloody war!
More tearful sight than mighty Hector's end
The walls of Troy must see.

ULYSSES: Now stay thy tears,
For mighty grief no bound or respite finds.

ANDROMACHE: Small space for tears, Ulysses, do I ask;
Some scanty moments yet, I pray thee, grant,
That I may close his eyes though living still,
And do a mother's part.
                    (*To* ASTYANAX)
                                        Lo, thou must die,
For, though a child, thou art too greatly feared.
Thy Troy awaits thee: go, in freedom's pride,
And see our Trojans, dead yet unenslaved.

ASTYANAX: O mother, mother, pity me and save!

ANDROMACHE: My son, why dost thou cling upon my robes,
And seek the vain protection of my hand?
As when the hungry lion's roar is heard,
The frightened calf for safety presses close
Its mother's side; but that remorseless beast,
Thrusting away the mother's timid form,
With ravenous jaws doth grasp the lesser prey,
And, crushing, drag it hence: so shalt thou, too,

Be snatched away from me by heartless foes.
Then take my tears and kisses, O my son,
Take these poor locks, and, full of mother love,
Go speed thee to thy sire; and in his ear
Speak these, thy grieving mother's parting words:
"If still thy manes feel their former cares,
And on the pyre thy love was not consumed,
Why dost thou suffer thy Andromache
To serve a Grecian lord, O cruel Hector?
Why dost thou lie in careless indolence?
Achilles has returned."
                                    Take once again
These hairs, these flowing tears, which still remain
From Hector's piteous death; this fond caress
And rain of parting kisses take for him.
But leave this cloak to comfort my distress,
For it, within his tomb and near his shade,
Hath lain enwrapping thee. If to its folds
One tiny mote of his dear ashes clings,
My eager lips shall seek it till they find.

ULYSSES: Thy grief is limitless. Come, break away,
                And end our Grecian fleet's too long delay.
                (*He leads the boy away with him.*)

                     Act Three.   Scene III

CHORUS: Where lies the home of our captivity?
                        On Thessaly's famed mountain heights?
                    Where Tempe's dusky shade invites?
                    Or Phthia, sturdy warriors' home,
                    Or where rough Trachin's cattle roam?
                    Iolchos, mistress of the main,
                    Or Crete, whose cities crowd the plain?
                    Where frequent flow Mothone's rills,
                    Beneath the shade of Oete's hills,
                    Whence came Alcides' fatal bow
                    Twice destined for our overthrow?
                But whither shall our alien course be sped?
                    Perchance to Pleuron's gates we go,
                    Where Dian's self was counted foe;

Perchance to Troezen's winding shore,
The land which mighty Theseus bore;
Or Pelion, by whose rugged side
Their mad ascent the giants tried.
Here, stretched within his mountain cave,
Once Chiron to Achilles gave
The lyre, whose stirring strains attest
The warlike passions of his breast.
What foreign shore our homeless band invites?
Must we our native country deem
Where bright Carystos' marbles gleam?
Where Chalcis breasts the heaving tide,
And swift Euripus' waters glide?
Perchance unhappy fortune calls
To bleak Gonoessa's windswept walls;
Perchance our wondering eyes shall see
Eleusin's awful mystery;
Or Elis, where great heroes strove
To win the Olympic crown of Jove.
Then welcome, stranger lands beyond the sea!
Let breezes waft our wretched band,
Where'er they list, to any land;
If only Sparta's curséd state
(To Greeks and Trojans common fate)
And Argos, never meet our view,
And bloody Pelops' city too;
May we ne'er see Ulysses' isle,
Whose borders share their master's guile.
But thee, O Hecuba, what fate,
What land, what Grecian lord await?

Act Four.   Scene I

(*Enter* HELEN.)

HELEN (*aside*): Whatever wedlock, bred of evil fate,
Is full of joyless omens, blood and tears,
Is worthy Helen's baleful auspices.
And now must I still further harm inflict
Upon the prostrate Trojans: 'tis my part
To feign Polyxena, the royal maid,

Is bid to be our Grecian Pyrrhus' wife,
And deck her in the garb of Grecian brides.
So by my artful words shall she be snared,
And by my craft shall Paris' sister fall.
But let her be deceived; 'tis better so;
To die without the shrinking fear of death
Is joy indeed. But why dost thou delay
Thy bidden task? If aught of sin there be,
'Tis his who doth command thee to the deed.

       (*To* POLYXENA)

O maiden, born of Priam's noble stock,
The gods begin to look upon thy house
In kinder mood, and even now prepare
To grant thee happy marriage; such a mate
As neither Troy herself in all her power
Nor royal Priam could have found for thee.
For lo, the flower of the Pelasgian lords,
Whose sway Thessalia's far-extending plains
Acknowledge, seeks thy hand in lawful wedlock.
Great Tethys waits to claim thee for her own,
And Thetis, whose majestic deity
Doth rule the swelling sea, and all the nymphs
Who dwell within its depths. As Pyrrhus' bride
Thou shalt be called the child of Peleus old,
And Nereus the divine.
                  Then change the garb
Of thy captivity for festal robes,
And straight forget that thou wast e'er a slave.
Thy wild, disheveled locks confine; permit
That I, with skilful hands, adorn thy head.
This chance, mayhap, shall place thee on a throne
More lofty far than ever Priam saw.
The captive's lot full oft a blessing proves.

ANDROMACHE: This was the one thing lacking to our woes—
That they should bid us smile when we would weep.
See there! Our city lies in smouldering heaps;
A fitting time to talk of marriages!
But who would dare refuse? When Helen bids,
Who would not hasten to the wedding rites?
Thou common curse of Greeks and Trojans too,
Thou fatal scourge, thou wasting pestilence,
Dost thou behold where buried heroes lie?

And dost thou see these poor unburied bones
That everywhere lie whitening on the plain?
This desolation hath thy marriage wrought.
For thee the blood of Asia flowed; for thee
Did Europe's heroes bleed, whilst thou, well pleased,
Didst look abroad upon the warring kings,
Who perished in thy cause, thou faithless jade!
There! Get thee gone! Prepare thy marriages!
What need of torches for the solemn rites?
What need of fire? Troy's self shall furnish forth
The ruddy flames to light her latest bride.
Then come, my sisters, come and celebrate
Lord Pyrrhus' nuptial day in fitting wise:
With groans and wailing let the scene resound.

HELEN: Though mighty grief is ne'er by reason swayed,
And oft the very comrades of its woe,
Unreasoning, hates; yet can I bear to stand
And plead my cause before a hostile judge,
For I have suffered heavier ills than these.
Behold, Andromache doth Hector mourn,
And Hecuba her Priam; each may claim
The public sympathy; but Helena
Alone must weep for Paris secretly.
Is slavery's yoke so heavy and so hard
To bear? This grievous yoke have I endured,
Ten years a captive. Doth your Ilium lie
In dust, your gods o'erthrown? I know 'tis hard
To lose one's native land, but harder still
To fear the land that gave you birth. Your woes
Are lightened by community of grief;
But friend and foe are foes alike to me.
Long since, the fated lot has hung in doubt
That sorts you to your lords; but I alone,
Without the hand of fate am claimed at once.
Think you that I have been the cause of war,
And Troy's great overthrow? Believe it true
If in a Spartan vessel I approached
Your land; but if, sped on by Phrygian oars,
I came a helpless prey; if to the judge
Of beauty's rival claims I fell the prize
By conquering Venus' gift, then pity me,
The plaything of the fates. An angry judge

Full soon my cause shall have—my Grecian lord.
Then leave to him the question of my guilt,
And judge me not.
                    But now forget thy woes
A little space, Andromache, and bid
This royal maid—but as I think on her
My tears unbidden flow.
       (She stops, overcome by emotion.)

ANDROMACHE *(in scorn)*:   Now great indeed
Must be the evil when our Helen weeps!
But dry thy tears, and tell what Ithacus
Is plotting now, what latest deed of shame?
Must this poor maid be hurled from Ida's heights,
Or from the top of Ilium's citadel?
Must she be flung into the cruel sea
That roars beneath this lofty precipice,
Which our Sigeum's rugged crag uprears?
Come, tell what thou dost hide with mimic grief.
In all our ills there's none so great as this,
That any princess of our royal house
Should wed with Pyrrhus. Speak thy dark intent;
What further suffering remains to bear?
To compensate our woes, this grace impart,
That we may know the worst that can befall.
Behold us ready for the stroke of fate.

HELEN: Alas! I would 'twere mine to break the bonds
Which bind me to this life I hate; to die
By Pyrrhus' cruel hand upon the tomb
Of great Achilles, and to share thy fate,
O poor Polyxena. For even now,
The ghost doth bid that thou be sacrificed,
And that thy blood be spilt upon his tomb;
That thus thy parting soul may mate with his,
Within the borders of Elysium.

ANDROMACHE *(observing the joy with which* POLYXENA *receives these
        tidings)*: Behold, her soul leaps up with mighty joy
At thought of death; she seeks the festal robes
Wherewith to deck her for the bridal rites,
And yields her golden locks to Helen's hands.
Who late accounted wedlock worse than death,

Now hails her death with more than bridal joy.
(*Observing* HECUBA)
But see, her mother stands amazed with woe,
Her spirit staggers 'neath the stroke of fate.
(*To* HECUBA)
Arise, O wretched queen, stand firm in soul,
And gird thy fainting spirit up.
(HECUBA *falls fainting*)
                        Behold,
By what a slender thread her feeble life
Is held to earth. How slight the barrier now
That doth remove our Hecuba from joy.
But no, she breathes, alas! she lives again,
For from the wretched, death is first to flee.

HECUBA (*reviving*): Still dost thou live, Achilles, for our bane?
    Dost still prolong the bitter strife? O Paris,
    Thine arrow should have dealt a deadlier wound.
    For see, the very ashes and the tomb
    Of that insatiate chieftain still do thirst
    For Trojan blood. But lately did a throng
    Of happy children press me round; and I,
    With fond endearment and the sweet caress
    That mother love would shower upon them all,
    Was oft forespent. But now this child alone
    Is left, my comrade, comfort of my woes,
    For whom to pray, in whom to rest my soul.
    Hers are the only lips still left to me
    To call me mother. Poor, unhappy soul,
    Why dost thou cling so stubbornly to life?
    Oh, speed thee out, and grant me death at last,
    The only boon I seek. Behold, I weep;
    And from my cheeks, o'erwhelmed with sympathy,
    A sudden rain of grieving tears descends.

ANDROMACHE: We, Hecuba, oh, we should most be mourned,
    Whom soon the fleet shall scatter o'er the sea;
    While *she* shall rest beneath the soil she loves.

HELEN: Still more wouldst thou begrudge thy sister's lot,
    If thou didst know thine own.

ANDROMACHE: Remains there still
    Some punishment that I must undergo?

HELEN: The whirling urn hath given you each her lord.

ANDROMACHE: To whom hath fate allotted me a slave?
                  Proclaim the chief whom I must call my lord.

HELEN: To Pyrrhus hast thou fallen by the lot.

ANDROMACHE: O happy maid, Cassandra, blest of heaven,
                  For by thy madness art thou held exempt
                  From fate that makes us chattels to the Greeks.

HELEN: Not so, for even now the Grecian king
                  Doth hold her as his prize.

HECUBA (*to* POLYXENA):   Rejoice, my child.
                  How gladly would thy sisters change their lot
                  For thy death-dooming marriage.
                      (*To* HELEN)
                               Tell me now,
                  Does any Greek lay claim to Hecuba?

HELEN: The Ithacan, though much against his will,
                  Hath gained by lot a short-lived prize in thee.

HECUBA: What cruel, ruthless providence hath given
                  A kingly slave as slave to kingly men?
                  What hostile god divides our captive band?
                  What heartless arbiter of destiny
                  So carelessly allots our future lords,
                  That Hector's mother is assigned to him
                  Who hath by favour gained th' accursed arms
                  Which laid my Hector low? And must I then
                  Obey the Ithacan? Now conquered quite,
                  Alas, and doubly captive do I seem,
                  And sore beset by all my woes at once.
                  Now must I blush, not for my slavery,
                  But for my master's sake. Yet Ithaca,
                  That barren land by savage seas beset,
                  Shall not receive my bones.
                             Then up, Ulysses,
                  And lead thy captive home. I'll not refuse
                  To follow thee as lord; for well I know
                  That my untoward fates shall follow me.
                  No gentle winds shall fill thy homeward sails,
                  But stormy blasts shall rage; destructive wars,
                  And fires, and Priam's evil fates and mine,

Shall haunt thee everywhere. But even now,
While yet those ills delay, hast thou received
Some punishment. For I usurped thy lot,
And stole thy chance to win a fairer prize.

(*Enter* PYRRHUS.)

But see, with hurried step and lowering brow,
Stern Pyrrhus comes.
                    (*To* PYRRHUS)
                              Why dost thou hesitate?
Come pierce my vitals with thy impious sword,
And join the parents of Achilles' bride.
Make haste, thou murderer of agéd men,
My blood befits thee too.
                    (*Pointing to* POLYXENA)
                              Away with her;
Defile the face of heaven with murder's stain,
Defile the shades.—But why make prayer to you?
I'll rather pray the sea whose savage rage
Befits these bloody rites; the selfsame doom,
Which for my ship I pray and prophesy,
May that befall the thousand ships of Greece,
And so may evil fate engulf them all.
            (PYRRHUS *departs with* POLYXENA.)

                    Act Four.   Scene II

CHORUS: 'Tis sweet for one in grief to know
                    That he but feels a common woe;
                    And lighter falls the stroke of care
                    Which all with equal sorrow bear;
            For selfish and malign is human grief
            Which in the tears of others finds relief.

                    Remove all men to fortune born,
                    And none will think himself forlorn;
                    Remove rich acres spreading wide,
                    With grazing herds on every side:
            Straight will the poor man's drooping soul revive,
            For none are poor if all in common thrive.

The mariner his fate bewails,
Who in a lonely vessel sails,
And, losing all his scanty store,
With life alone attains the shore;
But with a stouter heart the gale he braves,
That sinks a thousand ships beneath the waves.

When Phrixus fled in days of old
Upon the ram with fleece of gold,
His sister Helle with him fared
And all his exiled wanderings shared;
But when she fell and left him quite alone,
Then nothing could for Helle's loss atone.

Not so they wept, that fabled pair,
Deucalion and Pyrrha fair,
When 'midst the boundless sea they stood
The sole survivors of the flood;
For though their lot was hard and desolate,
They shared their sorrow—'twas a common fate.

Too soon our grieving company
Shall scatter on the rolling sea,
Where swelling sails and bending oars
Shall speed us on to distant shores.
Oh, then how hard shall be our wretched plight,
When far away our country lies,
And round us heaving billows rise,
And lofty Ida's summit sinks from sight.

Then mother shall her child embrace,
And point with straining eyes the place
Where Ilium's smouldering ruins lie,
Far off beneath the eastern sky:
"See there, my child, our Trojan ashes glow,
Where wreathing smoke in murky clouds
The distant, dim horizon shrouds."
And by that sign alone our land we know.

Act Five

(*Enter a* MESSENGER.)

MESSENGER (*entering*): Oh, cruel fate, oh, piteous, horrible!
What sight so fell and bloody have we seen
In ten long years of war? Between thy woes,
Andromache, and thine, O Hecuba,
I halt, and know not which to weep the more.

HECUBA: Weep whosesoe'er thou wilt—thou weepest mine.
While others bow beneath their single cares,
I feel the weight of all. All die to me;
Whatever grief there is, is Hecuba's.

MESSENGER: The maid is slain, the boy dashed from the walls.
But each has met his death with royal soul.

ANDROMACHE: Expound the deed in order, and display
The twofold crime. My mighty grief is fain
To hear the gruesome narrative entire.
Begin thy tale, and tell it as it was.

MESSENGER: One lofty tower of fallen Troy is left,
Well known to Priam, on whose battlements
He used to sit and view his warring hosts.
Here in his arms his grandson he would hold
With kind embrace, and bid the lad admire
His father's warlike deeds upon the field,
Where Hector, armed with fire and sword, pursued
The frightened Greeks. Around this lofty tower
Which lately stood, the glory of the walls,
But now a lonely crag, the people pour,
A motley, curious throng of high and low.
For some, a distant hill gives open view;
While others seek a cliff, upon whose edge
The crowd in tiptoed expectation stand.
The beech tree, laurel, pine, each has its load;
The whole wood bends beneath its human fruit.
One climbs a smouldering roof; unto another
A crumbling wall precarious footing gives;
While others (shameless!) stand on Hector's tomb.
Now through the thronging crowd with stately tread

Ulysses makes his way, and by the hand
He leads the little prince of Ilium.
With equal pace the lad approached the wall;
But when he reached the lofty battlement,
He stood and gazed around with dauntless soul.
And as the savage lion's tender young,
Its fangless jaws, all powerless to harm,
Still snaps with helpless wrath and swelling heart;
So he, though held in that strong foeman's grasp,
Stood firm, defiant. Then the crowd of men,
And leaders, and Ulysses' self, were moved.
But he alone wept not of all the throng
Who wept for him. And now Ulysses spake
In priestly wise the words of fate, and prayed,
And summoned to the rite the savage gods;
When suddenly, on self-destruction bent,
The lad sprang o'er the turret's edge, and plunged
Into the depths below.—

ANDROMACHE: What Colchian, what wandering Scythian,
What lawless race that dwells by Caspia's sea
Could do or dare a crime so hideous?
No blood of helpless children ever stained
Busiris' altars, monster though he was;
Nor did the horses of the Thracian king[18]
E'er feed on tender limbs. Where is my boy?
Who now will take and lay him in the tomb?

MESSENGER: Alas, my lady, how can aught remain
From such a fall, but broken, scattered bones,
Dismembered limbs, and all those noble signs
In face and feature of his royal birth,
Confused and crushed upon the ragged ground?[19]
Who was thy son lies now a shapeless corse.

ANDROMACHE: Thus also is he like his noble sire.

MESSENGER: When headlong from the tower the lad had sprung,
And all the Grecian throng bewailed the crime
Which it had seen and done; that selfsame throng
Returned to witness yet another crime
Upon Achilles' tomb. The seaward side
Is beaten by Rhoeteum's lapping waves;
While on the other sides a level space,

And rounded, gently sloping hills beyond,
Encompass it, and make a theatre.
Here rush the multitude and fill the place
With eager throngs. A few rejoice that now
Their homeward journey's long delay will end,
And that another prop of fallen Troy
Is stricken down. But all the common herd
Look on in silence at the crime they hate.
The Trojans, too, attend the sacrifice,
And wait with quaking hearts the final scene
Of Ilium's fall. When suddenly there shone
The gleaming torches of the wedding march;
And, as the bride's attendant, Helen came
With drooping head. Whereat the Trojans prayed:
"Oh, may Hermione be wed like this,
With bloody rites; like this may Helena
Return unto her lord." Then numbing dread
Seized Greeks and Trojans all, as they beheld
The maid. She walked with downcast, modest eyes,
But on her face a wondrous beauty glowed
In flaming splendour, as the setting sun
Lights up the sky with beams more beautiful,
When day hangs doubtful on the edge of night.
All gazed in wonder. Some her beauty moved,
And some her tender age and hapless fate;
But all, her dauntless courage in the face
Of death. Behind the maid grim Pyrrhus came;
And as they looked, the souls of all were filled
With quaking terror, pity, and amaze.
But when she reached the summit of the mound
And stood upon the lofty sepulchre,
Still with unfaltering step the maid advanced.
And now she turned her to the stroke of death
With eyes so fierce and fearless that she smote
The hearts of all, and, wondrous prodigy,
E'en Pyrrhus' bloody hand was slow to strike.
But soon, his right hand lifted to the stroke,
He drove the weapon deep within her breast;
And straight from that deep wound the blood burst forth
In sudden streams. But still the noble maid
Did not give o'er her bold and haughty mien,
Though in the act of death. For in her fall
She smote the earth with angry violence,

As if to make it heavy for the dead.
Then flowed the tears of all. The Trojans groaned
With secret woe, since fear restrained their tongues;
But openly the victors voiced their grief.
And now the savage rite was done. The blood
Stood not upon the ground, nor flowed away;
But downward all its ruddy stream was sucked,
As if the tomb were thirsty for the draught.

HECUBA: Now go, ye Greeks, and seek your homes in peace.
With spreading sails your fleet in safety now
May cleave the welcome sea; the maid and boy
Are slain, the war is done. Oh, whither now
Shall I betake me in my wretchedness?
Where spend this hateful remnant of my life?
My daughter or my grandson shall I mourn,
My husband, country—or myself alone?
O death, my sole desire, for boys and maids
Thou com'st with hurried step and savage mien;
But me alone of mortals dost thou fear
And shun; through all that dreadful night of Troy,
I sought thee 'midst the swords and blazing brands,
But all in vain my search. No cruel foe,
Nor crumbling wall, nor blazing fire, could give
The death I sought. And yet how near I stood
To agéd Priam's side when he was slain!

MESSENGER: Ye captives, haste you to the winding shore;
The sails are spread, our long delay is o'er.

MILLER'S TRANSLATION has been slightly modified in the following lines: 555, 633, 663, 982.

1. This refers to Rhesus, king of Thrace. Seneca confuses the river Don (Tanais) with the Danube.

2. This was the home of Memnon, son of Tithonus and Aurora, a warrior who also came to help the Trojans.

3. Cassandra, beloved by Apollo, rejected him after she had received the gift of prophecy; she was thereafter doomed to have her predictions disbelieved.

4. The "Ithacan" was Ulysses; his "comrade of the night" was Diomedes.

5. This refers to Pyrrhus, son of Achilles, and remote descendant of Aeacus.

6. Hercules rescued Hesione, daughter of King Laomedon of Troy, from a sea monster; when the king refused the promised reward, Hercules took Troy. After the death of Hercules, his bow and arrows passed to the possession of Philoctetes. When the Greeks learned from an oracle that the aid of Hercules' arrows would be necessary to take Troy, they sent for Philoctetes and the arrows. In this way "Hercules' darts" twice contributed to the fall of the city.

7. Achilles was the son of Thetis, a goddess of the sea.

8. Achilles defeated Cisseus, Hecuba's father, who was leading his Thracian forces to the relief of Troy.

9. Cycnus, son of Neptune, was changed into a swan when slain by Achilles.

10. The sacrifice of Iphigenia was made at Aulis that the Greek fleet might be permitted to sail to Troy to recover Helen.

11. Priam went to Achilles to ransom the body of Hector; the scene is described by Homer in the *Iliad*, Book XXIV.

12. This refers to the embassy to Achilles described in the *Iliad*, Book IX. Agamemnon offered gifts but did not himself go. The envoys were Ulysses and Ajax, who were accompanied by the aged Phoenix.

13. Pyrrhus alludes to the tragic feast prepared for Thyestes by Atreus, Agamemnon's father. Cf. Seneca's *Thyestes*.

14. The "feigned Peleus' son" refers to Patroclus who went into battle in the borrowed armour of Achilles and was slain by Hector.

15. This is apparently an allusion to the sacrifice of Iphigenia by Agamemnon.

16. Ulysses tricked Clytemnestra into letting Iphigenia go to Aulis, and he also discovered Achilles when the latter had been hidden away by Thetis.

17. Andromache under oath tells the literal truth but seems to say the opposite.

18. The Thracian king was Diomedes, who was conquered by Hercules.

19. Two verses were omitted by the translator at this point: "His neck was broken by the fall upon the rock, his skull was crushed, and his brains were dashed out."

III]
THE PHOENICIAN WOMEN

Characters in the Play

OEDIPUS, *late king of Thebes*
ANTIGONE, *daughter of* OEDIPUS
A MESSENGER
JOCASTA, *wife and mother of* OEDIPUS
A THEBAN GUARD
POLYNICES
ETEOCLES } *sons of* OEDIPUS *and rivals for the throne*

INTRODUCTION

The Phoenician Women is incomplete. Although the title implies that the tragedy contained a chorus of Phoenician women, the play as it has come down to us contains no chorus; it is in fact not a play at all, but merely two fragments dealing with the same general theme. The passages have been considered excerpts from two different dramas which may or may not have been completed; it has also been suggested that the two parts were brief dramatic sketches which were never intended to be worked up into play-form. N. T. Pratt, Jr., believes, however, that "the fragments manifest a well-knit coherence which seems to indicate that they together form part of a play by Seneca either imperfectly preserved or, more probably, never completed."

The action takes place three years after Oedipus' discovery of his parentage. The Theban king, self-blinded and self-exiled, has wandered in rough and trackless places, attended only by his faithful daughter Antigone. Meanwhile his sons are about to meet in strife. Eteocles, whose year of royal power is at an end, refuses to give up the throne, and Polynices, who has married the daughter of Adrastus, king of Argos, is marching against Thebes to enforce his rights. The conflict and death of Eteocles and Polynices provided material for Aeschylus' *The Seven Against Thebes,* Sophocles' *Antigone,* and Euripides *The Phoenissae.* One striking feature of the Euripidean drama was the portrayal of both Oedipus and Jocasta as still alive at the time of the conflict. Since Seneca presents this same version of the legend, it seems likely that Euripides' play was his main model, however much he may have been influenced by the other tragedies.

In the first fragment (Acts One and Two) the aged Oedipus is being guided by Antigone who has promised never to desert him. The situation is not unlike that of Sophocles' *Oedipus at Colonus,* but Seneca's Oedipus lacks the grandeur of the Sophoclean character. He declaims at length in rhetorical phrases on his desire for suicide—a desire that betrays the Stoical thought of the Roman playwright. There is a marked resemblance here to the scene in the *Mad Hercules,* where Hercules is determined to die after his crimes are known to him. As Amphitryon persuades him to yield, so in *The Phoenician Women* Oedipus accedes

555

to Antigone's demand that he live. When the news comes of the outbreak of the strife, he prays that the crimes of his sons will surpass his own. Seneca's Oedipus is far from being purified by his suffering.

The second fragment (Acts Three and Four) portrays the situation at Thebes and at the battle front. Jocasta rushes to her sons to persuade them to lay down their arms. "He who would his brother slay must slay his mother first," she cries. She will either end the strife or meet her own death. There is a temporary cessation of hostilities, and the brothers listen to her eloquent appeal. As the fragment ends Eteocles expresses sentiments which are tyrannical and unbending and which show how slight is the possibility of any reconciliation.

Although *The Phoenician Women* is no more than a fragment of a play, it provided, curiously enough, the model for the first English tragedy. *Gorboduc,* written by Norton and Sackville and produced in 1561, was, as F. L. Lucas states, "the first English play in the Senecan form, the first regular English tragedy, the first English drama in blank verse." Gorboduc divided Britain between his two sons, Ferrex and Porrex, who were rivals as were Eteocles and Polynices. The elder son was murdered by the younger, who was in turn slain by his mother, and both she and Gorboduc were slain by the people. In its plot of jealousy and fratricide and in the sententious speeches of the characters, the play followed closely the Senecan formula, and was far more dramatic than anything produced in England up to that date.

THE PHOENICIAN WOMEN

(SCENE:—*Acts One and Two, in the country; Act Three, in Thebes;*
Act Four, in the plain before Thebes.)

Act One

(Enter OEDIPUS, *led by* ANTIGONE.)

OEDIPUS: O guide of thy blind father, only cheer
To one sore wearied, daughter well-beloved
Though got at such a heavy price, forsake
Thy wretched parent. Wherefore shouldst thou lead
His wandering steps? Oh, let him stumble on!
'Tis better I should find the way I seek,
Alone—the path that takes me out of life
And frees from sight of this crime-laden head
The earth and sky. How little have I done!
The daylight, conscious of my evil deeds,
I do not see, indeed; but I am seen!
O child, unclasp the hand that clings to mine,
Where'er my blind steps lead me let me roam.
I go, I go, where high Cithaeron lifts
Its rugged summit, where Actaeon swift,
Roaming among the rocks, was made a prey
By his own dogs; where through the shadowy groves
And dusky woodlands of the bosky vales
The mother,[1] god-inspired, led forth her band,
And on her waving thyrsus lifted up
That head transfixed, rejoicing in ill deeds;
Where Zethus' bullock ran and dragged along
The shattered body—on the bristling thorns
Blood marked the course of the swift bullock's flight;
Or where with lofty summit Ino's cliff
Rises beside the sea, where fleeing crime

557

But finding crime the mother sought to drown
Her son with her, and leaped into the waves.
Thrice happy he whose better fortune gave
So good a mother! In these woods of ours
There lies another place that calls to me,
My footstep shall not falter, I will go
Thither without a guide, why hesitate
To take my rightful place? Oh, give me death,
Cithaeron, give me back my former lodge,
That where in infancy I should have died,
There in my age I may breathe out my life.
O ever savage, ruthless, cruel, fell,
Whether thou slay or spare, long, long ago
This lifeless trunk was due thee, now at last
Fulfil my father's mandate, mother's will.
My spirit longs to see accomplished now
The deed so long delayed. Why hold me clasped
With fatal love, my child? Why hold me so?
My father calls, I follow! Follow thee!
Yet spare! Behold where angry Laius comes,
Bearing the bloodstained standard of the realm
Snatched from him. With his hands he seeks to tear
My eyeballs' empty sockets. Dost thou see
My father, child? I see him!
        (To himself)
                       Now at last
Spew out thy baneful life, O coward soul,
Brave to destroy thy eyesight, not thyself!
Leave off thy long atonements, weak delays!
Why longer drag along thy life's slow length?
Why live? No crime remains for thee to do.
Ah, wretch! I here proclaim I still may sin!—
        (To ANTIGONE*)*
Go, virgin, leave thy father; for her sake—
Thy mother's—fear I all.

ANTIGONE: No power on earth,
O father, can unknit my hand from thine,
And none shall ever snatch me from thy side.
My brothers may with drawn sword seek to gain
The opulent realm and th' illustrious home
Of Labdacus, but mine the better part
Of all my father's realm—my father's self.

That brother who now holds in captured Thebes
The Theban sceptre cannot take from me
This share, nor can that other who now leads
Argolic hosts;[2] though Jupiter should speak
With thunderous voice out of the riven sky,
Although his bolt should fall to break our bond,
I will not let thee go. Though thou forbid,
Yet will I guide thee; though thou wish it not,
I will against thy will direct thy steps.
Seekst thou the plain? I go. The rugged heights?
I do not bar the way, but go before.
Whatever path thou treadst, make me thy guide,
We choose the selfsame road. Thou canst not die
Without me, with me thou mayst find thy death.
Here rises with steep sides the lofty cliff,
And views wide reaches of the sea that lies
Below; wilt thou go thither? There o'erhangs
The barren rock, there yawns the gaping jaws
Of the rent earth; shall I direct thee there?
There fall the hungry torrents, rolling down
The sundered rocks from off the broken hills;
Shall we rush headlong in? Lo, I go first,
I go where'er thou wilt, I do not urge,
I would not hinder. Father, wouldst thou cut
Thy thread of life? Is death thy dearest wish?
I go before thee if thou seekest death,
I follow if thou live. Yet change thy mind,
Call to thy aid thy will, so strong of old,
With force heroic master thy distress.
To die is to be conquered by thy woes.
Oh, be courageous still.

OEDIPUS: From so base home
Whence comes such noble growth? Whence comes
          this maid
So different from her race? Canst thou believe,
O fate, that this is true? Has any good
Been born of me? It never yet has been
That fortune smiled on me except to harm.
Nature obeys new laws; the streams, reversed,
Bear back swift waters to their fountain-head,
The torch of Phoebus ushers in the night,
And Hesperus brings the day; that I may find

Some increase of my woe, I, even I,
Shall have a loyal child. In death alone
Can Oedipus be safe. I may avenge
My father, unavenged till now; why cease
To mete out punishment, inert right hand?
Whatever hitherto was measured out
Was given for a mother. Dauntless maid,
Let go thy father's hand. Thou dost prolong
My death; thy living father's funeral rites,
Already all too long, thou lengthenest.
Cover the hateful body with the earth.
Thou errest, though with nobleness of aim,
And deemst it loyalty to drag about
A father who lacks yet his burial rites.
Who hinders one in haste to find his death
Equals in guilt the one who forces death
On one unwilling. Yet he equals not!
The first I deem, indeed, the greater sin.
I rather would be hurried to my end
Than be from death's jaws snatched away. My child,
No longer strive; in my own hands I hold
The right to live or die. I laid aside
Freely my sovereign power, but still retain
Sovereignty o'er myself. If thou indeed
Art loyal, give again thy father's sword,
The sword with parent's slaughter infamous.
Thou giv'st it? Do my children also hold
This with the realm? Wherever there is need
Of crime, there that should be; I give it up,
My sons shall have it, yea both sons. Prepare
The torches rather and a heap of wood;
On the high funeral pyre I'll cast myself,
Embrace the flames and 'neath the desolate pile
Will hide this too firm heart; set free at last,
Will give to ashes all that lives in me.
Where is the pitiless sea? Where jutting crags
O'erhang, where swift Ismenus' savage shoals
Roll downward, lead me, if thou leader art.
Where on the high cliff sat the Sphinx, half brute,
Proposing riddles, there I'll go to die.
Thither direct my steps, oh, place me there!
Not empty should that baleful seat be left,
Let it be by the greater monster filled.

There sitting on the rocks I will propose
The riddle of our fortune none can solve.
Whoe'er thou art who plow'st th' Assyrian fields,
Whoe'er, a suppliant, offerest up thy prayers
Where dwelt the far-famed dragon, ye who drink
Eurotas or inhabit Sparta, famed
For the twin brothers, husbandmen who reap
Elis, Parnassus, and the fertile fields
Of rich Boeotia, listen; what like this
Could she propose—Thebes' savage curse who wove
Dark, baneful riddles? What so hard to loose?
His father's father's son-in-law, yet found
His father's rival, brother to his sons,
And father of his brothers; at one birth
The father's mother bore the husband sons,
And grandsons to herself. Who can search out
This prodigy? I, even I, who bore
The trophies from the conquered Sphinx, perplexed,
Am slow to read my riddle. Why waste words?
Why strive with prayers to soften my hard heart?
Fixed is my purpose to pour out this life,
Too long with death contending, and to seek
The land of shadows, for the blackest night
Is all too little for this crime of mine.
Hide me in Tartarus, or if beyond
Aught lies, there hide me; what I should have done
Long since, I now will do. It cannot be;
Death is forbidden. Wilt thou keep the sword?
Wilt thou close up the way that leads to death,
Nor grant a halter? Wilt thou take away
Poisonous herbs? What profits all thy care?
In every place is death, most graciously
God ordered this; one may destroy man's life,
But none can snatch death from him, countless gates
To this lie open. I have need of nought;
Wont am I to employ my brave right hand.
Come, hand, with all thy force, with all thy guile,
With all thy strength; I purpose not to wound
One place alone, I am all black with sin.
Deal death in whatsoever part thou wilt.
Lay wide the bosom, tear away the heart
So filled with crime, the inmost parts lay bare,
Let my weak throat sound with redoubled blows,

And let my veins, by wounding nails torn through,
Bleed; or where thou art wont direct thy wrath:
Open again these wounds, with putrid gore
Wet them, and drag this unsubdued, hard heart
By this gate forth. O father, wheresoe'er
Thou mayst be found, judge of my penalty,
I have not thought by any punishment
Ever to fully expiate my sin;
I was not satisfied with death alone,
I have not paid my ransom with my eyes,
I wished to perish for thee limb by limb.
At length exact the penalty I owe.
Now I atone, 'twas then but sacrifice
I offered; oh, be present, inward urge
My feeble hand; oh, plunge it deeper still!
A timid, slight libation then I poured,
Hardly drew forth the eyes that eagerly
Followed my hand. My spirit even now
Falters, is loth with trembling hand to tear
These sockets. Oedipus, now hear the truth:
Less bold than thou hast purposed thou hast been,
In plucking out thine eyes; deep in thy brain
Bury thy hand, and perfect thou the death
Where I began to die.

ANTIGONE: I pray thee show
Some pity, great-souled father; calmly hear
Thy daughter's words. I would not lead thee back
To the old home, nor to the kingly throne
With all its splendour, would not have thee bear
With weak, untroubled breast the wrath of God
Which time has not yet softened, but 'tis meet
So strong a man should not be crushed by grief,
Or fly, o'ercome by manifold distress.
It is not, father, as thou deemst it, brave
To be afraid of life; 'tis brave to face
The greatest ills, nor flinch, nor turn the back.
He who has trampled on his destiny,
He who has rent life's good and cast it by,
And made his own life heavier, who has need
No more of God, why should he wish to die?
Why seek his death? Either were cowardly.
No one who longs for death despises it.

The man whose evil fate is at its worst
Is safe. Although he would, what god could make
Thy trouble heavier? Nor canst thou thyself
Unless in deeming thou art worthy death.
Thou art not, for no sin has touched thy heart.
Thou canst more surely call thyself guilt free,
Since thou art innocent, although the gods
Willed otherwise. What maddens thee? What adds
New stings to misery? What urges thee
Into the land of death? What drives thee hence?
Wouldst thou shun day? Thou hast. Or wouldst thou
        flee
Thy lofty palace and thy native land?
For thee, although thou livest, native land
Is dead. Or wouldst thou fly thy mother, sons?
Fate has removed thee from the sight of these.
What death from others takes, life takes from thee.
The tumult of the throne? At thy command
The press of crowding fortune fell away.
What wouldst thou fly, my father?

OEDIPUS: Ah! My self!
I flee a bosom conscious of all crimes,
I flee this hand, this sky, I flee the gods.
Do I yet touch the earth where Ceres grows
Fruitful and fair? With noxious life still breathe
The vital air? Or satisfy my thirst
With water? Or enjoy in any way
The gifts of mother Nature? Base, defiled,
Detestable, do I yet feel the touch
Of thy pure hand? Or can I yet perceive
Voices which speak the names of father, son?
Oh, could I with destroying hand throw wide
Those paths where enter sound! Might I destroy
These narrow pathways for the human voice!
O child, thy wretched father would have fled
Long, long ago, the knowledge that thou art,
Thou, part of my great sin. My crimes stick fast,
Repeated o'er and o'er. O eyes and ears,
Let all ye gave me pass away from me!
O'erwhelmed with blackest shadows, why not go
Into the everlasting shades of Dis?
Why keep my spirit here? Why weight the world?

Why wander yet among the souls that live?
What crime is left? Realm, parents, children, all,
Valour, the glory of sagacious mind,
Have perished; fate has taken from me all.
Tears still were left, these from myself I snatched.
Go, for my soul will listen to no prayers,
New penalties and equal to my crimes
I seek. Yet what can ever equal those?
I was condemned to death in infancy.
Who ever drew so bad a lot? Ere yet
I saw the light, ere from my mother's womb
I was set free, already I was feared!
Night seizes many, just when they are born,
And carries them away from the new day;
Death found me even ere I saw the light.
Some meet an early death within the womb,
But have they also sinned? Still hidden close,
Secreted in the womb, not knowing yet
That I should be the doer of great crimes,
A god impelled; my father at his word
Condemned me, pierced with steel my tender feet,
And left me in the forest, food for beasts
And savage birds (oft wet with blood of kings)
Which dark Cithaeron breeds. Yet whom the gods
Sentenced, and whom a father cast away,
Death also fled. I have fulfilled the word
Spoken at Delphi: I attacked and slew
My father. This might be by love made good.
My father I have slain, but I have loved
My mother—of our marriage torch to speak
Is loathsome, yet against my will I'll pay
This penalty, will tell the beastly crime,
Unheard-of, strange, at thought of which men shrink,
The crime which makes ashamed the man who slew
His father. This right hand, with father's blood
Made wet, even to my father's marriage bed
I took, and found sin's wages—greater sin.
My father's murder was a slight offence
Compared with this. Lest all too small should be
My guilt, my mother in my marriage bed
Was made a mother. Nature cannot yield
A greater crime than this, but should there be
A greater, those to whom 'twere possible

Have been by me created. From my hand
I cast aside the patricide's reward,
The sceptre, with it armed another hand.
I knew right well my kingdom's destiny,
Without the sacrifice of sacred blood
No man can hold it. Nameless ills to come
My father heart presages. Seeds are sown
Of future slaughter. He who holds the realm
Will not resign it, he who wishes it
Calls upon justice and the gods who see
The violated pact; exiled, he moves
Argos and all the cities of the Greeks
To arms; destruction comes to wretched Thebes;
The flying spear, flames, slaughter 'gainst her rise,
And greater ills, if greater ills there be,
That none may doubt I have begotten sons.

ANTIGONE: If thou no other reason hadst to live,
This were enough: that thou shouldst fatherlike
Control thy maddened sons. Thou canst avert,
And thou alone, the threats of impious war,
Thou only canst restrain those youths insane,
Give to the people peace, to Thebes repose,
And, to the broken compact, faith renewed.
If thou thyself shouldst to thyself refuse
The right to live, thou tak'st from many more
The right of life.

OEDIPUS: For empire and for blood.
For war and treachery athirst, base, vile,
In short my own, can these or can their like
Feel filial love? They joy in doing ill,
And deem naught sacred when rage drives them forth.
Those baseborn ones consider nothing base,
Their wretched father's shame affects them not,
Nor does their native country: they are mad
For sovereignty; whither they tend I know,
How much they strive to do; therefore I seek
A speedy way of death, make haste to die
While none is guiltier in my house than I.
Why, daughter, dost thou weep and clasp my knees?
Why strive with prayers to guide my untamed heart?
Elsewhere invulnerable, here alone
Can fortune wound me; thou alone canst warm

My frozen love, in all our house but thou
Canst teach me goodness. Nought to me is hard
Or grievous if I know it is thy wish.
If thou shouldst bid him, Oedipus would cross
Th' Aegean straits, would take between his lips
The flame earth belches from Sicilia's mount,
Would cast himself before the fiery snake
That rages for the fruit that Hercules
Stole from the grove, at thy command he'd bare
His bosom to the birds, at thy command
Would live.

(The first act seems to be complete here, except for the chorus which would naturally follow.)

Act Two

(Enter a MESSENGER[3] *from Thebes.)*

MESSENGER: O noble scion of a royal stock,
     Thebes, trembling at the brothers' hostile arms,
     Invokes thee, prays that thou wouldst turn aside
     The torch of war that threats thy father's land.
     Nor threats alone, the danger nearer comes.
     A brother claims the promised interchange
     Of royal power, into war would force
     The Grecian cities, seven camps invest
     The walls of Thebes. Make haste to bring her aid,
     Prevent at once impiety and war.

OEDIPUS: Am I the man should put an end to crime,
     Or teach the hand to keep itself unstained
     With blood of kindred? Have I learned the laws
     Of justice and of duteous love? They seek
     To follow the example of my crimes.
     Gladly I recognise and praise their deed,
     Exhort them do some action worthy me.
     Dear offspring, forward! Prove your noble birth
     By deeds, surpass my glory and my fame,
     Do something that shall make thy father glad
     That he has lived till now! I know you will,
     Your ancestry assures me that you will;

Such greatness cannot with poor, common crimes
Content itself. Bring weapons, cast the torch
Into the sacred temples of the gods,
Mow down with flames thy native country's grain,
Throw all into disorder, ruin all,
Destroy the city walls, and to the dust
Level the city, with their shrines destroy
The great divinities, and bring to naught
The household gods become so infamous;
Burn up the city, lay thy whole house low,
And to my marriage bed put first the torch.

ANTIGONE: Thy passionate, wild sorrow put aside;
The public sorrow urges thee to be
The bringer of sweet peace between thy sons.

OEDIPUS: Thinkst thou thou seest here a meek old man,
And that thou callest to aid thee one who loves
Sweet peace? This heart of mine with wrath is swelled,
Rage burns within me, greater war I seek
Than aught that destiny or youth desires.
I am not satisfied with cruel war,
Brother with brother wars—'tis not enough.
Crimes that are due, crimes that are like my own,
Crimes that become our bed,—let these be done.
Give weapons to the mother. From the woods
No one shall drag me, in the hollow cliffs
I'll lurk, or in dense thickets hide myself,
There will I wait on wandering Rumour's words,
And hear whate'er I can of brothers' war.

Act Three.   Scene I

(The scene is now Thebes. Enter JOCASTA.)

JOCASTA *(to herself)*: Happy Agave! The wild crime she did,
She herself bore; a blood-stained bacchanal,
She carried forth the dreadful spoil, her son
Dismembered; guilt was hers, yet naught of crime
Beyond her own great sin was brought to pass.
'Tis light to bear the burdens of the crimes
Myself have done. I have made others sin;

This also, even this is light to bear.
I have brought forth the guilty, to my woes
This bitterness still lacked—that I should love
An enemy. Three times the winter snows
Have fallen and three times the summer grain
Before the bending sickle been laid low,
Since, of his land deprived, my son has roamed
An exile, and, a fugitive, has craved
Aid from the Grecian kings. He has become
Adrastus' son-in-law—that king who rules
The waters the Corinthian Isthmus cuts,
Who now to aid his son-in-law leads forth
His hosts, and with him seven other kings.
I know not what I ought to wish or think;
He claims the kingdom; reason good he has
For claiming, yet he seeks it by ill means.
Alas, whose part shall I, the mother, take?
Each is my son, I cannot safely show
My love for either. If I wish one well,
I wish the other ill. With equal love
I love them both, and yet my spirit yearns,
Favouring still the weakest, towards the son
Whose lot is heaviest though his cause is just.
His evil fortune binds me to his side.

Act Three. Scene II

(Enter a THEBAN GUARD, *followed by* ANTIGONE.*)*

THEBAN GUARD: Queen, while in weeping and in wild lament
Thou wastest time, the battle line is here,
Drawn up in open war, the trumpet calls
To arms, th' advancing eagle calls to war.
Drawn up in serried ranks the kings prepare
Seven battlefields, and Cadmus' sons go forth
With equal courage; swiftly here and there
The soldiers rush; see how black clouds of dust
Obscure the day. There rises from the field
Clouds dark as smoke, raised by the hurrying feet
Of horsemen and, if those who fear see true,
The hostile standards shine, the foe's first ranks

Are present, and the golden banners bear
Illustrious names of well-known generals.
Go, to the brothers bring fraternal love,
Give peace to all and with a mother's voice
Forbid the war.

ANTIGONE: Haste, mother, haste, fly fast,
Hold back the weapons, from the brothers' hands
Strike down the sword, between the hostile spears
Set thy brave breast! O mother, stop the war,
Or perish first.

JOCASTA: I go, I go, my head
I'll offer to their swords, between the swords
I'll stand, and he who would his brother slay
Must slay his mother first. At my request
The duteous son will lay his weapon down;
The son who is not duteous shall begin
His war with me. Though old, I may restrain
The fiery youths; no impious crime shall be
While I am witness, or if impious crime
Can be committed and I witness it,
One crime were not enough.

ANTIGONE: The fight is on,
The neighbouring banners gleam, the noise of war
Resounds. O mother, now employ thy prayers.
But see, as though prevailed on by thy tears,
Slowly, with spears at rest, the line draws near.

THEBAN GUARD: The line moves slowly, but the leaders haste.

JOCASTA (*hurrying towards the conflict*): What winged wind will sweep
          me through the air,
With the mad rushing of the tempest driven?
Would that the Sphinx or the Stymphalian birds
That darken like a heavy cloud the day
Would bear me swiftly on their eager wings!
Or that the Harpies, seeing the fierce rage
Of the two cruel kings, would snatch me hence
And cast me down between the battle lines.

THEBAN GUARD (*looking after her*): Like one insane she moves, she's
          mad, indeed!
As the swift Parthian arrow from the bow

Is driven, as the raft is swept along
By the wild winds, or as a falling star
Drops from the skies, when with swift fires it breaks
A path unswerving, so her maddened flight
She takes, and stands between the hostile lines.
The fight a moment fails, compelled to yield
Before a mother's prayers, on either side
The warriors, eager to begin the work
Of mutual slaughter, in their right hands hold
The weapons poised, but motionless as yet
Both armies stand, at peace. The swords of all
Are sunk to earth, or hidden in the sheath,
Only the brothers' hands still brandish them.
The mother shows her loose hair, white and torn;
She supplicates, but they deny; she wets
Their knees with tears—who hesitates so long
Can in the end deny a mother's prayers.

Act Four

(JOCASTA *is between the battle lines. She kneels between her two hostile*
   sons, POLYNICES *and* ETEOCLES.)

JOCASTA: Against me turn your weapons and your fires,
                  Attack me only, valorous youths who come
                  From Argive cities; and ye warriors fierce,
                  Who from the Theban citadel descend,
                  Fall upon me alone. Let friend and foe
                  Alike attack this womb, which bore these sons—
                  My husband's brothers. Tear these limbs apart,
                  Scatter them far and wide. I bore you both.
                  Do you more quickly lay aside the sword?
                  And shall I say who fathered you, my sons?
                  Give me your hands, give them while yet unstained;
                  Till now ye have unwittingly done wrong;
                  Each crime was fortune's that against us sinned.
                  This is the first base act brought forth between
                  Those conscious of their guilt. In my hand lies
                  Whate'er you will: if holy piety
                  Be pleasing to you, give your mother peace;
                  If crime be pleasing, greater is prepared.

A mother stands between you, make an end
Of war or of the hinderer of war.
Whom with alternate prayers and anxious words
Shall I first strive to touch, whom first embrace?
With equal love am I to each one drawn.
One was far off—but if the brother's pact
Should hold, the other soon would be far off.
Shall I then never see the two at once
Except as now? Embrace me first, my son,
Who hast endured misfortunes manifold
And labours manifold, and now, foredone
By a long exile, dost at last behold
Thy mother. Nearer draw, within its sheath
Put up thy impious sword, and in the earth
Bury thy spear that trembles, poised to slay.
Thy shield prevents thy breast from meeting mine,
Lay it aside; loose from thy brow the bands
And from its warlike covering free thy head,
That I may see thy face. Where dost thou look?
Dost thou observe thy brother's battle line
With timid glance? I'll hide thee in my arms,
Through me must be the pathway to thy blood.
Why hesitate? Art thou afraid to trust
Thy mother?

POLYNICES: Yea, I am afraid. No more
Do nature's laws avail. Since I have known
A brother's faithlessness, I cannot trust
Even a mother's promise.

JOCASTA: Put again
Thy hand upon thy sword, bind on once more
Thy helmet, take thy shield, retain thy arms
Until thy brother shall have been disarmed.
          (*To* ETEOCLES)
Thou who first used the sword, put down the sword.
If peace is odious, if thou seekest war,
Thy mother asks thee for a short delay
That she may kiss the son from flight returned,
Whether it be the first kiss or the last.
Listen unarmed while I entreat for peace.
Thou fearest him, he thee? I fear thee both,
But for the sake of each. Why willst thou not
Lay down the sword? Be glad at these delays;

You seek to wage a war in which 'twere best
To be o'ercome. Thy hostile brother's guile
Fearst thou? 'Tis often needful to deceive
Or be oneself deceived, yet is it best
To suffer rather than commit a crime.
Fear not, a treacherous thrust from either side
Thy mother will receive. Do I prevail?
Shall I be envious of thy father's fate?
Have I come hither to prevent a crime,
Or see it nearer? See, he sheathes his sword,
He drops his spear, he lays aside his arms.

       (*To* POLYNICES)

And now to thee thy mother turns with prayers
And tears. I see again thy face, long sought.
Thee, from thy native land a fugitive,
A foreign king's penates long kept safe.
By divers seas and by a changeful fate
Thou hast been driven. Followed by her train,
Thy mother did not to thy marriage bed
Conduct thee, nor adorn the festal halls
Herself, nor with the sacred fillets bind
The happy torches; thy bride's father gave
No gift of gold, a treasure for a king,
Nor fields, nor towns; thy bridal gift is war.
Thou of a foe art made the son-in-law,
Far from thy land, the guest of alien laws,
Sought by a stranger, driven from thine own,
An exile through no crime that thou hast done.
Lest thou shouldst taste not all thy parents' fate,
This too thou hadst from them: to wed amiss.
O son, sent back to me from many lands;
O son, thy anxious mother's hope and fear;
For whose return I often prayed the gods,
Though thy return would snatch away as much
As it would give; how long, I asked, how long,
Before I cease to fear on his account?
The mocking god replied, till thou shalt fear
Himself. Thou hadst been far, but for this war;
Hadst thou been far I should have known no war.
The sight of thee is given at a price
Heavy to pay, but to thy mother's eyes
The sight is welcome. Now, ere cruel Mars
Dares some dread crime, let the two hosts withdraw;

Great sin it is that they have come so near.
I am amazed, I shudder, when I see
Two brothers stand so near the edge of crime.
My limbs are weak, how nearly had I seen
A crime of greater infamy than aught
Thy wretched father ever looked upon.
I am set free from fear of such a crime,
Such now I shall not see; and yet I feel
Unhappy that so nearly I have seen.
Oh! By the ten months' labour of my womb,
And by thy noble sister's piety,
And by thy father's eyes which he dragged forth,
Enraged against himself and from himself
Exacting the hard penalty of crime,
Though innocent of any guilt; I pray:
Save from the cursed torch thy country's walls,
Turn back the standards of the hostile lines;
Though thou turnst back, great portion of thy crime
Already is complete—thy land has seen
Its open plains o'errun by hordes of foes,
Has seen afar the shining troops, has seen
The Cadmean meadows trampled by the horse,
And princes in their chariots of war
Advancing, and the blaze of lighted beams
Prepared to burn our homes, and—even for Thebes
An unaccustomed crime—two brothers roused
To war against each other. All the host
Saw, the whole people saw, thy sister saw,
And I, thy mother. That he saw it not,
Thy father to his mangled eyeballs owes.
Ah, what if Oedipus should see thee now,
That judge who even for error would exact
The penalty? Ah, waste not with the sword
Thy country and thy home, nor overthrow
The Thebes thou eagerly dost wish to rule.
What madness has possession of thy mind?
Wilt thou by wild assault destroy the land?
That it may be thine own wouldst make it naught?
Thou dost but to thine own cause injury,
When thou inflam'st thy land with hostile arms,
Layest the ripe grain low, and far and wide
Spreadst terror. None thus devastate their own.
Thou must believe it but an alien land,

Which thou commandest to be seized by fire
And taken by the sword. Decide which one
Shall be the king, but let the kingdom stand.
Wilt thou with fire and spear destroy these roofs?
Or canst thou shake Amphion's mighty work?
Wouldst shake these walls, not builded by man's hand
That lifts with noisy crane the slow-moved weight,
But called together by the cither's sound
And singing—of themselves the stones moved up
Into the highest turrets—wouldst thou break
These walls in pieces? Wouldst thou bear away
A victor's spoil, thy father's vanquished peers
Lead hence, and shall the cruel soldiers drag
Mothers in chains, snatched from their husband's
    arms?
Shall Theban maidens, mingled with the herd
Of captives, go as gifts to Argive maids?
Shall I myself, with hands behind me bound,
The plunder of fraternal triumph be?
Canst thou behold thy fellow citizens
On all sides given o'er to death and flight?
Canst thou against these dear walls lead the foe?
Hast thou a heart so savage and so wild,
So cruel in its wrath? Thou are not yet
A king, what will thy sceptred hand perform?
I do beseech thee, put aside thy rage
And swelling anger, give to duteous love
Again thy heart.

POLYNICES: That I a fugitive
May wander? That I may afar from Thebes
Be kept? May ever as a guest desire
The aid of strangers? Had I broken faith,
Had I foresworn myself, what had I borne?
Shall I to aliens pay the penalty
Of treachery, and he alone enjoy
The profit of the crime? Thou bidst me go,
I would indeed obey a mother's word;
Where shall I go? My royal halls would be
My haughty brother's dwelling, a poor hut
Would cover me: give to the exiled that,
Let me exchange a realm for that poor home.
But shall I, given to my wife, a slave,

Bear the harsh judgments of a wealthy bride
And as a mean and humble follower
Obey the royal parents of my wife?
'Tis hard to fall from power to servitude.

JOCASTA: If thou dost now desire to be a king
Nor canst from the harsh sceptre free thy hand,
Many there are in the world's circle wide
That thou canst seize. Where Tmolus lifts its heights
Sacred to Bacchus, where wide stretches lie
Of fruitful soil, where rich Pactolus flows
And inundates the country with its gold.
Nor does Maeander with its wandering stream
Through meadowlands less happy wind its way;
Swift Hermus rolls through fertile fields; there lies
Gargara, loved by Ceres, and the land
Which Xanthus, swoll'n with Ida's snows, makes wet.
There lies the shore where the Ionian sea
Changes its name; across the narrow strait,
Opposite to Abydos, Sestos stands;
Or, farther east, with safe and frequent ports,
Lies Lycia: seek these kingdoms with the sword,
Let thy bride's father bear his hostile arms
Against these peoples, and betray these lands,
And give them to thee to be ruled by thee.
Think that thy father hitherto has held
This kingdom. Better far for thee would be
Exile than this return. Exiled thou art
Through guilt not thine; through crime thyself
    must do
Thou wilt return. 'Twere better thou shouldst seek
With these thy warriors a new realm, unstained
By any crime. The sharer of thy war,
Thy brother, will himself then fight for thee.
Go wage a war where we may wish thee well.
A kingdom won by crime is heavier far
Than any exile. Weigh the ills of war,
Think on uncertain Mars' vicissitudes.
Though thou shouldst lead with thee the flower of
    Greece,
Though far and wide thy countless hosts should
    spread,
Yet doubtful were the fortune of the war—

'Tis as Mars wills, he makes of equal strength
Two swords, although they were before ill matched;
Blind chance brings hope or fear. Though all the gods
Favoured thy vows, they have withdrawn from thee
And, put to flight, have sought the Theban side.
The soldiery, in awful overthrow
Lying, are scattered over all the field.
Say thou wage war, from thy slain brother bear
A victor's spoils, thy palms would soon be crushed;
Thinkst thou such war can bring the conqueror joy
When he commits in it accursed crime?
Him whom thou seekest now to overthrow,
Him, conquered, wretched one, thou wilt bewail.
Go, put an end to this disastrous war,
From terror free thy native land, from grief
Set free thy parents.

POLYNICES: Shall no punishment
For all his crime and treachery be borne
By my base brother?

JOCASTA: Fear not. He shall pay
Hard penalty indeed, for he shall reign;
This is his penalty. And shouldst thou doubt,
Look on his father's, his grandfather's fate;
Cadmus and Cadmus' offspring tell thee this:
Never unpunished did a Theban hold
The sceptre, none shall hold it who break faith,
And even now among such sinful ones
Thou numberest a brother.

ETEOCLES: Be it so!
'Tis worth so much to be among Thebes' kings.
          (*To* POLYNICES)
Thee, place I mid the throng of exiled ones.

JOCASTA: Reign hated by the people.

ETEOCLES: He who fears
Hatred can never wish to be a king.
God, the creator of the universe,
Has bound together hate and kingly power.
A great king, I believe, will overcome
Hatred itself. Their peoples' love prevents
Many from ruling; most is possible

Where hate abides. Who wishes to be loved
Rules with a languid hand.

JOCASTA: Not long maintained
Will be unwelcome empire.

ETEOCLES: Kings may give
The laws of empire with a better grace;
Speak thou of exiles. For my realm I wish—

JOCASTA: To give thy native land, thy household gods,
Thy wife, to the destroying flames?

ETEOCLES: Hard price
Is ever for imperial power paid.

Miss Harris' translation has been slightly modified in the following lines: 25, 178, 479, 556, 599.

1. The mother was Agave who, in a frenzy inspired by Bacchus, slew her son Pentheus. The story is found in Euripides' *The Bacchae*.

2. Antigone refers here to her two brothers, Eteocles who now rules in Thebes, and Polynices who leads the enemy against him.

3. Some editors assign the messenger's speech to Antigone; it belongs more fittingly to one who has just arrived, since it gives fresher information from Thebes than Antigone would possess.

IV
MEDEA

CHARACTERS IN THE PLAY

MEDEA, *daughter of Aeetes, king of Colchis, and wife of* JASON
CHORUS OF CORINTHIANS, *friendly to* JASON *and hostile to* MEDEA
NURSE *of* MEDEA
CREON, *king of Corinth*
JASON, *son of Aeson, and nephew of Pelias; organizer and leader of the
Argonautic expedition*
A MESSENGER
TWO SONS *of* MEDEA *and* JASON

INTRODUCTION

THE WELL-KNOWN myth of the Argonautic expedition provides the background of the *Medea*. At the instigation of his uncle Pelias, Jason sailed with his comrades to Colchis in quest of the golden fleece. Aeetes, king of Colchis, imposed three deadly labours upon Jason before the fleece could be won—the yoking of the fire-breathing bulls, the contest with the warriors who sprang from the serpent's teeth, and the overcoming of the sleepless dragon which guarded the fleece. Medea, the daughter of Aeetes, fell in love with Jason and by her magic enabled him to accomplish the labours and secure the fleece. She fled from Colchis with the Argonauts, and, to retard pursuit, slew her brother Absyrtus and scattered his mangled remains in the sea. Later, in Thessaly, she tricked the daughters of Pelias into slaying their aged father; this act made it necessary for Jason and Medea to flee to Corinth. Here they lived happily with their two sons until Jason, deserting Medea, planned to marry Creusa, daughter of Creon, king of Corinth. His faithlessness arouses Medea's fury and leads to the horrible vengeance described in the tragedy.

The romantic story of Jason and Medea has appealed to many dramatists from ancient times to the present. Euripides, Ennius, Accius, Ovid, and Seneca presented their conceptions of the alliance and its tragic outcome. In modern times the story has been treated by De la Péruse (1553), Corneille (1635), Longepierre (1694), Pellegrin (1713), Glover (1792), Grillparzer in his trilogy *Das Goldene Vliess* (1818), and Mendes (1898). Maxwell Anderson's *The Wingless Victory* (1936) presents a situation not unlike that of the Medea-dramas—the story of Oparre, an Eastern princess, who saves her lover from death and returns with him to his country; the common-law marriage, the repudiation of Oparre, and the slaying of the children are features strikingly similar to the details of the legend of Medea.

Of the plays of antiquity dealing with Medea only those of Euripides and Seneca are extant. Although the general structure of the two tragedies is similar, Seneca has introduced many innovations. For some of these he may well have been indebted to Ovid; many are doubtless the product of his own originality, for they betray both his strength and his weakness as a dramatist.

One of the most important changes in Seneca's play is a definite shift of sympathy towards Jason, who had been portrayed by Euripides as primarily ambitious for power and desirous of security. His plea that he was marrying Creusa for the welfare of Medea and the children could hardly ring true when the children as well as Medea were to be exiled. In Seneca's play the children are to remain in Corinth—an innovation which gives more support to Jason's claim that his act is motivated by paternal love. In both plays Medea's actions are the result of her love for Jason, for whom she had committed all her past crimes; Seneca, however, stresses her magical powers and recalls her earlier deeds again and again. His insertion of a long description of her incantations has been criticised not only for halting the action of the drama but for making her too much of an enchantress. It is significant also that the chorus, which in Euripides' play favoured Medea, has in the Senecan drama cast its sympathies to Jason and is definitely hostile to Medea. Seneca makes his portrayal of Medea more a study of criminal psychology than of human suffering, and so loses something of the emotional and psychological power of the Greek play.

Seneca omitted the Aegeus scene, for which Euripides has often been criticised both in ancient and modern times, but criticised wrongly, since it is the childlessness of Aegeus which apparently suggested to the Euripidean Medea the ultimate form of her vengeance. The Senecan tragedy does not suffer from this omission, for it is Jason's own statement about his love for his children that leads Medea to her decision. She says,

> "Doth he thus love his sons? 'Tis well;
> Then is he bound, and in his armoured strength this flaw
> Reveals the place to strike."

The killing of the children is the culmination of her revenge and leaves Jason completely desolate, since both Creon and Creusa meet their horrible death first.

A striking feature of Seneca's play is the brevity of the messenger's speech announcing the death of the king and the princess. C. W. Mendell says, "It is tempting to suspect, in this instance, a case of incompleteness of text or failure on the part of Seneca to finish the play for publication, but it is more probably simply another case of crude workmanship." H. E. Butler is more explicit in his condemnation of the messenger scene: "If we had not read Euripides we should scarcely understand the connexion between the gifts and the mysterious fire. Seneca . . . finds no room to give what might be a really dramatic description of the all-important catastrophe in which Medea's vengeance finds issue." One may well suggest that in this instance it is the critics who err, for Seneca's workmanship seems far from crude. It is unnecessary for the messenger to give a detailed description of the deaths of Creon and Creusa since Medea's description of the poisoned robe has already foreshadowed its dire effects. Seneca here presents the catastrophe by anticipation, as does Aeschylus in the *Agamemnon,* when Cassandra prophesies the death of the king. Furthermore, to add a detailed description of the deaths of Creon and Creusa might well detract from the climax of the play. The death of the children is the all-important catastrophe, as Medea's words make clear:

"But still how small a portion of thy just revenge
Is this which gives thee present joy? Not yet has love
Been banished from thy maddened heart if 'tis enough
That Jason widowed be."

From the standpoint both of structure and delineation of character the *Medea* is one of Seneca's better plays. The tragedy of Medea is the tragedy of a woman to whom love is everything; when deserted by Jason to whom love is secondary, her desire for vengeance becomes all-powerful and makes her commit the most terrible of crimes. The conflict between her love for her children and her passion for revenge is effectively portrayed in the final Act and it is here that Seneca treats her most sympathetically. His play lacks the emotional depth of Euripides' great tragedy, but it is a far better play than many critics admit.

MEDEA

SCENE:—*Before the house of* JASON *in Corinth. The palace of* CREON *is near.*)

Act One. Scene I

(*Enter* MEDEA.)

MEDEA:
>Ye gods of wedlock, thou the nuptial couch's guard,
>Lucina, thou from whom that tamer of the deep,
>The Argo's pilot, learned to guide his pristine bark,
>And Neptune, thou stern ruler of the ocean's depths,
>And Titan, by whose rays the shining day is born,
>Thou triformed maiden Hecate, whose conscious beams
>With splendour shine upon the mystic worshippers—
>Upon ye all I call, the powers of heaven, the gods
>By whose divinity false Jason swore; and ye
>Whose aid Medea may more boldly claim, thou world
>Of endless night, th' antipodes of heavenly realms,
>Ye damnéd ghosts, thou lord of hades' dark domain,
>Whose mistress was with trustier pledge won to thy
>   side—
>Before ye all this baleful prayer I bring: Be near!
>Be near! Ye crime-avenging furies, come and loose
>Your horrid locks with serpent coils entwined, and grasp
>With bloody hands the smoking torch; be near as once
>Ye stood in dread array beside my wedding couch.
>Upon this new-made bride destruction send, and death
>Upon the king and all the royal line! But he,
>My husband, may he live to meet some heavier doom;
>This curse I imprecate upon his head; may he,
>Through distant lands, in want, in exile wander, scorned
>And houseless. Nay, may he once more my favour woo;
>A stranger's threshold may he seek where now he walks

584

A well-known guest; and—this the blackest curse I
    know—
May children rise to him to emulate their sire,
Their mother's image bear.—Now won is vengeance,
    won!
For I have children borne.—Nay, nay, 'tis empty
    plaints
And useless words I frame. Shall I not rather rush
Against the foe and dash the torches from their hands,
The light from heaven? Does Father Phoebus suffer
    this?
Do men behold his face, as, seated in his car,
He rolls along th' accustomed track of sky serene?
Why does he not return to morning's gates, the law
Of heaven reversing? Grant that I be borne aloft
In my ancestral car! Give me the reins, O sire,
Thy fiery team grant me to guide with lines of flame.
Then Corinth, though with double shore delaying ships,
Herself consumed with fire, shall light two seas with
    flame.
But no, this course alone remains, that I myself
Should bear the wedding torch, with acquiescent
    prayers,
And slay the victims on the altars consecrate.
Thyself inspect the entrails, and seek there the way
By prayer, if still, O soul, thou livest, if there still
Remaineth aught of old-time strength in thee! Away
With woman's fears! Put on thy heart a breastplate
    hard
And chill as Caucasus! Then all the wizard arts
That Phasis knew, or Pontus, shall be seen again
In Corinth. Now with mad, unheard of, dreadful deeds,
Whereat high heaven and earth below shall pale and
    quake,
My pregnant soul is teeming; and my heart is full
Of pictured wounds and death and slaughter.—Ah, too
    long
On trifling ills I dwell. These were my virgin deeds.
Now that a mother's pains I've felt, my larger heart
Must larger crimes conceive. Then passion, gird thyself,
Put on thy strength, and for the issue now prepare!
Let my rejection pay as dread a fee as when,
Of old, through impious deeds of blood, I came to him.

Come, break through slow delay, and let the home once
     won
By crime, by equal deeds of crime be done away!

Act One.   Scene II

(Enter the CHORUS OF CORINTHIANS.*)*

CHORUS *(chanting the epithalamium for the nuptials of* JASON *and*
     CREUSA):

Now on our royal nuptials graciously smiling,
Here may the lords of heaven and the deeps of the ocean
Come while the people feast in pious rejoicing!

First to the gods who sway the sceptre of heaven,
Pealing forth their will in the voice of thunder,
Let the white bull his proud head bow in tribute.

Then to the fair Lucina, her gift we offer,
White as the driven snow, this beautiful heifer,
Still with her neck untouched by the yoke of bondage.

Thou who alone canst rule the heart of the war-god,
Thou who linkest in peace the opposing nations,
Out of thy generous hand abundance pouring—
Thee we offer a daintier gift, O Concord!

Thou[1] who, on the marriage torches attending,
Night's dark gloom with favouring hand dispellest,
Hither come with languishing footstep drunken,
Binding thy temples fair with garlands of roses!

Star of the evening, thou who to twilight leadest
The day, and hailest again the dawn of the morning,
All too slowly thou com'st for lovers impatient,
Eager to see thy sign in the glow of the sunset.

          The fairest of girls is she,
          The Athenian maids outshining,
     Or the Spartan maiden with armour laden,
          No burden of war declining.

          Not by Alpheus' sacred stream,
          Nor Boeotia's musical water,

Is there any fair who can compare
With our lovely Corinthian daughter.

Our Thessalian prince excels,
In beauty of form and face,
Even Bacchus, the son of the fierce-flaming one,
Who yokes the wild tigers in place.

The murmuring tripod's lord,
Though the fairest in heavenly story,
The twins with their star bright gleaming afar—
All yield to our Jason in glory.

When in her train of courtly maidens she mingles—
Like the bright sunshine paling the starry splendour,
Or the full moonlight quenching the Pleiads' brilliance,
So does she shine, all peerless, of fair ones the fairest.

Now, O Jason, freed from the hateful wedlock
That held thee bound to the barbarous Colchian woman,
Joyfully wed the fair Corinthian maiden,
While at last her parents' blessings attend thee.

Ho then, youths, with licensed jest and rejoicing,
Loud let the songs of gladness ring through the city;
Rarely against our lords such freedom is given.

Fair and noble band of Bacchus, the thyrsus-bearer,
Now is the time to light the glittering torches of pinewood.
Shake on high the festal fire with languishing fingers;

Now let the bold and merry Fescennine laughter and jesting[2]
Sound through our ranks. Let Medea fare in silence and darkness,
If perchance another lord she shall wed in her exile.

Act Two.   Scene I

(*Enter the* NURSE.)

MEDEA: We are undone! How harsh upon mine ears doth grate
The song! And even now I cannot comprehend
The vast extent of woe that hath befallen me.
Could Jason prove so false? Bereft of native land,
And home, and kingdom, could he leave me here alone

On foreign shores? Oh, cruel, could he quite reject
My sum of service, he who saw the fire and sea
With crime o'ercome for his dear sake? And does he
    think
That thus the fatal chapter can be ended? Wild,
Devoid of reason, sick of soul, my swift mind darts
In all directions seeking whence revenge may come!
I would he had a brother! But his wife—'gainst her
Be aimed the blow! Can thus my wrongs be satisfied?
Nay, nay—to meet my sum of woe must be heaped high
The crimes of Greece, of strange barbaric lands, and
    those
Which even thy hands have not known. Now lash thy
    soul
With memory's scourge, and call thy dark deeds in re-
    view:
The glory of thy father's kingdom reft away;[3]
Thy brother, guiltless comrade of thy guilty flight,
All hewn in pieces and his corpse strewn on the deep,
To break his royal father's heart; and, last of crimes,
Old Pelias by his daughters slain at thy command.
O impious one, what streams of blood have flowed to
    work
Thy ends! And yet, not one of all my crimes by wrath
Was prompted. Love, ill-omened love, suggested all.
Yet, what could Jason else have done, compelled to serve
Another's will, another's law? He should have died
Before he yielded to the tyrant's will. Nay, nay,
Thou raging passion, speak not so! For, if he may,
I would that Jason still may live and still be mine,
As once he was; if not, yet may he still live on,
And, mindful of my merits, live without my aid.
The guilt is Creon's all, who with unbridled power
Dissolves the marriage bond, my children separates
From me who bore them, yea, and makes the strongest
    pledge,
Though ratified with straightest oath, of none effect.
Let him alone sustain my wrath; let Creon pay
The debt of guilt he owes! His palace will I bring
To utter desolation; and the whirling fire
To far-off Malea's crags shall send its lurid glare.

NURSE: Be silent now, I pray thee, and thy plaints confine

To secret woe! The man who heavy blows can bear
In silence, biding still his time with patient soul,
Full oft his vengeance gains. 'Tis hidden wrath that
    harms;
But hate proclaimed oft loses half its power to harm.

MEDEA: But small the grief is that can counsel take and hide
Its head; great ills lie not in hiding, but must rush
Abroad and work their will.

NURSE: Oh, cease this mad complaint,
My mistress; scarce can friendly silence help thee now.

MEDEA: But fortune fears the brave, the faint of heart o'er-
    whelms.

NURSE: Then valour be approved, if for it still there's room.

MEDEA: But it must always be that valour finds its place.

NURSE: No star of hope points out the way from these our woes.

MEDEA: The man who hopes for naught at least has naught to
    fear.

NURSE: The Colchians are thy foes; thy husband's vows have
    failed;
Of all thy vast possessions not a jot is left.

MEDEA: Yet I am left. There's left both sea and land and fire
And sword and gods and hurtling thunderbolts.

NURSE: The king must be revered.

MEDEA: My father was a king.

NURSE: Dost thou not fear?

MEDEA: Not though the earth produced the foe.

NURSE: Thou'lt perish.

MEDEA: So I wish it.

NURSE: Flee!

MEDEA: I'm done with flight.

NURSE: Medea—

MEDEA: I shall be.

NURSE: Thy children!

MEDEA: Whose, thou know'st.

NURSE: And dost thou still delay?

MEDEA: I go, but vengeance first.

NURSE: Th' avenger will pursue.

MEDEA: Perchance I'll stop his course.

NURSE: Nay, hold thy words, and cease thy threats, O foolish
              one.
              Thy temper curb; 'tis well to yield to fate's decrees.

MEDEA: Though fate may strip me of my all, myself am left.
              But who flings wide the royal palace doors? Behold,
              'Tis Creon's self, exalted high in Grecian sway.
              (*The* NURSE *goes into the house.*)

Act Two.   Scene II

(*Enter* CREON.)

CREON (*to himself*): Medea, baleful daughter of the Colchian king,
              Has she not taken her hateful presence from our realm?
              On mischief is she bent. Well known her treach'rous
              power.
              For who escapes her? Who may pass his days in peace?
              This cursèd pestilence at once would I have stayed
              By force of arms; but Jason's prayers prevailed. She
              still
              May live, but let her free my borders from the fear
              Her presence genders, and her safety gain by flight.
              (*He sees* MEDEA *approaching*)
              But lo, she comes, with fierce and threatening mien, to
              seek
              An audience with us.
                   (*To attendants*)
                              Slaves defend us from her touch
              And pestilential presence! Bid her silence keep,
              And learn to yield obedience to the king's commands.
                   (*To* MEDEA)
              Go, speed thy flight, thou thing of evil, fell, and mon-
              strous!

MEDEA: But tell me what the crime, my lord, or what the guilt
          That merits exile?

CREON: Let the guiltless question thus.

MEDEA: If now thou judgest, hear me; if thou reign'st, com-
          mand.

CREON: The king's command thou must abide, nor question
          aught.

MEDEA: Unrighteous sovereignty has never long endured.

CREON: Go hence, and to the Colchians complain.

MEDEA: I go,
          But let him take me hence who brought me to thy shores.

CREON: Thy prayer has come too late, for fixed is my decree.

MEDEA: Who judges, and denies his ear to either side,
          Though right his judgment, still is he himself unjust.

CREON: Didst lend thine ear to Pelias, ere thou judgedst him?
          But come, I'll give thee grace to plead thy goodly cause.

MEDEA: How hard the task to turn the soul from wrath, when
          once
          To wrath inclined; how 'tis the creed of sceptred kings
          To swerve not from the purposed course they once have
          taken,
          Full well I know, for I have tasted royalty.
          For, though by present storms of ill I'm overwhelmed,
          An exile, suppliant, lone, forsaken, all forlorn,
          I once in happier times a royal princess shone,
          And traced my proud descent from heavenly Phoebus'
          self.
          My father's realm extended wide o'er all the land
          Where Phasis' gentle waters flow, o'er Scythia's plains
          Whose rivers sweeten Pontus' briny waves; where, too,
          Thermodon's banks enclose the race of warlike maids,
          Whose gleaming shields strike terror to their foes. All
          this
          My father held in sway. And I, of noble birth,
          And blessed of heaven, in royal state was high upraised.
          Then princes humbly sought my hand in wedlock, mine,
          Who now must sue. O changeful fortune, thou my throne

Hast reft away, and given me exile in its stead.
Trust not in kingly realms, since fickle chance may
     strew
Their treasures to the winds. Lo, this is regal, this
The work of kings, which time nor change cannot undo:
To succour the afflicted, to provide at need
A trusty refuge for the suppliant. This alone
I brought of all my Colchian treasure, this renown,
This very flower of fame, that by my arts I saved
The bulwark of the Greeks, the offspring of the gods.
My princely gift to Greece is Orpheus, that sweet bard
Who can the trees in willing bondage draw, and melt
The crag's hard heart. Mine too are Boreas' wingéd
     sons,[4]
And Leda's heaven-born progeny,[5] and Lynceus, he,
Whose glance can pierce the distant view—yea, all the
     Greeks,
Save Jason; for I mention not the king of kings,
The leader of the leaders; he is mine alone,
My labour's recompense; the rest I give to you.
Nay, come, O king, arraign me, and rehearse my crimes.
But stay! I shall confess them all. The only crime
Of which I stand accused is this—the Argo saved.
Suppose my maiden scruples had opposed the deed;
Suppose my filial piety had stayed my hand:
Then had the mighty chieftains fall'n, and in their fate
All Greece had been o'erwhelmed; then this, thy son-
     in-law,
Had felt the bull's consuming breath, and perished there.
Nay, nay, let fortune, when she will, my doom decree;
I glory still that kings have owed their lives to me.
But what reward I reap for all my glorious deeds
Is in thy hands. Convict me, if thou wilt, of sin,
But give him back for whom I sinned. O Creon, see,
I own that I am guilty. This much thou didst know,
When first I clasped thy knees, a humble suppliant,
And sought the shelter of thy royal clemency.
Some little corner of thy kingdom now I ask,
In which to hide my grief. If I must flee again,
Oh, let some nook remote within thy broad domain
Be found for me!

CREON: That I my power in mercy wield,

And spurn not those who seek my aid, let Jason's self
My witness be, who, exiled, overwhelmed by fate,
And smitten sore with fear, a refuge found with me.
For lo, Thessalia's monarch,[6] bent on vengeance dire,
Seeks Jason at my hand. The cause, indeed, is just:
For that his sire, o'erburdened with the weight of years,
Was foully taken off, while by thy wicked guile
His guileless sisters' hands were nerved to do the deed.
If now our Jason can unlink his cause from thine,
'Tis easy his defence to make, for on his hands
No stain of blood is found. His arm no sword upraised,
And he has had no part nor lot in this thy crime.
No, thou and thou alone the arch contriver art,
Uniting in thy person woman's fertile wit
And man's effective strength; while in thy reckless heart
No thought of reputation dwells to check thy hand.
Then go thou hence and purge our kingdom of its stain;
Bear hence thy deadly poisons; free the citizens
From fear; abiding in some other land than this,
Outwear the patience of the gods.

MEDEA: Thou bid'st me flee?
Then give me back my bark wherein to flee. Restore
The partner of my flight! Why should I flee alone?
I came not thus. Or if avenging war thou fear'st,
Then banish both the culprits; why distinguish me
From Jason? 'Twas for him old Pelias was o'ercome;
For him the flight, the plunder of my father's realm,
My sire forsaken and my infant brother slain,
And all the guilt that love suggests; 'twas all for him.
Deep dyed in sin am I, but on my guilty soul
The sin of profit lieth not.

CREON: Why seek delay
By speech? Too long thou tarriest.

MEDEA: I go, but grant
This last request: let not the mother's fall o'erwhelm
Her hapless babes.

CREON: Then go in peace. For I to them
A father's place will fill, and take them to my heart.

MEDEA: Now by the fair hopes born upon this wedding day,
And by thy hopes of lasting sovereignty secure

From changeful fate's assault, I pray thee grant from
    flight
A respite brief, while I upon my children's lips
A mother's kiss imprint, perchance the last.

CREON:
                              A time
Thou seek'st for treachery.

MEDEA:
                    What fraud can be devised
In one short hour?

CREON:
                To those on mischief bent, be sure,
The briefest time is fraught with mischief's fatal power.

MEDEA: Dost thou refuse me, then, one little space for tears?

CREON: Though deep-ingrafted fear would fain resist thy plea,
A single day I'll give thee ere my sentence holds.

MEDEA: Too gracious thou. But let my respite further shrink,
And I'll depart content.

CREON:
                    Thy life shall surely pay
The forfeit if tomorrow's sun beholds thee still
In Corinth. But the voice of Hymen calls away
To solemnise the rites of this his festal day.
(CREON *departs.* MEDEA *goes into her house.*)

Act Two.   Scene III

CHORUS:
    Too bold the man who first upon the seas,
The treacherous seas, his fragile bark confided;
Who, as the well-known shore behind him glided,
    His life intrusted to the fickle breeze;

    And, as his unknown seaward course he sped
Within his slender craft with foolish daring,
Midway 'twixt life and death went onward faring,
    Along the perilous narrow margin led.

    Not yet were sparkling constellations known,
Or sky, all spangled with the starry glory;
Not yet could sailors read the warning story
    By stormy Hyades upon the heavens thrown.

Not yet was Zeus's foster-mother famed,
Nor slow Bootes round the north star wheeling;
Nor Boreas nor Zephyr gently stealing,
    Each feared or welcomed, though as yet un·
      named.

    First Tiphys dared to spread his venturous
      sail,
The hidden lesson of the breezes learning,
Now all his canvas to the Zephyrs turning,
    Now shifting all to catch the changing gale.

Now midway on the mast the yard remains,
Now at the head with all its canvas drawing,
While eager sailors lure the breezes blowing,
    And over all the gleaming topsail strains.

The guiltless golden age our fathers saw,
When youth and age the same horizon bounded;
No greed of gain their simple hearts confounded;
    Their native wealth enough, 'twas all they
      knew.

    But lo, the severed worlds have been brought
      near
And linked in one by Argo's hand uniting;
While seas endure the oar's unwonted smiting,
    And add their fury to the primal fear.

This impious bark its guilt in dread atoned
When clashing mountains were together driven,
And sea from sea in mighty conflict riven,
    The stars besprinkled with the leaping foam.

Amid these perils sturdy Tiphys paled,
And from his nerveless hand the vessel bounded;
While stricken Orpheus' lyre no more resounded,
    And tuneful Argo's warning message failed.

What sinking terror filled each quaking breast,
When near the borders of sea-girt Pelorus,
There smote upon their ears the horrid chorus
    Of Scylla's baying wolves around them pressed.

What terror when they neared the Sirens' lair,
Who soothe the troubled waves with witching meas-
    ures!

But Orpheus filled their souls with nobler pleasures,
And left the foe in impotent despair.

And of this wild adventure what the prize,
That lured the daring bark with heroes laden?
The fleece of gold, and this mad Colchian maiden,
Well fit to be the first ship's merchandise.

The sea, subdued, the victor's law obeys;
No vessel needs a goddess' art in framing,
Nor oars in heroes' hands, the ocean taming:
The frailest craft now dares the roughest waves.

Now, every bound removed, new cities rise
In lands remote, their ancient walls removing;
While men of Ind by Caspian shores are roving,
And Persia's face now greets the western skies.

The time will come, as lapsing ages flee,
When every land shall yield its hidden treasure;
When men no more shall unknown courses measure,
For round the world no "farthest land" shall
be.

Act Three.   Scene I

(MEDEA *is rushing out to seek vengeance, while the* NURSE *tries in vain to restrain her.*)

NURSE: My foster-daughter, whither speedest thou abroad?
                Oh, stay, I pray thee, and restrain thy passion's force.
(MEDEA *hastens by without answering. The* NURSE *soliloquises*)
                As some wild Bacchanal, whose fury's raging fire
                The god inflames, now roams distraught on Pindus'
                  snows,
                And now on lofty Nysa's rugged slopes; so she,
                Now here, now there, with frenzied step is hurried on,
                Her face revealing every mark of stricken woe,
                With flushing cheek and sighs deep drawn, wild cries,
                  and tears,
                And laughter worse than tears. In her a medley strange
                Of every passion may be seen: o'ertopping wrath,
                Bewailings, bitter groans of anguish. Whither tends

This overburdened soul? What mean her frenzied
    threats?
When will the foaming wave of fury spend itself?
No common crime, I fear, no easy deed of ill
She meditates. Herself she will outvie. For well
' I recognise the wonted marks of rage. Some deed
Is threatening, wild, profane, and hideous.
        (*Re-enter* MEDEA)

                       Behold
Her face betrays her madness. O ye gods, may these
Our fears prove vain forebodings!

MEDEA (*not noticing the* NURSE's *presence*): For thy hate, poor soul,
Dost thou a measure seek? Let it be deep as love.
And shall I tamely view the wedding torches' glare?
And shall this day go uneventful by, this day,
So hardly won, so grudgingly bestowed? Nay, nay,
While, poised upon her heights, the central earth shall
    bear
The heavens up; while seasons run their endless round,
And sands unnumbered lie; while days, and nights, and
    sun,
And stars in due procession pass; while round the pole
The ocean-fearing bears revolve, and tumbling streams
Flow downward to the sea; my grief shall never cease
To seek revenge, and shall forever grow. What rage
Of savage beast can equal mine? What Scylla famed?
What sea-engulfing pool? What burning Aetna placed
On impious Titan's heaving breast? No torrent stream,
Nor storm-tossed sea, nor breath of flame fanned by the
    gale,
Can check or equal my wild storm of rage. My will
Is set on limitless revenge!

              Will Jason say
He feared the power of Creon and Acastus' threats?
True love is proof against the fear of man. But grant
He was compelled to yield, and pledged his hand in fear:
He might at least have sought his wife with one last
    word
Of comfort and farewell. But this, though brave in heart,
He feared to do. The cruel terms of banishment
Could Creon's son-in-law not soften? No. One day
Alone was giv'n for last farewell to both my babes.

But time's short space I'll not bewail; though brief in
    hours,
In consequence it stretches out eternally.
This day shall see a deed that ne'er shall be forgot.
But now I'll go and pray the gods, and move high
    heaven
But I shall work my will!

NURSE:
                           Thy heart all passion-tossed,
I pray thee, mistress, soothe, and calm thy troubled
    soul.

MEDEA:
My troubled soul can never know a time of rest
Until it sees all things o'erwhelmed in common doom.
All must go down with me! 'Tis sweet such death to die.

NURSE:
Oh, think what perils thou must meet if thou persist!
No one with safety may defy a sceptred king.

Act Three.   Scene II

(Enter JASON.*)*

JASON:
O heartless fate, if frowns or smiles bedeck thy brow,
How often are thy cures far worse than the disease
They seek to cure! If, now, I wish to keep the troth
I plighted to my lawful bride, my life must pay
The forfeit; if I shrink from death, my guilty soul
Must perjured be. I fear no power that man can wield;
But in my heart paternal love unmans me quite;
For well I know that in my death my children's fate
Is sealed. O sacred Justice, if in heaven thou dwell'st,
Be witness now, that for my children's sake I act.
Nay, sure am I that even she, Medea's self,
Though fierce she is of soul and brooking no restraint,
Will see her children's good outweighing all her wrongs.
With this good argument my purpose now is fixed,
In humble wise to brave her wrath.
                          At sight of me
Her raging fury flames anew! Hate, like a shield,
She bears, and in her face is pictured all her woe.

MEDEA: Thou see'st, Jason, that we flee. 'Tis no new thing
           To suffer exile, but the cause of flight is strange;
           For with thee I was wont to flee, not from thee. Yes,
           I go. But whither dost thou send me whom thou driv'st
           From out thy home? Shall I the Colchians seek again,
           My royal father's realm, whose soil is steeped in blood
           My brother shed? What country dost thou bid me seek?
           What way by sea is open? Shall I fare again
           Where once I saved the noble kings of Greece, and thee,
           Thou wanton, through the threatening jaws of Pontus'
               strait,
           The blue Symplegades? Or shall I hie me back
           To fair Thessalia's realms? Lo, all the doors which I,
           For thee, have opened wide, I've closed upon myself.
           But whither dost thou send me now? Thou bid'st me
               flee,
           But show'st no way or means of flight.
                                              But 'tis enough!
           The king's own son-in-law commands and I obey.
           Come, heap thy torments on me; I deserve them all.
           Let royal wrath oppress me, wanton that I am,
           With cruel hand, and load my guilty limbs with chains;
           And let me be immured in dungeons black as night:
           Still will my punishment be less than my offence.
           O ingrate! Hast thou then forgot the brazen bull,
           And his consuming breath? The fear that smote thee,
               when,
           Upon the field of Mars, the earth-born brood stood forth
           To meet thy single sword? 'Twas by my arts that they,
           The monsters, fell by mutual blows. Remember, too,
           The long-sought fleece of gold I won for thee, whose
               guard,
           The dragon huge, was lulled to rest at my command;
           My brother slain for thee. For thee old Pelias fell,
           When, taken by my guile, his daughters slew their sire,
           Whose life could not return. All this I did for thee.
           In quest of thine advantage have I quite forgot
           Mine own.
                        And now, by all thy fond paternal hopes,
           By thine established house, by all the monsters slain
           For thee, by these my hands which I have ever held
           To work thy will, by all the perils past, by heaven
           And sea that witnessed at my wedlock, pity me!

Since thou art blessed, restore me what I lost for thee:
That countless treasure plundered from the swarthy
    tribes
Of India, which filled our goodly vaults with wealth,
And decked our very trees with gold. This costly store
I left for thee, my native land, my brother, sire,
My reputation—all; and with this dower I came.
If now to homeless exile thou dost send me forth,
Give back the countless treasures which I left for thee.

JASON: Though Creon in a vengeful mood would have thy life,
I moved him by my tears to grant thee flight instead.

MEDEA: I thought my exile punishment; 'tis now, I see,
A gracious boon!

JASON: Oh, flee while still the respite holds;
Provoke him not, for deadly is the wrath of kings.

MEDEA: Not so. 'Tis for Creusa's love thou sayest this;
Thou wouldst remove the hated wanton once thy wife.

JASON: Dost thou reproach me with a guilty love?

MEDEA: Yea, that,
And murder too, and treachery.

JASON: But name me now,
If so thou canst, the crimes that I have done.

MEDEA: Thy crimes—
Whatever I have done.

JASON: Why then, in truth, thy guilt
Must all be mine, if all thy crimes are mine.

MEDEA: They are,
They are all thine; for who by sin advantage gains,
Commits the sin. All men proclaim thy wife defiled.
Do thou thyself protect her, and condone her sin.
Let her be guiltless in thine eyes who for thy gain
Has sinned.

JASON: But life which sin has bought 'twere shame to take.

MEDEA: Why keep'st thou then the life which it were shame to
    take?

JASON: Nay, curb thy fiery soul! Thy children—for their sake
Be calm.

MEDEA: My children! Them I do refuse, reject,
Renounce! Shall then Creusa brothers bear to these
My children?

JASON: But the queen can aid thy wretched sons.

MEDEA: May that day never dawn, that day of shame and woe,
When in one house are joined the low born and the high,
The sons of that foul robber Sisyphus, and these,
The sons of Phoebus.

JASON: Wretched one, and wilt thou then
Involve me also in thy fall? Begone, I pray.

MEDEA: Creon hath heard my prayer.

JASON: What wouldst thou have me do?

MEDEA: For me? I'd have thee dare the law.

JASON: The royal power
Doth compass me.

MEDEA: A greater than the king is here:
Medea. Set us front to front and let us strive;
And of this royal strife let Jason be the prize.

JASON: O'erwearied by my woes I yield. But be thou ware,
Medea, lest too often thou shouldst tempt thy fate.

MEDEA: Yet fortune's mistress have I ever been.

JASON: But see,
With hostile front Acastus comes, on vengeance bent,
While Creon threatens instant death.

MEDEA: Then flee them both.
I ask thee not to draw thy sword against the king
Nor yet to stain thy pious hands with kindred blood.
Come, flee with me.

JASON: But what resistance can we make,
If war with double visage rear his horrid front,
If Creon and Acastus join in common cause?

MEDEA: Add, too, the Colchian armies with my father's self
To lead them; join the Scythian and Pelasgian hordes:
In one deep gulf of ruin will I whelm them all.

JASON: Yet on the sceptre do I look with fear.

MEDEA: Beware,
Lest not the fear, but lust of power prevail with thee.

JASON: Too long we strive; have done, lest we suspicion breed.

MEDEA: Now Jove, throughout thy heavens let the thunders roll!
Thy mighty arm in wrath make bare! Thy darting
     flames
Of vengeance loose, and shake the lofty firmament
With rending storms! At random hurl thy vengeful bolts,
Selecting neither me nor Jason with thy aim;
That thus whoever falls may perish with the brand
Of guilt upon him; for thy hurtling darts can take
No erring flight.

JASON: Recall thee and in calmness speak
With words of peace and reason. Then if any gift
From Creon's royal house can compensate thy woes,
Take that as solace of thy flight.

MEDEA: My soul doth scorn
The wealth of kings. But let me have my little ones
As comrades of my flight, that in their childish breasts
Their mother's tears may flow. New sons await thy
     home.

JASON: My heart inclines to yield to thee, but love forbids.
For these my sons shall never from my arms be reft,
Though Creon's self demand. My very spring of life,
My sore heart's comfort, and my joy are these my sons;
And sooner could I part with limbs or vital breath,
Or light of life.

MEDEA (*aside*):   Doth he thus love his sons? 'Tis well;
Then is he bound, and in his armoured strength this flaw
Reveals the place to strike.
                    (*To* JASON)
                              At least, ere I depart,
Grant me this last request: let me once more embrace

My sons. E'en that small boon will comfort my sad
　　heart.
And this my latest prayer to thee: if, in my grief,
My tongue was over bold, let not my words remain
To rankle in thy heart. Remember happier things
Of me, and let my bitter words be straight forgot.

JASON: 　　Not one shall linger in my soul; and curb, I pray,
Thy too impetuous heart, and gently yield to fate.
For resignation ever soothes the woeful soul.
　　　　　(JASON *departs*.)

MEDEA (*to herself*): He's gone! And can it be? And shall he thus depart,
Forgetting me and all my service? Must I drop,
Like some discarded toy, out of his faithless heart?
It shall not be. Up then, and summon all thy strength
And all thy skill! And, this the fruit of former crime,
Count nothing criminal that works thy will. But lo,
We're hedged about; scant room is left for our designs.
Now must the attack be made where least suspicion
　　wakes
The least resistance. Now Medea, on! And do
And dare thine utmost, yea, beyond thine utmost power!
　　　　　(*To the* NURSE)
Do thou, my faithful nurse, the comrade of my grief,
And all the devious wanderings of my checkered course,
Assist me now in these my plans. There is a robe,
The glory of our Colchian realm, the precious gift
Of Phoebus' self to king Aeetes as a proof
Of fatherhood; a gleaming circlet, too, all wrought
With threads of gold, the yellow gold bespangled o'er
With gems, a fitting crown to deck a princess' head.
These treasures let Medea's children bear as gifts
To Jason's bride. But first infuse them with the power
Of magic, and invoke the aid of Hecate;
The woe-producing sacrifices then prepare,
And let the sacred flames through all our courts resound.
　(MEDEA *and the* NURSE *go into the house*.)

Act Three.   Scene III

CHORUS:

No force of flame or raging gale,
Or whizzing bolt so fearful is,
As when a wife, by her lord betrayed,
    Burns hot with hate.

Not such a force is Auster's blast,
When he marshals forth the wintry storms;
Nor Hister's headlong rushing stream,
Which, wrecking bridges in its course,
    Pours reckless on;

Nor yet the Rhone, whose current strong
Beats back the sea; nor when the snows,
Beneath the lengthening days of spring
And the sun's warm rays, melt down in streams
    From Haemus' top.

Blind is the rage of passion's fire,
Will not be governed, brooks no reins,
And scoffs at death; nay, hostile swords
    It gladly courts.

Spare, O ye gods, be merciful,
That he[7] who tamed the sea may live.
But much we fear, for the lord of the deep
Is wroth that his realm of the second lot
    Should be subdued.

The thoughtless youth[8] who dared to drive
His father's sacred chariot,
Was by those fires, which o'er the heavens
He scattered in his mad career,
    Himself consumed.

The beaten path has never proved
The way of danger. Walk ye then
Where your forefathers safely trod,
And keep great nature's holy laws
    Inviolate.

Whoever dipped the famous oars
Of that bold bark in the rushing sea;
Whoe'er despoiled old Pelion

Of the thick, dark shade of his sacred groves;
Whoever dared the clashing rocks,
And, after countless perils passed,
His vessel moored on a barbarous shore,
Hoping to fare on his homeward way
The master of the golden fleece,
All by a fearful end appeased
    The offended sea.

First Tiphys, tamer of the deep,
Abandoned to an untrained hand
His vessel's helm. On a foreign shore,
Far from his native land he died;
And now within a common tomb,
'Midst unknown ghosts, he lies at rest.
In wrathful memory of her king
Lost on the sea, did Aulis then
Within her sluggish harbour hold
    The impatient ships.

Then he, the tuneful Muse's son,[9]
At whose sweet strains the streams stood still
The winds were silent, and the birds,
Their songs forgotten, flocked to him,
The whole wood following after—he,
Over the Thracian fields was hurled
In scattered fragments; but his head
Down Hebrus' grieving stream was borne.
The well-remembered Styx he reached,
And Tartarus, whence ne'er again
    Would he return.

The wingéd sons of Boreas[4]
Alcides slew, and Neptune's son[10]
Who in a thousand changing forms
Could clothe himself. But after peace
On land and sea had been proclaimed,
And after savage Pluto's realm
Had been revealed to mortal eyes,
Then did Alcides' self,[11] alive,
On burning Oeta's top lie down,
And give his body to the flames;
For sore distressed was he, consumed

By Deïanira's deadly gift,
   The double blood.

A savage boar Ancaeus slew;
Thou, Meleager, impiously
Thy mother's brother in wrath didst slay,
And by that angry mother's hand
Didst die. All these deserved their death.
But for what crime did Hylas die,
A tender lad whom Hercules
Long time but vainly sought? For he,
'Mid waters safe was done to death.
Go then, and fearlessly the deep
Plow with your daring ships; but fear
   The peaceful pools.

Idmon, though well he knew the fates,
A serpent slew on Afric sands;
And Mopsus, to all others true,
False to himself, died far from Thebes.
If he with truth the future sang,
Then Nauplius, who strove to wreck
The Argive ships by lying fires,
Shall headlong fall into the sea.
And for his father's daring crime
Shall Ajax, that Oileus' son,
Make full atonement, perishing
   'Midst flame and flood.

And thou, Admetus' faithful mate,
Shalt for thy husband pay thy life,
Redeeming his from death. But he,
Who bade the first ship sail in quest
Of the golden spoil, King Pelias,
Seethed in a boiling cauldron, swam
'Mid those restricted waves. Enough,
O gods, have ye avenged the sea;
Spare him, we pray, who did but go
   On ordered ways.

Act Four.   Scene I

(Enter the NURSE.*)*

NURSE *(alone)*: My spirit trembles, for I feel the near approach
Of some unseen disaster. Swiftly grows her grief,
Its own fires kindling; and again her passion's force
Hath leaped to life. I oft have seen her, with the fit
Of inspiration in her soul, confront the gods
And force the very heavens to her will. But now,
A monstrous deed, of greater moment far than these,
Medea is preparing. For, but now, did she
With step of frenzy hurry off until she reached
Her stricken home. There, in her chamber, all her stores
Of magic wonders are revealed; once more she views
The things herself hath held in fear these many years,
Unloosing one by one her ministers of ill,
Occult, unspeakable, and wrapt in mystery;
And, grasping with her hand the sacred altar-horn,
With prayers, she straightly summons all destructive
          powers,
The creatures bred in Libya's sands, and on the peaks
Of frigid Taurus, clad in everlasting snows.
Obedient to her potent charms, the scaly brood
Of serpents leave their darksome lairs and swarm to her;
One savage creature rolls his monstrous length along,
And darts his forkéd tongue with its unvenomed sting,
Death-dealing; at the charming sound he stops amazed,
And fold on fold his body writhes in nerveless coils.
"But these are petty ills; unworthy of my hand,"
She cries, "are such weak, earth-born weapons. Potent
          charms
Are bred in heaven. Now, now 'tis time to summon
          powers
Transcending common magic. Down I'll draw from
          heaven
That serpent huge whose body lies athwart the sky
Like some great ocean stream, in whose constricting
          folds
The greater and the lesser Bears are held enthralled,
The greater set as guide for Grecian ships, the less
For Sidon's mariners! Let Ophiuchus loose

His hand and pour forth venom from his captive thrall!
And let the Python huge, that dared to rear its head
Against the heavenly twins, be present at my prayer!
Let Hydra's writhing heads, which by Alcides' hand
Were severed, all return to life and give me aid!
Thou too be near and leave thy ancient Colchian home,
Thou watchful dragon, to whose eyes the first sleep
    came
In answer to my incantations."
                                   When she thus
Had summoned all the serpent brood, she cast her store
Of baleful herbs together; all the poisons brewed
Amid the rocky caves of trackless Eryx; plants
That flourish on the snowy peaks of Caucasus,
Whose crags were spattered with Prometheus' gore; the
    herbs
Within whose deadly juice the Arab dips his darts,
And the quiver-bearing Mede and fleeing Parthian;
Those potent juices, too; which, near the shivering pole,
The Suabian chieftains gather in Hyrcanian groves.
The seasons, too, have paid their tribute to her stores:
Whatever earth produces in the nesting time,
And when the stiff'ning hand of winter's frost has
    stripped
The glory from the trees and fettered all the land
With icy bonds; whatever flow'ring plant conceals
Destruction in its bloom, or in its twisted roots
Distils the juice of death, she gathers to her use.
These pestilential herbs Haemonian Athos gave;
And these on lofty Pindus grew; a bloody knife
Clipped off these slender leaves on Macedonia's heights;
Still others grew beside the Tigris, whirling on
His flood to meet the sea; the Danube nourished some;
These grew on bright gem-starred Hydaspes' tepid
    stream;
And these the Baetis bore, which gave the land its name,
Displacing with its languorous tide, the western sea.
These felt the knife when early dawn begins to break;
The fruit of these was cut in midnight's gloomy hour;
This fatal crop was reaped with sickle magic-edged.
These deadly, potent herbs she takes and sprinkles o'er
With serpent venom, mixing all; and in the broth
She mingles unclean birds: a wailing screech owl's heart,

A ghastly vampire's vitals torn from living flesh.
Her magic poisons all she ranges for her use.
The ravening power of hidden fire is held in these,
While deep in others lurks the numbing chill of frost.
Now magic runes she adds more potent far.
                                              But lo!
Her voice resounds! And, as with maddened step she
     comes,
She chants her charms, while heaven and earth convul-
     sive rock.

Act Four.   Scene II

(Enter MEDEA, *chanting her incantations.)*

MEDEA: I supplicate the silent throng, and you, the gods
                Of death's sad rites, and groping chaos, and the home
                Of gloomy Pluto, and the black abyss of death
                Girt by the banks of Tartarus! Ye storied shades,
                Your torments leave and haste to grace the festival
                At Hymen's call! Let stop the whirling wheel that holds
                Ixion's limbs and let him tread Corinthian ground;
                Let Tantalus unfrighted drink Pirene's stream.
                On Creon's stock alone let heavier torments fall,
                And backward o'er the rocks let Sisyphus be hurled.
                You too, the seed of Danaus, whose fruitless toil
                The ever-empty urns deride, I summon you;
                This day requires your helping hands. Thou radiant
                     moon,
                Night's glorious orb, my supplications hear and come
                To aid; put on thy sternest guise, thou goddess dread
                Of triple form![12] Full oft have I with flowing locks,
                And feet unsandaled, wandered through thy darkling
                     groves
                And by thy inspiration summoned forth the rain
                From cloudless skies; the heaving seas have I subdued,
                And sent the vanquished waves to ocean's lowest depths.
                At my command the sun and stars together shine,
                The heavenly law reversed; while in the Arctic sea
                The Bears have plunged. The seasons, too, obey my will:
                I've made the burning summer blossom as the spring,

And hoary winter autumn's golden harvests bear.
The Phasis sends his swirling waves to seek their source,
And Ister, flowing to the sea with many mouths,
His eager water checks and sluggish rolls along.
The billows roar, the mad sea rages, though the winds
All silent lie. At my command primeval groves
Have lost their shade; the sun, abandoning the day,
Has stood in middle heaven; while falling Hyades
Attest my charms.

     But now thy sacred hour is come,
O Phoebe. Thine these bonds with bloody hand entwined
With ninefold serpent coils; these cords I offer thee,
Which on his hybrid limbs Typhoeus bore, who shook
The throne of Jove. This vessel holds the dying blood
Of Nessus, faithless porter of Alcides' bride.
Here are the ashes of the pyre on Oeta's top
Which drank the poisoned blood of dying Hercules;
And here the fatal billet that Althaea burned
In vengeance on her son. These plumes the Harpies left
Within their caverned lair when Zetes drove them forth;
And these the feathers of that vile Stymphalian bird
Which arrows, dipped in Lerna's deadly poison, pierced.

  But lo! Mine altar fires resound!
While in the tripod's answering voice
Behold the present deity!
I see the car of Trivia,
Not full and clear as when she drives
The livelong night to meet the dawn;
But with a baleful, lurid glare,
As, harried by Thessalian cries,
She holds a more restricted course.
Send such uncanny light abroad!
Fill mortals with a dread unknown;
And let our Corinth's priceless bronze
Resound, Dictynna, for thy aid!
To thee a solemn sacrifice
On bloody altar do we pay!
To thee, snatched from the mournful tomb,
The blazing torch nocturnal burns;
On thee I call with tossing head,
And many a frantic gesture make;
Corpselike upon the bier I lie,
My hair with priestly fillet bound;

Before thy awful shrine is waved
The branch in Stygian waters dipped.
And, calling on thy name, with gleaming shoulders
    bared,
Like Bacchus' mad adorers, will I lash my arms
With sacrificial knife. Now let my lifeblood flow!
And let my hands be used to draw the deadly sword,
And learn to shed belovéd blood!

(She cuts her arm and lets the blood flow upon the altar)

Behold, self-stricken have I poured the sacrifice!
    But if too oft upon thy name I call,
      I pray forgive this importunity!
    The cause, O Hecate, of all my prayers
    Is ever Jason; this my constant care.
          (To attendants)
Take now Creusa's bridal robe, and steep in these,
My potent drugs; and when she dons the clinging folds,
Let subtle flames go stealing through her inmost heart.
The fire that in this tawny golden circlet lurks
Prometheus gave, who, for his daring heavenly theft
In human aid, endured an ever-living death.
'Twas Vulcan showed the fires concealed in sulphur's
    veins;
While from my brother Phaethon I gained a flame
That never dies; I have preserved Chimera's breath,
And that fierce heat that parched the fiery, brazen bull
Of Colchis. These dread fires commingled with the gall
Of dire Medusa have I bidden keep the power
    Of lurking evil. Now, O Hecate,
    Give added force to these my deadly gifts.
    And strictly guard the hidden seeds of flame.
    Let them deceive the sight, endure the touch;
    But through her veins let burning fever run;
    In fervent heat consume her very bones,
    And let her fiercely blazing locks outshine
    Her marriage torches! Lo, my prayer is heard:
    Thrice have replied the hounds of Hecate,
    And she has shown her baleful, gleaming fires.
    Now all is ready: hither call my sons,
    And let them bear these presents to the bride.
          (Enter the sons)
Go, go, my sons, of hapless mother born,
And win with costly gifts and many prayers

The favour of the queen, your father's wife.
Begone, but quick your homeward way retrace,
That I may fold you in a last embrace.
(*The sons depart towards the palace,* MEDEA *in the opposite direction.*)

Act Four.   Scene III

CHORUS: Where hastes this Bacchic fury now,
All passion-swept? What evil deed
Does her unbridled rage prepare?
Her features are congealed with rage,
And with a queenly bearing, grand
But terrible, she sets herself
Against e'en Creon's royal power.
An exile who would deem her now?
Her cheeks anon with anger flush,
And now a deadly pallor show;
Each feeling quick succeeds to each,
While all the passions of her heart
Her changing aspect testifies.
She wanders restless here and there,
As a tigress, of her young bereft,
In frantic grief the jungle scours.
Medea knows not how in check
To hold her wrath nor yet her love;
If love and wrath make common cause,
What dire results will come?
When will this scourge of Corinth leave
Our Grecian shores for Colchis' strand,
And free our kingdom from its fear?
Now, Phoebus, hasten on thy course
With no retarding rein.
Let friendly darkness quickly veil the light,
And this dread day be buried deep in night.

Act Five.   Scene I

(*Enter* MESSENGER, *running in from the direction of the palace.*)

MESSENGER: Lo, all is lost! The kingdom totters from its base!
The daughter and the father lie in common dust!

CHORUS: By what snare taken?

MESSENGER: By gifts, the common snare of kings.

CHORUS: What harm could lurk in them?

MESSENGER: In equal doubt I stand;
                 And, though my eyes proclaim the dreadful deed is done,
                 I scarce can trust their witness.

CHORUS: What the mode of death?

MESSENGER: Devouring flames consume the palace at the will
                 Of her who sent them; there complete destruction reigns,
                 While men do tremble for the very city's doom.

CHORUS: Let water quench the fire.

MESSENGER: Nay here is added wonder:
                 The copious streams of water feed the deadly flames;
                 And opposition only fans their fiery rage
                 To whiter heat. The very bulwarks feel their power.

(*Enter* MEDEA *in time to hear that her magic has been successful.*)

NURSE (*to* MEDEA): Oh, haste thee, leave this land of Greece, in head-
                 long flight!

MEDEA: Thou bid'st me speed my flight? Nay rather, had I fled,
                 I should return for this. Strange bridal rites I see!
                 (*Absorbed in her own reflections*)
                 Why dost thou falter, O my soul? 'Tis well begun;
                 But still how small a portion of thy just revenge
                 Is that which gives thee present joy? Not yet has love
                 Been banished from thy maddened heart if 'tis enough
                 That Jason widowed be. Pursue thy vengeful quest
                 To acts as yet unknown, and steel thyself for these.
                 Away with every thought and fear of God and man;
                 Too lightly falls the rod that pious hands upbear.
                 Give passion fullest sway; exhaust thy ancient powers;
                 And let the worst thou yet hast done be innocent
                 Beside thy present deeds. Come, let them know how
                     slight
                 Were those thy crimes already done; mere training they
                 For greater deeds. For what could hands untrained in
                     crime
                 Accomplish? Or what mattered maiden rage? But now,

I am Medea; in the bitter school of woe
My powers have ripened.

(*In an ecstacy of madness*)

Oh, the bliss of memory!
My infant brother slain, his limbs asunder rent,
My royal father spoiled of his ancestral realm,
And Pelias' guiltless daughters lured to slay their sire!
But here I must not rest; no untrained hand I bring
To execute my deeds. But now, by what approach
Or by what weapon wilt thou threat the treacherous
    foe?
Deep hidden in my secret heart have I conceived
A purpose which I dare not utter. Oh, I fear
That in my foolish madness I have gone too far—
I would that children had been born to him of this
My hated rival. Still, since she hath gained his heart,
His children too are hers—
That punishment would be most fitting and deserved.
Yes, now I see the final deed of crime, and thou,
My soul, must face it. You, who once were called my
    sons,
Must pay the penalty of these your father's crimes—
My heart with horror melts, a numbing chill pervades
My limbs, and all my soul is filled with sinking fear.
Now wrath gives place, and, heedless of my husband's
    sins,
The tender mother-instinct quite possesses me.
And could I shed my helpless children's blood? Not so,
Oh, say not so, my maddened heart! Far from my hand
And thought be that unnameable and hideous deed!
What sin have they that shedding of their wretched
    blood
Would wash away?

Their sin—that Jason is their sire,
And, deeper guilt, that I have borne them. Let them
    die;
They are not mine. Nay, nay! They are my own, my
    sons,
And with no spot of guilt. Full innocent they are,
'Tis true—my brother, too, was innocent. O soul,
Why dost thou hesitate? Why flow these streaming
    tears,

While with contending thoughts my wavering heart is
    torn?
As when conflicting winds contend in stubborn strife,
And waves, to stormy waves opposed, the sea invade,
And to their lowest sands the briny waters boil;
With such a storm my heart is tossed. Hate conquers
    love,
And love puts impious hate to flight. Oh, yield thee,
    grief,
To love! Then come, my sons, sole comfort of my heart,
Come, cling within your mother's close embrace. Un-
    harmed
Your sire may keep you, while your mother holds you
    too.

        (*Embraces her sons*)

But flight and exile drive me forth! And even now
My children must be torn away with tears and cries.
Then let them die to Jason since they're lost to me.
Once more has hate resumed her sway, and passion's
    fire
Is hot within my soul. Now fury, as of yore,
Reseeks her own. Lead on, I follow to the end!
I would that I had borne twice seven sons, the boast
Of Niobe! But all too barren have I been.
Still will my two sufficient be to satisfy
My brother and my sire.

(*Sees a vision of the furies and her brother's ghost*)

                        But whither hastes that throng
Of furies? What their quest? What mean their bran-
    dished fires?
Whom threats this hellish host with horrid, bloody
    brands?
I hear the writhing lash resound of serpents huge.
Whom seeks Megaera with her deadly torch? Whose
    shade
Comes gibbering there with scattered limbs? It is my
    brother!
Revenge he seeks, and we will grant his quest. Then
    come,
Within my heart plunge all your torches, rend me, burn;
For lo, my bosom open to your fury's stroke.
O brother, bid these vengeful goddesses depart
And go in peace down to the lowest shades of hell.

And do thou leave me to myself, and let this hand
That slew thee with the sword now offer sacrifice
Unto thy shade.
>   (*Slays her first son*)
>   What sudden uproar meets my ear?
'Tis Corinth's citizens on my destruction bent.
Unto the palace roof I'll mount and there complete
This bloody sacrifice.
>   (*To her remaining son*)
>   Do thou come hence with me.
But thee, poor senseless corse, within mine arms I'll
>   bear.
Now gird thyself, my heart, with strength. Nor must
>   this deed
Lose all its just renown because in secret done;
But to the public eye my hand must be approved.

(MEDEA *takes her children inside.*)

Act Five. Scene II

(*Enter* JASON.)

JASON (*shouting to citizens*): Ho, all ye loyal sons, who mourn the
>   death of kings!
>   Come, let us seize the worker of this hideous crime.
>   Now ply your arms and raze her palace to the ground.

(MEDEA *appears on the housetop with her two sons.*)

MEDEA: Now, now have I regained my regal state, my sire,
>   My brother! Once again the Colchians hold the spoil
>   Of precious gold! And by the magic of this hour
>   I am a maid once more. O heavenly powers, appeased
>   At length! O festal hour! O nuptial day! On, on!
>   Accomplished is the guilt, but not the recompense.
>   Complete the task while yet thy hands are strong to act!
>   Why dost thou linger still? Why dost thou hesitate
>   Upon the threshold of the deed? Thou canst perform it.
>   Now wrath has died within me, and my soul is filled
>   With shame and deep remorse. Ah me, what have I
>   done,

Wretch that I am? Wretch that thou art, well mayst
    thou mourn,
For thou hast done it!
                    At that thought delirious joy
O'ermasters me and fills my heart which fain would
    grieve.
And yet, methinks, the act was almost meaningless,
Since Jason saw it not; for naught has been performed
If to his grief be added not the woe of sight.

JASON (*discovering her*): Lo, there she stands upon the lofty battle-
    ments!
Bring torches! Fire the house, that she may fall en-
    snared
By those devices she herself hath planned.

MEDEA (*derisively*):   Not so,
But rather build a lofty pyre for these thy sons;
Their funeral rites prepare. Already for thy bride
And father have I done the service due the dead;
For in their ruined palace have I buried them.
One son of thine has met his doom; and this shall die
Before his father's face.

JASON: By all the gods, and by the perils of our flight,
And by our marriage bond which I have ne'er betrayed,
I pray thee spare the boy, for he is innocent.
If aught of sin there be, 'tis mine. Myself I give
To be the victim. Take my guilty soul for his.

MEDEA: 'Tis for thy prayers and tears I draw, not sheathe the
    sword.
Go now, and take thee maids for wives, thou faithless
    one;
Abandon and betray the mother of thy sons.

JASON: And yet, I pray thee, let one sacrifice atone.

MEDEA: If in the blood of one my passion could be quenched,
No vengeance had it sought. Though both my sons I
    slay,
The number still is all too small to satisfy
My boundless grief.[13] If in my womb there still should
    lurk

A pledge of thee, I'll search my vitals with a sword
And hale it forth.

JASON: Then finish what thou hast begun—
I ask no more—and grant at least that no delay
Prolong my helpless agony.

MEDEA (*to herself*): Now hasten not,
Relentless passion, but enjoy a slow revenge.
This day is in thy hands; its fertile hours employ.

JASON: Oh, take my life, thou heartless one.

MEDEA: Thou bid'st me pity—
Well! (*Slays the second child*)—'Tis done!
No more atonement, passion, can I offer thee.
Now hither lift thy tearful eyes, ungrateful one.
Dost recognise thy wife? 'Twas thus of old I fled.
The heavens themselves provide me with a safe retreat.
(*A chariot drawn by dragons appears in the air*)
Twin serpents bow their necks submissive to the yoke.
Now, father, take thy sons; while I, upon my car,
With wingéd speed am borne aloft through realms of air.
(*Mounts her car and is borne away.*)

JASON (*calling after her*): Speed on through realms of air that mortals
never see:
But, witness heaven, where thou art gone no gods can
be!

MILLER'S TRANSLATION has been slightly modified in the following lines: 35, 171, 176, 180, 237, 504, 505.

1. This refers to Hymen, the god of marriage.

2. The Fescennine verses were originally a semi-dramatic verse form characterised by crude jests and abuse. In Seneca's time they were used primarily at weddings.

3. This refers to the golden fleece which Jason and Medea took away with them from Colchis.

4. Calais and Zetes, the sons of Boreas, accompanied Jason on the Argonautic expedition.

5. This is an allusion to Castor and Pollux.

6. Acastus, the son and successor of Pelias, wished to avenge his father's death.

7. This refers to Jason, whose ship, the Argo, is said to have been the first to sail the sea.

8. The reference is to Phaethon, son of Apollo.

9. This refers to Orpheus, who had visited the lower world once before.

10. Periclymenus, like Proteus, had the power to change his form.

11. The death of Hercules is described in Sophocles' *The Trachiniae* and in Seneca's *Hercules on Oeta*.

12. Hecate, the goddess of triple form, was identified with Luna in heaven, with Diana (or Phoebe) on earth, and with Proserpina in the underworld.

13. The remainder of this speech, omitted by Miller, has been added by the editor.

V
PHAEDRA

Characters in the Play

HIPPOLYTUS, *son of* THESEUS *and Antiope, an Amazon*
PHAEDRA, *wife of* THESEUS *and stepmother of* HIPPOLYTUS
NURSE *of* PHAEDRA
CHORUS OF ATHENIAN CITIZENS
THESEUS, *king of Athens*
A MESSENGER
Slaves and attendants

INTRODUCTION

EURIPIDES' tragedy, the *Hippolytus,* was the second of his two plays on the same theme, and was probably a reworking of the first version which is now lost. His vivid portrayal of the love of Phaedra, wife of Theseus, for her stepson Hippolytus with its tragic outcome on the lives of the three persons is deservedly famous. Euripides' *Hippolytus* is considered by many critics to be his finest play. Seneca's dramatisation of the story of Phaedra differs strikingly from the extant Greek play, particularly in the manner in which Phaedra's love is revealed; Seneca was undoubtedly influenced by the first version which is said to have portrayed Phaedra as less chaste and less restrained.

In the Greek play which we have, Hippolytus and Phaedra are exceedingly complex characters, and the conflict between the two is symbolised by the opposition of Aphrodite and Artemis, who appear at the beginning and the end of the play respectively. Hippolytus is a true tragic character—the victim of overweening pride in his own purity. Phaedra has a fatal weakness against which she struggles bravely. Although Euripides is primarily interested in the emotional states of his characters, the introduction of the two goddesses gives the play a religious significance that is lacking in Seneca's play. The Roman playwright, by omitting Artemis and Aphrodite from the action, keeps the play entirely on the human level and stresses the psychology of his main characters. It is doubtless for this reason that Léon Herrmann, who believes that Seneca's greatest contribution to drama was the development of a psychological tragedy, considers the *Phaedra* and the *Medea* as his most successful plays.

Euripides centred his tragedy on the character of Hippolytus; Seneca, like Racine in his *Phèdre,* makes Phaedra the protagonist and portrays her passion in the most realistic terms. Hippolytus is far less mystical than the youth in Euripides' play; although here too it is his chastity that leads him to reject the advances of Phaedra, the Euripidean emphasis upon his devotion to Artemis and the arrogance that resulted from that devotion have disappeared. Seneca omits the scene between Hippolytus and his father, so effective in the Greek play, and adds a scene between Phaedra and Hippolytus, in which she reveals her love to him. Seneca shows brilliantly the shame and embarrassment she feels when Hippolytus fails to understand her meaning; it is an intensely human scene and one that brings out fully the pathos of Phaedra's situation. The Senecan Phaedra does not kill herself immediately after Hippolytus has scorned her love, but remains to denounce him to his father. It is not until the mangled remains of Hippolytus are brought back after his horrible death that she commits suicide, and before doing so she confesses the truth and clears Hippolytus of the supposed crime. In Euripides' play the dying Hippolytus was the centre of attention at the end, and it was the goddess Artemis who revealed the truth. In few plays has Seneca revealed more clearly his conception of tragedy and his interest in the delineation of human passion. As in Euripides, the heaviest burden of the tragedy falls upon Theseus, who pays the penalty for his hasty condemnation of his son. The conclusion, often criticised for its excessive gruesomeness, stresses his paternal love and consciousness of his own guilt:

> "I realise
> My depth of crime, for I have murdered thee. . . .
> O childlessness, a bitter loss art thou
> For broken age!"

Racine's famous tragedy, the *Phèdre,* contains many details that have their counterpart in Euripides' play. In certain respects, however, the French play seems far more Senecan than Euripidean; Phèdre and not Hippolyte is the central figure of the tragedy; Phèdre lives on to the end of the play and admits her guilt before her death; the action takes place entirely on the human level. John Gassner says, comparing Racine and Euripides in their treatment of the story, "Gone in the French tragedy is the provocative symbolic conflict between the two human instincts respectively represented by Artemis and Aphrodite. Gone, too, is the deep psychological symbolism of a young man destroyed by the love instinct or the Aphrodite he has denied in himself." Although Seneca eliminates the goddesses and makes Hippolytus subordinate to Phaedra, he still keeps something of the Euripidean conception of a youth devoted to a life of chastity. Racine's innovation of Hippolyte's love for Aricie changes the whole conception of the tragedy and has a profound effect on the delineation of both Hippolyte and Phèdre. An entirely different motivation is given to the actions and the decisions of the youth, and Phèdre is not merely a passionate woman struggling vainly against overpowering emotion, but she is a jealous woman who remains silent when she knows Hippolyte is doomed to death. Racine's *Phèdre* is a powerful tragedy, but its basic conception is very unlike that of Seneca's *Phaedra* and Euripides' more famous play on the same theme.

PHAEDRA[1]

(SCENE:—*Before the palace of* THESEUS *at Athens.*)

Act One.   Scene I

(*Enter* HIPPOLYTUS, *accompanied by huntsmen. He assigns various duties to his followers.*)

HIPPOLYTUS: Up comrades, and the shadowy groves
With nets encircle; swiftly range
The heights of our Cecropian hills;
Scour well those coverts on the slopes
Of Parnes, or in Thria's vale
Whose chattering streamlet roars along
In rapid course; go climb the hills
Whose peaks are ever white with snows
Of Scythia. Let others go
Where woods with lofty alders stand
In dense array; where pastures lie
Whose springing grass is waked to life
By Zephyr's breath, dew-laden. Go,
Where calm Ilissus flows along
The level fields, a sluggish stream,
Whose winding course the barren sands
With niggard water laps. Go ye
Along the leftward-leading way,
Where Marathon her forest glades
Reveals, where nightly with their young
The suckling mothers feed. Do you,
Where, softened by the warming winds
From southern lands, Acharnae melts
His snows, repair; let others seek
Hymettus' rocky slopes, far famed
For honey; others still the glades

625

Of small Aphidnae. All too long
That region has unharried lain
Where Sunium with its jutting shore
Thrusts out the curving sea.
If any feels the forest's lure,
Him Phlye calls, where dwells the boar
Now scarred and known by many a wound,
The farmers' fear.
Now free the dogs from straining leash,
That hunt in silence; but the hounds
Of keen Molossian breed hold fast
In check; let the savage Cretans strain
With chaffing necks upon their chains;
The Spartans hold in strongest curb,
With caution bind, for bold their breed,
And eager for the prey.
The time will come when their baying loud
Through the hollow rocks shall echo; now
Let them snuff the air with nostrils keen,
And with lowered muzzles seek the tracks
Of beasts, while yet the dawn is dim,
And while the dewy earth still holds
The marks of treading feet. Let some
On burdened necks the wide nets bear,
And others haste to bring the snares
Of smooth-wrought cords. Let feathers, dyed
With crimson, hedge the timid deer
With terrors vain. Do thou use darts
Of Crete, and thou the heavy spear
By both hands wielded. Thou shalt sit
In hiding and with clamours loud
Drive out the frightened beasts; and thou,
When all is done, with curving blade
Shalt break the victims.
And thou, be with thy worshipper,
O goddess of the chase,[2] whose rule
Extends o'er all the secret haunts
Of earth; whose darts unerring pierce
The flying prey; whose thirst is quenched
By cool Araxes' distant stream,
Or for whose sport the Ister spreads
His frozen waves. Thy hand pursues
Gaetulian lions, Cretan deer;

And now the swiftly fleeing does
With lighter stroke are pierced. To thee
The spotted tigers yield, to thee
The bisons, shaggy backed, and the wild,
Broad-hornéd oxen of the woods.
Whatever feeds upon the plains
In desert pasture lands; whate'er
The needy Garamantian knows,
Whate'er the Arab rich in woods,
Or wild Sarmatian, wandering free
Across the lonely wilderness;
Whate'er the rugged Pyrenees
Or deep Hyrcanian glades conceal:
All fear thy bow, thou huntress queen.
If any worshipper of thine
Takes to the hunt thy favouring will,
His nets hold fast the struggling prey;
No birds break from his snares; for him
The groaning wagons homeward come
With booty rich; the hounds come back
With muzzles deeply dyed in blood,
And all the rustic throng returns
In shouting triumph home.
But lo, the goddess hears. The hounds
Are baying loud and clear to announce
The start. I'm summoned to the woods.
Here, here I'll hasten where the road
Most quickly leads away.

(HIPPOLYTUS *and the huntsmen depart.*)

Act One.   Scene II

(*Enter* PHAEDRA *and the* NURSE.)

PHAEDRA: O mighty Crete, thou mistress of the deep,
Whose ships uncounted sail through every sea
Wherever Nereus shows their beaks the way,
E'en to Assyria's shores; why dost thou here
Compel me thus in woe and tears to live,
A hostage given to the hated foe,
And to a foeman wed? Behold my lord,

Deserting me, his bride, is far away,
And keeps his wonted faith. Through shadows deep
Of that dark pool which may not be recrossed,
This doughty follower of a madcap prince[3]
Has gone, that from the very throne of Dis
He might seduce and bear away his queen.
With such mad folly linked he went away,
Restrained by neither fear nor shame. And so,
In deepest Acheron, illicit love
This father of Hippolytus desires.
But other, greater griefs than this oppress
My sorrowing soul; no quiet rest by night,
No slumber deep comes to dissolve my cares;
But woe is fed and grows within my heart,
And there burns hot as Aetna's raging fires.
My loom stands empty and my listless hands
Drop idly from their tasks. No more I care
To make my votive offerings to the gods,
Nor, with the Athenian women mingled, dance
Around their sacred shrines, and conscious brands
Toss high in secret rites. I have no heart
With chaste and pious prayers to worship her,
That mighty goddess who was set to guard
This Attic land. My only joy is found
In swift pursuit of fleeing beasts of prey,
My soft hands brandishing the heavy spear.
But what will come of this? Why do I love
The forest glades so madly? Ah, I feel
The fatal malady my mother[4] felt;
For both have learned within the forest depths
To sin in love. O mother, now my heart
Doth ache for thee; for, swept away by sin
Unspeakable, thou boldly didst conceive
A shameful passion for the savage lord
Of the wild herd. Untamable was he,
That stern and lustful leader of the flock;
And yet he loved. But in my passion's need
What god can help me? Where the Daedalus
Who can my love relieve? Should he return
Who shut our monster in the labyrinth,
He could not by his well-known Attic skill
Avail to save me from this dire mischance.
For Venus, filled with deadly hate of us,

The stock of Phoebus, seeks through me to avenge
The chains which fettered her in shame to Mars,
And all our house with direful love she fills.
No princess of our race has ever loved
In modest wise, but always monstrously.

NURSE: O wife of Theseus, glorious child of Jove,
Drive from thy modest breast these shameful thoughts,
Put out these flames; and give thyself no hope
Of such dire love as this. Whoe'er at first
Has set himself to fight and conquer love,
A safe and easy victory finds. But he,
Who dallies with its evil sweets, too late
Refuses to endure the galling yoke
Which he himself has placed upon his neck.
I know full well how scornful of the truth,
How harsh the swollen pride of princesses,
How it refuses to be bent aright.
Whatever outcome chance allots, I'll bear;
For dawning freedom makes the agéd brave.
To will to live uprightly nor to fall
From virtue's ways is best; but next to this
Is sense of shame, the knowing when to stop
A sinful course. What, pray, will be the end
For thee, poor mistress? Why dost heap thy house
With further infamy? Wouldst thou outsin
Thy mother? For thy impious love is worse
Than her unnatural and monstrous love.
The first you would impute to character,
The last to fate. If, since thy husband sees
No more the realms of earth, thou dost believe
That this thy sin is safe and free from fear,
Thou art in error. Grant that he is held
Imprisoned fast in Lethe's lowest depths,
And must forever feel the bonds of Styx;
Would he, thy sire, who by his spreading sway
Encroaches on the sea, who gives their laws
Unto a hundred peoples, e'er permit
So great a crime as this to lie unknown?
Keen is a parent's watchful care. And yet,
Suppose that by our craft and guile we hide
This crime from him: what of thy mother's sire,
Who floods the earth with his illuming rays?

And what of him who makes the earth to quake,
The bolts of Aetna flashing in his hand,
The father of the gods? And dost thou think
That it can be that thou couldst hide thy sin
From these thy grandsires, all-beholding ones?
But even should the favour of the gods,
Complaisant, hide thy shame from all the world;
Though to thy lust alone should fall that grace
Denied to other crimes: still must thou fear.
What of that ever-present punishment,
The terror of the soul that knows its guilt,
Is stained with crime and fearful of itself?
Some women have with safety sinned, but none
With peace of soul. Then quench these flames, I pray,
Of impious love, and shun this monstrous crime
Which no barbaric land has ever done,
No Getan wandering on his lonely plains,
No savage Taurian, no Scythian.
Expel from thy chaste soul this hideous thing,
And, mindful of thy mother's sin, avoid
Such monstrous unions. Wouldst in marriage give
Thyself to son and father? Wouldst thou take
In thine incestuous womb a progeny
So basely mixed? Then go the length of sin;
O'erthrow all nature with thy shameful fires.
Why should the monsters cease? Why empty stands
Thy brother's labyrinth? Shall all the world
Be shocked with prodigies, shall nature's laws
Be scorned, whene'er a Cretan woman loves?

PHAEDRA: I know that what thou say'st is true, dear nurse;
But raging passion forces me to take
The path of sin. Full consciously my soul
Goes headlong on its downward way, ofttimes
With backward glance, sane counsel seeking still,
Without avail. So, when the mariner
Would sail his ship against the boisterous waves,
His toil is all in vain, and, vanquished quite,
The ship drifts onward with the hurrying tide.
For what can reason do when passion rules,
When love, almighty, dominates the soul?
The wingéd god is lord through all the earth,
And with his flames unquenchable the heart

Of Jove himself is burned. The god of war
Has felt his fire; and Vulcan too, that god
Who forges Jove's three-forkéd thunderbolts;
Yea, he, who in the hold of Aetna huge
Is lord of ever-blazing furnaces,
By this small spark is burned. Apollo, too,
Who sends his arrows with unerring aim,
Was pierced by Cupid's still more certain darts.
For equally in heaven and earth the god
Is powerful.

NURSE: The god! 'Tis vicious lust
That hath his godhead framed; and, that its ends
More fully may be gained, it has assigned
To its unbridled love the specious name,
Divinity! 'Tis Venus' son, in sooth,
Sent wandering through all the earth! He flies
Through empty air and in his boyish hands
His deadly weapon bears! Though least of gods,
He holds the widest sway! Such vain conceits
The love-mad soul adopts, love's goddess feigns,
And Cupid's bow. Whoe'er too much enjoys
The smiles of fortune and in ease is lapped,
Is ever seeking unaccustomed joys.
Then that dire comrade of a high estate,
Inordinate desire, comes in. The feast
Of yesterday no longer pleases; now
A home of sane and simple living, food
Of humble sort, are odious. Oh, why
Does this destructive pest so rarely come
To lowly homes, but chooses rather homes
Of luxury? And why does modest love
Beneath the humble roof abide, and bless
With wholesome intercourse the common throng?
Why do the poor restrain their appetites,
Whereas the rich, on empire propped, desire
More than is right. Who wields too much of power
Desires to gain what is beyond his power.
What is befitting to thy high estate
Thou knowest well. Then fitting reverence show
To thy returning husband's sovereignty.

PHAEDRA: The sovereignty of love is over me,
The highest rule of all. My lord's return,

I fear it not; for never more has he,
Who once within the silent depths of night
Has plunged, beheld again the light of day.

NURSE: Trust not the power of Dis; for though his realm
He closely bar, and though the Stygian dog
Keep watch and ward upon the baleful doors,
Theseus can always walk forbidden ways.

PHAEDRA: Perchance he'll give indulgence to my love.

NURSE: But he was harsh e'en to a modest wife;
His heavy hand Antiope has known.
But grant that thou canst bend thy angry lord:
Canst bend as well the stubborn soul of him,
Hippolytus, who hates the very name
Of womankind? Inexorable his resolve
To spend his life unwedded. He so shuns
The sacred rites of marriage, thou wouldst know
That he of Amazonian stock was born.

PHAEDRA: Though on the tops of snowy hills he hide,
Or swiftly course along the ragged cliffs,
Through forests deep, o'er mountains, 'tis my will
To follow him.

NURSE: And will he turn again,
And yield himself unto thy sweet caress?
Or will he lay aside his modesty
At thy vile love's behest? Will he give o'er
His hate of womankind for thee alone,
On whose account, perchance, he hates them all?
He can not be by any prayers o'ercome.

PHAEDRA: He's wild, but even beasts are tamed by love.

NURSE: He'll flee.

PHAEDRA: Through Ocean's self I'll follow him.

NURSE: Thy sire remember.

PHAEDRA: And my mother too.

NURSE: Women he hates.

PHAEDRA: Then I'll no rival fear.

NURSE: Thy husband comes.

PHAEDRA: With him Pirithous!

NURSE: Thy sire!

PHAEDRA: To Ariadne he was kind.

NURSE: O child, by these white locks of age, I pray,
              This care-filled heart, these breasts that suckled thee,
              Put off this rage; to thine own rescue come.
              The greater part of life is will to live.

PHAEDRA: Shame has not wholly fled my noble soul.
              I yield; let love, which will not be controlled,
              Be conquered. Nor shalt thou, fair fame, be stained.
              This way alone is left, sole hope of woe:
              Theseus I'll follow, and by death shun sin.

NURSE: Oh, check, my child, this wild, impetuous thought;
              Be calm. For now I think thee worthy life,
              Because thou hast condemned thyself to death.

PHAEDRA: I am resolved to die, and only seek
              The mode of death. Shall I my spirit free
              By twisted rope, or fall upon the sword,
              Or shall I leap from yonder citadel?

NURSE: Shall my old age permit thee thus to die
              Self-slain? Thy deadly, raging purpose stay.
              No one may easily come back to life.

PHAEDRA: No argument can stay the will of one
              Who has resolved to die, and ought to die.
              Quick, let me arm myself in honour's cause.

NURSE: Sole comfort of my weary age, my child,
              If such unruly passion sways thy heart,
              Away with reputation! 'Tis a thing
              Which rarely with reality agrees;
              It smiles upon the ill-deserving man,
              And from the good withholds his meed of praise.
              Let us make trial of that stubborn soul.
              Mine be the task to approach the savage youth,
              And bend his will relentless to our own.
                        (*They go into the house.*)

Act One.   Scene III

(*Enter the* CHORUS OF ATHENIAN CITIZENS.)

CHORUS:

Thou goddess, child of the foaming sea,
Thou mother of love, how fierce are the flames,
And how sharp are the darts of thy petulant boy;
How deadly of aim his bow.
Deep to the heart the poison sinks
When the veins are imbued with his hidden flame;
No gaping wound upon the breast
Does his arrow leave; but far within
It burns with consuming fire.
No peace or rest does he give; world wide
Are his flying weapons sown abroad:
The shores that see the rising sun,
And the land that lies at the goal of the west;
The south where raging Cancer glows,
And the land of the cold Arcadian Bear
With its ever-wandering tribes—all know
And have felt the fires of love.
The hot blood of youth he rouses to madness,
The smouldering embers of age he rekindles,
And even the innocent breasts of maids
Are stirred by passion unknown.
He bids the immortals desert the skies
And dwell on the earth in forms assumed.
For love, Apollo kept the herds
Of Thessaly's king,[5] and, his lyre unused,
He called to his bulls on the gentle pipe.
How oft has Jove himself put on
The lower forms of life, who rules
The sky and the clouds. Now a bird he seems,
With white wings hovering, with voice
More sweet than the song of the dying swan;
Now with lowering front, as a wanton bull,
He offers his back to the sport of maids;
And soon through his brother's waves he floats,
With his hoofs like sturdy oars, and his breast
Stoutly opposing the waves, in fear
For the captured maid he bears. For love,
The shining goddess of the night

Her dim skies left, and her glittering car
To her brother allotted to guide. Untrained
In managing the dusky steeds,
Within a shorter circuit now
He learns to direct his course. Meanwhile
The nights no more their accustomed space
Retained, and the dawn came slowly back,
Since 'neath a heavier burden now
The axle trembled. Love compelled
Alcmena's son to lay aside
His quiver and the threat'ning spoil
Of that great lion's skin he bore,
And have his fingers set with gems,
His shaggy locks in order dressed.
His limbs were wrapped in cloth of gold,
His feet with yellow sandals bound;
And with that hand which bore but now
The mighty club, he wound the thread
Which from his mistress' spindle fell.[6]
The sight all Persia saw, and they
Who dwell in Lydia's fertile realm—
The savage lion's skin laid by,
And on those shoulders, once the prop
For heaven's vast dome, a gauzy cloak
Of Tyrian manufacture spread.
Accursed is love, its victims know,
And all too strong. In every land,
In the all-encircling briny deep,
In the airy heavens where the bright stars course,
There pitiless love holds sway.
The sea-green band of the Nereids
Have felt his darts in their deepest waves,
And the waters of ocean cannot quench
Their flames. The birds know the passion of love,
And mighty bulls, with its fire inflamed,
Wage furious battle, while the herd
Look on in wonder. Even stags,
Though timorous of heart, will fight
If for their mates they fear, while loud
Resound the snortings of their wrath.
When with love the striped tigers burn,
The swarthy Indian cowers in fear.
For love the boar whets his deadly tusks

And his huge mouth is white with foam.
The African lions toss their manes
When love inflames their hearts, and the woods
Resound with their savage roars.
The monsters of the raging deep,
And those great beasts, the elephants,
Feel the sway of love; since nature's power
Claims everything, and nothing spares.
Hate perishes when love commands,
And ancient feuds yield to his touch.
Why need I more his sway approve,
When even stepdames yield to love?

Act Two.   Scene I

(*Enter* NURSE *from the palace.*)

CHORUS: Speak, nurse, the news thou bring'st. How fares the
    queen?
Do her fierce fires of love know any end?

NURSE: I have no hope that such a malady
Can be relieved; her maddened passion's flames
Will endless burn. A hidden, silent fire
Consumes her, and her raging love, though shut
Within her heart, is by her face betrayed.
Her eyes dart fire; anon, her sunken gaze
Avoids the light of day. Her restless soul
Can find no pleasure long in anything.
Her aimless love allows her limbs no rest.
Now, as with dying, tottering steps, she goes,
And scarce can hold her nodding head erect;
And now lies down to sleep. But, sleepless quite,
She spends the night in tears. Now does she bid
Me lift her up, and straight to lay her down;
To loose her locks, and bind them up again.
In restless mood she constantly demands
Fresh robes. She has no care for food or health.
With failing strength she walks, with aimless feet.
Her old-time strength is gone; no longer shines
The ruddy glow of health upon her face.

Care feeds upon her limbs; her trembling steps
Betray her weakness, and the tender grace
Of her once blooming beauty is no more.
Her eyes, which once with Phoebus' brilliance shone,
No longer gleam with their ancestral fires.
Her tears flow ever, and her cheeks are wet
With constant rain; as when, on Taurus' top,
The snows are melted by a warming shower.
But look, the palace doors are opening,
And she, reclining on her couch of gold,
And sick of soul, refuses one by one
The customary garments of her state.

PHAEDRA (*within*): Remove, ye slaves, those bright and gold-wrought
          robes;
          Away with Tyrian purple, and the webs
          Of silk whose threads the far-off eastern tribes
          From leaves of trees collect. Gird high my robes;
          I'll wear no necklace, nor shall snowy pearls,
          The gift of Indian seas, weigh down my ears.
          No nard from far Assyria shall scent
          My locks; thus loosely tossing let them fall
          Around my neck and shoulders; let them stream
          Upon the wind, by my swift running stirred.
          Upon my left I'll wear a quiver girt,
          And in my right hand will I brandish free
          A hunting-spear of Thessaly; for thus
          The mother of Hippolytus was clad.
          So did she lead her hosts from the frozen shores
          Of Pontus, when to Attica she came,
          From distant Tanais or Maeotis' banks,
          Her comely locks down flowing from a knot,
          Her side protected by a crescent shield.
          Like her would I betake me to the woods.

CHORUS: Cease thy laments, for grief will not avail
          The wretched. Rather seek to appease the will
          Of that wild virgin goddess of the woods.

NURSE (*to Diana*): O queen of forests, thou who dwell'st alone
          On mountain tops, and thou who only art
          Within their desert haunts adored, convert,
          We pray, to better issue these sad fears.
          O mighty goddess of the woods and groves,

Bright star of heaven, thou glory of the night,
Whose torch, alternate with the sun, illumes
The sky, thou three-formed Hecate—Oh, smile,
We pray, on these our hopes; the unbending soul
Of stern Hippolytus subdue for us.
Teach him to love; our passion's mutual flame
May he endure. May he give ready ear
To our request. His hard and stubborn heart
Do thou make soft to us. Enthral his mind.
Though stern of soul, averse to love, and fierce,
May he yet yield himself to Venus' laws.
Bend all thy powers to this. So may thy face
Be ever clear, and through the rifted clouds
Mayst thou sail on with crescent shining bright;
So, when thou driv'st thy chariot through the sky,
May no Thessalian mummeries prevail
To draw thee from thy nightly journey down;
And may no shepherd boast himself of thee.
I pray thee, come in answer to our prayer.
    (HIPPOLYTUS *is seen approaching*)
I see Hippolytus himself, alone,
Approaching to perform the yearly rites
To Dian due.
        (*To herself*)
           Why dost thou hesitate?
Both time and place are given by fortune's lot.
Use all thy arts. Why do I quake with fear?
It is no easy task to do the deed
Enjoined on me. Yet she, who serves a queen,
Must banish from her heart all thought of right;
For sense of shame ill serves a royal will.

Act Two.   Scene II

(*Enter* HIPPOLYTUS.)

HIPPOLYTUS: Why dost thou hither turn thine agéd feet,
            O faithful nurse? Why is thy face so sad,
            Thy brow so troubled? Truly is my sire
            In safety, Phaedra safe, and their two sons.

NURSE: Thou need'st not fear for them; the kingdom stands
In prosperous estate, and all thy house
Rejoices in the blessings of the gods.
But now do thou with greater kindness look
Upon thy fortune. For my heart is vexed
And anxious for thy sake; for thou thyself
With grievous sufferings dost bruise thy soul.
If fate compels it, one may be forgiven
For wretchedness; but if, of his own will,
A man prefers to live in misery,
Brings tortures on himself, then he deserves
To lose those gifts he knows not how to use.
Be mindful of thy youth; relax thy mind.
Lift high the blazing torch on festal nights;
Let Bacchus free thee from thy weighty cares;
Enjoy this time which speeds so swiftly by.
Now is the time when love comes easily,
And smiles on youth. Come, let thy soul rejoice.
Why dost thou lie upon a lonely couch?
Dissolve in pleasures that grim mood of thine,
And snatch the passing joys; let loose the reins.
Forbid that these, the best days of thy life,
Should vanish unenjoyed. Its proper hue
Has God allotted to each time of life,
And leads from step to step the age of man.
So joy becomes the young, a face severe
The agéd. Why dost thou restrain thyself,
And strangle at their birth the joys of life?
That crop rewards the farmer's labour most
Which in the young and tender sprouting-time
Runs riot in the fields. With lofty top
That tree will overspread the neighbouring grove,
Which no begrudging hand cuts back or prunes.
So do our inborn powers a richer fruit
Of praise and glory bear, if liberty,
Unchecked and boundless, feed the noble soul.
Thou, harsh, uncouth, and ignorant of life,
Dost spend thy youth to joy and love unknown.
Think'st thou that this is man's allotted task,
To suffer hardships, curb the rushing steeds,
And fight like savage beasts in bloody war?
When he beheld the boundless greed of death,
The mighty father of the world ordained

A means by which the race might be renewed.
Suppose the power of Venus over men
Should cease, who doth supply and still renew
The stream of life, then would this lovely world
Become a foul, unsightly thing indeed:
The sea would bear no fish within its waves,
The woods no beasts of prey, the air no birds;
But through its empty space the winds alone
Would rove. How various the forms of death
That seize and feed upon our mortal race:
The wrecking sea, the sword, and treachery!
But say that these are lacking: still we fall
Of our own gravity to gloomy Styx.
Suppose our youth should choose a mateless life,
And live in childless state; then all this world
Of teeming life which thou dost see, would live
This generation only, and would fall
In ruins on itself. Then spend thy life
As nature doth direct; frequent the town,
And live in friendly union with thy kind.

HIPPOLYTUS: There is no life so free, so innocent,
Which better cherishes the ancient rites,
Than that which spurns the crowded ways of men
And seeks the silent places of the woods.
His soul no maddening greed of gain inflames
Who on the lofty levels of the hills
His blameless pleasures finds. No fickle breath
Of passing favour frets him here, no sting
Of base ingratitude, no poisonous hate.
He fears no kingdom's laws; nor, in the quest
Of power, does he pursue the phantom shapes
Of fame and wealth. From hope and fear alike
Is he removed. No black and biting spite
With base, malicious tooth preys on him here.
He never hears of those base, shameful things
That spawn amid the city's teeming throngs.
It is not his with guilty heart to quake
At every sound; he need not hide his thoughts
With guileful words; in pride of sinful wealth
He seeks to own no lordly palace propped
Upon a thousand pillars, with its beams
In flaunting arrogance incased with gold.

No streams of blood his pious altars drench;
No hecatombs of snowy bullocks stand
Foredoomed to death, their foreheads sprinkled o'er
With sacred meal; but in the spacious fields,
Beneath the sky, in fearless innocence,
He wanders lord of all. His only guile,
To set the cunning snare for beasts of prey;
And, when o'erspent with labours of the chase,
He soothes his body in the shining stream
Of cool Ilissus. Now swift Alpheus' banks
He skirts, and now the lofty forest's deep,
Dense places treads, where Lerna, clear and cool,
Pours forth her glimmering streams.
Here twittering birds make all the woods resound,
And through the branches of the ancient beech
The leaves are all a-flutter in the breeze.
How sweet upon some vagrant river's bank,
Or on the verdant turf, to lie at length,
And quaff one's fill of deep, delicious sleep,
Whether in hurrying floods some copious stream
Pours down its waves, or through the vernal flowers
Some murmuring brook sings sweetly as it flows.
The windfall apples of the wood appease
His hunger, while the ripening berries plucked
From wayside thickets grant an easy meal.
He gladly shuns the luxuries of kings.
Let mighty lords from anxious cups of gold
Their nectar quaff; for him how sweet to catch
With naked hand the water of the spring!
More certain slumber soothes him, though his couch
Be hard, if free from care he lay him down.
With guilty soul he seeks no shameful deeds
In nooks remote upon some hidden couch,
Nor timorous hides in labyrinthine cell;
He courts the open air and light of day,
And lives before the conscious eye of heaven.
Such was the life, I think, the ancients lived,
Those primal men who mingled with the gods.
They were not blinded by the love of gold;
No sacred stone divided off the fields
And lotted each his own in judgment there.
Nor yet did vessels rashly plow the seas;
But each his native waters knew alone.

Then cities were not girt with massive walls,
With frequent towers set; no soldier there
To savage arms his hands applied, nor burst
The close-barred gates with huge and heavy stones
From ponderous engines hurled. As yet the earth
Endured no master's rule, nor felt the sway
Of labouring oxen yoked in common toil;
But all the fields, self-fruitful, fed mankind,
Who took and asked no more. The woods gave wealth,
And shady grottoes natural homes supplied.
Unholy greed first broke these peaceful bonds,
And headlong wrath, and lust which sets aflame
The hearts of men. Then came the cruel thirst
For empire; and the weak became the prey
Of strong, and might was counted right. At first
Men fought with naked fists, but soon they turned
Rough clubs and stones to use of arms. Not yet
Were cornel spears with slender points of iron,
And long, sharp-pointed swords, and crested helms.
Such weapons wrath invented. Warlike Mars
Produced new arts of strife, and forms of death
In countless numbers made. Thence streams of gore
Stained every land, and reddened every sea.
Then crime, o'erleaping every bound, ran wild;
Invaded every home. No hideous deed
Was left undone; but brothers by the hand
Of brothers fell, parents by children's hands,
Husbands by wives', and impious mothers killed
Their helpless babes. Stepmothers need no words;
The very beasts are kind compared with them.
Of all these evils woman was the cause,
The leader she. She with her wicked arts
Besets the minds of men; and all for her
And her vile, lustful ways, unnumbered towns
Lie low in smoking heaps; whole nations rush
To arms; and kingdoms, utterly o'erthrown,
Drag down their ruined peoples in their fall.
Though I should name no other, Aegeus' wife[7]
Would prove all womankind a cursèd race.

NURSE: Why blame all women for the crimes of few?

HIPPOLYTUS: I hate them all. I dread and shun and curse
                 Them all. Whether from reason, instinct, blind

And causeless madness, this I know—I hate.
And sooner shall you fire and water wed;
Sooner shall dangerous quicksands friendly turn
And give safe anchorage; and sooner far
Shall Tethys from her utmost western bounds
Bring forth the shining day, and savage wolves
Smile kindly on the timid does, than I,
O'ercome, feel ought but hate to womankind.

NURSE: But oft doth love put reins on stubborn souls,
And all their hatred to affection turns.
Behold thy mother's realm of warlike dames;
Yet even they the sway of passion know.
Of this thy birth itself is proof enough.[8]

HIPPOLYTUS: My comfort for my mother's loss is this,
That now I'm free to hate all womankind.

NURSE (*aside*): As some hard crag, on every side unmoved,
Resists the waves, and dashes backward far
The opposing floods, so he doth spurn my words.
But hither Phaedra comes with hasty step,
Impatient of delay. What fate is hers?
Or to what action doth her madness tend?

Act Two.   Scene III

(PHAEDRA *enters and falls fainting to the earth.*)

NURSE: But see, in sudden fainting fit she falls,
And deathlike pallor overspreads her face.
(HIPPOLYTUS *hastens to raise her up in his arms*)
Lift up thy face, speak out, my daughter, see,
Thine own Hippolytus embraces thee.

PHAEDRA (*recovering from her faint*): Who gives me back to griefs, and
                  floods again
My soul with heavy care? How well for me
Had I sunk down to death!

HIPPOLYTUS: But why, poor soul,
Dost thou lament the gift of life restored?

PHAEDRA (*aside*): Come dare, attempt, fulfil thine own command.
Speak out, and fearlessly. Who asks in fear
Suggests a prompt refusal. Even now
The greater part of my offence is done.
Too late my present modesty. My love,
I know, is base; but if I persevere,
Perchance the marriage torch will hide my sin.
Success makes certain sins respectable.
Come now, begin.
            (*To* HIPPOLYTUS)
                              Bend lower down thine ear,
I pray; if any comrade be at hand,
Let him depart, that we may speak alone.

HIPPOLYTUS: Behold, the place is free from witnesses.

PHAEDRA: My lips refuse to speak my waiting words;
A mighty force compels my utterance,
A mightier holds it back. Ye heavenly powers,
I call ye all to witness, what I wish—

HIPPOLYTUS: Thy heart desires and cannot tell its wish?

PHAEDRA: Light cares speak out, the weighty have no words.

HIPPOLYTUS: Into my ears, my mother, tell thy cares.

PHAEDRA: The name of mother is too proud and high;
My heart dictates some humbler name than that.
Pray call me sister—slave, Hippolytus.
Yes, slave I'd be. I'll bear all servitude;
And shouldst thou bid me tread the driven snows,
To walk along high Pindus' frozen peaks,
I'd not refuse; no, not if thou shouldst bid
Me go through fire, and serried ranks of foes,
I would not hesitate to bare my breast
Unto the naked swords. Take thou the power
Which was consigned to me. Make me thy slave.
Rule thou the state, and let me subject be.
It is no woman's task to guard this realm
Of many towns. Do thou, who in the flower
Of youth rejoicest, rule the citizens
With strong paternal sway. But me receive
Into thy arms, and there protect thy slave
And suppliant. My widowhood relieve.

HIPPOLYTUS: May God on high this omen dark avert!
              My father will in safety soon return.

PHAEDRA: Not so: the king of that fast-holding realm
              And silent Styx has never opened back
              The doors of earth to those who once have left
              The realms above. Think'st thou that he will loose
              The ravisher of his couch? Unless, indeed,
              Grim Pluto has at last grown mild to love.

HIPPOLYTUS: The righteous gods of heaven will bring him back.
              But while the gods still hold our prayers in doubt,
              My brothers will I make my pious care,
              And thee as well. Think not thou art bereft;
              For I will fill for thee my father's place.

PHAEDRA (*aside*): Oh, hope of lovers, easily beguiled!
              Deceitful love! Has he not said enough?
              I'll ply him now with prayers.
                          (*To* HIPPOLYTUS)
                                        Oh, pity me.
              Hear thou the prayers which I must only think.
              I long to utter them, but am ashamed.

HIPPOLYTUS: What is thy trouble then?

PHAEDRA: A trouble mine,
              Which thou wouldst scarce believe could vex the soul
              Of any stepdame.

HIPPOLYTUS: Speak more openly;
              In doubtful words thy meaning thou dost wrap.

PHAEDRA: My maddened heart with burning love is scorched;
              My inmost marrow is devoured with love;
              And through my veins and vitals steals the fire,
              As when the flames through roomy holds of ships
              Run darting.

HIPPOLYTUS: Surely with a modest love
              For Theseus thou dost burn.

PHAEDRA: Hippolytus,
              'Tis thus with me: I love those former looks
              Of Theseus, which in early manhood once
              He wore, when first a beard began to show
              Upon his modest cheeks, what time he saw

The Cretan monster's hidden lurking-place,
And by a thread his labyrinthine way
Retraced. Oh, what a glorious sight he was!
Soft fillets held in check his flowing locks,
And modesty upon his tender face
Glowed blushing red. His soft-appearing arms
But half concealed his muscles' manly strength.
His face was like thy heavenly Phoebe's face,
Or my Apollo's, or 'twas like thine own.
Like thee, like thee he was when first he pleased
His enemy. Just so he proudly held
His head erect; still more in thee shines out
That beauty unadorned; in thee I find
Thy father all. And yet thy mother's stern
And lofty beauty has some share in thee;
Her Scythian firmness tempers Grecian grace.
If with thy father thou hadst sailed to Crete,
My sister would have spun the thread for thee
And not for him. O sister, wheresoe'er
In heaven's starry vault thou shinest, thee,
Oh, thee I call to aid my hapless cause,
So like thine own. One house has overthrown
Two sisters, thee the father, me the son.
      (*To* HIPPOLYTUS)
Behold, as suppliant, fallen to thy knees,
A royal princess kneels. Without a spot
Of sin, unstained and innocent, was I;
And thou alone hast wrought the change in me.
See, at thy feet I kneel and pray, resolved
This day shall end my misery or life.
Oh, pity her who loves thee—

HIPPOLYTUS: God in heaven,
Great ruler of all gods, dost thou this sin
So calmly hear, so calmly see? If now
Thou hurlest not thy bolt with deadly hand,
What shameful cause will ever send it forth?
Let all the sky in shattered ruins fall,
And hide the light of day in murky clouds.
Let stars turn back, and trace again their course
Athwart their proper ways. And thou, great star
Of stars, thou radiant Sun, let not thine eyes
Behold the impious shame of this thy stock;

But hide thy face, and to the darkness flee.
Why is thy hand, O king of gods and men,
Inactive? Why by forkéd lightning's brands
Is not the world in flames? Direct thy bolts
At me; pierce me. Let that fierce darting flame
Consume me quite, for mine is all the blame.
I ought to die, for I have favour found
In my stepmother's eyes.

(*To* PHAEDRA)

                      Did I seem one
To thee to do this vile and shameful thing?
Did I seem easy fuel to thy fire,
I only? Has my virtuous life deserved
Such estimate? Thou, worse than all thy kind!
Thou woman, who hast in thy heart conceived
A deed more shameful than thy mother's sin,[4]
Whose womb gave monstrous birth; thou worse than
    she!
She stained herself with vilest lust, and long
Concealed the deed. But all in vain: at last,
Her two-formed child revealed his mother's crime,
And by his fierce bull-visage proved her guilt.
Of such a womb and mother art thou born.
Oh, thrice and four times blesséd is their lot
Whom hate and treachery give o'er and doom
To death. O father, how I envy thee!
Thy stepdame was the Colchian; but this,
This woman is a greater curse than she.

PHAEDRA: I clearly see the destiny of my house:
We follow ever what we should avoid.
But I have given over self-control;
I'll follow thee through fire, through raging sea,
O'er ragged cliffs, through roaring torrents wild—
Wherever thou dost go, in mad pursuit
I shall be borne. Again, O haughty one,
I fall in suppliance and embrace thy knees.

HIPPOLYTUS: Away from my chaste body with thy touch
Impure! What more? She falls upon my breast!
I'll draw my sword and smite as she deserves.
See, by her twisted locks, I backward bend
Her shameless head. No blood more worthily

Was ever spilled, O goddess of the bow,
Upon thy altars.

PHAEDRA: Now, Hippolytus,
Thou dost fulfil the fondest wish of mine;
Thou sav'st me from my madness; greater far
Than all my hopes, that by the hands I love,
By thine own hands, I perish ere I sin.

HIPPOLYTUS: Then live, be gone! Thou shalt gain naught from me.
And this my sword, defiled by thy base touch,
No more shall hang upon my modest side.
        (*He throws his sword from him*)
What Tanais will make me clean again?
Or what Maeotis rushing to the sea,
With its barbaric waves? Not Neptune's self,
With all his ocean's waters could avail
To cleanse so foul a stain. O woods! O beasts!
(*He rushes off into the depths of the forest.*)

NURSE (*in soliloquy, while* PHAEDRA *seems to have fallen in a fainting
        fit*): Now is her fault discovered. Soul of mine,
Why dost thou stand in dumb amaze? This crime
We must throw back upon the man himself,
And charge him with a guilty love, ourselves.
Sin must be hid by sin. The safest way
Is to go straight forward on the course you fear.
Who is to know, since no one saw the deed,
Whether we dared, ourselves, or suffered ill?
        (*Raising her voice in a loud cry*)
Help! Help! Ye dames of Athens! Faithful band
Of slaves, bring aid! Behold Hippolytus,
With vile adultery, attacks the queen!
He has her in his power! He threatens death!
At point of sword he storms her chastity!
There, he has gone in haste, and left behind
His sword in trembling, panic-stricken flight.
This proof of guilt we'll keep. But first restore
The stricken queen to life. Let all remain
Just as they are, her locks disheveled, torn,
To show how great a wrong she has endured.
Back to the city bear her now. Revive,
My mistress. Why dost seek to harm thyself
And shun thy comrades' eyes. For be thou sure

Not circumstance but will can make impure.
(PHAEDRA *goes into the palace.*)

Act Two.   Scene IV

CHORUS: He fled away like the storm-blast wild,
                     More swift than cloud-compelling winds;
                     And swifter than the comet's torch,
                     When, driven before the wind, it speeds
                     With long-drawn, trailing fires.
                     Let fame, that boasts of her olden times,
                     Compare with thine all ancient charms:
                     Beyond compare does thy beauty shine,
                     Clear and bright as the full-orbed moon,
                     When, with waxing hours in splendour joined,
                     Night long she speeds her shining car,
                     And her ruddy face so brightly gleams,
                     That the fires of the lesser stars are dimmed.
                     He is fair as the messenger of night,
                     When he leads the evening shadows in,
                     Himself new bathed in the ocean's foam;
                     Or when, the darkness put to flight,
                     He heralds the dawn—bright Lucifer.
                     And thou of the thyrsus, Indian Bacchus,
                     With the flowing locks of endless youth,
                     With thine ivy-clad spear the tigers driving,
                     And thy turban set on thy hornéd head:
                     Not thus will thy glorious locks outshine
                     The unadorned hair of Hippolytus.
                     And admire not thy beauty over much,
                     For fame has spread the story far,
                     How Phaedra's sister preferred to thee,
                     O Bromius, a mortal man.[9]
                     Ah beauty, a doubtful boon art thou,
                     The gift of a fleeting hour! How swift
                     On flying feet thou glidest away!
                     So flowery meadows of the spring
                     The summer's burning heat devours,
                     When midday's raging sun rides high,
                     And night's brief round is hurried through.
                     As the lilies languish on their stems,

So pleasing tresses fail the head;
And swiftly is the radiance dimmed
Which gleams from the tender cheeks of youth!
Each day hath its spoil from the lovely form;
For beauty flees and soon is gone.
Who then would trust a gift so frail?
Nay, use its joys, while still thou mayst;
For silent time will soon destroy thee,
And hours to baser hours steal on.
Why seek the desert wilds? Thy form
Is no more safe in pathless ways.
If in the forest's depths thou hide,
When Titan brings the noonday heat,
The saucy Naids will surround thee,
Who are wont in their clear springs to snare
The lovely youth; and 'gainst thy sleep
The wanton goddesses of groves,
The Dryads, who the roving Pans
Drive in pursuit, will mischief plot.
Or else that glowing star, whose birth
The old Arcadians beheld,
Will see thee from the spangled sky,
And straight forget to drive her car.
Of late she blushed a fiery red,
And yet no staining cloud obscured
Her shining disk. But we, in fear
For her troubled face, clashed cymbals loud,
Deeming her harried by the charms
Of Thessaly. But for thee alone
Was all her toil; thou wast the cause
Of her long delay; for, seeing thee,
The night's fair goddess checked her course.
If only winter's blasts would beat
Less fiercely on that face of thine;
If less it felt the sun's hot rays,
More bright than Parian marble's gleam
Would it appear. How beautiful
The manly sternness in thy face,
Thy brow's dark frowning majesty!
Compare with Phoebus' that fair neck.
His hair o'er his shoulders flowing free,
Unbound by fillet, ornaments
And shelters him. A shaggy brow

Becomes thee best; thee, shorter locks,
In tossing disarray. 'Tis thine
The rough and warlike gods to meet
In strife, and by thy mighty strength
To overcome them. Even now,
The muscles of a Hercules
Thy youthful arms can match. Thy breast
Is broader than the breast of Mars.
If on a horny-footed steed
Thou'rt pleased to mount, not Castor's self
More easily could hold in check
The Spartan Cyllarus.
Take thong in hand; with all thy strength
Discharge the javelin: not so far,
Though they be trained to hurl the dart,
Will Cretans send the slender reed.
Or if it please thee into air,
In Parthian style, to shoot thy darts,
None will descend without its bird,
Fixed deep within the throbbing breast;
From out the very clouds thy prey
Thou wilt regain.
By few has beauty been possessed
(The voice of history proclaims)
Without some loss or suffering.
But thee, unharmed, may God pass by
More merciful, and may thy form,
Now famous for its beauty, show
At last the marks of ugly age.
What crime would woman's fury leave undared?
She plans against this harmless youth some fraud.
Behold her scheme! For by her tumbled hair,
All torn, she seeks sure credence for her tale.
She wets her cheeks with tears; and every art
That woman's shrewdness knows, does she employ.

(*A man is seen approaching, who proves to be* THESEUS)

But who is that who comes with grace of kings
Displayed upon his face, his lofty head
Held high in kingly pride? In countenance,
How like the young Pirithous he seems,
Were not his cheeks too deadly pale and wan,
And if his hair fell not in locks unkempt.
Behold, 'tis Theseus' self returned to earth.

Act Three.   Scene I

(*Enter* THESEUS.)

THESEUS: At last have I escaped from endless night,
              That shadowy realm which close confines the dead.
              And now my eyes can scarce endure the light
              Which I have long desired. Eleusin now
              Has four times reaped her ripened grain, the gift
              Triptolemus bestowed; thrice and again
              Has Libra measured equal day and night,
              Since dubious battling with an unknown fate
              Has held me in the toils of life and death.
              To me, though dead to all things else, one part
              Of life remained, the consciousness of ill.
              Alcides was the end. When he came down
              To bring the dog by force from Tartarus,
              He brought me also to the upper world.
              But ah, my wearied frame has lost the strength
              It had of old; I walk with faltering steps.
              Alas! How great a task it was to reach
              The world of light from lower Phlegethon,
              To flee from death and follow Hercules!
                    But why this sound of wailing in my ears?
              Let someone tell; for agonies of woe
              And grief and lamentations sad I meet
              Upon the very threshold of my home—
              A fitting welcome to a guest from hell.

NURSE: The queen is obstinately bent on death,
              And scorns the strong remonstrance of our tears.

THESEUS: Why should she die, her husband safe returned?

NURSE: That very cause compels her speedy death.

THESEUS: Thy words are dark and hide some weighty truth.
              Speak out and tell what grief weighs down her soul.

NURSE: She tells her grief to none. Some secret woe
              She hides within her heart, and is resolved
              To take her secret with her to the grave.
              But speed thee to her; there is need of haste.

THESEUS: Unbar the close-shut portals of my house.

Act Three.   Scene II

(The doors are opened and THESEUS *encounters his wife just within.)*

THESEUS (*to* PHAEDRA): My queen, is't thus thou dost receive thy lord,
    And welcome back thy husband long desired?
    Nay, put away the sword from thy right hand,
    And give me heart again. Reveal to me
    The cause that forces thee to flee from life.

PHAEDRA: Alas, great Theseus, by thy kingly power,
    And by thy children's souls, by thy return,
    And by my ashes, suffer me to die.

THESEUS: What cause compels thy death?

PHAEDRA: The fruit of death
    Would perish if I let its cause be known.

THESEUS: None else shall hear it save myself alone.

PHAEDRA: A chaste wife fears her husband most of all.

THESEUS: Speak out; I'll hide thy secret in my heart.

PHAEDRA: The secret thou wouldst have another guard,
    First guard thyself.

THESEUS: No chance of death thou'lt find.

PHAEDRA: Death cannot fail the heart that's bent on death.

THESEUS: Confess what sin must be atoned by death.

PHAEDRA: My life.

THESEUS: Will not my tears avail with thee?

PHAEDRA: That death is best which one's own friends lament.

THESEUS: She still persists in silence. By the lash
    And chains shall her old nurse be forced to tell
    What she will not declare. Put her in chains.
    Now let the lash lay bare her hidden thoughts.

PHAEDRA: Hold, stay thy hand, for I myself will speak.

THESEUS: Why dost thou turn thy grieving face away,
    And hide the quickly rising shower of tears
    Behind thy robe?

PHAEDRA:
                 Thee, thee do I invoke,
O father of the gods, and thee, O Sun,
Thou shining glory of the heavenly dome,
On whom as founder doth our house depend,
I call ye both to witness that I strove
Against his prayers, though sorely tried. To threats
Of death my spirit did not yield; but force
O'ercame my body. This the shameful stain
Upon my honour which my blood must cleanse.

THESEUS: Come, tell, who hath defiled our honour so?

PHAEDRA: Whom thou wouldst least expect.

THESEUS:
                      But who is he?
I wait to hear his name.

PHAEDRA:
                   This sword shall tell,
Which in his terror at our loud laments,
The adulterer left, fearing the citizens.

THESEUS: Ah me! What villainy do I behold?
What monstrous deed is this? The royal sword,
Its ivory hilt with tiny signs engraved,
Shines out, the glory of the Athenian race.
But he—where has he gone?

PHAEDRA:
                  These slaves have seen
How, borne on speeding feet, he fled away.

THESEUS: Oh, holy piety! O thou who reign'st
In heaven, and thou who rulest in the seas,
Whence came this base infection of our race?
Was he of Grecian birth, or did he spring
From Scythian Taurus or some Colchian stream?
The type reverts to its ancestral stock,
And blood ignoble but repeats its source.
This is the madness of that savage race,
To scorn all lawful love, and prostitute
At last the long-chaste body to the crowd.
Oh, loathsome race, restrained by no good laws
Which milder climes revere! The very beasts
Shun love incestuous, and keep the laws
Of nature with instinctive chastity.
Where is that face, that feigned austerity,
That rough and careless garb that sought to ape

The ancient customs? Where that aspect stern,
That sour severity which age assumes?
O life, two-faced! How thou dost hide thy thoughts!
For fairest faces cover foulest hearts;
The chaste demeanour hides inchastity;
The gentle, boldness; seeming goodness, sin.
False men approve the truth; the faint of heart
Affect a blustering mood. O thou, of woods
Enamoured, savage, rough and virgin pure,
Didst thou reserve thyself for me alone?
On my couch first and with so fell a crime
Wast thou inclined to try thy manly powers?
Now, now I thank the kindly gods of heaven
That long ago I slew Antiope;
That, when I went below to Stygian caves,
I did not leave thy mother for thy lust.
Go, get thee far away to unknown lands;
And there, though to her utmost bounds removed,
The earth should hem thee off by ocean's wastes;
Though thou shouldst dwell at the Antipodes;
Though to the frigid northern realms thou go,
And deep within her farthest caverns hide;
Or, though beyond the reach of winter placed,
And drifting snows, thou leave the boisterous threats
Of frosty Boreas in mad pursuit:
Thou still shalt meet thy fitting punishment.
Persistent shall I chase thee in thy flight
Through all thy hiding-places. Ways remote,
Hemmed in, secluded, hard and trackless ways,
I'll traverse in pursuit. No obstacle
Shall block my way. Thou know'st whence I return.
And whither spears cannot be hurled at thee
I'll hurl my prayers. My father of the sea
Once promised me that thrice I might prevail
With him in prayer, and ratified the boon
By oath upon the inviolable Styx.
             (*To Neptune*)
      Thou ruler of the sea, the boon bestow,
And grant my prayer: let not Hippolytus
Live to behold another sun's bright rays,
But may he go to meet those shades of hell
Enraged at my escape. O father, now
I pray that aid which still I deprecate.

This last of thy three boons I would not use,
If I were not beset by grievous ills.
Amidst the depths of hell and dreadful Dis,
Amidst the infernal king's pursuing threats,
I did not call on thee. But now I claim
Thy promise, father. Why delay thine aid?
Why are thy waves inactive? Let the winds
That drive the blackening clouds bring darkness on;
Snatch stars and sky from sight; pour forth the sea;
Arouse thy watery monsters, and let loose
On him from ocean's depths thy swelling waves.

Act Three.   Scene III

CHORUS: Great nature, mother of the gods,
                   And thou, fire-girt Olympus' lord,
                   Who speedest through the flying skies
                   The scattered stars, the wandering ways
                   Of constellations, and the heavens
                   Upon their whirling axes turn'st:
                   Why is thy care so great to keep
                   The annual highways of the air,
                   That now the hoary frosts may strip
                   The woods of leaves, and now the trees
                   May spread once more their pleasant shade;
                   That now the summer's fervent heat
                   May ripen Ceres' gift, and soon
                   Her strength the Autumn may subdue?
                   But why, though thou dost rule so wide,
                   Though in thy hand the ponderous worlds
                   Are poised, and calmly wheel along
                   Their appointed ways, why dost thou shun
                   The affairs of men and have no care
                   For them? Art not solicitous
                   That good should prosper, and that sin
                   Receive its just deserts? But no!
                   Blind Fortune rules the affairs of men,
                   Dispensing with unthinking hand
                   Her gifts, oft favouring the worst.
                   And so the violent oppress
                   The innocent; and fraud holds sway

In highest places. To the hands
Of brutish men the rabble most
Rejoice to trust their government;
The same they honour and they hate,
With fickle will. Sad virtue finds
Her recompense for righteousness
All gone away; and poverty,
Relentless, follows innocence;
While, deep intrenched in wickedness,
The adulterer sits secure, and reigns.
O modesty—an empty name!
And worth—a glorious cheat!
But what would yonder messenger announce,
Who comes in haste, with woeful countenance?

Act Four.   Scene I

(*Enter* MESSENGER.)

MESSENGER: O slavery, thou hard and bitter lot,
Why must I voice these woes unspeakable?

THESEUS: Fear not, but boldly tell the worst mischance;
I bear a heart not unprepared for grief.

MESSENGER: My tongue can find no words to voice its woe.

THESEUS: But speak, what evil fortune still besets
My shattered house?

MESSENGER: Hippolytus is dead!

THESEUS: The father knew long since his son had died;
But now the adulterer has met his end.
Tell me, I pray, the manner of his death.

MESSENGER: When, fleeing forth, he left the city's walls,
With maddened speed he hurried on his way,
And quickly yoked his chargers to his car,
And curbed them to his will with close-drawn reins.
And then, with much wild speech, and cursing loud
His native land, oft calling on his sire,
He fiercely shook the reins above his steeds;
When suddenly, far out the vast sea roared,

And heaved itself to heaven. No wind was there
To stir the sea, no quarter of the sky
Broke in upon its peace; the rising waves
Were by their own peculiar tempest raised.
No blast so great had ever stirred the straits
Of Sicily, nor had the deep e'er swelled
With such wild rage before the north wind's breath,
When high cliffs trembled with the shock of waves,
And hoary foam smote high Leucate's top.
The sea then rose into a mighty heap,
[And, big with monstrous birth, was landward borne.][10]
For no ship's wrecking was this swelling pest
Intended; landward was its aim. The flood
Rolled shoreward heavily, something unknown
Within its laden bosom carrying.
What land, new born, will lift its head aloft?
Is some new island of the Cyclades
Arising? [Now the rocky heights are hid,
Held sacred to the Epidaurian god,
And those high crags well known for Sciron's crime;
No longer can be seen that land whose shores
Are washed by double seas.][10] While in amaze
We look in fear and wonder, suddenly
The whole sea bellows, and on every side
The towering cliffs re-echo with the roar;
While all their tops the leaping spray bedews.
The deep spouts forth and vomits up its waves
In alternating streams, like some huge whale
Which roves the ocean, spouting up the floods.
Then did that mound of waters strongly heave
And break itself, and threw upon the shore
A thing more terrible than all our fears.
The sea itself rushed landward, following
That monstrous thing. I shudder at the thought.
What form and bearing had the monster huge!
A bull it was in form, with dark-green neck
Uplifted high, its lofty front adorned
With verdant mane. Its ears with shaggy hair
Were rough; its horns with changing colour flashed,
Such as the lord of some fierce herd would have,
Both earth and ocean-born. He vomits flames;
With flames his fierce eyes gleam. His glossy neck
Great couch-like muscles shows, and as he breathes,

His spreading nostrils quiver with the blast
Of his deep panting. Breast and dewlap hang
All green with clinging moss; and on his sides
Red lichens cling. His hinder parts appear
In monstrous shape, and like some scaly fish
His vast and shapeless members drag along;
As are those monsters of the distant seas
Which swallow ships, and spout them forth again.
The countryside was panic-stricken; herds
In frenzied terror scattered through the fields;
Nor did the herdsmen think to follow them.
The wild beasts in the forest pastures fled
In all directions, and the hunters shook
With deadly fear. Hippolytus alone
Was not afraid, but curbed his frantic steeds
With close-drawn reins, and with his well-known voice
He cheered them on. The road to Argos runs
Precipitous along the broken hills,
On one side bordered by the roaring sea.
Here does that massive monster whet himself
And kindle hot his wrath; then, when he felt
His courage strong within his breast, and when
His power to attempt the strife he had rehearsed,
He charged Hippolytus with headlong course,
The ground scarce touching with his bounding feet;
And, fearful, stopped before the trembling steeds.
But this thy son, with savage countenance,
Stood steadfast, threatening, before the foe.
His features changed not, while he thundered loud:
"This empty terror cannot daunt my soul,
For 'twas my father's task to vanquish bulls."
But straightway, disobedient to the reins,
The horses hurried off the car. And now,
The highway leaving, maddened by their fear,
They plunged along where'er their terror led,
And took their way among the rocky fields.
But he, their driver, as some captain strong
Holds straight his bark upon the boisterous sea,
Lest she oppose her side against the waves,
And by his art escapes the yawning floods;
Not otherwise he guides the whirling car.
For now with tight-drawn reins he curbs his steeds,
And now upon their backs he plies the lash.

But doggedly that monster kept along,
Now running by their side, now leaping straight
Upon them as they came, from every hand
Great fear inspiring. Soon all further flight
Was checked; for that dread, hornéd, ocean beast
With lowering front charged full against their course.
Then, truly, did the horses, wild with fear,
Break loose from all control; and from the yoke
They madly struggled to withdraw their necks,
Their master hurling to their stamping feet.
Headlong among the loosened reins he fell,
His form all tangled in their clinging strands.
The more he struggled to release himself
The tighter those relentless fetters bound.
The steeds perceived what they had done, and now,
With empty car, and no one mastering them,
They ran where terror bade. Just so, of old,
Not recognising their accustomed load,
And hot with anger that the car of day
Had been entrusted to a spurious sun,
The steeds of Phoebus hurled young Phaethon
Far through the airs of heaven in wandering course.
Now far and wide he stains the fields with blood,
His head rebounding from the smitten rocks.
The bramble thickets pluck away his hair,
And that fair face is bruised upon the stones.
His fatal beauty which had been his bane,
Is ruined now by many a wound. His limbs
Are dragged along upon the flying wheels.
At last, his bleeding trunk upon a charred
And pointed stake is caught, pierced through the groin;
And for a little, by its master held,
The car stood still. The horses by that wound
Were held awhile, but soon they break delay—
And break their master too. While on they rush,
The whipping branches cut his dying form,
The rough and thorny brambles tear his flesh,
And every bush retains its part of him.
Now bands of servants scour those woeful fields,
Those places where Hippolytus was dragged,
And where his bloody trail directs the way;
And sorrowing dogs trace out their master's limbs.
But not as yet has all this careful toil

Of grieving friends sufficed to gather all.
And has it come to this, that glorious form?
But now the partner of his father's realm,
And his acknowledged heir, illustrious youth,
Who shone refulgent like the stars—behold
His scattered fragments for the funeral pile
They gather up and heap them on the bier!

THESEUS: O mother Nature, all too potent thou!
How firmly dost thou hold me by the ties
Of blood! How thou dost force me to obey
Thy will! I wished to slay my guilty son,
While yet he lived; but now I mourn his loss.

MESSENGER: One may not rightly mourn what he has willed.[11]

THESEUS: This is indeed the crowning woe, I think,
When chance fulfils the prayers we should not make.

MESSENGER: If still you hate your son, why weep for him?

THESEUS: Because I slew, not lost my son, I weep.

Act Four.   Scene II

CHORUS: How on the wheel of circumstance
We mortals whirl! 'Gainst humble folk
Does fate more gently rage, and God
More lightly smites the lightly blest.
A life in dim retirement spent
Insures a peaceful soul; and he
Who in a lowly cottage dwells
May live to tranquil age at last.
The mountain tops that pierce the skies,
Feel all the stormy winds that blow,
Fierce Eurus, Notus, and the threats
Of Boreas, and Corus too,
     Storm bringer.
The vale low lying seldom feels
The thunder's stroke; but Caucasus,
The huge, and the lofty Phrygian groves
Of mother Cybele have felt
The bolts of Jove the Thunderer.

For Jupiter in jealousy
Attacks the heights too near his skies;
But never is the humble roof
Uptorn by jealous heaven's assaults.
Round mighty kings and homes of kings
    He thunders.
The passing hour on doubtful wings
Flits ever; nor may any claim
Swift Fortune's pledge. Behold our king,
Who sees at last the glowing stars
And light of day, the gloom of hell
Behind him left, a sad return
Laments; for this his welcome home
He finds more sorrowful by far
Than dismal, dark Avernus' self.
O Pallas, by the Athenian race
In reverence held, that once again
Thy Theseus sees the light of day,
 And has escaped the pools of Styx,
Thou owest naught to greedy Dis;
For still the number of the shades
Within the infernal tyrant's power
    Remains the same.
But why the sounds of wailing that we hear?
And what would Phaedra with her naked sword?

Act Five

(*Enter* PHAEDRA *with a drawn sword in her hand.*)

THESEUS (*to* PHAEDRA): What madness pricks thee on, all wild with
      grief?
      What means that sword? Or why these loud laments?
      Why weepest thou above the hated corpse?

PHAEDRA: Me, me, O savage ruler of the deep,
      Attack; against me send the monstrous shapes
      That breed within the caverns of the sea,
      Whatever Tethys in her heart conceals,
      And ocean hides within his wandering waves.
      O Theseus, always ill of omen thou!

Oh, never to thy loved ones safe returned,
Since son and father[12] by their death have paid
For thy homecoming. Thou of thine own house
Art the destroyer; ever baneful thou,
Whether in love or hatred of thy wives.

(Turning to the mangled corpse)

Hippolytus, is this thy face I see?
Have I brought thee to this? What Sinis wild,
What pitiless Procrustes mangled thee?
What Cretan bull-man, filling all the cave
Of Daedalus with his vast bellowings,
Has rent thee thus upon his savage horns?
Ah me! Where now is fled thy beauty bright,
Thy eyes, my stars? Dost thou all lifeless lie?
Come back a little while and hear my words.
'Tis nothing base I speak. With my own hand
I'll make the full atonement, and will plunge
The avenging sword within my sinful breast,
And so be free from life and guilt at once.
Thee will I follow through Tartarean pools,
Across the Styx, through streams of liquid fire.
Let me appease the spirit of the dead.
Accept the spoils I offer, take this lock
Torn from my bleeding forehead. 'Twas not right
To join our souls in life; but surely now
We may by death unite our fates.

(To herself)

                                    Now die,
If thou art undefiled, to appease thy lord;
But if defiled, die for thy lover's sake.
Is't meet that I should live and seek again
My husband's couch, by such foul incest stained?
This wrong was lacking still, that, as if pure,
Thou shouldst enjoy that union, justified.
O death, thou only cure for evil love,
For injured chastity the last resort:
I fly to thee; spread wide thy soothing arms.
Hear me, O Athens; thou, O father, hear,
Thou worse than stepdame: I have falsely sworn.
The crime, which I myself within my heart,
With passion mad, conceived, I basely charged
To him. An empty vengeance hast thou wrought
Upon thy son; for he in chastity,

Through fault of the unchaste, lies there, unstained
And innocent.
                    (*To* HIPPOLYTUS)
                    Regain thine honour now;
Behold my impious breast awaits the stroke
Of justice, and my blood makes sacrifice
Unto the spirit of a guiltless man.
                    (*To* THESEUS)
How thou mayst recompense thy murdered son,
Learn now from me—and seek the Acheron.
(*She falls upon her sword and dies.*)

THESEUS: Ye jaws of wan Avernus, and ye caves
Of Taenara, ye floods of Lethe's stream,
A soothing balm to hearts o'ercome with grief,
Ye sluggish pools: take ye my impious soul
And plunge me deep in your eternal woes.
Now come, ye savage monsters of the deep,
Whatever Proteus hides within his caves,
And drown me in your pools, me who rejoice
In crime so hideous. O father, thou
Who ever dost too readily assent
Unto my wrathful prayers, I merit not
An easy death, who on my son have brought
A death so strange, and scattered through the fields
His mangled limbs; who, while, as austere judge,
I sought to punish evil falsely charged,
Have fallen myself into the pit of crime.
For heaven, hell, and seas have by my sins
Been peopled; now no further lot remains;
Three kingdoms know me now. Was it for this
That I returned? Was heaven's light restored
To me that I might see two funerals,
A double death? That I, bereft of wife
And son, should with one torch upon the pyre
Consume them both? Thou giver of the light
Which has so baleful proved, thou, Hercules,
Take back thy boon, and give me up again
To Dis; restore me to the cursèd shades
Whom I escaped. Oh, impious, in vain
I call upon that death I left behind.
Thou bloody man, well skilled in deadly arts,
Who hast contrived unwonted ways of death

And terrible, now deal unto thyself
The fitting punishment. Let some great pine
Be bent to earth and hurl me high in air;
Or let me headlong leap from Sciron's cliff.
More dreadful punishments have I beheld,
Which Phlegethon upon the guilty souls
Encircled by his fiery stream inflicts.
What suffering awaits me, and what place,
Full well I know. Make room, ye guilty shades;
On me, me only, let that rock be placed,
The everlasting toil of Sisyphus,
And let these wearied hands upbear its weight;
Let cooling waters lap and mock my lips;
Let that fell vulture fly from Tityus,
And let my vitals ever living be
For punishment. And thou, Ixion, sire
Of my Pirithous, take rest awhile,
And let the wheel that never stops its flight
Bear these my limbs upon its whirling rim.
Now yawn, O earth, and chaos dire, receive,
I pray, receive me to your depths; for thus
'Tis fitting that I journey to the shades.
I go to meet my son. And fear thou not,
Thou king of dead men's souls; I come in peace
To that eternal home, whence ne'er again
Shall I come forth.
               My prayers move not the gods.
But if some impious plea I made to them,
How ready would they be to grant my prayer!

CHORUS: Theseus, thou hast unending time to mourn.
Now pay the funeral honours due thy son,
And bury these poor torn and scattered limbs.

THESEUS: Then hither bring the pitiful remains
Of that dear corpse, and heap together here
That shapeless mass of flesh, those mangled limbs.
Is this Hippolytus? I realise
My depth of crime, for I have murdered thee.
And lest but once and I alone should sin,
A parent, bent to do an impious thing,
My father did I summon to my aid.
Behold, my father's boon do I enjoy.
O childlessness, a bitter loss art thou

For broken age! But come, embrace his limbs,
Whatever of thy hapless son is left,
And clasp them, wretched father, to thy breast.
Arrange in order those dismembered parts,
And to their proper place restore them. Here
His brave right hand should be. Place here the left,
Well trained to curb his horses with the reins.
The marks of his left side I recognise;
And yet how large a part is lacking still
Unto our tears. Be firm, ye trembling hands,
To do the last sad offices of grief;
Be dry, my cheeks, and stay your flowing tears,
While I count o'er the members of my son,
And lay his body out for burial.
What is this shapeless piece, on all sides torn
With many a wound? I know not what it is,
Save that 'tis part of thee. Here lay it down.
Not in its own, but in an empty place.
That face, that once with starry splendour gleamed,
That softened by its grace e'en foemen's eyes,
Has that bright beauty come to this? O fate,
How bitter! Deadly favour of the gods!
And is it thus my son comes back to me
In answer to my prayers? These final rites
Thy father pays, receive, O thou my son,
Who often to thy funeral must be borne.
And now let fires consume these dear remains.
Throw open wide my palace, dark with death,
And let all Athens ring with loud laments.
Do some of you prepare the royal pyre,
And others seek yet farther in the fields
His scattered parts.
　　　　(*Pointing to* PHAEDRA'S *corpse*)
　　　　　　　　　　Let earth on her be spread,
And may it heavy rest upon her head.

MILLER'S TRANSLATION has been slightly modified in the following lines: 239-240, 423, 437, 994, 1217.

1. The better attested title of the tragedy is *Phaedra*, although *Hippolytus* also occurs as the title.

2. The goddess of the chase is Diana.

3. This refers to Pirithous who attempted to steal Proserpina from Hades. Theseus accompanied him on his mad adventure.

4. The mother of Phaedra was Pasiphae, who was afflicted with an unnatural passion for a bull.

5. The reference is to King Admetus.

6. Hercules went into voluntary servitude to Omphale, queen of Lydia.

7. This refers to Medea, who fled to Athens after her horrible vengeance on Jason (cf. Euripides' and Seneca's *Medea*) and married Aegeus.

8. The Amazons were said to kill all boys born to them. Hippolytus, the son of Theseus and Antiope, had been spared.

9. Ariadne fell in love with Theseus, who deserted her.

10. This passage is deleted by Leo and bracketed by Peiper and Richter.

11. The translator reads here *haud quisquam honeste flere, quod voluit, potest.*

12. Theseus was the cause of the death of his father Aegeus, since he did not display white sails on his return from Crete as a signal of his safety. Aegeus, believing that his son had perished, threw himself into the sea.

VI
OEDIPUS

CHARACTERS IN THE PLAY

OEDIPUS, *king of Thebes; the son, as he supposed, of Polybus and Merope, king and queen of Corinth, but found to be the son of Laius and* JOCASTA

JOCASTA, *wife and mother of* OEDIPUS

CHORUS OF THEBAN ELDERS

CREON, *brother of* JOCASTA

TIRESIAS, *a celebrated prophet of Thebes, now old and blind*

MANTO, *his daughter*

OLD MAN, *sent from Corinth to announce the death of Polybus*

PHORBAS, *head-shepherd of the royal flocks of Thebes*

A MESSENGER

INTRODUCTION

THE *Oedipus* of Seneca is not one of his most successful plays and suffers by comparison with *Oedipus the King,* Sophocles' masterpiece and one of the greatest tragedies in dramatic literature. Although several Greek playwrights wrote dramas about the story of Oedipus, Sophocles' play is usually considered Seneca's model; if this be true, the dramatic power of the Greek original, its superb irony, and its presentation of Oedipus as an ideal tragic hero are lost to a considerable degree in the Latin adaptation.

The events of the story antecedent to the opening of the play are gradually unfolded as the action of the drama advances. An oracle related to Laius, king of Thebes, that he was destined to perish by the hands of his own son. When a son was born, he gave the infant to a shepherd to be exposed on Mt. Cithaeron. The shepherd disobeyed the order and gave the baby to a herdsman from Corinth. Oedipus grew to manhood as the reputed son of Polybus and Merope, king and queen of Corinth. Hearing an oracle that doomed him to kill his father and marry his mother, he fled from Corinth to escape his fate. As he journeyed northward, he met and slew King Laius. Arriving at Thebes he solved the riddle of the Sphinx, became king, and married Jocasta, the recently widowed queen. Sons and daughters were born to the royal pair. Some time later a dreadful pestilence came upon the city of Thebes, and Oedipus sent Creon, Jocasta's brother, to consult the oracle and learn how the state might be delivered from the scourge. It is at this point that both the Sophoclean and Senecan versions of the story begin. During the course of the action Oedipus and Jocasta discover the horrible truth that Oedipus has killed his father and married his mother.

Seneca's tragedy differs in many respects from the Greek play. The omissions and additions which he made are valuable for the light they throw upon his conception of tragedy and his attitude towards his original. He saw in the legend of Oedipus an opportunity for both declamation and weird necromancy. The prophecy of Tiresias was developed into the sacrifice which Manto, the daughter of Tiresias, describes at length. Her words foreshadow with vivid allegory not only

Oedipus' self-inflicted blindness and Jocasta's death but also the later events, the civil strife of Polynices and Eteocles. In addition to this, Seneca inserted a long passage in which Creon describes the calling up of the spirit of King Laius. The ghost of Laius denounces Oedipus as the guilty man:

> "But 'tis thy bloody king,
> Who, as the prize of savage murder done,
> Hath seized his father's sceptre and his bed."

Oedipus, believing that his father is Polybus, king of Corinth, refuses to accept Creon's story and accuses him of plotting with Tiresias to seize the throne. Seneca attempted here to avoid some of the improbabilities of the Greek play. Although the Sophoclean Oedipus failed to realise the truth until the final revelation was made, he had nevertheless been suspicious enough of his supposed parentage to consult the oracle of Apollo. Seneca, wishing to make Oedipus' attitude more credible, removed this doubt concerning his birth; Oedipus therefore has less reason to link his own fate with that of the former king of Thebes. But in such changes as this Seneca destroyed part of the complexity of the Sophoclean Oedipus which makes him one of the great characterisations of all time.

That the purpose of the two dramatists was different is obvious. Less than half of Seneca's play is devoted to dramatic dialogue; the remainder consists of lyric songs and the long scenes of sacrifice and necromancy. In other words, Seneca gives less than 500 lines to the gradual revelation of a complicated dramatic plot. Omission and compression were inevitable and the play has suffered thereby, not merely structurally, but in the delineation of the characters as well. Oedipus is a suspicious and somewhat tyrannical king, and lacks the dignity and grandeur of the Sophoclean character. He seems less a master of his destiny than an individual doomed by Fate to the most horrible of crimes. Yet, like the Greek Oedipus, he accepts responsibility for his crimes at the end; when Jocasta stabs herself and falls dead before him, he cries to Apollo:

> "O fate-revealer, thee do I upbraid,
> Thou god and guardian of the oracles.
> My father only was I doomed to slay;
> But now, twice parricide and past my fears,
> Have I been guilty, and my mother slain.
> For 'tis by sin of mine that she is dead."

In spite of Seneca's excessive rhetoric and his horror-raising descriptions, there are passages of real power in the play. The tragic irony in

Oedipus' curse on the murderer of King Laius, the sudden reversal that comes when the Corinthian attempts to reassure Oedipus with the news that he is not the son of Merope—passages such as these retain something of the greatness of the Greek original. The messenger's description of the blinding of Oedipus, for all its horror, reveals a care for psychological analysis that is characteristic of the Roman playwright. As Oedipus debates with himself whether to die or to live a lingering death in life, the tears stream down his face, and the very tears he sheds suggest to him the form his self-inflicted punishment must take.

OEDIPUS

(SCENE:—*Before the royal palace of Thebes.*)

Act One.   Scene I

(*Enter* OEDIPUS.)

OEDIPUS: Now night has fled; and with a wavering gleam
Returns the sun; all wrapped in murky clouds
His beams arise, and with their baleful light
Shall soon look forth upon our stricken homes,
And day reveal the havoc of the night.
Does any man rejoice in power? Fate,
That seemest good, how many ills lie hid
Behind thy smiling face! As lofty peaks
Most feel the winds' abuse; and as the cliff,
That with its rocky front divides the deep,
The waves of e'en a quiet sea assail;
So is the loftiest power the most exposed
To hostile fate's assaults.
                    'Twas well conceived
That I should flee the kingdom of my sire,
Old Polybus, and from my fears be freed,
A homeless exile, dauntless, wandering.
Be heaven and all the gods my witnesses,
I chanced upon this realm. Yet even now
The dreadful fear remains that by my hand
My sire shall die. Thus spoke the Delphic god.
And still another, greater sin he showed.
And can there be a blacker crime than this,
A father slain? Oh, cursed impiety!
'Twere shame to tell the hideous oracle:
For Phoebus warned me of my father's couch,
And impious wedlock. 'Twas the fear of this

674

That drove me headlong from my father's realm,
And for no sin I left my native land.
All self-distrustful did I well secure
Thy sacred laws, O mother Nature; still,
When in the heart a mighty dread abides,
Though well assured it cannot be fulfilled,
The fear remains. I fear exceedingly,
Nor can I trust myself unto myself.
And even now the fates are aimed at me.
For what am I to think, when this fell pest,
Although it lays its blighting hand on all,
Spares me alone? For what new horror now
Am I reserved? Amidst my city's woes,
'Mid funeral pyres that ever must be wet
With tears of grief afresh, 'mid heaps of slain,
I stand unscathed. And couldst thou hope that thou,
A culprit at the bar of God, shouldst gain
For guilt a wholesome kingdom in return?
Nay, rather, I myself infect the air.
For now no breeze with its soft breath relieves
Our spirits suffocating with the heat;
No gentle zephyrs breathe upon the land;
But Titan with the dog-star's scorching fires
Doth parch us, pressing hard upon the back
Of Nemea's lion. From their wonted streams
The waters all have fled, and from the herbs
Their accustomed green. Now Dirce's fount is dry;
While to a trickling rill Ismenus' flood
Hath shrunk, and barely laves the naked sands.
Athwart the sky doth Phoebus' sister glide
With paling light, and, 'mid the lowering clouds,
The darkling heavens fade. No starlight gleams
Amid the gloomy silence of the night,
But heavy mists brood low upon the earth;
And those bright mansions of the heavenly gods
Are sicklied over with the hues of hell.
The full-grown harvest doth withhold its fruit;
And, though the yellow fields stand thick with corn,
Upon the stalk the shriveled grain is dead.
No class is free from this destructive plague,
But every age and sex falls equally;
Where youth with age, and sire with son are joined,
And wife and husband are together burned.

Now funerals claim no more their wonted grief;
The magnitude of woe hath dried our eyes;
And tears, the last resource of woeful hearts,
Have perished utterly. The stricken sire
Here bears his son unto the funeral flames;
And there the mother lays her dead child down,
And hastes to bring another to the pyre.
Nay, in the midst of grief a new woe springs;
For, while they minister unto the dead,
Themselves need funeral rites. Anon they burn
With others' fires the bodies of their friends.
The fire is stol'n, for in their wretchedness
No shame remains. No separate tombs receive
The hallowed bones; mere burning is enough.
How small a covering their ashes need!
And yet the land does not suffice for all;
And now the very woods have failed the pyre.
Nor prayers nor skill avail to serve the sick,
For even they who own the healing art
Are smitten down. The baleful pestilence
Removes the check that would restrain its force.
    So, prostrate at the altar, do I fall
And, stretching suppliant hands, I pray the gods
To grant a speedy end; that in my death
I may anticipate my falling throne,
Nor be myself the last of all to die,
The sole surviving remnant of my realm.
O gods of heaven, too hard! O heavy fate!
Is death to be denied to me alone,
So easy for all else? Come, fly the land
Thy baleful touch has tainted. Leave thou here
The grief, the death, the pestilential air,
Which with thyself thou bring'st. Go speed thy flight
To any land, e'en to thy parents' realm.

(*Enter* JOCASTA *in time to hear her husband's last words.*)

JOCASTA: What boots it, husband, to augment thy woes
With lamentations? For I think, indeed,
This very thing is regal, to endure
Adversity, and all the more to stand,
With heart more valiant and with foot more sure,
When the weight of empire totters to its fall.

For 'tis not manly to present thy back
To fortune's darts.

OEDIPUS:　　　　　　　　　　Not mine the guilt of fear;
My valour feels no such ignoble throes.
Should swords be drawn against me, should the power,
The dreadful power of Mars upon me rush,
Against the very giants would I stand.
The Sphinx I fled not when she wove her words
In mystic measures, but I bore to look
Upon the bloody jaws of that fell bard,
And on the ground, all white with scattered bones.
But when, from a lofty cliff, with threatening mien,
The baleful creature poised her wings to strike,
And, like a savage lion, lashed her tail,
In act to spring; still did I dare my fate
And ask her riddle. Then with horrid sound
Of deadly jaws together crashed, she spake;
The while her claws, impatient of delay,
And eager for my vitals, rent the rock.
But the close-wrought words of fate with guile entwined,
And that dark riddle of the wingéd beast
Did I resolve.

JOCASTA:　　　　　　　What meant'st then thou by these
Thy maddened prayers for death? Thou mightst have
　　　died.
But no; the very sceptre in thy hand
Is thy reward for that fell Sphinx destroyed.

OEDIPUS:　Yea that, the artful monster's cruel shade,
Doth war against me still. Now she alone,
In vengeance for her death, is wasting Thebes.
But now, one only way of safety still is left,
If Phoebus show us not of safety all bereft.

Act One.　Scene II

(*Enter the* CHORUS OF THEBAN ELDERS, *deploring the violence of the
　plague.*)

CHORUS:　　　　　How art thou fall'n, O glorious stock
　　　　　　　　Of Cadmus, thou and Thebes in one!

How dost thou see, poor ruined Thebes,
Thy lands laid waste and tenantless.
And thou, O Theban Bacchus, hear:
That hardy soldiery of thine,
Thy comrades to the farthest Ind,
Who dared invade the Eastern plains,
And plant thy banners at the gates of dawn—
Behold, destruction feeds on them.
They saw the blessed Arabes,
'Mid spicy groves; and the fleeing steeds
Of the Parthian, deadliest when he flees;
They trod the marge of the ruddy sea,
Where Phoebus his rising beams displays,
And the day reveals; where his nearer fires
Darken the naked Indians.
Yea we, that race invincible,
Beneath the hand of greedy fate
Are falling fast.
The gloomy retinue of death
In march unceasing hurries on;
The grieving line unending hastes
To the place of death. Space fails the throng.
For, though seven gates stand open wide,
Still for the crowding funerals
'Tis not enough; for everywhere
Is carnage seen, and death treads hard
Upon the heels of death.
The sluggish ewes first felt the blight,
For the woolly flock the rich grass cropped
To its own doom. At the victim's neck
The priest stood still, in act to strike;
But while his hand still poised the blow,
Behold, the bull, with gilded horns,
Fell heavily; whereat his neck,
Beneath the shock of his huge weight,
Was broken and asunder yawned.
No blood the sacred weapon stained,[1]
But from the wound dark gore oozed forth.
The steed a sudden languor feels,
And stumbles in his circling course,
While from his downward-sinking side
His rider falls.
The abandoned flocks lie in the fields;

The bull amid his dying herd
Is pining; and the shepherd fails
His scanty flock, for he himself
'Mid his wasting kine is perishing.
The stag no more fears the ravenous wolf;
No longer the lion's roar is heard;
The shaggy bear has lost her rage,
And the lurking serpent his deadly sting;
For parched and dying now he lies,
With venom dried.
No more do the woods, with leafage crowned,
Spread out their shade in the mountain glens;
No more are fields with verdure clad;
No vines bend low with laden arms;
For the very earth has felt the breath
Of our dire pestilence.
Through the riven bars of Erebus,
With torches lit in Tartara,
The raging band of the Furies troop;
Dark Phlegethon has changed his course,
And forced the waters of the Styx
To mingle with our Theban streams.
Grim Death opes wide his greedy jaws,
And all his baleful wings outspreads.
And he who plies that swollen stream
In his roomy skiff, though his age is fresh
And hardy, scarce can raise his arms,
O'erwearied with his constant toil
And the passage of the endless throng.
'Tis even rumoured that the dog
Hath burst the chains of Taenara,
And through our fields is wandering.
Now dreadful prodigies appear:
The earth gives out a rumbling sound,
And ghosts go stealing through the groves,
Larger than mortal forms; and twice
The trees of our Cadmean woods
Have trembled sore and shed their snows;
Twice Dirce flowed with streams of blood;
And in the stilly night we heard
The baying of Amphion's hounds.
Oh, cruel, strange new form of death,
And worse than death! The sluggish limbs

Are with a weary languor seized;
The sickly cheek with fever burns,
And all the head with loathsome sores
Is blotched. Now heated vapours rise
And scorch with fever's flames the brain
Within the body's citadel,
And the throbbing temples swell with blood.
The eyeballs start; the accursèd fire
Devours the limbs; the ears resound,
And from the nostrils dark blood drips
And strains apart the swelling veins.
Now quick convulsions rend and tear
The inmost vitals.
Now to their burning hearts they strain
Cold stones to soothe their agony;
And they, whom laxer care permits,
Since they who should control are dead,
The fountains seek, and feed their thirst
With copious draughts. The smitten throng
All prostrate at the altars lie
And pray for death; and this alone
The gods, compliant, grant to them.
Men seek the sacred fanes, and pray,
Not that the gods may be appeased,
But glutted with their feast of death.

Act Two. Scene I

(CREON *is seen approaching.*)

OEDIPUS: But who with hasty step the palace seeks?
Is this our Creon, high in birth and deed,
Or does my sickened soul see false for true?

CHORUS: 'Tis Creon's self, in answer to our prayer.

(*Enter* CREON.)

OEDIPUS: I quake with horror, and I fear to know
The tendency of fate. My trembling soul
Strives 'neath a double load; for joy and grief
Lie mingled still in dark obscurity.

I shrink from knowing what I long to know.
Wherefore, O brother of my consort, speak;
And if to weary hearts thou bring'st relief,
With quickened utterance thy news proclaim.

CREON: In dark obscurity the answer lies.

OEDIPUS: Who gives me doubtful succour grants me none.

CREON: It is the custom of the Delphic god
In dark enigmas to conceal the fates.

OEDIPUS: Yet speak; however dark the riddle be
'Tis given to Oedipus alone to solve.

CREON: Apollo doth ordain that banishment
Be meted out to him who slew our king,
And so our murdered Laius be avenged;
For only thus shall we again behold
The day's clear light, and drink safe draughts of air.

OEDIPUS: Who was the slayer of the noble king?
Tell who is designated by the god,
That he th' allotted punishment may pay.

CREON: May it be granted me to tell the things
To sight and hearing dreadful. At the thought,
Numb horror holds my limbs, my blood runs cold.
When to Apollo's hallowed shrine I came
With reverent feet, and pious hands upraised,
Parnassus' double-crested, snowy peak
Gave forth a fearful crash, the laurels shook,
And fair Castalia's waters ceased to flow.
The priestess of the son of Leto then
Began to spread her bristling locks abroad,
And felt the inspiration of the god.
Scarce had she reached the sacred inner shrine,
When with a roar, beyond the voice of man,
There sounded forth this doubtful oracle:
"Kind shall the stars return to the Theban city of Cadmus,
If, O fugitive guest, Ismenian Dirce thou leavest,
Stained with the blood of a king, from infancy known to Apollo.
Brief shall be thy joys, the impious joys of slaughter.
With thee war thou bringest, and war to thy children thou leavest,
Foul returned once more to the impious arms of thy mother."

OEDIPUS:　What I at heaven's command now meditate,
Long since should have been rendered to the king,
That none by craft might violate the throne.
And most doth it become a sceptred king
To guard the life of kings; for none laments
The death of him whose safety breedeth fear.

CREON:　Our care for him a greater fear removed.

OEDIPUS:　What fear so great that duty to prevent?

CREON:　The Sphinx and her accurséd riddle's threats.

OEDIPUS:　Then now at heaven's command shall be atoned
That impious deed.
　　　　　　　　　Whoever of the gods
Dost look with kindly eye upon our realm;
And thou, whose hand doth guide the rolling sphere;
And thou, O glory of the smiling sky,
Who in thy wandering course dost rule the stars,
And with thy flying wheels dost measure out
The slow procession of the centuries;
Thou sister of the sun, night-wanderer,
Who ever dost reflect thy brother's fires;
And thou, great ruler of the boisterous winds,
Who o'er the level deep dost drive thy car;
And thou, who dost allot the sunless homes:
May he, by whose right hand king Laius fell,
No peaceful home, no trusty lares find;
And may no land in hospitality
Receive his cheerless, exiled wanderings.
O'er shameful marriage may he live to grieve,
And monstrous progeny. May he his sire
By his own hand destroy; and may he do
(What doom more dreadful can I imprecate?)
The deed which by my flight I did not do.
No room for pardon shall be given him;
By this my regal sceptre do I swear,
Both by the sway which I as stranger hold,
And that I left behind; by my household gods,
And thee, O Neptune, who with shorter waves
And twofold current dost disport thyself
Upon my native Corinth's double shores.
And thou thyself be witness to my words,

Who dost inspire the fate-revealing lips
Of Cirrha's priestess: so may Polybus,
My royal father, spend a quiet age,
And end his days in peace upon the throne;
And so may Merope, my mother, know
The marriage of her Polybus alone,
As from my grasp no favouring power shall snatch
That guilty one, who basely slew the king.
But tell me, where was that foul murder done?
In open fight, or was he basely snared?

CREON: In quest of cool Castalia's sacred fount
And leafy woods, along the way he fared,
On either side with tangled thickets hedged.
'Twas where the road, three-forked, spreads to the plain.
One leads through Phocian land, to Bacchus dear,
Where high Parnassus, by a gentle slope
The lowlands leaving, lifts his double peak
Into the heavens; and one leads off to where
Two oceans bathe the land of Sisyphus;
A third path, passing through Olenian fields,
Along a hollow valley's winding way,
Attains the vagrant waters and divides
The chilling current of the Elean stream.
'Twas here he journeyed, safe 'mid general peace,
When on a sudden, lo, a robber band
Fell on him with the sword and slew him there.
          (TIRESIAS *is seen approaching*)
But in the nick of time, by Phoebus roused,
Tiresias, agéd and with trembling limbs,
Hastes to our presence with what speed he may;
And, as his faithful comrade, Manto comes,
Her sightless father leading by the hand.

Act Two.   Scene II

(*Enter* TIRESIAS, *led by his daughter* MANTO.)

OEDIPUS: O priest of heaven, thou next to Phoebus' self,
Explain the oracle which he hath sent,
And tell on whom the penalty is laid.

TIRESIAS: Because my tongue is slow and seeks delay,
                Thou shouldst not wonder, great-souled Oedipus;
                Much truth is hidden when the eye is dimmed.
                But when my country, when Apollo calls,
                I will obey. Then let me search the fates.
                If in my veins still flowed the blood of youth,
                I would myself sustain the god and speak.
                Now to the altar drive a pure-white bull,
                A heifer, too, upon whose tender neck
                The curvéd yoke of toil hath never pressed.
                And thou, my child, who guid'st my darkened steps,
                Describe the omens which Apollo sends.

(The victims are stationed before the altar as directed.)

MANTO: A perfect victim at the altar stands.

TIRESIAS: With prayer invoke the presence of the gods,
                And heap the altar high with frankincense.

MANTO: Lo, on the sacred fire the spice is heaped.

TIRESIAS: What of the flame? Did it with vigour seize
                The generous feast?

MANTO: With sudden gleam it leaped
                Into the air, and quickly fell again.

TIRESIAS: And did the sacred fire burn bright and clear,
                And point its gleaming summit straight to heaven,
                And, spreading outward, to the breeze unfold;
                Or crawl, with course uncertain, near the ground,
                And, flickering, die away in gloomy smoke?

MANTO: Not one appearance only had the flame.
                As when the tempest-bringing Iris spreads
                Her varying colours on the vault of heaven,
                And with her painted bow adorns the sky;
                So to the sacred fire thou wouldst not tell
                What hue is wanting there and what prevails.
                Dark blue it flickered first, with yellow spots;
                Then bloody red, and then it vanished quite.
                But see! The flame is rent in rival parts,
                And the glowing embers of one sacred pile
                Are cleft in double heaps and fall apart!
                O father, horror fills me as I gaze;
                For, as I pour the sacred liquid forth,

It changes straight to blood—Oh, horrible!
And stifling smoke surrounds the royal head.
And now in denser gloom it settles down
Upon his face, and, with its veiling cloud,
It shuts away from him the fading light.[2]
Oh, speak, and tell us what it doth portend.

TIRESIAS: How can I speak, who halting stand amazed
Amid conflicting voices of the soul?
What shall I say? Dire ills are here, indeed,
But hidden yet in deepest mystery.
With signs well known the wrath of heaven is wont
To be made manifest: but what is that
Which now they would disclose, and then, again,
With changing and destructive purpose hide?
Some deed so vile, it shameth heaven to tell.
But quickly set the chosen victims here,
And sprinkle salted meal upon their heads.
With peaceful face do they endure the rites,
And hands outstretched to smite?

MANTO: His lofty head
The bull uplifted to the eastern sky,
Then shunned the light of day, and quickly turned
In terror from the newly risen sun.

TIRESIAS: With one blow, smitten, do they fall to earth?

MANTO: The heifer threw herself upon the steel,
And with one blow has fallen; but the bull,
Though smitten by a double deadly blow,
Distracted wanders here and there in pain,
And scarce can force his struggling life away.[3]

TIRESIAS: Driven through a narrow opening spurts the blood,
Or, sluggish, does it water deeper wounds?

MANTO: The blood of one, through that same welcome thrust,
Doth flow in generous streams; but of the bull,
Those yawning wounds are stained with scanty drops,
While, turning backward, through his eyes and mouth
The plenteous current flows.

TIRESIAS: These unblest rites
Some dreadful ills portend. But come, describe
The trusty markings of the viscera.

MANTO: Oh, what is this? For not, as is their wont,
With gentle motion do the entrails quake,
But, rather, strongly throb beneath the touch,
While from the veins the blood leaps forth anew.
The sickly heart is shriveled up and lies
Deep hidden in the breast; the veins appear
Of livid hue. The entrails suffer lack;
And from the wasting liver oozes slow
A stream of black corruption. Nay, behold
(A sign of dark foreboding to a king
Who holdeth single sway), two swelling points
Of equal elevation rise to view;
But both are lopped and covered with a veil.
Refusing lurking-place to things unseen,
The hostile side uprears itself with strength
And shows seven swelling veins; [4] but these, again,
An intersecting line cuts straight across,
Preventing their return. The natural law
And order of the parts has been reversed,
And nothing lies within its proper place.
All on the right the blood-filled lungs appear,
Incapable of air; the heart no more
Is found upon the left, its 'customed place.
The fatty walls, with their soft covering,
No longer richly fold the entrails in.
The ways of nature are in all things changed;
The womb itself is most unnatural.
Look close, and see what impious thing is this:
Oh, monstrous! 'Tis the unborn progeny
Of a heifer still unmated! Stranger still,
It lies not in the wonted place, assigned
By nature's laws, but fills its mother's side.
It moves its members with a feeble groan;
Its unformed limbs with trembling rigours twitch.
Black blood has stained the darkened entrails all;
The mangled bodies strive e'en yet to move,
Make show to rise, and menace with their horns
The priestly hands. The entrails shun the touch.
Nor is that lowing which has frightened thee
The deep-voiced roar of bulls, nor do the calls
Of frightened cattle sound upon our ears:
It is the lowing of the altar fires,
It is the frightened muttering of the shrine!

OEDIPUS: What meaning have these monstrous signs? Declare;
And with no timid ears will I attend.
For he who has the dregs of fortune drained
Fears nothing more.

TIRESIAS: The time will come to thee,
When these thy ills, for which thou seekest aid,
Will blessings seem.

OEDIPUS: But tell me then, I pray,
The one thing which the gods would have me know:
Whose hands are stained with murder of the king?

TIRESIAS: Neither the birds can summon up the name,
Who cleave the depths of heaven on fleeting wing,
Nor yet the vitals plucked from living breasts.
But we must seek it in another way:
The murdered king himself must be recalled
From realms of everlasting night, that thus,
Released from Erebus, he may declare
His murderer. The earth must be unsealed;
The pitiless divinity of Dis
Must be implored, and hither brought the shades
Who live beyond the Styx.
Now do thou tell
To whom thou giv'st the sacred embassy;
For 'tis not right for thee who hold'st the reins
Of government to seek the gloomy shades.

OEDIPUS: O Creon, thee this task demands, to whom,
As next in power, my kingdom looks for aid.

TIRESIAS: And while we loose the bars of deepest hell,
Do ye the praises of our Bacchus tell.
(*Exeunt* CREON, TIRESIAS, *and* MANTO.)

Act Two.   Scene III

THE CHORUS (*in dithyrambic strain sings in praise of Bacchus*): Bind
ye now your flowing locks with the swaying ivy,
Brandish aloft with your languishing arms the Nysaean thyrsus!
O glorious light of heaven, attend the prayers
Which noble Thebes, thy Thebes, O beautiful Bacchus,

With suppliant hands outstretched here offers thee.
          Turn hither thy smiling virgin face,
Dispel the clouds with thy starry glance,
The gloomy threats of Erebus,
          And ravenous fate.
Thee it becomes to crown thy locks with flowers of the
          springtime,
Thee to bind thy head with the Tyrian fillet;
Or with the clinging ivy, gleaming with berries,
          Softly to wreathe thy brow;
Now thy hair to unbind and spread in confusion,
Now in close-drawn knot to collect and confine it;
Just as when thou, fearing the wrath of Juno,
Didst conceal thyself in the guise of maidens.
Virgin, too, thou seemedst with golden ringlets,
Binding up thy robe with a saffron girdle.
So the softer graces of living please thee,
Robes ungirt and flowing in long profusion.
When in thy golden car thou wast drawn by lions,
Clad in flowing garments, the East beheld thee,
All the vast expanse of the Indian country,
They who drink the Ganges and cleave the surface
          Of snowy Araxes.
Seated on humble beast the old Silenus attends thee,
Binding his throbbing brows with a waving garland of ivy;
While the wanton priests lead on the mysterious revels.
          And then a troop of Bassarids
          With dancing step conducted thee,
          Now ranging o'er Pangaeus' foot,
          And now on Thracian Pindus' top.
          Soon, 'mid the noble dames of Thebes,
          A furious Maenad, the comrade of Bacchus,
          In garment of fawn-skin, conducted the god.
          The Theban dames, by Bacchus excited,
          With streaming locks and thyrsus uplifted
          In high-waving hands, now join in the revels,
          And wild in their madness they rend Pentheus
               Limb from limb.
          Their fury spent, with weary frame,
          They look upon their impious deed,
               And know it not.
Ino the sea realms holds, the foster-mother of Bacchus;
Round her the daughters of Nereus dance, Leucothoe singing;

Over the mighty deep, though new to its waves, Palaemon,
Brother of Bacchus, rules, a mortal changed to a sea-god.
When in childhood a band of robbers assailing
Bore thee away in their flying vessel a captive,
Nereus quickly calmed the billowy ocean;
When lo! To rolling meadows the dark sea changes;
Here stands in vernal green the flourishing plane-tree,
There the groves of laurel dear to Apollo;
While resounds the chatter of birds in the branches.
Now are the oars enwreathed with the living ivy,
While at the masthead hang the clustering grape vines;
There on the prow loud roars a lion of Ida,
At the stern appears a terrible tiger of Ganges.
Filled with terror the pirates leap in the ocean.
Straight in their plunging forms new changes appear;
For first their arms are seen to shrink and fall,
Their bodies' length to shorten; and on their sides
The hands appear as fins; with curving back
They skim the waves, and, lashing their crescent tails,
    They dash through the water.
Changed to a school of dolphins now, they follow the vessel.
Soon did the Lydian stream with its precious waters receive thee,
Pouring down its golden waves in a billowy current.
Loosed was the vanquished bow and Scythian darts of the savage
Massagetan who mingles blood in his milky goblets.
The realm of Lycurgus, bearer of axes, submitted to Bacchus;
The land of the Dacians untamable felt his dominion,
The wandering tribes of the north by Boreas smitten,
And whom the Maeotis bathes with its frozen waters.
Where the Arcadian star looks down from the zenith,
Even there the power of Bacchus extended;
Conquered too the scattered Gelonian peoples.
From the warlike maidens their arms he wrested;
Down to the earth they fell in desperate conflict,
The hardy bands of Amazonian maidens.
Now, at last, their arrows swift are abandoned,
    And Maenads have they become.
Holy Cithaeron too has streamed with slaughter,
Where was spilt the noble blood of Ophion.[5]
Proetus' daughters the forests sought; and Argos,
Juno at last consenting, paid homage to Bacchus.
The island of Naxos, girt by the broad Aegean,
Gave to Bacchus the maid[6] whom Theseus abandoned,

Compensating her loss by a better husband.
Out of the rock there gushed Nyctelian liquor;
Babbling streams at his word clove the grassy meadows;
Deep the earth drank in the nectarean juices;
Streams of snowy milk burst forth from the fountains,
Mingled with Lesbian wine all fragrant with spices.
Now is the bride to her place in the heavens conducted;
Phoebus, with flowing locks, sings a stately anthem;
Love, in honour of both, bears the wedding torches;
Jove lays down the deadly darts of his lightning,
Hating his bolts of flame at the coming of Bacchus.
While the gleaming stars in their boundless pasturage wander,
While the sea shall gird th' imprisoned earth with its waters,
While the full-orb'd moon shall gather her lost refulgence,
While the morning star shall herald the coming of Phoebus,
While in the north the Bear shall fear the cerulean ocean,
Still shall we worship the shining face of the beautiful Bacchus.

Act Three.   Scene I

(*Enter* CREON, *returned from the rites of necromancy.*)

OEDIPUS: Although thy face displays the marks of grief,
Declare whose death an angry heaven demands.

CREON: Thou bid'st me speak where fear would silence keep.

OEDIPUS: If Thebes, to ruin falling, move thee not,
Regard the sceptre of thy kindred house.

CREON: Thou wilt repent the knowledge which thou seek'st.

OEDIPUS: A useless cure for ills is ignorance.
And wilt thou still obstruct the public weal?

CREON: Where foul the cure, 'tis grievous to be cured.

OEDIPUS: Thy tidings speak; or, by thy pains subdued,
Thou soon shalt know what angered kings can do.

CREON: Kings hate the words whose speech they would compel.

OEDIPUS: In Hades shalt thou pay thy life for all,
Unless thou tell the secrets of the fates.

CREON: Nay, let me hold my peace. No smaller boon
            Was ever sought.

OEDIPUS: More often than by speech,
            Have kingdoms by the boon of silence fall'n.

CREON: When silence is denied what can be given?

OEDIPUS: He sins who silence holds when speech is best.

CREON: Then hear in peace the words which I must speak.

OEDIPUS: Was ever punishment for speech compelled?

CREON: Afar from Thebes there is a frowning grove
            Near the well-watered vale of Dirce's fount.
            And there a cypress lifts its giant head
            And holds within its evergreen embrace
            The trees around. Here stands an ancient oak
            And spreads its branches dark with clustering mould.
            One side is torn by time's destructive hand;
            The rest, with roots decayed and falling, hangs
            Supported on a neighbour's trunk. Here stand
            The bitter laurel, rustling linden trees,
            The myrtle, and the alder destined soon
            To sweep its oarage on the boundless sea.
            Midway, a mighty pine its smooth trunk lifts
            Against the rays of Phoebus and the winds,
            And with its heavy shade it overwhelms
            The lesser trees; for, with its spreading boughs,
            It stands, the giant guardian of the wood.
            Beneath this pine there springs a gloomy pool
            That never saw the sun nor light of day.
            An oozy swamp surrounds the sluggish pool.
            Here did the agéd priest direct his steps;
            Nor was there need to wait; the gloomy spot
            Supplied the shades of night. A trench is dug,
            Where brands are kindled, pluck'd from funeral pyres.
            The priest is shrouded in a mourning pall,
            And waves the bough; his dark robe sweeps the earth.
            And now, in squalid garb and wrapped in gloom,
            The priest advances, with his hoary locks
            Encircled by the yew-tree's deadly leaves.
            Black sheep and sable oxen, backward driven,
            Are sacrificed. The fire devours the food,

And the living entrails quiver in the flames.
The shades he calls, and him who rules the shades,
And him who guards the dark Lethaean stream.
A magic rune he mutters o'er and o'er
And fiercely chants the charm which either lures
The shifting ghosts, or forces them to come.
He burns the victims whole, and fills the trench
With sacrificial blood, and snowy milk,
And, with his left hand pouring, mingles wine;
Again he chants, and, bending to the earth,
With stronger words and frantic, summons up
The manes. Loudly bayed the hounds of hell;
And thrice the hollows gave a mournful sound;
The whole earth trembled and the solid ground
Was rent asunder. Then the priest exclaimed:
"I have prevailed, for strong the words I spoke;
The deep and gloomy realm of chaos yawns,
And for the dwellers in the home of Dis
A way is opened to the world of light."
The whole wood shrank away; its leaves erect
In horror stood, the mighty trunks were split,
And all the grove was smitten with amaze.
The frightened earth crouched back with hollow groans,
As if unwillingly she saw the deeps
Of Acheron assailed; or else herself,
That back to life the dead might find a way,
With crashing sound her close-wrought barriers burst;
Or threefold Cerberus in angry rage
Clanked loud his heavy chains. Then suddenly
The earth yawned wide, and at our very feet
A deep abyss appeared. I saw, myself,
The sluggish pools amidst the dusky shades;
I saw the shadowy gods, and that black gloom
No earthly night can give. At that dread sight
My blood ran cold and froze within my veins.
And then there hurried forth a dreadful band,
And stood in armed array, that viper brood,
The troop of brothers sprung from dragon's teeth;
And that fell pestilence, the curse of Thebes.
Then grim Erinys raised her piercing cry,
Blind Fury, Dread, and all the ghastly forms
Which spawn and lurk within the endless shades:
Grief, in her madness, tearing out her hair;

Disease, scarce holding up her weary head;
Age, burdened with itself, and brooding Fear.
Our spirits died within us at the sight.
Even the prophet's daughter stood amazed,
Though well she knew her father's mystic arts.
But he, undaunted, since he saw them not,
Convoked the bloodless throng of gloomy Dis.
Like clouds the shadowy forms come trooping up,
And snuff the air of unrestricted heaven.
Not lofty Eryx in his mountain glades
As many falling leaves, nor Hybla's slopes
As many flowers produce, in sunny spring,
When greedy bees in teeming bunches swarm;
As many waves break not upon the shore;
As many birds deserting Strymon's streams,
Exchange not wintry blasts and Arctic snows,
And seek the milder valley of the Nile;
As were the shades the prophet summoned forth.
In eager haste the shivering spirits seek
The hiding-places of the leafy grove.
From out the cave, his right hand by the horns
A raging bull restraining, Zethus came,
And next Amphion, with that famous shell
Whose magic strains insensate rocks allured.
Here haughty Niobe, in safety now,
Amongst her children lifts her head in scorn
And proudly counts her shades. And worse than she,
That mother, mad Agave, next appears,
With all the impious band who rent the king.
Then Pentheus' self, all torn and bleeding, comes,
In rage pursuing those wild Bacchanals.
At length, when often summoned, Laius comes
In shame, and, skulking, flees the shadowy throng,
And hides himself away; but still the seer,
With unrelenting purpose pressing on,
Repeats his strong compelling exorcisms,
Until he brings the ghost to open view.
I shudder as I tell it. There he stood,
A fearful sight, his body drenched with blood,
His matted locks o'erspread with horrid filth.
And now, with raging tongue, the spectre spoke:
"O wild and savage house of Cadmus, thou
Who ever dost rejoice in brother's blood!

The thyrsus wave, in madness rend thy sons.
The greatest crime of Thebes is mother's love.
O fatherland, 'tis not the wrath of heaven,
But sin of man by which thou art undone.
No plague-fraught south wind with its deadly blast,
Nor yet the parchéd earth with its dry breath,
Is harming thee; but 'tis thy bloody king,
Who, as the prize of savage murder done,
Hath seized his father's sceptre and his bed.
An impious son (but far more impious,
The mother who in most unhallowed womb
Bore children once again), he forced his way
Back to his source of life, and there begot
Upon his mother offspring horrible,
Got brothers to himself, a custom base,
Whence e'en the very beasts of prey are free.
Oh, base entanglement, more monstrous far
Than that fell Sphinx which he himself hath slain.
Thee, thee, who dost the bloody sceptre hold,
Thee will thy sire, still unavenged, pursue,
With all thy town; and with me will I bring
Th' attendant fury of my wedding night—
I'll bring her with her loud-resounding lash!
Thy house, polluted, will I overthrow,
And thy Penates will I trample down
In fratricidal strife! Then quickly drive
Thy king, O Thebes, from out thy boundaries!
For when his baleful step shall leave the land,
In vernal green shall it renew itself,
The air shall give again pure springs of life,
And to the woods their beauty shall return.
Destruction, Pestilence and Death, Distress,
Disease, Despair—his fitting company—
Shall all depart with him. And he, indeed,
Will seek with eager haste to flee his realm,
But him will I hedge round with barriers,
And hold him back. Uncertain of his way,
And with his staff to guide his faltering steps,
He'll creep along his sad and darkened path.
Do ye the land deny him; I, his sire,
Will take away from him the light of heaven."

OEDIPUS: A chilling tremor penetrates my bones;

The very thing which I have feared to do,
They say that I have done it. But the charge
That in unholy wedlock I am joined,
My mother Merope refutes, for she
To Polybus, my sire, is wedded still;
And my hands from stain of father's blood are clean,
Since Polybus in safety lives and reigns.
Since both my parents free me from the guilt
Of murder and that base, incestuous crime,
What room is there for accusation more?
And as for Laius, Thebes his death deplored
Long 'ere I set my feet upon her soil.
What shall we say then? Was the seer deceived,
Or does the hand of God afflict the state?
No! Now we see these two confederates
Deep in a crafty plot: that priest of thine
With lying tongue pretends the will of heaven,
And promises my sovereignty to thee.

CREON: Would I expel my sister from the throne?
But if that sacred fealty which I owe
Unto my kindred house restrained me not,
Yet fortune would herself affright me sore,
For with care and danger is she ever fraught.
But be thyself content to lay aside,
While still thou safely mayst, the cares of state,
Lest, borne too long, they may o'erwhelm thee quite
In a humbler state more safely shalt thou dwell.

OEDIPUS: And dost thou bid me, then, of mine own will
To lay aside the heavy cares of state?

CREON: Thus would I counsel those to whom the way
Is open yet to choose the path he will.
But the lot that fortune sends thee thou must bear.

OEDIPUS: When one desires to reign, 'tis ever thus,
That humble life he praises, and the joys
Of ease and sleep are ever in his mouth.
A peaceful face oft hides a restless heart.

CREON: Does my long loyalty defend me not?

OEDIPUS: To traitors, loyalty's a cloak to crime.

CREON: Free from the burdens of a kingly state,
I still enjoy the fruits of royalty;
My house is honoured by our citizens;
And day by day thy royal gifts o'erflow,
And fill my kindred home with luxury.
Rich food and clothing, gifts of every sort,
And safety flow to many through my aid.
Why should I think aught lacking to my lot?

OEDIPUS: Because there is a lack. Prosperity
Ne'er halts at any bounds.

CREON: And shall I fall,
Prejudged, and have no right to plead my cause?

OEDIPUS: Hadst thou consideration for *my* life?
Did old Tiresias listen to my cause?
And yet I am condemned. My pattern, thou;
I do but follow in the way thou lead'st.

CREON: But what if I am guiltless?

OEDIPUS: Kings are wont
To fear alike the doubtful and the true.

CREON: Who quakes at empty fears, hath true in store.

OEDIPUS: Who in a fault is taken, and forgiven,
Is filled with hate. Let all such dubious faith
Be far from me.

CREON: But thus is hatred bred.

OEDIPUS: Nay, he who feareth hatred overmuch,
Knows not the art of ruling like a king;
For 'tis by fear that kings are guarded most.

CREON: Who holds the sceptre with tyrannic sway,
Doth live in fear of those who fear his power;
For terror ever doth return to him
Who doth inspire it.

OEDIPUS (*to attendants*): Hence, away with him;
Deep in some rocky dungeon let him stay,
While I unto the palace take my way.
(CREON *is led away by the attendants, while* OEDIPUS *retires into the palace.*)

Act Three.   Scene II

CHORUS:

Not thou the cause of these our ills;
And not on thy account hath fate
Attacked the house of Labdacus;
But 'tis the ancient wrath of heaven
That still pursues our race.
Castalia's grove once lent its shade
Unto the Tyrian wanderer,[7]
And Dirce gave her cooling waves,
What time the great Agenor's son,
O'er all the earth the stolen prey
Of Jove pursuing, worn and spent,
Within these forests knelt him down
And adored the heavenly ravisher.
Then by Apollo's bidding led,
A wandering heifer following,
Upon whose neck the dragging plow,
Nor the plodding wagon's curving yoke
Had never rested, he his quest
At last gave over, and his race
From that ill-omened heifer named.[8]
From that time forth, the land of Thebes
Strange monsters hath engendered: first,
That serpent, sprung from the valley's depths,
Hissing, o'ertopped the agéd oaks
And lofty pines; and higher still,
Above Chaonia's woods, he reared
His gleaming head, though on the ground
His body lay in many coils.
And next the teeming earth produced
An impious brood of arméd men.
The battle call resounded loud
From the curving horn, and the piercing notes
Of the brazen trumpet shrill were heard.
Their new-created, nimble tongues,
And voices strange, they first employ
In hostile clamour; and the fields,
The plains, their kindred soil, they fill.
This monster brood, consorting well
With that dire seed from which they sprung,
Their life within a day's brief span

Enjoyed; for after Phoebus rose
They had their birth, but ere he set
They perished. At the dreadful sight
Great terror seized the wanderer;
And much he feared to face in war
His new-born foes. Until, at length
The savage youth in mutual strife
Fell down, and mother earth
Beheld her sons, but now produced,
Returned again to her embrace.
And oh, that with their fall might end
All impious strife within the state!
May Thebes, the land of Hercules,
Such fratricidal strife behold
No more!   Why sing Actaeon's fate,
Whose brow the new-sprung antlers crowned
Of the long-lived stag, and whom his hounds,
Though their hapless master still, pursued?
In headlong haste through the mountains and woods,
He flees in fear, and with nimble feet
He scours the glades and rocky passes,
In fear of the wind-tossed feathers hung
Among the trees; but most he shuns
The snares which he himself has set;
Until at last in the still, smooth pool
He sees his horns and his features wild,
The pool where the goddess, too sternly chaste,
Had bathed her virgin limbs.

Act Four.   Scene I

(*Enter* OEDIPUS *and* JOCASTA.)

OEDIPUS: My soul is filled with dark, foreboding fear;
              For the gods in heaven and Hades join the charge
              That by my guilty hand King Laius fell.
              And yet my soul, in conscious innocence,
              And knowing better than the gods themselves
              Its secret deeds, denies the charge.
                                      But now,

Along the shadowy vistas of the past,
My memory beholds an agéd man who fell
Beneath the heavy stroke of my stout staff.
But first the elder strove with haughty words
To drive the younger traveler from the path.
But that was far from Thebes, in Phocis' realm,
Where the forkéd road in three directions leads.
But thou, my faithful wife, dispel my care:
What span of life had Laius at his death?
Fell he in manhood's bloom, or spent with age?

JOCASTA: Midway 'twixt youth and age, but nearer age.

OEDIPUS: Did courtiers, thronging round, protect his course?

JOCASTA: The many lost him on the winding way;
A few by faithful toil kept near his side.

OEDIPUS: Did any fall as comrade of his fate?

JOCASTA: One comrade in his death did valour give.

OEDIPUS: Alas, I stand convicted, for the place
And number tally. Tell me now the time.

JOCASTA: Since Laius fell, ten harvests have been reaped.

Act Four.   Scene II

(*Enter an* OLD CORINTHIAN MAN, *a messenger from Merope.*)

OLD MAN (*to* OEDIPUS): The state of Corinth calls thee to the throne,
For Polybus has gained his lasting rest.

OEDIPUS: See how a heartless fate doth compass me!
But tell me how my father met his end.

OLD MAN: In gentle sleep he breathed his life away.

OEDIPUS: My sire is dead, and not by violence!
I call the gods to witness that to heaven
I now in piety may lift my hands,
And fear no stain of impious slaughter more.
And yet a still more fearful fate remains.

OLD MAN: Thy father's kingdom will dispel thy fears.

OEDIPUS: My father's kingdom would I seek, but still
I fear my mother.

OLD MAN: Fear'st thou her who waits
With anxious heart, imploring thy return?

OEDIPUS: 'Tis piety itself that bids me flee.

OLD MAN: And wouldst thou leave her in her widowhood?

OEDIPUS: Thou speak'st the very essence of my fears.

OLD MAN: Speak out the fear that doth oppress thy soul;
For 'tis my wont in trusty confidence
To counsel kings.

OEDIPUS: By Phoebus' word forewarned,
From wedlock with my mother do I flee.

OLD MAN: Then cease thy empty fears, and lay aside
Thy base forebodings; for I tell thee here
That thou art not the son of Merope.

OEDIPUS: Why did she wish to rear a spurious son?

OLD MAN: Because the proud security of kings
Is by a son established.

OEDIPUS: Tell me now
How thou dost know the secrets of the court.

OLD MAN: With my own hands I gave thee to the king.

OEDIPUS: Thou gavest me? But who gave me to thee?

OLD MAN: A shepherd on Cithaeron's snowy slopes.

OEDIPUS: How camest thou within that sacred wood?

OLD MAN: My sheep upon that mountain did I seek.

OEDIPUS: Now on my body name some well-known mark.

OLD MAN: Behold, thy feet in infancy were pierced,
And from thy swollen ankles art thou named.

OEDIPUS: Who was the man who gave me as a gift
Into thy hands?

OLD MAN: He fed the royal flocks,
And under him the hireling shepherds served.

OEDIPUS: But tell his name.

OLD MAN: An old man's memory
Grows faint and weakly falters with disuse.

OEDIPUS: But wouldst thou know the features of the man?

OLD MAN: I might recall him, for a slender clue
Ofttimes awakens memory of things
Long buried and forgot.

OEDIPUS: Then hasten, slaves,
Let all the master-shepherds drive their flocks
Before the altar here, yea, summon all
On whom depends the guidance of the flocks.
                (The slaves depart.)

OLD MAN: Or chance or providence has kept thy fate
In darkness hid. What long hath lain concealed,
I bid thee suffer to remain in doubt.
For often truth, when brought into the light,
Becomes the bane of him who seeks for her.

OEDIPUS: Can any ills be worse than those I fear?

OLD MAN: Oh, be thou sure the truth is big with fate,
Whose meaning must be sought with toil and pain.
The public weal calls there, and here thine own,
And both with equal voice. Direct thy steps
Along a middle course! Provoke not fate;
Permit thy fortune to unfold itself.
It profits naught to change a happy state.

OEDIPUS: A change is well when all is at the worst.

OLD MAN: What better canst thou ask than royal birth?
No further seek, lest thou thy sire repent.

OEDIPUS: Though I should prove to be of shameful blood,
My purpose still is fixed to know the truth.

Act Four.   Scene III

(*Enter* PHORBAS, *the head-shepherd.*)

OEDIPUS: But see, the agéd man, old Phorbas, comes,
'Neath whose control the royal flocks are kept.
Dost thou remember still his face or name?

OLD MAN: His form eludes my mind; not fully known,
And yet again not all unknown his face.
(*To* PHORBAS)
Old man, while Laius still was king, didst thou,
His shepherd, ever drive the royal flocks
To pasture here upon Cithaeron's slopes?

PHORBAS: On fair Cithaeron's sunny slopes my flocks
Have ever found the greenest pasturage.

OLD MAN: Dost thou know me?

PHORBAS: But dim and indistinct
My memory.

OEDIPUS: Didst thou at any time
An infant boy deliver to this man?
(PHORBAS *falters and turns pale*)
Come then, speak out! Why dost thou hesitate?
And why does pallor overspread thy cheeks?
Why seek for words? The truth no respite needs.

PHORBAS: Thou speak'st of things long buried and forgot.

OEDIPUS: But speak, or pain shall drive thee to confess.

PHORBAS: I gave a boy to him, a useless gift;
He never could have lived or known the light.

OLD MAN: The gods forbid! The child is living still;
And may his life be long on earth, I pray.

OEDIPUS: Why dost thou think the child did not survive?

PHORBAS: A slender rod of iron his ankles pierced,
And bound his limbs. This wound produced a sore,
Which by contagion spread o'er all his frame.

OLD MAN: Why question more? The fatal truth draws near.
Who was that infant boy?

PHORBAS: My lips are sealed.

OEDIPUS: Bring hither fire! Its flames shall loose thy speech.

PHORBAS: Must truth be sought along such cruel paths?
I pray thy grace.

OEDIPUS: If I seem harsh to thee,
Or headstrong, thy revenge is in thy hand—
The truth revealed. Then speak: who was the child?
Of what sire gotten? Of what mother born?

PHORBAS: *He was the son of her who is thy—wife.*

OEDIPUS: Then yawn, O earth! And thou, O king of shades,
Into the lowest depths of Hades hurl
This vile confounder of the son and sire!
Ye citizens, on my incestuous head
Heap crushing rocks! With weapons slaughter me!
Let husbands, fathers, sons, and brothers—all
Whose name I have defiled, against me arm!
And let the poor, plague-smitten populace
Hurl blazing brands from off their funeral pyres!
The plague spot of the age, I wander here,
Heaven-cursed polluter of all sacred ties;
Who, in the day when first I breathed the air,
Was doomed to death.
                    (*To himself*)
                          Call up thy courage now,
And dare some deed befitting these thy crimes.
Haste to thy palace and congratulate
Thy mother's house increased by children's sons.
(OEDIPUS *goes into the palace.*)

Act Four.   Scene IV

CHORUS: If it were mine to choose my fate
            And fashion as I would,
I'd trim my sails to the gentle breeze,
Lest, by the raging blasts o'erwhelmed,
            My spars should broken be.

May soft and gently blowing winds
 My dauntless bark lead on;
And ever on the middle course,
Where safely runs the path of life,
 May I be travelling.
Fearing the Cretan king, 'tis said,
 And trusting in strange arts,
Young Icarus essayed the stars,
And strove to conquer birds in flight,
 On false wings balancing.
He fell into the raging sea
 And his name alone survived.
But, wiser far, old Daedalus
A safer course midst the clouds pursued,
 Awaiting his wingéd son.
As the timid bird flees the threat'ning hawk,
 And collects her scattered young;
So the father watched till he saw his son
Plying his hands in the gulfing sea,
 Enmeshed in his useless wings.
So does he stand in treacherous ways,
Whoever goes beyond the bounds
 Ordained by nature's law.
But what is this? The palace gates resound;
Behold, it is the royal messenger.
With wild and woeful mien he seems to come.
Speak out, and tell us what the news thou bring'st.

Act Five. Scene I

(*Enter* MESSENGER *from the palace.*)

MESSENGER: When Oedipus his impious race perceived,
And saw the warning fates had been fulfilled;
When on a hideous charge he stood condemned;
Then, with a deadly purpose in his breast,
Did he approach his palace, and in haste
Beneath those hated battlements he went.
And as a lion rages o'er the sands,
And, threat'ning, tosses back his tawny mane;
So Oedipus advanced with blazing eyes,

And stern, mad face, while hollow groans burst forth,
And from his limbs there dripped a chilling sweat.
He foams and vents a stream of threat'ning words,
And from his heart his mighty grief o'erflows.
He in his madness seeks against himself
Some heavy penalty and like his fate.
"Why do I wait for punishment?" he cries;
"Let my guilty heart with hostile sword be pierced,
Or overwhelmed with flames or crushing rocks!
Oh, for a tiger or some bird of prey,
To rend my tender flesh! Do thou thyself,
Who hast beheld full many deeds of blood,
O cursed Cithaeron, from thy forests send
Thy wild beasts 'gainst me or thy greedy dogs.
Oh, that Agave were returned to earth!
But thou, my soul, why dost thou shrink from death?
For death alone can make thee innocent."
So spake he, and his impious hand he laid
Upon the hilt and drew his glittering sword.
"And dost thou, then, with this brief punishment
Expect to pay thy mighty debt of guilt,
And with one blow wilt balance all thy sins?
Thy death would satisfy thy murdered sire;
But what to appease thy mother wilt thou do,
And those thy children, shamefully begot?
What recompense canst make unto thy land,
Which for thy sin is smit with pestilence?
Such debts as these thou canst not pay by death.
Let Nature, who, in Oedipus alone,
Strange births devising, hath her laws o'erturned,
Subvert herself again to punish him.
Let it be mine, in never-ending round,
To live and die, and to be born again,
That for my crimes by never-ending pain
I may atone. Now use thy wit, poor soul.
Since by repeated death thou canst not die,
Choose then some form of lingering death in life,
Some way by which, not numbered with the dead,
Nor yet the living, thou mayst linger on.
So die, that in thy death thou mayst remain
Without the land wherein thy father dwells.
O soul, why dost thou hesitate?" And then
A sudden stream of tears o'erspread his face,

And wet his cheeks. "And can my tears suffice?
Too long my eyes these useless showers have poured;
Nay, let them follow where the tears have flowed,
From out their sockets driven. O gods of wedlock,
Is this enough? These eyes must be removed."
He spoke with frenzied rage; and all the while
His cheeks were flaming with a dangerous light,
And his starting eyeballs strained to leave their seats.
His face was full of passion, fierce resolve.
Groaning he thrust his hands into his eyes;
And those fierce eyes stood forth to meet his hands,
And eager followed of their own accord
Their kindred hands, as courting that deep wound.
Deep in with hookéd fingers he explores,
And rends his eyeballs from their deepest roots.
Still stays his hands within those empty seats,
And tears the hollow sockets with his nails,
With savage joy, with vain and endless rage;
So great his fear and hatred of the light.
He lifts his head, and with those empty eyes
The heavens surveying, tests his darkened sight.
Whatever from his mangled eyes still hangs,
He tears away, and now in triumph cries
To all the gods: "Oh, spare my country now,
I pray; for I have done what must be done,
And I have paid the penalty I owed.
Now have I found at last a fitting night
To match my impious wedlock." As he speaks,
His face is watered by a hideous shower,
As the blood flows streaming from his ruptured veins.

Act Five.   Scene II

CHORUS: By fate we're driven; then yield to fate.
No anxious, brooding care can change
The thread of destiny that falls
From that grim spindle of the Fates.
Whate'er we mortals suffer here,
Whate'er we do, all hath its birth
In that deep realm of mystery.
Stern Lachesis her distaff whirls,

Spinning the threads of mortal men,
But with no backward-turning hand.
All things in ordered pathways go;
And on our natal day was fixed
Our day of death. Not God himself
Can change the current of our lives,
Which bears its own compelling force
Within itself. Each life goes on
In order fixed and absolute,
Unmoved by prayer. Nay, fear itself
Has been by many found a bane;
For, while they sought to shun their fate,
They came upon it in their flight.
But now the palace gates resound, and see,
The sightless king himself, with none to guide,
Takes hitherward his blind and groping way.

Act Five.   Scene III

(*Enter* OEDIPUS.)

OEDIPUS: Now all is well and finished; to my sire
I've paid the debt I owed. How sweet these shades!
What god, at length appeased, hath wrapped my head
In a pall of darkness, and my crimes forgiven?
Now have I 'scaped the conscious eye of day;
And nothing dost thou owe, O parricide,
To thine avenging hand. Thy sight is gone,
And such a countenance becomes thee well.

(*Enter* JOCASTA.)

CHORUS: See where with hurried step Jocasta comes,
Beside herself and overcome with grief;
As when in maddened rage that Theban dame[9]
Her son's head tore away and realised
What she had done. She wavers, longs to speak
To that afflicted one, and fears to speak.
Now shame at last has yielded to her grief,
And with a faltering tongue she speaks to him.

JOCASTA: What shall I call thee? Son? Dost shun that name?
Thou art my son; thy shame confesseth it.

And yet, O son, though all unwilling, speak.
Why dost thou turn away thy sightless face?

OEDIPUS: Who now forbids me to enjoy my night?
Who gives me back mine eyes? My mother's voice!
Oh, awful sound! Now is my labour vain.
Stay where thou art! Each step is impious.
Let boundless seas our guilty souls divide,
And lands remote; and if beneath this land
Some other hangs, beholding other stars,
May that far country one of us receive.

JOCASTA: What thou deplorest is the fault of fate.
A fated crime can leave no stain of sin.

OEDIPUS: Now cease thy words, O mother, spare my ears,
By these poor remnants of my mangled form,
By that unhallowed offspring of my blood,
And all that in the double names we bear
Is right and wrong!

JOCASTA (*to herself*): Why art thou listless now,
O soul of mine? Since thou hast shared his guilt,
Why hesitate to share his punishment?
The beauty of all human intercourse
Has fallen into ruin for thy sake,
Confused and lost, O wretch incestuous.
Not if the father of the gods himself
Should hurl at me his glittering thunderbolts,
Could I for my foul crimes atonement make,
Since I the name of mother have profaned.
Now death is welcome, but the way of death
Must I consider.
(*To* OEDIPUS)
Come, thou parricide,
And lift thy hand against thy mother too.
This act is wanting to complete thy work.
(*To herself*)
Now let the sword be drawn. By this good blade
Was Laius, my husband, slain—not so;
My husband's father, by his rightful name!
Shall I this weapon plunge into my breast,
Or thrust it deep within my waiting neck?
Nay, nay: thou know'st not how to choose a place.

Strike here, O hand, through this capacious womb,
Which (horrible!) the son and husband bore.
(*She stabs herself and falls dead.*)

CHORUS: She lies in death, her failing hand relaxed;
And spouting streams of blood drive out the sword.

OEDIPUS: O fate-revealer, thee do I upbraid,
Thou god and guardian of the oracles.
My father only was I doomed to slay;
But now, twice parricide and past my fears,
Have I been guilty, and my mother slain.
For 'tis by sin of mine that she is dead.
O lying Phoebus, now have I outdone
The impious fates.
                              With apprehensive feet
Let me go out upon my darkened way,
Planting my footsteps with a faltering tread,
And through the darkness grope with trembling hands.
Stay not thy flight, speed thy uncertain steps—
But hold! Lest on thy mother's corse thou tread.
O Thebans, weak and smitten sore with ills,
Whose hearts are fainting in your breasts, behold,
I flee, I go: lift up your drooping heads.
A milder sky and sweeter air shall come
When I am gone. Whoever still retains
His feeble life may now inhale the air
In deep, life-giving draughts. Go, lend your aid
To those who were to certain death resigned;
For with me in my exile do I bear
All pestilential humours of the land.
Then come, ye blasting Fates and mad Despair,
Thou deadly Pestilence, come, come with me;
With such a company 'tis sweet to flee!

MILLER'S TRANSLATION has been revised in line 6.

1. This is the second victim. The first bull fell before he was struck; the second was struck with the axe, but no blood flowed.

2. This apparently alludes to the punishment which Oedipus inflicts upon himself after the disclosure of his crimes.

3. Seneca in this speech clearly foreshadows the suicide of Jocasta and the self-inflicted blindness of Oedipus and his lingering death.

4. This passage alludes to the civil strife between Eteocles and Polynices, the sons of Oedipus and Jocasta; the seven veins symbolise the expedition of the seven armies against Thebes.

5. This refers to the death of Pentheus.

6. The maiden deserted by Theseus was Ariadne.

7. This is an allusion to Cadmus, the founder of Thebes.

8. The region about Thebes was named Boeotia, from *boûs* (cow).

9. This refers to Agave, who, in a Bacchic frenzy, tore to pieces her son Pentheus.

VII
AGAMEMNON

Characters in the Play

GHOST OF THYESTES, *father of* AEGISTHUS

CHORUS OF ARGIVE WOMEN

CLYTEMNESTRA, *wife of* AGAMEMNON

NURSE *of* CLYTEMNESTRA

AEGISTHUS, *son of* THYESTES *and paramour of* CLYTEMNESTRA

EURYBATES, *messenger of* AGAMEMNON

CHORUS OF CAPTIVE TROJAN WOMEN

CASSANDRA, *daughter of Priam, captive of* AGAMEMNON

AGAMEMNON, *king of Argos, and leader of the Greeks against Troy*

ELECTRA, *daughter of* AGAMEMNON *and* CLYTEMNESTRA

STROPHIUS, *king of Phocis*

ORESTES, *son of* AGAMEMNON

PYLADES, *son of* STROPHIUS

INTRODUCTION

AESCHYLUS' *Agamemnon,* the first play in his great trilogy, the *Oresteia,* is apparently the chief source of Seneca's *Agamemnon,* although the Roman playwright may have drawn material also from plays by Sophocles, Livius Andronicus, and Accius. Aeschylus' play is one of the most powerful tragedies of all time; it is famed for the symbolic imagery of its choral odes, for its masterly delineation of Clytemnestra, and for the emotional tension of Cassandra's prophecy; it is, moreover, one of the most spectacular of ancient tragedies. Seneca is as unfortunate here as in the case of his *Oedipus;* in each instance, his attempt to rework a Greek masterpiece has resulted in a play not only inferior to the Greek model but less successful than most of his other tragedies. It has been suggested that the *Agamemnon* was Seneca's first attempt at drama and that the *Oedipus* was his second play.

The *Agamemnon* tells of the return of the victorious king and his reception by his wife Clytemnestra. Clytemnestra is enraged because Agamemnon sacrificed her daughter Iphigenia at Aulis, and is filled with jealousy because he is bringing back Cassandra as a possible rival; she is estranged also by her own guilty love for Aegisthus, with whom she is plotting to slay Agamemnon on his return. Aeschylus subordinated the motive of Clytemnestra's passion until late in the play. Seneca stresses it early in the action in a scene between the queen and her lover. Léon Herrmann suggests that Seneca's primary interest here is criminal psychology—the analysis of the guilty natures of Aegisthus and Clytemnestra. But, although her love for Aegisthus is brought into the play early, Seneca avoids making her too unsympathetic as a character; he portrays her as willing to give up Aegisthus and the plan of vengeance and to return to her husband; it is Aegisthus who strengthens her resolve, and who later strikes the first blow. This version of the story in which Aegisthus plays the leading part resembles the account of Agamemnon's death as found in Homer's *Odyssey* rather than the Aeschylean treatment, and Seneca's Clytemnestra as a result is a weaker and less noble character. Aeschylus' heroine never falters in her resolution and is calm and collected when the deed is done. Her final speech to Aegisthus,

713

"I and thou will rule the palace and will order all things well."

is on a very different plane from Clytemnestra's final words to Cassandra in Seneca's play,

"O maddened wretch, thy death I wait to see."

The two sentiments epitomise, as it were, the varying conceptions of the two dramatists.

Many of Seneca's other changes and innovations are significant, and are motivated in part by a desire for expansion rather than simplification, as was his more usual procedure. Aeschylus' play had a relatively simple plot and structure, but his long choral odes were an integral part of the action. Since Seneca's lyrics had little bearing on the plot, the Roman dramatist apparently felt the need of enriching his play. He added several characters: the ghost of Thyestes, which, like the ghost of Tantalus in the *Thyestes,* creates anticipation of the tragedy to come and lends an atmosphere of horror to the play at its beginning; the nurse, whose function is to provide a foil for the heroine, as do the nurses in the *Medea* and the *Phaedra;* Electra and Strophius at the end, who make possible the escape of Orestes; the effect of these two characters seems somewhat anticlimactic, although Electra's noble nature brings out more strongly the baseness and weakness of Clytemnestra after the crime has been committed. The play contains two choruses, as do the *Hercules on Oeta* and the *Octavia,* but the choral songs express the usual lyric commonplaces, so reminiscent of Horace, and give a description of the final days of Troy that owes much to Vergil's *Aeneid,* Book II; the deep religious significance of the Greek choral passages is utterly lacking. Eurybates' description of the storm serves to maintain suspense by delaying the arrival of Agamemnon, but it resembles Theseus' description of the underworld in the *Mad Hercules;* it is too long, and, as rhetorical narrative, brings the action of the drama to a temporary halt. Cassandra's account of the murder of Agamemnon is a description, not a prophecy as in Aeschylus, and so loses much of the dramatic effectiveness of the latter. On the whole, the play suffers from Seneca's fondness for declamation and for the supernatural, but above all from the fact that Aeschylus' masterpiece, with its poetic imagery, its symbolism, its theological import, was unsuited by its very nature to Seneca's talents. Seneca was at his best when analysing and depicting human passions and human sufferings, and it is significant that his most successful tragedies were those modelled chiefly on plays by Euripides.

AGAMEMNON

(SCENE:—*Before the palace of* AGAMEMNON *at Mycenae or Argos.*)

Act One. Scene I

(*The* GHOST OF THYESTES *appears.*)

GHOST:

Escaped from gloomy Pluto's murky realm
And leaving Tartara's deep pit I come,
All doubting which abode I hate the more;
That world I flee, but this I put to flight.
My soul shrinks back, my limbs do quake with fear.
I see my father's house—my brother's too!
Here is the ancient seat of Pelops' race;
In this proud hall it is Pelasgians' wont
To crown their kings; here sit those overlords
Whose hands the kingdom's haughty sceptre wield;
Here is their council chamber—here they feast!
Let me go hence. Were it not better far
To sit beside the dark, sad pools of Styx,
And see the hell-hound's black and tossing mane?[1]
Where one, bound fast upon a whirling wheel,
Back to himself is borne; where fruitless toil
Is mocked forever by the rolling stone;
Where living vitals glut the vulture's greed,
Consumed but e'er renewed; and one old man,
By mocking waves surrounded, seeks in vain
To sate his burning thirst, dire punishment
For that he strove to trick th' immortal gods.
But, ranked with mine, how slight that old man's sin!
Take count of all whose impious deeds on earth
Make them to tremble at the bar of hell:
By my dread crimes will I outdo them all—
But not my brother's crimes. Three sons of mine
Lie buried in me, yea, mine own dear flesh

715

Have I consumed.[2] Nor this the only blot
With which dire fortune's hand hath stained my soul;
But, daring greater sin, she bade me seek
(Oh, foul impiety!) my daughter's arms.
Bold for revenge, I dared and did the deed,
And so the fearful cycle was complete:
As sons the sire, so sire the daughter filled.
Then were the laws of nature backward turned:
I mingled sire with grandsire, sons with grandsons;
Yea, monstrous! Husband and father did I join,
And drove the day back to the shades of night.
But fate at last, though doubtful, long deferred,
Hath had regard unto my evil plight,
And brought the day of vengeance near; for lo,
This king of kings, this leader of the Greeks,
This Agamemnon comes, whose royal flag
A thousand Grecian vessels following
Once filled the Trojan waters with their sails.
Now ten bright suns have run their course, and Troy
Has been o'erthrown, and he is close at hand—
To place his neck in Clytemnestra's power.
Now, now, this house shall flow again with blood,
But this of Atreus' stock! Swords, axes, darts
I see, and that proud head with murderous stroke
Asunder cleft; now impious crimes are near,
Now treachery, slaughter, blood; the feast is spread.
The cause, Aegisthus, of thy shameful birth,
Is come at last.[3] But why hangs down thy head
In shame? Why hesitates thy faltering hand
And sinks inactive? Why dost counsel take
Within thy heart, and turn away, and ask
Whether this deed become thee? Do but think
Upon thy mother; then wilt thou confess
It doth become thee well. But what drags out
In long delay this summer night's brief span
To winter's hours of darkness? And what cause
Prevents the stars from sinking in the sky?
The sun shrinks from my face. I must away,
That so he may bring back the light of day.

(*The* ghost *vanishes.*)

Act One.   Scene II

(*Enter* CHORUS OF ARGIVE WOMEN.)

CHORUS:

On fortune's headlong brink they stand
  Who hold the sceptre in their hand;
  No safe assurance can they know
  Who on too lofty pathways go:
But care on care pursues them to the last,
Their souls assailed and vexed by every blast.

  As seas on Libya's sandy shore
  Their waves in ceaseless billows pour;
  As Euxine's swelling waters rise
  Beneath the lowering northern skies,
  Where bright Bootes wheels his team
  High o'er the ocean's darksome stream:
With such assaults, by such wild tempests blown,
Does fortune batter at a kingly throne!

  Who would be feared, in fear must live.
  No kindly night can refuge give;
  Nor sleep, that comforts all the rest,
  Can bring care-freedom to his breast.
What throne so safe, on such foundation stands,
That may not be destroyed by impious hands?

  For justice, shame, the virtues all,
  E'en wifely faith, soon flee the hall
  Where courtiers dwell. Within, there stands
  Bellona dire with bloody hands;
  Erinys too, the dogging fate,
  Of them who hold too high estate,
Which any hour from high to low may bring.
  Though arms be lacking, wiles be none,
  Still is the will of fortune done:
By force of his own greatness falls the king.

  'Tis ever thus: the bellying sail
  Fears the o'erstrong though favouring gale;
  The tower feels rainy Auster's dread
  If to the clouds it rear its head;
  Huge oaks most feel the whirlwind's lash;
  High mountains most with thunder crash;

And while the common herd in safety feeds,
Their mighty leader, marked for slaughter, bleeds.

Fate places us on high, that so
To surer ruin we may go.
The meanest things in longest fortune live.
Then happy he whose modest soul
In safety seeks a nearer goal;
Fearing to leave the friendly shore,
He rows with unambitious oar,
Content in low security to thrive.

Act Two. Scene I

(*Enter* CLYTEMNESTRA *and her* NURSE.)

CLYTEMNESTRA: Why, sluggish soul, dost thou safe counsel seek?
Why hesitate? Closed is the better way.
Once thou couldst chastely guard thy widowed couch,
And keep thy husband's realm with wifely faith;
But now, long since has faith thy palace fled,
The homely virtues, honour, piety,
And chastity, which goes, but ne'er returns.
Loose be thy reins, swift speed thy wanton course;
The safest way through crime is by the path
Of greater crime. Consider in thy heart
All woman's wiles, what faithless wives have done,
Bereft of reason, blind and passion-driven;
What bloody deeds stepmother's hands have dared;
Or what she dared, ablaze with impious love,
Who left her father's realm for Thessaly:[4]
Dare sword, dare poison; else in stealthy flight
Must thou go hence with him who shares thy guilt.
But who would talk of stealth, of exile, flight?
Such were thy sister's deeds:[5] some greater crime,
Some mightier deed of evil suits thy hand.

NURSE: O Grecian queen, illustrious Leda's child,
What say'st thou there in whispered mutterings?
Or what unbridled deeds within thy breast,
By reckless passion tossed, dost meditate?

Though thou be silent, yet thy face declares
Thy hidden pain in speech more eloquent.
Whate'er thy grief, take time and room for thought.
Time often cures what reason cannot heal.

CLYTEMNESTRA: Too dire my grief to wait time's healing hand.
My very soul is scorched with flaming pains:
I feel the goads of fear and jealous rage,
The throbbing pulse of hate, the pangs of love,
Base love that presses hard his heavy yoke
Upon my heart, and holds me vanquished quite.
And always, 'mid those flames that vex my soul,
Though faint indeed, and downcast, all undone,
Shame struggles on. By shifting seas I'm tossed:
As when here wind, there tide impels the deep,
The waves stand halting 'twixt the warring powers.
And so I'll strive no more to guide my bark.
Where wrath, where grief, where hope shall bear me on,
There will I speed my course; my helmless ship
I've giv'n to be the sport of winds and floods.
Where reason fails 'tis best to follow chance.

NURSE: Oh, rash and blind, who follows doubtful chance.

CLYTEMNESTRA: Who fears a doubtful chance, if 'tis his last?

NURSE: Thy fault may find safe hiding if thou wilt.

CLYTEMNESTRA: Nay, faults of royal homes proclaim themselves.

NURSE: Dost thou repent the old, yet plan the new?

CLYTEMNESTRA: To stop midway in sin is foolishness.

NURSE: His fears increase, who covers crime with crime.

CLYTEMNESTRA: But iron and fire oft aid the healer's art.

NURSE: Yet desperate measures no one first attempts.

CLYTEMNESTRA: The path of sin is headlong from the first.

NURSE: Still let thy wifely duty hold thee back.

CLYTEMNESTRA: What long-deserted wife regards her lord?

NURSE: Your common children—hast no thought of them?

CLYTEMNESTRA: I do think on my daughter's wedding rites,
Highborn Achilles, and my husband's lies.[6]

NURSE: She freed our Grecian fleet from long delay,
                 And waked from their dull calm the sluggish seas.

CLYTEMNESTRA: Oh, shameful thought! That I, the heaven-born child
                 Of Tyndarus, should give my daughter up
                 To save the Grecian fleet! I see once more
                 In memory my daughter's wedding day,
                 Which *he* made worthy of base Pelops' house,
                 When, with his pious face, this father stood
                 Before the altar fires—Oh, monstrous rites!
                 E'en Calchas shuddered at his own dread words
                 And backward-shrinking fires. O bloody house,
                 That ever wades through crime to other crime!
                 With blood we soothe the winds, with blood we war.

NURSE: Yet by that blood a thousand vessels sailed.[7]

CLYTEMNESTRA: But not with favouring omens did they sail;
                 The port of Aulis fairly drave them forth.
                 So launched in war, he still no better fared.
                 Smit with a captive's love, unmoved by prayer,
                 He held as spoil the child of Phoebus' priest,
                 E'en then, as now, a sacred maiden's thrall.
                 Nor could the stern Achilles bend his will,
                 Nor he whose eye alone can read the fates
                 (A faithful seer to us, to captives mild),
                 Nor his pest-smitten camp and gleaming pyres.
                 When baffled Greece stood tottering to her fall,
                 This man with passion pined, had time for love,
                 Thought ever on amours; and, lest his couch
                 Should be of any Phrygian maid bereft,
                 He lusted for Achilles' beauteous bride,[8]
                 Nor blushed to tear her from her lover's arms.
                 Fit foe for Paris! Now new wounds he feels,
                 And burns, inflamed by mad Cassandra's love.
                 And, now that Troy is conquered, home he comes,
                 A captive's husband, Priam's son-in-law!
                 Arise, my soul; no easy task essay;
                 Be swift to act. What dost thou, sluggish, wait
                 Till Phrygian rivals wrest thy power away?
                 Or do thy virgin daughters stay thy hand,
                 Or yet Orestes, image of his sire?
                 Nay, 'tis for these thy children thou must act,
                 Lest greater ills befall them; for, behold,

A mad stepmother soon shall call them hers.
Through thine own heart, if so thou must, prepare
To drive the sword, and so slay two in one.
Let thy blood flow with his; in slaying, die.
For death is sweet if with a foeman shared.

NURSE: My queen, restrain thyself, check thy wild wrath,
And think how great thy task. Atrides comes,
Wild Asia's conqueror and Europe's lord;
He leads Troy captive, Phrygia subdued.
'Gainst him wouldst thou with sly assault prevail,
Whom great Achilles slew not with his sword,
Though he with angry hand the weapon drew;
Nor Telamonian Ajax, crazed with rage;
Nor Hector, Troy's sole prop and war's delay;
Nor Paris' deadly darts; nor Memnon black;
Nor Xanthus, choked with corpses and with arms;
Nor Simois' waves, empurpled with the slain;
Nor Cycnus, snowy offspring of the sea;
Nor warlike Rhesus with his Thracian band;
Nor that fierce maid who led the Amazons,
Armed with the deadly battle-axe and shield?
This hero, home returned, dost thou prepare
To slay, and stain thy hearth with impious blood?
Would Greece, all hot from conquest, suffer this?
Bethink thee of the countless steeds and arms,
The sea a-bristle with a thousand ships,
The plains of Ilium soaked with streams of blood,
Troy taken and in utter ruin laid:
Remember this, I say, and check thy wrath,
And bid thy thoughts in safer channels run.

Act Two.   Scene II

(*Enter* AEGISTHUS.)

AEGISTHUS (*to himself*): The fatal day which I was born to see,
Towards which I've ever looked with dread, is here.
Why dost thou fear, my soul, to face thy fate,
And turn away from action scarce begun?
Be sure that not thy hand is ordering

These dire events, but the relentless gods.
Then put thy shame-bought life in pawn to fate
And let thy heart drain suffering to the dregs.
To one of shameful birth death is a boon.
(*To* CLYTEMNESTRA)
Thou comrade of my perils, Leda's child,
Be with me still in this; and thy false lord,
This valiant sire, shall pay thee blood for blood.
But why does pallor blanch thy trembling cheeks?
What bodes this softened face, this listless gaze?

CLYTEMNESTRA: My husband's love has met and conquered me.
Let us retrace our steps, while still there's room,
To that estate whence we should ne'er have come;
Let even now fair fame be sought again;
For never is it over late to mend.
Who grieves for sin is counted innocent.

AEGISTHUS: What madness this? Dost thou believe or hope
That Agamemnon will be true to thee?
Though no grave fears, of conscious guilt begot,
Annoyed thy soul with thoughts of punishment;
Still would his swelling, o'er-inflated pride,
Create in him a dour and headstrong mood.
Harsh was he to his friends while Troy still stood;
How, think'st thou, has the fall of Troy pricked on
His soul, by nature harsh, to greater harshness?
Mycenae's king he went; he will return
Her tyrant. So doth fortune foster pride.
With how great pomp this throng of rivals comes!
But one of these, surpassing all the rest,
Apollo's priestess, holds the king in thrall.
And wilt thou meekly share thy lord with her?
But she will not. A wife's last infamy—
To see her rival ruling in her stead.
No throne nor bed can brook a rival mate.

CLYTEMNESTRA: Aegisthus, why dost drive me headlong on,
And fan to flames again my dying wrath?
For if the victor has his right employed,
To work his will upon a captive maid,
His wife should not complain or reck of this.
The law that binds the man fits not the king.
And why should I, myself in conscious guilt,

Make bold to sit in judgment on my lord?
Let her forgive who most forgiveness needs.

AEGISTHUS: In very truth there's room for mutual grace.
But thou know'st naught of royal privilege.
Thee will the king judge harshly, to himself
A milder law in gentler mood apply.
And this they deem the highest pledge of power,
If, what to common mortals is denied,
Is given by general will to them alone.

CLYTEMNESTRA: He pardoned Helen; home is she returned,
To Menelaus joined, though East and West
Have been engulfed for her in common woe.

AEGISTHUS: But Menelaus nursed no secret love,
Which closed his heart unto his lawful wife.
Thy lord seeks charge against thee, cause of strife.
Suppose thy heart and life were free from guilt:
What boots an honest life, a stainless heart,
When hate condemns the suppliant unheard?
Wilt thou seek Sparta's shelter, and return
Unto thy father's house? No shelter waits
The scorned of kings; that hope were false indeed.

CLYTEMNESTRA: None knows my sin save one most faithful friend.

AEGISTHUS: In vain: no faith is found in royal courts.

CLYTEMNESTRA: But surely gifts will buy fidelity.

AEGISTHUS: Faith bought by gifts is sold for other gifts.

CLYTEMNESTRA: My strength and purity of soul revive.
Why wouldst thou thwart me? Why, with cozening
     words,
Wouldst thou persuade me to thy evil course?
Dost think that I would leave a king of kings
And stoop to wed an outcast wretch like thee?

AEGISTHUS: What? Seem I less than Atreus' son to thee,
Who am Thyestes' son?

CLYTEMNESTRA: Why, so thou art,
And grandson too.

AEGISTHUS: My getting shames me not;
For Phoebus' self is voucher for my birth.

CLYTEMNESTRA: Name Phoebus not with thine incestuous stock,
Who checked his flying steeds and fled the sky,
Withdrawn in sudden night, lest he behold
Thy father's feast. Wouldst thou besmirch the gods,
Thou, trained to revel in unlawful love?
Then get thee gone in haste, and rid mine eyes
Of that which doth disgrace this noble house;
This home is waiting for its king and lord.

AEGISTHUS: Exile is naught to me, for I am used
To woe. At thy command I'll farther flee
Than from this house: I but await thy word
To plunge my dagger in this woeful breast.

CLYTEMNESTRA (*aside*): Shall I in cruel scorn desert him now?
Who sin in company should suffer so.
(*To* AEGISTHUS)
Nay, come with me; we will together wait
The issue of our dark and dangerous fate.
(*They go into the palace.*)

Act Two.   Scene III

CHORUS: Sing Phoebus' praise, O race renowned;
With festal laurel wreathe your heads;
And let your virgin locks flow free,
    Ye Argive maids.
And ye who drink of the cold Erasinus,
Who dwell by Eurotas,
Who know the green banks of the silent Ismenus,
Come join in our singing;
And do ye swell our chorus, ye far Theban daugh-
    ters,
Whom the child of Tiresias, Manto the seer,
Once taught to bow down to the Delian gods.
    Now peace has come:
Unbend thy victorious bow, O Apollo,
Lay down from thy shoulder thy quiver of arrows,
And let thy tuneful lyre resound
To the touch of thy swift-flying fingers.
No lofty strain be thine today,
But such as on thy milder lyre

Thou art wont to sound when the learnéd muse
    Surveys thy sports.
And yet, an' thou wilt, strike a heavier strain,
As when thou didst sing of the Titans o'ercome
    By Jupiter's hurtling bolts;
When mountain on lofty mountain piled,
Pelion, Ossa, and pine-clad Olympus,
Built high to the sky for the impious monsters
    Their ladder's rocky rounds.
Thou too be with us, Juno, queen,
Who sharest the throne of heaven's lord.
Mycenae's altars blaze for thee.
    Thou alone dost protect us,
    Anxious and suppliant;
    Thou art the goddess of peace,
    And the issues of war are thine;
And thine are the laurels of victory twined
On the brow of our king Agamemnon.
To thee the boxwood flute resounds
    In solemn festival;
To thee the maidens strike the harp
      In sweetest song;
To thee the votive torch is tossed;
The gleaming heifer, all unmarred
    By the plow's rough touch
      Falls at thy shrine.
And thou, child of the Thunderer,
    Pallas illustrious, hear;
Before whose might the Dardanian walls
    Have trembled and fallen to dust.
Thee maidens and matrons in chorus united
Exalt and adore; at thy approach
Thy temple doors swing open wide,
While the welcoming throng, with garlands be-
    decked,
    Rejoice at thy coming;
And feeble, tottering elders come
To pay their vows of thanks and praise,
And pour their offerings of wine
    With trembling hands.
And to thee with mindful lips we pray,
Bright Trivia, Lucina called.
Thy native Delos didst thou bid

Stand fast upon the sea, and float
No more, the wandering mock of winds.
And now, with firmly fixéd root,
It stands secure, defies the gale,
And, wont of old to follow ships,
   Now gives them anchorage.
Proud Niobe thy vengeance felt
Who thy divinity defied.
Now, high on lonely Sipylus,
She sits and weeps in stony grief;
Though to insensate marble turned,
Her tears flow fresh forevermore.
And now both men and women join
In praise to the twin divinities.
But thee, above all gods, we praise;
Our father and our ruler thou,
Lord of the hurtling thunderbolt,
At whose dread nod the farthest poles
   Do quake and tremble.
O Jove, thou founder of our race,
Accept our gifts, and have regard
Unto thy faithful progeny.
But lo, a warrior hither comes in haste,
With wonted signs of victory displayed;
For on his spear a laurel wreath he bears—
Eurybates, our king's own messenger.

Act Three.   Scene I

(*Enter* EURYBATES *with laurel-wreathed spear.*)

EURYBATES: Ye shrines and altars of the heavenly gods,
Ye Lares of my fathers, after long
And weary wanderings, scarce trusting yet
My longing eyes, I give ye grateful thanks.
Pay now your vows which you have vowed to heaven,
Ye Argive people; for behold, your king,
The pride and glory of this land of Greece,
Back to his father's house as victor comes.

(*Enter* CLYTEMNESTRA *in time to hear the concluding words of the
herald.*)

CLYTEMNESTRA: Oh, joyful tidings that I long to hear!
But where delays my lord, whom I with grief
For ten long years have waited? Doth the sea
Still stay his course, or hath he gained the land?

EURYBATES: Unharmed, by glory crowned, increased in praise,
He hath set foot upon the long-sought shore.

CLYTEMNESTRA: Then hail this day with joy, and thank the gods
Who, though their favouring aid was late bestowed,
At last have smiled propitious on our cause.
But tell me thou, doth yet my brother live?
Say, too, how fares my sister Helena?

EURYBATES: If prayer and hope prevail, they yet survive;
No surer tidings is it given to speak
Of those who wander on the stormy sea.
Scarce had the swollen highways of the deep
Received our fleet, when ship from kindred ship
Was driven, and lost amid the gathering gloom.
E'en Agamemnon's self in doubt and fear
Went wandering upon the trackless waste,
And suffered more from Neptune's buffetings
Than he had e'er endured in bloody war.
And now, a humble victor, home he comes,
With but a shattered remnant of his fleet.

CLYTEMNESTRA: But say what fate has swallowed up my ships,
And scattered our great chieftains o'er the sea?

EURYBATES: A sorry tale 'twould be: thou bid'st me mix
The bitter message with the sweet. But I,
Alas, am sick at heart, and cannot tell
For very horror our most woeful tale.

CLYTEMNESTRA: But tell it even so; for he who shrinks
From knowledge of his woe has greater fear.
And ills half seen are worse than certainty.

EURYBATES: When Troy lies smouldering 'neath our Grecian fires
We quickly lot the spoil, and seek the sea
In eager haste. And now our weary sides
Are eas'd of the falchion's wonted load;
Our shields along the vessels' lofty sterns
Unheeded hang, and once again our hands,
Long used to swords, are fitted to the oar;

And all impatiently we wait the word.
Then flashed from Agamemnon's ship the sign
That bade us homeward speed, and clear and loud
The trumpet pealed upon our joyful ears;
The flagship's gilded prow gleamed on ahead,
The course directing for a thousand ships.
A kindly breeze first stole into our sails
And urged us softly on; the tranquil waves
Scarce rippled with the Zephyr's gentle breath;
The sea was all a-glitter with the fleet
Which lit e'en while it hid the watery way.
'Tis sweet to see the empty shores of Troy,
The broad plains left in lonely solitude.
The eager sailors ply the bending oars,
Hands aiding sails, and move their sturdy arms
With rhythmic swing. The furrowed waters gleam,
And sing along the sides, while rushing prows
Besprinkle all the sea with hoary spray.
When fresher breezes fill our swelling sails,
We cease from toil, and, stretched along the thwarts,
We watch the far-off shores of Ilium,
Fast fleeing as our vessels seaward fare;
Or tell old tales of war: brave Hector's threats,
His corpse dishonoured, and again restored
To purchased honours of the funeral pyre;
And Priam sprinkling with his royal blood
The sacred altar of Hercean Jove.
Then to and fro amid the briny sea
The dolphins sport, and leap the heaving waves
With arching backs; now race in circles wide,
Now swim beside us in a friendly band,
Now dash ahead or follow in our wake;
Anon in wanton sport they smite our prows,
And so our thousand rushing barks surround.
Now sinks the shore from view, the spreading plains;
And far-off Ida seems a misty cloud.
And now, what but the sharpest eye can see,
Troy's rising smoke blurs dim the distant sky.
The sun was bringing weary mortals rest,
And waning day was giving place to night;
When clouds began to fill the western sky,
And dim the lustre of the sinking sun—
The grim prognostic of a rising gale.

Young night had spangled all the sky with stars,
And empty sails hung languid on the masts;
When low, foreboding sighings of the wind
Spring from our landward side; the hidden shore
Resounds afar with warning mutterings;
The rising waves anticipate the storm;
The moon is blotted out, the stars are hid,
The sea leaps skyward, and the sky is gone.
Gloom broods o'er all, but not of night alone;
For blinding mists add blackness to the night,
And murky waves with murky sky contend.
Then in concerted rush from every hand
The winds fall roughly on the ravished sea,
And heave its boiling billows from the depths;
While east with west wind struggles, south with north.
Each wields his wonted arms to lash the sea:
The fierce Strymonian blast with rattling hail
Roars on, and Libyan Auster heaps the waves
Upon the seething sands. Nor those alone
Provoke the strife: for raving Notus first
Grows big with bursting clouds and swells the waves;
And boisterous Eurus shakes the Orient,
The far Arabian realms and morning seas.
What dire disaster did fierce Corus work,
His dark face gleaming forth upon the deep?
We thought the very heavens would be rent,
The gods fall down from out the riven sky,
And all revert to chaos as of old.
The waves opposed the winds, the winds in turn
Hurled back the warring waves. Nor was the sea
Within itself contained; but, lifted high,
It mingled with the streaming floods of heaven.
Nor were we solaced in our dreadful plight
By open view and knowledge of our ills;
For darkness like the murky night of Styx
Hedged in our view. Yet was this darkness rent,
When flashing lightnings cleft the inky clouds
With crashing bolts. Yet e'en this fearful gleam
Was welcome to our eyes: so sweet it is
To those in evil plight to see their ills.
The fleet assists its own destruction, too,
Prow dashing hard on prow, and side on side;
Now sinks it headlong in the yawning flood,

And now, belched forth, it sees the air again.
One plunges down, of its own weight compelled;
Another, through its gaping side, invites
Destruction from the raging floods; a third
Is smothered by the tenth and mightiest wave.
Here idly floats a mangled, shattered thing,
Of all its boastful decoration shorn;
And there a ship sans sails and oars and all.
No lofty mast with hanging spars remains,
But, helpless hulks, the shattered vessels drift
Upon the boundless sea. Amid such ills,
Of what avail the hardy sailor's art?
Cold horror holds our limbs. The sailors stand
In dumb amaze, and all their tasks forget;
While all, in abject terror, drop their oars,
And turn their wretched souls to heaven for aid.
Now (marvel of the fates!) with common vows
The Greeks and Trojans supplicate the skies.
Now Pyrrhus envies great Achilles' fate;
Ulysses, Ajax'; Menelaus, Hector's;
And Priam seems to Agamemnon blest:
Yea all who perished on the plains of Troy,
Whose lot it was to die by human hand,
Are counted blest of heaven, secure in fame,
For they rest safely in the land they won.
"Shall winds and waves engulf in common fate
The faint of heart who nothing noble dare,
And those brave souls who quit themselves like men?
Must we for naught resign ourselves to death?
O thou of gods who art not even yet
With these our evil fortunes satisfied,
At last have pity on our woeful plight,
Which Ilium itself would weep to see.
If still thine anger holds, and 'tis decreed
That we of Greece must perish utterly,
Why doom these Trojans, for whose sake we die,
To share our fate? Allay the raging sea:
For this our fleet bears Greeks and Trojans too."
So prayed we, but in vain; our suppliant words
Were swallowed by the raging storm. And lo,
Another shape of death! For Pallas, armed
With those swift bolts her angry father wields,
Essays what ruin dire her threatening spear,

Her aegis set with stony Gorgon's head,
And these her father's thunderbolts, can work.
Unconquered by his ills, with daring soul,
Bold Ajax⁹ struggles on. Him, shortening sail
With halyards strained, a falling thunderbolt
Smote full; again the goddess poised her bolt
With hand far backward drawn, like Jove himself,
And hurled it true with shock impetuous.
Straight fell the bolt, and, piercing man and ship,
It strewed them both in ruin on the sea.
Still undismayed, he overtops the waves,
All charred and blasted like some rugged cliff,
And bravely breasts the wildly raging sea.
Still gleaming with the lightning's lurid glare,
He shines amid the blackness like a torch
Which sheds its beams afar upon the deep.
At length a jutting rock he gains, and shouts
In madness: "Now have I o'ercome the sea,
The flames; 'tis sweet to conquer sky, and waves,
The thunderbolts, and her who brandished them.
I've braved the terrors of the god of war;
With my sole arm I fronted Hector, huge,
Nor did the darts of Phoebus frighten me.
Those gods, together with their Phrygians,
I set at naught; and shall I quake at thee?
Thou hurl'st with weakling's hand another's bolts:
But what if Jove himself—"
When madly thus he dared blaspheme the gods,
Great Neptune with his trident smote the rock,
And whelmed its tottering bulk beneath the sea.
So, falling with its fall, the madman lies
By earth and fire and billows overcome.
        But us, poor shipwrecked, hopeless mariners,
A worse destruction waits. There is a reef,
Low lying, treacherous with ragged shoals,
Where false Caphereus hides his rocky foot
Beneath the whirling waters of the sea.
Above this reef the billows heave and dash,
And madly seethe with each recurring wave.
High o'er this spot a frowning crag projects,
Which views on either side the spreading sea.
There distant lie thine own Pelopian shores,
And there the curving Isthmus, deep withdrawn.

Shielding the broad Aegean from the west.
There blood-stained Lemnos looms; here Chalcis lies;[10]
And yonder wind-locked Aulis' peaceful port.
This lofty cliff old Nauplius occupied,
With hate inspired for Palamedes' sake.
There his accurséd hand a beacon raised
And lured us onward to the fatal spot.
Now hang our barks by jagged rocks transfixed,
Or founder, wrecked and wrecking in the shoals;
And where but now our vessels sought to land,
They flee the land and choose the angry waves.
With dawn the sea's destructive rage was spent,
And full atonement had been made to Troy.
Then came the sun again; and brightening day
Revealed the awful havoc of the night.

CLYTEMNESTRA: I know not which were better, grief or joy.
I do rejoice to see my lord again,
And yet my kingdom's losses counsel tears.
O father Jove, at whose august command
The sounding heavens quake, regard our race,
And bid the angry gods be merciful.
Let every head be decked with festal wreath,
The flute resound, and at the stately shrine
Let snowy victims fall in sacrifice.
        But lo, a grieving throng, with locks unkempt,
The Trojan women come; and at their head,
With step majestic, queenly, heaven inspired,
Apollo's bride, with his own laurel tired.

Act Three.   Scene II

(*Enter* CHORUS OF TROJAN WOMEN, *led by* CASSANDRA.)

CHORUS OF TROJAN WOMEN: Alas, how bitter, yet how sweet a thing,
        This love of life we mortals cherish so!
        What madness, when the door stands open wide
        That frees us from our ills, and death calls loud
        And welcomes us to everlasting rest!
            Who finds that refuge, fears no more
            These nameless terrors, these assaults.

These insolent assaults of fate,
And sidelong-glancing bolts of Jove.
        Deep peace of death!
No frenzied burgher-throng to fear,
No victor's threatening madness here;
No wild seas ruffled by the blast;
No hosts in serried battle massed,
Where whirling clouds of dust disclose
The savage riders to their foes;
No nation falling with its city's fall,
'Mid smouldering battlement and crumbling wall;
        No wasting fires,
        No burning pyres,
And all the horrors impious war inspires.
        They from the servile bonds of fate
        This human life emancipate,
        Who fickle fortune dare to brave,
        And face the terrors of the grave;
        Who joyful view the joyless Styx,
        And dare their mortal span to fix.
How like a king, how like a god on high
Is he who faces death nor fears to die!
In one dark night we saw our city doomed,
When Doric fires the Dardan homes consumed;
But not in battle, not by warlike arts,
As once it fell beneath Alcides' darts.
        No son of Thetis dealt the blow
        Which wrought our final overthrow,
        Nor his loved friend, Patroclus hight,
        When once, in borrowed armour dight,
        He put our Trojan chiefs to flight;
        Nor when Pelides' self gave o'er
        The fierce resentment that he bore,
        And sped him forth on vengeance bent—
        Not even in such evils pent,
        Did Troy to cruel fortune bend,
        But struggled bravely to the end.
Her bitter fate—for ten long years to stand,
And fall at last by one vile trickster's hand.
In memory still we see the monstrous bulk
Of that pretended and most fatal gift,
The Grecian horse, which we, too credulous,
With our own hands into our city led.

The noisy-footed monster stumbled oft
Upon the threshold of the city gate,
While in its roomy hold crouched kings and war.
And we might well have turned their crafty arts
To work their own destruction. But alas,
We neither saw nor heeded. Oftentimes
The sound of clashing shields smote on our ears,
And low and angry mutterings within
Where Pyrrhus 'gainst the shrewd Ulysses strove.
    Now free from fear our Trojan youth
    Crowd round to touch the sacred cords
    With joyous hands. Astyanax
    Here leads his youthful playmates on,
    While 'midst the maidens gaily comes
    The maid Polyxena, foredoomed
    To bleed upon Achilles' tomb.[11]
    Mothers in festal garments bring
    Their votive offerings to the gods,
    And sires press gaily round the shrines.
    Throughout the town all faces tell
    One tale of joy; e'en Hecuba,
    Who, since her Hector's fatal pyre,
    Had never ceased her tears, was glad.
    But now, unhappy grief, what first,
    What last, dost thou prepare to weep?
    Our city walls in ruin laid,
    Though built by heavenly hands? Our shrines
    Upon their very gods consumed?
    Nay, nay; long since our weary eyes
    Have dried their tears for these. But now
    We weep, O father, king, for thee.
    We saw, with our own eyes we saw,
The old man slain by Pyrrhus' impious hand,
Whose scanty blood scarce stained the gleaming
    brand.

CASSANDRA: Restrain your tears which lingering time awaits,
Ye Trojan dames; weep not for me and mine.
Let each bewail her several woes; but I
For my own heavy grief have tears enough.

CHORUS: Yet 'tis a balm of grief to know
    That our own tears with others' flow;

More sharply gnaws the hidden care
Which we with others may not share:
And thou, though strong of soul, inured to grief,
Canst not in thine own weeping find relief.
    Though Philomel for Itys sing
    Her sad, sweet notes in wakening spring;
    Though Procne, with insistent din,
    Bewail her husband's hidden sin;
Not these, with all their passionate lament,
Can voice the sorrows in thy bosom pent.
    Let Cycnus raise his dying song,
    And its soft, plaintive strains prolong;
    Let Halcyon mourn her Ceyx brave,
    A-flutter o'er the tossing wave;
    Let priests of tower-crowned Cybele
    Their tears for Attis share with thee:
Still would our tears in no such measure flow,
For sufferings like these no limits know.

    (CASSANDRA *lays aside her fillets*)
But why dost lay aside the sacred wool?
Most by the wretched should the gods be feared.

CASSANDRA: But ills like mine o'erleap the bounds of fear.
I'll supplicate the heavenly gods no more,
For now am I beyond their power to harm,
And I have drained to dregs the cup of fate.
No country have I left, no sister, sire;
For tombs and altars have my blood consumed.
Where is that happy throng of brothers now?
Departed all! And only weak old men
Remain within the lonely palace walls
To serve the wretched king; and these, alas,
Throughout those stately chambered halls behold,
Save Spartan Helen, none but widowed wives.
And Hecuba, proud mother of a race
Of kings, herself the queen of Phrygia,
Fecund for funeral pyres, became the mock
Of fickle fate; and now in bestial form,
Barks madly round the ruins of her home,
Surviving Troy, son, husband, and herself.

CHORUS: Why falls this sudden silence on her? See,
Her cheeks are pale, and fits of trembling fear

Possess her frame; her locks in horror rise,
And we can hear, though pent within her breast,
The loud pulsations of her fluttering heart.
Her glance uncertain wanders; and anon
Her eyes seem backward turned into herself,
Then fix again and harshly stare abroad.
Now higher than her wont she lifts her head
And walks with stately step; and now she strives
To open her reluctant lips. At last,
Though struggling still against th' inspiring god,
The maddened priestess speaks with muttered words.

CASSANDRA: Why prick me on with fury's goads anew,
Ye sacred slopes of high Parnassus? Why
Must I, insensate, prophesy afresh?
Away, thou prophet god! I am not thine.
Subdue the fires that smoulder in my breast.
Whose doom yet waits my frenzied prophecy?
Now Troy is fallen—must I still rave on,
And speak unheeded words? Oh, where am I?
The kindly light has fled, and deepest night
Enshrouds my face, and all the heavens lie wrapped
In deepest gloom. But see, with double sun,
The day shines forth again; and doubled homes
In doubled Argos seem to stand. Again
I see Mount Ida's groves. The shepherd sits
Amid those awful goddesses to judge
(Oh, fatal judgment!) twixt their rival charms.
Ye mighty kings, I warn ye, fear the fruit
Of stolen love; that rustic foundling soon
Shall overthrow your house.
                                        Beware the queen!
Why does she madly in her woman's hand
Those naked weapons bear? Whom does she seek
With brandished battle-ax, though Spartan bred,
Like some fierce warrior of the Amazons?
What horrid vision next affronts mine eyes?
A mighty Afric lion, king of beasts,
Lies low, death-smitten by his cruel mate;
While at his mangled neck a low-born beast
Gnaws greedily.
                        Why do ye summon me,
Saved only of my house, ye kindred shades?

I'll follow thee, my father, buried deep
Beneath the stones of Troy; and thee, O prop
Of Phrygia, the terror of the Greeks,
I see, though not in brave and fair array,
As once thou cam'st, still flushing with the glow
Of burning ships; but with thy members torn
And foully mangled by the dragging thongs.
And thee, O Troilus, I follow too,
Alas, too quickly met with Peleus' son!
I see thy face, my poor Deiphobus,
Past recognition scarred. Is this the gift
Of thy new wife?
      Ah me, 'tis sweet to go
Along the borders of the Stygian pool;
To see the savage hound of Tartarus,
The realms of greedy Dis, and Charon old,
Whose dusky skiff shall bear two royal souls
Across the murky Phlegethon today,
The vanquished and the vanquisher. Ye shades,
And thee, dread stream, by which the gods of heaven
Do swear their straightest oaths, I pray ye both:
Withdraw the curtain of your hidden realm,
That so yon shadowy throng of Phrygians
May look upon Mycenae's woes. Behold,
Poor souls; the wheel of fortune backward turns.

 See, see! The squalid sisters come,
 Their bloody lashes brandishing,
 And smoking torches half consumed.
 A sickly pallor overspreads
 Their bloated cheeks; and dusky robes
 Of death begird their hollow loins.
 The gloomy night with fearsome cries
 Resounds, and to my startled eyes
 Dread sights appear: there lie the bones
 Of that huge giant, far outstretched,
 Upon a slimy marsh's brink
 All white and rotting. Now I see
 That old man, wan with suffering,
 Forget awhile the mocking waves,
 Forget his burning thirst, to grieve
 For this disaster hovering
 About his house;
 But Dardanus exults to see

His foeman's baleful destiny.

CHORUS:　　Now has her rage prophetic spent itself,
And fall'n away; like some devoted bull,
Which sinks with tottering knees before the shrine
Beneath the sacrificial axe's stroke.
Let us support her ere she faint and fall.
But see, our Agamemnon comes at last
To greet his gods, with bay of victory crowned;
And, all in festal garb, with glad accord,
His consort welcomes her returning lord.

Act Four. Scene I

(*Enter* AGAMEMNON. *He is met and greeted by his wife, who returns into the palace.*)

AGAMEMNON:　　At last in safety am I home returned.
Oh, hail, belovéd land! I bring thee spoil
From many barbarous tribes; and Troy at length,
So long the mistress of the haughty east,
Submits herself as suppliant to thee.
But see, Cassandra faints, and trembling falls
With nerveless form. Ye slaves with speed uplift her;
Revive her drooping spirits with the chill
Of water on her face. Her languid eyes
Again behold the light of day. Arise,
Cassandra, and recall thy sluggish sense.
That shelter from our woes, so long desired,
Is here at last. This is a festal day.

CASSANDRA:　　Remember Ilium's festal day. ·

AGAMEMNON:　　　　　　　　　　　　But come,
We'll kneel before the shrine.

CASSANDRA:　　　　　　　　　　　　Before the shrine
My father fell.

AGAMEMNON:　　　　　　　　We will together pray
In thankfulness to Jove.

CASSANDRA:　　　　　　　　　　　Hercean Jove?

AGAMEMNON: Thou think'st of Ilium?

CASSANDRA: And Priam too.

AGAMEMNON: This is not Troy.

CASSANDRA: Where a Helen is, is Troy.

AGAMEMNON: Fear not thy mistress, though in captive's bonds.

CASSANDRA: But freedom is at hand.

AGAMEMNON: Live on secure.

CASSANDRA: I think that death is my security.

AGAMEMNON: For thee there's naught to fear.

CASSANDRA: But much for thee.

AGAMEMNON: What can a victor fear?

CASSANDRA: What least he fears.

AGAMEMNON: Keep her, ye faithful slaves, in careful guard,
               Till she shall throw this mood of madness off,
               Lest in unbridled rage she harm herself.
               To thee, O father, who the blinding bolt
               Dost hurl, at whose command the clouds disperse,
               Who rul'st the starry heavens and the lands,
               To whom triumphant victors bring their spoils;
               And thee, O sister of thy mighty lord,
               Argolic Juno, here I offer now
               All fitting gifts—and so fulfil my vow.
               (AGAMEMNON *goes into the palace.*)

Act Four.   Scene II

CHORUS OF ARGIVE WOMEN: O Argos, famed for thy worthy sons,
               And dear to the jealous Juno's heart,
               How mighty the children who feed at thy breast!
               Thou hast added a god to the ranks of immortals;
               For Alcides has won by his labours heroic
               The right to be named with the lords of the sky.
               Alcides the great! At his birth were the laws
               Of the universe broken; for Jove bade the night

To double the dew-laden hours of the darkness.
At his command did the god of the sun
To a sluggish pace restrain his car;
And slow of foot around their course,
O pale, white moon, thy horses paced.
He also checked his feet, the star,
Which hails the dawn, but glows as oft
In the evening sky; and he marveled that he
Should be called Hesperus. 'Tis said that Aurora
Roused to her wonted task, but again
Sank back to her sleep on the breast of Tithonus:
For long must the night be, and tardy the morning,
That waits for the birth of a hero divine.
The swift-whirling vault of the sky stood still
To greet thee, O youth to the heavens appointed.
Thy labours how many and mighty! Thy hand
Has the terrible lion of Nemea felt,
The fleet-footed hind, and the ravaging boar
That Arcadia feared. Loud bellowed the bull
    When torn from the fields of Crete;
Thou didst conquer the Hydra, which fed on de-
    struction,
And severed the last of its multiplied heads.
The dread giant, Geryon, three monsters in one,
Fell slain with one blow of thy crashing club;
But his oxen, the famous Hesperian herds,
Were driven away as the spoils of the east.
The terrible steeds of the Thracian king,[12]
Which their master fed not on the grass of the
    Strymon,
Or the green banks of Hebrus (but, cruel and
    bloody,
With flesh of the hapless wayfarer he fed them),
These steeds did our Hercules take, and in venge-
    ance,
As their last gory feast gave the flesh of their
    master.
The spoil of her girdle Hippolyte saw
    A-gleam on her conqueror's breast.
The Stymphalian bird fell down from the clouds
    By his arrows death-smitten,
And the tree which bears the fruit of gold
Feared his approach, but, despoiled of its treasures,

Lifted high in the air its burdenless branches.
Forth from the ravished grove he strode
With its golden fruit full laden; in vain
Did the deadly, sleepless dragon guard
Hear the sound of the musical metal.
By triple chains to the upper world
The hound of hell was meekly dragged;
His three great mouths in silence gaped,
  Amazed by the light of day.
And, greatest of toils, beneath his might,
The lying house of Dardanus
Was overthrown, and felt the force
Of that dread bow which it was doomed
In far-off time to feel again.[13]
Ten days sufficed for Troy's first overthrow;
As many years her second ruins know.
  (*The* CHORUS *departs.*)

Act Five.   Scene I

CASSANDRA (*alone upon the stage, standing where she can see the interior of the palace, describes what is going on there; or else she sees it by clairvoyant power*):

Great deeds are done within, the cruel match
For ten long years of suffering at Troy.
Alas, what do they there? Arise, my soul,
And take reward for thy mad prophecies.
The conquered Phrygians are victors now.
'Tis well! O Troy, thou risest from the dust,
For thou hast now to equal ruin brought
Mycenae too. Low lies thy conqueror.
Oh, ne'er before has my prophetic soul
So clearly seen the things of which it raved.
I see, and no false image cheats my sight,
I see it plainly: there, within the hall,
A royal feast is spread, and thronged with guests,
Like that last fatal feast of ours at Troy.
The couches gleam with Trojan tapestries;
Their wine they quaff from rare old cups of gold

That once cheered great Assaracus; and see,
The king himself, in 'broidered vestment clad,
Sits high in triumph at the table's head,
With Priam's noble spoils upon his breast.
Now comes his queen and bids him put away
The garment which his enemy has worn,
And don instead the robe which she has made
With loving thoughts of him.

　　　　　　　　　　　　Oh, horrid deed!
I shudder at the sight. Shall that base man,
That exile, smite a king? The paramour
The husband slay? The fatal hour has come.
The second course shall flow with royal blood,
And gory streams shall mingle with the wine.
And now the king has donned the deadly robe,
Which gives him bound and helpless to his fate.
His hands no outlet find; the clinging gown
Enwraps his head in dark and smothering folds.
With trembling hand the coward paramour
Now smites the king, but not with deadly wound;
For in mid stroke his nerveless hand is stayed.
But, as some shaggy boar in forest wilds,
Within the net's strong meshes caught, still strives
And strains to burst his bonds, yet all in vain:
So Agamemnon seeks to throw aside
The floating, blinding folds. In vain; and yet,
Though blind and bound, he seeks his enemy.
Now frenzied Clytemnestra snatches up
A two-edged battle-ax; and, as the priest,
Before he smites the sacrificial bull,
Marks well the spot and meditates his aim:
So she her impious weapon balances.
He has the blow. 'Tis done. The severed head
Hangs loosely down, and floods the trunk with gore.
Nor do they even yet their weapons stay:
The baseborn wretch hacks at the lifeless corpse,
While she, his mate, pursues her bloody task.
So each responds to each in infamy.
Thyestes' son in very truth is he,
While she to Helen proves her sisterhood.
The sun stands doubtful on the edge of day;
Shall he go on or backward bend his way?
　　　(*Remains beside the altar.*)

Act Five.   Scene II

(*Enter* ELECTRA, *leading her little brother,* ORESTES.)

ELECTRA: Flee, sole avenger of my father's death,
                Oh, flee, and shun these impious butchers' hands.
                Our royal house is utterly o'erthrown,
                Our kingdom gone.
                            But see, a stranger comes,
                His horses driven to their utmost speed;
                Come, brother, hide thyself beneath my robe.
                But, O my foolish heart, whom dost thou fear?
                A stranger? Nay, thy foes are here at home.
                Put off thy fears, for close at hand I see
                The timely shelter of a faithful friend.

Act Five.   Scene III

(*Enter* STROPHIUS *in a chariot, accompanied by his son* PYLADES.)

STROPHIUS: I, Strophius, had left my Phocian realm,
                And now, illustrious with th' Olympic palm,
                I home return. My hither course is bent
                To 'gratulate my friend, by whose assault
                Has Ilium fallen after years of war.
                    (*Noticing* ELECTRA'S *distress*)
                But why these flowing tears and looks of woe?
                And why these marks of fear? I recognise
                In thee the royal house. Electra! Why,
                When all is joyful here, dost thou lament?

ELECTRA: My father lies within the palace, slain
                By Clytemnestra's hand. His son is doomed
                To share his father's death. Aegisthus holds
                The throne which he through guilty love has gained.

STROPHIUS: Oh, happiness that never long endures!

ELECTRA: By all thy kindly memories of my sire,
                By his proud sceptre, known to all the earth,
                And by the fickle gods, I pray thee take
                My brother hence, and hide him from his foes.

STROPHIUS: Although dead Agamemnon bids me fear,
I'll brave the danger and thy brother save.
Good fortune asks for faith; adversity
Compels us to be true.
    (*Takes* ORESTES *into the chariot*)
               My lad, attend:
Wear this wild-olive wreath upon thy brow,
The noble prize I won on Pisa's plain;
And hold above thy head this leafy branch,
The palm of victory, that it may be
A shield and omen of success to thee.
And do thou too, O Pylades, my son,
Who dost as comrade guide thy father's car,
From my example faith in friendship learn.
Do you, swift steeds, before the eyes of Greece
Speed on in flight, and leave this faithless land.
    (*They depart at great speed.*)

ELECTRA (*looking after them*): So is he gone. His car at reckless pace
Fast vanishes from sight. And now my foes,
With heart released from care, will I await,
And willingly submit my head to death.
Here comes the bloody conqueror of her lord,
And bears upon her robes the stains of blood.
Her hands still reek with gore, and in her face
She bears the witness of her impious crime.
I'll hie me to the shrine; and, kneeling here,
I'll join Cassandra in our common fear.

Act Five. Scene IV

(*Enter* CLYTEMNESTRA, *fresh from the murder of her husband.*)

CLYTEMNESTRA (*to* ELECTRA): Thou base, unfilial, and froward girl,
Thy mother's foe, by what authority
Dost thou, a virgin, seek the public gaze?

ELECTRA: Because I am a virgin have I left
The tainted home of vile adulterers.

CLYTEMNESTRA: Who would believe thee chaste?

ELECTRA: I am thy child.

CLYTEMNESTRA: Thou shouldst thy mother speak with gentler tongue.

ELECTRA: Shall I learn filial piety of thee?

CLYTEMNESTRA: Thou hast a mannish soul, too puffed with pride;
              But tamed by suffering thou soon shalt learn
              To play a woman's part.

ELECTRA: A woman's part!
              Yea, truly, 'tis to wield the battle-ax.

CLYTEMNESTRA: Thou fool, dost think thyself a match for us?

ELECTRA: "For us?" Hast thou another husband then?
              Speak thou as widow, for thy lord is dead.

CLYTEMNESTRA: As queen I soon shall curb thy saucy tongue,
              And break thy pride. But meanwhile quickly tell,
              Where is my son, where is thy brother hid?

ELECTRA: Far from Mycenae fled.

CLYTEMNESTRA: Then bring him back.

ELECTRA: Bring back my father too.

CLYTEMNESTRA: Where lurks the boy?

ELECTRA: In safety, where he fears no rival's power.
              This will content a loving mother.

CLYTEMNESTRA: Yes,
              But not an angry one. Thou diest today.

ELECTRA: Oh, let me perish by thy practiced hand!
              Behold, I leave the altar's sheltering side;
              Wilt plunge the knife into my tender throat?
              I yield me to thy will. Or dost prefer
              At one fell stroke to smite away my head?
              My neck awaits thy deadly aim. Let crime
              By other crime be purged. Thy hands are stained
              And reeking with thy murdered husband's blood.
              Come, cleanse them in the fresher stream of mine.

                    (*Enter* AEGISTHUS.)

CLYTEMNESTRA: Thou partner of my perils and my throne,
              Aegisthus, come; this most unnatural child
              Assails her mother and her brother hides.

AEGISTHUS: Thou mad and foolish girl, restrain thy tongue,
For such wild words offend thy mother's ears.

ELECTRA: Thou arch contriver of most impious crime,
Wilt thou admonish me? Thou baseborn wretch,
Thou sister's son, and grandson of thy sire!

CLYTEMNESTRA: Aegisthus, how canst thou restrain thy hand
From smiting off her head? But hear my word:
Let her give up her brother or her life.

AEGISTHUS: Nay, rather, in some dark and stony cell
Let her be straight confined; and there, perchance,
By cruel tortures racked, will she give up
Whom now she hides. Resourceless, starving there,
In dank and loathsome solitude immured,
Widowed, ere wedded, exiled, scorned of all—
Then will she, though too late, to fortune yield.

ELECTRA: Oh, grant me death.

AEGISTHUS: If thou shouldst plead for life,
I'd grant thee death. A foolish ruler he,
Who balances by death the score of sin.

ELECTRA: Can any punishment be worse than death?

AEGISTHUS: Yes! Life for those who wish to die. Away,
Ye slaves, seek out some dark and lonely cave,
Far from Mycenae's bounds; and there in chains,
Confine this bold, unmanageable maid,
If haply prison walls may curb her will.
        (ELECTRA *is led away*.)

CLYTEMNESTRA (*indicating* CASSANDRA): But she shall die, that rival of my couch,
That captive bride. Go, drag her hence at once,
That she may follow him she stole from me.

CASSANDRA: Nay, drag me not; for I with joy will go,
Outstripping your desire. How eagerly
I hasten to my Phrygians, to tell
The news: the ocean covered with the wrecks
Of Argive ships; Mycenae overthrown;
The leader of a thousand leaders slain
(And thus atoning for the woes of Troy)
By woman's gift of wantonness and guile.

Make haste! I falter not, but thank the gods,
That I have lived to see my land avenged.

CLYTEMNESTRA: O maddened wretch, thy death I wait to see.

CASSANDRA: A fateful madness waits as well for thee.[14]

1. In the passage which follows Thyestes calls to mind the stock punishments of the lower world; the sufferers are, respectively, Ixion, Sisyphus, Tityus, and Tantalus.

2. This horrible crime is the subject of Seneca's *Thyestes*.

3. In this and the following lines Thyestes addresses his son Aegisthus as if he were present.

4. This refers to Medea's flight with Jason from Colchis.

5. Clytemnestra's sister was Helen, who fled with Paris to Troy.

6. This refers to Iphigenia, sacrificed by Agamemnon at Aulis.

7. This verse is assigned to Clytemnestra in the earlier Mss.

8. The "bride" was Briseis, whom Achilles gave up to Agamemnon at the time of the quarrel which Homer describes in the first book of the *Iliad*.

9. This is Ajax, son of Oileus. The greater Ajax, son of Telamon, committed suicide after the award of Achilles' armour to Ulysses.

10. Miller reads here *hinc et Chalcida*.

11. The deaths of Astyanax and Polyxena are described in Seneca's *The Trojan Women*.

12. The Thracian king was Diomedes, whose man-eating horses were captured by Hercules.

13. Troy was first captured by Hercules in the time of Laomedon; the bow and arrows of Hercules, brought to Troy by Philoctetes, assisted in the final fall of Troy under Priam. Cf. *The Trojan Women*, note 6.

14. This probably refers to the madness of Orestes, who later slays both Aegisthus and Clytemnestra.

VIII
THYESTES

CHARACTERS IN THE PLAY

GHOST OF TANTALUS
MEGAERA, *a Fury*
CHORUS OF MEN OF MYCENAE
ATREUS, *king of Argos, grandson of* TANTALUS
AN ATTENDANT *of* ATREUS
THYESTES, *brother of* ATREUS, *in exile from his fatherland*
THREE SONS *of* THYESTES, *only one of whom,* TANTALUS, *takes part in the dialogue*
A MESSENGER

INTRODUCTION

SENECA's *Thyestes* depicts the fiendish vengeance wrought by Atreus upon his brother Thyestes. Atreus, upon the death of his father Pelops, had taken possession of the kingdom of Argos; Thyestes, too, had claimed the throne and sought to gain it by foul means; he had seduced his brother's wife and with her assistance had stolen a magical ram with golden fleece. The right to rule was said to belong to him who possessed the ram. Thyestes was exiled for his crime, but Atreus planned a more complete revenge upon his brother. The play relates how Atreus, pretending friendship, recalls Thyestes, murders his sons, and serves their bodies to the father at a banquet. The *Thyestes* is the most gruesome of Seneca's tragedies, and in many respects one of the most famous. It provided the model for later plays of revenge, such as Kyd's *The Spanish Tragedy,* and has perhaps exerted a greater influence than Seneca's other plays. F. L. Lucas says,

"The Revenge play after its first success in *The Spanish Tragedy* was long to continue both popular and Senecan. The lost original Hamlet, probably by Kyd (1587), his *Soliman and Persida* (1588), *Titus Andronicus* (1585-90), *Lust's Dominion* (1590), *The True Tragedie of Richard III* (1591) and Shakespeare's *Richard III* (1593), Marston's *Antonio and Mellida* (1599), Chettle's *Hoffmann* (1602), Shakespeare's *Hamlet* (1602), the four main plays of Tourneur and Webster, Chapman's *Revenge of Bussy d'Ambois* (1604), *Macbeth* (1605-6), Beaumont and Fletcher's *Triumph of Death* (1608) all belong to this particular genre, and most of them, especially Marston and Chapman, show definite Senecan influence."

Before the time of Seneca tragedies on the story of Thyestes had been written by Sophocles, Euripides, Ennius, Accius, and by Varius, the friend and contemporary of Horace and Vergil. No one of these plays has survived, and it is therefore impossible to compare Seneca's treatment with the earlier versions. There seems little doubt, however, that the distinctive features of the play are Seneca's own contribution. The scene between the ghost of Tantalus and the Fury gives an atmosphere of gloom to the play at its opening. The terrible events to come are foreshadowed, and the reluctance of the ghost to be a party to the crime intensifies the horror of the situation. The foreboding of disaster which

751

Thyestes is unable to shake off on his return, and the presentiment of evil that hovers over him at the banquet are typically Senecan devices to make the effect of the crime more appalling. Few tragedies contain more hideous irony.

Atreus is a masterpiece of villainy and, as such, is one of Seneca's most striking characterisations. He demands of his people not only submission but hypocrisy as well; he sums up his theory of power in his speech to his attendant,

> "Herein is greatest good of royal power;
> The populace not only must endure
> Their master's deeds, but praise them."

A more damning self-revelation is found in his words,

> "Mild tyrants slay;
> Death is a longed-for favour in my realm."

His own hypocrisy and cruelty are apparent in the delight he pretends to feel at his brother's return. Upon the killing of the children, vividly described by the messenger, Atreus becomes an inhuman monster; he delights in the slaughter, and in his cold-blooded revelation of the truth to Thyestes. As the latter, overcame with forebodings of disaster, asks for his sons, Atreus replies with overpowering irony,

> "Yea, I will give them back, and never more
> Shalt thou be parted from them."

Even when he discloses that the children are dead, he withholds for a time the more terrible aspect of his vengeance and keeps Thyestes in uncertainty concerning the whereabouts of their bodies. Atreus has been called "a criminal maniac" and the play "mental pathology" rather than drama. Seneca has been successful in his desire to depict one of the most hideous villains in dramatic literature.

THYESTES

(SCENE:—*Before the palace of* ATREUS.)

Act One.   Scene I

(*Enter the* GHOST OF TANTALUS *and* MEGAERA.)

GHOST:　　Who drags me from my place among the shades,
Where with dry lips I seek the flying waves?
What hostile god again shows Tantalus
His hated palace? Has some worse thing come
Than thirst amid the waters or the pangs
Of ever-gnawing hunger? Must the stone,
The slippery burden borne by Sisyphus,
Weigh down my shoulders, or Ixion's wheel
Carry my limbs around in its swift course,
Or must I fear Tityus' punishment?
Stretched in a lofty cave he feeds dun birds
Upon his vitals which they tear away,
And night renews whatever day destroyed,
And thus he offers them full feast again.
Against what evil have I been reserved?
Stern judge of Hades, whosoe'er thou art
Who metest to the dead due penalties,
If something can be added more than pain,
Seek that at which the grim custodian
Of this dark prison must himself feel fear,
Something from which sad Acheron shall shrink,
Before whose horror I myself must fear;
For many sprung from me, who shall outsin
Their house, who, daring deeds undared by me,
Make me seem innocent, already come.
Whatever impious deed this realm may lack
My house will bring; while Pelops' line remains,
Minos shall never be unoccupied.

MEGAERA: Go, hated shade, and drive thy sin-stained home
            To madness; let the sword try every crime,
            And pass from hand to hand; nor let there be
            Limit to rage and shame; let fury blind
            Urge on their thoughts; let parents' hearts be hard
            Through madness, long iniquity be heaped
            Upon the children, let them never know
            Leisure to hate old crimes, let new ones rise,
            Many in one; let sin while punished grow;
            From the proud brothers let the throne depart,
            Then let it call the exiled home again.
            Let the dark fortunes of a violent house
            Among unstable kings be brought to naught.
            Let evil fortune on the mighty fall,
            The wretched come to power; let chance toss
            The kingdom with an ever-changing tide
            Where'er it will. Exiled because of crime,
            When god would give them back their native land
            Let them through crime reach home, and let them hate
            Themselves as others hate them. Let them deem
            No crime forbidden when their passions rage;
            Let brother greatly fear his brother's hand,
            Let parents fear their sons, and let the sons
            Feel fear of parents, children wretched die,
            More wretchedly be born. Let wife rebel
            Against her husband, wars pass over seas,
            And every land be wet with blood poured forth.
            Let lust, victorious, o'er great kings exult
            And basest deeds be easy in thy house;
            Let right and truth and justice be no more
            'Twixt brothers. Let not heaven be immune—
            Why shine the stars within the firmament
            To be a source of beauty to the world?
            Let night be different, day no more exist.
            O'erthrow thy household gods, bring hatred, death,
            Wild slaughter, with thy spirit fill the house,
            Deck the high portals, let the gates be green
            With laurel, fires for thy arrival meet
            Shall glow, crimes worse than Thracian shall be done.
            Why idle lies the uncle's stern right hand?
            Thyestes has not yet bewept his sons;
            When will they be destroyed? Lo, even now
            Upon the fire the brazen pot shall boil,

The members shall be broken into parts,
The father's hearth with children's blood be wet,
The feast shall be prepared. Thou wilt not come
Guest at a feast whose crime is new to thee:
Today we give thee freedom; satisfy
Thy hunger at those tables, end thy fast.
Blood mixed with wine shall in thy sight be drunk,
Food have I found that even thou wouldst shun.
Stay! Whither dost thou rush?

GHOST: To stagnant pools,
Rivers and waters ever slipping by,
To the fell trees that will not give me food.
Let me go hence to my dark prison-house,
Let me, if all too little seems my woe,
Seek other shores; within thy channels' midst
And by thy floods of fire hemmed about,
O Phlegethon, permit me to be left.
O ye who suffer by the fates' decree
Sharp penalties, O thou who, filled with fear,
Within the hallowed cave dost wait the fall
Of the impending mountain, thou who dreadst
The ravening lion's open jaws, the hand
Of cruel furies that encompass thee,
Thou who, half burned, dost feel their torch applied,
Hear ye the voice of Tantalus who knows:
Love ye your penalties! Ah, woe is me,
When shall I be allowed to flee to hell?

MEGAERA: First into dread confusion throw thy house,
Bring with thee battle and the sword and love,
Strike thou the king's wild heart with frantic rage.

GHOST: 'Tis right that I should suffer punishment,
But not that I myself be punishment.
Like a death-dealing vapour must I go
Out of the riven earth, or like a plague
Most grievous to the people, or a pest
Widespread, I bring my children's children crime.
Great father of the gods, our father too—
However much our sonship cause thee shame—
Although my too loquacious tongue should pay
Due punishment for sin, yet will I speak:
Stain not, my kinsmen, holy hands with blood.

The altars with unholy sacrifice
Pollute not. I will stay and ward off crime.
(*To* MEGAERA)
Why dost thou terrify me with thy torch,
And fiercely threaten with thy writhing snakes?
Why dost thou stir the hunger in my reins?
My heart is burning with the fire of thirst,
My parched veins feel the flame.

MEGAERA: Through all thy house
Scatter this fury; thus shall they, too, rage,
And, mad with anger, thirst by turns to drink
Each other's blood. Thy house thy coming feels
And trembles at thy execrable touch.
It is enough; depart to hell's dark caves
And to thy well-known river. Earth is sad
And burdened by thy presence. Backward forced,
Seest thou not the waters leave the streams,
How all the banks are dry, how fiery winds
Drive the few scattered clouds? The foliage pales,
And every branch is bare, the fruits are fled.
And where the Isthmus has been wont to sound
With the near waters, roaring on each side,
And cutting off the narrow strip of land,
Far from the shore is heard the sound remote.
Now Lerna's waters have been backward drawn,
Sacred Alpheus' stream is seen no more,
Cithaeron's summit stands untouched with snow,
And Argos fears again its former thirst.
Lo, Titan's self is doubtful—shall he drive
His horses upward, bring again the day?
It will but rise to die.
(*They vanish.*)

Act One.   Scene II

(*Enter the* CHORUS OF MEN OF MYCENAE.)

CHORUS: If any god still cherish love for Greece,
Argos, and Pisa for her chariots famed,
If any cherishes the Isthmian realm,

And the twin havens, and the parted seas,
If anẏ love Taygetus' bright snows
That shine afar, which northern winter lays
Upon its highest summits and the breath
Of summer trade winds welcome to the sails
Melts, let him whom Alpheus' ice-cold stream
Touches, well known for his Olympic course,
Wield the calm influence of his heavenly power,
Nor suffer crimes in constant series come.
Let not a grandson, readier for that crime
E'en than his father's father, follow him,
Nor let the father's error please the sons.
Let thirsty Tantalus' base progeny,
Wearied at length, give up their fierce attempts;
Enough of crime! No more is right of worth,
And common wrongs of little moment seem;
The traitor Myrtilus betrayed his lord
And slew him—by such faith as he had shown
Himself dragged down, he gave the sea a name;
To ships on the Aegean never tale
Was better known. Met by the cruel sword,
Even while he ran to gain his father's kiss,
The little son[1] was slain; he early fell
A victim to the hearth, by thy right hand,
O Tantalus, cut off that thou mightst spread
Such feasts before the gods. Eternal thirst
And endless famine followed on the feast;
Nor can a worthier punishment be found
For savage feast like that. With empty maw
Stands weary Tantalus, above his head
Hangs ready food, more swift to take its flight
Than Phineus' birds; on every side it hangs;
The tree beneath the burden of its fruit
Bending and trembling, shuns his open mouth;
He though so eager, brooking no delay,
Yet oft deceived, neglects to touch the tree,
And drops his head and presses close his lips,
And shuts his hunger in behind clenched teeth.
The ripe fruit taunts him from the languid boughs,
And whets his hunger till it urges him
To stretch again his hand oft stretched in vain.
Then the whole harvest of the bended boughs
Is lifted out of reach. Thirst rises then,

More hard to bear than hunger, when his blood
Is hot within him and his eyes aflame;
Wretched he stands striving to touch his lips
To the near waters, but the stream retreats,
Forsakes him when he strives to follow it,
And leaves him in dry sands; his eager lips
Drink but the dust.

Act Two. Scene I

(*Enter* ATREUS *and an* ATTENDANT.)

ATREUS (*to himself*): O slothful, indolent, weak, unavenged
(This last I deem for tyrants greatest wrong
In great affairs), after so many crimes,
After thy brother's treachery to thee,
After the breaking of all laws of right,
Dost thou, O angry Atreus, waste the time
In idle lamentations? All the world
Should echo with the uproar of thy arms,
And either sea should bear thy ships of war;
The fields and cities should be bright with flame;
The flashing sword should everywhere be drawn;
All Greece shall with our horsemen's tread resound;
Woods shall not hide the foe nor towers built
Upon the highest summits of the hills;
Mycenae's citizens shall leave the town
And sing the warsong; he shall die hard death
Who gives that hated head a hiding-place.
This palace even, noble Pelops' home,
Shall fall, if it must be, and bury me
If only on my brother too it fall.
Up, do a deed which none shall e'er approve,
But one whose fame none shall e'er cease to speak.
Some fierce and bloody crime must now be dared,
Such as my brother seeing shall wish his.
A wrong is not avenged but by worse wrong.
What deed can be so wild 'tis worse than his?
Does he lie humbled? Does he feel content
When fortune smiles, or tranquil when she frowns?
I know the tameless spirit of the man,

Not to be bent but broken, therefore seek
Revenge before he makes himself secure,
Renews his strength, lest he should fall on me
When I am unaware. Or kill, or die!
Crime is between us to be seized by one.

ATTENDANT: Fearest thou not the people's hostile words?

ATREUS: Herein is greatest good of royal power:
The populace not only must endure
Their master's deeds, but praise them.

ATTENDANT: Fear shall make
Those hostile who were first compelled to praise;
But he who seeks the fame of true applause
Would rather by the heart than voice be praised.

ATREUS: The lowly oft enjoy praise truly meant,
The mighty ne'er know aught but flattery.
The people oft must will what they would not.

ATTENDANT: The king should wish for honesty and right;
Then there is none who does not wish with him.

ATREUS: When he who rules must wish for right alone
He hardly rules, except on sufferance.

ATTENDANT: When reverence is not, nor love of law,
Nor loyalty, integrity, nor truth,
The realm is insecure.

ATREUS: Integrity,
Truth, loyalty, are private virtues; kings
Do as they will.

ATTENDANT: Oh, deem it wrong to harm
A brother, even though he be most base.

ATREUS: No deed that is unlawful to be done
Against a brother but may lawfully
Be done against this man. What has he left
Untainted by his crime? Where has he spared
To do an impious deed? He took my wife
Adulterously, he took my realm by stealth,
The earnest of the realm he gained by fraud,
By fraud he brought confusion to my home.
There is in Pelops' stalls a noble sheep,

A magic ram, lord of the fruitful herd;
O'er all his body hangs the golden fleece.
In him each king sprung from the royal line
Of Tantalus his golden sceptre holds,
Who has the ram possesses too the realm,
The fortunes of the palace follow him.
As fits a sacred thing, he feeds apart,
In a safe meadow which a wall surrounds
Hiding the pasture with its fateful stones.
The faithless one, daring a matchless crime,
Stole him away and with him took my wife,
Accomplice in his sin. From this has flowed
Every disaster; exiled and in fear
I've wandered through my realm; no place is safe
From brother's plots; my wife has been defiled,
The quiet of my realm has been disturbed,
My house is troubled, and the ties of blood
Are insecure, of nothing am I sure
Unless it be my brother's enmity.
Why hesitate? At length be strong to act.
Look upon Tantalus, on Pelops look;
To deeds like theirs these hands of mine are called.
          (*To* SLAVE)
Tell me, how shall I slay that cursed one?

ATTENDANT: Slain by the sword let him spew forth his soul.

ATREUS: Thou tellest the end of punishment, I wish
The punishment itself. Mild tyrants slay;
Death is a longed-for favour in my realm.

ATTENDANT: Hast thou no piety?

ATREUS: If e'er it dwelt
Within our home, let piety depart.
Let the grim company of Furies come,
Jarring Erinys and Megaera dread
Shaking their torches twain. My breast burns not
With anger hot enough. I fain would feel
Worse horrors.

ATTENDANT: What new exile dost thou plot,
In thy mad rage?

ATREUS: No deed that keeps the bounds
Of former evils. I will leave no crime
Untried, and none is great enough for me.

ATTENDANT: The sword?

ATREUS: 'Tis poor.

ATTENDANT: Or fire?

ATREUS: 'Tis not enough.

ATTENDANT: What weapon then shall arm such hate as thine?

ATREUS: Thyestes' self.

ATTENDANT: This ill is worse than hate.

ATREUS: I own it. In my breast a tumult reigns;
It rages deep within, and I am urged
I know not whither, yet it urges me.
Earth from its lowest depths sends forth a groan,
It thunders though the daylight is serene,
The whole house shakes as though the house were rent,
The trembling Lares turn away their face.
This shall be done, this evil shall be done,
Which, gods, ye fear.

ATTENDANT: What is it thou wilt do?

ATREUS: I know not what great passion in my heart,
Wilder than I have known, beyond the bounds
Of human nature, rises, urges on
My slothful hands. I know not what it is,
'Tis something great. Yet be it what it may,
Make haste, my soul! Fit for Thyestes' hand
This crime would be; 'tis worthy Atreus, too.
And both shall do it. Tereus' house has seen
Such shocking feasts. I own the crime is great,
And yet it has been done; some greater crime
Let grief invent. Inspire thou my soul
O Daulian Procne, thou wast sister too;
Our cause is like, assist, impel my hand.
The father, hungrily, with joy shall tear
His children, and shall eat their very flesh;
'Tis well, it is enough. This punishment
Is so far pleasing. But where can he be?

And why is Atreus so long innocent?
Already all the sacrifice I see,
As in a picture, see the morsels placed
Within the father's mouth. Wherefore, my soul,
Art thou afraid? Why fail before the deed?
Forward! It must be done. Himself shall do
What is in such a deed the greater crime.

ATTENDANT: But captured by what wiles, will he consent
To put his feet within our toils? He deems
That all are hostile.

ATREUS: 'Twere not possible
To capture him but that he'd capture me.
He hopes to gain my kingdom; through this hope
He will make haste to meet the thunderbolts
Of threatening Jove, in this hope will endure
The swelling whirlpool's threats, and dare to go
Within the Libyan Syrtes' doubtful shoals,
To see again his brother, last and worst
Of evils deemed; this hope shall lead him on.

ATTENDANT: Who shall persuade him he may come in peace?
Whose word will he believe?

ATREUS: Malicious hope
Is credulous, yet I will give my sons
A message they shall to their uncle bear:
"The wandering exile, leaving chance abodes,
May for a kingdom change his misery,
May reign in Argos, sharer of my throne."
But if Thyestes sternly spurn my prayers,
His artless children, wearied by their woes
And easily persuaded, with their plea
Will overcome him; his old thirst for rule,
Beside sad poverty and heavy toil,
With weight of evil, will subdue his soul
However hard it be.

ATTENDANT: Time will have made
His sorrow light.

ATREUS: Thou errest; sense of ills
Increases daily. To endure distress
Is easy, but to bear it to the end
Is hard.

ATTENDANT: Choose others for thy messengers
In this dread plan.

ATREUS: Youth freely dares the worst.

ATTENDANT: What now thou teachest them in enmity
Against their uncle, they may later do
Against their father; evil deeds return
Full oft upon their author.

ATREUS: If they learned
The way of treachery and crime from none,
Possession of the throne would teach it them.
Art thou afraid their natures will grow base?
So were they born. That which thou callest wild
And cruel, and deemst hardly to be done,
Ruthless, nor showing honour for god's laws,
Perchance is even now against ourselves
Attempted.

ATTENDANT: Shall thy sons know what they do?

ATREUS: Discretion is not found with so few years.
They might perhaps discover all the guile;
Silence is learned through long and evil years.

ATTENDANT: The very ones through whom thou wouldst deceive
Another thou deceivest?

ATREUS: That themselves
May be exempt from crime or fault of mine.
Why should I mix my children in my sins?
My hatred shall unfold itself in me.
Yet say not so, thou doest ill, my soul;
If thine thou sparest, thou sparest also his.
My minister shall Agamemnon be,
And know my plan, and Menelaus too
Shall know his father's plans and further them.
Through this crime will I prove if they be mine;
If they refuse the contest nor consent
To my revenge, but call him uncle, then
I'll know he is their father. It shall be.
But oft a frightened look lays bare the heart,
Great plans may be unwillingly betrayed;
They shall not know how great affairs they aid.
Hide thou our undertaking.

ATTENDANT: Scarce were need
That I should be admonished; in my breast
Both fear and loyalty will keep it hid,
But loyalty the rather.

(ATREUS *and the* ATTENDANT *go into the palace.*)

Act Two.   Scene II

CHORUS: The ancient race of royal Inachus
At last has laid aside fraternal threats.[2]
What madness drove you, that by turns you shed
Each other's blood and sought to mount the throne
By crime? You know not, eager for high place,
What kingly station means. It is not wealth
That makes the king, nor robes of Tyrian dye,
'Tis not the crown upon the royal brow,
Nor gates made bright with gold; a king is he
Whose hard heart has forgotten fear and pain,
Whom impotent ambition does not move,
Nor the inconstant favour of the crowd,
Who covets nothing that the west affords,
Nor aught that Tagus' golden waves wash up
From its bright channels, nor the grain thrashed out
Upon the glowing Libyan threshing-floors,
Who neither fears the falling thunderbolt,
Nor Eurus stirring all the sea to wrath,
Nor windy Adriatic's swelling rage;
Who is not conquered by a soldier's lance,
Nor the drawn sword; who, seated on safe heights,
Sees everything beneath him; who makes haste
Freely to meet his fate, nor grieves to die.
Let kings who vex the scattered Scythians come,
Who hold the Red Sea's shore, the pearl-filled sea,
Or who intrenched upon the Caspian range
To bold Sarmatians close the way, who breast
The Danube's waves, or those who dare pursue
And spoil the noble Seres where'er they dwell.
The mind a kingdom is; there is no need
Of horse, or weapon, or the coward dart
Which from afar the Parthian hurls and flees—

Or seems to flee, no need to overthrow
Cities with engines that hurl stones afar,
When one possesses in himself his realm.
Whoever will may on the slippery heights
Of empire stand, but I with sweet repose
Am satisfied, rejoice in gentle ease,
And, to my fellow citizens unknown,
My life shall flow in calm obscurity,
And when, untouched by storm, my days have passed,
Then will I die, a common citizen,
In good old age. Death seemeth hard to him
Who dies but too well known to all the world,
Yet knowing not himself.

Act Three.   Scene I

(*Enter* THYESTES, *accompanied by* TANTALUS *and two other sons.*)

THYESTES (*to himself*): The longed-for dwelling of my native land
            And, to the wretched exile greatest boon,
            Rich Argos and a stretch of native soil,
            And, if there yet be gods, my country's gods
            I see at last; the Cyclop's sacred towers,
            Of greater beauty than the work of man;
            The celebrated race-course of my youth
            Where oft, well known, I drove my father's car
            And carried off the palm. Argos will come
            To meet me, and the people come in crowds,
            Perchance my brother Atreus too will come!
            Rather return to exile in the woods
            And mountain pastures, live the life of brutes
            Among them. This bright splendour of the realm
            With its false glitter shall not blind my eyes.
            Look on the giver, not the gift alone.
            In fortunes which the world deemed hard I lived
            Joyous and brave, now am I forced to fear,
            My courage fails me, fain would I retreat,
            Unwillingly I go.

TANTALUS (*aside*):   What see I here?
            With hesitating step my father goes,
            He seems uncertain, turns away his head.

THYESTES (*to himself*): Why doubt, my soul? Or why so long revolve
  Deliberations easy to conclude?
  In most uncertain things dost thou confide
  And in thy brother's realm, and stand in fear
  Of ills already conquered and found mild?
  Dost fly the troubles thou hast learned to bear?
  Now to be wretched with the shades were joy,
  Turn while thou yet hast time.

TANTALUS: Why turn away
  From thy loved country? Why deny thyself
  So much of happiness? His wrath forgot,
  Thy brother gives thee back the kingdom's half
  And to the jarring members of his house
  Brings peace, restores thee once more to thyself.

THYESTES: Thou askest why I fear; I do not know.
  I see not aught to fear and yet I fear.
  Fain would I go and yet with slothful feet
  I waver and am borne unwillingly
  Whither I would not; thus the ship propelled
  By oar and sail is driven from its course
  By the opposing tide.

TANTALUS: Whatever thwarts
  Or hinders thee, o'ercome; see what rewards
  Are waiting thy return. Thou mayst be king.

THYESTES: Since I can die.

TANTALUS: The very highest power—

THYESTES: Is naught, if thou hast come to wish for naught.

TANTALUS: Thy sons shall be thy heirs.

THYESTES: No realm can have
  Two kings.

TANTALUS: Does one who might be happy choose
  Unhappiness?

THYESTES: Believe me, with false name
  Does power deceive; and vain it is to fear
  Laborious fortunes. High in place, I feared,
  Yea, feared the very sword upon my side.
  How good it is to be the foe of none,

To lie upon the ground, in safety eat.
Crime enters not the cottage; without fear
May food be eaten at the humble board,
Poison is drunk from gold. I speak known truth—
Ill fortune is to be preferred to good.
The humble citizen fears not my house;
It is not on the mountain summit placed,
Its high roofs do not shine with ivory;
No watchman guards my sleep; we do not fish
With fleets, nor drive the ocean from its bed
With massive walls, nor feed vile gluttony
With tribute from all peoples; not for me
Are harvested the fields beyond the Getes
And Parthians; men do not honour me
With incense, nor are altars built for me
Instead of Jove; upon my palace roofs
No forests nod, no hot pools steam for me;
Day is not spent in sleep nor night in crime
And watching. Aye, none fears me and my home,
Although without a weapon, is secure.
Great peace attends on humble circumstance;
He has a kingdom who can be content
Without a kingdom.

TANTALUS: If a favouring god
Give thee a realm, it should not be refused,
Nor should it be desired. Thy brother begs
That thou wouldst rule.

THYESTES: He begs? Then I must fear.
He seeks some means whereby he may betray.

TANTALUS: Full often loyalty that was withdrawn
Is given back, and true affection gains
Redoubled strength.

THYESTES: And shall his brother love
Thyestes? Rather shall the ocean wet
The northern Bear, and the rapacious tides
Of the Sicilian waters stay their waves,
The harvest ripen in Ionian seas,
And black night give the earth the light of day;
Rather shall flame with water, life with death,
The winds with ocean join in faithful pact.

TANTALUS: What fraud dost thou still fear?

THYESTES: All. Where may end
              My cause for fear? His hate is as his power.

TANTALUS: What power has he to harm thee?

THYESTES: For myself
              I do not fear; my sons, for you I dread
              My brother Atreus.

TANTALUS: Dost thou fear deceit?

THYESTES: It is too late to seek security
              When one is in the very midst of ill.
              Let us begone. This one thing I affirm:
              I follow you, not lead.

TANTALUS: God will behold
              With favour thy design; boldly advance.

Act Three.   Scene II

(Enter ATREUS.*)*

ATREUS *(aside)*: At last the wild beast is within my toils:
              Lo, I behold him with his hated brood.
              My vengeance now is sure, into my hands
              Thyestes has completely fall'n; my joy
              Scarce can I temper, scarcely curb my wrath.
              Thus when the cunning Umbrian hound is held
              In leash, and tracks his prey, with lowered nose
              Searching the ground, when from afar he scents
              By slightest clue the bear, he silently
              Explores the place, submitting to be held,
              But when the prey is nearer, then he fights
              To free himself, and with impatient voice
              Calls the slow huntsman, straining at the leash.
              When passion hopes for blood it will not own
              Restraint; and yet my wrath must be restrained!
              See how his heavy, unkempt hair conceals
              His face, how loathsome lies his beard. Ah, well!
              Faith shall be kept.

(*To* THYESTES)

                        To see my brother's face
How glad I am! All former wrath is past.
From this day loyalty to family ties
Shall be maintained, from this day let all hate
Be banished from our hearts.

THYESTES (*aside*):   Oh, wert thou not
    Such as thou art, all could be put aside.
              (*To* ATREUS)
    Atreus, I own, I own that I have done
All thou believest; this day's loyalty
Makes me seem truly base: he sins indeed
Who sins against a brother good as thou.
Tears must wash out my guilt. See at thy feet
These hands are clasped in prayer that ne'er before
Entreated any. Let all anger cease,
Let swelling rage forever be dispelled;
Receive these children, pledges of my faith.

ATREUS: No longer clasp my knees, nay, rather seek
My warm embrace. Ye, too, the props of age,
So young, my children, cling about my neck.
And thou, put off thy raiment mean and coarse;
Oh, spare my sight, put on these royal robes
Like mine, and gladly share thy brother's realm.
This greater glory shall at last be mine:
To my illustrious brother I give back
His heritage. One holds a throne by chance,
To give it up is noble.

THYESTES: May the gods
Give thee, my brother, fair return for all
Thy benefits. Alas, my wretchedness
Forbids me to accept the royal crown,
My guilty hand shrinks from the sceptre's weight;
Let me in lesser rank unnoted live.

ATREUS: This realm recovers its two kings.

THYESTES: I hold,
    O brother, all of thine the same as mine.

ATREUS: Who would refuse the gifts that fortune gives?

THYESTES: He who has learned how swiftly they depart.

ATREUS: Wouldst thou refuse thy brother such renown?

THYESTES: Thy glory is fulfilled, but mine still waits:
               Firm is my resolution to refuse
               The kingdom.

ATREUS: I relinquish all my power
               Unless thou hast thy part.

THYESTES: I take it then.
               I'll wear the name of king, but law and arms
               And I shall be thy slaves, for evermore.

ATREUS: Wear then upon thy head the royal crown.
               I'll give the destined victim to the gods.
                 (ATREUS, THYESTES, *and the sons of* THYESTES *depart.*)

                         Act Three.   Scene III³

CHORUS: Who would believe it? Atreus, fierce and wild,
               Savage and tameless, shrank and was amazed
               When he beheld his brother. Stronger bonds
               Than nature's laws exist not. Wars may last
               With foreign foes, but true love still will bind
               Those whom it once has bound. When wrath, aroused
               By some great quarrel, has dissevered friends
               And called to arms, when the light cavalry
               Advance with ringing bridles, here and there
               Shines the swift sword which, seeking fresh-shed blood,
               The raging war-god wields with frequent blows;
               But love and loyalty subdue the sword,
               And in great peace unite unwilling hearts.
               What god gave sudden peace from so great war?
               Throughout Mycenae rang the crash of arms
               As though in civil strife, pale mothers held
               Their children to their bosoms, and the wife
               Feared for her steel-armed husband, when the sword,
               Stained with the rust acquired in long peace,
               Unwillingly obeyed his hand. One sped
               To strengthen falling walls, to build again
               The tottering towers, to make fast the gates
               With iron bars; and on the battlements

The pale watch waked through all the anxious night.
The fear of war is worse than war itself.
But threatenings of the cruel sword have ceased,
The trumpet's deep-toned voice at last is stilled,
The braying of the strident horn is hushed,
And to the joyous city peace returns.
So when the northwest wind beats up the sea
And from the deep the swelling waves roll in,
Scylla from out her smitten caverns roars
And sailors in the havens fear the flood
That ravening Charybdis vomits forth,
And the fierce Cyclops, dwelling on the top
Of fiery Aetna, dreads his father's rage,
Lest whelmed beneath the waves, the fires that roar
Within his immemorial chimney's throat
Should be profaned, and poor Laertes thinks,
Since Ithaca is shaken, that his realm
May be submerged; then, if the winds subside,
More quiet than a pool the ocean lies,
Scattered on every side gay little skiffs
Stretch the fair canvas of their spreading sails
Upon the sea which, late, ships feared to cut;
And there where, shaken by the hurricane,
The Cyclades were fearful of the deep,
The fishes play. No fortune long endures:
Sorrows and pleasures each in turn depart,
But pleasure soonest; from the fairest heights,
An hour may plunge one to the lowest depths;
He who upon his forehead wears a crown,
Who nods and Medians lay aside the sword,
Indians, too, near neighbours of the sun,
And Dacians that assail the Parthian horse,
He holds his sceptre with an anxious hand,
Foresees the overthrow of all his joy,
And fears uncertain time and fickle chance.
Ye whom the ruler of the earth and sea
Has given power over life and death,
Be not so proud, a stronger threatens you
With whatsoever ills the weaker fears
From you; each realm is by a greater ruled.
Him whom the rising sun beholds in power
The setting sees laid low. Let none confide
Too much in happiness, let none despair

When he has fallen from his high estate,
For Clotho blends the evil with the good;
She turns about all fortunes on her wheel;
None may abide. Such favouring deities
No one has ever found that he may trust
Tomorrow; on his flying wheel a god
Spins our swift-changing fortunes.

Act Four.   Scene I

(*Enter the* MESSENGER *in breathless haste.*)

MESSENGER: Oh, who will bear me headlong through the air,
Like a swift wind, and hide me in thick cloud
That I no longer may behold such crime?
O house dishonoured, whose base deeds disgrace
Pelops and Tantalus!

CHORUS: What news is thine?

MESSENGER: What region can it be that I behold?
Argos and Sparta to which fate assigned
Such loving brothers? Corinth or the shores
Of the two seas? The Danube that compels
The fierce Alani frequently to flee?
Hyrcania underneath eternal snows?
Is it the wandering Scythians' changing home?
What land is this that knows such monstrous deeds?

CHORUS: Speak and declare the ill whate'er it be.

MESSENGER: If I have courage, if cold fear relax
Its hold upon my members. Still I see
Th' accomplished slaughter. Bear me far from hence,
O driving whirlwind; whither day is borne
Bear me, torn hence!

CHORUS: Control thy fear, wrung heart.
What is the deed that makes thee quake with fear?
Speak and declare its author, I ask not
Who it may be, but which. Now quickly tell.

MESSENGER: Upon the heights a part of Pelops' house
Faces the south; the further side of this

Lifts itself upward like a mountain top
And overlooks the city; thence their kings
May hold the stubborn people 'neath their sway.
Here shines the great hall that might well contain
An army, vari-colored columns bear
Its golden architraves; behind the room
Known to the vulgar, where the people come,
Stretch chambers rich and wide, and far within
Lie the arcana of the royal house,
The sacred penetralia; here no tree
Of brilliant foliage grows, and none is trimmed;
But yews and cypress and black ilex trees
Bend in the gloomy wood, an ancient oak
Rises above the grove and, eminent
Over the other trees, looks down on all
From its great height. Here the Tantalides
Are consecrated kings, and here they seek
Aid in uncertain or untoward events
Here hang their votive offerings, clear-toned trumps,
And broken chariots,[4] wreckage of the sea,
And wheels that fell a prey to treachery,
And evidence of every crime the race
Has done. Here Trojan Pelops' crown is hung,
Here the embroidered robe from barbarous foes
Won. In the shade trickles a sluggish rill
That in the black swamp lingers lazily,
Like the unsightly waters of black Styx
By which the gods make oath. 'Tis said that here
The gods of the infernal regions sigh
Through all the dark night, that the place resounds
With rattling chains, and spirits of the dead
Go wailing up and down. Here may be seen
All dreadful things; here wanders the great throng
Of spirits of the ancient dead sent forth
From antique tombs, and monsters fill the place
Greater than have been known, and oft the wood
With threefold baying echoes, oftentimes
The house is terrible with mighty forms.
Nor does the daylight put an end to fear,
Night is eternal in the grove, and here
The sanctity of the infernal world
Reigns in the midst of day. Here sure response
Is given those who seek the oracle;

From the adytum with a thundering noise
The fatal utterance finds a passage out,
And all the grot reechoes the god's voice.
Here raging Atreus entered, dragging in
His brother's sons; the altars were adorned—
Ah, who can tell the tale? The noble youths
Have their hands bound behind them and their brows
Bound with the purple fillet; incense too
Is there, and wine to Bacchus consecrate,
And sacrificial knife, and salted meal;
All things are done in order, lest such crime
Should be accomplished without fitting rites.

CHORUS: Whose hand took up the sword?

MESSENGER: He is himself
The priest. He sang himself with boisterous lips
The sacrificial song, those given to death
He placed, he took the sword and wielded it;
Nothing was lacking to the sacrifice.
Earth trembled, all the grove bent down its head,
The palace nodded, doubtful where to fling
Its mighty weight, and from the left there shot
A star from heaven, drawing a black train.
The wine poured forth upon the fire was changed
And flowed red blood; the royal diadem
Fell twice, yea thrice; within the temple walls
The ivory statues wept. All things were moved
At such a deed; himself alone unmoved,
Atreus stood firm and faced the threatening gods.
And now delay at last was put aside;
He stood before the altar, sidelong, fierce
In gaze. As by the Ganges, in the woods,
The hungry tiger stands between two bulls,
Uncertain which one first shall feel his teeth—
Eager for both, now here now there he turns
His eyes and in such doubt is hungry still—
So cruel Atreus gazes on the heads,
Devoted sacrifices to his rage;
He hesitates which one shall first be slain,
And which be immolated afterward;
It matters not and yet he hesitates,
And in the order of his cruel crime
Takes pleasure.

CHORUS: Which is first to feel the sword?

MESSENGER: Lest he should seem to fail in loyalty
             First place is given to his ancestor—
             The one named Tantalus is first to fall.

CHORUS: What courage showed the youth? How bore he death?

MESSENGER: He stood unmoved, no useless prayers were heard.
             That cruel one hid in the wound the sword,
             Pressing it deep within the victim's neck,
             Then drew it forth. The corpse was upright still;
             It hesitated long which way to fall,
             Then fell against the uncle. Atreus then,
             Dragging before the altar Plisthenes,
             Hurried him to his brother. With one blow
             He cut away the head; the lifeless trunk
             Fell prone and with a whispered sound the head
             Rolled downward.

CHORUS: Double murder thus complete,
             What did he then? Spared he the other boy?
             Or did he heap up crime on crime?

MESSENGER: Alas!
             As crested lion in Armenian woods
             Attacks the herd, nor lays aside his wrath
             Though sated, but with jaws that drip with blood
             Follows the bulls, and satisfied with food
             Threatens the calves but languidly; so threats
             Atreus, so swells his wrath, and holding still
             The sword with double murder wet, forgets
             Whom he attacks; with direful hand he drives
             Right through the body and the sword, received
             Within the breast, passes straight through the back.
             He falls and with his blood puts out the fires;
             By double wound he dies.

CHORUS: O savage crime!

MESSENGER: Art horrified? If there the work had ceased,
             It had been pious.

CHORUS: Could a greater crime
             Or more atrocious be by nature borne?

MESSENGER: And dost thou think this was the end of crime?
'Twas its beginning.

CHORUS: What more could there be?
Perchance he threw the bodies to wild beasts
That they might tear them, kept from funeral fire?

MESSENGER: Would he had kept, would that no grave might hide
The dead, no fire burn them, would the birds
And savage beasts might feast on such sad food!
That which were torment else is wished for here.
Would father's eyes unburied sons might see!
O crime incredible to every age!
O crime which future ages shall deny!
The entrails taken from the living breast
Tremble, the lungs still breathe, the timid heart
Throbs, but he tears its fibre, ponders well
What it foretells and notes its still warm veins.
When he at last has satisfied himself
About the victims, of his brother's feast
He makes secure. The mangled forms he cuts,
And from the trunk he separates the arms
As far as the broad shoulders, savagely
Lays bare the joints and cleaves apart the bones;
The heads he spares and the right hands they gave
In such good faith. He puts the severed limbs
Upon the spits and roasts them by slow fire;
The other parts into the glowing pot
He throws to boil them. From the food the fire
Leaps back, is twice, yea thrice, replaced and forced
At last reluctantly to do its work.
The liver on the spit emits shrill cries,
I cannot tell whether the flesh or flame
Most deeply groaned. The troubled fire smoked,
The smoke itself, a dark and heavy cloud,
Rose not in air nor scattered readily;
The ugly cloud obscured the household gods.
O patient Phoebus, thou hast backward fled
And, breaking off the light of day at noon,
Submerged the day, but thou didst set too late.
The father mangles his own sons, and eats
Flesh of his flesh, with sin-polluted lips;
His locks are wet and shine with glowing oil;
Heavy is he with wine; the morsels stick

Between his lips. Thyestes, this one good
Amid thy evil fortunes still remains:
Thou knowest it not. But this good too shall die.
Let Titan, turning backward on his path,
Lead back his chariot and with darkness hide
This foul new crime, let blackest night arise
At midday, yet the deed must come to light.
All will be manifest.

Act Four.   Scene II

(Unnatural darkness has come over the world.)

CHORUS: Oh, whither, father of the earth and sky,
Whose rising puts the glory of the night
To flight, oh, whither dost thou turn thy path,
That light has fled at midday? Phoebus, why
Hast thou withdrawn thy beams? The evening star,
The messenger of darkness, has not yet
Called forth the constellations of the night,
Not yet the westward turning course commands
To free thy horses that have done their work,
The trumpet has not yet its third call given,
The signal of declining day, new night.
The plowman is amazed at the swift fall
Of supper-time, his oxen by the plow
Are yet unwearied. From thy path in heaven
What drives thee, O Apollo? What the cause
That forces from their wonted way thy steeds?
Though conquered, do the giants strive again
In war, hell's prison being opened wide?
Or does Tityus in his wounded breast
Renew his ancient wrath? The mountains rent,
Does Titan's son, Typhoeus, stretch again
His giant body? Is a pathway built
By Macedonian giants to the sky,
On Thracian Ossa is Mount Pelion piled?
The ancient order of the universe
Has perished! Rise and setting will not be!
Eos, the dewy mother of the dawn,
Wont to the god of day to give the reins,

Sees with amaze her kingdom overthrown,
She knows not how to bathe the wearied steeds,
Nor dip the smoking horses in the sea.
The setting sun himself, amazed, beholds
Aurora, and commands the darkness rise
Ere night is ready. The bright stars rise not,
Nor do the heavens show the faintest light,
Nor does the morn dissolve the heavy shades.
Whate'er it be would it were only night!
Shaken with mighty fear my bosom quakes,
Lest all the world to ruin should be hurled,
And formless chaos cover gods and men,
And nature once again enfold and hide
The land and sea and starry firmament.
With the upspringing of its deathless torch
Bringing the seasons, never more shall come
The king of stars and give the waiting world
Changes of summer and of winter's cold;
No more shall Luna meet the sun's bright flame
And take away the terror of the night,
And running through a briefer circuit pass
Her brother's car; into one gulf shall fall
The heaped-up throng of gods.
The zodiac, pathway of the sacred stars,
Which cuts the zones obliquely, shall behold
The falling stars and fall itself from heaven.
Aries, who comes again in early spring
And with warm zephyr swells the sails, shall fall
Headlong into the sea through which he bore
Timorous Helle; and the Bull, that wears
The Hyades upon its shining brow,
Shall with himself drag down the starry Twins
And Cancer's claws; the Lion, glowing hot,
That Hercules once conquered, shall again
Fall from the skies; and to the earth she left
The Virgin[5] too shall fall, and the just Scales,
And with them drag the churlish Scorpion.
Old Chiron, who holds fixed the feathered dart
In the Thessalian bow, shall loose his shaft
From the snapped bowstring, and cold Capricorn
Who brings the winter's cold shall fall, and break
For thee, whoe'er thou art, thy water-jug,
Thou Water-bearer; with thee too shall fall

The Fishes, last of stars; and Charles' Wain,
That never yet has sunk below the sea,
Falling shall plunge beneath the ocean wave.
The slippery Dragon, that between the Bears
Winds like a winding river, shall descend;
And, with the Dragon joined, the Lesser Bear
So icy cold, and slow Bootes too,
Already tottering to his overthrow,
Shall fall from heaven with his heavy wain.
Out of so many do we seem alone
Worthy to be beneath the universe
Buried, when heaven itself is overthrown?
In our day has the end of all things come?
Created were we for a bitter fate,
Whether we've banished or destroyed the sun.
Let lamentation cease, depart base fear;
Eager for life is he who would not die
Even though with him all the world should fall.

Act Five.   Scene I

(*Enter* ATREUS.)

ATREUS: High above all and equal to the stars
I move, my proud head touches heaven itself;
At last I hold the crown, at last I hold
My father's throne. Now I abandon you,
Ye gods, for I have touched the highest point
Of glory possible. It is enough.
Ev'n I am satisfied. Why satisfied?
No shame withholds me, day has been withdrawn;
Act while the sky is dark. Would I might keep
The gods from flight, and drag them back by force
That all might see the feast that gives revenge.
It is enough the father shall behold.
Though daylight be unwilling to abide,
Yet will I take from thee the dark that hides
Thy miseries; too long with merry look
Thou liest at thy feast: enough of wine,
Enough of food, Thyestes. There is need,
In this thy crowning ill, thou be not drunk

With wine. Slaves, open wide the temple doors,
And let the house of feasting open lie.
I long to see his colour when he sees
His dead sons' heads, to hear his words that flow
With the first shock of sorrow, to behold
How, stricken dumb, he sits with rigid form.
This is the recompense of all my toil.
I do not wish to see his wretchedness
Save as it grows upon him.
(*The doors are thrown open, showing* THYESTES *at the banquet-table*)
                                        The wide hall
Is bright with many a torch; supine he lies
On gold and purple, his left hand supports
His head that is so heavy now with wine;
He vomits. Mightiest of the gods am I,
And king of kings! My wish has been excelled!
Full is he, in the silver cup he lifts
The wine. Spare not to drink, there still remains
Some of the victims' blood, the old wine's red
Conceals it; with this cup the feast shall end.
His children's blood mixed with the wine he drinks;
He would have drunken mine. Lo, now he sings,
Sings festal songs, his mind is dimmed with wine.

Act Five.   Scene II

(THYESTES *sits alone at the banquet-table, half overcome with wine; he
     tries to sing and be gay, but some premonition of evil weighs upon
     him.*)

THYESTES (*to himself*): By long grief dulled, put by thy cares, my heart,
                    Let fear and sorrow fly and bitter need,
                    Companion of thy timorous banishment,
                    And shame, hard burden of afflicted souls.
                    Whence thou hast fallen profits more to know
                    Than whither; great is he who with firm step
                    Moves on the plain when fallen from the height;
                    He who, oppressed by sorrows numberless
                    And driven from his realm, with unbent neck
                    Carries his burdens, not degenerate
                    Or conquered, who stands firm beneath the weight

Of all his burdens, he is great indeed.
Now scatter all the clouds of bitter fate,
Put by all signs of thy unhappy days,
In happy fortunes show a happy face,
Forget the old Thyestes. Ah, this vice
Still follows misery: never to trust
In happy days; though better fortunes come,
Those who have borne afflictions find it hard
To joy in better days. What holds me back,
Forbids me celebrate the festal tide?
What cause of grief, arising causelessly,
Bids me to weep? What art thou that forbids
That I should crown my head with festal wreath?
It does forbid, forbid! Upon my head
The roses languish, and my hair that drips
With ointment rises as with sudden fear,
My face is wet with showers of tears that fall
Unwillingly, and groans break off my song.
Grief loves accustomed tears, the wretched feel
That they must weep. I would be glad to make
Most bitter lamentation, and to wail,
And rend this robe with Tyrian purple dyed.
My mind gives warning of some coming grief,
Presages future ills. The storm that smites
When all the sea is calm weighs heavily
Upon the sailor. Fool! What grief, what storm,
Dost thou conceive? Believe thy brother now.
Be what it may, thou fearest now too late,
Or causelessly. I do not wish to be
Unhappy, but vague terror smites my breast.
No cause is evident and yet my eyes
O'erflow with sudden tears. What can it be,
Or grief, or fear? Or has great pleasure tears?

Act Five.   Scene III

ATREUS (*approaching* THYESTES): Brother, let us together celebrate
This festal day; this day it is which makes
My sceptre firm, which binds the deathless pact
Of certain peace.

THYESTES: Enough of food and wine!
This only could augment my happiness,
If with my sons I might enjoy my bliss.

ATREUS: Believe thy sons are here in thy embrace.
Here are they and shall be, no single part
Of thy loved offspring shall be lost to thee.
Ask and whate'er thou wishest I will give,
I'll satisfy the father with his sons;
Fear not, thou shalt be more than satisfied.
Now with my own thy young sons lengthen out
The joyous feast: they shall be sent for; drink
The wine, it is an heirloom of our house.

(He hands THYESTES *the cup filled with mingled blood and wine.)*

THYESTES: I take my brother's gift. Wine shall be poured
First to our fathers' gods, then shall be drunk.
But what is this? My hands refuse to lift
The cup, its weight increases and holds down
My right hand, from my lips the wine retreats,
Around my mouth it flows and will not pass
Within my lips, and from the trembling earth
The tables leap, the fire scarce gives light,
The air is heavy and the light is dim
As between day and darkness. What is this?
The arch of heaven trembles more and more,
To the dense shadows ever thicker mist
Is added, night withdraws in blacker night,
The constellations flee. Whate'er it is,
I pray thee spare my sons, let all the storm
Break over my vile head. Give back my sons!

ATREUS: Yea, I will give them back, and never more
Shalt thou be parted from them.
(ATREUS departs.)

THYESTES *(to himself)*: What distress
Seizes my reins? Why shake my inward parts?
I feel a burden that will forth, my breast
Groans with a groaning that is not my own.
Come, children, your unhappy father calls;
Come, might I see you all this woe would flee.
Whence come these voices?

(Re-enter ATREUS *with a covered platter in his hands.)*

ATREUS: Father, spread wide thy arms, they come, they come.
            Dost thou indeed now recognise thy sons?
            (*The platter is uncovered.*)

THYESTES: I recognise my brother! Canst thou bear
            Such deeds, O earth? O Styx, wilt thou not break
            Thy banks and whelm in everlasting night
            Both king and kingdom, bearing them away
            By a dread path to chaos' awful void?
            And, plucking down thy houses, fallest thou not,
            O city of Mycenae, to the ground?
            We should already be with Tantalus!
            Earth, ope thy prisons wide on every side;
            If under Tartarus, below the place
            Where dwell our kinsmen, rests a lower deep,
            Within thy bosom let a chasm yawn
            Thitherward, under all of Acheron
            Hide us; let guilty souls roam o'er our heads,
            Let Phlegethon that bears its fiery sands
            Down through its glowing channels, flow o'er me!
            Yet earth unmoved lies but a heavy weight,
            The gods have fled.

ATREUS: Take, rather, willingly
            Those whom thou hast so long desired to see;
            Thy brother does not hinder thee. Rejoice;
            Kiss them, divide thy love between the three.

THYESTES: This is thy compact? This a brother's faith?
            Is this thy favour? Layst thou thus aside
            Thy hate? I do not ask to see my sons
            Unharmed; what wickedness and deathless hate
            May give, a brother asks: grant to my sons
            Burial; give them back, thou shalt behold
            Straightway their burning. Lo, I ask thee naught,
            The father will not have but lose his sons.

ATREUS: Thou hast whate'er remains, whate'er is lost.

THYESTES: And do they furnish food for savage birds?
            Are they destroyed by monsters, fed to beasts?

ATREUS: Thyself hast banqueted upon thy sons,
            Am impious feast.

THYESTES:
'Tis this that shamed the gods!
This backward drove the daylight whence it came!
Unhappy me! But what cry shall I make,
What wailing? What words will suffice my woe?
I see the severed heads, the hands cut off,
Greedy and hungry, these I did not eat!
I feel their flesh within my bowels move;
Prisoned, the dread thing struggles, tries to flee,
But has no passage forth; give me the sword,
Brother, it has already drunk my blood;
The sword shall give a pathway to my sons.
It is denied? Then rending blows shall sound
Upon my breast. Unhappy one, refrain
Thy hand, oh, spare the dead! Who e'er beheld
Such hideous crime? Not wandering tribes that dwell
On the unkindly Caucasus' rough cliffs,
Or fierce Procrustes, dread of Attica.
Behold, the father feasts upon his sons,
The sons lie heavy in him—is there found
No limit to thy base and impious deeds?

ATREUS:
Crime finds a limit when the crime is done,
Not when avenged. Even this is not enough.
Into thy mouth I should have poured the blood
Warm from the wounds; thou shouldst have drunk the blood
Of living sons. My hate betrayed itself
Through too much haste. I smote them with the sword,
I slew them at the altar, sacrificed
A votive offering to the household gods.
From the dead trunks I cut away the heads,
And into tiniest pieces tore the limbs;
Some in the boiling pot I plunged, and some
I bade should be before a slow flame placed;
I cut the flesh from the still living limbs,
I saw it roar upon the slender spit,
And with my own right hand I plied the fire.
All this the father might have better done:
All of my vengeance falls in nothingness!
He ate his sons with impious lips indeed,
Alas, nor he nor they knew what he did!

THYESTES:
Hear, O ye seas, stayed by inconstant shores;
Ye too, ye gods, wherever ye have fled,

Hear what a deed is done! Hear, gods of Hell,
Hear, Earth, and heavy Tartarean night
Dark with thick cloud! Oh, listen to my cry!
Thine am I, Hell, thou only seest my woe,
Thou also hast no star. I do not make
Presumptuous prayer, naught for myself I ask—
What could be given me? I make my prayer
For you, my sons. Thou ruler of the heavens,
Thou mighty king of the ethereal courts,
Cover the universe with horrid clouds,
Let winds contend on every side, send forth
Thy thunders everywhere; not with light hand,
As when thou smitest with thy lesser darts
Innocent homes; but as when mountains fell
And with their threefold ruin overwhelmed
The Giants—use such power, send forth such fires,
Avenge the banished day, where light has fled
Fill up the darkness with thy thunderbolts.
Each one is evil,—do not hesitate—
Yet if not both, I sure am base; seek me
With triple dart, through this breast send this brand;
If I would give my sons a funeral pyre
And burial, I must give myself to flames.
If nothing moves the gods, if none will send
His darts against this sinful head, let night,
Eternal night, abide and hide the crime
In everlasting shadows. If thou, Sun,
No longer shinest, I have naught to ask.

ATREUS: Now in my work I glory, now indeed
I hold the victor's palm. I would have lost
My crime's reward unless thou thus wert grieved.
I now believe my sons were truly mine—
Now may I trust again in a chaste bed.

THYESTES: What evil have my children done to thee?

ATREUS: They were thy sons.

THYESTES: The children of their sire—

ATREUS: Undoubted sons; 'tis this that makes me glad.

THYESTES: I call upon the gods who guard the right
To witness.

ATREUS: Why not call upon the gods
Who guard the marriage-bed?

THYESTES: Who punishes
A crime with crime?

ATREUS: I know what makes thee mourn:
Another first accomplished the grim deed,
For this thou mournest; thou art not distressed
Because of thy dread feast, thou feelest grief
That thou hast not prepared such feast for me.
This mind was in thee: to provide like food
For thy unconscious brother, and to slay
My children with their mother's aid. One thing
Withheld thee—thou believedst they were thine.

THYESTES: Th' avenging gods will come and punish thee;
To them my prayers commit thee.

ATREUS: To thy sons
I give thee over for thy punishment.

NOTES

1. This refers to Tantalus' son, Pelops, who was slain by his father and served to the gods in a banquet, but later restored to life.

2. The first sentence of the choral ode is deleted by Richter. The attitude of the chorus here seems strange if it is supposed to have overheard Atreus' plan of vengeance; see note 3.

3. The chorus in this scene is apparently ignorant of Atreus' real intention. The best solution is to assume that the chorus was not supposed to be on the stage during Act Two, Scene I.

4. Pelops agreed to a chariot race with Oenomaus in order to marry Hippodamia, the daughter of Oenomaus. He won the race by trickery, since Myrtilus, Oenomaus' charioteer, was bribed by Pelops to wreck his master's chariot. Pelops rewarded Myrtilus by throwing him into the sea.

5. This refers to Astraea, the goddess of Justice.

IX
HERCULES ON OETA

Characters in the Play

HERCULES, *son of Jupiter and* ALCMENA
CHORUS OF OECHALIAN MAIDENS
IOLE, *daughter of Eurytus, king of Oechalia*
NURSE *of* DEIANIRA
DEIANIRA, *wife of* HERCULES
CHORUS OF AETOLIAN WOMEN
HYLLUS, *son of* HERCULES *and* DEIANIRA
ALCMENA, *mother of* HERCULES
PHILOCTETES, *son of Poeas, and faithful friend of* HERCULES

INTRODUCTION

THE *Hercules on Oeta* is Seneca's longest and most ambitious tragedy. Longer by two hundred lines than any other ancient play, it has been suspected of being in part spurious, or of being an unfinished draft which would have been shortened in the final revision. The explanation of the unusual length is probably to be sought in the subject of the play—the death and deification of Hercules. Seneca, the Stoic philosopher, naturally found in Hercules, the ideal Stoic hero, a congenial subject and devoted himself to a full portrayal of the hero's victory over physical suffering and death. The play relates how Hercules captured Iole and aroused the jealousy of his wife Deianira, who endeavoured to win back his love by sending him a robe poisoned with the blood of the centaur Nessus. The centaur had been slain by Hercules in an attempt to carry off Deianira and, as he died, had given her the clotted blood from his wound as a love-charm. The story of Deianira's love for Hercules, the sending of the robe, and the tragic death of Hercules was the theme of Sophocles' *The Trachiniae*—a tragedy to which Seneca was doubtless indebted, in spite of the numerous differences between the two plays. The story of Hercules and Deianira as related by Ovid (in the *Heroides* and the *Metamorphoses*) may have suggested to Seneca certain features of his play, and particularly his delineation of Deianira.

The charm and power of Sophocles' tragedy lay chiefly in the superb portrayal of Deianira—the loving and devoted wife whose attempt to win back her husband's love resulted in catastrophe. Sophocles' play has been criticised for its lack of unity and for its division of interest between Deianira and Hercules, whose physical agony is treated in the latter part of the drama. Seneca by his many changes has completely altered the nature of the tragedy; he presents the victorious Hercules in the first scene and so subordinates Deianira, who does not appear until Act Two in the Roman play. Furthermore, by depicting her as violent in her jealousy and her hatred of her rival, he makes her far less appealing than Sophocles' heroine. His tragedy gains in unity, for Hercules is the protagonist throughout the play. The characters introduced into the action by Seneca help to keep the spotlight on the hero: Alcmena, Hercules' mother, laments his sufferings, and it is to her that the deified Hercules appears after his death; Philoctetes plays the part of a messenger in describing the death of Hercules, but is a close friend of the hero and receives his far-famed bow and arrows.

Seneca thus concentrates his interest on Hercules whose suffering, death, and deification are symbolic of the victory of the virtuous Stoic over folly and evil. As Hercules in the *Mad Hercules* conquered remorse and mental anguish, so at his death the hero rises triumphant over the most excruciating physical agony. Hercules realises that this is a fitting conclusion to his life of toil—that he be slain by the hand of one he had conquered;

> "I make no plaint, 'twas right this end be given
> Lest anyone should live to boast himself
> Alcides' conqueror. Now comes at length
> A noble death, of great and wide renown,
> And worthy me."

At the end of the play Hercules is victorious over death itself, and the playwright successfully points out the contrast between the human and the divine nature of the hero. After his courageous death on the funeral pyre, the deified Hercules speaks from heaven to his mother:

> "Forbear thy mourning, mother; once indeed
> I saw the land of death, whate'er of man
> I may have had was purged away by fire.
> The part my father gave is borne to heaven;
> Thy part was given to the flames. . . .
> 'Tis meet that I should seek celestial climes;
> Alcides once again has conquered hell."

HERCULES ON OETA

(SCENE:—*Act One, in Euboea; Acts Two to Five, before the palace of* HERCULES *in Trachin.*)

Act One.   Scene I

(*Enter* HERCULES *with* LICHAS *and servants.*)

HERCULES: O father of the gods, whose thunderbolt
Both homes of Phoebus, east and west, do know,
Reign now secure, for I have brought thee peace
Wherever Nereus checks the spread of land.
There is no need to thunder, perjured kings
And cruel tyrants lie o'erthrown. I've slain
Whatever might have felt thy thunderbolt.
But father, why is heaven to me denied?
In all things, surely, I have worthy proved
Of Jove, my stepdame even witnesses
My heavenly birth. Why longer make delay?
Dost fear? Could Atlas not support the skies
If Hercules were there? Why still refuse
The star? Death sent me back to thee, all ills
That earth or sea or air or hell bring forth
Have yielded: through Arcadian streets no more
The lion wanders; the Stymphalian birds
Are dead; there is no stag of Maenalus;
The dying dragon sprinkled with his blood
The golden groves; the Hydra yields his life;
Beside the river Hebrus I destroyed
That well-known herd, with blood of slaughtered guests
Made fat; and from Thermodon bore away
The spoils of war; [1] I saw the silent shades,
Nor thence returned alone. The trembling day
Beheld black Cerberus. He saw the sun.
Busiris was before his altars slain;

By this one hand fell Geryon, and by this
The bull, the terror of a hundred lands;
Whatever hostile thing the earth brought forth
Has perished, by my right hand overcome.
If earth denies wild beasts to Juno's wrath,
Give back, I pray, a father to thy son,
Or give a constellation to the brave.
I do not ask that thou shouldst show the road,
If thou permit me, I will find a way;
Or if thou fear'st lest earth conceive wild beasts,
Then speed the evil while she has and sees
Thy Hercules: who else would dare assail
Such foes, or be, in any Argive town,
Worthy of Juno's hate? There is no land
That does not speak my fame, the frost-bound race
Of Scythians in the north, the men of Ind
Exposed to Phoebus' rays, the Libyans, too,
Beneath the constellation of the crab,
Have felt my hand; bright Titan, thee I call
To witness, I have gone with thee where'er
Thou sheddest light—thy light could not pursue
My triumphs, for beyond the sun's bright world
I passed: day was not where my metes were set,
Nor nature, earth was wanting to my steps,
She first was wearied. Night assailed my eyes,
And utmost chaos. I have come again
From whence none other ever has returned.
The threats of ocean I have borne, no storms
Could wreck my boat, wherever I have gone.
The empty ether cannot now suffice
The hatred of thy wife; earth fears to yield
Wild beasts for me to conquer, does not give
New monsters, none remain, and Hercules
Stands in their place. How many evil things
Have I, unarmed, destroyed. All dreadful forms
That rose against me, I, alone, o'erthrew,
Nor feared as babe or boy to meet wild beasts.
The toils commanded me seemed light, no day
Shone fruitless for me. Oh, how many ills
I vanquished, when no king commanded me,—
My valour drove me more than Juno's wrath.
What profit to have made the race secure?
Gods have not peace; the earth is free, but sees

All things it had to fear secure in heaven.
Juno translates the brutes: the crab, though slain,
Moves in a burning pathway, has been made
A Libyan constellation, ripening
The grain; the lion to Astraea gives
The flying year, he shakes his fiery mane,
Dries up the moist south wind, dispels the clouds,
Behold even now has each wild beast attained
The skies, and so outstripped me. From the earth
I still, though victor, must behold my foes.
To brutes and monsters Juno gives a star
That she may make the skies a dreaded place
For me. Aye, let her waste the earth and make
The heav'ns more terrible than earth or hell,
Yet still Alcides shall be given room.
If after war, if after conquered beasts
And Stygian dog, I still am deemed unmeet
For heavenly heights, Hesperia shall touch
Pelorus,[2] and the two lands be but one;
I'll put the seas to flight—or dost thou bid
That they be joined? Let Isthmus no more part
The waves, and on united seas let ships
Be borne by new-found paths to Attica.
Let earth be changed: the Ister flow along
Through channels new, the Tanais find new ways.
Grant, Jupiter, at least, that I may guard
The gods; thou needst not hurl thy thunderbolt
Where I shall be the guardian. Though thou bid
That I protect the realms of heat and cold,
Believe, the gods are safe in that abode.
The dragon slain, Apollo merited
A Delphian temple and a heavenly home,—
How many Pythons in the Hydra lay!
Bacchus and Perseus have attained the skies,
How small a region was the east he quelled!
How many monsters in the Gorgon lived?
What son of thine, of Juno born, deserved
A constellation by his glorious deeds?
The realm I on my shoulders bore I seek.

                    (*To* LICHAS)

But thou, O Lichas, comrades of my toils,
Herald my triumph, of the conquered home
And fallen realm of great Eurytus tell.

(*To his servants*)
Drive ye the victims quickly to the fanes
Built to Cenaean Jove where wild with storms
The feared Euboean ocean hurls its waves.
(HERCULES *and his attendants depart.*)

Act One.   Scene II

(*Enter* IOLE *and the* CHORUS OF OECHALIAN MAIDENS.)

CHORUS: The equal of immortal gods is he
                 Whose life and fortune travel hand in hand;
                 But he who slowly drags his life along
                 With heavy groans, believes it worse than death.
                 He who beneath his feet put eager fates,
                 And steered the boat on the dark river's flood,
                 Shall never give to chains his captive arms,
                 Nor ever grace the tyrant's triumph car.
                 He to whom death is easy never finds
                 Life wretched: though his vessel in mid seas
                 Desert him, when old Boreas in his might
                 Drives back the south wind, or when Eurus strives
                 With Zephyr, when the waters seem to part,—
                 He may not gather up the broken beams
                 Of his wrecked ship that, in the waters' midst,
                 He may yet hope for land; he cannot know
                 Shipwreck, who freely can forgo his life.
                   Base weakness, tears, locks sordid with the dust
                 Of my dear fatherland are mine, not flames
                 Nor crash of fortune strike me down. O Death,
                 Thou comest to the happy; wretched men
                 Thou fleest. Still I live; my fatherland,
                 Alas! shall lapse to wilderness and woods,
                 Its fallen temples yield to sordid huts,
                 The cold Dolopian thither lead his flock
                 Where yet Oechalia's growing ashes lie;
                 Thessalian shepherds, to the very town
                 Bringing their unskilled pipes, in doleful lays
                 Retell the mournful story of our times,
                 And ere a few more generations pass
                 The world shall seek in vain the place where stood

My country. Happy once, I made my home
By no unfruitful hearth nor dwelt among
Thessalia's barren acres; now I go
To Trachin, land of rocks and heavy brakes,
Parched mountain summits, groves the mountain goat
Scarce loves to haunt. But if a milder fate
Await the slave, if Inachus' swift stream
Shall bear him on its bosom, if he dwell
By Dirce's fountain where the languid stream
Ismenos flows, a slender thread—'twas there
The mother of proud Hercules was wed.

    False is the fable of the double night,
When longer in the heavens shone the stars,
When Hesperus arose for Lucifer,
And slow Diana long delayed the sun.
What rocks or cliffs or Scythia nourished thee?
Did Rhodope's wild mountain bring thee forth
A Titan; or Mount Athos' rugged steeps;
Or the stern mountains by the Caspian shore?
What tiger's spotted breast has suckled thee?
He cannot feel a wound, the spear grows dull,
The steel is softened, shattered is the sword
That smites his naked body, and the stones
Fly back; he does not fear the fates, invites
With flesh unconquerable death itself;
Spears may not pierce him, nor the Scythian shafts
From the tense bowstring shot, nor any dart
The cold Sarmatians bear, nor can they wound
Who eastward, near the Nabataeans, dwell,
Where arrows truer than the Cretan's fly—
The Parthian's. With his body he o'erthrew
Oechalia's walls, against him naught can stand.
What he prepares to conquer is o'ercome.
His hostile face brings death, to have but seen
The wrath of Hercules is woe enough.
Could vast Briareus, or could Gyas huge,
Who, standing on Thessalian mountains, stormed
The skies with snake-armed hands, make him afraid?
Beside great evils lie his great rewards,
No more of ill is left, we have beheld—
Unhappy we—great Hercules in wrath.

IOLE: Me miserable! Not that temples lie

With gods and homes o'erthrown, that in the flames
Fathers with sons, divinities with men,
The temple with the tombs, are burned to dust—
We mourn no common woe; my tears are caused
By other sorrows, fortune bids me weep
For other ruins. What first shall I mourn?
What most demands my tears? All equally!
Earth hath not breasts enough to sound with blows
Worthy these sorrows. O ye gods above,
Make me a mournful Sipylean rock;³
Or place me by the banks of Po where sounds
The murmur of the trees, the sisters sad
Of Phaethon, or on Sicilian rocks
Where I, a siren, may lament the fate
Of Thessaly; or to the Thracian woods
Bear me, where like a swallow Procne sits
Beneath Ismarian shade and mourns her son.
Give me a form fit for my bitter tears,
And let harsh Trachin echo with my woe.
Still Cyprian Myrrha weeps, and Ceyx' wife
Grieves for her husband, Niobe outlives
Herself, and Thracian Philomela flees
And, a sad nightingale, laments her son.
Oh, happy, happy were I, if my home
Might be the woods, if I, a bird, might rest
Within my country's meadows and bemoan
My fate with querulous murmur, and fame tell
Of winged Iole. I saw, I saw
My father's wretched fate, when smitten down
By Hercules' death-dealing club, he lay
Through all the courtyard scattered. If the fates
Had given thee a tomb, where had I sought,
O father, for thy members? Have I borne
To see thy death, O Toxeus, when not yet
Thy tender cheeks with manly beard were decked,
Nor yet man's blood was coursing through thy veins?
But why, my parents, should I mourn your fate
Whom friendly death holds safe? My fate demands
My tears. A captive, I am forced to drive
The distaff and the spindle for my lord.
Oh, cruel beauty, comeliness of form
That brought me death! My home for this alone
Fell ruined, since my father would not give

His daughter to Alcides, feared to be
Akin by marriage to great Hercules.
But I must seek my mistress' proud abode.

CHORUS: Why foolishly recall thy father's realm
And thy sad fate? Forget thy former lot,
He only can be happy who has learned
To keep, as king or slave, an equal mind,
And suffer varying fortunes. He has snatched
The heaviness from ill, strength for himself,
Who bears whate'er befalls with steadfast soul.
            (IOLE *and the* CHORUS *depart.*)

Act Two.   Scene I

(*Enter the* NURSE *of* DEIANIRA. *The scene is now before the palace of*
DEIANIRA *in Trachin, after the arrival of the captives.*)

NURSE: What cruel raging seizes woman's heart
When one roof covers wife and concubine!
Charybdis, Scylla, in Sicilian straits,
Need less be feared; less wild the savage beast.
For when the beauty of the captive shone,
And Iole was bright as cloudless day,
Or like the stars that shine in nights serene,
The wife of Hercules like one insane,
With fierce look stood. As lying with her young
Within a cavern in Armenia's land,
The tigress, at an enemy's approach,
Springs forth, or as the maenad, god-inspired,
When bidden wave the thyrsus, for a time
Stands doubtful whither she shall turn her steps,
So rages through the house of Hercules
His wife, nor does the house give room enough;
She rushes up and down, roams to and fro,
Then pauses, in her cheeks all sorrows burn,
Naught is within her bosom hid; swift tears
Follow her threats, nor does one mood endure,
Nor is she with a single phase of wrath
Contented: now her cheeks are like a flame,
Now pallor drives away the red, her grief

Takes every form, she weeps, laments, implores.
The door creaks, see, with headlong steps she comes,
Telling with words confused her inmost thoughts.

Act Two.   Scene II

(*Enter* DEIANIRA *and* CHORUS OF AETOLIAN WOMEN.)

DEIANIRA: O wife of Jove, wherever thou may'st be
Within thy airy home, send thence, I pray,
Against Alcides such a savage beast
As may suffice me. If a dragon lives
Unconquered, vaster, with more fruitful head;
If any beast exists so huge and dire,
So terrible, that Hercules himself
Averts his eyes, let this from some vast cave
Come forth; or if wild beasts must be denied,
I pray thee to some terror change this form—
With this mind I can do whatever ill
Thou wouldst. Oh, make my form express my woe!
My bosom will not hold the wrath I feel.
Why searchest thou the ends of earth? Why turn
The world about? Why seek for plagues in Dis?
Within this bosom wilt thou find all ills
Which need be feared, with this shaft arm thy hate;
I too may be a stepdame. Thou canst slay
Alcides, use this hand for what thou wilt.
Why pause? Use me, the mad one, what new crime
Dost thou command? Say on, why hesitate?
'Tis well that thou shouldst rest, this wrath does all.

NURSE: O foster-child, a little calm thyself.
Restrain thy plaints, control thy fiery rage,
And curb thy grief, now show thyself indeed
The wife of Hercules.

DEIANIRA: Shall Iole,
The captive maid, give brothers to my sons,
The slave become the daughter of great Jove?
Not in one bed can flame and torrent flow,
The northern bear may not in ocean's blue
Be wet—not unavenged will I remain.

What though thy shoulders bore the sky, though earth
Must thank thee for its peace? There yet remains
A greater terror than the Hydra's rage:
The anger of an injured wife. Burn thus
The flames of glowing Etna? This my wrath
Can conquer all thy conquests, shall a slave
Seize on my marriage-bed? Till now I feared.
Dread monsters, none remain, those plagues are gone,
In place of beasts there comes the hated slave.
By Titan, by the ruler of the gods,
I was Alcides' wife but while he feared!
The prayers I made the gods, they grant the slave;
I was successful for the concubine!
Ye heard my prayers, ye gods, but for her sake,
And for her sake he came again unharmed.
O anguish that no vengeance can assuage,
Seek some revenge unthought, unspeakable,
And dreadful, teach great Juno how to hate;
She knows not how to rage. For me he warred,
For me made red the Achelous' waves
With his own blood, he overcame the snake,
He turned his threats against the bull, and slew
A thousand foes in one. But now no more
He finds me pleasing, and a captive maid
Has been preferred to me—but shall not be!
The day that ends our marriage ends his life.
Yet what is this? My courage fails, my wrath
Declines, my anger ceases, wretched one,
Why languid? Wherefore lose thy rage? Wouldst keep
A woman's patient constancy? What law
Forbids add fuel to the flame? What force
Subdues the fire? O strength of wrath, abide!
Peers shall we be, I have no need of vows,
A stepdame will be with me who will guide
My hands aright, though she be uninvoked.

NURSE: What crime preparest thou, O heart insane?
Wouldst slay thy husband, him whose glory spreads
From east to west, his fame from earth to heaven?
The land of Greece would rise 'gainst such a deed,
His father's house, the whole Aetolian race
Would grieve, and all the earth avenge his death.
What canst thou do alone? Though thou shouldst think

T' escape the vengeance of the earth and man,
The father of Alcides wields his bolts.
See, see his threatening torches in the sky,
The thunder-riven heavens! Fear death itself,
In which thou hop'st thou yet mayst safety find.
There rules the uncle of thy Hercules;
Wherever thou wouldst turn, unhappy one,
Thou findest there thy husband's kindred gods.

DEIANIRA: The crime is great, I own, but grief impels,

NURSE: Thou'lt die.

DEIANIRA: But yet the wife of Hercules.
No day shall rise to find me widowed wife,
No captive concubine enjoy my couch.
The day shall sooner rise from out the west,
The Indian beneath the northern sky
Shall sooner pale, and sooner Phoebus' rays
Make dark the Scythian, than Thessalian maids
See me deserted; with my blood I'll quench
Their marriage torches. He shall die or I;
To savage beings slain he yet may add
A wife, and I among his mighty deeds
Be numbered. Yet in death I'll still embrace
The couch of Hercules. Alcides' wife
May freely pass among the shades, but goes
Not unavenged; should Iole conceive
A child by Hercules, these hands of mine
Shall tear it from her womb, yea through the blaze
Of marriage torches I will seize the maid.
What though in anger, on his wedding day,
He make of me the victim, if I fall
Above the lifeless form of Iole?
Who falls upon the forms of those he hates
Dies happy.

NURSE: Why add fuel to the flame?
Why feed thy boundless sorrow? Wretched one,
Why needlessly afraid? He chose the maid
While yet her father reigned; he sought in her
The daughter of a king, but when the queen
Declined into a slave, love lost its force
And her misfortune took away her charm:

Forbidden things are loved, what one may have
One willingly foregoes.

DEIANIRA: Her lowered state
Inflames a greater love; he loves her still.
Although she lacks a home, although her hair
Hangs unadorned with gold or precious gems.
Perchance his pity loves her very grief.
This is his wont, to love his captive ones.

NURSE: Dardanian Priam's sister,[4] whom he loved,
He gave away; recall how many wives,
How many virgins he has loved before,
Inconstant ever. While she wove the dance
In Pallas' honour, the Arcadian maid,
Augeia, suffered from Alcides' lust—
She died and Hercules remembered not
His former love. Need I of others speak?
The muses have no lover, brief the flame
Which burned for them within Alcides' breast.
A guest upon Timolus, he caressed
The Lydian maid,[5] and, still the slave of love,
He sat beside the wheel and lightly turned
With unaccustomed hand the moistened thread;
He laid from off his neck the lion's spoil,
The Lydian fillet bound his shaggy locks
That dripped with myrrh from Saba. Everywhere
He feels the heat of love, but brief the flame.

DEIANIRA: A gallant ever follows wandering flames.

NURSE: Could he prefer a slave, a foeman's child,
To thee?

DEIANIRA: As when the early sunshine clothes
The grove's bare boughs, the joyous woods put forth
New buds, but when the cold north wind drives back
The south wind and harsh winter cuts away
The leaves, and one beholds the bare brown trunks,
So we in running life's long journey lose
Some beauty ever and less lovely grow.
That way has love departed, what in us
He loved is gone, and pain and motherhood
Have robbed me of him. Seest thou not the slave
Has not yet lost her pristine comeliness?

Rich ornaments indeed she lacks, and sits
In squalor, yet her beauty shines through all,
And time and chance have taken from her naught
Except her kingdom. Therefore grief slays sleep.
I was the wife most honoured everywhere,
And every woman looked with envious eyes
Upon my marriage; when Argolic maids
Made prayers for aught to any of the gods,
I was the measure of the good they asked.
What father shall I have that equals Jove?
What husband under heaven equals mine?
Should he who gave Alcides his commands,
Eurystheus' self, espouse me, he is less.
To have been severed from a prince's bed
Were little; she indeed is sorely reft
Who feels herself bereft of Hercules.

NURSE: The children oft win back the husband's love.

DEIANĪRA: Her child, perchance, will draw him from my couch.

NURSE: Perchance he brought her to thee for a gift.

DEIANĪRA: The man thou seest pass among the towns,
Illustrious, and bearing on his back
The tawny lion's skin, who from the proud
Takes realms and gives them to the sore distressed,
Who in his dread hand bears a mighty club,
Whose triumphs by the farthest lands are sung,
Are sung by all the peoples of the earth,
Is most inconstant; nor does glory's grace
Incite him, through the world he wanders still,
Not as the peer of Jove, nor as the great
Should pass through Argive cities, but he seeks
One he may love, would gain a virgin's bed.
He ravishes whatever is denied,
Against the people's anger, from their wreck,
Procures his brides, and raging passion gains
The name of courage. Famed Oechalia fell;
One day, one sun beheld the city safe
And ruined, Love the only cause of war.
As often as a father shall refuse
To give his daughter to great Hercules,
So oft he needs to fear. Who will not be

Alcides' father is Alcides' foe,
And if he be not made a son, he slays.
Why keep I then my hands in innocence,
Till, feigning madness, with his savage hands
He bends his bow and slays his son and me?
So Hercules is wont to cast aside
His wives, so wont to break his marriage bond.
Nor can one count him guilty; to the world
Juno appears the cause of all his crimes.
Why should inactive anger pause amazed?
Anticipate his crime—up, hands, and smite,
While yet my wrath burns hot within my breast.

NURSE: Wouldst slay a husband?

DEIANIRA: Yes, of concubines!

NURSE: The Jove-begotten?

DEIANIRA: Of Alcmena's race.

NURSE: Not with the sword?

DEIANIRA: The sword.

NURSE: But if too weak?

DEIANIRA: By guile I'll kill him.

NURSE: Oh, what madness this!

DEIANIRA: My husband was the teacher.

NURSE: Wilt thou slay
The man whom Juno could not?

DEIANIRA: Whom the gods
Most hate they render wretched, whom men hate
They bring to nothing.

NURSE: Spare him, wretched one,
And fear.

DEIANIRA: Who does not stand in fear of death
Fears nothing. I rejoice to meet his sword.

NURSE: O foster-child, thy grief is heavier
Than's meet, the fault demands an equal hate
Oh, why so harshly judge his light offence?
Measure thy grieving by thy injury.

DEIANIRA: And is a mistress then a slight offence
Against a wife? Whatever else she bears,
This is indeed too heavy.

NURSE: Has thy love
For great Alcides fled?

DEIANIRA: Nay, nurse, not fled.
Believe, it lives deep fixed within my heart,
But angered love is anguish infinite.

NURSE: By magic arts and prayers have wives oft bound
Their husbands. I have made the winter groves
Grow green, the hurtling thunderbolt stand still,
Have made the dry earth glad; the rocks gave place,
The gates of hell flew back, the dead stood still,
The gods infernal spoke at my command,
The dog of hell was silent, midnight saw
The sun, and day was overwhelmed in night,
The earth and sea, the sky and Tartarus,
Obeyed me, nothing kept its ancient seat
Before my incantations. Let us seek
To bend his will, my songs will find a way.

DEIANIRA: What plants does Pontus nourish, or what grows
On Pindus underneath Thessalian rocks?
Where shall I find a charm to conquer him?
Though Luna at the magic of thy songs
Should leave the stars and hide within the earth,
And winter see the harvest; though the flash
Of Jove's swift lightning pause at thy command;
Though nature's order be reversed, and day
Should shine with many stars, he will not bend.

NURSE: Love conquers even the immortal gods.

DEIANIRA: This too, perchance, he'll conquer, gain this spoil,
And love may be Alcides' last great task.
By the divinity of all the gods,
By this my fear, I pray thee: keep concealed
Whate'er I do in secret, hide it well.

NURSE: What is it thou wouldst hide?

DEIANIRA: Not spears, nor swords,
Nor yet avenging fires.

NURSE: I can and will
            Keep silence, if such silence be not sin.

DEIANIRA: I pray thee look around, lest any hear
            And keep a watchful eye on every side.

NURSE: The place is safe from any prying one.

DEIANIRA: In a far corner of this realm there lies
            A hidden cave that keeps our secret well.
            That place sees not the sun at morning's prime
            Nor yet when Titan, bringer of the light,
            Sinks with the spent day in the crimson sea.
            There lies assurance of Alcides' love,
            The charm from Nessus comes, whom Nephele
            Conceived by the Thessalian king and bore
            Where Pindus lifts its head among the stars,
            Where rising o'er the clouds bald Othrys stands.
            For when, exposed to dread Alcides' club,
            Achelous took lightly every form,
            But, having passed through all, stood forth at last
            Subdued, with broken horns and wounded head,
            The victor Hercules to Argos went
            With me, his wife. Evenus' wandering stream
            Swift through the meadows to the ocean bore
            Its floods of waters, its impetuous waves
            Already almost reached the line of woods.
            The centaur Nessus, used to crossing floods,
            Was eager for a prize, and bearing me
            Upon his back where join the horse and man,
            He stemmed the swelling water's threatening waves.
            Alcides still was wandering in their midst
            Cutting the eager depths with mighty strides.
            Then when he saw Alcides still afar:
            "My spoil art thou," he said, "my wife shalt be,
            The waves are passed." Then holding me embraced,
            His steps he hastened. But the waves no more
            Detained great Hercules. "Base ferryman,"
            He said, "though Ister and the Ganges flow
            With mingled currents, I will conquer both,
            My shafts will check thy flight." More swift his bow
            Than words; the arrow, flying to the wound,
            Transfixed the centaur, ending flight in death.
            Already searching blindly for the light

He caught the poison flowing from the wound,
And in his hoof, which with his savage hand
He boldly tore away, he gave it me.
Then spake he dying words: "This charm," he said,
"Can fix a wavering lover, so the brides
Of Thessaly were by Mycale taught—
She was the mage at whose command the moon
Deserted starry heaven to follow her,
A garment smeared with this, this very blood,"
He said, "give thou to fickle Hercules,
If e'er a hated mistress should usurp
Thy marriage rights, and he should give great Jove
Another daughter. It must see no light,
In darkness most remote lie things like this.
So only shall this blood retain its strength."
Then did the sleep of death cut short his words,
And brought his weary members long repose.
O thou, to whom I trust, with whom I share
This secret, quickly go and bring the charm,
That, smeared upon his shining robe, its force
May enter through his heart and limbs, and pierce
His inmost marrow.

NURSE: Quickly I obey
Thy will, dear foster-child; do thou invoke
With earnest prayer the god invincible
Who shoots with youthful hand his certain shafts.
(*The* NURSE *goes into the palace.*)

Act Two.   Scene III

DEIANIRA (*invoking Cupid*): O thou whom earth and sea and heavenly
          powers
Adore in fear, who shakest Etna's fires,
I make my prayer to thee, O winged child,
Feared of thy ruthless mother; with true aim
Make ready thy swift dart, no common shafts;
I pray thee, choose the keenest, which not yet
Thy hands have aimed at any, there is need
Of such that Hercules may learn to love.
With firm hand draw the bow till both horns meet,

Shoot now the shaft that wounded once dread Jove
When casting down his thunderbolt, the god
Put on a horned and swelling front, and cleft
The raging seas, and as a bull bore off
The fair Assyrian maid. Oh, pierce with love,
A love more keen than any yet have felt!
Let Hercules learn love for me his wife.
And if the charms of Iole should set
The fire of love aflame within his heart,
Oh, let it drink the love of me and die.
Thou oft hast conquered thunder-bearing Jove,
And him who in the land of shadows wields
The dusky sceptre, ruler of the Styx
And leader of the great majority.
More strong than angered stepdame, take, O god,
This triumph—thou alone—quell Hercules.

Act Two.   Scene IV

(Re-enter NURSE *with robe and charm.)*

NURSE: The charm is ready, and the shining web
That wearied all thy damsels' hands to weave.
Smear now the poison, let Alcides' robe
Drink in the blood, I'll strengthen with my prayers
Its magic power. But see where Lichas comes;
The charm must be concealed, nor our device
Be known.

Act Two.   Scene V

(Enter LICHAS.*)*

DEIANIRA: In palaces of kings is rarely found
A faithful servant; faithful Lichas, take
This garment which with my own hands I spun
While Hercules was wandering through the world,
Or drunk with wine was holding on his breast
The Lydian maid, or seeking Iole.

Yet peradventure, having well deserved,
I may win back the rugged hero's heart,
For merit often overcometh ill.
Command my husband not to wear the robe
Until with incense he has fed the flames,
And reconciled the gods, and on wet locks
Has bound a wreath of silver poplar leaves.
    (LICHAS *departs with the robe.*)
Within the palace I will make my prayers
To Venus, mother of unconquered love.
Ye Calydonian women, friends who came
From home with me, lament my mournful fate.
    (DEIANIRA *and the* NURSE *go inside.*)

Act Two. Scene VI

CHORUS: O daughter of Oineus, thy childhood's friends,
We weep thy hapless marriage, honoured one.
We, who with thee were wont to wade the shoals
Of Achelous, when with passing spring
Its swollen waters ebbed, and with slow sweep
Its slender current wound, and when no more
The yellow waters of Lycormas rolled,
A headlong, turgid river; we were wont
To seek Minerva's altars, and to join
The virgin chorus; we with thee were wont
To bear the holy emblems treasured up
Within the Theban ark,⁶ when winter's cold
Had passed, and thrice the sun called summer forth,
When the grain-giver Ceres' sacred seat
Eleusis shut the priest within her shrines.
Whatever fate thou fearest, let us still
Remain the faithful sharers of thy lot.
When happier fortune smiles, fidelity
Is rare. Though all the people throng thy courts,
Though hundreds cross thy threshold, though thou pass
Surrounded by a crowd of followers,
Yet hardly shalt thou find among them all
One faithful friend; the dread Erinnyes hold
The gilded portals, and when great men's gates
Are opened fraud and craft and treachery

And lurking murder enter, and abroad
Thou goest among the people companied
By envy. Oft as morning drives out night,
Believe, so often is a monarch born.
Few serve the king and not his kingly power,
The glory of the court is dear to most:
One seeks to be the nearest to the king
And pass illustrious through the city streets;
And one with glory's lust is burnt, and one
Would sate his thirst with gold—nor all the tracts
Of Ister, rich in gems, suffice his greed,
Nor Lydia quench his thirst, nor all the land
Where Zephyr sighs and golden Tagus flows;
Nor were the Hebrus his, flowed through his fields
The rich Hydaspes, if the Ganges' flood
Within his borders ran; the world itself
Is all too small to serve the covetous.
Kings and kings' palaces one cultivates,
Not that to drive the plough with bended back
The ploughmen never cease, or thousands till
The fields—he only longs for heaped-up wealth.
One serves the king that he may trample all,
May ruin many and may strengthen none;
He longs for power but to use it ill.
How few death finds at fulness of their fame;
Whom Cynthia beholds in happiness,
The new-born day sees wretched; rare it is
To grow old happy. Softer is the sod
Than Tyrian robe and brings a fearless sleep,
But golden roofs disturb repose, and kings
Must lengthen out the watches of the night.
Oh, if the rich man's heart were visible,
How many fears fair fortune stirs within!
The Bruttian waters, tossed by northwest winds,
Are port more peaceful. With untroubled heart
The poor may rest, his cup and plate, indeed,
Are only birchwood, but with fearless hand
He holds them; easily his simple food
Is gathered, and he fears no waiting sword;
In cup of gold the drink is mixed with blood.
The wife who weds a man of humble means
May wear no costly necklace nor be decked
With Red Sea's gift, nor carry in her ears

The choicest gems of eastern waves, nor wear
Soft wool twice dipped in rich Sidonian dyes,
Nor with Maeonian needle broider it—
The Seres, dwelling near the rising sun,
To eastward, made the needle from the trees.
What though with common plants she dye the weft
Her unskilled hands have woven, she enjoys
Untroubled marriage. Whom the people praise
The dread Erinnys follows with her scourge,
And poverty itself is scarcely glad
Until it sees the fortunate o'erthrown.
The man who will not keep the middle course
Ne'er finds his pathway safe. When once he sought
To drive his father's car and bring the day,
The boy[7] kept not the wonted road, but found
With wandering wheel a way among the stars
Unknown to flaming Phoebus—in his fall
The world was ruined. While he ploughed through heaven
A middle course, bold Daedalus steered safe
Through peaceful climes, nor gave the sea a name,
But Icarus despised his father's flight
And dared to fly beyond the birds themselves,
Close to the sun. He gave an unknown sea
His name. Great deeds are recompensed by ill.
Be others known as fortunate and great,
But let no crowd hail me as powerful,
Let no great gale compel my slender ships
To sail broad seas, small boats should keep near shore;
Misfortune passes by the quiet ports
And seeks the ships that ride the deep, whose sails
Knock at the clouds. But why with pallid face,
Like maenad drunk with Bacchus, stands the queen?
Speak, wretched one, what grief does Fortune's wheel
Roll round for thee? Though thou refuse to speak
Thy face would tell the sorrows thou wouldst hide.

Act Three.   Scene I

(*Enter* DEIANIRA *and the* NURSE *from the palace.*)

DEIANIRA: A trembling shakes my terror-smitten limbs,
My hair with horror stands erect, and fear
Benumbs the soul till now so madly tossed;
Aghast and terrified, my heart leaps up,
With throbbing veins my liver palpitates;
As when the storm-blown sea still tosses high,
Although the day has calmed and languid airs
Breathe softly, so my mind that hitherto
Has swelled with fear is still with dread oppressed;
When once god turns against the fortunate,
Misfortune follows fast. Such end awaits
Performance of great deeds.

NURSE: What cruel fate
Turns now the wheel for thee, O wretched one?

DEIANIRA: When I had smeared the robe with Nessus' blood
And sent it, and had sadly turned to seek
My chamber, sudden fear, I know not why,
Assailed me—fear of fraud. I'll test the charm.
Fierce Nessus bade me keep the charmed blood
From flame or sun, this artifice itself
Foreboded treachery. Undimmed by cloud,
The glowing sun was ushering in bright day;
Fear hardly yet permits me speak! I cast
Within the fiery beams of Titan's light
The blood with which the garment had been wet,
The vestments smeared. The blood I threw away
Quivered, and, hardly yet by Phoebus' beams
Made warm, blazed up. I scarce can tell the tale!
As Eurus or warm Notus melts the snow
That slips from sparkling Mimas in the spring;
As the Leucadian headland breaks the waves
That roll against it from the Ionian sea,
And all the wearied surf breaks into foam;
Or as the bitter incense melts away
Upon the glowing altar of the gods,
So all the wool was withered and destroyed,
And while I wondered, that which gave me cause

For wonder vanished, but the earth was moved
Like foam, and everything the poison touched
Shrank into nothingness. But swift of foot
And terrified, I see my son approach.

Act Three.   Scene II

(*Enter* HYLLUS.)

DEIANIRA: What tidings dost thou bring me? Speak, I pray.

HYLLUS: Fly, fly, if any hiding-place remains
On earth, or sea, or ocean, in the skies
Or Hades, mother, fly beyond the hand
Of Hercules.

DEIANIRA: 'Tis what my soul presaged!

HYLLUS: Oh, seek the realm of the victorious one,
Seek Juno's shrine, this still is free to thee,
All sanctuaries else are snatched away.

DEIANIRA: Oh, speak, what fate awaits me innocent?

HYLLUS: That glory of the earth, the only guard
The fates have given to a stricken world
In place of Jove himself, is gone; there burns
Within the trunk and limbs of Hercules
Some plague, I know not what. Who ruled the beasts,
That victor now is conquered, moans, laments.
What further wouldst thou ask?

DEIANIRA: The wretched seek
To know their misery; speak, what the fate
That presses on our home? O household gods!
Unhappy household gods! I am indeed
Now widowed, exiled, overwhelmed by fate!

HYLLUS: Thou weepest not alone for Hercules,
The world must mourn him with thee, do not deem,
O mother, that the grief is thine alone;
Already all the race lifts up its voice.
Lo, all the world laments with heavy grief
The man thou mournest; thou but sufferest

A sorrow that the whole earth shares with thee,
Thou mourn'st Alcides first, O wretched one,
But not alone.

DEIANIRA: Yet tell me, tell, I pray,
How near to death lies now my Hercules.

HYLLUS: Death, whom in his own realm he conquered once,
Flies from him, nor dares fate permit the wrong.
Dread Clotho throws aside the threads, perchance,
And fears to end the fates of Hercules.
O fatal day! O day calamitous!
Shall great Alcides see no other day?

DEIANIRA: What? Dost thou say that he has gone before
To death, the shadow realm, the dark abode?
May I not be the first to die? Oh, speak,
If he not yet has fall'n.

HYLLUS: Euboea's land,
That swells with mighty headlands, on all sides
Is beaten by the sea; the Hellespont
Smites Caphereus; this side the south wind blows,
But there Aquilo's snowy storm-winds threat,
Euripus turns the restless, wandering tides
That seven times roll up and seven times
Drop back ere Titan in the ocean's flood
Merges his weary head. Upon the isle,
High on a cliff which many clouds surround,
An ancient temple of Cenaean Jove
Shines forth. When on the altars he had placed
The votive offering and all the grove
Was filled with lowing of the gilded bulls,
He threw aside his tawny lion's skin
All foul with putrid gore, laid down his club
And freed his shoulder from the quiver's weight,
Then shining in thy robe, his shaggy locks
With silver poplar bound, he lit the fire
Upon the altar. "Take," he said, "this gift,
O father, let thy sacred fires shine bright
With plenteous incense, which from Saba's trees
The Arabs, wealthy servants of the sun,
Collect. The earth," he said, "the sky, the sea,
Are all at peace; all savage beasts subdued,

And I have come a victor. Lay aside
Thy thunderbolt." But even as he prayed,
He groaned, and wondering at himself fell prone.
A horrid clamour filled the air, such noise
As when the bull attempts to fly the wound
Inflicted by the two-edged ax, and feels
The sting of steel, and with his mighty roar
Fills all the holy place; or, as Jove's bolt
From heaven thunders, so this groaning rolled
Skyward and seaward; Chalcis heard the sound,
It woke the echoes of the Cyclades,
The crags of Caphereus and all the groves
Gave back Alcides' voice. I saw him weep;
The people thought him mad as once he was;
His servants fled; he turned with fiery glance
And sought for one alone among them all—
Sought Lichas. He with trembling fingers grasped
The altars, died of fear, and left small room
For vengeance. With his hand the hero grasped
The quivering corpse. "By this hand, this," he cried,
"O fates, have I at last been overcome?
Has Lichas conquered Hercules? Behold
Another conquest: Lichas overwhelmed
By Hercules. My deeds grow poor and mean.
Be this my latest labour." 'Mid the stars
He flung him, sprinkled with his blood the clouds.
So flies the Getic arrow from the bow
Towards heaven, so the Cretan archer shoots
His shaft, but not so far the arrow flies.
The head was shattered on the cliffs, the trunk
Fell into ocean, there they both abide.
"Stay, madness has not seized my mind," he said,
"This ill is worse than madness or than wrath,
I rage against myself." He spoke and raged.
He rent apart his joints, with cruel hand
He tore his giant limbs and wounded them;
He sought in vain to pluck away the robe.
In this alone I saw Alcides fail,
Yet striving still to tear it off he tore
His limbs themselves, the robe had grown a part
Of Hercules' dread body, with the flesh
The garment mingled, nor could one detect
The dread disaster's cause, though cause there is.

Now hardly able to endure his pain,
Wearied he lies and presses with his face
The earth, then longs for ocean, his distress
The waves soothe not; he seeks the sounding shore
And leaps into the deep, his servants' hands
Hold back the wandering one. O bitter fate!
We were the equal of great Hercules!
Now from Euboea's shore a vessel bears
The hero back, a gentle south wind wafts
Alcides' giant weight; life leaves his limbs,
Night sits upon his eyes.

DEIANIRA: Why faint, my soul?
Why art thou so amazed? The crime is done.
Can Jove demand again his son of thee,
Or Juno ask her rival? To the world
Thou must atone, render then what thou canst.
The sword shall smite me. Thus it shall be done.
Suits such light punishment such heavy guilt?
O father, with thy thunderbolts destroy
Thy sinful child, nor let thy hand be armed
With common weapons. Send that thunderbolt
With which, had not Alcides been thy son,
Thou wouldst have burned the Hydra; as a scourge
Destroy me, as an evil dreaded more
Than angry stepdame. Such a bolt send forth
As once at wandering Phaethon was hurled.
I ruined, in Alcides, all the world.
Why ask a weapon of the gods? Now spare
Thy son, O Jove; the wife of Hercules
Should be ashamed to beg for death, this hand
Shall give the gift I ask for. Seize the sword:
Yet why a sword? Whatever drags to death
Is sword sufficient. From some soaring cliff
I'll cast me down. This Oeta will I choose,
This Oeta where first shines the newborn day;
From this I'll fling myself, the rugged rocks
Shall cut me into pieces, every stone
Shall take a part of me, my wounded hands
Shall hang upon them, all the mountain side
Be crimsoned with my blood. A single death
Is nothing.—Nothing? Can I make it more?
Canst thou not choose the weapon, O my soul,

On which to fall? Oh, might Alcides' sword
Become my couch! 'Twere well to die on this.
Is it enough that by my own right hand
I die? Assemble nations of the earth,
Hurl rocks and flaming brands, let no hand fail,
So have I found at last my punishment.
Already cruel kings bear rule unchecked;
Now unrestrained, are savage monsters born;
Again the accustomed altars seek to take
A brother's blood for sacrificial gift.
My hand has opened up a path for crime,
Has snatched away the punisher of kings,
Of tyrants, beasts, and monsters, 'gainst the gods
I set myself. O wife of thundering Jove,
Dost stay thy hand? Why spare thy lightning's shaft,
Nor imitate thy brother, sending forth
The thunder snatched from Jove? Why slay me not?
From thee great glory, honour infinite,
I snatched, O Juno, in thy rival slain.

HYLLUS: Why wouldst thou overthrow a tottering house?
             If crime is here it is of error sprung;
             And he who sins unwittingly scarce sins.

DEIANIRA: Who would remit his fate and spare himself
             Deserves to err. 'Tis well that I should die.

HYLLUS: Who longs for death seems guilty.

DEIANIRA: Death alone
             Makes guiltless those deceived.

HYLLUS: From Titan's beams
             First fleeing—

DEIANIRA: Titan flees, himself, from me.

HYLLUS: Wouldst part with life?

DEIANIRA: Alcides would I seek.

HYLLUS: He breathes, he yet takes in the vital air.

DEIANIRA: When Hercules was conquered, he was dead!

HYLLUS: Wouldst leave thy son? Thyself cut short thy life?

DEIANIRA: She whom her own son buries has lived long.

HYLLUS: Follow thy husband.

DEIANIRA: Ah, the faithful wife
Is wont to go before.

HYLLUS: Unhappy one,
If thou condemn thyself, thou seemst indeed
To prove thyself the guilty.

DEIANIRA: He who sins
May not himself annul the punishment.

HYLLUS: The life of many a one is spared whose sin
Was done in error, not by his own hand.
Who blames his lot?

DEIANIRA: Whoever draws a lot
Unfavouring.

HYLLUS: The man, forsooth, whose darts
Pierced Megara, whose fiercely raging hand
Sent the Lernaean shaft that slew his sons,[8]
Though thrice a murderer, yet forgives himself.
In Cinyphs' stream, beneath the Libyan skies,
He bathed his hands and washed away his guilt.
Oh, whither art thou driven, wretched one?
Why blame thy hands?

DEIANIRA: The conquered Hercules
Himself condemns them—one should punish crime.

HYLLUS: If I have known Alcides, he will be
Again the victor; treachery, o'erwhelmed,
Will bow before thy Hercules.

DEIANIRA: His joints
Are wasted by the Hydra's venomed gore,
The poison eats my husband's giant limbs.

HYLLUS: Thou deemst the poison of the strangled snake
Can slay the one who took its evil life?
He killed the dragon, though its teeth were fixed
Within his flesh; and, though his limbs were wet
With flowing venom, as a victor stood.
Can Nessus' blood destroy the one who slew
Dread Nessus' self?

DEIANIRA: In vain wouldst thou detain
One doomed to die. The sentence has gone forth
That I must leave the light, enough of life
Has he who meets his death with Hercules.

NURSE: By these white hairs, I ask thee; by this breast
That like a mother's nourished thee, I pray,
Put by thy wounded spirit's heavy threats;
Thrust out the fearful thoughts of dreaded death.

DEIANIRA: He who persuades the wretched not to die
Is cruel; death is sometimes punishment,
But, oft a blessing, has to many brought
Forgiveness.

NURSE: Yet unhappy one, restrain
Thy hand, that he may know the crime to be
Not thine, but error's.

DEIANIRA: There I'm free indeed!
I think the gods infernal will absolve.
I am by my own self condemned; these hands
Let Pluto purge. Forgetful, by thy banks,
O Lethe, let me stand, a mournful shade,
Receive my husband! Whosoe'er was bold
For crime, his sin was less than my mistake:
Not Juno's self had dared to snatch from earth
Great Hercules. Some worthy penalty
Prepare; let Sisyphus desert his stone
And let my shoulders roll its heavy weight.
Me let the wandering waters fly, my thirst
The faithless waves delude; I have deserved
That thou shouldst roll me round, O flying wheel
Whereon the king of Thessaly is racked.
Let eager vultures on my entrails feed;
One child of Danaus there lacks—the tale
Of fifty I will fill. O Colchian wife,[9]
Take me as thy companion, with worse crime
Than thine this hand is stained, though thou didst slay
Thy children and thy brother. Take thy child,
Mother Althaea, take thy child indeed!
Yet no such deed was thine! Ye faithful wives,
Who in the sacred woodland stretches dwell,
Shut me from fields Elysian. If one there

Has sprinkled with her husband's blood her hands,
Unmindful of chaste marriage torch has stood,
A bloody child of Belus, with drawn sword,
She as her own will know me, praise my deed;
That company of wives I well may join;
But they, too, shun my hands so basely stained.
O husband, strong, invincible, my soul
Is innocent, my hands alone are stained.
O mind too credulous! O Nessus, false
And of half beastly guile! A concubine
I sought to ruin, but destroyed myself!
Bright Titan, life, that flattering still dost hold
The wretched in the light of day, depart!
Where Hercules is not the light is vile.
I will discharge the penalty for thee,
Will give my life. Shall I prolong that life
Till at thy hand, O husband, I meet death?
Hast any strength? Can thy right hand make tense
The bowstring for the sending of the shaft?
Or do the weapons fall, thy languid hands
No longer draw the bow? O husband brave,
If thou art able still to slay, I wait
Thy hand, I wait for death; as thou didst dash
In pieces guiltless Lichas, slay me now,
In other cities scatter me, in worlds
To thee unknown; as monstrous things did cease
In Arcady, destroy me. Yet from those
Thou didst return, O husband!

HYLLUS: Mother, cease.
Excuse thy deed, an error is not crime.

DEIANIRA: If filial piety be truly thine,
O Hyllus, smite thy mother. Wherefore now
Trembles thy hand? Why turn away thy face?
This crime were filial piety indeed.
O dastard, dost thou hesitate? This hand
Snatched from thee Hercules, destroyed the one
Who gave thee for a grandsire thundering Jove;
I snatched from thee a glory far more great
Than e'er I gave thee when I gave thee light.
If crime is new to thee, then learn of me,
Hew with the sword my throat, let iron pierce

The womb that bore thee, an intrepid soul
Thy mother gave thee. Such deed were not crime
For thee; by my will, though by thy right hand,
I die. Dost fear, O son of Hercules?
Wilt thou not, like thy father, crush out ill,
Perform great deeds? Prepare thy good right hand!
Behold a bosom full of misery
Lies bared: strike, I proclaim thee free from crime:
The dread Eumenides themselves will spare,
I hear their scourges singing. Who is that
Whose viperous locks upon her forehead writhe,
Who brandishes her sword and shakes her wings?
Why dost thou follow me with flaming torch,
Megaera? Dost demand the vengeance due
For Hercules? I give it. Awful one,
Have hell's dread arbiters judged yet my cause?
Behold I see the dreadful prison doors.
What aged one is he who strives to lift
The giant rock upon his wounded back?
Behold already does the conquered stone
Roll back! Whose members tremble on the wheel?
Lo, pallid, dread Tisiphone appears,
She charges murder; spare thy blows, I pray!
Megaera, spare! Thy Stygian torches stay!
The crime was caused by love. But what is this?
Earth shakes, the smitten roofs crack, whence these
    threats?
The whole world falls upon me, everywhere
The nations groan, the universe demands
Its great defender. O ye cities spare!
Ah, whither can I fly? In death alone
I find a harbour for my shipwrecked soul.
I call to witness shining Phoebus' wheel
Of flame, the heavenly ones to witness call:
I die and leave great Hercules on earth.
        (DEIANIRA *departs*.)

HYLLUS: Ah, me, she flies amazed; the mother's part
Is finished, she resolved to die, my part
Remains—to snatch her from the shock of death.
O pitiable filial piety!
If I should stay my mother's death, my crime
Is great against my father; yet I sin

Against my mother, suffering her death;
Crime presses either way, yet she must be
Prevented—I must snatch her from this crime.
(HYLLUS *and the* NURSE *depart.*)

Act Three. Scene III

CHORUS: What Orpheus sang, Calliope's blest son,
When 'neath the heights of Thracian Rhodope
He struck his lute Pierian, is true:
Nothing abides. The rushing waterfall
Silenced its thunder at his music's sound,
The waters ceased their flow, forgot their haste,
And while the rivers thus delayed their course,
The far-off Thracian thought the Hebrus failed.
The woodland brought the winged kind, they came
Resting within the groves, or if a wing
That, roaming, flew through upper air the while,
Was wanting, when it heard the song it dropped.
Mount Athos tore away its crags and came,
Bearing the Centaurs as it moved along,
And stood by Rhodope; its snowy crown
Was melted by the song; the dryad fled
Her oak and hasted to the prophet's side;
The wild beasts at thy singing with their dens
Drew near; the Afric lion sat beside
The fearless flock, nor did the timid does
Tremble before the wolves; the serpent came
From gloomy den, its poisoned sting forgot.
  Nay more, he passed the gates of Taenarus
Among the silent phantoms, bearing there
His mournful lute, and with his doleful song
He overcame the melancholy gods
Of Erebus, nor feared the Stygian lake
By which the gods make oath; the restless wheel
Stood still, its languid whirling forced to cease;
The heart of Tityus began to grow
The while the vultures listened to the song;
Thou also heardst, O oarsman, and thy boat
Came oarless over the infernal stream;

Then first the aged Phrygian forgot
His raging thirst although the waves stood still,
Nor did he stretch a hand to reach the fruit.
When Orpheus seeking thus the lower world
Poured forth his singing and the restless stone
Was conquered, following the prophet's song,
The Goddesses restored the severed thread
Of fair Eurydice. But Orpheus looked
Behind, forgetful or not deeming true
Restored Eurydice was following him.
He lost the song's reward, she died again
Who hardly had been given back to life.
Then seeking comfort in his song, he sang
These words to Getan folk in mournful strains:
Unchanging laws are given by the gods,
And he who rules the seasons ordereth
Four fleeting changes for the changing year.
Dead Hercules compels us to believe
The Thracian Seer. The Parcae tie again
The thread of life for none, however much
He may desire; all that has been born
Or shall be dies. When to the world shall come
The time when law is not, the southern sky
Shall bury Libya, and on Afric's sands
Shall fallen lie; the northern sky o'erwhelm
Whatever lies beneath the poles, whate'er
Cold Boreas smites; pale Titan blot the day
From heaven; the royal palace of the sky
In its own ruin drag the rising sun
And setting; death and chaos overtake
The gods; death find at last within itself
Its end. What place will then receive the world?
Shall Tartarus spread wide her doors to take
The shattered heavens? Or is there space enough
Between the earth and heaven—perchance too much?
What place can hold such crime? A single place
Will hold the three realms—earth, and sea, and sky.

But what great clangour moves the wondering air?
It is the sounding voice of Hercules.

Act Four.　Scene I

(Enter HERCULES *in agony.)*

HERCULES:　Bright Titan, turn again thy wearied steeds,
　　　　　Send night, let perish to the world that day
　　　　　Whereon I fell, let black cloud shadow day,
　　　　　So thwart my stepdame. Father, now command
　　　　　Black chaos to return; their union rent,
　　　　　The poles should here and there be torn apart;
　　　　　Why spare the stars? O father, thou hast left
　　　　　Thy Hercules! Scan well on every side
　　　　　The sky, O Jove, lest any Gyas hurl
　　　　　Thessalian crags, and Othrys' weight be made
　　　　　Too light for great Enceladus. The gates
　　　　　Of Hell's black prison now are opened wide
　　　　　By haughty Pluto, and his father's chains
　　　　　Are broken—to the sky he leads him back.
　　　　　That son who stood in place of thy dread torch
　　　　　And thunder, as avenger of the world,
　　　　　Returns to Styx; and fierce Enceladus
　　　　　Shall rise and hurl against the gods the weight
　　　　　With which he now is held to earth. My death
　　　　　Shall make thy heavenly throne, O father, shake.
　　　　　Before the giants make thy heavens their spoil,
　　　　　Beneath the ruins of the universe,
　　　　　O father, bury me in whom thou losest
　　　　　The firmament itself.

CHORUS:　　Not empty are thy threats, O son of Jove.
　　　　　Now on Thessalian Ossa Pelion stands,
　　　　　And Athos piled on Pindus lifts its groves
　　　　　Amid the starry ether, Typhoeus thence
　　　　　Shall overcome the cliffs and raise on high
　　　　　From out the Tuscan sea Inarime.
　　　　　Enceladus, by lightning not yet slain
　　　　　Shall rend his chimneys in the mountain side
　　　　　And lift aloft great Etna. Even now
　　　　　The realm of heaven is in thee destroyed.

HERCULES:　I, I, who conquered death and scorned the Styx
　　　　　And came again through stagnant Lethe's midst,
　　　　　With spoil at sight of which bright Titan shrank

And from his fleeing horses almost fell;
Yes, I, whose power the gods' three realms have felt,
I die although no sword has pierced my side,
Although Mount Othrys did not bring my death,
Although no giant form with fierce wide jaws
Has overwhelmed me with all Pindus' ridge.
I fell without a foe and worst of all—
O wretched valour!—Hercules' last day
Shall see no monster prostrate! Woe is me,
I lost my life, but not in noble deeds!
O judge of earth, ye gods who oft have seen
My labours, and thou earth, is it your will
To smite your Hercules with death? O shame
Unmatched! O bitter fate! A woman's hand
To be the author of Alcides' death!
If fate unchanging willed my fate should be
By woman's hand, if such base threads run out
My last of life, ah me, why might I not
By Juno's hatred fall? By woman's hand
I should have fallen, but by one divine.
If this had been too much to ask, ye gods,
An Amazon brought forth 'neath Scythian skies
Might well have vanquished me. What woman's hand
Could conquer me, great Juno's foe? Ah, worse
Thy shame in this, my stepdame! Wherefore call
This day a glad one? What has earth brought forth
To satisfy thy wrath? A woman's hate,
A mortal's, was more powerful than thine.
Till now thou hadst to tolerate the shame
Of finding thou wast not Alcides' peer,
Now thou art by two mortals overcome,
The gods should be ashamed of such revenge!
Would the Nemaean lion with my blood
Had satisfied his thirst, or I, brought low,
Surrounded by the hundred-headed snake,
Had trembled; would that I had been the prey
Of Nessus, or that I might wretched sit
Forever on an everlasting rock
Conquered among the shades. Fate stood amazed,
While I dragged forth my latest prey and came
From Stygian depths again to light, and broke
The chains of Dis: Death fled me everywhere
That I might lack in death a glorious fate.

O monsters, conquered monsters! Not the dog
Of hell, at sight of day, has dragged me back
To Styx, not underneath the western sky
Has the Iberian Geryon's savage rout
O'ercome me, not twin dragons; woe is me,
How often have I lost a noble death!
What fame shall be my last?

CHORUS: Dost see how courage, conscious of itself,
Shrinks not at Lethe's stream? He does not grieve
At death, but feels ashamed before its cause,
He fain would end his final day of life
Beneath some swelling giant's mighty form,
Of mountain-bearing Titan feel the weight,
Or owe his death to ravening wild beast.
O wretched one, thy hand itself the cause
Why no wild beast or savage monster lives;
What worthy author of Alcides' death
Remains, unless it be thy own right hand?

HERCULES: Alas, what scorpion within my breast,
What cancer from the burning plains turned back
And fixed within my bosom, burns my reins?
My lungs once full of swelling blood are dry,
With burning venom is my heart aflame,
Slow fever dries my blood. The pest first eats
My skin, thence makes an entrance to my limbs;
The poison takes away my sides, it gnaws
My joints and ribs, my very marrow wastes;
Within my empty bones the venom stays,
The bones themselves may not for long endure,
Torn from the ruptured joints the mighty mass
To ruin falls, my giant body fails,
The limbs of Hercules are not enough
To satisfy the pest. How great the ill
That I own great. O dreadful infamy!
Behold, ye cities, see what now remains,
See what remains of that great Hercules!
O father, dost thou recognise thy son?
Did these arms hold to earth the conquered neck
Of the dread lion? Did the mighty bow,
By this hand strung, bring down Stymphalian birds
From out the very stars? Did I o'ertake

With steps of mine the fleet-foot stag that bore
The branching gold upon his radiant front?
Did Calpe, dashed to pieces by these hands,
Let out the sea? By these hands overcome,
Lie low so many beasts, so many crimes,
So many kings? Sat once the dome of heaven
Upon these shoulders? Is this body mine?
This neck? Have I against a falling sky
Stretched forth these hands? Or was the Stygian dog
Dragged by my hand beyond the river Styx?
What sepulchre contains my early strength?
Why call I Jove my father? Why through him
Claim I, unhappy one, my right to heaven?
Already is Amphitryon deemed my sire.
Whatever venom lurks within my veins,
Come forth! Why seek me with a secret wound?
Wast thou within the Scythian sea brought forth,
Beneath the frozen sky? Was Tethys slow,
Or Spanish Calpe on the Moorish shore
Thy author? O dread ill, didst thou come forth
As serpent lifting up thy crested head?
Or something evil, yet unknown to me?
Wast thou from blood of the Lernaean snake
Produced, or wast thou left upon the earth
By Stygian dog? Thou art all ills and none.
What face is thine? Grant me at least to know
By what I die; whatever evil thing
Or savage beast thou art, fight openly.
Who makes for thee a place within my bones?
Lo, from my mangled flesh my hand draws forth
My entrails; deeper yet the way is found
Within the seat of life. O malady,
Alcides' peer! Whence come these bitter groans?
Whence come these tears I feel upon my cheeks?
My eyes unconquerable once, nor wont
To show a tear before my enemies,
At last have learned to weep. O bitter shame!
What day, what land e'er saw Alcides' tears?
How many evils have I borne dry-eyed,
To thee alone that courage yields which slew
So many monsters, thou alone, thou first,
Hast made me weep! More hard than frowning rock,
Or Chalybean steel, or wandering isles,

The stern Symplegades, thy might has crushed
My power, has forced my eyes at last to weep.
O mighty ruler of the skies, the earth
Beholds me weeping, groaning, worst of all,
My stepdame sees me. Ah, once more it burns
My fibres; lo, the fever glows again.
Where now is found for me a thunderbolt?

CHORUS: What cannot suffering conquer? Once more firm
Than Getic Haemus, than Parrhasian skies
Not milder, to the bitter pain he yields;
He bows his wearied head upon his breast,
From side to side he moves his ponderous weight,
His valour often overcomes his tears.
So with however warm a beam he shine,
Titan can never melt the arctic snows;
The radiance of the ice outshines the torch
Of blazing Phoebus.

HERCULES: Father, turn thy face
To my complaint, Alcides ne'er before
Asked aid; not when the fruitful Hydra wound
Its fold about my limbs; between hell's lakes
Where black night reigns I stood with death, nor sought
Thy aid; dread monsters, tyrants, kings, I slew,
Nor skyward turned my face. This hand of mine
Was still my pledge, for me no thunderbolt
E'er flashed from out Jove's heaven. This day compels
A prayer from me; it is the first, last time
That he shall hear me pray: one thunderbolt
I ask, one only, but a giant one.
I might have stormed the heavens, but since I deemed
Thou wert my father, I have spared the skies.
O father, whether thou art merciful
Or cruel, to thy son stretch forth thy hand,
Speed now his death and give thyself this fame.
Or if it grieve thee, and thy hand refuse
To do the deed, from the Sicilian peak
Send for the Titans, bearing in their hands
Mount Pindus, or let Ossa with its weight
O'erwhelm me; burst the doors of Erebus
And let Bellona with drawn sword attack:
Send forth fierce, rushing Mars, against me arm

That terrible swift one; he is indeed
My brother, yet my stepdame Juno's son.
Thou too, Athena, by one parent born
The sister of Alcides, hurl thy spear
Against thy brother; supplicating hands
I stretch toward thee, my stepdame; hurl at length
A dart, I pray, against me; I would still
By woman's hand be slain; already calmed,
Already satisfied, why nourish wrath,
Why seek for further vengeance? Suppliant here
Thou seest Hercules; no savage beast,
No land, e'er saw me praying thus to thee.
Now that I need indeed a stepdame's wrath,
Now, does thy anger cease? Dost put aside
Thy hatred? Since I wish for death, thou sparest.
O earth, O cities of the earth, does none
Yield torch or weapon now for Hercules?
Ye rob me of my arms? When I am gone
May no land bring forth monsters wild, the world
Long never for my hand if evil rise,
Or hate be born. Cast at my hapless head
Great stones, and end at last my misery.
O world ungrateful, dost thou now desert?
Hast thou forgot? Thou wouldst have been the prey
Of beasts and monsters, hadst thou not borne me.
Ye nations, now snatch hence the rescuer;
This time is given you to recompense
My benefits, death be their great reward.

Act Four.   Scene II

(Enter ALCMENA.*)*

ALCMENA: Where shall Alcides' wretched mother go?
Where seek her son? If sure my sight, lo, there
With throbbing heart he lies and passion-tossed.
He groans, 'tis finished. Let me, O my son,
For the last time embrace thee, let me take
Thy fleeting breath. Receive my last embrace.
But where are now thy limbs? Where now that neck
That bore the firmament with all its stars?

Who is it leaves to thee so small a part
Of all thy powers?

HERCULES: O mother, thou indeed
Dost look on Hercules, but on his shade.
O mother, recognise thy son. Why weep,
With eyes turned from me? Wherefore veil thy face?
Dost blush that Hercules is called thy son?

ALCMENA: What land brought forth this new calamity?
What fearful thing has triumphed over thee?
Who is the conqueror of great Hercules?

HERCULES: Thou seest Alcides slain by woman's guile.

ALCMENA: What guile is great enough to conquer him?

HERCULES: A woman's anger, mother, is enough,

ALCMENA: Whence flowed the poison in thy bones and joints?

HERCULES: Her venom found its way through poisoned robe.

ALCMENA: But where the robe? I see thy naked limbs.

HERCULES: With me it is consumed.

ALCMENA: Can such things be?

HERCULES: Mother, the Hydra and a thousand beasts
Invade my vitals. What flame like to these
Divides Sicilian skies or Lemnos' isles,
Or heaven's burning plain whose fiery zone
Forbids the day to move? Oh, cast me, friends,
Into the channel or the river's midst.
The Ister is not deep enough for me,
Nor mighty ocean's self could quench my flames;
All water fails me, every stream dries up.
Why didst thou send me back again to Jove,
O lord of Erebus? 'Twas right to keep.
Give back thy darkness, show to conquered hell
Alcides; nothing will I carry thence,
Why be afraid again of Hercules?
Death, fear not, come; now Hercules can die.

ALCMENA: Restrain thy tears; at least control thy woe,
Be still invincible before such ills.
As thou art wont, smite death and conquer hell.

HERCULES: If rugged Caucasus should offer me,
Bound by his chains, a feast for eager birds,
In Scythia that echoes with their cries,
No lamentations would be heard from me;
Or if the wandering Symplegades
Returning crush me 'midst their cliffs, I'd wait
Unmoved their threatened ruin. Should the weight
Of Pindus lie upon me, Haemus too,
And Athos, where the Thracian seas break high,
And Mimas smitten by Jove's thunderbolts;
My mother, should this universe itself
Fall on me, and above my body blaze
The burning wheel of Phoebus' flaming car,
Ignoble clamour should not overcome
Alcides' courage. Should a thousand beasts
Attack and tear me—here Stymphalian birds
With clangour wild fly at me from the air,
And there the threatening bull with all his force;
All monsters that have been! Or should the groves
Rise everywhere, and cruel Sinis hurl
His mighty limbs against me, scattering me,
I still were silent; savage beasts, nor crimes,
Nor aught that I could meet in open fight
Could force from me a groan.

ALCMENA: Perchance, my son,
No woman's poison scorches now thy limbs,
But all thy heavy tasks, thy labours long,
Now make thee tremble with some dread disease.

HERCULES: Where is the sickness, where? Does any ill
Exist upon the earth with me till now?
Let it come hither, hand me now a bow.
These naked hands suffice. Come on! Come on!

ALCMENA: Ah, me, his overwhelming pain destroys
His senses. Take away his darts, I pray,
Snatch hence his murderous arrows, I beseech.
His cheeks suffused with fire threat dreadful crime.
What place of hiding can I, aged one,
Seek out? This rage is madness. Hercules
Alone can rule himself. Why, foolish one,
Seek flight or hiding? By a hero's hand
Alcmena merits death; so let me die,

E'er anything ignoble bids me fall,
E'er evil hands may triumph over me.
But see, by troubles weakened, pain binds up
His wearied limbs with sleep, his bosom heaves
With heavy sighs. Be merciful, ye gods!
If ye refuse me my illustrious son,
At least preserve its saviour to the world.
Drive out his bitter pain, let Hercules
Renew his ancient strength.

Act Four.   Scene III

(*Enter* HYLLUS.)

HYLLUS: O cruel light! O day so full of crime!
The thunderer's daughter dies,[10] his son lies low,
The grandchild only lives. He lost his life,
Slain by my mother's hand, by treachery
Was she deceived. Alas, what man grown old
Through all the changes of the years has known
In all his life such sorrows? One day snatched
Both parents from me. But of other ills
I will not speak: great Hercules is dead.

ALCMENA: Be silent, noble son of Hercules,
Grandson of sad Alcmena—for perchance
Long sleep will overcome Alcides' ills.
But see, repose deserts his wearied mind,
He is recalled to sickness, I to grief.

HERCULES (*awakening in delirium*): What see I? Trachin with its
                    rugged cliffs?
Or, placed among the stars, have I at length
Escaped mortality? Who opens heaven?
I see thee, father; thee behold I too,
My stepdame, reconciled. What heavenly sound
Strikes on my ear? Great Juno calls me son.
I see bright heaven's shining realm, I see
The sun's encircling road with Phoebus' car.
But what is this? Who closes heaven to me?
Who drives me from the stars? But now I felt
The breath of Phoebus' car, almost I stood

In heaven itself. 'Tis Trachin that I see,
Who brings me back to earth? I see night's couch,
The shadows call me hither. Only now
Mount Oeta stood below me; all the world
Was spread beneath. How happily, O pain,
Thou wast forgot! Thou forcest me to speak,
Oh, spare me! Take away this voice from me!
                    (*To* HYLLUS)
This gift, this benefit, thy mother gave,
O Hyllus. Would that with my lifted club
I might have beaten out her wicked life,
As once beside the snowy Caucasus
I tamed the Amazon. O Megara,
Much loved, wast thou my wife when I was mad?
Give back my bow and club; my hand is stained,
I will with glory wipe away the spot,
And Hercules' last toil shall by his wife
Be given.

HYLLUS: Father, curb thy wrathful threats;
'Tis finished, she has suffered, she has paid
The penalty thou fain wouldst from her claim.
Dead lies my mother, by her own hand dead.

HERCULES: Thou, trouble, still abidest at my side;
She by the hand of wrathful Hercules
Deserved to perish, Lichas is bereft
Of fitting comrade; wrath compels me rage
Against her lifeless body. Why should that
Escape my vengeance? Let the wild beasts take
Their food.

HYLLUS: She suffered most, thou wouldst have wished
Somewhat to lighten that her load of woe;
Grieving for thee, she died by her own hand.
A heavier penalty than thou wouldst ask,
She suffered. But thou liest overcome
Not by the baseness of thy cruel wife,
Not by my mother's treachery; thy pain
Was heaped on thee by Nessus whom thy shaft
Deprived of life; the robe was dipped in blood
Of that half beast, half man, and Nessus now
Demands revenge.

HERCULES: He has it, 'tis complete.
My life is finished, this day is my last,
The prophet oak foretold this fate to me,
And the Parnassian grot that with its groans
Shook the Cirrhean temple: "Thou shalt fall,
Alcides, conquered by the hand of one
Whom thou hast conquered; this shall come to pass
When earth and sea and hell are overcome."
I make no plaint, 'twas right this end be given
Lest any one should live to boast himself
Alcides' conqueror. Now comes at length
A noble death, of great and wide renown,
And worthy me. This day shall I see feared.
Let all the woods be cut, let Oeta's groves
Be dragged together that a mighty pyre
Receive me; but before I come to die,
Thou, Poeas' son, perform for me, dear youth,
The melancholy office, let the day
Be set ablaze with the Herculean flames.
To thee, I make, O Hyllus, my last prayer:
There is, within, a noble captive maid,
She bears her kingly lineage in her face,
The virgin Iole, Eurytus' child;
Receive her for thy bride. I, stained with blood,
Victorious, bore her from her home and land.
To the unhappy maid I've given naught
But Hercules, and he is snatched away.
Jove's grandchild she shall wed, Alcides' son,
And find a recompense for all her woes.
Whatever seed she has conceived by me
To thee she shall bring forth.
                    (*To* ALCMENA)
                                          O mother dear,
Forbear thy grief, Alcides lives for thee.
My courage makes thy rival to be deemed
A stepdame; either certainly is known
The night on which Alcides was begot,
Or else my father was a mortal man.
Yet though, perchance, my lineage be feigned,
I have deserved such noble parentage;
My glorious deeds brought honour to the skies,
My mother to Jove's glory brought me forth.
And if my father, though great Jove himself,

Rejoices in his fatherhood, restrain
Thy tears, O mother, proudest shalt thou be
Among Argolic mothers; no such son
Has she who wields the sceptre of the skies,
Great Juno, wife of thundering Jove, brought forth;
She envied mortal though the heaven was hers,
She longed to call great Hercules her son.
Now Titan, thou must run alone thy course,
I who have been thy comrade everywhere
Seek now the manes and Tartarean shades;
Yet to the depths of hell I bear this fame:
No evil slew Alcides openly,
Alcides conquered openly all ill.

(All depart.)

Act Four.   Scene IV

CHORUS: O radiant Titan, glory of the world,
At whose first shining wearied Hecate leaves
Her night-dark car, say to the Sabean lands
That lie beneath thy dawning, say to Spain
That lies beneath thy setting, say to all
That suffer underneath the Greater Bear,
Or palpitate beneath the burning wheel:
Alcides hastes to everlasting shades
And to the kingdom of the sleepless dog
Whence he has once returned. Let clouds surround
Thy brightness, look upon the mourning lands
With pallid face and veil thy head with mists;
When, where, beneath what sky, mayst thou behold
Another Hercules? Whose hand shall earth
Invoke, if e'er in Lerna should arise
A hundred-headed Hydra scattering bane,
Or any Erymanthian boar disturb
The quiet of Arcadia's ancient race;
Or any child of Thracian Rhodope,
More harsh than snowy Helice, make wet
With human blood its stables? Who will give
Peace to a timorous people if the gods
Be angry and command new monsters rise?
Like other mortals now he lies whom earth

Produced the equal of the Thunderer.
Let all the world reecho sounds of woe;
Your bare arms beat, ye women, let your hair
Fall loose; and let the temples of the gods
Shut fast their portals, open not their gates
But for my fearless stepdame; to the shores
Of Styx and Lethe goest thou, from whence
No keel shall bring thee back; unhappy one,
Thyself a shade, thou goest with fleshless arms,
Pale face, and drooping shoulders, to the shades
From whence thou camest once victorious,
When thou hadst conquered death. Nor thee alone
Shall that ship bear. Yet not with common shades,
With the twin Cretan kings and Aeacus
Shalt thou be judge of men, smite tyrants down.
Spare, O ye mighty ones, refrain your hands;
'Tis great indeed to keep your swords unstained,
And while you reign to keep the realm in peace.
But valour has a place among the stars.
Wilt thou thy seat to northward find, be placed
Where Titan carries fervid heat? Wilt shine
Within the mild west whence thou mayest hear
Calpe reecho with the sounding waves?
Where in the heavens serene wilt thou be set?
What place will be secure among the stars
When Hercules has come? O father, grant,
A seat from the dread lion far removed
And from the burning cancer, lest the stars
Should tremble at thy coming and forsake
Their ancient laws, and Titan be afraid.
While flowers blossom with the spring's warm days,
While winter cuts the foliage from the groves,
Or warmth calls back the foliage to the groves;
While with the flying autumn falls the fruit,
No flight of time shall snatch thee from the world:
Thou shalt be mate to Phoebus and the stars.
Sooner shall cornfields flourish in the deep,
The straits shall sooner whisper with soft waves,
The constellation of the icy bear
Shall sooner leave the heavens and enjoy
Forbidden seas than nations shall forget
To sing thy praises. Father of the world,
We wretched ones entreat thee, let no beasts

Be born, no monsters, nor the troubled world
Fear cruel leaders, let us not be ruled
By any court that deems the dignity
Of empire lies in ever-threatening sword.
If any monster rise again on earth,
We seek a saviour for the orphaned world.
Ah, hear! Heaven thunders, does his father mourn
Alcides? Is the cry the voice of gods,
Or timid stepdame? Does great Juno flee
At sight of Hercules? Or 'neath his load
Does Atlas tremble? Are the dreaded shades
Now shaken by the sight of Hercules?
Or does the hell-hound rend away his chains
And fly in fear that face? We are deceived,
Behold with joyous look comes Poeas' son,
Alcides' follower; on his shoulder clangs
The well-known shafts and quiver.

Act Five.   Scene I

(*Enter* PHILOCTETES.)

CHORUS: Tell, youth, I pray, the fate of Hercules,
                Say with what mien Alcides met his death.

PHILOCTETES: With such a mien as no one e'er met life.

CHORUS: So gladly did he mount his funeral pyre?

PHILOCTETES: He showed that flames are naught; what is there left
                On earth which Hercules has not o'ercome?
                Lo, all is conquered.

CHORUS: 'Midst the flames what place
                For mighty deeds?

PHILOCTETES: One evil in the world
                He had not yet o'ercome, but he has ruled
                The fire, this also to the savage beasts
                He adds, among the tasks of Hercules
                Shall fire be placed.

CHORUS: I pray thee, now unfold
                The way in which the flames were overcome.

PHILOCTETES: Each sorrowing hand cut Oeta's forests down,
The beech-tree lost its wealth of shade, and lay
Hewn from its base; one strong hand felled the pine
Whose top reached heaven, and called it from the
    clouds,
Falling it moved the rocks and with it bore
The lesser trees. An oak with spreading top,
Like that which whispers in Chaonia,
Shut out the sun and stretched on either side
Its boughs; the great tree, pierced by many wounds,
Cried out and broke the wedges, the dulled steel
Recoiled, the ax was injured, nor was found
Inflexible enough; but, stirred at length,
The oak bore ruin with it in its fall,
And everywhere the place admits the sun.
The birds are driven from their resting-place
And eddying through the sunlight where the grove
Has fallen, querulous, on wearied wing
They seek their homes. Already every tree
Resounds, the sacred oak-trees even feel
The hand that holds the dreaded ax, the grove
Is no avail to save the holy place.
The forest forms a mound, alternate beams
Raise to the skies a pyre all too small
For Hercules. The pine and hardy oak
And shorter ilex carry up the flames,
And poplars wont to ornament the brow
Of Hercules fill up the funeral pyre.
As roars a mighty lion lying sick
In Afric forests, he is borne along;
Who will believe him carried to the flames?
His glance was seeking for the stars, not fires.
As Oeta's soil he pressed and with his glance
Scanned all the pyre, mounting upon the beams
He broke them. For his bow he asked, then said:
"Take this, O son of Poeas, take the gift
Of Hercules; the Hydra felt these shafts,
By these were slain the foul Stymphalian birds,
And every evil that from far I slew.
O youth, be happily victorious,
Nor ever send without avail these shafts
Against a foe. Or, shouldst thou wish to bring
The birds from out the clouds, let birds descend,

Let slaughter always follow thy sure shaft,
Nor ever let this bow thy right hand fail;
Well has it learned to free the shaft and give
A sure direction to the arrow's flight,
Sent from the string the dart shall never fail
To find the way. I pray thee, bring the fire,
And light for me the funeral torch. This club,"
He said, "which never hand but mine shall bear,
Shall burn with me; this mighty weapon go
With Hercules. This too thou mightest have,"
He said, "if thou couldst wield it; it may aid
Its master's funeral pyre." And then he asked
That with him might be burned the shaggy spoil
Of the Nemaean lion; with the spoil
The pyre was hid. The throng about him groaned,
And sorrow filled the eyes of all with tears.
His mother, raging with her grief, laid bare
Her ample bosom, even to the womb,
And smote with heavy blows her naked breasts,
And, moving with her cries the gods themselves
And Jove, with woman's shrieks the place she filled.
"O mother, thou mak'st base Alcides' death,
Restrain thy tears, and let thy woman's grief
Turn inward. Why shall Juno know one day
Of joy because thou weepest? She is glad
To see her rival's tears. Thy feeble heart
Control, O mother, it is sin that thou
Shouldst tear the womb and breast that nourished me."
Then roaring mightily, as when he led
The dreaded hell-hound through Argolic streets,
What time he came again from conquered Dis
And trembling death, a victor over hell,
Upon his funeral pyre he laid him down.
What conqueror at his triumph ever stood
So joyous in his car? What tyrant prince
With such a glance e'er gave the nations laws?
How calmly did he bear his fate! Our tears
Were dried, our sorrow, smitten, fell away;
None raised lament for him who was to die.
'Twere shame to weep. Although sex bade her mourn,
Alcmena stood with cheeks unwet with tears,
A mother almost equal to her son.

CHORUS: And did he, on the point of death, lift up
                 To heaven no invocation to the gods,
                 Nor look towards Jove in prayer?

PHILOCTETES: Secure he lay
                 And, scanning heaven with his eyes, he sought
                 The part from whence his father should look down.
                 Then stretching forth his hand he said; "That one
                 For whom the night was joined to night, and day
                 Deferred, is father to me. Whencesoe'er,
                 O father, thou dost look upon thy son,
                 Since either mete of Phoebus, and the race
                 Of Scythians, and every burning strand
                 Where glows the day now praise me; since the earth
                 Has peace, no lands cry out, and none pollute
                 The altars, since no evil thing remains,
                 I pray thee, take this spirit to the stars.
                 Not death, nor hell, nor mournful realm of Dis
                 Could fright me; but to be a shade and pass
                 To those divinities that I o'ercame,
                 O father, makes me blush. Divide the clouds,
                 Lay wide the day that eyes of gods may see
                 Alcides burning. Thou canst close to him
                 The stars and heaven: vainly would one seek
                 To force thy will, O father, but if grief
                 May lift one prayer, then ope the Stygian lake
                 And give me back to death; but prove me first
                 Thy son, let this day make it evident
                 That I am worthy of the stars. All deeds
                 Till now are poor, this day shall bring to light
                 Alcides, or reject him." Having said,
                 He asked for fire. "Up, friend of Hercules,"
                 He said, "be swift, snatch the Oetaean torch.
                 Why trembles thy right hand? What, timorous one,
                 Dost shrink before the dreaded infamy?
                 Give back the quiver, coward, slow, and weak!
                 That hand bend bow of mine? Why pales thy cheek?
                 With face and courage such as thou dost see
                 Alcides wear, apply the torch; base one,
                 Consider him who is about to die.
                 Lo, now my father calls, he opens heaven.
                 I come!" His face was changed; with trembling hand
                 I placed the glowing torch, the flames fled back,

The torches shrank away and shunned his limbs,
But Hercules pursued the flying flames.
Thou wouldst have thought that Athos, Caucasus,
Or Pindus was ablaze; no groan was heard,
But loudly roared the flames. O iron heart!
Huge Typhon placed upon that funeral pyre
Had groaned, and fierce Enceladus himself
Who tore from earth and on his shoulders bore
Mount Ossa. But from out the hot flames' midst
He rose half burned and mangled, gazed unawed.
"Now, mother, thou dost show thyself indeed
Alcides' parent," said he, "thus to stand
Beside his pyre; 'tis meet to mourn him thus."
Amid the smoke and threatening flame he stood
Unmoved and steadfast, shrinking not, but bright,
And spoke encouraging and warning words.
To every ministrant he gave new strength,
You would have thought him eager to be burned.
The people stood amazed and hardly deemed
The flames were flames indeed, so calm his front,
Such majesty was his. He did not seek
To speed his burning, but when he believed
Sufficient fortitude in death was shown,
Into the hottest blaze he dragged the beams
That seemed the least afire, and where the flame
Was brightest there the fearless hero stood.
He veiled his face with flames, his heavy beard
Was bright with fire, the threatening blaze leaped up
And shone about his head; [11] Alcmena groaned
And tore her loosened hair.

Act Five.   Scene II

(Enter ALCMENA *carrying a funeral urn.)*

ALCMENA: Ye gods, stand now in awe of death! So few
                Alcides' ashes, to this little dust
                Has shrunk that giant! Ah, how great a one
                Has fallen, Titan, into nothingness!
                Ah, me, this aged bosom shall receive
                Alcides, here his tomb. Lo, Hercules

Scarce fills his urn, how light for me the weight
Of him who lightly bore the vault of heaven.
O son, to that far realm and Tartarus
Once hast thou journeyed and returned from thence;
Wilt thou perchance again from Styx return?
Not that again with spoil thou mayst return,
And Theseus owe again the light to thee,
But yet, perchance, alone? Can all the world
Placed o'er thy shades suffice to hold thee down?
Or Cerberus be able to constrain?
Wilt thou smite down the gates of Taenarus?
Within what portals shall thy mother pass?
Which way shall death be found? Thou goest now
To Hades, never more to come again.
Why waste the day in tears? Why, wretched life,
Dost thou still bide with me? Why wish for light?
Can I bear Jove another Hercules?
Or will Alcmena by another son
Like him be mother called? O happy, thou,
My Theban husband, thou didst enter in
The realm of Tartarus while still thy son
Was flourishing; perchance the gods of hell
Fear'd when thou camest, since, though not indeed
Alcides' father, thou wast known as such.
What country can I seek in this my age—
I, whom harsh tyrants hate (if any such
Still live)? Me miserable! If a son
Laments a father, let him seek revenge
On me. Let all attack me; if a child
Of wild Busiris or Antaeus lives
And terrifies the tropic zone, I stand
A ready prey; if any seek revenge
For cruel Diomedes' Thracian herd,
Upon my members let the dread flock feed.
Perchance an angered Juno seeks revenge.
All cause for wrath is gone, secure at last,
She shall be free from conquered Hercules.
Her rival yet remains. I cannot pay
The penalty she seeks. My mighty son
Has made his mother terrible. What place
Is left? What land, what kingdom, or what zone
In all the universe will dare defend,
Or to what hiding can a mother go

Who is through thee so famed? Shall I seek out
My land and fallen home? Eurystheus rules
In Argos. Shall I seek the Theban realm?
Ismenus' stream? The couch where chosen once
I once saw Jove? Oh, happy had I felt
Jove's bolt! Oh, would Alcides had been torn
Untimely from my womb! Now comes the hour
To see my son Jove's son through glory gained.
Would that this too were given: to know what fate
Might snatch me hence. O son, what nation lives
That thinks on thee? Ungrateful every race!
Shall I seek Cleon? The Arcadian realm?
The lands ennobled by thy glorious deeds?
There fell the serpent, there the savage birds,
There fell the cruel king, there was o'ercome
By thee the lion which, since thou art dead,
Now dwells in heaven. If earth had gratitude,
All would defend Alcmena for thy sake.
Shall I repair to Thrace and Hebrus' shores?
Those lands were also by thy merits saved,
The stables and the realm were overcome,
The cruel king is prostrate, peace is there.
What land indeed enjoys not peace through thee?
Where shall I seek for thee a sepulchre,
Unhappy, agéd woman that I am?
Let all the world contend for thy remains.
What people, or what temple, or what race
Seek now the ashes of great Hercules?
Who asks, who wishes this, Alcmena's load?
What sepulchre, O son, suffices thee?
What tomb? This whole round world to which thy fame
Shall give thee title! Why afraid, my soul?
Thou hast Alcides' ashes, hast his bones.
Thy aid, thy all-sufficing aid, shall be
His ashes, and his death make kings afraid.

PHILOCTETES: O mother of illustrious Hercules,
Although thy sorrow for thy son is due,
Restrain thy tears; he must not be bewailed,
Nor deeply mourned, whose valour banished death;
His valour is eternal and forbids
That Hercules be mourned.[12]

ALCMENA: My saviour lost,
    Shall I, his mother, cease to mourn for him?

PHILOCTETES: Thou dost not mourn alone, the earth and sea,
    And every place where purple day looks down
    On either ocean from her shining car
    Mourns too.

ALCMENA: O wretched mother! In one son
    How many have I lost! I lacked a realm,
    Yet might have given one. I had no prayer,
    I only of all mothers earth brought forth;
    I asked the gods for nothing while my son
    Still lived. What was there that Alcides' zeal
    Could not bestow? What god could aught deny?
    In that hand lay fulfilment of each wish;
    Whatever Jove refused Alcides gave.
    What mortal mother e'er bore such a child?
    One mother was transformed to stone[3] who stood
    Cut off from all her offspring and bewailed
    Twice seven children. To how great a band
    My son was equal! Until now there lacked
    A great example of sad motherhood:
    Alcmena gives it. Mothers, mourn no more,
    Although persistent grief till now compelled
    Your tears; though heavy sorrow turn to stone,
    Give place to my misfortunes. Up, sad hand,
    Smite now the aged breast! Canst thou enough,
    Thou humbled, aged woman, mourn his loss
    Whom all the world laments? Yet beat thy breast,
    Although thy arms are weary. Though the gods
    Be jealous of thy mourning, call the race
    To mourn with thee.
    Go smite your bosoms for Alcmena's son
    And Jove's; for his conception one day died
    And Eos was delayed for two long nights.
    One greater than the light itself has died.
    All nations, smite your breasts; your tyrants harsh
    He forced to penetrate the Stygian realm
    And put aside the dripping sword; mourn now
    His merits, let the whole world cry aloud.
    Blue Crete, dear land of Thundering Jove, lament
    Alcides, let thy hundred peoples mourn.

Curetes, Corybantes, in your hands
Clash now Idaean weapons, it is right
To mourn him thus; now beat your breasts indeed,
For Hercules is dead; he is not less,
O Crete, than is thy Thunderer himself.
Weep ye Alcides' death, Arcadian race,
A race ere Dian's birth. Reecho blows,
Parrhasian and Nemaean mountain tops,
Let Menala give back the heavy sound.
The bristles scattered on your field demand
Groans for the great Alcides, and the birds
Whose feathers veiled the day, whom his shaft slew.
Argolic peoples weep; Cleonae, weep—
There once my son's right hand the lion slew
That terrified your city. Beat your breasts,
Bistonian matrons, let cold Hebrus' stream
Give back the sound, lament for Hercules;
Your children are no longer born to feed
The bloody stables, on your flesh no more
Shall feast the savage herd. Weep, all ye lands
From fierce Antaeus freed, the region snatched
From cruel Geryon. Beat with me your breasts,
Ye wretched nations, let the blows be heard
By either Tethys. Weep Alcides' death,
O company divine of heaven's swift vault;
My Hercules upon his shoulders bore
Your sky, O gods, when from his load set free
The giant Atlas, who was wont to bear
Olympus and its shining stars, had rest.
Where now, O Jove, thy lofty seat, where now
Thy promised dwelling in the skies? Alas!
Alcides as a mortal died; alas,
As mortal is consumed. How oft he spared
Thy fires, how oft he spared thy thunderbolt!
Ah, deem me Semele and hurl at me
Thy torch! Hast thou, O son, already found
The fields Elysian whither nature calls
The nations? Or does black Styx close the way,
Because of captured Cerberus, and fate
Detain thee at the outer gate of Dis?
What tumult now possesses all the shades?
Flees now the boatman with receding skiff?
Through all the wondering realm of death flees now

Thessalia's Centaur? Does the Hydra fear
And hide its serpents underneath the waves?
Do all thy labours fear thee, O my son?
Ah, no; I am deceived, am mad, I rave;
Nor shades nor manes fear thee, thy left arm
No longer bears th' Argolic lion's spoil,
The fearful pelt with all its tawny mane,
Nor do the wild beast's teeth entrench thy brows;
Thy quiver is another's and thy shafts
A weaker hand lets fly; unarmed thou goest,
O son, through Hades, never to return.

Act Five.   Scene III

(The voice of HERCULES *is heard from above.)*

HERCULES: I hold a seat within the heavenly realm;
Why with thy mourning dost thou bid me feel
Once more the pang of death? I pray thee, spare!
Already had my valour made a way
Up to the stars, yes, to the very gods.

ALCMENA: Whence, whence the sound that strikes our startled ear?
Whence comes the sound forbids my tears? I know
That Chaos is o'ercome. Dost thou return,
O son, again from Styx? Not once alone
Is cruel death subdued? Hast thou again
Been conqueror over death, and Charon's boat.
And hell's sad pools? Does languid Acheron
Afford a passage and permit return
To thee alone? Nor even after death
The fates constrain thee? Or does Pluto close
For thee the way, and tremble for his throne?
I surely saw thee on the blazing woods,
When raged the giant flames against the sky;
Why does the far abode no longer hold
Thy shade? Why do the phantoms feel dread fear?
Art thou a shade too terrible for Dis?

HERCULES (*as his form takes shape above*): The fear of dark Cocytus
        held me not,
The dread boat has not borne my shade across;

Forbear thy mourning, mother; once indeed
I saw the land of death, whate'er of man
I may have had was purged away by fire.
The part my father gave is borne to heaven;
Thy part was given to the flames. Weep not
As one who weeps a deedless son, 'tis meet
To mourn th' unworthy; valour starward tends,
But fear towards death. O mother, from the stars
Alcides speaks. To thee the cruel king,
Eurystheus, soon shall pay due penalty;
Borne in thy car thou shalt lift up proud head.
'Tis meet that I should seek celestial climes;
Alcides once again has conquered hell.
                    (HERCULES *vanishes.*)

ALCMENA: Stay, but a moment stay! He's passed from sight,
He has departed, he is starward borne.
Am I deceived, or do I dream I saw
My son? My sad heart is incredulous.
Thou art a god, the heavens evermore
Shall hold thee; in thy triumph I believe.
The Theban realm I'll seek and there will sing
The glory of the new divinity.

CHORUS: Never shall glorious valour be borne down
To Stygian shades, the brave forever live,
Nor shall the cruel fates through Lethe's stream
E'er drag them; but when comes the final hour
Of life's last day, then glory shall lay wide
The pathway to the gods. Be present still,
Thou mighty victor over savage beasts,
Thou who hast given peace to all the world;
Now from whatever place, behold our land,
And if a monster with new face should shake
The world with terror, with thy three-forked bolts
Break him in pieces, hurl thy lightning shafts
More boldly than thy father Jove himself.

Miss Harris' translation has been slightly modified in the following lines: 896, 950, 980-981, 1485, 1490, 1604, 1744, 1821-1823, 1961.

1. This refers to the girdle of the Amazon queen, Hippolyte, which Hercules secured as one of his labours. The Amazons dwelt on the river Thermodon.

2. Pelorus was a promontory in Sicily opposite Italy (Hesperia).

3. This refers to Niobe who was changed to stone on Sipylus, a mountain in Asia Minor.

4. The sister of Priam was Hesione, rescued from a sea-monster by Hercules and captured by him when he took Troy; he later gave her to Telamon.

5. The Lydian maid was Omphale, queen of Lydia; Hercules was in bondage to her for three years.

6. This is an allusion to the Bacchic mysteries.

7. The boy who drove his father's car was Phaethon, son of Apollo.

8. The tragic story of Hercules' slaying of his wife Megara and his sons is the theme of Seneca's *Mad Hercules*.

9. This refers to Medea, the wife of Jason, whose deeds are related in Seneca's *Medea*.

10. This refers to Deianira who has just killed herself offstage.

11. Miss Harris follows Leo in deleting two verses at this point. The conclusion of Philoctetes' speech is as follows (Miller's translation):

> "He did not close his eyes. But what is this?
> 'Tis sad Alcmena. With what signs of woe
> She makes her way, while in her breast she bears
> The pitiful remains of Hercules."

12. Peiper and Richter assign this and the following speech of Philoctetes to Hyllus.

X
OCTAVIA

Characters in the Play

OCTAVIA, *stepsister and wife of* NERO
NURSE *of* OCTAVIA
CHORUS OF ROMANS, *sympathetic with* OCTAVIA
SENECA, *former tutor of* NERO, *and later one of his chief counselors*
NERO, *emperor of Rome*
PREFECT *of Roman soldiers*
GHOST OF AGRIPPINA, *mother of* NERO, *slain by him*
NURSE *of* POPPAEA
POPPAEA, *mistress and afterward wife of* NERO
CHORUS OF WOMEN, *attached to the interests of the court*
A MESSENGER

INTRODUCTION

THE *Octavia* enjoys a unique distinction, for it is the only *fabula praetexta,* or Roman historical play, which has survived to our day. Historical dramas had been written by Naevius, Ennius, Pacuvius, Accius, and others, but the fragments of these plays are too brief to give an adequate idea of their character or content. The *Clastidium* of Naevius celebrated the victory of Marcellus over the Gauls in 222 B.C.; the *Paulus* of Pacuvius honoured the exploits of Lucius Aemilius Paulus who conquered Perseus, king of Macedonia, in the battle of Pydna in 168 B.C.; the *Brutus* of Accius dealt with the expulsion of the Tarquins and the establishment of the republic, and may have been written in honour of Decimus Junius Brutus, consul in 138 B.C. Apparently these earlier historical dramas were plays of occasion, for the most part, written to honour outstanding Romans, and acted either at their triumphs or at their funerals.

The *Octavia* gives in dramatic form a picture of historical events of the year 62 A.D.—Nero's divorce of his wife Octavia and his marriage to Poppaea. There are numerous references also to the reign of the emperor Claudius, who, after the disgraceful conduct and death of his wife Messalina, married his niece Agrippina and adopted her son by a former marriage. Agrippina was a woman of unscrupulous ambition; she had her son Nero preferred to Claudius' own son Britannicus, and Claudius' daughter Octavia was married to Nero when she was only a child. Upon the sudden death of Claudius in 54 A.D. Nero became emperor. Britannicus, a potential rival to the throne, was killed soon after. The first five years of Nero's reign were quiet and peaceful, for Nero submitted to the guidance of his counselors, Seneca and Burrus. He was unwilling, however, to endure the personal domination of his mother and in 59 A.D. had her killed. As the influence of his mistress Poppaea increased, the rejection of his wife who detested him became inevitable and led to the situation described in the play. Both the action of the drama itself and the frequent references to the events of the preceding decade seem historically accurate and parallel with amazing fidelity the accounts of the period given by Tacitus and other ancient historians.

Although the *Octavia* has come down with the tragedies of Seneca, it seems extremely doubtful if Seneca is the author of the play. Several arguments have been advanced against Senecan authorship: Seneca would hardly have put himself into the play as a character; it would have been dangerous to portray Nero in such an unfavourable light; the ghost of Agrippina alludes to Nero's death in terms that could only have been written after his downfall in 68 A.D. and therefore could not have been foreseen by Seneca who committed suicide in 65 A.D. None of these arguments is necessarily conclusive; the so-called anachronisms in particular do not bear careful scrutiny, for Agrippina's ghost seems merely to be foreshadowing dire punishment for the tyrant both in this world and the next. In many respects the play is very Senecan—the ghost, the tyrant, the two nurses, the stichomythia, the Stoic thought, the lengthy lamentations are all features that are characteristic of Senecan tragedy, but these features could equally well be the result of imitation by an admirer of Seneca. In language and style, in the metrical simplicity of the choral odes, the play is less similar to Seneca's tragedies; also, there are fewer rhetorical devices and fewer mythological allusions. Another unusual feature of the play is the presence of several recurring themes, e.g. the power of Cupid, the fatal ship of Agrippina, the comparison of Octavia, sister-wife of Nero, to Juno, sister-wife of Jupiter. It is not impossible that Seneca wrote the play, which could have been published after his death, and, presumably, after the death of Nero. But it seems preferable to assume, as do most scholars, that the *Octavia* was composed soon after Nero's death by a dramatist who had been an eye-witness of the events described, and who, in his portrayal of the pitiful fate of Octavia, imitated the technique and structure of Senecan tragedy.

The play has been severely criticised: D. C. Stuart writes, "It offends almost every canon of dramatic art. The protagonists and antagonists never meet on the stage. . . . There is no obligatory scene. The play is a succession of elegiac scenes, ghost scenes, vengeance scenes, and messengering." A careful reading of the play will reveal the injustice of such a sweeping criticism. The subject is not an undramatic one, as Léon Herrmann points out. The divorce of Octavia leads to an uprising of the people against Nero and Poppaea, and genuine suspense is aroused concerning the outcome of the revolt. The fears and forebodings of Poppaea serve to heighten the tension. In the favour of the citizens for Octavia there is the germ of a real dramatic conflict which the playwright could have developed far more successfully, had he not devoted so much space to the lamentations of Octavia concerning her fate. C. L. Thompson says, in the introduction to her edition of the *Octavia*, "The vitalising theme of the play is justice, the rights of individuals and of the people to a square deal. It is not given them in the play; the tragic denial of it to the chief character, and the dismal failure of the people to make their protest heard make the appeal of the play carry as no successful consummation could." Furthermore, we should guard against viewing Octavia merely as a victim or martyr and Nero as a villain or "a heartless monster," as J. W. Duff calls him. Octavia was unbending in her hatred of Nero and should perhaps bear some responsibility for her tragic fate. It is possible to view Nero also as a tragic character. He lived in constant fear of conspiracy and assassination, and his own words in the play give the keynote to his character:

"Let him be just whose heart is free from fear."

The author of the *Octavia,* whoever he may have been, has failed to make the most of the possibilities of his theme, but his play is more successful as a tragedy than many critics admit.

OCTAVIA

(SCENE:—NERO'S *palace in Rome.*)

Act One.   Scene I

(*Enter* OCTAVIA.)

OCTAVIA: Now doth the flushing dawn from heaven drive
             The wandering stars; the sun mounts into sight
             With radiant beams, and brings the world once more
             The light of day. Up, then, my heavy soul,
             With grievous cares o'erburdened, and resume
             Thy woe; out-wail the sea-bred Halcyons,
             And those sad birds of old Pandion's house;
             For this thy lot is heavier far than theirs.
             O mother, constant source of tears to me,
             Hear now thy woeful daughter's sad complaints,
             If aught of sense remains among the shades.
             Oh, that the grizzly Clotho long ago,
             With her own hand had clipt my thread of life!
             Through blinding tears I saw thy bleeding wounds,
             Thy features sprinkled with defiling blood.
             Oh, light of day, abhorrent to my eyes!
             From that dread hour I hate the day's pure light
             More than the night's dark gloom; for daily now
             Must I endure a cruel stepdame's rule,
             Must daily bear her hateful looks and words.
             She, she the baleful fury fiend it was
             Who at my marriage rites bore torches lit
             With hellish fires; 'twas she who wrought thy death,
             O wretched father, whom but yesterday
             The whole world owned as lord on land and sea;
             To whom the Britain bowed, though ne'er before
             Had he a Roman master known or owned.

Alas, my father, by thy wife's fell plots
Thou liest low, and I and all thy house
Like captives groan beneath the tyrant's sway.
(OCTAVIA *departs to her chamber.*)

Act One.   Scene II

(*Enter the* NURSE.)

NURSE: Who stands in wonder, smitten by the gloss
And splendour of a princely court, amazed
At sight of easy-won prosperity,
Let him behold how, at the stroke of fate,
The house of Claudius is overthrown,
To whose control the world was subjugate,
Whose rule an ocean, long to sway unknown,
Obeyed, and bore our ships with subject will.
Lo, he, who first the savage Britains curbed,
And filled an unknown ocean with his fleet,
And passed in safety 'mid barbaric tribes—
By his own wife's impiety was slain.
And she was destined by her son to fall,
Whose hapless brother lies already slain
By poison's hand, whose sister-wife alone
Is left to mourn.[1] Nor may she hide her grief,
By bitter wrath impelled to speak. She shuns
Her cruel lord's society, and, fired
With equal hate, with mutual loathing burns.
Our pious faithfulness in vain consoles
Her grieving heart; her cruel woes reject
Our aid; the noble passion of her soul
Will not be ruled, but grows on ills renewed.
Alas, my fears forebode some desperate deed,
Which may the gods forbid!

Act One.   Scene III

OCTAVIA (*heard speaking from within her chamber*): O fate of mine,
that can no equal know!
Thy woes, Electra, were no match for these;

For thou couldst soothe with tears the grief thou hadst
For thy dear father's fall; thou couldst avenge
The murder by thy brother's ready hand,[2]
Who by thy piety was saved from death,
And whom thy faith concealed. But me base fear
Forbids to weep my parents reft away
By cruel fate; forbids to weep the death
Of him, my brother, who my sole hope was,
My fleeting comfort of so many woes.
And now, surviving but to suffer still,
I live, the shadow of a noble name.

NURSE: Behold, the voice of my sad foster-child
Falls on my list'ning ears. Slow steps of age,
Why haste ye not within her chamber there?
(Starts to enter the chamber, but is met by OCTAVIA *coming forth.)*

OCTAVIA: Within thy bosom let me weep, dear nurse,
Thou ever trusty witness of my grief.

NURSE: What day shall free thee from thy woes, poor child?

OCTAVIA: The day that sends me to the Stygian shades.

NURSE: May heaven keep such dark omens far away!

OCTAVIA: 'Tis not thy prayers, but fate that shapes my life.

NURSE: But God will bring thy life to better days.
Do thou but be appeased, and win thy lord
With mild obedience.

OCTAVIA: I'll sooner tame
The savage lion's heart, the tiger's rage,
Than curb that brutal tyrant's cruel soul.
He hates all sons of noble blood, and gods
And men he sets at naught; nor can he bear
That high estate to which along the paths
Of shameful crime his impious mother led;
For though it shames him now, ungrateful one,
To hold the sceptre which his mother gave;
And though by death he has requited her:
Still will the glory of the empire won
Belong to her for centuries to come.

NURSE: Restrain these words that voice thy raging heart,
And check thy tongue's too rash and thoughtless speech.

OCTAVIA: Though I should bear what may be borne, my woes,
            Save by a cruel death, could not be ended.
            For, since my mother was by murder slain,
            And my father taken off by crime most foul,
            Robbed of my brother, overwhelmed with woe,
            Oppressed with sadness, by my husband scorned,
            Degraded to the level of my slave,[3]
            I find this life no more endurable.
            My heart doth tremble, not with fear of death,
            But slander base, employed to work my death.[4]
            Far from my name and fate be that foul blot.
            For death itself—Oh, 'twould be sweet to die;
            For 'tis a punishment far worse than death,
            To live in contact with the man I loathe,
            To see the tyrant's face all passion puffed,
            And fierce with rage, to kiss my deadliest foe.
            That I should fear his nod, obey his will,
            My grief, resentful, will not suffer me,
            Since by his hand my brother was destroyed,
            Whose kingdom he usurps, and boasts himself
            The author of that shameful deed. How oft
            Before my eyes does that sad image come,
            My brother's ghost, when I have gone to rest,
            And sleep has closed my eyelids faint with tears!
            Now in his weakling hand he brandishes
            The smoking torch, and violently assails
            His brother to his face; now, trembling sore,
            He flees for refuge to my sheltering arms.
            His foe pursues, and, as his victim clings
            Convulsively to me, he thrusts his sword
            With murderous intent through both our sides.
            Then, all a-tremble, do I start awake,
            And in my waking sense renew my fear.
            Add to these cares a rival,[5] arrogant,
            Who queens it in the spoils of this our house;
            At whose behest the mother was enticed
            To that fell ship which should have carried her
            To Orcus' depths; but when o'er ocean's waves
            She triumphed, he, than ocean's waves more harsh
            And pitiless, despatched her with the sword.
            Amid such deeds, what hopes of peace have I?
            O'erblown with hate, triumphant, doth my rival
            Within my very chamber's hold defy me;

With deadly malice doth she blaze against me,
And as the price of her adulterous sweets,
Doth she demand that he, my husband, give
My life, his lawful wife's, in sacrifice.
Oh, rise thou, father, from the gloomy shades,
And help thy daughter who invokes thine aid;
Or else cleave wide the earth to Stygian depths,
And let me plunge at last to shelter there.

NURSE: In vain dost thou invoke thy father's soul,
Poor child, in vain; for there among the shades
He little thinks upon his offspring here;
Who, when in life, unto his own true son
Preferred the offspring of another's blood,
And to himself in most incestuous bonds
And rites unhallowed joined his brother's child.
From this foul source has flowed a stream of crime:
Of murder, treachery, the lust of power,
The thirst for blood. Thy promised husband fell,
A victim slain to grace that wedding feast,
Lest, joined with thee, he should too mighty grow.
Oh, monstrous deed! Silanus, charged with crime,
Was slain to make a bridal offering,
And stained the household gods with guiltless blood.
And then this alien comes, oh, woe is me,
And by his mother's wiles usurps the house,
Made son-in-law and son to the emperor,
A youth of temper most unnatural,
To impious crime inclined, whose passion's flame
His mother fanned, and forced thee at the last
In hated wedlock into his embrace.
Emboldened by this notable success,
She dared to dream of wider sovereignty.
What tongue can tell the changing forms of crime,
Her impious hopes, her cozening treacheries,
Who seeks the throne along the ways of sin?
Then Piety with trembling haste withdrew,
And Fury through the empty palace halls
With baleful tread resounded, and defiled
The sacred images with Stygian brands.
All holy laws of nature and of heaven
In mad abandon did she set at naught.
She mingled deadly poison for her lord,

And she herself by the impious mandate fell
Of her own son. Thou too dost lifeless lie,
Poor youth, forever to be mourned by us,
Ill-starred Britannicus, so late, in life,
The brightest star of this our firmament,
The prop and stay of our imperial house;
But now, oh, woe is me, a heap of dust,
Of unsubstantial dust, a flitting shade.
Nay, even thy stepmother's cruel cheeks
Were wet with tears, when on the funeral pyre
She placed thy form and saw the flames consume
Thy limbs and face fair as the wingéd god's.

OCTAVIA: Me, too, he must destroy—or fall by me.

NURSE: But nature has not given thee strength to slay.

OCTAVIA: Yet anguish, anger, pain, distress of soul,
The ecstasy of grief will give me strength.

NURSE: Nay, by compliance, rather, win thy lord.

OCTAVIA: That thus he may restore my brother slain?

NURSE: That thou thyself mayst go unscathed of death;
That thou by thine own offspring mayst restore
Thy father's falling house.

OCTAVIA: This princely house
Expects an heir, 'tis true; but not from me,[6]
For I am doomed to meet my brother's fate.

NURSE: Console thy heart with this, that thou art dear
Unto the populace, who love thee well.

OCTAVIA: That thought doth soothe, but cannot cure my grief.

NURSE: Their power availeth much.

OCTAVIA: The prince's more.

NURSE: He will regard his wife.

OCTAVIA: My foe forbids.

NURSE: But she is scorned by all.

OCTAVIA: Yet loved by him.

NURSE: She is not yet his wife.

OCTAVIA: But soon will be,
           And mother of his child, his kingdom's heir.

NURSE: The fire of youthful passion glows at first
           With heat impetuous; but soon abates,
           And vanishes like flickering tongues of flame.
           Unhallowed love cannot for long endure;
           But pure and lasting is the love inspired
           By chaste and wifely faith. She who dared first
           To violate thy bed, and held so long
           Thy husband's heart in thrall, herself a slave,
           That same one feared—

OCTAVIA: One placed above herself.

NURSE: Subdued and crushed she builds memorials
           That show how deep her fear.[7] Poppaea, too,
           Shall wingéd Cupid, false and fickle god,
           Abandon and betray. Though face and form
           Be passing fair, though beauty vaunt herself,
           And boast her power, still are her triumphs brief,
           Her joys a passing dream.
                                  Nay, Juno's self,
           Though queen of heaven, endured such grief as thine,
           When he, her lord, and father of the gods,
           Stole from her side to seek in mortal forms
           The love of mortal maids. Now, in his need,
           He dons the snowy plumage of a swan;
           Now hornéd seems, like a Sidonian bull;
           And now a glorious, golden shower he falls,
           And rests within the arms of Danaë.
           Nor yet is Juno's sum of woe complete:
           The sons of Leda glitter in the sky
           In starry splendour; Bacchus proudly stands
           Beside his father on Olympus' height;
           Divine Alcides hath to Hebe's charms
           Attained, and fears stern Juno's wrath no more.
           Her very son-in-law hath he become
           Whom once she hated most. Yet in her heart
           Deep down she pressed her grief, and wisely won,
           By mild compliance to his wayward will,
           Her husband's love again. And now the queen,
           Secure at last from rivalry, holds sway
           Alone, within the Thunderer's heart. No more,

By mortal beauty smitten, does he leave
His royal chambers in the vaulted sky.
Thou, too, on earth, another Juno art,
The wife and sister of our mighty lord.
Then be thou wise as she, make show of love,
And hide thy crushing sorrows with a smile.

OCTAVIA: The savage seas shall sooner mate with stars,
And fire with water, heav'n with gloomy hell,
Glad light with shades, and day with dewy night,
Than shall my soul in amity consort
With his black heart, most foul and impious:
Too mindful I of my poor brother's ghost.
And oh, that he who guides the heavenly worlds,
Who shakes the realms of earth with deadly bolts,
And with his dreadful thunders awes our minds,
Would whelm in fiery death this murderous prince.
Strange portents have we seen: the comet dire,[8]
Shining with baleful light, his glowing train
Far gleaming in the distant northern sky,
Where slow Bootes, numb with arctic frosts,
Directs his ponderous wagon's endless rounds.
The very air is tainted by the breath
Of this destructive prince; and for his sake
The stars, resentful, threaten to destroy
The nations which so dire a tyrant rules.
Not such a pest was impious Typhon huge,
Whom earth, in wrath and scorn of heaven, produced.
This scourge is more destructive far than he.
He is the bitter foe of gods and men,
Who drives the heavenly beings from their shrines,
And from their native land the citizens;
Who from his brother took the breath of life,
And drained his mother's blood.
                              And does he live,
This guilty wretch, and draw his tainted breath?
O Jove, thou high-exalted father, why
Dost thou so oft with thine imperial hand
Thy darts invincible at random hurl?
Why from his guilty head dost thou withhold
Thy hand of vengeance? Oh, that he might pay
For all his crimes the fitting penalty,
This grafted scion of Domitius,

This Nero, heartless tyrant of the world,
Which he beneath the yoke of bondage holds,
This moral blot upon a noble name!

NURSE: Unworthy he to be thy mate, I know;
But, dearest child, to fate and fortune yield,
Lest thou excite thy savage husband's wrath.
Perchance some god will come to right thy wrongs,
And on thy life some happier day will dawn.

OCTAVIA: That may not be. Long since, our ill-starred house
Has groaned beneath the heavy wrath of heaven.
That wrath at first my hapless mother felt,
Whom Venus cursed with lust insatiate;
For she, with heedless, impious passion fired,
Unmindful of her absent lord, of us,
Her guiltless children, and the law's restraints,
In open day another husband wed.[9]
To that fell couch avenging Fury came
With streaming locks and serpents intertwined,
And quenched those stolen wedding fires in blood.
For with destructive rage, on murder bent,
She fired the prince's heart; and at his word,
Ah, woe is me, my ill-starred mother fell,
And, dying, doomed me to perpetual grief.
For after her in quick succession came
Her husband and her son; and this our house,
Already falling, was to ruin plunged.

NURSE: Forbear with pious tears to renew thy grief,
And do not so disturb thy father's shade,
Who for his rage has bitterly atoned.
(OCTAVIA *and the* NURSE *go into the palace.*)

Act One.   Scene IV

(*Enter the* CHORUS OF ROMANS, *sympathetic with* OCTAVIA.)

CHORUS: False prove the rumour that of late
To our ears has come! May its vaunted threats
Fall fruitless out and of no avail!
May no new wife invade the bed

Of our royal prince; may Octavia, born
Of the Claudian race, maintain her right
And bear us a son, the pledge of peace,
In which the joyful world shall rest,
And Rome preserve her glorious name.
Most mighty Juno holds the lot
By fate assigned—her brother's mate;
But this our Juno, sister, wife
Of our august prince, why is she driven
From her father's court? Of what avail
Her faith, her father deified,
Her love and spotless chastity?
We, too, of our former master's fame
Have been unmindful, and his child
At the hest of cringing fear betrayed.
Not so of old: then Rome could boast
Of manly virtue, martial blood.
There lived a race of heroes then
Who curbed the power of haughty kings
And drove them forth from Rome; and thee,
O maiden,[10] slain by thy father's hand,
Lest thou shouldst in slavery's bonds be held,
And lest foul lust its victorious will
Should work on thee, did well avenge.
Thee, too, a bloody war avenged,
O chaste Lucretia; for thou,
By the lust of an impious tyrant stained,
With wretched hand didst seek to cleanse
Those stains by thy innocent blood.
Then Tullia with her guilty lord,
Base Tarquin, dared an impious deed,
Whose penalty they paid; for she
Over the limbs of her murdered sire,
A heartless child, drove cruel wheels,
And left his corpse unburied there.
Such deeds of dire impiety
Our age has known, our eyes have seen,
When the prince on the mighty Tyrrhene deep
In a fatal bark his mother sent,
By guile ensnared.[11]
The sailors at his bidding haste
To leave the peaceful harbour's arms;
And soon the rougher waves resound

Beneath their oars, and far away
Upon the deep the vessel glides;
When suddenly the reeling bark
With loosened beams yawns open wide,
And drinks the briny sea.
A mighty shout to heaven goes,
With women's lamentations filled,
And death stalks dire before the eyes
Of all. Each seeks to save himself.
Some naked cling upon the planks
Of the broken ship and fight the floods,
While others swimming seek the shore.
But most, alas, a watery death
By fate awaits. Then did the queen
In mad despair her garments rend;
Her comely locks she tore, and tears
Fell streaming down her grieving cheeks.
At last, with hope of safety gone,
With wrath inflamed, by woes o'ercome,
"Dost thou, O son, make this return,"
She cried, "for that great boon I gave?
Such death I merit, I confess,
Who bore such monstrous child as thou,
Who gave to thee the light of day,
And in my madness raised thee high
To Caesar's name and Caesar's throne.
Oh, rise from deepest Acheron,
My murdered husband, feast thine eyes
Upon my righteous punishment;
For I brought death to thee, poor soul,
And to thy son. See, see, I come,
Deep down to meet thy grieving shade;
And there, as I have merited,
Shall I unburied lie, o'erwhelmed
By the raging sea." Even as she spoke,
The lapping waves broke o'er her lips,
And deep she plunged below. Anon
She rises from the briny depths,
And, stung by fear of death, she strives
With frenzied hands to conquer fate;
But, spent with fruitless toil at last,
She yields and waits the end. But lo,
In hearts which in trembling silence watch,

Faith triumphs over deadly fear,
And to their mistress, spent and wan
With fruitless buffetings, they dare
To lend their aid with cheering words
And helping hands.
                    But what avails
To escape the grasp of the savage sea?
By the sword of the son is she doomed to die,
Whose monstrous deed posterity
Will scarce believe. With rage and grief
Inflamed, he raves that still she lives,
His mother, snatched from the wild sea's jaws,
And doubles crime on impious crime.
Bent on his wretched mother's death,
He brooks no tarrying of fate.
His willing creatures work his will,
And in the hapless woman's breast
The fatal sword is plunged; but she
To that fell minister of death
Appeals with dying tongue: "Nay here,
Here rather strike the murderous blow,
Here sheathe thy sword, deep in the womb
Which such a monster bore."
So spake the dying queen, her words
And groans commingling. So at last
Through gaping wounds her spirit fled
In grief and agony.

Act Two.   Scene I

(*Enter* SENECA.)

SENECA (*alone*): Why hast thou, potent Fate, with flattering looks,
            Exalted me, contented with my lot,
            That so from this great height I might descend
            With heavier fall, and wider prospect see
            Of deadly fears? Ah, better was I, hid
            Far from the stinging lash of envy's tongue,
            Amid the lonely crags of Corsica.
            There was my spirit free to act at will,
            Was master of itself, had time to think

And meditate at length each favourite theme.
Oh, what delight, than which none greater is,
Of all that mother nature hath produced,
To watch the heavens, the bright sun's sacred rounds,
The heavenly movements and the changing night,
The moon's full orb with wandering stars begirt,
The far-effulgent glory of the sky!
And is it growing old, this structure vast,
Doomed to return to groping nothingness?
Then must that final doomsday be at hand,
That shall by heaven's fall o'erwhelm a race
So impious, that thus the world may see
A newer race of men, a better stock,
Which once the golden reign of Saturn knew.
Then virgin Justice, holy child of heaven,
In mercy ruled the world; the race of men
Knew naught of war, the trumpet's savage blare,
The clang of arms; not yet were cities hedged
With ponderous walls; the way was free to all,
And free to all the use of everything.
The earth, untilled, spread wide her fertile lap,
The happy mother of a pious stock.
Then rose another race of sterner mould;
Another yet to curious arts inclined,
But pious still; a fourth of restless mood,
Which lusted to pursue the savage beasts,
To draw the fishes from their sheltering waves
With net or slender pole, to snare the birds,
To force the headstrong bullocks to endure
The bondage of the yoke, to plow the earth
Which never yet had felt the share's deep wound,
And which in pain and grief now hid her fruits
Within her sacred bosom's safer hold.
Now deep within the bowels of the earth
Did that debased, unfilial age intrude;
And thence it dug the deadly iron and gold,
And soon it armed its savage hands for war.
It fixed the bounds of realms, constructed towns,
Fought for its own abodes, or threat'ning strove
To plunder those of others as a prize.
Then did abandoned Justice, heavenly maid,
In terror flee the earth, the bestial ways
Of men, their hands with bloody slaughter stained,

And, fixed in heaven, now shines among the stars.
Then lust of war increased, and greed for gold,
Throughout the world; and luxury arose,
That deadliest of evils, luring pest,
To whose fell powers new strength and force were given
By custom long observed, and precedent
Of evil into worser evil led.
This flood of vice, through many ages dammed,
In ours has burst its bounds and overflowed.
By this dire age we're fairly overwhelmed—
An age when crime sits regnant on the throne,
Impiety stalks raging, unrestrained;
Foul lust, with all unbridled power, is queen,
And luxury long since with greedy hands
Has snatched the boundless riches of the world,
That she with equal greed may squander them.
But see, with frenzied step and savage mien,
The prince approaches. How I fear his will.

Act Two.   Scene II

(*Enter* NERO, *followed by the* PREFECT.)

NERO (*to* PREFECT): Speed my commands: send forth a messenger
Who straight shall bring me here the severed heads
Of Plautus and of Sulla.

PREFECT: Good, my lord;
Without delay I'll speed me to the camp.
(*The* PREFECT *departs.*)

SENECA: One should not rashly judge against his friends.

NERO: Let him be just whose heart is free from fear.

SENECA: But mercy is a sovereign cure for fear.

NERO: A ruler's part is to destroy his foes.

SENECA: A ruler's better part, to save his friends.

NERO: A mild old man's advice is fit for boys.

SENECA: Still more does hot young manhood need the rein—

NERO: I deem that at this age we're wise enough.

SENECA: That on thy deed the heavenly gods may smile.

NERO: Thou fool, shall I fear gods myself can make?[12]

SENECA: Fear this the more, that so great power is thine.

NERO: My royal fortune grants all things to me.

SENECA: But trust her cautiously; she may deceive.

NERO: A fool is he who does not what he may.

SENECA: To do, not what he may, but ought, wins praise.

NERO: The crowd spurns sluggish men.

SENECA: The hated, slays.

NERO: Yet swords protect a prince.

SENECA: Still better, faith.

NERO: A Caesar should be feared.

SENECA: And more be loved.

NERO: But men must fear.

SENECA: Enforced commands are hard.

NERO: Let them obey our laws.

SENECA: Make better laws—

NERO: I'll be the judge.

SENECA: Which all men may approve.

NERO: The sword shall force respect.

SENECA: May heaven forbid!

NERO: Shall I then tamely let them seek my blood,
That suddenly despised and unavenged,
I may be taken off? Though exiled far,
The stubborn spirits are not broken yet
Of Plautus and of Sulla. Still their rage
Persistent spurs their friends to seek my death;
For still have they the people's love in Rome,
Which ever nourishes the exile's hopes.
Then let the sword remove my enemies;

My hateful wife shall die, and follow him,
That brother whom she loves. The high must fall.

SENECA: How fair a thing it is to be the first
Among great men, to think for fatherland,
To spare the weak, to hold the hand of power
From deeds of blood, to give wrath time to think,
Give rest to a weary world, peace to the age.
This is the noblest part; by this high path
Is heaven sought. So did Augustus first,
The father of his country, gain the stars,
And as a god is worshipped at the shrines.
Yet he was long by adverse fortune tossed
On land and sea, in battle's deadly chance,
Until his father's foes he recompensed.
But fortune hath to thee in peaceful guise
Bent her divinity; with unstained hand
Hath she the reins of government bestowed,
And given world-dominion to thy nod.
Sour hate is overcome, and in its stead
Is filial harmony; the senate, knights,
All orders yield obedience to thy will;
For in the fathers' judgment and the prayers
Of humbler folk, thou art the arbiter
Of peace, the god of human destinies,
Ordained to rule the world by right divine.
Thy country's father thou. This sacred name
Doth suppliant Rome beseech thee to preserve,
And doth commend her citizens to thee.

NERO: It is the gift of heaven that haughty Rome,
Her people, and her senate bow to me,
And that my terror doth extort those prayers
And servile words from their unwilling lips.
To save the citizens! Seditious men,
Who ever 'gainst their land and prince conspire,
Puffed up with pride of race—sheer madness that,
When all my enemies one word of mine
Can doom to death. Base Brutus raised his hand
To slay that prince from whom he had his all;
And he, who never 'mid the shock of arms
Had been o'ercome, the world's great conqueror,
Who trod, a very Jove, the lofty paths
Of honour, he was slain by impious hands—

Of *citizens*! What streams of blood hath Rome,
So often rent by civil strife, beheld!
That very saint of thine, Augustus' self,
Who, as thou said'st but now, did merit heaven
By piety—how many noble men
Did he destroy, in lusty youth, in age,
At home, abroad, when, spurred by mortal fear,
They fled their household gods and that fell sword
Of the Triumvirate,[13] consigned to death
Upon those mindful tablets' fatal lists.
The grieving parents saw their severed heads
Upon the rostra set, but dared not weep
Their hapless sons; the forum reeked with blood,
And gore down all those rotting faces dripped.
Nor this the end of slaughter and of death:
Long did the plains of grim Philippi feed
The ravenous birds and prowling beasts of prey;
While ships and men, in deadly conflict met,
Beneath Sicilia's waters were engulfed.
The whole world trembled with the shock of arms;
And now, when all was lost, with fleeing ships,
That mighty leader sought the distant Nile,
Doomed soon himself to perish there. And thus,
Once more incestuous Egypt drank the blood
Of Rome's great captains.[14] Now his flitting shade
Is hovering there; and there is civil strife,
So long and impious, at last interred.
Now did the weary victor sheathe his sword,
All blunted with the savage blows he gave,
And held his empire with the rein of fear.
He lived in safety 'neath the ample shield
Of loyal guards; and when his end was come,
The pious mandate of his son proclaimed
Him god, and at the temples' sacred shrines
Was he adored. So shall the stars expect
My godhead too, if first I seize and slay
With sword relentless all who bear me hate,
And on a worthy offspring found my house.

SENECA: But she will fill thy house with noble sons,
That heaven-born glory of the Claudian stock,
Who by the will of fate was wed to thee,
As Juno to her brother Jove was given.

NERO: A child of hers would stain my noble line,
            For she herself was of a harlot born;
            And more—her heart was never linked to me.

SENECA: In tender years is faith not manifest,
            When love, by shame o'ercome, conceals its fires.

NERO: This I myself long trusted, but in vain,
            Though she was clearly of unloving heart,
            And every look betrayed her hate of me.
            At length, in angry grief, I sought revenge;
            And I have now a worthy wife obtained,
            In race and beauty blessed, before whose charms
            Minerva, Venus, Juno—all would bow.

SENECA: But honour, wifely faith, and modesty—
            These should the husband seek, for these alone,
            The priceless treasures of the heart and soul,
            Remain perpetual; but beauty's flower
            Doth fade and languish with each passing day.

NERO: On her has heaven all its charms bestowed,
            And fate has given her from her birth to me.

SENECA: But love will fail; do not too rashly trust.

NERO: Shall he give way, that tyrant of the skies,
            Whom Jove, the Thunderer, cannot remove,
            Who lords it over savage seas, the realms
            Of gloomy Dis, and draws the gods to earth?

SENECA: 'Tis by our human error that we paint
            Love as a god, wingéd, implacable,
            And arm his sacred hands with darts and bow,
            Assign him blazing torches, count him son
            Of fostering Venus and of Vulcan. Nay,
            But love is of the heart's compelling power,
            A fond and cozening passion of the soul;
            Of hot youth is it born, and in the lap
            Of ease and luxury, 'midst fortune's joys,
            Is fostered. But it sickens straight and dies
            When you no longer feed and fondle it.

NERO: I deem the primal source of life is this,
            The joy of love; and it can never die,
            Since by sweet love, which soothes e'en savage breasts,

The human race is evermore renewed.
This god shall bear for me the wedding torch,
And join me with Poppaea in his bonds.

SENECA: The people's grief could scarce endure to see
That marriage, nor would piety permit.

NERO: Shall I alone avoid what all may do?

SENECA: The state from loftiest souls expects the best.

NERO: I fain would see if, broken by my power,
This rashly cherished favour will not yield.

SENECA: 'Tis better calmly to obey the state.

NERO: Ill fares the state, when commons govern kings.

SENECA: They justly chafe who pray without avail.

NERO: When prayers do not avail, should force be sought?

SENECA: Rebuffs are hard.

NERO: 'Tis wrong to force a prince.

SENECA: He should give way.

NERO: Then rumour counts him forced.

SENECA: Rumour's an empty thing.

NERO: But harmful too.

SENECA: She fears the strong.

NERO: But none the less maligns.

SENECA: She soon can be o'ercome. But let the youth,
The faith and chastity of this thy wife,
The merits of her sainted sire prevail
To turn thee from thy will.

NERO: Have done at last,
For wearisome has thy insistence grown;
One still may do what Seneca condemns.
And I myself have now too long delayed
The people's prayers for offspring to the throne.
Tomorrow's morn her wedding day shall prove,
Who bears within her womb my pledge of love.
(NERO *and* SENECA *depart.*)

Act Three.   Scene I

(Enter the GHOST OF AGRIPPINA, *bearing a flaming torch.)*

GHOST OF AGRIPPINA: Through cloven earth from Tartarus I come,
    To bring in bloody hands this torch of hell
    To light these cursèd rites; with such dire flames
    Let this Poppaea wed my son, which soon
    His mother's grief and vengeful hand shall turn
    To funeral fires. And ever 'mid the shades
    My impious murder in my memory dwells,
    A heavy weight upon my grieving soul
    Still unavenged; for, oh, ingratitude
    He gave me in return for all my gifts,
    E'en for the gift of empire did he give
    A murderous ship designed to work my death.
    I would have wept my comrades' plight, and more,
    My son's most cruel deed; no time for tears
    Was given, but even higher did he heap
    His sum of crime. Though I escaped the sea,
    I felt the keen sword's thrust, and, with my blood
    The very gods defiling, poured my soul
    In anguish forth. But even yet his hate
    Was not appeased. Against my very name
    The tyrant raged; my merits he obscured;
    My statues, my inscriptions, honours—all,
    On pain of death he bade to be destroyed
    Throughout the world—that world my hapless love,
    To my own direful punishment, had given
    To be by him, an untried boy, controlled.
    And now my murdered husband's angry ghost
    Shakes vengeful torches in my guilty face,
    Insistent, threat'ning; blames his death on me,
    His murdered son, and loud demands that now
    The guilty cause be given up. Have done:
    He shall be given, and that right speedily.
    Avenging furies for his impious head
    Are planning even now a worthy fate:
    Base flight and blows, and fearful sufferings,
    By which the raging thirst of Tantalus
    He shall surpass; the cruel, endless toil
    Of Sisyphus; the pain that Tityus feels,

And the dread, racking anguish of the wheel
On which Ixion's whirling limbs are stretched.
Let gold and marble deck his palace walls;
Let arméd guards protect him; let the world
Be beggared that its treasures vast may flow
Into his lap; let suppliant Parthians bend
To kiss his hands, and bring rich offerings:
The day and hour will come when for his crimes
His guilty soul shall full atonement make,
When to his enemies he shall be given,
Deserted and destroyed and stripped of all.
Oh, to what end my labours and my prayers?
Why did thy frenzied madness, O my son,
And fate impel thee to such depths of crime
That e'en thy mother's wrath, whom thou didst slay,
Is all too small to match her sufferings?
Oh, would that, ere I brought thee forth to light,
And suckled thee, my vitals had been rent
By savage beasts! Then senseless, innocent,
And mine wouldst thou have perished; joined to me
Wouldst thou forever see the quiet seats
Of this abode of souls, thy mighty sire,
And grandsires too, those men of glorious name,
Whom now perpetual shame and grief await
Because of thee, thou monster, and of me.
But why delay in hell to hide my face,
Since I have proved a curse to all my race?
(*The* GHOST *vanishes.*)

Act Three.   Scene II

(*Two nights and a day have passed.* NERO *has divorced* OCTAVIA *and
married* POPPAEA. OCTAVIA *enters and addresses the grieving*
CHORUS.)

OCTAVIA: Restrain your tears; put on a face of joy,
As on a festal day, lest this your love
And care for me should stir the royal wrath,
And I be cause of suffering to you.
This wound is not the first my heart has felt;
Far worse have I endured; but all shall end,

Perchance in death, before this day is done.
No more upon my brutal husband's face
Shall I be forced to look; that hateful couch,
Long since consigned to slavish uses, base,
I shall behold no more.
For now Augustus' sister shall I be,
And not his wife. But oh, be far from me
All cruel punishments and fear of death.
Poor, foolish girl! And canst thou hope for this?
Bethink thee of his former sins—and hope.
Nay, he has spared thy wretched life till now,
That thou mayst at his marriage altars fall.
But why so often turn thy streaming eyes
Upon thy home? Now speed thy steps away,
And leave this bloody prince's hall for aye.

                    (OCTAVIA *departs.*)

CHORUS: Now dawns at last the day we long have feared
And talked of. Lo, our Claudia, driven forth
By cruel Nero's threats, leaves that abode
Which even now Poppaea calls her own;
While we must sit and grieve with sluggish woe,
By heavy fear oppressed.
Where is that Roman people's manhood now,
Which once the pride of mighty leaders crushed,
Gave righteous laws to an unconquered land,
Gave powers at will to worthy citizens,
Made peace and war, fierce nations overcame,
And held in dungeons dark their captive kings?
Behold, on every side our eyes are grieved
By this Poppaea's gleaming statues joined
With Nero's images—a shameful sight.
Come, overturn them with indignant hands,
Too like in feature to her living face.
And her we'll drag from off that royal couch;
And then, with flaming brand and deadly sword,
Attack the princely palace of her lord.

                    (*The* CHORUS *departs.*)

Act Four.   Scene I

(*Enter* POPPAEA *and her* NURSE. POPPAEA *appears distraught.*)

NURSE:

Why dost thou from thy husband's chamber come,
Dear child, with hurried step and troubled face?
Why dost thou seek a lonely place to weep?
For surely has the day we long have sought
With prayers and promised victims come at last.
Thou hast thy Caesar, firmly joined to thee
By ties of marriage, whom thy beauty won,
Whom Venus gave to thee in bonds of love,
Though Seneca despised and flouted her.[15]
How beautiful, upon the banquet couch
Reclining in the palace, didst thou seem!
The senate viewed thy beauty in amaze
When thou didst offer incense to the gods,
And sprinkle wine upon the sacred shrines,
Thy head the while with gauzy purple veiled.
And close beside thee was thy lord himself;
Amid the favouring plaudits of the crowd
He walked majestic, in his look and mien
Proclaiming all his pride and joy in thee.
So did the noble Peleus lead his bride
Emerging from the ocean's snowy foam,
Whose wedding feast the heavenly gods adorned,
With equal joy the sea divinities.
What sudden cause has clouded o'er thy face?
Tell me, what mean thy pallor and thy tears!

POPPAEA:

Dear nurse, this night I had a dreadful dream;
And even now, as I remember it,
My mind is troubled and my senses fail.
For when the joyful day had sunk to rest,
And in the darkened sky the stars appeared,
I lay asleep within my Nero's arms.
But that sweet sleep I could not long enjoy;
For suddenly a grieving crowd appeared
To throng my chamber—Roman matrons they,
With hair disheveled and loud cries of woe.
Then 'midst the oft-repeated, strident blasts
Of trumpets, there appeared my husband's mother,

And shook before my face with threat'ning mien
A bloody torch. Compelled by present fear,
I followed her; when suddenly the earth
Seemed rent asunder to its lowest depths.
Headlong to these I plunged, and even there
In wonder I beheld my wedding couch,
Whereon I sank in utter weariness.
Then with a throng of followers I saw
My son and former husband drawing near.
Straightway Crispinus hastened to my arms,
And on my lips his eager kisses fell:
When suddenly within that chamber burst
My lord the king with frantic, hurrying steps,
And plunged his sword into that other's throat.
A mighty terror seized me, and at last
It roused me from my sleep. I started up
With trembling limbs and wildly beating heart.
Long was I speechless from that haunting fear,
Until thy fond affection gave me tongue.
Why do the ghosts of Hades threaten me?
Or why did I behold my husband's blood?

NURSE: All things which occupy the waking mind,
Some subtle power, swift working, weaves again
Into our web of dreams. Small wonder then,
Thy sleeping thoughts were filled with marriage beds
And husbands, when thy newly mated lord
Held thee in his embrace. Does it seem strange
That thou shouldst dream tonight of sounds of woe,
Of breasts hard beaten and of streaming hair?
Octavia's departure did they mourn
Within her brother's and her father's house.
The torch which thou didst follow, borne aloft
By Agrippina's hand, is but a sign
That hate shall win for thee a mighty name.
Thy marriage couch, in realms infernal seen,
Portends a lasting state of wedded joy.
Since in Crispinus' neck the sword was sheathed,
Believe that no more wars thy lord shall wage,
But hide his sword within the breast of peace.
Take heart again, recall thy joys, I pray,
Throw off thy fears, and to thy couch return.

POPPAEA: Nay, rather will I seek the sacred shrines,
And there make sacrifice unto the gods,
That they avert these threats of night and sleep,
And turn my terrors all upon my foes.
Do thou pray for me and the gods implore
That in this happy state I may endure.
(POPPAEA *and the* NURSE *depart.*)

Act Four. Scene II

(*Enter the* CHORUS OF WOMEN *in sympathy with* POPPAEA.)

CHORUS: If babbling rumour's tales of Jove,
His secret joys in mortal love,
Are true, he once, in plumage dressed,
Was to the lovely Leda pressed;
And as a savage bull he bore
Europa from her native shore:
But should he once thy form, Poppaea, see,
He would leave his shining stars to dwell with thee.
For thou than Leda many fold
Art fairer, or that maid of old
Whom Jove embraced in showers of gold.[16]
Let Sparta boast her lovely dame,
Who, as his prize, to Paris came:
Though Helen's beauty drove the world to arms,
She still must yield to our Poppaea's charms.
But who comes here with hurried step and wild?
What tidings bears he in his heaving breast?

Act Four. Scene III

(*Enter a* MESSENGER.)

MESSENGER: Whoever guards our noble prince's house,
Let him defend it from the people's rage.
Behold, the prefects lead their men in haste,
To save the city from the furious mob
Whose reckless passion grows, unchecked by fear.

CHORUS: What is the madness that inflames their hearts?

MESSENGER: The people for their loved Octavia
               Are wild with rage and grief; and now in throngs
               Are rushing forth in mood for any deed.

CHORUS: What are they bent to do, or with what plan?

MESSENGER: To give Octavia back her father's house,
               Her brother's bed, and her due share of empire.

CHORUS: But these Poppaea holds as Nero's wife.

MESSENGER: 'Tis even she 'gainst whom the people's rage
               Burns most persistent, and to reckless deeds
               Is driven headlong on. Whate'er they see,
               Of noble marble wrought, or gleaming bronze,
               The hated image of Poppaea's face,
               They cast it to the earth with wanton hands
               And crushing bars. The shattered parts they drag
               Along the streets, and with insulting heel
               Deep in the filthy mud they trample them.
               These savage deeds are mingled with such words
               As I should fear to utter in your ears.
               Soon will they hedge the royal house with flames,
               Unless the prince his new-made wife give up
               To sate the people's wrath, and then restore
               To noble Claudia her father's house.
               That he himself may know these threatened deeds,
               I'll haste to tell him as the prefect bade.
                    (*The* MESSENGER *departs.*)

                    Act Four.   Scene IV

CHORUS: Why vainly strive against the powers above?
               For Cupid's weapons are invincible.
               Your puny fires by those fierce flames he'll dim
               By which he oft has quenched the bolts of Jove,
               And brought the Thunderer captive from the sky.
               For this offence you shall dire forfeit pay,
               E'en with your blood; for hot of wrath is he,
               And may not be o'ercome. At his command
               Did fierce Achilles strike the peaceful lyre;

He forced the Greeks and Agamemnon proud
To do his will. Illustrious cities, too,
And Priam's realm he utterly destroyed.
And now my mind in fear awaits to see
What Cupid's cruel penalties will be.

(*The* CHORUS *departs.*)

Act Five.   Scene I

(*Enter* NERO.)

NERO: Too slow my soldiers' hands, too mild my wrath,
When citizens have dared such crimes as these.
Those torches that they kindled 'gainst their prince
Their blood shall quench; and Rome, who bore such men,
Shall be bespattered with her people's gore.
Yet death is far too light a punishment
For such atrocities; this impious mob
Shall suffer worse than death. But she, my wife
And sister, whom I hate with deadly fear,
For whose sole sake the people rage at me,
Shall give her life at last to sate my grief,
And quench my anger in her flowing blood.
Soon shall my flames enwrap the city's walls,
And in the ruins of her falling homes
The people shall be buried; squalid want,
Dire hunger, grief—all these shall they endure.
Too fat upon the blessings of our age
Has this vile mob become, and know not how
To bear our clemency and relish peace;
But, rash and reckless, are they ever borne
By shifting tides of passion to their hurt.
They must be held in check by suffering,
Be ever pressed beneath the heavy yoke,
Lest once again they dare assail the throne,
And to the august features of my wife
Dare lift again their vulgar eyes. O'erawed
By fear of punishment must they be taught
To yield obedience to their prince's nod.
But here I see the man whose loyalty
Has made him captain of my royal guards.

Act Five.   Scene II

(*Enter the* PREFECT.)

PREFECT: The people's rage by slaughter of a few,
          Who most resistance made is overcome.

NERO: Is that enough? Was that my word to thee?
          "Is overcome?" Where then is my revenge?

PREFECT: The guilty leaders of the mob are dead.

NERO: Nay, but the mob itself, which dared to assail
          My house with flames, to dictate laws to me,
          To drag my noble wife from off my bed,
          And with unhallowed hands and angry threats
          To affront her majesty—are they unscathed?

PREFECT: Shall angry grief decide their punishment?

NERO: It shall—whose fame no future age shall dim.

PREFECT: Which neither wrath nor fear shall moderate?[17]

NERO: She first shall feel my wrath who merits it.

PREFECT: Tell whom thou mean'st. My hand shall spare her not.

NERO: My wrath demands my guilty sister's death.

PREFECT: Benumbing horror holds me in its grasp.

NERO: Wilt not obey my word?

PREFECT: Why question that?

NERO: Because thou spar'st my foe.

PREFECT: A woman, foe?

NERO: If she be criminal.

PREFECT: But what her crime?

NERO: The people's rage.

PREFECT: But who can check their rage?

NERO: The one who fanned its flame.

PREFECT: But who that one?

NERO: A woman she, to whom an evil heart
               Hath nature given, a soul to fraud inclined.

PREFECT: But not the power to act.

NERO: That she may be
               Without the power to act, that present fear
               May break her strength, let punishment at once,
               Too long delayed, crush out her guilty life.
               Have done at once with arguments and prayers,
               And do my royal bidding: let her sail
               To some far distant shore and there be slain,
               That thus at last my fears may be at rest.
               (NERO *and the* PREFECT *depart.*)

                      Act Five.   Scene III

      (*Enter the* CHORUS OF ROMANS, *sympathetic with* OCTAVIA.)

CHORUS: Oh, dire and deadly has the people's love
               To many proved, which fills their swelling sails
               With favouring breeze, and bears them out to sea;
               But soon its vigour languishes and dies,
               And leaves them to the mercy of the deep.
               The wretched mother of the Gracchi wept
               Her murdered sons, who, though of noble blood,
               Far famed for eloquence and piety,
               Stout-hearted, learnèd in defence of law,
               Were brought to ruin by the people's love
               And popular renown. And Livius,[18] thee
               To equal fate did fickle fortune give,
               Who found no safety in thy lictors' rods,
               No refuge in thy home. But grief forbids
               To tell more instances. This hapless girl,
               To whom but now the citizens decreed
               The restoration of her fatherland,
               Her home, her brother's couch, is dragged away
               In tears and misery to punishment,
               With citizens consenting to her death!
               Oh, blessèd poverty, content to hide
               Beneath the refuge of a lowly roof!
               For lofty homes, to fame and fortune known,
               By storms are blasted and by fate o'erthrown!

Act Five.   Scene IV

(*Enter* OCTAVIA *in the custody of the palace guards, who are dragging
her roughly out into the street.*)

OCTAVIA: Oh, whither do ye hurry me? What fate
              Has that vile tyrant or his queen ordained?
              Does she, subdued and softened by my woes,
              Grant me to live in exile? Or, if not,
              If she intends to crown my sufferings
              With death, why does her savage heart begrudge
              That I should die at home? But now, alas,
              I can no longer hope for life; behold,
              My brother's bark, within whose treacherous hold
              His mother once was borne; and now for me,
              Poor wretch, his slighted sister-wife, it waits.
              No more has right a place upon the earth,
              Nor heavenly gods. Grim Fury reigns supreme.
              Oh, who can fitly weep my evil plight?
              What nightingale has tongue to sing my woes?
              Would that the fates would grant her wings to me!
              Then would I speed away on pinions swift,
              And leave my grievous troubles far behind,
              Leave these unholy haunts of savage men.
              There, all alone, within some forest wide,
              Among the swaying branches would I sit,
              And let my grieving spirit weep its fill.

CHORUS: The race of men is by the fates controlled,
              And none may hope to make his own secure;
              And o'er the ever-shifting ways of life
              The day which most we fear shall come to us.
              But comfort now thy heart with thought of those
              Of thine own house who suffered ill, and ask:
              In what has fortune been more harsh to thee?
              Thee first I name, Agrippa's noble child,[19]
              The famous mother of so many sons,
              Great Caesar's wife, whose name throughout the world
              In flaming glory shone, whose teeming womb
              Brought forth so many hostages of peace:
              E'en thee did exile wait, and cruel chains,
              Blows, bitter anguish, and at last a death

Of lingering agony. And Livia, thou,
Though fortunate in husband and in sons,
Didst walk the way of sin—and punishment.
And Julia, too, endured her mother's fate;
For, though no evil deed was charged to her,
She fell a victim to the sword at last.
What could not once thy mighty mother do
Who ruled supreme the house of Claudius,
By him beloved, and in her son secure?
Yet she at last was subject to a slave,
And fell beneath a brutal soldier's sword.
For what exalted heights of royalty
Might not our Nero's mother once have hoped?
Mishandled first by vulgar sailors' hands,
Then slain and mangled by the bungling sword,
She lay the victim of her cruel son.

OCTAVIA: Me, too, the tyrant to the world of shades
Is sending. Why delay? Then speed my death,
For fate hath made me subject to your power.
I pray the heavenly gods—what wouldst thou, fool?
Pray not to gods who show their scorn of thee.
But, O ye gods of hell, ye furies dire,
Who work your vengeance on the crimes of men,
And thou, my father's restless spirit, come
And bring this tyrant fitting punishment.
                (To her guards)
The death you threaten has no terrors now
For me. Go, set your ship in readiness,
Unfurl your sails, and let your pilot seek
The barren shores of Pandataria.
            (OCTAVIA *departs with the guards.*)

CHORUS: Ye gentle breezes and ye zephyrs mild,
Which once from savage Dian's altar bore
Atrides' daughter[20] in a cloud concealed,
This child of ours, Octavia too, we pray,
Bear far away from these too cruel woes,
And set her in the fane of Trivia.
For Aulis is more merciful than Rome,
The savage Taurian land more mild than this:
There hapless strangers to their gods they feed,
But Rome delights to see her children bleed.

1. This passage refers to the murders of Claudius, Agrippina, and Britannicus respectively. There are numerous allusions to these three deaths throughout the play. The sister-wife is Octavia.

2. Orestes, brother of Electra, killed his mother Clytemnestra in order to avenge the murder of his father Agamemnon.

3. This refers to Acte, who was Nero's mistress before he transferred his affections to Poppaea.

4. Nero accused Octavia of adultery with Anicetus, his freedman.

5. The rival was Poppaea, who is here accused of responsibility for Nero's murder of his mother Agrippina.

6. Octavia refers to the expected child of Nero and Poppaea.

7. Lines 193-198 have been revised to bring out the distinction between Acte, the former favourite, and Poppaea, whom Cupid will also desert. Miller assumed that Poppaea was meant throughout the passage. A Latin inscription has been found dedicated by Acte to Ceres as goddess of divorce. This is perhaps the memorial to which the nurse refers.

8. A comet was supposed to denote a change of government. The appearance of a comet in 60 A.D. led some Romans to think of the possibility of a successor to Nero.

9. This refers to Messalina's marriage to Gaius Silius in 48 A.D.

10. This refers to Virginia, slain by her father to avoid the lust of Appius Claudius.

11. The detailed description of the death of Agrippina which follows should be compared with the account given by Tacitus in his *Annals*, XIV, 4-8.

12. Nero here doubtless refers to the deification of Claudius.

13. The second triumvirate was composed of Octavian, Antony, and Lepidus.

14. The "mighty leader" is Antony; Pompey had also met his death in Egypt.

15. The text of this line is uncertain.

16. This refers to Jupiter's love for Danae.

17. Miller reads *quam temperet non ira*.

18. This refers to the tribune Marcus Livius Drusus, who met his death in 91 B.C.

19. This refers to the elder Agrippina, wife of Germanicus.

20. The chorus alludes to Iphigenia, daughter of Agamemnon and Clytemnestra.

APPENDIX

QUEROLUS

CHARACTERS IN THE PLAY

HOUSEHOLD GOD *of the house of* QUEROLUS
QUEROLUS, *the son of Euclio*
MANDROGERUS, *a parasite and self-styled magician*
A SWINDLER, *an accomplice of* MANDROGERUS
SARDANAPALLUS, *another accomplice of* MANDROGERUS
PANTOMALUS, *slave of* QUEROLUS
A WITNESS, *a friend and neighbour of* QUEROLUS

INTRODUCTION

THE *Querolus,* an English translation of which appears here for the first time, is a comedy that is known to very few. When we speak of Roman Comedy, we think of the great period of dramatic activity in the second century B.C. and the twenty-six extant plays of Plautus and Terence; it is seldom realised that a twenty-seventh comedy has come down from Roman times, a full-length play that in many respects is very different from the others. The title of the comedy appears in the Mss. in a double form, *Querolus* or *The Pot of Gold.* The misinterpretation of a passage in the prologue is doubtless responsible for the second title, which in turn has led to needless confusion with Plautus' comedy, *The Pot of Gold.* The traditional view of the *Querolus,* one that has contributed not a little to its neglect in modern times, is that the play is a direct adaptation or reworking of the Plautine comedy. Nothing is farther from the truth, as even a rapid reading of the two plays will show. Both comedies have a household god as one of the characters, and in each a miser named Euclio has buried a pot of gold. These are the only points of similarity. The author of the *Querolus* knew Plautus' play, but developed his own plot along original lines.

The identity of the author is not known. The language and style of the play, as well as the numerous allusions in it to other Latin writers, indicate that the date of composition belongs late in the Roman empire. If Rutilius, to whom the play is dedicated, is the poet Rutilius Claudius Namatianus, as many scholars believe, the play must be dated in the early part of the fifth century A.D. In this case, it is almost six centuries later than the comedies of Plautus and Terence.

The plot deals with the attempt of the parasite Mandrogerus and his two accomplices to secure the pot of gold they know to be in the home of Querolus. By means of a display of religious and astrological lore and a feigned ceremony of purification they gain access to the house and steal an urn in which they believe the gold to be buried. Upon examination the urn appears to contain only ashes. Mandrogerus, not realising that the gold is hidden beneath the ashes, hurls the urn back through the window. In this way Querolus receives his inheritance from his father, and the trickster is the victim of his own deception. The final act, which has wrongly been condemned as an unnecessary addition to the plot, shows the parasite's attempt to secure a share of the gold as joint heir with Querolus of the estate of the deceased Euclio.

Much of the dialogue is witty and amusing, especially in the scenes which deal with the fate of the buried treasure. The structure of the play as a whole, however, is far from faultless. There are several long digressions which delay the course of the action. While the plot of the play may go back to a Greek original, the Latin author has not hesitated to enrich it with philosophical, religious, social, and legal satire. The opening scenes of the play present a study of the character of Querolus, the man who complains about everything; he sums up his unhappy situation with the question: why do the wicked flourish and the righteous suffer? The household god, in his lengthy debate with Querolus, proves that Querolus, if he is miserable, deserves to be so, but that actually he is far more fortunate than he realises. Throughout the play runs the moral that man can accomplish nothing without the favour of an all-powerful Deity. Men are rewarded according to their merits, but, on the other hand, it is often the righteous who suffer the most. Léon Herrmann considers the author a fatalist and a conservative, and believes that in many passages he was attacking Christianity, now the official religion of the Empire; he sees also in the religious satire an attack on various governmental and administrative abuses. We must be on our guard against reading too much into what may be meant merely as an entertaining and satirical comedy. But it is undoubtedly true that the play contains far more philosophical and religious thought than is to be found in any play of Plautus or Terence. It has been pointed out that the *Querolus* betrays its mediaeval character by putting the moral first and using the story to illustrate the moral.

When and how the play was produced we do not know, nor can we be sure that it ever was produced. The only clue is the statement in the dedication that the comedy was written for production at a banquet in the home of Rutilius. It would obviously have had a greater appeal to a select literary group than to a larger and more general public. The play has come down as prose, but a kind of rhythmical prose, with iambic and trochaic clausulae. The author may have believed that he was following the metres of Plautus and Terence which were but imperfectly understood in his day. Attempts such as that of Louis Havet to restore the text to a fixed metrical form by means of radical emendation and transposition have proved unsuccessful.

The *Querolus* is thus the only extant Roman play of the late empire. It is of interest for its language and style and for its philosophical, religious, and social content, and it has far more intrinsic value as a comedy than has often been realised. The author, whoever he may have been, was a man of moderate talents, but of considerable originality. The play is not an imitation of a Plautine comedy, but a new creation which is wholly characteristic of the age in which the dramatist lived.

The *Querolus* was well known in the Middle Ages and was adapted into Latin elegiacs in the twelfth century by Vital de Blois. The false astrology of Mandrogerus was quoted by the historian Liudprand in the tenth century and was apparently as proverbial at that time as the similar astronomical explanations of Sganarelle in Molière's *Le Médecin Malgré Lui* are in French literature today.

QUEROLUS

(SCENE:—*In front of the house of* QUEROLUS.)

Dedication and Prologue

O RUTILIUS,[1] you should always be honoured with great praise, for you provide me with a noble leisure which I can devote to the writing of plays. You deem me worthy of honour among your nearest and most intimate friends, and I acknowledge the twofold benefit you bestow upon me: the honour I receive, the associations I enjoy; this is true distinction. Since my debt is so great, what fitting repayment can I make? Money, the source of power and the cause of worry, is neither plentiful with me nor of value in your sight. My trifling literary efforts have caused me no small labour; from this source comes my renown and my recompense; from this same source I shall repay my debt to you. And that my work may have a bit of added charm, I have taken some material from that philosophical discourse of yours. Do you recall that a favourite theme of yours was to ridicule those who complained of their own fortune? And that you were accustomed to develop the theme in true philosophical fashion by means of argument and refutation? How much is taken from this source only he will know who is acquainted with your writings. I have written this little work for the discussions at your banquet table.

The plot is as follows: the father of our hero Querolus was the miser Euclio. This same Euclio some time ago concealed a treasure of gold in an urn, and, just as if it were the ashes of his father, he poured incense over it and wrote an epitaph on the outside. Being about to set sail from home, he buried the urn in his house and told no one about it. On his travels, finding himself on the point of death, he chose a parasite, a chance acquaintance, to be joint heir with his son, and gave him a secret document to that effect, on condition that he reveal the buried treasure to the son without trickery. The old man disclosed only the location of the treasure. Not suspecting any guile, the parasite sets sail and comes to Querolus; thereupon he breaks his promise and pretends to be a magician, an astrologer, and anything else that a thief can invent. As though a fortuneteller he speaks about the intimate details of the household of Querolus, which he has learned from his patron; Querolus puts his trust in him and asks his aid. The parasite in his role as magician cleanses the house, and cleans it out, as well. But as soon as he is free to examine the urn, he is deceived by Euclio's old trick; he is convinced that it really contains ashes, as it appeared to do, and he believes he has been deceived. In order to get some sort of revenge he cunningly and silently stole back to Querolus' house and hurled the urn through the window; the urn was shattered to bits and the ashes turned to gold. Thus, contrary to logic and belief, the parasite discovered the treasure when it was hidden and returned it when he had found it. Later, when he learns the truth, he hurries back and demands his share of the inheritance; however, since he admits what he has stolen and cannot prove what he has returned, he is accused first of theft and then of violating a burial-place. The outcome is this: as a result of fate and their own merit, the master and the parasite both receive their due reward.

Rutilius, illustrious sir, this play is dedicated to you. May you live with good health and fortune and thus fulfill our prayers and yours.

Grant us peace and quiet, spectators! This is the demand of our poetic composition, which relates to you in barbarian speech the wisdom of the Greeks and revives in your age ancient Latin literature. Moreover, it prays and hopes in polished speech that, in return for his labours in your behalf, the author may receive your kind favour. We are going to present today *The Pot of Gold*,[2] but not an old and crude one, following the footsteps of Plautus. This is the gist of the play: we present here a fortunate man saved by his destiny and, on the other hand, a trickster cheated by his own trickery. Querolus, who will appear presently, will be the main character. He is that disagreeable hero of ours; he will be fortunate. On the contrary, Mandrogerus will prove to be deceitful and miserable. The household god, who will be the first to enter, will explain everything. The subject will amuse you, even if the manner of presentation wearies you. As to our jests and jokes, we desire the freedom of bygone days; no one should take personally what we say to everyone, nor should anyone be offended by a joke meant for the general public. No one should find a resemblance to reality, for we are making the whole story up.[3] Whether this play should be named *Querolus* or *The Pot of Gold* is for you to judge; the decision will rest in your hands. Furthermore, we should hesitate to come forward with a halting rhythm[4] in presenting our play, were it not that in this respect we are following the example of great and renowned predecessors.

Act One.   Scene I

(Enter the HOUSEHOLD GOD *from the home of* QUEROLUS.)

HOUSEHOLD GOD *(to the audience)*: I am the inhabitant and guardian
of the home to which I have been assigned. I now control this house
from which I have just come forth. I modify the decrees of fate; if
there is anything in the nature of a blessing, I speed its approach; anything that is too severe I make mild. I now control the fate of Querolus;
he is a disagreeable person, but not a wicked one. So far he has had
enough to live on—the best of blessings; but now he will even become
extremely wealthy. He has deserved it. For if you think that good people
ought not to be rewarded according to their deserts, you are grievously
mistaken.

And now I'll set forth briefly the order and arrangement of the story:
the father of Querolus here was Euclio, a miserly and shrewd old man.
A long time ago he buried a tremendous amount of gold in an urn.
Honouring the gold as though it were his father's ashes, he concealed it
quite openly. Setting out on a trip abroad, he buried the urn in his
house and left it in front of my altar. To his household he entrusted a
grave, to me a treasure. The old man departed and failed to return; as
he was dying abroad, he revealed the truth to only one person, a tricky
and deceitful fellow. But either being forgetful, or deeming it unnecessary, he said nothing concerning the burial ashes and the inscription.
As far as the interests of Querolus are concerned, this is sufficient. And
thus it is that the treasure remains unknown to all, and yet it is known.
It would have been quite easy for me to reveal the gold to its master
by means of prophecy or dream. But mortals must learn that no one
can be deprived of a gift from a god; and so the gold which has been
exposed to dishonesty will be preserved by theft. The thief will soon
appear, by whom our wealth will be saved. When he finds the urn, he
will think it contains ashes; the old man took precautions for this very
thing. After stealing the plunder, the parasite will bring it back and
restore the whole amount; he should have been satisfied to seek his
share. And so it turns out well that the treacherous man who tries to
cheat another ruins himself.

However, that you may not have seen me here in vain, I have certain explanations to make. That friend of ours, Querolus, as you know,
is disagreeable to everyone, even to a god, if it is right to say so; the
fellow's absurdly hotheaded, and therefore all the more ridiculous. I
wish to have a debate with him and show how worthless his knowledge is. And so you will now hear Destiny on one side, a mortal on the

other, and you spectators shall judge between us. I shall confess that I am his guardian spirit, but with the greatest possible caution, so that he will do me no harm. He never ceases to heap abuse on me night and day. (*Listening*) But there, I hear his voice; he's damning his fate and his fortune. (*Looking down the street*) He's coming towards me, he's heard that his father died abroad. Whew! How deeply he grieves; that's the way human nature is: he's learned that nothing was left him, I suppose. What am I to do now? I can't fly away from here at once. I've been far too bold. (*Looking about him*) Ah, this is fortunate! I see here a trident with hooks; not a bad protection for me, by Jove! If Querolus doesn't cease being troublesome today, I'll give him something to be querulous about. I wonder where this came from; I saw some fishermen pass by here this morning; perhaps one of them dropped it. (*The* HOUSEHOLD GOD *picks up the trident and steps back.*)

Act One.   Scene II

(*Enter* QUEROLUS.)

QUEROLUS (*to himself, not seeing the* HOUSEHOLD GOD): O Fortune! O Favouring Fortune! O accursed and impious Fate! If anyone should now show me your whereabouts, I'd produce and prepare for you a fate from which you couldn't extricate yourself.

HOUSEHOLD GOD (*aside*): I must put trust in this trident today. But why hesitate to interrupt and address him? (*To* QUEROLUS) Good day, Querolus.

QUEROLUS (*to himself, not looking*): Here's this wearisome phrase again, "Good day, Querolus." What's the advantage of greeting so many men on this side and that? Even if there were any point to it, it would still be tiresome.

HOUSEHOLD GOD (*aside*): By heavens, he's a true misanthrope; he sees one person and thinks it's a crowd.

QUEROLUS (*to the* HOUSEHOLD GOD): Pray tell me, friend, what's your business with me? Are you demanding payment of a debt, or seeking a thief?

HOUSEHOLD GOD: You're very irritable, Querolus.

QUEROLUS (*aside*): Ha! I've rejected his courtesies; now he's adding abuse. (*He moves away.*)

HOUSEHOLD GOD: Wait a moment.

QUEROLUS: I haven't time.

HOUSEHOLD GOD: It's necessary. Wait.

QUEROLUS (*aside*): This looks like force. (*Aloud*) Come, tell me what you want.

HOUSEHOLD GOD: Do you know why I'm carrying this trident?

QUEROLUS: I don't, by Jove! Except that I suppose it was first invented for troublesome persons.

HOUSEHOLD GOD: I'm carrying it so that I can prick your heels for you, if you touch me.

QUEROLUS (*aside*): Didn't I say this would happen? A greeting can't even be given with impunity. (*Aloud*) Gad, here is a good proposition! I won't touch you and don't you touch me. Good-bye. Go and make your friendships! What good was your first greeting?

HOUSEHOLD GOD: Wait! I am he whom you seek and whom you curse, you manikin! (*Threatening* QUEROLUS *with the trident.*)

QUEROLUS: Oh! Oh! I want to take my heels away in safety.

HOUSEHOLD GOD (*severely*): Weren't you cursing your fate just now?

QUEROLUS: I do curse it and hunt for it.

HOUSEHOLD GOD: Well, come here, then. I am it.

QUEROLUS: You? My fate?

HOUSEHOLD GOD: I am your Household God, whom you mortals call fate.

QUEROLUS: I have been seeking you for a long time. (*Coming nearer*) You won't take a step from here today.

HOUSEHOLD GOD (*again threatening*): I warned you about this trident; look out for it.

QUEROLUS (*pursuing the* HOUSEHOLD GOD): You're the one to look out!

HOUSEHOLD GOD: I've already taken precautions. (*His costume gradually becomes white and a bright light surrounds his body.*)

QUEROLUS: What the devil kind of hocus-pocus is this?

HOUSEHOLD GOD: Away from me, you idiot! There's no hocus-pocus here. (*As* QUEROLUS *approaches*) Stop, unless you want to get three jabs at once.

QUEROLUS (*aside*): Aha! This fellow seems to be someone from the spirits or the mysteries. He appears half naked and clad in white, and his whole body gleams with light. (*Aloud*) Hurrah, Household God! You've done well for yourself today. But there's something I don't understand. I can see why you're half naked; but I don't know where you got your white garments. I've long been of the opinion that you were living in the coalbin; but now you come from the flour mill.

HOUSEHOLD GOD: Well, you can even thank me for being able to make such clever jokes in the midst of your misfortunes. Listen to me now; your complaint touches me, Querolus, even though it is unfounded. And that's why I have come, that I might render a complete accounting to you, a favour that never before has been granted a mortal.

QUEROLUS: What? An accounting of human affairs? Are you permitted to know them and to reveal them?

HOUSEHOLD GOD: I know them and will explain them. Tell me today, therefore, everything you were complaining about.

QUEROLUS: The day will be too short.

HOUSEHOLD GOD: Tell me a few in brief, and I'll explain everything about them.

QUEROLUS: Well, there's one thing that I'd like to have made clear to me: why do the wicked prosper and the good suffer?

HOUSEHOLD GOD: First of all, as is the usual procedure among you mortals, there is the question of the person involved. In whose behalf do you speak? For yourself, or people in general?

QUEROLUS: Both for the people and myself.

HOUSEHOLD GOD: Since you are accusing yourself, how do you plan to defend so many others?

QUEROLUS: I know that I'm not being accused.

HOUSEHOLD GOD: Well, the charge will disappear, then, if we abolish the person involved. Where do you place yourself, among good citizens or bad?

QUEROLUS: Do you really ask what I think of myself, when I complain about wicked men?

HOUSEHOLD GOD: If I prove that you belong to the group you are accusing, namely the wicked, in whose behalf will you speak hereafter?

QUEROLUS: If you convince me that I'm a scoundrel, I'll have to adapt my ideas to my merits.

HOUSEHOLD GOD: Now, Querolus, answer me this quickly: how many serious crimes do you think you've committed?

QUEROLUS: None, to be sure, so far as I know.

HOUSEHOLD GOD: What, none? Have you then forgotten all your deeds?

QUEROLUS: No, I remember almost all of them, but I don't know of any crime.

HOUSEHOLD GOD: What, Querolus? Have you never committed a theft?

QUEROLUS: Never a one—since the time I stopped.

HOUSEHOLD GOD: Ha, ha, ha! Is that the same as never committing one?

QUEROLUS: I don't deny what is true. In my youth, I admit, I committed certain deeds which are usually praised.

HOUSEHOLD GOD: Why, then, did you cease from such praiseworthy crime? But let's pass over that. What are we to say about falsehood?

QUEROLUS: Humph! Who ever tells the truth? That's a common weakness. Forget it.

HOUSEHOLD GOD: No crime involved there, then? What about adultery?

QUEROLUS: What? Even that? That's no crime.

HOUSEHOLD GOD: When did it begin to be lawful, then?

QUEROLUS: A fine question! As if you didn't know! That's a thing that can neither be permitted nor prevented.

HOUSEHOLD GOD: What about this, Querolus? Don't you see that you are living a lawless life?

QUEROLUS: If you charge me with this, there isn't anyone who is free of sin.

HOUSEHOLD GOD: And yet I haven't asked you if you remembered everything.

QUEROLUS: There isn't anything more.[5]

HOUSEHOLD GOD: Well, have you desired anyone's death?

QUEROLUS: Not a person's.

HOUSEHOLD GOD: But if I prove it?

QUEROLUS: I'd have nothing to say.

HOUSEHOLD GOD: Tell me. Have you ever had a father-in-law or a mother-in-law?

QUEROLUS: There you go again, talking about something that's universal.

HOUSEHOLD GOD: Then you admit everything on all these points?

QUEROLUS: Why not, since you put your questions this way?

HOUSEHOLD GOD: If these matters seem so trifling to you, I don't know what you would consider a crime. But answer me again. How often have you sworn falsely? (*As* QUEROLUS *hesitates*) Tell me quickly.

QUEROLUS: As I hope to have a happy hour, I swear I've always been innocent of that crime.

HOUSEHOLD GOD: What I want to know is this: how many times over and above a thousand have you sworn falsely? Tell me that, at least.

QUEROLUS: Oho! Now you mean those everyday joking remarks.

HOUSEHOLD GOD: I don't quite understand what a joking lie is. But let's pass over that, since I see that common practice has made it seem trifling. Now, then! Have you never consciously and intentionally broken your oath? For instance, have you never sworn to love a person and then, after your oath, proceeded to hate him?

QUEROLUS (*aside*): I'm a poor wretch! What misfortune this fellow has brought me today! (*Aloud*) I have often sworn an oath, I admit, that has been observed in the letter, but not in the spirit.

HOUSEHOLD GOD: Clever fellow! Then you *have* sworn falsely. That's the usual way. How I'd prefer to have the letter broken and the spirit observed! Querolus, do you think you have cleared yourself by observing the letter? Often a person swears falsely by keeping still. And it's just as bad to refrain from telling the truth as it is to utter a falsehood.

QUEROLUS (*disgruntled*): You've completed your proof, then. I've deserved my misfortune. (*Turning to go*) Good-bye.

HOUSEHOLD GOD: Wait! I've accomplished nothing, Querolus, unless I achieve these two results: in the first place, to prove that you deserve to be miserable; in the second place, to make you realise that even now you are fortunate.

QUEROLUS: What? Am I not overwhelmed with woe?

HOUSEHOLD GOD: You are, I admit,[6] but it's your own fault. Now that I may refute you on all points, tell me briefly what you have particularly to complain about.

QUEROLUS: Well, first of all, most excellent God, I complain about my friends.

HOUSEHOLD GOD (*aside*): Blessed Hope! What will he do about his enemies? (*To* QUEROLUS) In what way has your trust in your friends ever injured you?

QUEROLUS: No one is more disagreeable to me than an intimate friend, and no one is more obliging than a slight acquaintance.

HOUSEHOLD GOD: And why is it strange if the person who knows you well despises you, while the person who doesn't know you loves you?

QUEROLUS (*bitterly*): Thanks, Household God! You honour me in all respects!

HOUSEHOLD GOD: Now I know why you are complaining. Would you like a quick remedy?

QUEROLUS: Most certainly.

HOUSEHOLD GOD: Don't give your friendship and your trust to fools. For it's easier to endure the hatred of silly and sinful persons than their companionship.

QUEROLUS: But if there isn't any person of good sense?

HOUSEHOLD GOD: Then govern the fools by your own intelligence.

QUEROLUS: How?

HOUSEHOLD GOD: Do you wish to avoid being deceived?

QUEROLUS: Of course.

HOUSEHOLD GOD: Don't put your trust in anyone. It's in your own power to avoid deception. Why accuse the disloyalty of others? Do you wish to be honoured?

QUEROLUS: By all means.

HOUSEHOLD GOD: Then live among those who are wretched.

QUEROLUS: That sounds like the truth.

HOUSEHOLD GOD: Do you wish particularly not to be deceived by your own folks?

QUEROLUS: I'd like it, if it were possible.

HOUSEHOLD GOD: I'll repeat what I've already said. Don't be too friendly with anyone, Querolus. It's a very strange thing that man cannot put up with his equal. You all scorn your inferiors, you envy your betters, you disagree with your equals.

QUEROLUS: Please tell me then what I ought to do.

HOUSEHOLD GOD: Learn what must be done in accordance with the character and vices of men. Avoid companions, parties, wine, crowds. The more you wish to attach someone to yourself, the lighter you should make the bond. I don't expect crowds, orgies, frivolous amusements to produce friendship, and I pray that they produce no hatred!

QUEROLUS: Why is it that many people get great enjoyment from society of this sort?

HOUSEHOLD GOD: I understand perfectly. You speak of those individuals who keep everything concealed. The men you mean are either very careful or very lucky. But this has nothing to do with Querolus.

QUEROLUS: I have another complaint to make. I am a poor man, as you know—perhaps you are responsible for it—but I can bear that. What I can't endure is to have no one respect my slender circumstances or admit that a certain person is poor—

HOUSEHOLD GOD: What next?

QUEROLUS: Alas! What charges they add! Folly, carelessness, laziness, gluttony! Patience is called indifference, impatience is considered cruelty. Thus everything is changed around. No one has any regard for ability, no one respects a person's means. The rich man is always industrious, the poor man is always shiftless.

HOUSEHOLD GOD: Save these complaints for the censors, Querolus. Now, tell me what it is that grieves and distresses you particularly. The things that you have mentioned so far are ancient and universal disadvantages of poverty. Besides, you're neither rich nor poor. If you only realised this, you'd be happy.

QUEROLUS: Don't you know that I've just lost my father?

HOUSEHOLD GOD (*with sarcasm*): You've followed my instructions. Here is certainly an individual misfortune, such as has befallen no one before this time! Well then? Isn't it proper for a son to bury his father?

QUEROLUS: I admit it is; but my father left nothing.

HOUSEHOLD GOD: A bitter complaint! You mourn because the funeral brings you nothing? This is vexation, not grief! Your father certainly lacked nothing, and you lack nothing today. This is no small inheritance. Are you angry at the old man even on his deathbed? Did he live for himself, when he always lived for you? I hope you leave as much to your heirs as Euclio left. Speak of something else, now, for I won't hear a word about this.

QUEROLUS: I have a slave I can't endure, Pantomalus, and his character fits his name.[7]

HOUSEHOLD GOD: Lucky you are, Querolus, if you have only one; many people have several Pantomaluses.

QUEROLUS: But don't I hear many men even praising their slaves?

HOUSEHOLD GOD: Their slaves are still worse.

QUEROLUS: Why do they praise them, then?

HOUSEHOLD GOD: Because they don't know what they lose by them.

QUEROLUS (*trying another approach*): Bad weather destroyed my crops; that isn't a universal disaster, is it?

HOUSEHOLD GOD: There's more than one way of punishing men. Bad weather has injured you; another person has suffered something else.

QUEROLUS: Really? My comrades have suffered no misfortune for a long time.

HOUSEHOLD GOD: Well, you're stupidly mistaken there.

QUEROLUS (*ironically*): Please pardon me; I didn't know that you had a particular regard for my comrades. But I still have a complaint to make: I have a bad neighbour.

HOUSEHOLD GOD: Here's a bad business, to be sure! But consider even here, Querolus, how much I have favoured you with that neighbour. You have only one bad neighbour to put up with. What do those people do who have many?

QUEROLUS (*dryly*): Just keep him safe, please, Household God; I want you to watch the one you favoured me with, so there won't be two of them.

HOUSEHOLD GOD: And what if I refute you even concerning this fellow? Tell me now, I beg of you: whom do you consider happier, yourself or the man you're complaining about?

QUEROLUS: What sort of comparison is this? How can there be any doubt that the person who makes another complain is happier than the one who takes refuge in complaint?

HOUSEHOLD GOD: Well, Querolus, do you wish me to prove to you that he is the unhappier?

QUEROLUS: I certainly do.

HOUSEHOLD GOD: But I'll merely give you a hint. Bring your ear a bit nearer.

QUEROLUS: Why not speak openly? You're not afraid of anything, are you?

HOUSEHOLD GOD (*with irony*): How can I help being afraid when I live with you? Give me your ear.

QUEROLUS: All right, speak. (*He approaches the* HOUSEHOLD GOD *who whispers in his ear;* QUEROLUS *bursts out laughing*) Ha, ha, ha! I don't envy him that possession—he can have it, and good riddance.[8] Gad, teacher, you treat me well.

HOUSEHOLD GOD: Isn't that true?

QUEROLUS: I certainly make no complaint now.

HOUSEHOLD GOD: Well, Querolus? You'll think so for a little while, then you'll return to your true nature. But since you are unable to show that you're wretched, it remains for me to prove that you're fortunate. Tell me, please, Querolus; are you in good health?

QUEROLUS: I believe so.

HOUSEHOLD GOD: How much do you think this is worth?

QUEROLUS: Does this enter into your calculation?

HOUSEHOLD GOD: Oh, Querolus, you're in good health and you deny your good fortune? Take care lest you realise too late that you have had it.

QUEROLUS: I admitted it a little while ago; my life by itself is good, but bad when compared to others.

HOUSEHOLD GOD: Everything certainly goes well with you, does it not?

QUEROLUS: I admit that.

HOUSEHOLD GOD: Then what more do you want?

QUEROLUS: Why are others better off?

HOUSEHOLD GOD: This smacks of envy!

QUEROLUS: But the envy is justified, for I am worse off than those who are my inferiors.

HOUSEHOLD GOD: What if I prove you're more fortunate than those of whom you're about to speak?

QUEROLUS: Then you'll accomplish this, that Querolus hereafter will permit no one to complain.

HOUSEHOLD GOD: To make the business shorter and clearer, I'll leave aside the arguments. You tell me the fortune that would please you, and I'll give you what you want immediately. But remember this one thing: don't think that you can have any regrets or withdraw from the choice you make.

QUEROLUS: I'd like the opportunity to choose. Give me wealth and military honours, at least in moderation.

HOUSEHOLD GOD: I can bestow this upon you. But consider if you're able to fulfill the duties you seek.

QUEROLUS: What do you mean?

HOUSEHOLD GOD: Are you able to wage war? To parry a sword-thrust? To break the enemy's line?

QUEROLUS: That's something I've never been able to do.

HOUSEHOLD GOD: Then leave the rewards and honours to those who can.

QUEROLUS: Give me something at least of a civil and administrative nature.

HOUSEHOLD GOD: You wish to collect and pay out money?

QUEROLUS: Alas! That's gone! I don't care for either. If you have the ability, Household God, make me a private citizen and one of power.

HOUSEHOLD GOD: What sort of power do you wish?

QUEROLUS: That I may plunder those who owe me nothing, beat strangers, and as for my neighbours, I'd like both to plunder and beat them.

HOUSEHOLD GOD (*laughing*): Ha, ha, ha! It's brigandage you're asking for, not power. I certainly don't know how this can be granted to you. (*Reflecting a moment*) Wait, I've found it! You have your wish. Go live along the Loire.

QUEROLUS: What then?

HOUSEHOLD GOD: There people live according to natural law;[9] there you will find no trickery; there capital sentences are pronounced from under oak trees and are written on the bones of animals. There the peasants are lawyers and private citizens are judges. There everything is permitted. If you are rich, you will be called Nabob;[10] that's what the Greeks say. O forests, O solitude! Who said that you were free? There are many other things I could mention, but this is enough for the present.

QUEROLUS: But I'm not rich, and I don't care to use the oak tree this way. I'm not interested in these forest laws.

HOUSEHOLD GOD: Then seek something more gentle and more noble, if you're not able to enter into disputes.

QUEROLUS: Give me such honour as that official receives on whom you particularly bestow favours.

HOUSEHOLD GOD: Now you've asked for something very easy. Even if I have no power, I can still do that. Do you wish me to grant it to you?

QUEROLUS: There's nothing that I'd like more.

HOUSEHOLD GOD: I'll omit the serious disadvantages. Put on clothing that is too short in winter and too thick in summer; put on woollen buskins which are always run down and torn and which will be rotted by rain, filled with dust, stuck together with mud and sweat; put on cheaply covered boots which stick to the ground and are barely distinguishable in colour from the mud. Spend the summer with your knees covered, the winter with your legs bare; wear slippers in winter, tight boots in hot weather. Be ready to endure irregular toil, meetings before daybreak, an early lunch or an afternoon banquet for a judge, whether it be heated or cold, whether it be crazy or serious. Sell your voice, sell your tongue; hire out your anger and your hatred. In short, be a poor man and bring home a little money, but more ill will. I could add more, but with people like that—it's better to pronounce their funeral oration[11] than denounce them.

QUEROLUS: I don't care for that either. Give me wealth such as those acquire who keep accounts.

HOUSEHOLD GOD: Then receive the lack of sleep and the labours of those you envy. In your youth seek gold; when you're old seek a land in which to dwell; be a beginner on your farm instead of a veteran of the forum; be a skilled bookkeeper, but an inexperienced owner. Be well-known to strangers, but a stranger to your neighbours. Be the object of hatred all your life in order to attain a sumptuous funeral. Heaven will provide heirs for you, to be sure. Querolus, I don't want you to envy people like that. Often what the wolf has stored away becomes the plunder of the fox.

QUEROLUS: Aha! No accounts for me! Give me merely the purse of the foreigner, that merchant who trades across the sea.

HOUSEHOLD GOD: Go, then! Set sail on the sea and entrust yourself and your possessions to the mercy of the waves and the winds.

QUEROLUS: Oh, I never wanted to do that. Give me at least the treasure box of Titus.

HOUSEHOLD GOD: Then take the gout of Titus along with it.

QUEROLUS: Not at all.

HOUSEHOLD GOD: Then you won't receive the treasure box of Titus.

QUEROLUS: Well, I don't want it, anyway. Give me some music girls and sweet little concubines, such as that greedy moneylender from abroad has.

HOUSEHOLD GOD: Now you certainly shall have just what you ask for. Take a whole band of dancers, if you wish; take Paphie, Cytheris, Briseis, but along with them take the burden of old Nestor.[12]

QUEROLUS: Ha, ha, ha! Why so?

HOUSEHOLD GOD: That's the way the man is whose fortune you desire. Oho, Querolus, haven't you ever heard the saying: "Everyone must pay for his fun"? Either you must accept the disadvantages with the advantages, or give up the advantages with the disadvantages.

QUEROLUS: I still think of something I'd like to have; give me merely shamelessness.

HOUSEHOLD GOD: My word, a clever fellow! Now you desire everything I've just refused you. If you want to have the world at your feet, be shameless; but then you'll have to give up all wisdom.

QUEROLUS: Why?

HOUSEHOLD GOD: Because no man of wisdom is ever shameless.

QUEROLUS (*annoyed*): Oh, get out, Household God, you and your argumentations!

HOUSEHOLD GOD: And you get out, Querolus, you and your lamentations!

QUEROLUS: Then will my bad fortune never be changed?

HOUSEHOLD GOD: Not so long as you live.

QUEROLUS (*gloomily*): Then there are no happy persons.

HOUSEHOLD GOD: Oh, yes, a few, but not the ones you think.

QUEROLUS: How's that? If I point out to you right now some person that's both healthy and rich, will you deny that he is happy?

HOUSEHOLD GOD: You can recognise a rich man, but what do you think constitutes good health?

QUEROLUS: For a man to have a sound body.

HOUSEHOLD GOD: But what if he is mentally sick?

QUEROLUS: That's something I don't know about.

HOUSEHOLD GOD: O Querolus, you think only in terms of bodily ailments; how much greater are the ailments of the mind! Hope, fear, desire, avarice, despair—these do not permit a man to be happy. What if that person you refer to isn't the same in mind as he is in appearance? What if he is gay in public and wretched in private? To pass over more serious points—what if he doesn't love his wife? Or what if he loves her too much?

QUEROLUS: If no one is fortunate, is then no one righteous?[13]

HOUSEHOLD GOD: I can answer that, too. There are some men who are almost righteous, I admit, but their lot is the most wretched of all.[14] Is there anything now that you wish?

QUEROLUS (*convinced*): No, damn it, not a thing. Let me have my own fortune, since I have discovered nothing better.

HOUSEHOLD GOD: Then it is agreed that you are happy. But even so, I want you to realise now that your good fortune will increase. Today you shall acquire a large amount of gold.

QUEROLUS: You're making fun of me; that just isn't possible.

HOUSEHOLD GOD: Why not?

QUEROLUS: Because there's no way that it can happen.

HOUSEHOLD GOD: It surely isn't difficult for me to do things and discover things that you don't understand.

QUEROLUS (*with irony*): Tell me, please. A rich patron isn't going to give me any wealth, is he?

HOUSEHOLD GOD: By no means.

QUEROLUS: Some friend going to give me something as a gift?

HOUSEHOLD GOD: By no means.

QUEROLUS: No one will make me his heir unexpectedly, will he?

HOUSEHOLD GOD: That's even less possible.

QUEROLUS: Will a treasure be dug up somewhere and appear before my eyes?

HOUSEHOLD GOD (*mysteriously*): Even if a treasure were hidden in your own house, another person would have to discover it before you.

QUEROLUS: And how am I going to have something that no one will give me?

HOUSEHOLD GOD: Go now and do whatever is contrary to your own interests.

QUEROLUS: Why so?

HOUSEHOLD GOD (*more mysteriously*): This is the way to benefit yourself. Put your trust in the man that deceives you; give aid and assistance to the man who plots against you; if thieves come to your house, welcome them eagerly.

QUEROLUS: Then, if someone applies a torch to my house, would you advise me to pour oil on the fire?

HOUSEHOLD GOD: I was sure that you wouldn't believe me.

QUEROLUS: Thieves and robbers—what good are they to me?

HOUSEHOLD GOD: So that, if you still have any hopes or resources, they can carry them off entirely.

QUEROLUS: What for?

HOUSEHOLD GOD: That you may be rich.

QUEROLUS: How?

HOUSEHOLD GOD: By losing your possessions.

QUEROLUS: What for?

HOUSEHOLD GOD: That you may be happy.

QUEROLUS: How?

HOUSEHOLD GOD: By being miserable.

QUEROLUS (*aside*): This is certainly an example of the old saying, "to wrap the truth in riddles." (*To the* HOUSEHOLD GOD) But what do you advise me to do?

HOUSEHOLD GOD: What you consider to your disadvantage.

QUEROLUS: Then tell me what that is, so that in my ignorance I won't happen to do something to my advantage.

HOUSEHOLD GOD: Whatever you do or accomplish today will be to your advantage.

QUEROLUS: What if I'm unwilling?

HOUSEHOLD GOD: Good fortune will enter your house, whether you're willing or not.

QUEROLUS: What if I lock up the house?

HOUSEHOLD GOD: It will flow in through the window.

QUEROLUS: And if I close the window?

HOUSEHOLD GOD: You fool! The windows will open and the earth itself will gape apart before you can shut out or drive away that which cannot be changed.

QUEROLUS: And so, as I understand it, this is no gift to me, because it must happen whether I wish it or not.

HOUSEHOLD GOD: I didn't expect you to thank me, but to make it clear that you were "querulous" in every respect. (*The* HOUSEHOLD GOD *moves towards the house of* QUEROLUS.)

QUEROLUS: Where are you going now?

HOUSEHOLD GOD: I'm returning to your house, or rather, to mine. From there I'll go wherever I wish. But wherever I wander, I'll see to it that I never desert you. (*He enters the house of* QUEROLUS.)

QUEROLUS (*to himself*): I've been more confused today than ever before in my life. What in the world am I to do with such answers as these? To what person has such an oracle ever been given, that he should seek misery for himself and should not shut out the misfortune that threatened him, even if it were possible to do so? "Lose," says he, "whatever you have at home, that you may acquire much more." But if my own property is taken away, who will give me some other person's property, or when? "Come," says he to me, "seek thieves, receive robbers into your home." First of all, suppose that this could be known and proved, wouldn't a judge quite properly condemn me as an accomplice of robbers? (*Reflecting*) But where on earth can I find these thieves? I don't know where to look for them. Where is that sooty, smoky, dirty regiment that lives underground in the daytime and prowls around houses by night? Where are those men who are clever at unclasping buckles and cutting belts? (*Pausing and looking down the street*) If I'm not mistaken, I see one of them now. Yes, there he is ready for business. (*Calling*) Hey there, you pickpocket, you, I mean! Look out! Stop right there! (*To himself*) Excellent! My buckle is safe. (*Reflecting*) Damn! I'm lost now! I forgot my instructions. I was forbidden to oppose the thieves. But not to shut them out is damned stupid; I certainly don't like that. (*Pausing again*) And yet, if I'm not mistaken, the fellow that spoke with me is a mighty clever person. But what have I done to deserve this special favour, a heavenly apparition? There's some sort of trickery here. Heavens, I'm afraid that he's already finished the thievery that he announced to me. I'll go back inside and if I find him there, I'll drag him out here at once. (QUEROLUS *hurries into his house.*)

Act Two.   Scene I

(*Enter* MANDROGERUS, *followed by his two accomplices, the* SWINDLER *and* SARDANAPALLUS.)

MANDROGERUS: Many men pride themselves upon their ability in dealing with swift-fleeing animals or ferocious wild beasts, either in tracking them down, or catching them in their lairs, or overpowering them by chance. How much greater is my talent and my profit, for I hunt men in the sight of all! And what men? Why, particularly the rich, the powerful, and the cultured. (*Proudly*) I am Mandrogerus, the most pre-eminent by far of all parasites. There lies near here a certain pot, and the breeze has wafted its scent to me across the seas. Away, you mixers of sauces! Away, you concoctions of cooks! Away, you recipes of Apicius![15] The secrets[16] of this pot were known to Euclio alone. Why are you surprised? It is gold that I follow; it is gold that sends its odour across seas and lands. What do you say to this now, my novices and my beginners? When can you learn these methods? When will you have such understanding? And the ability to give such instruction?

SWINDLER: Oh, my dear Mandrogerus, if you only knew the dream I had last night!

MANDROGERUS: Tell me about it, please, if there's any good in it.

SWINDLER: Last night I saw the hoped-for treasure already in our hands.

MANDROGERUS: What then?

SWINDLER: I saw that part of it was gold coin.

MANDROGERUS: Ah! Part, eh? I don't like that.

SWINDLER: Moreover, there were some little barbed hooks in it, and some neck-chains and little shackles.

MANDROGERUS (*ironically*): Tell me, I beg of you, didn't you dream of fetters and floggings also?

SARDANAPALLUS (*interrupting*): A damned unlucky dreamer! The only thing he missed seeing was a prison! (*To the* SWINDLER) Oho, you man of marvels! To hell with you and your words! (*To* MANDROGERUS) Now I saw a funeral in *my* sleep last night.

MANDROGERUS: The gods bless you well!

SARDANAPALLUS: And we ourselves were taking out the ashes somewhere.

MANDROGERUS: Excellent!

SARDANAPALLUS: And in addition to that we were shedding tears for the dead man; and yet he seemed a stranger to us.

MANDROGERUS (*to the* SWINDLER): Do you hear that, you fool? I prefer clear dreams like this to such dreams as yours. (*To both*) The funeral means happiness; the tears are a sign of joy; the fact that we carried out the dead man—that's out-and-out rejoicing. Now I'll tell you about my dream—and it's quite the clearest one of all. Someone told me in my dream last night that gold was being saved for me beyond the shadow of a doubt and that no other person except myself would have the chance to find it. But he added this also: from this wealth only so much would benefit me as went down my gullet.

SWINDLER: Why, that's a damned fine dream! What else are we looking for except enough to satisfy our bellies and our gullets?

SARDANAPALLUS: Jove! You've had a beautiful dream; you're lucky, Mandrogerus, and so are we, your companions.

MANDROGERUS (*halting suddenly in front of* QUEROLUS' *house*): Look here, my dear swindler, if my information doesn't mislead me, we've arrived.

SARDANAPALLUS (*looking about*): This is the very street you're looking for.

SWINDLER: Quick now, look at your directions.[17]

MANDROGERUS (*referring to his notes*): There's a shrine on one side, and a banker's booth opposite.

SWINDLER: They're both here.

SARDANAPALLUS: We have arrived. What next?[18]

MANDROGERUS: A high house.

SWINDLER: That's obvious.

MANDROGERUS: With oaken doors.

SARDANAPALLUS: The very one.

MANDROGERUS (*examining the house carefully*): Oh! Oh! How low the windows are! Wonderful! No need here to shut the doors. Then, too, those feeble bars—how far apart they are! Gad, a fine layout I have here, a place where thieves are not feared! But I get a whiff of the gold inside. Now we must try a different means. Look here now, Swindler, and you too, Sardanapallus; if you have any ability, charm, and courage, now's the time to display it all. Like the master of the hunt, I'll discover and deliver into your hands the captured prey; you watch the nets while I drive him from his lair. Keep in mind now what we've been saying for a long time and what we've been rehearsing night and day.

SWINDLER (*as though reciting*): There's a gallery off the hall.

MANDROGERUS: You've got it straight.

SARDANAPALLUS: And three little statues in the shrine.

MANDROGERUS: Correct.

SWINDLER: A small altar in the middle.

MANDROGERUS: That's just the way everything is.

SARDANAPALLUS: In front of the altar is the gold.

MANDROGERUS: And that's ours now. Well, do you know the description of Querolus?

SWINDLER: Yes, a lot better than we know yours. You see if you have the ability to be a fortuneteller; we know how to lie.

MANDROGERUS (*pointing down the street*): Well, I'll go for a walk now in that direction; I'll watch from there and return here instantly when the situation demands it. (MANDROGERUS *departs.*)

SWINDLER (*to* SARDANAPALLUS): Let us withdraw a bit, too, so that there won't be any suspicion of crooked work. (*They go a little distance from the house of* QUEROLUS.)

Act Two. Scene II

(*Enter* QUEROLUS *from his house.*)

QUEROLUS (*to himself, not seeing the others*): That fellow who was talking to me completely disappeared, and he didn't steal anything in the house. He certainly wasn't a mortal.

SARDANAPALLUS (*aside to the* SWINDLER): There! That's our man. (*Aloud*) Gad, if I wouldn't like to have that person show up, the one I saw a while ago! I know about magicians and astrologers, but I never saw one like this. This is real fortunetelling, not the sort that certain people are in the habit of doing in jest.

QUEROLUS (*to himself, overhearing*): Hm-m! What fortuneteller are they talking about?

SARDANAPALLUS (*to the* SWINDLER): But what I've just seen is amazing! When the man sees you, first of all he calls you by your own name, then he describes your parents, your slaves, your entire household; he explains everything, just as if he knows what you've done all your life and what you're going to do next.

QUEROLUS (*aside*): Heavens! What a splendid person this somebody must be! I mustn't miss any of their conversation.

SWINDLER: Listen, please. Why not go to the man, no matter what the pretext?

SARDANAPALLUS: I was certainly a silly and stupid person not to consult him immediately.

SWINDLER: I'd like to very much, too, but as you know, I haven't time.

QUEROLUS (*aside, still more interested*): Why don't I find out everything about this? (*Aloud, as he approaches the two rogues*) Good day, my friends.

SWINDLER: The same to you, since you bid us good day.

QUEROLUS (*pretending ignorance*): What were you talking about? A secret, perhaps?

SARDANAPALLUS: A secret from the common classes, but not from wise men.

QUEROLUS: I heard you mention a certain magician.

SARDANAPALLUS: That's right; we were just talking about a man who foretells everything. But I don't know who the fellow is.

QUEROLUS: Is there really some such person?

SARDANAPALLUS: Of course. (*To the* SWINDLER) As I was saying, Swindler, I beg you by all you hold dear to come along with me.

SWINDLER: I told you already; I'd gladly go if I had the leisure. (*He pretends to depart.*)

SARDANAPALLUS: Stay here a while.

QUEROLUS: Please, my friend, don't dash away so quickly. I'm eager to know who that person is that you were just talking about.

SWINDLER: Damn it! I have some other business on hand. My relatives and friends have been waiting for me at home for a long time.

SARDANAPALLUS (*to* QUEROLUS): Heavens! What a difficult man to persuade! (*To the* SWINDLER) You don't have any friends or relatives waiting for you. Stay here a while.

QUEROLUS: Please, my friend, if you don't object to my presence, I'd like to consult him along with you.

SARDANAPALLUS: I'm really afraid that he will be hard to approach, if he sees several people.

SWINDLER (*to* SARDANAPALLUS): Quite right, to be sure. Look, please, here is the companion you were seeking. Don't bother me about it.

QUEROLUS (*to* SARDANAPALLUS): My friend, please let him go if it is his wish. You and I will go there together.

SARDANAPALLUS: But we need this fellow, since he has seen the fortuneteller and knows him well.

QUEROLUS (*to the* SWINDLER): It's right for you to give us your assistance today, since the situation really demands it.

SWINDLER (*with irony*): Why, this man knows him a lot better than I do, and the fortuneteller considers him an intimate friend.

QUEROLUS: But seriously now, on your word, who is the fellow? Where does he come from?

SWINDLER: So far as I've learned, he's named Mandrogerus; that's all I know.

QUEROLUS: Ah! It's a beautiful name, to be sure! Now I'm positive he[19] is a magician.

SWINDLER: First he sets forth the past. Then, if you admit everything, he discusses the future.

QUEROLUS: He must be wonderfully gifted—this man you're speaking of. And yet you don't wish to consult him?

SWINDLER: I really want to, but for the moment I haven't time.

QUEROLUS: Oh, come, oblige your friends; command the same of us when you want something.

SWINDLER: Thank you. I'll do it, since you both desire it. But mark my words: men of this sort are charlatans.

QUEROLUS: Ahem! The very thing I wanted to say. He certainly doesn't have a magic wand or walk about with a bunch of cronies.

SWINDLER: Ha, ha, ha! That's the sort that an inquisitive person like this (*indicating* SARDANAPALLUS) ought to consult.

SARDANAPALLUS: He can deceive us with his words as much as he wishes; but so far as I'm concerned, nothing more than that is possible.

SWINDLER: If this meets with your approval, let me put the questions to the man and scrutinise everything in every possible way. If he can answer me on every point, then you may be sure that he really is a fortuneteller or a magician.

SARDANAPALLUS: Well spoken. (*Looking down the street*) But there he is, passing by this way. It's happened just as I wished. What gravity in his step! What dignity in his countenance!

QUEROLUS: Let's approach and draw him aside, so that you can talk in secret.

Act Two.　Scene III

(*Enter* MANDROGERUS.)

QUEROLUS: Good day, Mandrogerus.

MANDROGERUS (*gravely*): Good health to all of you.

QUEROLUS: May you too have the best of health, O mightiest of priests, since you are greatly praised and beloved—as you deserve.

SWINDLER: Do you know, Mandrogerus, what we want to learn from you?

MANDROGERUS: What is it? Perhaps I can help you.

SWINDLER: We wish to consult you about certain matters and to become acquainted with your remarkable wisdom.

MANDROGERUS: I hadn't planned to do this; however, since you wish, give me your questions so that I can answer.

SWINDLER: We beg you to be generous with your assistance. We have need now of a lengthy discussion.

MANDROGERUS: Tell me what you wish.

SWINDLER: In the first place, we ask you to explain to us the best kinds of worship and the easiest to practise.

MANDROGERUS: There are two kinds of divinities; the one gives orders, the other carries them out; that's the way everything is managed. The power of the greater divinities is more distinguished, the favour of the lesser is more useful. Concerning these greater divinities, however, it is pointless for me to speak or for you to listen. And so, if you wish to avoid both ill will and expense, put your trust in the lesser deities.

SWINDLER: Who are these inferior powers to whom we must submit?

MANDROGERUS: I'll tell you quickly. There are three kinds, first of all: the powerful Planets, the troublesome Geese, and the ferocious Dog-heads. If you can pay attention to them and appease their images in all the shrines and chapels, there is nothing that can stand in your way.

SWINDLER: Tell me, please, do you mean those planets which make everything revolve in harmony?

MANDROGERUS: The very ones; they're neither easy to see nor friendly to talk to. They direct the course of the atoms, they count the stars, they weigh the seas. They can change everything except their own condition.

SWINDLER: I had heard they were the ones that governed the universe.

MANDROGERUS (*laughing*): Ha, ha, ha! If you consider this any sort of governing, I don't know what you'd call a shipwreck. When they learn that there is a shortage of supplies in a certain place, that's where they assemble men. Their chief remedy is to sweep other places clean in turn. With frightful storms they transfer harvests from one place to another, and a few worthless people get all the benefit.

SARDANAPALLUS: That's not a new thing to you [for harvests to be transferred],[20] is it?

MANDROGERUS (*continuing*): They have the power to change the appearance and shape of everything as they wish. And how many stages there are to their transformations! They turn this into that. You can see wine suddenly change to wheat, and wheat to wine. A yellow crop of barley is easily produced from any material and name whatsoever. For them to send mortal souls to Hades or to Heaven is no labour at all.

SARDANAPALLUS (*to the* SWINDLER): You see, then, don't you, that such powerful beings ought to be placated?

MANDROGERUS (*laughing*): Ha, ha, ha! That's permitted to only a few mortals; their sanctuaries are too magnificent and too expensive. If you want to follow my advice, pay your offerings in a modest little shrine.

SWINDLER: And oracles, where are they to be sought particularly?

MANDROGERUS: Wherever you wish, here and there, above, below, on land, on sea.

SWINDLER: And what unlucky fellow could discover or approach these wandering planets?

MANDROGERUS: It's not easy to approach them, and to depart from them is impossible.

SWINDLER: Why?

MANDROGERUS: Mysterious creatures guard the entrance, various secret ones that we alone know: Harpies, Dog-heads, Furies, Screech-owls, Night-owls. Persons who are absent are brought there with serpents; those who are there are driven away with blows. Thus there's no safety whether one comes near or stays away. They disperse crowds and yet they want them. In brief, if the gods love you, don't try to find out anything about them.

SWINDLER: My dear priest, this mysterious worship doesn't appeal to me. Explain about the second kind, the Geese, and tell us if they're good for anything.

MANDROGERUS: They are the creatures who plead in behalf of mortal men before the altars and shrines; they have the heads and necks of swans. Their practice is to eat what falls from the table. Of all fore-tellers of the future they are by far the most deceptive; they serve merely to explain men's desires, and they do it badly;[21] they utter prayers in their behalf, but they never gain from the gods an answer that is suitable.

SARDANAPALLUS: Do you say they're swans? I've seen many geese in the shrines near by, but never a swan. They stretch out their heads and enormous necks, and they use their wings as hands. They begin by darting out their three-forked tongues at each other and hissing. Then, when one of them has made a sound, they all flap their wings and make a dreadful clatter.

MANDROGERUS: They're not easily satisfied. They don't eat bread and don't want it; they're eager for barley that's cracked and soaked; some of them eat ears of grain, and certain ones even eat polenta and meat that's about to spoil.

SWINDLER: That's a silly expense.

MANDROGERUS: The great Cicero once said of them, "The geese are fed at the expense of the state and the dogs are nourished on the Capitol."[22]

SWINDLER: What a manifold and varied race of creatures! I suppose their mother was Circe, their father Proteus.

SARDANAPALLUS: Damn it! I don't like them either. Describe the Dog-heads now, if you think they're better.

MANDROGERUS: They are the ones that watch the curtains at the entrances of the temples and shrines. From the chest up they have the heads of dogs; they have fat bellies and crooked hands. They are guards and custodians of the temple. Once upon a time Hecuba, after she became a real dog, married our god Anubis the barker and then gave birth to the Dog-heads in litters of ten for all the temples and shrines. That's why they have two forms; men from the breast down, and wild beasts from the breast up. And so, when a strange worshipper comes to a temple, all the Dog-heads surround him on every side and bark loudly at him. To approach, you'll give so much; to be allowed to finish your prayers, you'll give so much more. They make a mysterious thing of worship, and they make a business arrangement of it. Everything that's common and free they sell at the entrance. You must make an offering to all of these; if you can't get off cheaply, do the best you can. Just consider the powers that human beings have and forgive us. Believe me, you can approach a god for less than a fair trial costs.

SWINDLER: That's enough! I don't care about them either. I don't think there's anything worse among all the gods you've described.

MANDROGERUS:[23] You're lucky in having nothing to do with the Dog-heads. Why, I saw Cerberus himself once, and if the golden bough hadn't been there, Aeneas wouldn't have escaped.[24]

SWINDLER: And the monkeys?

MANDROGERUS: They're the creatures that write down what will take place, the proceedings, as you men say. They unroll the fates of mortals on thin pages. These animals aren't really dangerous, but they're annoying and worthless. What grimaces, what clustering you'd see, if you scattered money in front of them! And if you give them nuts and apples besides, you'll catch the whole tribe.

SWINDLER: Pardon me, but you passed over the Harpies, who always plunder and devour.

MANDROGERUS: They are the ones who check on men's prayers and the honours paid to the gods. They insist upon not only the ordinary ceremonies, but also the unusual ones and funeral anniversaries. If something isn't ready on the appointed day they torture people until it's done. They fly over the earth, here, there, everywhere in the world. They sharpen their frightfully curved nails for purposes of plunder. They always fly over tables; what they touch they carry away, what they leave behind they pollute. I'd rather feed such monsters than make their acquaintance, but I don't care to do either.

SARDANAPALLUS: You didn't mention the swift, night-wandering, goat-footed prophets.

MANDROGERUS: These monsters are countless, but cowardly and worthless. There is only one god that they follow and worship, the great god Pan-loaf.[25]

SWINDLER: Well, you yourself have disapproved of all these religions. What do you advise?

MANDROGERUS: Since you make this straightforward request, I'll tell you; among all these worships, there's nothing better than to be born with good luck.

QUEROLUS: I suspect that's true. But that good luck you mention—how can it be worshipped and made favourable?

MANDROGERUS: I'll tell you. You have to worship Household Gods, since they control the decrees of Fate. You have to appease them and win them over, and, at the same time, if there's any Bad Fortune in the house, it must be tied up and bundled off.

QUEROLUS: Gad, what wonderful instruction! But so that we can follow you more easily on all these points, give us a sample of your power and your wisdom. You've just told us what you know; now, if you can, tell us what you don't know.

MANDROGERUS: I can't do that offhand very well. But here are a few things and you can judge the rest from these. (*With a wink at* SARDANAPALLUS) I certainly have had no opportunity to learn about your character and your position.

SARDANAPALLUS: That's true.

MANDROGERUS: Sardanapallus, you're a poor man.

SARDANAPALLUS: I know that; but I'm afraid that many people know it, too.

MANDROGERUS: A man of lowly birth.

SARDANAPALLUS: That's right.

MANDROGERUS: And that's why this royal name[26] was given to you, by way of contrast.

SARDANAPALLUS: So they say.

MANDROGERUS: You're a greedy and a disagreeable person; in fact, a most pernicious individual.

SARDANAPALLUS: Look here, Mandrogerus, I didn't ask you to tell me my faults, did I?

MANDROGERUS: I cannot tell a lie. Is there still something that you want me to tell you?

SARDANAPALLUS: I wish that you hadn't even said this much about me. If you have anything more to say, tell it to my friends here.

SWINDLER: Mandrogerus, I want you now to tell me my fortune, but only the things that are good.

MANDROGERUS: I can't do that unless I start from the beginning. You, swindler, were born of noble and illustrious parents.

SWINDLER: That's right.

MANDROGERUS: You were worthless from your earliest years.

SWINDLER (*brazenly*): I admit it. I haven't changed a bit.

MANDROGERUS: You suffer many losses.

SWINDLER: True.

MANDROGERUS: Dangers often threaten you: fire, steel, floods.

SWINDLER (*to* QUEROLUS): Damned if he hasn't told everything as accurately as if he had been living with me.

MANDROGERUS: Your destiny is to have no property of your own.

SWINDLER: I know that.

MANDROGERUS: But to have a lot of other people's property.

SWINDLER: Well, that's enough for me.[27] And now we want you to give your responses to our companion here (*pointing to* QUEROLUS) who isn't at all a bad fellow.

MANDROGERUS: I'm glad to. (*To* QUEROLUS) Look here, my friend, is your name Querolus?

QUEROLUS (*surprised*): The gods bless you! It is that.

MANDROGERUS: What hour do you say it is?

SWINDLER (*with a wink*): Between noon and mid-morning.[28]

MANDROGERUS: Such accuracy! You'd think the man had consulted a water-clock. (*Calculating*) Hm-m! Let me see. Mars in trigon, Saturn opposite Venus, Jupiter quadrate, Mercury angry at him, the Sun round, and the Moon in exaltation. Now I've got your entire horoscope, Querolus. Bad Fortune overwhelms you.

QUEROLUS: I know it.

MANDROGERUS: Your father left you nothing, your friends give you nothing.

QUEROLUS: True enough.

MANDROGERUS: You want to hear everything? You have an evil neighbour and a worthless slave.

QUEROLUS: I know all that.

MANDROGERUS: Do you want me now to tell you the names of your slaves?

QUEROLUS: I'd like to hear them.

MANDROGERUS: You have a slave named Pantomalus.

QUEROLUS: True.

MANDROGERUS: There's another named Geta.

QUEROLUS: Quite right.

SWINDLER (*with pretended awe*): O heavenly priest!

MANDROGERUS: Do you wish still more? You're sure that I'm not acquainted with your house, aren't you?

QUEROLUS: Of course.

MANDROGERUS: There's a gallery on the right as you enter, and a shrine opposite.

QUEROLUS (*impressed*): That's just the way they are.

MANDROGERUS: And in the shrine are three statues.

QUEROLUS: True.

MANDROGERUS: One is the statue of your Protecting Deity; the others are those of your attendant spirits.

QUEROLUS: That's enough to prove your power and your skill. Now set forth a remedy for my ills.

MANDROGERUS: I can give you advice for that quickly, without delay and expense. That shrine of yours is secret and apart, I suppose.

QUEROLUS: Yes.

MANDROGERUS: And there's nothing stored there, surely.

QUEROLUS: Nothing but the statues.

MANDROGERUS: A certain ceremony must be celebrated there, but its nature is such that you and your household must go outside.

QUEROLUS: As you wish.

MANDROGERUS: The ceremony must be carried on by strangers.

QUEROLUS: I'm willing.

MANDROGERUS (*looking about*): But whom can we find now without delay? (*Pauses*) It would be fine and fitting if these men were willing to give you their services.

QUEROLUS (*to* SWINDLER *and* SARDANAPALLUS): I beg of you, my friends, do now an act both dutiful and pious. I'll do the same thing for you if the need ever arises.

SWINDLER (*apparently somewhat unwilling*): Well, we don't know anything about this, but if it has to be done, all right.

SARDANAPALLUS (*piously*): It would be inhuman to reject your entreaties.

MANDROGERUS (*approvingly*): That's very kind of you; you're both good men.

QUEROLUS (*a bit uneasy*): Curses on it! Am I to be alone now, shut out of the plan? (*Calling to his slave within the house*) Hey, Pantomalus!

Quick, now! Run and find my neighbour, wherever he is, and bring him here as a witness. (*More severely*) I know the sort of person you are; go now and hire yourself out to the barkeepers for the day.

MANDROGERUS (*impatiently*): Don't you know, Querolus, that this is a deed and a decision for the present moment?

QUEROLUS: What do you mean?

MANDROGERUS: This is the hour decreed by the stars; this is the hour I want. If we don't act right now, we've come here in vain.

QUEROLUS (*convinced*): Let's go inside then.

MANDROGERUS: You go ahead; we'll follow you. (*Pauses*) Ha! One thing I forgot. Do you have an empty chest?

QUEROLUS: Several.

MANDROGERUS: One is sufficient; just so the object of the purification can be carried outside.

QUEROLUS: And I'll furnish the keys, so that this Bad Fortune can be shut up in it and put outside the house.

MANDROGERUS: Everything is done. May this home be happy and blessed and fortunate! We are ready. (*All enter the house of* QUEROLUS.)

Act Two. Scene IV

(*Enter* PANTOMALUS *from the house.*)

PANTOMALUS (*seating himself on a bench in front of the house and addressing the audience*): It's a well-established and self-evident fact that all masters are wicked. But I've found out to my own satisfaction that my master's worse than any of them. He isn't really a dangerous fellow, but he's damned ungrateful and sour. If a theft is committed in the house, he curses as if it were a horrible crime. If a person loses anything, just look at the instant clamour and evil abuse he pours out! If anyone pushes a chair, a table, a couch into the fire, as we often do in our haste, a regular trial is held about it. If the roof leaks, if the door is broken, he calls everybody in and holds an investigation. Gad, he's just unbearable! Furthermore, he writes down with his own hand the expenses and all the accounts; if something can't be shown to be an expense, he insists that the money be paid back to him.

And when he takes a trip then he's especially disagreeable and un-manageable. Whenever we have to start before dawn, first we gulp a bit of wine and then we snatch a nap; that's his first reason for finding fault. Then, while he is complaining about our sleeping and drinking,[29] he finds a lot of other things to rant about: the confusion of the crowd, the search for the animals, the flight of the drivers, poor pairing of the mules, twisted harness, the muleteer in no state to drive; from this source come new complaints on the journey. When another person makes a trip, he gradually takes care of all this with patience and delay. But Querolus, on the contrary, seeks one pretext after another, makes one complaint after another. He doesn't want a worn-out carriage or a sickly animal to be moved; straightway he shouts, "Why didn't you tell me about this?" Just as if he himself couldn't have seen it first? Oh, what an unjust master!

Moreover, if he happens to notice someone commit a fault, he conceals it and keeps quiet; then he begins to rave at a time when there's no longer an excuse on tap; then all one can say is, "That's what I wanted to do; that's what I wanted to say." And then, as often as we're pushed around hither and yon, we have to be back at the appointed time. And I'll tell you this, that you may completely realise the cunning of the wicked man: he always gives us one day more than necessary, so that we can get back on the prescribed day. Isn't he just looking for reasons for wrath? And no matter what happens the rest of the time, we always devote to our own enjoyment the very day on which we're to return; our master doesn't wish to be fooled or deceived, so he orders us to return the day before he wants us to be back.

Then, too, what sort of procedure is this, that he curses a drunken slave and spots him in a minute? At first sight he sees on his face and lips the amount and the quality of the wine. [He isn't willing to be cheated or deceived in the usual way.][30] Who could be a good slave to a master like this or obey him? He doesn't care for steaming hot water or for cups of ointment. What use are such luxuries? If a cup is dented or cracked, if a winejug is dirty or has lost its ears, if a bottle has lost its top, or is cracked and held together with a patch of wax, he doesn't merely look at it; he can hardly restrain his fury. I can't figure out what would satisfy such a depraved disposition.

Another thing: he knows immediately when wine has been weakened and diluted with water. We have the practice also of mixing wines to-gether. He can't say there's any falsification, can he, if we pour new wine into the old bottles that have been emptied? Querolus considers that this is an unpardonable crime; he's so wicked that he suspects it instantly.

And if a tiny bit of silverware is dented with the slightest of blows, he always thinks it's being filed away and altered, because it did happen once. But this doesn't make much difference, does it? The colour of the silver is the same, at any rate. Now in changing gold coins there are a thousand tricks. We say, "Change and change again," and we do so. Yet gold itself can't be changed. At least coins cast in the same mould ought not to differ, for what is more alike than one gold coin to another? And yet, even in gold there is a difference; profile, age and colour, true worth, letters, origin, exact weight to the fraction of an ounce—these are sought in the case of a gold coin more than in the case of a man. Also, if you have gold, you have everything. Querolus didn't know this formerly, but then the bad ruin the good.[31]

And this witness I'm going to get now—what an accursed villain he is! He gives his slaves less food and more work than is right. Heavens! He'd get a dishonest profit from an empty bushel basket, if he could. If these two men meet by chance or intention, they give each other advice. Still, by Jove, when everything's said and done, if I have to choose, I prefer my own master. Whatever his faults are, he's still our master, and he isn't stingy towards his own household. His only faults are beating us too frequently and complaining incessantly. And may God's anger be on both of them.

And yet we aren't as miserable and as stupid as certain people think. Some consider us sleepyheads because we sleep in the daytime. But we do this because of our watchfulness, since we keep watch by night. The slave who gets his rest in the daylight hours is wide awake when other people sleep.[32] And of all the things that Nature has done for mortals, nothing is better in my opinion than night. That is our daytime, that's when everything is done. We go to the baths at night, even though the daytime tempts us. Moreover, we bathe with the attendants and the maids; isn't this the life of a free man? A sufficient amount of light is provided, but not enough to make everything clear. I hold in my arms a naked girl; my master is hardly permitted to see her when she is clothed. I caress her sides, I run my hand through her loosened locks, I sit by her and embrace her, we fondle each other. What master can do that? And the high point of our happiness is that we slaves are not jealous of each other. We all steal and no one betrays us, since each of us does the same thing. We watch our masters and keep them out, for slaves and maids are all in league together. Woe to those slaves whose masters stay awake until late in the night! When you take part of the night away from a slave, you take away just so much of his life. How many freeborn men would like to have the gift of metamorphosis, so that they could be masters in the morning and slaves in the evening! Isn't it necessary for you, Querolus, to worry about paying taxes, while we slaves are enjoying ourselves in this fashion?[33] Why, every day we have weddings, birthdays, revelry, orgies, maids' holidays. That's why some of us don't even wish to be set free. Who can undergo such expense and enjoy such freedom when he is a free man?

But I've been sitting here too long. (*Arising from his bench*) My master will start shouting at me now, I suppose, as he usually does. I should have carried out his order—to go to his comrade's. (*With a shrug*) But what will happen? Abuse must be received in silence. They are our masters; let them say what they wish. One must put up with it as long as it pleases them. In the name of the gods, will I never gain the favour I have so long desired, that my stern and severe master win and lose standing as townsman, official, or chief of a bureau? Why do I say this? Well, loss of rank is more humiliating after enjoyment of it. What then should I desire but that he keep his present position? Let him live on as a candidate for office, an entertainer of judges, a frequenter of entrance halls, a servant of worthless servants, a busybody around the forum, a cunning investigator, a searcher and seizer of opportune moments, a morning man, a noonday man, an evening man. Let the impudent fellow greet those who scorn him, let him go to meet those who do not come, and I hope he has to wear boots in the heat of summer that are new and tight. (PANTOMALUS *departs.*)

Act Three.   Scene I

(*Enter* MANDROGERUS *and* QUEROLUS *from the house carrying a heavy chest between them. The* SWINDLER *and* SARDANAPALLUS *follow.*)

MANDROGERUS: Querolus, put down from your shoulders such a heavy weight. You've done enough for the ceremony in carrying your own Bad Fortune out of the house. (*They place the chest on the ground.*)

QUEROLUS: Oh, Mandrogerus, I never thought this would be possible, I admit. But the outcome proves your power and knowledge of religion. When I took this chest into the house, how light it was for me alone, and now how heavy it is for the two of us!

MANDROGERUS: Don't you know that nothing is heavier than Bad Fortune?

QUEROLUS: By Jove, I know it and realise it well.

MANDROGERUS: The gods bless you! What you praise me for has surpassed my hopes. I don't think any home has ever been so well purified. Whatever misfortune and misery the house contained we've shut up in this chest.

QUEROLUS: Gad, I still wonder where the weight comes from.

MANDROGERUS: That can't be explained in a moment. But often it happens that misfortune like this can't be moved by several teams of oxen. But enough! My helpers will hurl these impurities into the river. Now you must take to heart the directions that I shall give you. This Bad Fortune that we have removed will attempt to return home.

QUEROLUS: The gods forbid! I hope it stays away forever.

MANDROGERUS: You are in danger for the next three days; that's when this evil plague will attempt to return to you. And so the thing for you to do is to remain shut in your house night and day for these three days. Don't let anything out of your house and don't take anything in. Spurn all your neighbours, relatives, friends as though they were unclean. If Good Fortune herself should call to you and knock on the door, no one is to hear her today. When the three days are up, you'll never have in your house what you have just brought out of it. Go inside now.

QUEROLUS: I certainly shall, and with pleasure, provided that a wall always separates me from my Bad Fortune.

MANDROGERUS: Go in quickly. (*As* QUEROLUS *goes into his house*) Hey, Querolus! Close the door good and tight.

QUEROLUS (*from within*): It's done.

MANDROGERUS: Put on the bolts and chains.

QUEROLUS (*from within*): I'll do it as for myself.

Act Three.   Scene II

MANDROGERUS: Jove! Everything's gone beautifully! We found our man, robbed him, shut him up inside. But where are we to examine the urn? Where shall we smash this chest and conceal it so there'll be no trace of the theft?

SWINDLER: I don't know, to be sure, unless we drop it somewhere in the river.

SARDANAPALLUS: Do you believe it, Mandrogerus? I've been so overcome with joy that I haven't dared to look at the urn.

SWINDLER: Nor I.

MANDROGERUS: And you've acted as you should. Any haste would arouse suspicion.

SWINDLER: That's true.

MANDROGERUS: The most important thing was to find it. The rest follows; all is safe—

SWINDLER (*interrupting*): Whatever you have to say, Mandrogerus, let's get away somewhere. I won't believe myself until I've seen the gold with my own eyes.

MANDROGERUS: Nor I. Let's hurry away together.

SWINDLER: This way, that way; provided it's a secret place.

MANDROGERUS (*looking in every direction*): Damnation! All the streets are crowded and the river banks are filled with people. Let's find a place somewhere quickly. (MANDROGERUS *and his accomplices pick up the chest and hurry away.*)

Act Four. Scene I

(*Enter* PANTOMALUS *and the neighbour who is being brought as a* WITNESS.)

WITNESS: Well, Pantomalus, how goes it at home? How's your master behaving?

PANTOMALUS: Badly, as you know.

WITNESS: Complaining, eh?

PANTOMALUS: Not exactly; I hope he'll be well and favourably disposed towards us.

WITNESS: And yet, by Jove, he usually is disagreeable.

PANTOMALUS: What do you expect? That's the way things are. The sky isn't always the same, is it? Even the sun doesn't always shine.

WITNESS (*ironically*): Good, friend Pantomalus! You're the only one who speaks thus in behalf of masters.

PANTOMALUS (*virtuously*): I speak the same way to all of you whether you're absent or present.

WITNESS: I believe you, for I've always known that you were a good fellow.

PANTOMALUS: It's you who make us good and always happy, because you give good advice to our master.

WITNESS (*dryly*): I have and always do.

PANTOMALUS: Ah! I wish that he had your character and was as patient and kind to us as you are to your slaves.

WITNESS: I don't accept your praise, Pantomalus. You speak too highly of me.

PANTOMALUS: Heavens! We all know you well and praise you endlessly. I hope that everything happens to you as we poor slaves desire.

WITNESS (*sarcastic*): On the contrary, to you, confound it! I hope that what you have desired for me happens to your own hide and bones.

PANTOMALUS: Ah, why so suspicious? You don't make any accusation against us, do you?

WITNESS: No, but it's natural for you slaves always to hate masters without distinction.

PANTOMALUS: We heap curses on many, it's true, both frequently and sincerely, but they are deceitful and abusive, as you know well.

WITNESS: Come, come, I believe you. But what did you say your master was doing?

PANTOMALUS: He was beginning a religious ceremony. A magician and his attendants were here. They were all going into the house when I left.

WITNESS: But why is it that I see the door shut? They're engaged in the ceremony, I suppose. Call someone out here.

PANTOMALUS (*calling at the door*): Hey there, Theocles! Hey, Zeta! Someone come here instantly! (*As no one replies*) How am I to explain this? Absolute silence, no one there!

WITNESS: The doorkeepers were not in the habit of sleeping so soundly in that house.

PANTOMALUS: Confound it, I suppose it's on account of the ceremony! They don't want to have any troublesome visitors. Let's go around to the back door; you know the one I mean.

WITNESS: What if that's shut too?

PANTOMALUS: Don't worry when I lead the way. That's our regular entrance. They can shut it but they can't shut us out. (*They disappear behind the house.*)

Act Four. Scene II

(*Enter* MANDROGERUS, *the* SWINDLER, *and* SARDANAPALLUS, *all very dejected.* MANDROGERUS *carries a funeral urn.*)

MANDROGERUS: O miserable me!

SWINDLER: O ill-fated me!

SARDANAPALLUS: O stripped and shipwrecked me!

SWINDLER: O Mandrogerus, my master!

SARDANAPALLUS: O Swindler, my friend!

MANDROGERUS: O Sardanapallus, my aged comrade!

SARDANAPALLUS: Mourn, my unhappy companions; cover your heads with your hoods. Ah, this is worse than losing a friend; now we're mourning a real loss. With all your power, what will you do now? Why do you think of treasures? Our gold has turned to ashes. I wish all gold would do the same thing; then we'd be richer.

MANDROGERUS: Put down the poor empty weight. Let's shed tears for the sad occasion. O deceitful treasure, you're what I followed through seas and storms. (*Ironically*) You're the reason for my successful voyage, you're the reason for all my labours. To think that I studied astrology and magic, to be deceived by those long dead! I cast the horoscope of others, I couldn't tell my own fortune. Now I understand clearly the meaning of all these different visions. There was certainly good fortune here, but it was destined for another, not for me. Our fates have been changed around; we found a treasure, but for someone else.[34] What sort of perversity is this, anyway? I've never mourned for myself and here I am now weeping for a stranger. (*Looking towards the house*) Ah, Querolus, doesn't any righteous sorrow touch you?

SARDANAPALLUS: O cruel gold, what sickness carried you away? What funeral pyre reduced you to such ashes? What magician made off with you? Treasure, you have disinherited us. Where are we to turn now, disowned as we are? What spot will give us shelter? What pot will give us food?[35]

MANDROGERUS (*to the* SWINDLER): Come, friend, examine the urn again and again.

SWINDLER: You can go look for some other hope, my friend; this one isn't even warm.

MANDROGERUS (*handing the urn to* SARDANAPALLUS): Please read again the epitaph of the dead man and all the writing on it.

SARDANAPALLUS (*horrified*): I beg of you, I—I say, if you please, I—I can't bear to touch any sort of funeral object. There's nothing I fear more.

SWINDLER: You're a coward, Sardanapallus. I'll read it. (*He takes the urn and examines it carefully*) "Trierinus, the son of Tricipitinus, lies buried here." Oh, what an unhappy wretch I am! Oh, what an unhappy wretch I am!

MANDROGERUS (*noting the* SWINDLER'S *expression of disgust*): What's the matter with you?

SWINDLER: Oh! My breath is caught in my throat. I've heard it said that gold had an odour, but the smell of this is really strong.

MANDROGERUS: How's that?

SWINDLER: The lead cover is full of openings and it breathes forth foul odours. I never knew before this that gold could have such a rank smell. It ought to have a stench like this for moneylenders.

MANDROGERUS: What do the ashes smell like?

SWINDLER: Expense and grief, the sort of smell a wretched funeral demands.

MANDROGERUS (*dryly*): These ashes would seem to have had honourable treatment if they still have such a worthy smell.

SWINDLER: I wouldn't have had this misfortune if I had believed the jackdaw's song of warning.

SARDANAPALLUS: I wouldn't have fallen into a trap if I'd followed the advice of the short-tailed dog.

MANDROGERUS: And what sort of advice did the dog give you?

SARDANAPALLUS: He nipped my calves as I came into the street.

MANDROGERUS (*disgusted*): I wish he'd hamstrung you so that you couldn't have moved a step from there. O accursed Euclio! Didn't you deceive me enough when you were alive? Won't you cease after your death? (*Reflecting*) I've well deserved this misfortune for putting my trust in that treacherous *homme-sans-rire*. Even on the point of death he laughed at my fate.

SWINDLER: Well, what are we to do now?

MANDROGERUS: What can we do, except what we agreed on just now? We can exact a satisfactory vengeance from his son Querolus, at any rate. He's superstitious; let's profit by it and have some wondrous sport with him. Let's hurl the urn through the window without his knowing it, so that he can begin to grieve over it as we've already been mourning. (*To* SARDANAPALLUS) Approach on tiptoe and listen to what Querolus is doing.

SARDANAPALLUS: A good idea.

MANDROGERUS: Go near, confound you, but spy on them cleverly.

SARDANAPALLUS (*approaching the house and peering through the window*): Aha! What's this I see? The men are all there holding clubs and sticks.

MANDROGERUS: The trusting fools are waiting for Bad Fortune to return, I suppose. Go up and frighten them with a terrible noise. Declare that you are Bad Fortune and threaten to rush into the house.

SARDANAPALLUS (*calling out in a sepulchral voice*): Ho there, Querolus!

QUEROLUS (*from within*): Who are you?

SARDANAPALLUS: Quick, see to the door.

QUEROLUS (*from within*): Why?

SARDANAPALLUS: So that I can enter my home again.

QUEROLUS (*within*): Hey, Zeta! Hey, Pantomalus! Take your positions here and there.

SARDANAPALLUS: Ho! Querolus!

QUEROLUS (*from within*): I ask you, why do you keep calling my name?

SARDANAPALLUS: I am your Fortune, whose return the magician predicted.

QUEROLUS (*from within*): Go away from here at once, you Bad Fortune; stay where the priest took you. Get away from here! I won't receive any fortune today, not even good.

MANDROGERUS (*taking the urn*): Look here, Swindler, you lure the men over to the door, while I hurl these ashes through the window.

SWINDLER (*pounding on the door*): Open this door!

QUEROLUS (*within*): Run here quickly, all of you.

MANDROGERUS (*hurling the urn through the window*): There, Querolus, take your treasure that Euclio left you. I hope you always have such a treasure and leave such a treasure to your sons. (*In a lower tone to his accomplices*) Now everything's done. Away from here to the ship, quick, before some sudden evil comes upon us. (MANDROGERUS *departs, followed by the* SWINDLER.)

SARDANAPALLUS (*to himself*): Well, whatever happens today must be endured. I'm going back a little nearer to the house. The trick is spoiled unless I hear what Querolus says. He is such a superstitious and cowardly fellow. How horrified he'll be now when he sees the ashes! (*Listening at the window*) I'll apply my ear here gently. Heavens! What's this I hear? They're jumping up and down in glee. No hope for me there! I'll listen again. Oh, it's all up! Happiness has come to them; that means sorrow for us. Everybody inside is hunting for bags, satchels, boxes; it's gold they're handling; I hear the jingle of the coins. Oh, damn it all! It was life that was buried in the urn, and we thought it was death. To our sorrow we were deceived, but in no simple fashion; we were deceived, but not simply once. This is a case of metamorphosis. We took away ashes, we threw away gold. But what am I to do now? The one thing still in store for me is to be held as a thief. I'll join my fellow-conspirators so that I'll have someone to share my grief at such a miraculous occurrence and such a real funeral. (SARDANAPALLUS *departs in despair*.)

Act Five. Scene I

(*The* HOUSEHOLD GOD *appears.*)

HOUSEHOLD GOD (*to the audience*): At last the pregnant urn has given birth to masses of gold, and a mother without value has produced a precious offspring. It didn't deserve to be broken; its faithfulness merited a better reward. At one and the same time this large and remarkable urn kept faith with its master and robbed the robbers. O wise Euclio, we gods are not boastful; it's you who preserved the treasure during your life and released it after your death. All men should now realise that they can neither gain anything nor lose anything except with the favour of Him who has all power. As far as Querolus is concerned, everything is satisfactorily completed. But I wish now to ensnare that treacherous thief Mandrogerus; as soon as he hears this and learns what has happened, he'll return immediately to claim his share of the treasure. He'll even have the audacity to present the letter in which he was named joint heir on the condition that he reveal the pot of gold to Querolus without trickery. What would he deserve, except what shall now happen to him? Let him suffer for his intention; his action was the result of my endeavour. (*The* HOUSEHOLD GOD *disappears.*)

Act Five. Scene II

(*Enter* QUEROLUS *from his house, followed by the* WITNESS *and* PANTOMALUS.)

QUEROLUS: Friend witness, can you really believe what you've just seen?

WITNESS: Gad, I believe it; I'm sure of it.

QUEROLUS: What do you say, Pantomalus?

PANTOMALUS: What do I say? After this you can stop finding fault.

QUEROLUS: My mind is overwhelmed with joy. What should I do first? Be amazed or be delighted? Consider it the result of my father's wisdom or the gift of a god?

WITNESS: The gift of a god, first of all. Because, if you think of human intervention, it's quite obvious and evident that a thief gave you more assistance than your father.

QUEROLUS: What do you think of me for taking so long to recognise the fragments of an urn that I had known such a long time?

WITNESS: I wouldn't have believed my own eyes if I hadn't seen the spot where the earth had been moved. Before that I didn't think it possible.

PANTOMALUS: I didn't have the least doubt about it when I saw certain letters on the broken fragments.

QUEROLUS: Then is Mandrogerus responsible for all this?

WITNESS: What other explanation can there be?

QUEROLUS: The accursed wretch, who called himself a magician and an astrologer! Was I to take my father's treasure from the house with my own hands? Was I to lock myself up in the house? Was I to prevent the return of the treasure? This certainly fulfills the prophecy of the Household God, that even in spite of my opposition and my resistance all blessings would come to me.

WITNESS: What an amazing outcome, that the greed of this archde-ceiver was foiled!

QUEROLUS: Can you believe it, witness? You know my very generous nature. Damned if I wouldn't be willing to reward the wretch if I should meet him! His villainy was so laughable and he deceived himself so thoroughly.

WITNESS: The rogue deserves punishment, as we all know; but since he is responsible for everything turning out so well for you, we wish him well. But it's on the basis of the outcome, not his intention.

QUEROLUS (*looking down the street*): Aha! What's this? If I'm not mistaken, Mandrogerus is approaching yonder. Now what the devil is he coming back here for? He'll furnish us with some new sleight-of-hand trick, I suppose. Get inside quick, Pantomalus, and bring out here the pieces of the urn. (PANTOMALUS *goes into the house.*)

WITNESS: A good idea, by Jove!

QUEROLUS: My dear witness, how about our setting a trap for this dis-honest fellow? Let's demand that he return the treasure he stole from me, and let's pretend that the ashes he hurled into the house belong to a stranger.

WITNESS: An excellent plan!

QUEROLUS: We'll carry out the scheme then; the rest will follow.

Act Five.　Scene III

(*Enter* MANDROGERUS.)

MANDROGERUS: Good day, friend Querolus.

QUEROLUS: Do you greet me, you gallows bird, as if you haven't seen me today?

MANDROGERUS: Of course I've seen you, and I'm glad to see you again.

QUEROLUS (*angrily*): Well, as I live, I'll see that this is the last time.

MANDROGERUS (*with pretended innocence*): Why, what have I done?

QUEROLUS: You ask that, you rogue, when you plundered my home today?

MANDROGERUS: Oh, forget about that; I'm not a stranger. Why, I've looked after that home of yours for a long time.

QUEROLUS: More magic, eh? And you stole my gold from me today.

MANDROGERUS (*mysteriously*): Perhaps I did the right thing; didn't it belong to me too?

QUEROLUS: Gad, what a fine lie! Up to now I was the only heir here. (*Sarcastically*) Where have you come from, my brother, so young and yet so old? How did you suddenly get so old, when a short while ago you weren't even born? If you should claim to be my brother, you scoundrel, you should add that you're only two years old. Three years ago when my father Euclio left home, I was his one and only son.

MANDROGERUS: All this is unnecessary. I am your joint heir, not your brother.

QUEROLUS: That's not the right way to do it, confound you! I'd much prefer you to claim to be my brother than my joint heir.

MANDROGERUS: Why waste words, Querolus? (*Handing him a letter*) Read what's written here. Take it, I appreciate your good faith.

QUEROLUS: Damn it, you should, after today's experience! (*Taking the letter*) Hm-m! What's this? (*Reading*) "Greetings from aged Euclio to his son Querolus. Since I feared that you might be robbed either by a slave or by some stranger, I have sent to you my faithful friend Mandrogerus, with whom I became acquainted while abroad. He is to reveal to you without trickery what I have left. You will give him half of the treasure, if his loyalty and his labour deserve it." (*To the* WITNESS) Here, please! Come over here a bit. (QUEROLUS *takes the* WITNESS *aside and speaks in a lower tone*) The letter makes it perfectly clear that I don't owe this fellow anything; but, if I wish, I may spend something; it may please me to give him some reward. (*Returning to* MANDROGERUS) So you were my father's friend and companion while he was abroad?

MANDROGERUS: That's obvious.

QUEROLUS (*sarcastically*): I suppose that's why you're silent about these deeds that have been done in such good faith. Well, my friend, since you have been appointed heir along with me, give me the wealth that is to be divided.

MANDROGERUS: Why, I did discover the treasure for you, and I gave it to you uninjured and untouched.

QUEROLUS (*feigning surprise*): What's that? Did you ever give me a treasure?

MANDROGERUS: Do you deny it?

QUEROLUS: If you don't refresh my memory, some detail may escape me. What treasure are you talking about?

MANDROGERUS: The one Euclio left you, the one I handed over to you.

QUEROLUS: And just how did you get hold of the gold, when you were an utter stranger?

MANDROGERUS: I was only joking, so that you might realise fully my good faith.

QUEROLUS: Then you did take away the buried treasure that my father had left?

MANDROGERUS (*evasively*): In any case it's turned out well for you; another person wouldn't have returned it.

QUEROLUS: Come now, if you please; you've joked enough. Restore the treasure; then I'll really appreciate your good faith.

MANDROGERUS (*to the* WITNESS): Thank the gods, neighbour and witness, my hopes are secure. Didn't I just say a stranger wouldn't have done this? (*With irony*) I'm grateful for your aid.

QUEROLUS (*to* MANDROGERUS, *with equal irony*): The gods bless you, most excellent of friends, for keeping faith with my dead father and with me, his survivor! Tell me now, where have you concealed that pot of gold? Let's have everything done according to my father's instructions. Produce the treasure and we'll divide it; we're fortunate in having a witness here.

MANDROGERUS: No, you produce it and show your good faith. I've done my part.

QUEROLUS: Are you just tiring me out with words, Mandrogerus, or do you speak seriously?

MANDROGERUS: I assure you, I speak seriously and honestly. Why, I could have had the whole treasure, and I'm seeking only my share.

QUEROLUS: Then you did have in your possession the gold that belongs to me?

MANDROGERUS: Yes, I did, confound it!

QUEROLUS (*threateningly*): You won't take a single step from here unless you restore what you admit you stole; you can't deny it now. (*As* MANDROGERUS *hesitates*) Look here, I say, will you restore what you stole?

MANDROGERUS: I did restore it.

QUEROLUS: To whom? When? How?

MANDROGERUS: Today, through the window.

QUEROLUS (*laughing*): Ha, ha, ha! And where did you find the treasure?

MANDROGERUS: In your shrine.

QUEROLUS: How did you take it out?

MANDROGERUS: Through this front door of yours.

QUEROLUS: Then why did you return it through the window?

MANDROGERUS (*correcting himself*): But you're the one, I say, that brought the treasure out of the house.

QUEROLUS: That's a damned fine way of fulfilling the terms of the letter which specified that you should reveal the treasure to me without trickery! But I pass over this clause; I can use it if you should give the gold to me now. All this discussion is unnecessary, when the subject of it doesn't appear. Give back to me what you refuse to give.

MANDROGERUS (*tragically*): O times! O customs! O aged Euclio! Is this the good faith of your home that you spoke about? (*To* QUEROLUS) I did give it back to you, I swear by all the gods; I hurled the treasure into your house intact.

QUEROLUS (*turning to the* WITNESS): My good witness, this rascal has done more than we thought. If I'm not mistaken, he's the fellow that threw that urn of ashes into the house.

MANDROGERUS (*eagerly*): The gods bless you! That's the one I threw in. Now the truth is coming to light at last.

QUEROLUS: Tell me this, Mandrogerus, please. If you see the fragments, can you recognise them?

MANDROGERUS: Well enough to fit them all together again.

QUEROLUS (*calling at the door*): Ho there, Pantomalus, there's something I told you to bring out here. (PANTOMALUS *enters with the pieces of broken pottery.*)

WITNESS: These are certainly the parts that had the inscription on them.

QUEROLUS: Do you recognise them, Mandrogerus?

MANDROGERUS: I certainly do. Now we're finished with trickery and humbug.

QUEROLUS: If you really recognise them, read quickly what's written there.

MANDROGERUS: I have read it and I can read it now. Pantomalus, hand me those broken pieces. (PANTOMALUS *does so and* MANDROGERUS *reads*) "Trierinus, the son of Tricipitinus, lies buried here."

QUEROLUS: You see this, you villain? You not only had no regard for the good will of the living, but you even dared to lay your hands on the dead and make them an object of your mockery, eh? You weren't satisfied with digging up the urn with the ashes, you even had to throw these poor remains in through my window? (*As* MANDROGERUS *is silent*) What do you say to this? You stole a treasure, you dishonoured a tomb, you wretch! You not only plundered my home, you even polluted it with sacrilege. Do you deny it?

MANDROGERUS: Please! Since fortune has so deserted me, I ask for nothing more. Good-bye. (*Preparing to depart.*)

QUEROLUS (*barring his way*): But I ask for something more, confound you! You've overwhelmed me with evil, you rogue. (*To* PANTOMALUS) Hey, Pantomalus, don't move an inch from him. I'm going now without delay to find where the praetor is holding session and I shall take the whole matter to court.

MANDROGERUS (*to the* WITNESS): Please, friend witness, speak a word in my behalf. I ask for nothing but forgiveness.

WITNESS: O Querolus, never allow yourself to be carried to extremes so quickly. Pardon him and forgive his crime; to do so is true victory.

QUEROLUS: Well, the ashes of the dead man will be buried again. But what about the treasure?

WITNESS (*to* MANDROGERUS): Answer, Mandrogerus.

MANDROGERUS: I swear by the gods, I swear by the good faith that I broke, I have neither gold nor treasure.

QUEROLUS: Stop these idle words for a while. Let's suppose that we are in court. You certainly stole that urn.

MANDROGERUS: True.

QUEROLUS: Choose which you prefer, Mandrogerus; what was in the urn, ashes or gold? A case of this sort has more than one string in its bow.

MANDROGERUS (*aside*): I've got the wolf by the ears, as they say. I don't know whether to lie or to confess the truth. Whichever I say will be held against me, I see that. I'll speak, however. (*Aloud*) There was gold in it.

QUEROLUS: Return it then.

MANDROGERUS: I've already done so.

QUEROLUS: Prove it.

MANDROGERUS: Do you recognise the urn?

QUEROLUS: What do you want me to answer? First of all, I don't recognise the pot. Is this sufficient?

MANDROGERUS: What? You don't recognise the inscription?

QUEROLUS: Not a bit better than I do you, and I've never seen you before this day. But suppose now that I do recognise the pot and the inscription; give me back what was in the pot.

MANDROGERUS: It's your turn; what do you claim was in the pot?

QUEROLUS: Wait; I haven't told you yet. It's up to you to decide which you prefer.

MANDROGERUS: And how can you demand gold of me when it obviously contained funeral ashes?

WITNESS: Then you admit it was a funeral urn?

MANDROGERUS: Yes, I admit it; it's quite evident. (*Aside*) I haven't made much progress this way; I'll have to try a different road.

QUEROLUS: You fool, you confess to sacrilege and deny the robbery!

MANDROGERUS: What if there was nothing in the urn?

QUEROLUS: What in the world are you asking for, then? If there was gold there, you stole it; if you didn't take it away, there wasn't any there.

MANDROGERUS: Now you tell me in your turn, please: what the devil was in it?

QUEROLUS: It's sufficient for the present for me to defend myself and to repel attack. (*Aside*) I'm advancing properly; this is the way to go.

MANDROGERUS (*aside*): What strange sort of mystery is this? I did everything myself and yet I don't know a thing! (*Aloud*) Now, I beg of you, since neither object nor motive remains, tell me frankly whether I have committed theft or sacrilege. Unless perchance this unhappy fate is in store for me: that I, who was unable to commit theft and had no intention of sacrilege, be convicted of both crimes.

QUEROLUS: Are you still trying to get around it? The case is very simple; you stole away my gold and threw away the ashes. The one deed was dishonest, the other shameful. No one could believe that you desired the ashes and hurled away the gold.

MANDROGERUS: All this is set forth in plausible fashion, and even to me it seems likely. But it doesn't happen to be true, if you're willing to believe me.

QUEROLUS (*pleasantly*): Come now, cheer up. You've committed only sacrilege. There was no gold there.

MANDROGERUS: Then I'm not guilty of theft. The gods bless you! I win. At the moment I'd rather undergo punishment than owe money. But explain this one point, please; why the great weight?

QUEROLUS (*grinning*): What? You a magician, and you don't know that nothing is heavier than Bad Fortune?

MANDROGERUS (*sadly*): I realise it.

QUEROLUS: You still ask where the weight comes from? You didn't see that the cover of the urn was made of lead?

MANDROGERUS: Yes, everything agrees. But by such tricks as this couldn't even an experienced magician be deceived?

WITNESS: Don't you yet understand, stupid, that you were tricked by that good friend of yours? And besides, where would a man, almost a pauper, get a treasure? And if he had had one, would Querolus here have been ignorant of his father's secret? And would his father have revealed to you a secret that he didn't entrust to his own son? Then, too, if the father knew about the treasure, would he have concealed it in a place like that? And would you have had free access to it?

MANDROGERUS (*overwhelmed*): Good Lord! I don't know what to say.

WITNESS: You didn't know Euclio's nature, then? That old man was full of gay tricks like this; even now, after his death, he's laughing at you.

MANDROGERUS: Damn it! Now at last I understand everything; I realise clearly his villainy. Many a time he played similar tricks on me. (*To* QUEROLUS) Forgive me, please, for taking away the ashes; I thought it was gold.

WITNESS (*to* MANDROGERUS): You make a good plea, Mandrogerus. I see that you have a most ingenious nature; you're a true companion for Euclio. The old man always cherished[36] friends of this type.

MANDROGERUS: Let me go, please.

WITNESS: Look, Querolus, I know you've always been kind and compassionate; don't permit such an excellent fellow to leave. He's a man of many parts; you have here a magician and an astrologer; the only thing is, and it's of prime importance, he doesn't know how to commit a theft. So I urge you, take in the man both as an old and a new friend. He's the only property that your father Euclio left you.

QUEROLUS: Ah, but I'm afraid of robbery.

WITNESS: Why fear it now?[37] This fellow took away everything you had.

MANDROGERUS: Listen, Querolus; I had already devoted myself to your father; now I wish to serve you, since you've taken such pity on me today. You have granted me life, now give me something to live on.

QUEROLUS: Since the two of you wish it, I consent. Are you able to learn the new laws?

MANDROGERUS (*laughing*): Ha, ha, ha! Why I drafted part of them.

QUEROLUS: I mean the Servilian and Parasitian decree of the senate.

MANDROGERUS: Oho! You wish me to recite the sections of the prohibitions? You mean the Porkian Doggian Furian law passed in the consulship of Messrs. Neck-Chain and Bull's Hide?

QUEROLUS: Are you able to obey all the provisions?

MANDROGERUS: That's not difficult for me. You want me to learn them; why, I'm eager to instruct you.[38] (*Quoting the decree concerning parasites*) . . .[39] "The parasite if injured shall receive compensation for his wounds. If his garment be torn at the banquet, he shall receive from the master of ceremonies double the cost of the repairs. For bruises the penalty shall be three-twelfths of one gold piece, for swellings the penalty shall be four-twelfths. But if there be both bruise and swelling, he shall be entitled by law to receive eight-twelfths; we allow one-twelfth extra in consideration of the expense of the treatment. It is furthermore decreed that in the case of blows and open wounds the parasite be granted an examination by his friends without criminal proceedings; this is on condition that neither the favour of the examiners nor the generosity of the giver exceed nine-twelfths of one gold piece. In the case of dislocations and bones out of place it is decreed that the damages be increased to eleven-twelfths. Furthermore, in the case of broken bones it is decreed and ordered that one gold piece be paid immediately for minor bones, a pound of silver for major bones. A consultation of doctors shall decide which bones are to be considered major and which minor. If a parasite demand more than is prescribed, he is to be strangled on the charge of excessive demand. The master of ceremonies shall be compelled to pay the value of the injuries in the case of voluntary conflicts, on condition that the payment made by the guilty party exceed the damages paid to the wounded man. The law has made provision for parasites to this extent, that if one should succumb to his wound after bringing suit, his heirs shall not be deprived of the fruits of his labour and his value. But if the parasite, no matter how badly he has been mistreated, should die without making testamentary disposition of his 'evils,'[40] his heir shall not be permitted to bring suit. If the cause of the death be not shown, the corpse shall be cast forth without burial. The aforesaid regulations have been established to provide for violence committed during the sport of free and equal men. If a parasite suffer injury from his patron or a slave of his patron, he shall be granted full freedom to leave the house."

WITNESS (*to* QUEROLUS): Aha! We have here a man who wins all prizes. You must keep with you a person so versed in the fine points of the law. People usually pay a high price for one like this.

QUEROLUS: Well, I consent, since such is your wish. (*To* MANDROGERUS) But where are your companions, your accomplices?

Act Five. Scene IV

(*Enter the* SWINDLER *and* SARDANAPALLUS.)

SWINDLER: Here we are too, O master and patron.

QUEROLUS: O Swindler, O Sardanapallus, so this is your religious ceremony! Mandrogerus here has already given me the reasons for it. Go now wherever you wish.

SWINDLER (*sadly*): We know we must, Querolus; one house can't provide for three gluttons. But we beg you to grant us something for travelling expenses, since our plans have been foiled.

QUEROLUS: Travelling expenses for you? For what reason?

SWINDLER: Well, we came here with Mandrogerus.

QUEROLUS: A worthy reason, indeed!

(*The concluding lines of the play are lost.*)

THE TEUBNER TEXT of Rudolph Peiper (1875) has been used as the basis of this translation. The two more recent editions, those by Louis Havet (1880) and Léon Herrmann (1937) are too unsound to provide a safe text of the play. Havet emended and transposed far too freely in an effort to make the Latin conform to his own idea of the original metre, while Herrmann's text is not only filled with unnecessary conjectures and transpositions but is also marred by many inaccuracies. Peiper's edition, while not free from faults, remains the most accurate and the most readable. The notes indicate the few passages where it has seemed advisable to depart from Peiper's reading.

1. Rutilius, to whom the play is dedicated, is generally believed to have been Rutilius Claudius Namatianus, often called the last of the classical Latin poets. An extant poem on his return from Rome to his native Gaul was composed about 417 A.D.

2. The Latin word is *Aulularia,* the same as the Latin title of Plautus' *The Pot of Gold,* in which the miser Euclio played a leading role.

3. Note the similarity to the statement so frequently found in modern books; e.g. "The characters in this book are entirely imaginary and have no relation to any living person."

4. The problem of the metrical form is discussed briefly in the Introduction to the play.

5. Havet and Herrmann seem correct in considering this speech a statement. Peiper punctuates it as a question.

6. Thomas' reading, *es fateor,* has been adopted.

7. The hybrid name, *Pantomalus,* signifies "Wholly-evil."

8. The scandalous secret which the Household God whispers in the ear of Querolus may well have concerned the neighbour's wife.

9. This passage apparently refers to a state of lawlessness and confusion in Gaul, when country people were setting up their own local laws.

10. The Latin text has *patus* here, the significance of which is not clear. Herrmann considers it a Gallic word corresponding to the Greek *pachus,* "rich man."

11. The verb *efferre* here has the double meaning of "praise" and "bury."

12. Nestor here evidently typifies an aged man who is impotent.

Havet and Herrmann hold the opposite view, that Nestor's ailment was excessive virility.

13. The punctuation of Havet has been adopted. Peiper considers the speech a statement.

14. Herrmann sees here a trace of the influence of Christianity, the doctrine that God punishes those whom he loves best.

15. Apicius, a famous gourmet of the time of Tiberius, committed his recipes to writing. The work on cookery in ten books which passes under his name was compiled several centuries later.

16. There is possibly a play here between *condītum,* "flavour, seasoning," and *condĭtum,* "place of concealment."

17. *Indiculum,* the conjecture of G. Paris for *aediculum,* seems correct here and has been adopted by both Havet and Herrmann.

18. Peiper wrongly assigns this speech to Mandrogerus.

19. Thomas' reading, *hunc* in place of *hoc,* has been adopted.

20. Havet deletes *transferri messes* as a gloss which destroys the meaning.

21. *Male,* the reading of the Mss., seems preferable to *vale,* suggested by Scaliger and adopted by Peiper.

22. The sentence occurs in Cicero's oration *Pro Sexto Roscio Amerino,* 20, 56.

23. The Mss. give this speech to Sardanapallus; Klinkhamer seems correct in assigning it to Mandrogerus.

24. It was necessary for Aeneas to procure the golden bough before he could make his descent to the underworld; cf. Vergil, *Aeneid* VI, 136 ff., 406 f.

25. There is a play here upon Pan, the god, and *panis,* "bread."

26. Sardanapallus, a king of Assyria, was noted in Greek and Roman writings for his effeminacy and extravagance. He is largely a composite figure of legend and the traits assigned to him chiefly represent Assurbanipal.

27. There appears to be a double meaning here. "Other people's property" is sufficient for him, and also he has heard enough from Mandrogerus concerning his fortune.

28. This senseless reply seems to harmonise with the satirical tone of much of this scene and is probably correct. Some scholars have emended the text to read "between noon and one o'clock." It is all the more amusing that Mandrogerus apparently asks for the hour of the day instead of the hour of Querolus' birth.

29. *Merum,* the emendation of Thomas for *metum,* seems correct here.

30. Peiper brackets this sentence as spurious.

31. This is ambiguous and can refer both to men and to coins.

32. *Somni,* Thomas' conjecture for *omni,* is adopted here.

33. The text here is corrupt; Havet's emendation, *nos exerceant,* has been adopted.

34. That is, the ashes of his grandfather would be something for Querolus to treasure.

35. There is a play here upon *aula,* "dwelling," and *olla,* "pot."

36. *Dilexit,* the correction of *dixit* in the Palatine Ms., seems necessary here.

37. *Nunc,* the emendation of Thomas for *unum,* has been adopted.

38. Thomas inserts at this point the fragmentary decree concerning parasites which in the Mss. is found at the end of the play. This transposition is accepted by both Havet and Herrmann.

39. The first part of the decree is lost.

40. Ordinarily an individual disposes of his *bona,* "his goods," by his last will and testament; the property of a parasite, however, is assumed to consist of *mala,* "evils," the injuries he has suffered and for which recompense is due.

GLOSSARY

The following classes of proper names have been omitted from the Glossary:
1. Geographical names of purely ornamental or entirely obvious significance;
2. Names of fictitious characters in Roman comedy.

ABSYRTUS. Son of Aeetes and brother of Medea. He was slain by Medea when she fled with Jason from Colchis. She scattered his mangled remains in the sea, in order to retard her father's pursuit.

ACASTUS. Son of Pelias, king of Thessaly. He demanded Jason and Medea from Creon, king of Corinth, to avenge his father who had been murdered through the machinations of Medea.

ACHELOUS. A river in Greece. The god of the river fought with Hercules for possession of Deianira and was defeated.

ACHERON. A river in the Underworld.

ACHILLES. Son of Peleus and Thetis, father of Pyrrhus, and the greatest of the Greek warriors before Troy. Among his victims were Memnon, Penthesilea, and Hector, whose dead body he dragged around the walls of Troy. He was finally slain by Paris.

ACTAEON. A grandson of Cadmus who accidentally saw Diana bathing. The goddess in anger changed him into a stag and he was torn to pieces by his own hunting dogs.

ACTE. The mistress of Nero, whom he deserted for Poppaea.

ADMETUS. King of Pherae in Thessaly, husband of Alcestis. See ALCESTIS.

ADONIS. A handsome youth beloved by Venus.

ADRASTUS. King of Argos. He received the fugitive Polynices at his court, gave him his daughter in marriage, and headed the expedition of the Seven against Thebes in order to reinstate his son-in-law upon the throne.

AEACUS. Son of Jupiter and father of Peleus; so famous for his justice that he became one of the judges in the Underworld.

AEDILES. Roman magistrates who superintended trade, streets and buildings, the games, and the sanitation of the city.

AEETES. King of Colchis, son of Phoebus and Persa, and father of Medea and Absyrtus. He was despoiled of his realm through the theft of the golden fleece.

AEGEUS. An early king of Athens, the father of Theseus.

AEGISTHUS. Son of an incestuous union between Thyestes and his daughter, and cousin of Agamemnon. He lived in adultery with Clytemnestra, wife of Agamemnon, during the absence of Agamemnon at the Trojan War.

AEGYPTUS. A king of Egypt whose fifty sons sought to marry the fifty daughters of Danaus, the twin brother of Aegyptus. See DANAIDES.

AENEAS. The hero of Vergil's *Aeneid*. He led a band of Trojan survivors to Italy, where his descendants founded Rome.

AESCULAPIUS. A son of Apollo, who learned to heal the sick and revive the dead. Slain by Jupiter, he was later deified and became the god of

953

medicine. The chief seat of his worship was Epidaurus.

AETNA. A volcanic mountain in Sicily. It was considered the seat of the forge of Vulcan. One of the Titans was believed to have been buried beneath it by the victorious Jupiter.

AGAMEMNON. Son of Atreus, brother of Menelaus, king of Mycenae, leader of the Greek forces against Troy.

AGATHOCLES. King of Syracuse from 317 to 289 B.C.

AGAVE. Daughter of Cadmus and mother of Pentheus, king of Thebes. In a Bacchic frenzy she slew Pentheus and bore his head back to Thebes.

AGENOR. King of Phoenicia, son of Neptune, father of Cadmus.

AGRIPPINA. 1. Daughter of Marcus Vipsanius Agrippa and Julia, the daughter of Augustus. She married Germanicus and had nine children, among whom were the emperor Caligula and Agrippina, the mother of Nero. She died in exile on the island of Pandataria. 2. Daughter of Germanicus and Agrippina, wife of Gnaeus Domitius Ahenobarbus, and mother of Nero. She married the emperor Claudius, her uncle, and in 54 A.D. poisoned him to secure the succession for her son, who caused her to be assassinated in 59 A.D.

AJAX. 1. Son of Telamon and one of the bravest Greek heroes in the Trojan War. When the armour of the dead Achilles was awarded to Ulysses, Ajax, crazed with rage, committed suicide. 2. Son of Oileus. At Troy he often fought side by side with Ajax, son of Telamon. He was destroyed by Minerva and Neptune in the great storm which wrecked the Greek fleet on its homeward voyage.

ALATRIUM. A small town in Italy.

ALCESTIS. Wife of Admetus, king of Pherae. To preserve the life of her husband she gave up her own.

ALCIDES. A name of Hercules, as the grandson of Alcaeus.

ALCMAEON. Son of Amphiaraus and Eriphyle. On his return home from the expedition of the Seven against Thebes he slew his mother according to the injunction of his father. For this deed he became mad and was haunted by the Furies.

ALCMENA. Wife of Amphitryon and mother, by Jupiter, of Hercules.

ALCYONE. Wife of Ceyx. When her husband perished in a shipwreck she mourned him incessantly, until finally both husband and wife were changed into birds.

ALEXANDER. 1. Another name for Paris, son of Priam. 2. Son of Philip II. of Macedon. Called Alexander the Great as a result of his conquests in Asia Minor, Egypt, Persia, and India.

ALPHEUS. A river in the Peloponnesus, flowing through Arcadia and Elis, near Olympia.

ALTHAEA. Wife of Oeneus, king of Calydon, and mother of Meleager. In revenge for Meleager's slaughter of her two brothers, she burned the magic piece of wood on which her son's life depended and so brought about his death.

AMALTHEA. The goat of Olenus which fed with its milk the infant Jupiter, and was set as a constellation in the sky.

AMAZONS. A race of warlike women who dwelt on the river Thermodon. An attack on them was one of the exploits of Hercules. In the Trojan War they were allies of Troy; their queen, Penthesilea, was slain by Achilles.

AMBRACIA. A Greek city in Epirus, taken by the Romans in 189 B.C. Ennius wrote a historical play called *Ambracia* in honour of the victory.

AMPHION. Son of Jupiter and Antiope, and twin brother of Zethus. He and his brother captured Thebes and killed Lycus and Dirce because of their cruelty to Antiope. Amphion built the walls of Thebes by the magic of his lyre. He married Niobe and became the father of numerous children, all of whom were killed by Apollo and Diana.

AMPHITRYON. Son of Alcaeus and husband of Alcmena, who was beloved by Jupiter and gave birth to Hercules.

ANACTORIUM. A town in Acarnania, in western Greece.

ANCAEUS. An Arcadian hero, one of the Argonauts, slain by the Calydonian boar.

ANDROMACHE. Wife of Hector and mother of Astyanax.

ANTAEUS. Son of Neptune and Terra (Earth), a mighty giant, whose strength was invincible so long as he remained in contact with his mother earth. Hercules defeated him by holding him aloft in the air.

ANTIGONE. Daughter of Oedipus and Jocasta. She refused to desert her father in his blindness and exile.

ANTENOR. One of the wisest among the elders at Troy. He was spared by the Greeks when the city was captured.

ANTIOCHUS. Called Antiochus the Great. King of Syria 223-187 B.C.

ANTIOPE. I. Mother, by Jupiter, of Amphion and Zethus. 2. An Amazon, wife of Theseus and mother of Hippolytus.

ANTONIUS. Marcus Antonius, the triumvir, defeated by Octavian at the battle of Actium, 31 B.C.

ANUBIS. An Egyptian god, worshipped in the form of a human being with a dog's head. His worship was introduced at Rome in the first century B.C.

APELLES. A famous Greek painter of the fourth century B.C.

APOLLO. Son of Jupiter and Latona, twin brother of Diana. Apollo was the god of healing, of prophecy, and of music, and was worshipped as the sun god under the name of Phoebus.

APOLLODORUS. A poet of the Greek New Comedy.

ARABES. The inhabitants of Arabia.

ARCADIA. Anglicised into Arcady. The mountainous central region of the Peloponnesus, where the god Pan was worshipped. Seneca calls the Arcadians the most ancient race of men.

ARCADIAN BEARS. The constellation of the Great and Little Bears.

ARCADIAN BOAR. Captured by Hercules and brought alive to Eurystheus as his fourth labour.

ARCADIAN STAG. Captured by Hercules.

ARGO. The name of the ship in which the Greek heroes under Jason sailed to Colchis in quest of the golden fleece.

ARGOS. A city in the northeast corner of the Peloponnesus; also the region in which this city was situated.

ARGUS. The hundred-eyed guardian of Io after she had been transformed into a cow. Argus was slain by Mercury and his eyes were placed by Juno in the tail of the peacock, her favourite bird.

ARIADNE. Daughter of Minos, king of Crete, and Pasiphae, and sister of Phaedra. She fell in love with Theseus and helped him find his way out of the labyrinth. Theseus deserted her on the island of Naxos, where she was found by Dionysus who made her his wife and placed her in the heavens as a constellation.

ARIES. The ram with the golden fleece which bore Phrixus and Helle through the air, and which was afterwards set in the heavens as one of the signs of the zodiac.

ARISTARCHUS. A writer of Greek tragedy in the fifth century B.C.

ASSARACUS. An early king of Troy, grandfather of Anchises and great-grandfather of Aeneas.

ASTRAEA. The goddess of Justice who lived among men during the Golden Age, but left the earth because of the sins of man. She was placed among the stars, under the name Virgo.

ASTYANAX. Son of Hector and Andromache.

ATHENA. The Greek goddess of wisdom and peaceful arts, also thought of as a warrior goddess. She was the special protectress of Athens. The Romans identified her with Minerva.

ATLANTIDES. The seven daughters of Atlas and Pleione. They were transformed into the group of stars called Pleiades.

ATLAS. A high mountain in northwestern Libya, conceived as a giant who held the heavens on his shoulders.

ATREUS. Son of Pelops, brother of Thyestes, and father of Agamemnon and Menelaus.

ATRIDES. The son of Atreus. A patronymic referring to Agamemnon or Menelaus.

ATTALUS. King of Pergamus.

ATTICA. The district of Greece around Athens.

ATTIS. A young Phrygian shepherd mourned by the priests of Cybele.

AUGEAN STABLES. The stables of Augeas, king of Elis, which contained three thousand head of cattle. Although the stables had not been cleansed for thirty years, Hercules was able to clean them in a single day.

AUGEIA. An Arcadian maiden, loved by Hercules, and mother by him of Telephus.

AUGUSTUS. The first emperor of Rome, deified after his death in 14 A.D.

AULIS. A harbour in Boeotia from which the Greek expedition sailed against Troy. The death of Tiphys, king of Aulis, on the Argonautic expedition is given as a reason for the detention of the Greek fleet.

AURORA. The goddess of the dawn, wife of Tithonus, mother of Memnon.

AUSTER. The south or southwest wind.

AUTOLYCUS. Grandfather of Ulysses, renowned as the master-thief of antiquity.

AVERNUS. A lake near Cumae, celebrated for its connection with the Lower World.

BACCHANTES. Worshippers of Bacchus.

BACCHUS. Son of Jupiter and Semele, the daughter of Cadmus. He was the god of wine and of the productive powers of nature. See ARIADNE, LYCURGUS, PENTHEUS.

BASSARIDS. Female worshippers of Bacchus, so called because they were clad in fox-skins.

BEARS. The northern constellations of the Great and Little Bears.

BELLEROPHON. Son of Glaucus, king of Corinth. After the slaying of Belerus, he fled to Proetus, King of Argos. Antea, Proetus' wife, fell in love with Bellerophon. When her advances were scorned, she accused him to Proetus, who sent him to Lycia to his father-in-law with a letter requesting that the young man be put to death. Bellerophon was sent to kill the Chimaera, an apparently impossible task. With the aid of the winged steed Pegasus he was able to slay the monster.

BELLONA. Goddess of war.

BELUS. Father of Aegyptus and Danaus. His granddaughters were the Danaides.

BISTONIAN. Thracian. The Bistones were a people of Thrace.

BOEOTIA. The district around Thebes, named from the heifer which guided Cadmus to the place where he should found his city.

BOOTES. The constellation of the Little Bear.

BOREAS. The north wind. He carried off Orithyia, a daughter of Erechtheus, king of Attica, by whom he begot Zetes and Calais.

BRIAREUS. One of the giants who attempted to storm heaven.

BRISEIS. A captive maiden, beloved by Achilles and taken from him by Agamemnon.

BRITANNICUS. Son of the emperor Claudius and Messalina, brother of Octavia, and stepbrother of Nero. He was murdered by Nero.

BROMIUS. An epithet of Bacchus.

BRUTUS. The friend of Julius Caesar and one of the leaders of the conspiracy against him.

BUSIRIS. A king of Egypt who sacrificed strangers upon his altars. He was slain by Hercules.

CADMEIDS. Daughters of Cadmus, i.e. Agave, Autonoe, Ino, who in their madness tore Pentheus to pieces.

CADMUS. Son of Agenor, king of Phoenicia. After wandering over the earth in search of his lost sister, Europa, he came to the land which he called

Boeotia. There he killed the dragon, sacred to Mars, and sowed the dragon's teeth, from which armed men sprang up. He founded Thebes and was himself changed into a serpent.

CAECILIUS. Caecilius Statius, a Roman comic poet who flourished shortly before the time of Terence.

CALCHAS. A famous seer among the Greeks at Troy.

CALLIOPE. One of the Muses, the Muse of epic poetry.

CALPE. One of the so-called Pillars of Hercules, now Gibraltar.

CALYDON. An ancient town of Aetolia, in Greece, famed for the hunt of the Calydonian boar.

CANCER. A sign of the zodiac.

CAPHEREUS. A cliff on the coast of Euboea, where Nauplius lured the Greek fleet to destruction by displaying false fires.

CARIA. A district in Asia Minor.

CARTHAGE. A powerful city on the northern coast of Africa, founded by the Phoenicians. Carthage lost her power when defeated by the Romans in the second Punic war (218-201 B.C.).

CASSANDRA. Daughter of Priam and Hecuba. She received the gift of prophecy from Apollo, but refused to comply with his desires, whereupon the god ordained that no one should believe her prophecies.

CASTALIA. A fountain on Mt. Parnassus, sacred to Apollo and the Muses.

CASTOR. One of the twin sons of Jupiter and Leda, wife of Tyndareus, king of Sparta. His brother was Pollux. The twins were members of the Argonautic expedition. Castor was famed for his skill as a horseman, Pollux for his skill as a boxer. They were set in the sky as constellations and were a guide to sailors.

CAUCASUS. A range of mountains between the Black Sea and Caspian. Prometheus was chained on this mountain.

CENAEUM. The northwest promontory of Euboea, where there was a temple to Zeus (Jupiter). It was here that Hercules sacrificed to Cenean Jove and put on the poisoned robe sent by Deianira.

CENTAURS. A mythical race of creatures, half man and half horse, believed to dwell in Thessaly. The centaur Nessus was slain by Hercules.

CERBERUS. The three-headed dog stationed at the entrance to Hades to keep the living from getting in and the dead from getting out. Cerberus was brought to the Upper World by Hercules as one of his twelve labours.

CERES. Daughter of Saturn, sister of Jupiter, mother of Proserpina, and goddess of agriculture. See ELEUSIS, PROSERPINA, TRIPTOLEMUS.

CEYX. King of Trachis who suffered death by shipwreck. His wife Alcyone mourned him until both were changed into birds.

CHALCIS. The principal town of Euboea, situated on the Euripus.

CHAONIA. A region of Epirus in northwestern Greece. The Chaonian oaks were a sacred grove containing a temple and oracle of Jupiter.

CHARON. The aged man who ferried souls across the river Styx.

CHARYBDIS. A whirlpool between Italy and Sicily, opposite Scylla, which alternately sucked in and vomited up the sea.

CHIMAERA. A monster combining a lion, a dragon, and a goat, which vomited forth fire.

CHIRON. The wisest of the centaurs. He lived in a cavern on Mt. Pelion and was the teacher of gods and heroes, most notably Achilles.

CHRYSA. The home of Chryses, priest of Apollo. His daughter Chryseis was captured by Agamemnon, who was forced by a pestilence to give her up. Agamemnon then claimed Briseis, the captive maid of Achilles.

CINYPHS. A river in Libya.

CIRCE. Daughter of the Sun and sister of Aeetes, famed for her magic arts. She changed the companions of Ulysses into swine.

CIRRHA. A very ancient town in Phocis,

near Delphi, where the famous oracle of Apollo was located.

CISSEUS. A king in Thrace, and father of Hecuba.

CITHAERON. A mountain near Thebes where the infant Oedipus was exposed. See PENTHEUS.

CLAUDIA. Octavia, the daughter of Claudius and Messalina. See OCTAVIA.

CLAUDIUS. The fourth Roman emperor, father of Octavia. He was murdered by his second wife, Agrippina.

CLEONAE. An ancient town in Argolis, near Nemea, where Hercules killed the lion.

CLOTHO. One of the three Fates.

CLYTEMNESTRA. Daughter of Tyndareus and Leda, wife of Agamemnon, mother of Orestes, Iphigenia, and Electra. During the absence of her husband at the Trojan War, she conspired with Aegisthus to murder Agamemnon.

COCYTUS. A river in the Underworld.

COLCHIAN WOMAN. See MEDEA.

COLCHIS. The kingdom of Aeetes, to which Jason came in search for the golden fleece.

CORA. 1. A name of Proserpina. 2. A small town in Italy.

CORUS (or CAURUS). The northwest wind.

CORYBANTES. Priests of Cybele, who worshipped her in orgiastic dances.

CREON. 1. A Theban prince, brother of Queen Jocasta. He became king after the death of Eteocles and Polynices. He was slain by the usurper Lycus. 2. King of Corinth and father of Creusa. He and his daughter were slain by Medea by means of the magic robe.

CRETE. A large island in the Mediterranean Sea south of the Aegean.

CRETAN BULL. A bull which laid waste the island of Crete. It was captured alive by Hercules as one of his labours.

CREUSA. Daughter of Creon, king of Corinth. When Jason deserted Medea for her, she was burned to death by a poisoned robe which Medea sent to her.

CRISPINUS. A Roman knight, the husband of Poppaea.

CUPID. Son of Venus, and god of Love.

CURETES. Ancient inhabitants of Crete.

CYBELE. A goddess worshipped in Phrygia and identified with Rhea, the mother of the gods.

CYCLOPES. A race of one-eyed giants, who lived on the coast of Sicily. They were said to have built the walls of Mycenae.

CYCNUS. 1. A son of Mars, slain by Hercules. 2. A son of Neptune, slain by Achilles. Upon his death he was changed into a swan.

CYLLARUS. A famous horse which Juno received from Neptune and presented to Castor.

CYNTHIA. A name of Diana. Cynthus was a mountain in Delos, where Apollo and Diana were born.

CYPRUS. A large island in the Mediterranean Sea south of Cilicia and west of Syria. It was one of the chief seats of the worship of Aphrodite (Venus).

DAEDALUS. A mythical architect and inventor in the time of Theseus and Minos. He built the labyrinth for the Minotaur and escaped from Crete on wings which he had constructed. See ICARUS.

DANAE. Daughter of Acrisius, king of Argos, and mother of Perseus by Jupiter who visited her in a shower of gold. Acrisius shut mother and child in a chest and cast it into the sea, but both were rescued.

DANAIDES. The fifty daughters of Danaus, brother of Aegyptus. Being forced to marry the fifty sons of Aegyptus, all slew their husbands on their wedding night, with the single exception of Hypermnestra. For their crime the Danaides were punished in Hades with the task of carrying water in sieves.

DANAUS. Twin brother of Aegyptus. See DANAIDES.

DARDANUS. Son of Jupiter and Electra, and one of the ancestors of the royal house of Troy.

DARIUS. King of Persia, father of Xerxes.

DAULIS. An ancient town of Phocis, the residence of King Tereus. Daulis was celebrated as the scene of the tragic story of Philomela and Procne. See PHILOMELA.

DEIANIRA. Daughter of Oeneus, sister of Meleager, wife of Hercules, and mother of Hyllus. Ignorant of its real power, she sent a poisoned robe to Hercules to win back his love; the robe caused his death.

DEIDAMIA. Daughter of Lycomedes, king of Scyros. When Achilles was concealed in Scyros in maiden's attire, she became by him the mother of Pyrrhus.

DEIPHOBUS. Son of Priam and Hecuba, and husband of Helen after the death of Paris.

DELOS. A small island in the Aegean, birthplace of Apollo and Diana. The island was later famed for its temple of Apollo.

DELPHI. The site of the famous oracle of Apollo.

DEMETRIUS. Son of Antigonus and king of Macedon. He captured Athens in 307 B.C.

DEMOPHILUS. A writer of Greek New Comedy.

DEUCALION. Son of Prometheus and husband of Pyrrha. He and his wife were the only mortals saved from the flood.

DIAN. See DIANA.

DIANA. Daughter of Jupiter and Latona, twin sister of Apollo, the virgin goddess of the hunt. She was worshipped as Luna or Phoebe in heaven and as Hecate in Hades. When slighted by King Oeneus she sent a huge boar to ravage Calydon.

DICTYNNA. Another name for Diana.

DIOMEDES. 1. A king of the Bistones in Thrace, who fed his captives to fierce man-eating horses. Hercules, as one of his labours, captured the horses and killed Diomedes, whose body he threw to the horses. After eating the flesh of their master they became tame. 2. Son of Tydeus, and a Greek hero in the Trojan war. He and

Ulysseus carried off the Palladium from the city of Troy.

DIONYSIA. Festivals held at Athens in honour of Dionysus (Bacchus).

DIONYSUS. The Greek god of wine. See BACCHUS.

DIPHILUS. A poet of the Greek New Comedy, contemporary of Menander.

DIRCA. See DIRCE.

DIRCE. Wife of Lycus, king of Thebes. Because of her cruelty to their mother Antiope, Amphion and Zethus tied her to a wild bull, and she was dragged to death on Mt. Cithaeron. She was changed to a fountain of the same name.

DIS. A name given to Pluto, and also to the Lower World.

DOLOPIAN. Thessalian. The Dolopes were a people of Thessaly who fought in the war against Troy.

DOMITIUS. Gnaeus Domitius Ahenobarbus, who married Agrippina and was the father of the emperor Nero.

DRACHMA. A Greek coin, worth about eighteen cents. See MINA.

DRAGON. 1. The guardian of the apples of the Hesperides, slain by Hercules, and afterwards placed in the heavens as the constellation Draco. 2. The dragon killed by Cadmus near the site of later Thebes. 3. The dragon of Colchis, guardian of the golden fleece, put to sleep by the magic of Medea.

DRYADS. A race of wood-nymphs.

ECHO. A nymph whom Juno prevented from speaking except to repeat the last words that had been said in her hearing. She fell in love with Narcissus; when the love was not returned, she pined away to a mere voice.

EETION. King of Thebe, in Cilicia, and father of Andromache, the wife of Hector.

ELECTRA. Daughter of Agamemnon and Clytemnestra, and sister of Orestes.

ELECTRYON. Father of Alcmena, the wife of Amphitryon.

ELEUSIS or ELEUSIN. A town near Athens, where mysteries were held in honour of Ceres.

ELYSIUM. The abode of the blest in the Underworld.

ENCELADUS. One of the giants who attempted to dethrone Jupiter. He was killed and buried under Mt. Aetna.

ENNIUS. A Roman poet and playwright, famous for his tragedies and his great national epic, the *Annales*. He lived in the time of Plautus, and was regarded by the Romans as the father of their literature.

EPIDAMNUS. A town in Greek Illyria on the Adriatic Sea.

EPIDAURUS. A town in Argolis, famed for the worship of Aesculapius.

EPIUS. The builder of the Trojan horse.

EREBUS. The darkness surrounding the Underworld.

ERETRIA. A town in Euboea, situated on the Euripus.

ERINYES. The Furies.

ERYX. Son of Butes and Venus, and a famous boxer. He was overcome by Hercules. A mountain in Sicily was said to have been named after him.

ETEOCLES. One of the two sons of Oedipus and Jocasta. See POLYNICES.

EUMENIDES. "The Benevolent Ones," a euphemism for the Furies.

EURIPUS. The channel between Euboea and Boeotia.

EUROPA. Daughter of Agenor, king of Phoenicia, and sister of Cadmus. Jupiter fell in love with her and, in the form of a bull, swam to Crete carrying her on his back. There she became the mother of Minos, Rhadamanthus, and Sarpedon. The continent of Europe was named after her.

EURUS. The east or southeast wind.

EURYBATES. A messenger of Agamemnon who announced the return of the victorious hero.

EURYDICE. Wife of Orpheus, rescued by her husband from the Underworld, but lost again. See ORPHEUS.

EURYSTHEUS. King of Argos, enemy and master of Hercules, to whom he assigned the twelve labours.

EURYTUS. King of Oechalia and father of Iole.

EVENUS. A river in Aetolia.

FAVONIUS. The west wind.

FRASINONE. A small town in Italy.

FURIES. Avenging goddesses, dwelling in Hades.

GANYMEDE. A handsome Trojan youth whom Jupiter made cup-bearer to the gods. One version relates that Jupiter, in the form of an eagle, carried him off to heaven.

GARAMANTIAN. African. The Garamantes were a people of northern Africa.

GELONIAN. Scythian. The Geloni were a people of Scythia who tattooed themselves.

GERYON. A triple-bodied monster in Spain. Hercules killed him and drove his cattle back to Eurystheus as one of his labours.

GETES. A people of Thrace.

GIANTS. Monstrous sons of Earth who attacked the gods; they piled mountains (Pelion, Ossa, and Olympus) one on another, in order to scale heaven. They were overthrown by the gods, with the assistance of Hercules, and buried under Sicily.

GORGON. Medusa, one of the three daughters of Phorcys. Her head was covered with snaky locks, and anyone who looked upon her was turned to stone. She was killed by Perseus, and her head was presented to Minerva, who fixed it on her shield.

GRACCHI. Tiberius Sempronius Gracchus and Gaius Sempronius Gracchus, his brother. Both were leaders of the people and proposed numerous agrarian reforms.

GYAS. One of the hundred-handed giants who attempted to overthrow the gods.

HADES. The god of the Underworld. Also used as a name for the Underworld.

HALCYON. See ALCYONE.

HARPIES. Mythical monsters, half woman and half bird.

HEBE. Daughter of Jupiter and Juno, and goddess of youth. She married Hercules after he was received among the gods.

HEBRUS. The principal river in Thrace.

HECATE. A confusing divinity, often identified with Proserpina in the Underworld, Diana on earth, and Luna in heaven. As a divinity of the lower world she was the sender of visions and phantoms.

HECTOR. Son of Priam and Hecuba, husband of Andromache, the bravest warrior of the Trojans. He was slain by Achilles and his body was dragged around the walls of Troy, but was later ransomed by Priam.

HECUBA. Wife of Priam, and queen of Troy. After the fall of Troy she was carried away by the Greeks and was changed into a dog.

HELEN. Daughter of Jupiter and Leda, sister of Clytemnestra, Castor, and Pollux, wife of Menelaus. She was considered the most beautiful woman in Greece, and was given to Paris by Venus as a reward for his judgment in her favour. Helen's desertion of her husband Menelaus and flight to Troy with Paris precipitated the Trojan War.

HELENUS. Son of Priam and Hecuba, noted for his powers of prophecy.

HELLE. Sister of Phrixus, who fled with him on the ram with the golden fleece. She fell into the sea which thereafter bore her name (Hellespont).

HERCEAN JOVE. An epithet of Jupiter as the protector of the house.

HERCULES. The most celebrated of ancient heroes, later deified. He was the son of Jupiter and Alcmena. Through the trickery of Juno Eurystheus was given power over Hercules who was forced to perform various labours for his master. The twelve labours are usually arranged in the following order: (1) killing of the Nemean lion; (2) destruction of the hydra of Lerna; (3) capture of the Arcadian stag; (4) capture of the Erymanthian boar; (5) cleansing of the stables of Augeas; (6) killing of the Stymphalian birds; (7) capture of the Cretan bull; (8) capture of the man-eating horses of Diomedes, king

of Thrace; (9) securing of the girdle of Hippolyte, queen of the Amazons; (10) killing of Geryon and the capture of his oxen; (11) securing the golden apples of the Hesperides; (12) bringing Cerberus from the Underworld. Numerous other heroic deeds are related of Hercules: his fight with the centaurs, the killing of Nessus, Antaeus, Busiris, Cycnus, Zetes and Calais, the capture of Troy during the reign of Laomedon, the supporting of the heavens on his shoulders in place of Atlas. For extended recapitulations of the deeds of Hercules, see the following passages: Seneca's *Mad Hercules* 205-308, 524-560, *Agamemnon* 808-866, *Hercules on Oeta* 1-98, 1161-1206, 1218-1257, 1518-1606, 1872-1939.

HERMIONE. Daughter of Menelaus and Helen.

HESIONE. Daughter of Laomedon, king of Troy. She was rescued from a sea-monster by Hercules, and later captured by him when he took Troy.

HESPERIDES. Nymphs on a far western island who watched over the golden apples which Earth gave to Juno at her marriage with Jupiter. The apples were guarded also by a sleepless dragon. It was one of the labours of Hercules to obtain possession of the apples.

HESPERUS. The evening star.

HIERO. King of Syracuse from 265 to 215 B.C.

HIPPODAMIA. Daughter of Oenomaus, king of Pisa, and wife of Pelops.

HIPPOLYTE. Queen of the Amazons. She possessed a girdle given to her by Mars, her father. Hercules killed her and secured the girdle as one of his labours.

HIPPOLYTUS. Son of Theseus and Antiope, the sister of Hippolyte.

HYADES. Daughters of Atlas and sisters of the Pleiades. They formed a constellation supposed to bring rain.

HYBLA. A town in Sicily.

HYDASPES. A river in India.

HYDRA. A monster which infested the marsh of Lerna. It was slain by Hercules as one of his labours and its blood was used by the hero to poison his arrows.

HYLAS. A handsome youth who accompanied Hercules on the Argonautic expedition. He was seized by waternymphs when he stopped on the coast of Mysia for water.

HYLLUS. Son of Hercules and Deianira.

HYMEN. The god of marriage.

HYPERMNESTRA. One of the fifty daughters of Danaus. She alone refused to kill her husband on her wedding night (see DANAIDES) and did not suffer among her sisters in Hades.

ICARUS. The son of Daedalus, who attempted to escape from Crete on wings made by his father. He flew too near the sun, the wax of his wings melted, and he fell into the sea which thereafter was named after him.

IDA. A mountain range in Asia Minor, famed as the scene of the rape of Ganymede and of the judgment of Paris.

IDMON. Son of Apollo, a soothsayer, and a member of the Argonautic expedition.

ILISSUS. A small river in Attica, near Athens.

INACHUS. Father of Io and the first king of Argos. He gave his name to the river Inachus there.

INARIME. An island near the coast of Campania, now Ischia.

INO. Daughter of Cadmus, sister of Semele, wife of Athamas, the king of Thebes. When her husband, driven mad by Juno, attempted to slay her, she escaped him by leaping into the sea with her son Melicertes. She and her son were changed into divinities of the sea, Ino becoming Leucothoe, and Melicertes, Palaemon.

IO. Daughter of Inachus, beloved by Jupiter, and changed into a heifer, through fear of Juno. The goddess, aware of the change, placed her under the care of the hundred-eyed Argus, who was slain by Hermes. Juno then tormented Io with a gadfly and drove her from land to land.

IOLE. Daughter of Eurytus, king of Oechalia. She was captured by Hercules when her father refused to allow Hercules to marry her.

IPHIGENIA. Daughter of Agamemnon and Clytemnestra. She was taken to Aulis to be sacrificed to Diana, but was rescued by the goddess and became the priestess in her temple in the land of the Taurians.

IRIS. Goddess of the rainbow and messenger of Juno.

ISMENUS. A small river in Boeotia, near Thebes.

ISTER. The Danube.

ITYS. Son of Tereus and Procne, slain by his mother to punish Tereus for his outrage upon her sister, Philomela. The body of Itys was served to Tereus as a banquet.

IXION. A king of the Lapithae who tried to win the love of Juno. He was punished by being chained to a wheel in the Underworld which never ceased revolving.

JASON. 1. Son of Aeson, king of Thessaly, and nephew of the usurping king, Pelias. At the demand of Pelias, he organised the Argonautic expedition to bring back the golden fleece. He performed the tasks imposed by King Aeetes of Colchis and fled with Medea, who had aided him. 2. King of Pherae in Thessaly.

JOCASTA. Wife of Laius, king of Thebes, and mother of Oedipus. She committed suicide upon learning that she had married her son. According to another version of the story, she was living at the time of the strife of her sons, Eteocles and Polynices.

JUDGES IN HADES. See AEACUS, MINOS, and RHADAMANTHUS.

JULIA. Daughter of Drusus and Livia, exiled and later slain.

JUNO. Sister and wife of Jupiter. She was portrayed as jealous and hostile to the women loved by Jupiter, and to his irregular offspring.

JUPITER. Lord of Olympus, ruler of heaven and earth. He had love affairs with many mortal women: Alcmena,

Callisto, Danae, Europa, Latona, Leda, Semele.

JUSTICE. See ASTRAEA.

LABDACUS. A king of Thebes, father of Laius.

LACHESIS. One of the three fates. The other two were Clotho and Atropos.

LAERTES. Father of Ulysses.

LAIUS. A king of Thebes, the husband of Jocasta, and father of Oedipus. He was murdered by an unknown man who was later revealed as his son Oedipus.

LANUVINUS. Luscius Lanuvinus, a writer of Roman comedy and a bitter opponent and critic of Terence.

LAOMEDON. A king of Troy, father of Priam. Apollo and Neptune built the walls of Troy, but Laomedon refused to pay them the promised reward. When Neptune sent a sea-monster against Troy, Hercules killed the monster, but Laomedon again failed to pay the reward. The hero then captured Troy, killed Laomedon, and gave his daughter Hesione to Telamon.

LAPITHAE. A mythical people of Thessaly, famed for their battle with the Centaurs.

LAR. Household god. The spirit of a dead ancestor who watched over the home.

LATONA. Beloved by Jupiter, to whom she bore Apollo and Diana.

LAVERNA. The Roman goddess of thieves and impostors.

LEDA. Wife of Tyndareus, king of Sparta, and mother of Clytemnestra by Tyndareus, of Castor, Pollux, and Helen by Jupiter.

LEMNOS. A large volcanic island in the Aegean. Vulcan was said to have fallen there, when he was hurled from Olympus. A myth told that all the Lemnian women, except Hypsipyle, murdered their husbands.

LERNA. A district in Argolis where Hercules slew the hydra.

LETHE. A river in Hades. When the souls of the departed drank of its waters,

they were rendered oblivious of their past experiences.

LETO. See LATONA.

LEUCOTHOE. A sea goddess. See INO.

LIBRA. The zodiacal constellation of the Scales, marking the autumnal equinox.

LICHAS. An attendant of Hercules. He brought his master the poisoned robe and was hurled by him into the sea.

LICTORS. Attendants who carried the *fasces* (rods bound in a bundle and containing an axe) before Roman magistrates.

LINUS. The personification of a dirge or lamentation, and described as a son of Apollo. According to one tradition, he was killed by Hercules to whom he was giving instruction in music.

LION. The sign of the zodiac which represented the Nemean lion, slain by Hercules and set in the sky as a constellation.

LIVIA. Wife of Drusus, the son of Tiberius.

LIVIUS. Marcus Livius Drusus, tribune of the people in 91 B.C.

LOIRE. A river in France, called Liger by the Romans.

LUCIFER. The morning star.

LUCINA. The goddess who presided over the birth of children.

LUCRETIA. Daughter of Lucretius and wife of Collatinus. Her rape by Sextus Tarquinius led to the overthrow of Tarquinius Superbus and later to the establishment of the Roman republic.

LUNA. The goddess of the moon, identified with Diana; called also Phoebe as sister of Phoebus Apollo.

LYCORMAS. A river in Aetolia, in northwest Greece.

LYCURGUS. 1. A king of Thrace who opposed Bacchus. He was driven mad by the gods and later killed. 2. The Spartan legislator, celebrated for his wisdom.

LYCUS. A usurper who killed Creon, king of Thebes, and seized control of the city.

LYNCEUS. One of the Argonautic heroes,

noted for his extraordinary keenness of vision.

MAEANDER. A river of Phrygia, celebrated for its winding course.

MAENADS. Frenzied worshippers of Bacchus.

MAENALUS. A mountain in Arcadia.

MANES. The souls of the departed, worshipped by the Romans as gods.

MANTO. Daughter of the seer Tiresias.

MARS. God of war, son of Jupiter and Juno.

MEDEA. Daughter of Aeetes, king of Colchis. By means of her magic arts she enabled Jason to perform the deadly tasks set by her father. She fled with Jason to Greece, slew her brother Absyrtus, tricked the daughters of Pelias into killing their father. When Jason deserted her, she sent a poisoned robe to destroy her rival, Creusa, and killed her two sons.

MEDUSA. One of the Gorgons, slain by Perseus.

MEGAERA. One of the Furies.

MEGALENSIAN GAMES. The annual festival at Rome in honour of the Great Mother (Cybele).

MEGARA. Daughter of Creon, king of Thebes, and wife of Hercules, by whom she was slain in a fit of madness.

MELEAGER. Son of Oeneus and Althaea. See ALTHAEA.

MEMNON. Son of Aurora, slain by Achilles.

MENANDER. The most distinguished poet of the Greek New Comedy. Many of the comedies of Plautus and Terence were adapted from Menandrian originals.

MENELAUS. King of Sparta, son of Atreus, brother of Agamemnon, husband of Helen.

MERCURY. Son of Jupiter and Maia, and messenger of the gods. He was also the guide of the souls of the dead, and the god of trickery and thievery.

MEROPE. Wife of Polybus, king of Corinth, and the foster-mother of Oedipus.

MESSALINA. Wife of the emperor Claudius and the mother of Octavia and Britannicus. She openly married Gaius Silius during her husband's absence and was slain by the order of the emperor.

MIMAS. One of the giants who fought against the gods.

MINA. A Greek weight of silver, the equivalent of one hundred drachmae. The value of the mina was about eighteen dollars, but the purchasing power was many times greater.

MINERVA. The goddess of wisdom and the patroness of arts and trades, identified by the Romans with the Greek goddess Athena.

MINOS. King of Crete, husband of Pasiphae, father of Ariadne and Phaedra. Because of his righteousness on earth he was made one of the judges of the Underworld.

MINOTAUR. A Cretan monster, half man and half bull, born of a union between Pasiphae and a bull. He was confined in a labyrinth and slain by Theseus, with the assistance of Ariadne, the daughter of King Minos.

MOPSUS. A Thessalian soothsayer who went on the expedition of the Argonauts and perished from the bite of a serpent in Libya.

MYCALE. A celebrated witch of Thessaly.

MYCENAE. An ancient city in Argolis, the home of Agamemnon.

MYRRHA. Daughter of Cinyras who conceived an unnatural passion for her father. She was changed into a myrrh tree.

MYRTILUS. Son of Mercury and charioteer of Oenomaus. He was bribed by Pelops to wreck his master's chariot.

NABATAEAN. Arabian.

NAEVIUS. An early Latin poet who wrote both epic and dramatic poetry. He died about 202 B.C.

NAIDS. Nymphs who inhabited brooks and springs.

NAUPLIUS. King of Euboea, son of Neptune, father of Palamedes. To avenge the death of Palamedes, who had been slain by the Greeks, he lighted false beacon fires on the coast of Euboea and lured the Greek fleet to destruction as it sailed home from Troy. When Odysseus escaped, Nauplius threw himself from a cliff.

NEMEA. A valley in Argolis where Hercules slew the Nemean lion.

NEPHELE. The cloud form of Juno, devised by Jupiter, upon which Ixion begot the centaur, Nessus, in the belief that he was making love to Juno.

NEPTUNE. The god of the sea. He was the son of Saturn, brother of Jupiter and Pluto, and father of Theseus, Cyncus, and Periclymenus.

NEREIDS. Nymphs of the sea.

NEREUS. A sea god, father of the Nereids.

NERIENE. A daughter of Nereus.

NERO. Son of Gnaeus Domitius Ahenobarbus and Agrippina, adopted by Claudius after his mother's marriage to the emperor. He married Octavia, his stepsister, and became emperor in 54 A.D. upon the death of Claudius.

NESSUS. A centaur, son of Ixion and Nephele. He was slain by Hercules while attempting to carry off Deianira. As he was dying, he gave his poisoned blood to Deianira as a love charm.

NESTOR. King of Pylos, renowned for his wisdom and justice. He took part in the Trojan War.

NIOBE. Daughter of Tantalus and wife of Amphion, king of Thebes. Because of her fourteen children she considered herself superior to Latona. All her children were slain by Apollo and Diana, and Niobe herself was turned into a stone on Mt. Sipylus in Lydia.

NOTUS. The south or southwest wind.

NYCTELIUS. An epithet of Bacchus, because his mysteries were celebrated at night.

NYSAEAN. A term applied to Bacchus, whose birthplace was said to be Nysa, in India.

OCTAVIA. Daughter of the emperor Claudius and Messalina. Though previously betrothed to Silanus, she married her stepbrother Nero. In 62 A.D. Nero divorced her to marry his mistress, Poppaea. Octavia was exiled and soon after was put to death by Nero's order.

OEDIPUS. King of Thebes, son of Laius and Jocasta, father of Eteocles, Polynices, Antigone and Ismene. He saved Thebes from the Sphinx by answering her riddle. It was Oedipus' sad fate unwittingly to kill his father and marry his mother.

OENEUS. King of Calydon and Pleuron in Aetolia, husband of Althaea, father of Meleager and Deianira.

OILEUS. King of the Locrians and father of the lesser Ajax. He was one of the Argonauts.

OLENIAN. Of Olenus, a city in Aetolia.

OLYMPIA. A place in Elis, in the Peloponnesus, where the Olympic games were celebrated every four years. A famous temple of Jupiter was located there.

OLYMPUS. A mountain between Macedonia and Thessaly, regarded by the Greeks as the home of the gods. See PELION.

OMPHALE. A queen of Lydia under whom Hercules served in bondage for three years.

OPHION. Originally one of the companions of Cadmus, sprung from the serpent's teeth. In an adjectival form the word means simply Theban.

OPHIUCHUS. The northern constellation of the "Serpent Holder," representing a man holding a serpent.

OPS. Wife of Saturn, and the Roman goddess of plenty and fertility.

ORCUS. See HADES.

ORESTES. Son of Agamemnon and Clytemnestra, brother of Electra.

ORION. A handsome giant and hunter. After his death he was placed in the heavens as a constellation.

ORPHEUS. Son of Apollo and the muse Calliope, and one of the Argonauts. His sweet music could move rocks and trees. He descended to Hades and persuaded the gods of the Underworld to release his wife, Eurydice. He lost her again because he did not keep the condition imposed upon him. He met his death at the hands of Thracian women.

OSSA. A mountain in northern Thessaly. See PELION.

OTHRYS. A mountain in Thessaly.

PACTOLUS. A river of Lydia, celebrated for its golden sands.

PALAEMON. See INO.

PALAMEDES. Son of Nauplius, king of Euboea. He was put to death by the Greeks on false charges brought by Ulysses. See NAUPLIUS.

PALLADIUM. A statue of Pallas Athena (Minerva) which stood in Troy. Since the safety of the city depended on its preservation, it was stolen by Ulysses and Diomedes, and carried by the latter to Greece.

PALLAS. A name given to Athena.

PAN. The god of flocks and shepherds, originally an Arcadian god. Sudden terror (panic) was caused by him. In works of art Pan is represented as having horns and goat's feet.

PANDATARIA. An island near the bay of Naples, to which members of the imperial family were exiled.

PANDION. A king of Athens, father of Procne and Philomela, both of whom were changed to birds.

PARCAE. The three personified fates, Clotho, Lachesis, and Atropos.

PARIS. Son of Priam and Hecuba. Venus promised him the most beautiful woman for his wife, if he gave her the award for beauty in the contest with Juno and Minerva. Paris visited Menelaus, king of Sparta, and carried off Helen to Troy.

PARNASSUS. A mountain range in central Greece, sacred to Apollo and the Muses.

PARRHASIAN. Arcadian.

PARTHIA. A country of Asia, southeast of the Caspian Sea. The Parthians were famous for their archery.

PASIPHAE. Wife of Minos, king of Crete. She was the mother of the Minotaur, slain by Theseus.

PATROCLUS. A Greek hero in the Trojan War. He was Achilles' closest friend and was slain by Hector while fighting in Achilles' armour.

PAULUS. Lucius Aemilius Paulus, a Roman general who defeated Perseus, king of Macedonia, at Pydna in 168 B.C. He died in 160 B.C. and funeral games were presented in his honour.

PEGASUS. A winged horse, the offspring of Neptune and Medusa.

PELASGIANS. The Greeks, so named from Pelasgus, a mythical ancestor of the earliest inhabitants of Greece.

PELEUS. Son of Aeacus and king of Thessaly. Husband of Thetis and father of Achilles.

PELIAS. Usurping king of Iolcus, and father of Acastus. He drove out the rightful king, Aeson, and sent Aeson's son, Jason, on the quest for the golden fleece. On Jason's return, Medea deceitfully persuaded Pelias' daughters that they could restore their father's youth by cutting him to pieces and boiling him.

PELIDES. Achilles, son of Peleus.

PELION. A range of mountains in Thessaly, the home of the centaur, Chiron, who educated the young Achilles. The giants attempted to reach the heavens by piling Pelion, Ossa, and Olympus, one on another.

PELLIO. A comic actor in the time of Plautus.

PELOPS. Son of Tantalus. He was slain by his father and served as a banquet to the gods, but was restored by them to life. He married Hippodamia, and was the ancestor of the house of Atreus. The Peloponnesus takes its name from him.

PELORUS. A promontory of Sicily opposite the coast of Italy. The monster Scylla was said to dwell under this promontory.

PENATES. The household gods of the Romans.

PENELOPE. Wife of Ulysses, to whom she was faithful during his absence of twenty years.

PENTHESILEA. Queen of the Amazons. She came to the aid of the Trojans and was slain by Achilles.

PENTHEUS. King of Thebes, son of

Agave, grandson of Cadmus. He was torn to pieces on Mt. Cithaeron by his mother and her sisters after they had been driven mad by Bacchus.

PERICLYMENUS. A son of Neptune who had the power of changing into various forms. He was one of the Argonauts and was slain by Hercules.

PERSEUS. Son of Jupiter and Danae. He was the slayer of Medusa.

PHAEDRA. Daughter of Minos and Pasiphae, sister of Ariadne, wife of Theseus.

PHAETHON. Son of Apollo, who was allowed to drive his father's chariot. The youth could not control the horses, and was killed by Jupiter to prevent the earth from catching fire. His sisters mourned his death and were changed into poplar trees.

PHAON. A handsome youth, whom the poetess Sappho is said to have loved.

PHASIS. A river in Colchis.

PHERAE. An ancient town in Thessaly, the home of Admetus.

PHILEMON. A poet of the Greek New Comedy, contemporary of Menander.

PHILIP. Philip II of Macedon, father of Alexander the Great.

PHILIPPEAN. A gold coin first minted by Philip II of Macedon. The *philippus* was worth about twenty drachmae, or about three dollars and sixty cents. See MINA.

PHILIPPI. A city in Thrace, celebrated for the victory gained there by Antony and Octavian over Brutus and Cassius in 42 B.C.

PHILIPPIDES. A poet of Greek New Comedy.

PHILOCTETES. Son of Poeas and friend of Hercules, who bequeathed to him his bow and arrows. On the way to the Trojan war, Philoctetes was poisoned by the bite of a serpent and was left behind on the island of Lemnos. In the tenth year of the war he was brought to Troy by the Greeks, where he slew Paris and many other Trojans.

PHILOMELA. Daughter of Pandion, king of Athens, and sister of Procne, who had married Tereus, king of Thrace.

When Philomela was outraged by Tereus, she and Procne punished him by slaying his son Itys and serving him as a banquet to his father. She was changed into a nightingale and mourned constantly for Itys.

PHINEUS. King of Salmydessus in Thrace. He blinded his sons because of a false accusation made against them by their stepmother. The gods then blinded him and sent the Harpies to torment him. See ZETES.

PHLEGETHON. A river in the Underworld.

PHLEGRA. A valley in Thrace where the giants fought with the gods.

PHOEBUS. A name of Apollo as the god of the sun, who drives his fiery chariot across the sky.

PHOENIX. The aged guardian of Achilles. He brought the news of Achilles' death to Peleus, the hero's father.

PHORBAS. Shepherd of the royal flocks at Thebes.

PHRIXUS. Son of Athamas and Nephele and brother of Helle. Persecuted by his stepmother Ino, he fled through the air with his sister on the ram with the golden fleece. Helle fell into the sea and Phrixus made his way to Colchis where he sacrificed the ram and presented the fleece to Aeetes.

PHRYGIAN. Trojan. Phrygia was a country in northwestern Asia Minor.

PINDUS. A mountain between Thessaly and Epirus.

PIRENE. A famous fountain at Corinth, where Bellerophon caught Pegasus.

PIRITHOUS. Son of Ixion. Accompanied by Theseus, he went to the Underworld and attempted to steal Proserpina from Hades.

PISA. A city in Elis. The Olympian games were held nearby.

PLAUTUS. 1. Titus Maccius Plautus, the famous Roman comic poet (c. 254-184 B.C.). 2. Rubellius Plautus, son of Rubellius Blandus and Julia, granddaughter of the emperor Tiberius. He was exiled in 60 A.D. and killed by Nero's orders in 62.

PLEIADES. See ATLANTIDES.

PLISTHENES. A son of Thyestes, slain by Atreus.

PLUTO. Brother of Jupiter and Neptune, and god of the Underworld.

POLIORCETES. "The Besieger," a surname of Demetrius.

POLLUX. See CASTOR.

POLYBUS. King of Corinth, the fosterfather of Oedipus.

POLYNICES. Son of Oedipus and Jocasta, brother of Eteocles and Antigone. When Eteocles refused to give up the kingdom of Thebes, Polynices fled to Adrastus, king of Argos, who gave him refuge and made him his son-inlaw. To avenge Polynices, Adrastus marched against Thebes with an army led by seven famous chiefs.

POLYXENA. Daughter of Priam and Hecuba, who was sacrificed to appease the shade of Achilles.

PONTUS. 1. A country in northeastern Asia Minor, along the coast of the Black Sea. 2. The Black Sea.

POPPAEA. Wife of Rufus Crispinus, whom she abandoned for Otho. She left Otho to become the mistress of the emperor Nero, and the rival of Nero's wife, Octavia.

POSIDIPPUS. A poet of Greek New Comedy.

PRAENESTE. An ancient town in Latium, about twenty miles southeast of Rome.

PRAETOR. A Roman magistrate who administered justice. Magistrates of praetorian rank presided over the special courts of law.

PRIAM. King of Troy during the Trojan War. As a youth he had been spared by Hercules at the first taking of Troy. When Troy was captured and destroyed by the Greeks under Agamemnon, Priam was slain by Pyrrhus at the altar of Hercean Jove.

PROCNE. Daughter of Pandion and wife of Tereus. See PHILOMELA.

PROCRUSTES. A famous robber of Attica, who forced people to lie in beds which did not fit them; if they were shorter than the bed, he stretched their hands; if they were longer, he sawed off their limbs. He was finally slain by Theseus.

PROETIDES. Daughters of Proetus, king of Argos. They considered themselves more beautiful than Juno, and also refused to worship Bacchus. The god drove them mad and they wandered through the forests thinking themselves cows.

PROETUS. King of Argos. See BELLEROPHON, PROETIDES.

PROMETHEUS. One of the Titans, a great benefactor of mankind. He stole fire from heaven and gave it to mortals. Jupiter punished him by having him chained to a rock on Mt. Caucasus, where an eagle fed upon his everrenewed vitals. He was finally set free by Hercules.

PROSERPINA. Daughter of Jupiter and Ceres. She was stolen away by Pluto and made queen of the Underworld.

PROTEUS. The old man of the sea who had the gift of prophecy and the power to change his form. He was the shepherd and guardian of the sea-calves.

PTERELA. King of the Teleboans, defeated by Amphitryon.

PYLADES. Son of Strophius, king of Phocis, and friend of Orestes.

PYRRHA. Wife of Deucalion.

PYRRHUS. Son of Achilles and Deidamia. He took part in the destruction of Troy and slew King Priam.

PYTHON. A huge serpent slain by Apollo. The Pythian games were founded in commemoration of Apollo's victory.

RHADAMANTHUS. Son of Jupiter and Europa, and brother of Minos. He was one of the judges in the Underworld.

RHAMNUS. A deme, or district, of Attica.

RHESUS. A king of Thrace who came to the aid of the Trojans during the Trojan War. An oracle said that Troy could never be taken if the horses of Rhesus should drink the waters of the Xanthus and feed upon the Trojan plain. The oracle was frustrated by Ulysses and Diomedes, who killed Rhesus and captured his horses.

RHODES. A large island in the southeastern Aegean.

SARMATIANS. A nation dwelling north of the Black Sea.

SATURN. A Roman god who ruled in the Golden Age. Identified with the Greek Cronus, and hence made the father of Jupiter, Neptune, and Pluto. He was dethroned by his three sons who divided his kingdom among themselves. Saturn was then chained in Hades by Pluto.

SCALES. The constellation which marked the autumn equinox.

SCIRON. A robber in Attica, who threw his victims over the cliffs into the sea. He was slain by Theseus.

SCYLLA. A sea-monster, who lived in a cave in the straits between Italy and Sicily. See CHARYBDIS.

SCYROS. An island off Euboea. See DEIDAMIA.

SCYTHIA. A name given by the ancients to a portion of northern Asia.

SELEUCIA. There were cities of this name in Cilicia, Syria, and Babylonia. They were built by Seleucus I, king of Syria.

SEMELE. Daughter of Cadmus. Beloved by Jupiter, she became the mother of Bacchus. She was blasted by a thunderbolt before Bacchus was born; the unborn child was saved by Jupiter.

SENECA. Lucius Annaeus Seneca, the Roman philosopher and playwright (c. 4 B.C.-65 A.D.). He appears in the *Octavia* as one of the characters.

SERES. A people of Eastern Asia, believed identical with the Chinese.

SICYON. A town on the Corinthian Gulf, west of Corinth.

SIGAEUM (more correctly, SIGNIA). A small town in Latium.

SIGEUM. The northwestern promontory of the Troad, the site of the Greek camp in the Trojan War.

SILANUS. L. Junius Silanus, the betrothed husband of Octavia. He committed suicide when Octavia married Nero.

SILENUS. A satyr, the foster-father and constant companion of Bacchus.

SILIUS. See MESSALINA.

SILVANUS. A Latin divinity of the fields and forests.

SIMOIS. A river near Troy.

SINIS. A robber of the Isthmus of Corinth, who bent down treetops and, fastening his victims to these, shot them through the air. He was slain by Theseus.

SINON. A Greek warrior who deceived the Trojans as to the character and purpose of the wooden horse.

SIPYLUS. A mountain in Asia Minor. See NIOBE.

SIRENS. Sea-nymphs, who had the power of charming and luring to destruction all who heard their songs. The Argonauts passed them in safety because Orpheus played sweeter music.

SISYPHUS. Son of Aeolus and founder of the royal house of Corinth. For his wickedness in life he was punished in the Underworld by being compelled to roll a huge stone up a hill; it always rolled back and renewed his toil.

SOL. The sun, personified as the sun-god.

SOLON. Famous Athenian statesman and poet of the early sixth century B.C. He was one of the seven wise men of Greece.

SPES. The personification of hope, worshipped by the Romans as a goddess.

SPHINX. A monster, part lion, part woman. She proposed a riddle to the Thebans and killed all who could not solve it. Oedipus gave her the correct answer, whereupon she slew herself.

STRATONICUS. A celebrated musician of the time of Alexander the Great, who travelled from place to place in Greece and exhibited his art.

STROPHIUS. King of Phocis, father of Pylades.

STYMPHALIAN BIRDS. Monstrous birds which inhabited a pool near the town of Stymphalus in Arcadia. They were destroyed by Hercules.

STYX. The principal river of the Underworld, which the souls of the dead had to cross. From meaning the river of death, it came to mean death itself, and the land of the dead.

SUMMANUS. An old Roman deity, the god of lightning at night.

SULLA. Faustus Cornelius Sulla Felix, consul in 52 A.D., put to death by Nero in 62 A.D.

SYBARITE. An inhabitant of Sybaris, a Greek city in southern Italy which was noted for its luxury and voluptuousness.

SYMPLEGADES. Two islands or rocks at the entrance of the Black Sea which clashed together when ships attempted to pass between them. The Argo was the first ship to sail between them with success.

SYRACUSE. A large and powerful Greek city on the eastern coast of Sicily.

TAENARUS (or TAENARA). A promontory on the southernmost point of the Peloponnesus near which was an entrance to the Underworld.

TAGUS. A river of Spain, celebrated for its golden sands.

TALENT. A Greek term for a sum of money, the equivalent of sixty minae, or approximately eleven hundred dollars. See MINA.

TANAIS. A river in Sarmatia, now the Don.

TANTALIDES. Descendants of Tantalus.

TANTALUS. 1. Son of Jupiter, father of Pelops and Niobe. Because of his sin against the gods (see PELOPS) he was doomed to suffer endless hunger and thirst in the Underworld. 2. One of the sons of Thyestes, slain by Atreus.

TARENTUM. An important Greek city in southern Italy.

TARQUIN. Lucius Tarquinius Superbus, who married Tullia, daughter of Servius Tullius, king of Rome. Tarquin and his wife conspired to usurp the power of the king. Servius Tullius was killed and Tullia drove her chariot over his dead body as it lay in the road.

TARTARUS (also written TARTARA). The portion of the Underworld devoted to the punishment of the wicked, but often used of the Underworld in general.

TAURUS. The constellation of the Bull, said to be the bull in whose form Jupiter bore Europa from Phoenicia to Crete.

TAYGETUS. A lofty mountain range to the west of Sparta.

TELEMACHUS. Son of Ulysses and Penelope.

TELEPHUS. King of Mysia. Wounded by Achilles' spear, he was cured by application of the rust scraped from its point.

TELOBOANS. A people in Acarnania, in western Greece.

TENEDOS. A small island in the Aegean, off the coast of Troy.

TERENCE. Publius Terentius Afer, celebrated writer of Roman comedy.

TEREUS. A king of Thrace. See PHILOMELA.

TETHYS. Wife of Oceanus and goddess of the sea. The name is used frequently for the sea itself.

THALES. The earliest Greek philosopher and one of the seven wise men of Greece.

THEBES. The chief city of Boeotia, founded by Cadmus. See AMPHION, LYCUS, OEDIPUS.

THESEUS. King of Athens, son of Aegeus and Aethra, father of Hippolytus. He was also said to be the son of Neptune, who had granted him three wishes; the last of these he used against his son Hippolytus. Theseus was the most famous and most active of the legendary heroes of Attica. See ARIADNE, PIRITHOUS.

THETIS. A sea-goddess, daughter of Nereus, wife of Peleus, mother of Achilles.

THRACIAN CRIME. See PHILOMELA.

THYESTES. Son of Pelops, brother of Atreus, father of Aegisthus. Three other sons were slain by Atreus and their flesh served to their father.

TIPHYS. The pilot of the Argo.

TIRESIAS. The blind seer of Thebes, and father of Manto. Tiresias was one of the most renowned soothsayers in antiquity.

TISIPHONE. One of the Furies.

TITANS. Sons of Heaven and Earth, one of whom was Hyperion, identified with the sun. Seneca frequently uses Titan as equivalent to the sun or the sun-god. The Titans were confused with the Giants who attempted to overthrow Jupiter.

TITHONUS. Son of Laomedon, brother of Priam, husband of Aurora. At the request of his wife the gods granted to him eternal life but neglected to add eternal youth. He grew older but was unable to die; hence a decrepit old man was proverbially called Tithonus.

TITYUS. A giant, son of Earth, who attempted to assault Latona. For this he was punished in the Underworld, where a vulture kept feeding upon his ever-renewed vitals.

TMOLUS. A mountain range in Lydia.

TOXEUS. A youth slain by Hercules.

TRACHIS (or TRACHIN). A town of Thessaly, celebrated as the residence of Hercules.

TRIPTOLEMUS. Son of the king of Eleusis. In return for his kind treatment to Ceres when she was searching for her daughter, the goddess granted to Triptolemus the knowledge of agriculture; this he taught to mankind, thus becoming the originator of civilisation.

TRITONS. Sea-deities. They sang the marriage chorus of Achilles.

TRIVIA. An epithet of Diana, because she presided over places where three roads meet. See HECATE.

TROILUS. A son of Priam, slain by Achilles.

TROY. An ancient city of Troas, whose walls were built by Neptune and Apollo. First destroyed by Hercules during the reign of Laomedon. Its second fall was after ten years of siege by the Greeks under Agamemnon.

TULLIA. See TARQUIN.

TURPIO. Lucius Ambivius Turpio, manager of a troupe of actors, and himself one of the most famous of Roman actors.

TYNDAREUS. King of Sparta, husband of Leda, the actual father of Clytemnestra, and the reputed father of Castor, Pollux, and Helen.

TYNDARIDAE. Castor and Pollux, the sons of Jupiter and Leda, but falsely named from Tyndareus, the mortal husband of Leda. See CASTOR.

TYPHOEUS. One of the Giants who fought against Jupiter.

TYPHON. A monster or giant, apparently the same as Typhoeus.

TYRRHENE. The Tyrrhenian or Etruscan sea, the part of the Mediterranean between Italy and Corsica and Sardinia.

ULYSSES. One of the Greek heroes in the Trojan War, son of Laertes and Anticlea, husband of Penelope.

VENUS. The goddess of love; mother of Cupid, god of love.

VIRGIN. The constellation Virgo. See ASTRAEA.

VIRGINIA. Daughter of Lucius Virginius slain by her father to save her from the lust of Appius Claudius, the decemvir.

VULCAN. The god of fire, who forged the thunderbolts of Jupiter.

XANTHUS. A river near Troy.

ZACYNTHUS. An island off the northwest corner of the Peloponnesus.

ZEPHYRUS. The west wind.

ZETES. A winged son of Boreas. He and his brother Calais were members of the Argonautic expedition and drove away the Harpies from Phineus. The two brothers were slain by Hercules.

ZETHUS. A Theban prince, twin brother of Amphion. See AMPHION.

ZEUXIS. A famous Greek painter.

LIBRARY
JUNIOR COLLEGE DISTRICT
ST. LOUIS, MO.

LIBRARY
JUNIOR COLLEGE DISTRICT
ST. LOUIS, MO.